p 3⁵⁰

"EASILY THE MOST THOROUGHGOING
BIOGRAPHY OF MARILYN MONROE . . .
HER TRAGIC STORY IS TOLD IN DEPTH,
AMPLIFIED BY NUMEROUS PHOTOGRAPHS."
—*John Barkham Reviews*

"You'll know everything about Marilyn . . . her
involvement with the Kennedys and her possible
murder . . . her affair with Frank Sinatra, and her
naming the poodle he gave her 'Maf'—short for
Mafia . . . the note Yves Montand slipped under her
hotel door . . . the touching telegram she sent to
Robert Kennedy . . . the chilling poem she wrote
. . . her inability to have a climax (according to
one of her lovers, who may have been to blame)
. . . her obsessive fear of homosexuality . . .
juicy . . . controversial . . . *Goddess* dissects the
Monroe legend, and the people who spat on it,
with a surgeon's care."

—*Saturday Review*

"Packed to the hilt with revelations."

—*Buffalo News*

More . . .

"A MAJOR ACHIEVEMENT IN INVESTIGATIVE REPORTING."

—*Chattanooga Times*

"A REMARKABLE PERFORMANCE . . . The ghost of Marilyn Monroe cries out on these pages as poignantly as in any book yet written about her."

—*The New York Times*

"The book is neither sleaze nor sensation. It is a complicated patchwork of Monroe's strange and tormented life . . . with a cast of characters who include John Kennedy, Robert, actor Peter Lawford, Frank Sinatra, underworld figures Jimmy Hoffa and Sam Giancana, baseball star Joe DiMaggio, playwright Arthur Miller and hundreds of extras . . . leading to the final speculation that Monroe's life ended with an extraordinary coverup involving the President, his brother, their friends and possibly their enemies."

—*Newsday*

"A motherlode of material on the whole of Monroe's life . . . fascinating in the extreme."

—*Kirkus Reviews*

"Must reading . . . both a master detective work and riveting biography."

—*Los Angeles Weekly*

GODDESS

The Secret Lives of Marilyn Monroe

Anthony Summers

AN ONYX BOOK

ONYX
Published by the Penguin Group
Penguin Books USA Inc., 375 Hudson Street,
New York, New York 10014, U.S.A.
Penguin Books Ltd, 27 Wrights Lane,
London W8 5TZ, England
Penguin Books Australia Ltd, Ringwood,
Victoria, Australia
Penguin Books Canada Ltd, 10 Alcorn Avenue,
Toronto, Ontario, Canada M4V 3B2
Penguin Books (N.Z.) Ltd, 182–190 Wairau Road,
Auckland 10, New Zealand

Penguin Books Ltd, Registered Offices:
Harmondsworth, Middlesex, England

Published by arrangement with Macmillan Publishing Company

First Onyx Printing, December, 1986
14   13   12   11   10   9   8   7

Grateful acknowledgment is made to the following for permission to reprint previously
published material from:
The Letters of Nunnally Johnson, edited by Dorris Johnson and Ellen Leventhal.
Copyright © 1981 by Dorris Johnson. Reprinted by permission of Alfred A. Knopf, Inc.
"Joltin' Joe DiMaggio." Copyright Alan Court and Ben Homer 1941. Reprinted by
permission of the Estate of Alan Courtney.
"Never Give All the Heart" from *The Poems of W. B. Yeat,* edited by Richard J.
Finneran. Published by Macmillan Publishing Company, 1983.
Marilyn: An Untold Story by Norman Rosten. Copyright © 1967, 1972, 1973 by
Norman Rosten. Reprinted by permission of Harold Ober Associates Incorporated.
Published by Signet, 1973.

Photo credits appear on pages 526–527.

REGISTERED TRADEMARK—MARCA REGISTRADA

Printed in the United States of America

for Olga and Ronan

"She did originate something. She was the first person I know of who was truly unconventional. She was a sixties person before it started—way before it started—like ten years."

ARTHUR MILLER
1979

CONTENTS

ACKNOWLEDGMENTS

Work on this book lasted continuously from 1982 to spring 1986. It began when the Los Angeles District Attorney announced a review of the circumstances surrounding the death of Marilyn Monroe. Ron Hall, editor of London's *Sunday Express* magazine, commissioned me to write a short article, and I traveled to California. I soon realized it would be pointless to tackle the death issue without long research. I also discovered, to my astonishment, that not a single author had attempted an in-depth examination of the actress's personal life, coupled with serious inquiries into her death and the alleged connection with the Kennedys. In 1986, after the publication of the hardcover edition led to international furor and renewed calls for a new official investigation into Marilyn's death, I conducted further intensive research.

Some 650 people were interviewed. I thank them all—though many must regret having let me into their lives. A handful of interviewees asked to remain anonymous; I agreed in very few cases, when testimony was crucial to the story, and when it withstood hard scrutiny. My publishers have been briefed in each instance. Neither Joe DiMaggio nor Arthur Miller agreed to be interviewed—I doubt whether the baseball star will ever discuss his former wife and the playwright, I understand, is preparing his autobiography.

Of those who crossed paths with Marilyn Monroe, and who did talk to me, some were especially patient with my questions, and frank in their answers. They include Rupert Allan, Marilyn's press aide, her New York hosts, Amy Greene and her late husband, Milton, her psychiatrist's widow, Hildi Greenson, and his children, Danny and Joan. James Haspiel, once her teenage fan, today perhaps the most informed person on the planet about Marilyn, generously gave me access to his knowledge and his archives.

I thank the family of Fred Karger, whom Marilyn once hoped to marry, and especially Anne Batté. Author Richard

Meryman, a former *Life* reporter, proved that one writer's integrity can redeem a thousand column inches of the type of nonsense so often spewed out on Marilyn. Patricia Newcomb, the last close female intimate, granted me interviews where she has rebuffed others. She tried to be honest without compromising old loyalties to the Kennedy brothers.

Gordon Heaver and Gloria Romanoff, who both knew Marilyn, offered insights into the Los Angeles of thirty and more years ago. In New York, Ralph Roberts gave me his trust and a unique tape recording, and Norman Rosten opened up more than just the safe-deposit box in which he keeps Marilyn's fragments of poetry. Hal Schaefer, the quiet musician who suffered for his relations with Marilyn during the DiMaggio marriage, impressed me with his courage. Lynn Sherman brought to life for me the social games once played by the wealthy beach dwellers of Santa Monica. Steffi Sidney, daughter of Marilyn's friend Sidney Skolsky, gave me first access to her father's papers, following his death during the writing of this book. Skolsky's files are now lodged with the Academy of Motion Picture Arts and Sciences, where I was received with great tolerance.

Robert Slatzer, who claims to have been briefly married to Marilyn, took my interrogations with good humor, even though seriously ill, and he proved an invaluable source of vital documentation. Neil Spotts, one of the many former policemen interviewed, opened doors long tightly closed. Bobbette Butigan shared research done after Marilyn's death, and Nevada historian Bethel van Tassel told me about the Cal-Neva Lodge. Bill Woodfield told me of the only serious effort to report Marilyn's death at the time, and—together with his wife Lili—offered warm hospitality in a chilly town.

Maurice Zolotow's book about Marilyn, written while she was still alive, still stands as the best work to date. He kindly allowed me access to the Zolotow Collection, housed at the Humanities Research Center of the University of Texas at Austin. I am grateful to Paul M. Bailey of the Theater Arts Library there, and to Henry J. Gwiazda II, Curator of the Robert F. Kennedy Collection in the John F. Kennedy Library, who went out of his way to give honest answers to sensitive questions. Carl Rollyson allowed me to see parts of his manuscript, *The Replicated Life of Marilyn Monroe*. Edward Wagenknecht, a veteran Marilyn scholar, gave me the benefit of his collection of rare articles, and Roy Turner, who has labored to clarify Marilyn's ancestry, generously shared his knowledge.

For the third time in my writing career, I turned for assistance to the late Professor Keith Simpson, Britain's most distinguished forensic pathologist. He patiently analyzed the medical aspects of Marilyn's death along with Dr. Christopher Foster, pathologist at St. Bartholomew's Hospital in London. I am indebted to the psychiatrists of the Los Angeles Suicide Prevention Team, and especially Dr. Robert Litman, who allowed me to see materials hitherto sealed. I immensely enjoyed fencing with John Miner, former Deputy District Attorney in Los Angeles, a man of honor burdened with secrets he cannot divulge. Former FBI Assistant Director Courtney Evans, who had the daunting job of acting as liaison between J. Edgar Hoover and Attorney General Robert Kennedy, more than lived up to his nickname, "Courtly." I have tried not to disappoint Assistant Los Angeles District Attorney "Mike" Carroll, who conscientiously ran the limited 1982 review of Marilyn's death, and who believed that I would deal responsibly with a case that had left him troubled.

From its inception, this project included plans for a television documentary as well as a book. In that connection I joined forces with Ted Landreth, a former CBS executive, who tried for three years to find an American television network with the guts and the will to bring the story of Marilyn's final tragedy to a national audience. Those in power in American television were afraid to rock the historical boat. As described in the Postscript, ABC-TV's *20/20* producers eventually made a program, only to see it canceled by executives on the day of transmission.

Our efforts did bear fruit, however, thanks to the British Broadcasting Corporation and independent backers from several countries. Thanks are due, especially to Will Wyatt, George Carey, and the producer Christopher Olgiati at the BBC. The program they made, *Say Goodbye to the President,* has now been seen across the United States and around the world. It was the last film cut by a great BBC film editor and faithful friend to many producers, the late Ian Calloway.

I came to respect Landreth and his investigative team, especially Ed Tivnan and Anthony Cook, for their tenacious journalism. When America is poorly served by a timid establishment media, there is honor in being free-lance and determined.

Almost all important interviews were conducted by myself,

even when witnesses had first been approached by colleagues. However, I am indebted to researchers Kathy Castle and Gay Watson in England, Theresa Garofalo and Charlie Holland in New York, Larry Harris and Robert Ranftel in Washington, Jack Crane, Monica Gruler and Paul Hoch in California, and Mary Powers in Mexico City.

I owe a great deal to Lori Winchester in Los Angeles, without whose expertise many witnesses could never have been traced, and her partner, Bill Jordan, a retired lieutenant of the Los Angeles Police Department. They offered, virtually free, the help of WCJ Inc., which provides investigative and protection services to clients as diverse as politicians, celebrities, and—in 1984—the organizers of the Olympic Games.

Kitty Kelley, presently writing about Frank Sinatra in spite of efforts to deter her with litigation, generously exchanged information. Attorney James Lesar, a master of the labyrinth called the Freedom of Information Act, burned the midnight oil on my behalf. Mark Allen shared invaluable FBI documents. As the Postscript shows, his work paid off handsomely.

Cynthia Rowan once again supplied wisdom and helped construct the chronology on which the book is based. Jean Manship and Joan Withington dug me out from under mountains of paper, and Angie Carpenter looked after logistics. Angela Curtin served as vital liaison in California. In Ireland, Joanne Kett, Lesley Morrisson, and Anne Stearn coped with the author during the last stages of the hardcover edition. Alma Clissman, Caroline Burrell, and Denise FitzGerald helped pull the paperback together. Marathon runner Willie Henry has again been a faithful friend.

I am grateful to my agents, Anne McDermid in London and Peter Ginsberg in New York. I also thank my editors, publisher Hillel Black at Macmillan, Michaela Hamilton at Signet, Joanna Goldsworthy at Gollancz, and Barbara Boote at Sphere. Also at Macmillan, Brenda O'Brien worked tirelessly on the original manuscript.

Olga, my wife, committed the folly of telling me to write another book and supported me with hard labor of her own. Her family, who could be forgiven for thinking there was no life outside the subject of Marilyn Monroe, put up with both of us.

Heartfelt thanks to all.

—A.S.

Part I

INTO THE LAND OF THE SCORPIONS

"The Industry giveth, and the Industry taketh away. Hollywood, the dream factory, had created a dream girl. Could she awaken to reality? And what was the reality? Was there a life for her outside the dream?"

NORMAN ROSTEN, Poet and
Marilyn's long time friend

"In Hollywood, 'starlet' is the name for any woman under 30 not employed in a brothel."

BEN HECHT, with whom Marilyn
did her first major interviews

1

THE HOUR BEFORE MIDNIGHT, Saturday, August 4, 1962, in Los Angeles. In the auditorium of the Hollywood Bowl, under a sickle moon, the crowd was listening to the bittersweet strains of the Henry Mancini orchestra.

Abruptly, unnoticed by most of the concertgoers, there was a minor disturbance. An attendant, whispering apologetically, passed an urgent message to a man seated in one of the higher-priced seats. The man rose, walked to a telephone, and listened. Then he spoke a few terse sentences, summoned his wife, and hurried to his car.

In the night hours that followed, as Los Angeles slept, there would be other little incidents, more comings and goings. Telephones would jangle at bedsides around the city, rousing doctors, a prominent lawyer, leading figures in show business, and private detectives. A famous actor, brother-in-law of the President of the United States, would place a call to Washington. Some of the actor's neighbors, in their fine houses on the beach, would be roused from sleep by the clatter of a helicopter. An ambulance would be summoned to an unpretentious house in the suburbs, on a mission the driver says he cannot recall.

The public would learn nothing of these nocturnal events, nor, so far as we know, were they recorded by any official body. Yet the event that triggered them was the news story of the year, one that received more coverage than even the Missile Crisis, the near-nuclear war that followed a few weeks later. Marilyn Monroe was dead.

Exactly twenty years later, in 1982, the Los Angeles District Attorney reopened inquiries into a case that had never ceased to be the subject of rumor and controversy. His brief was limited. Was there sufficient evidence to open a criminal investigation? Could Monroe have been murdered? After four months the DA was advised that the evidence "fails to support any theory of criminal conduct." This, though, had been

3

only a "threshold investigation." It was indeed; the investigators did not even interview the detective who attended the scene of the death.

The 1982 report acknowledged that "factual discrepancies" and "unanswered questions" had surfaced during the Monroe inquiry. Privately, officials today make it clear that they felt they had stumbled into a morass of untruth and obfuscation. Marilyn Monroe may, they surmise, have died by her own hand. Yet they feel something was indeed covered up in 1962.

That something involved Monroe's relations with President John Kennedy and his brother Robert—and, in particular, Robert Kennedy's activities at the time Monroe died.

The DA's men shrug ruefully when they discuss the Kennedy angle. "We were not asked," says one, "to investigate a political cover-up." With far less excuse, the press at the time preferred the easy wallow in pathos to serious reporting. Since then, in all the profusion of writing about Marilyn Monroe, not one qualified writer has attempted a professional inquiry into the last days of the woman most firmly enthroned as the goddess of her century. Norman Mailer, who caused a stir with his book hinting at murder, today regrets "not giving it my best effort."

The failure to report the end of Marilyn Monroe is at least consistent. For all the millions of words tapped out on typewriters, kind and cruel, sophisticated and stupid, nobody has yet fully documented her life.

Who was the woman who turned herself into "Marilyn Monroe"? She had a body, in truth, not so unlike other female bodies. How did she make us notice her more than any other woman, in her time and on into the end of the century? How much of this alchemy was achieved by talent, how much in the carefully chosen embraces of powerful males? What was at the hidden center of the phenomenon that was Marilyn Monroe?

Behind the hyberbole and the hysteria there was a child who grew to be a woman, who was a symbol of love yet essentially lonely, who died famously but in folly at the age of thirty-six. She postured as the world's mistress, yet yearned for monogamy and motherhood. The profile was crude while the pursuit was for culture. The brilliance of the actress masked a seriously disturbed psyche. The private person read philosophy and planned gardens, yet drowned in drugs and alcohol. Marilyn Monroe anticipated a decade that trumpeted fulfillment and achieved only confusion.

She told her last interviewer: "When you're famous you kind of run into human nature in a raw kind of way. . . . People you run into feel that, well, who is she—who does she think she is, Marilyn Monroe? It's nice to be included in people's fantasies but you also like to be accepted for your own sake."

With another reporter, a few months earlier, she had mused, "I wonder how I'll feel when I'm fifty?" Then, her mind turning to birthdays, she mentioned that she was born under the sign of Gemini.

"What kind of people are Geminis?" the reporter asked.

"Jekyll and Hyde. Two in one," came the reply.

"And that's you?"

"More than two. I'm so many people. They shock me sometimes. I wish I was just *me*! I used to think I was going crazy, until I discovered some people I admired were like that, too."

Marilyn—and we may call her Marilyn because that is how she is known from Connecticut to the Congo—never saw her fortieth birthday, let alone her half-century. Were she alive today she would be nearly sixty. Yet her life remains as unfaithfully reported as was her death.

It is time to grant this goddess a measure of reality. Who do we think she was?

In 1983, unrecognized by passers-by, an elderly woman wearing a bucket hat regularly sallied forth into the streets of Gainesville, Florida, riding a tricycle with a red danger flag on the handle bars. The woman was a surprising survivor— Marilyn's octogenarian mother, living out her life in virtual anonymity.

Gladys Monroe—for Monroe was the name of Marilyn's maternal grandmother—was born in 1902, in Mexico, of American parents. By the age of twenty-four she had been married twice and borne two children, who were raised by relatives of her first husband. The second husband did not last long. He was gone by the time Marilyn was born on June 1, 1926, in Los Angeles General Hospital.

We do not know who Marilyn's father was. Her birth certificate identifies him as "Edward Mortenson," and her mother was married to a Martin E. Mortensen two years before Marilyn's birth. It appears he was a Norwegian immigrant, a baker who died in a motorcycle accident in 1929, but even that is disputed. At all events, although she used his name on official documents throughout her life, Marilyn later denied that Mortenson was her father.

Marilyn told one interviewer that her real father "used to live in the same apartment building where my mother lived—he walked out and left her while I was getting born." That scenario sits best with a man called Stanley Gifford. He worked for Consolidated Film Industries, where Marilyn's mother worked as a film cutter, and rumor had it that Gifford was Gladys' lover when her marriage to Mortenson collapsed.

The infant Marilyn had to make do with an imagined father. Once her mother pointed to a photograph and said, "That's your father." She remembered the face of a man in a slouch hat—"there was a lively smile in his eyes, and he had a thin moustache like Clark Gable."

It was the beginning of a lifelong fantasy. As a child, Marilyn would recall, she told gullible friends that Clark Gable actually had been her father. In her last months, after she had acted with Gable in *The Misfits*, she fell back on the old fantasy. The widow of Marilyn's psychiatrist, Hildi Greenson, says, "Marilyn had seen that photograph, and it looked like Gable, so sometimes she let herself believe her father was Gable."

In 1962, the year of her death, Marilyn had to fill out an entry for "Father's Name" on an official form. She wrote simply—and in her secretary's opinion, savagely—"Unknown."

If mystery surrounds Marilyn's father, the facts about her mother's side of the family are painfully well documented. Knowing what she knew of that history, Marilyn feared she was genetically prone to insanity. The fear was understandable.

Her maternal great-grandfather, Tilford Hogan, hanged himself at the age of eighty-two. Suicide among the aged is not uncommon. It is certainly not necessarily a sign of madness, but mental illness did run in the family.

The maternal grandfather, Otis Monroe, died in an institution of general paresis, according to the death certificate. Paresis, and specifically paretic dementia, is recognized as a form of insanity provoked by syphilis in its final stage.

Marilyn ran no risk of inheriting syphilis, but her maternal grandmother, Della, also died in an asylum, at age fifty-one, a year after Marilyn's birth. She had been something of a religious zealot. The cause of her death was given as heart disease, with "manic-depressive psychosis" as a contributory factor.

The adult Marilyn would claim that she remembered her grandmother trying to smother her shortly before she was sent to the mental hospital. Since Marilyn was only thirteen months old at the time, it is highly unlikely she really remembered any such thing. Her little horror story almost certainly belongs in the ragbag of fantasies from which Marilyn embroidered her youth.

Family life was virtually nonexistent. After Marilyn's birth, apparently feeling unable to cope with full-time motherhood, Gladys went back to her work as a film cutter. She provided for her baby, but left her most of the time in the care of foster parents. Gladys' older children had long since been taken away by relatives of her first husband.

Catastrophe came when Marilyn was seven and living with her mother for a while. Gladys suffered a period of deep depression, then an explosion of rage and frustration. Some reports say she attacked a friend with a knife. She was promptly committed to the very hospital in which her own mother had died.

Except for brief periods, Gladys would remain confined until after Marilyn's death. Inez Melson, Marilyn's former business manager, was eventually appointed Gladys' guardian. She spent more time with her than anyone else and considered her disturbed rather than insane.

"Marilyn's mother was overly taken up with her religion, Christian Science, and with evil," Melson said. "That was her area of disturbance. She figured she had done something wrong in her life, and was being punished for it."

In that obsession Gladys was following the pattern set by her own mother. Religious fixation, and the notion of atoning for unspecified sin, is a feature found both in manic disorders and schizophrenia.

Marilyn had religious zeal thrust at her during childhood by Gladys and by one of the women who cared for her, and she remained a wobbly adherent of Christian Science into adulthood. With her, however, it was not a fixation. Marilyn would one day convert to the Jewish faith to marry the playwright, Arthur Miller; but she later cheerfully described herself as an "atheist Jew."

Marilyn was not definitely doomed to psychiatric illness, but she was born at serious risk. Psychiatrists consulted for this book point out that—as heavily documented in manuals used as guidelines by American doctors and the World Health Organization—manic and schizophrenic disorders frequently run in families.

This book will be an investigation of Marilyn's adult life, not of her childhood—that desolate, dislocated period has been well charted by earlier biographers. It was a time that the grown woman would never forget nor allow her public to ignore—ten foster homes, two years in the Los Angeles Orphans' Home, another foster home, and finally four years with the guardian appointed by county authorities after her mother's departure to an asylum.

This saga of deprivation made a classic launching pad for future psychiatric disorder. Dr. Valérie Shikhverg, consultant psychiatrist at several New York hospitals, sees Marilyn as a prime candidate for what is today called a "borderline" personality—someone who hovers "on the border between psychotic and neurotic, with frequent fluctuations between the two."

"The problems of such a person," says Dr. Shikhverg, originate very early in life. 'Borderlines' tend to have had a mother who could not cope, or who suffered from overt psychosis. Their family histories typically feature separation or divorce, or the total absence of one or both parents during early childhood. Marilyn's background was tailormade to make her 'borderline.' "

The "borderline" person is likely to be emotionally unstable, excessively impulsive, and to show the world a mood that appears expansive and active. He or she is likely to be histrionic or seductive or overly concerned with good looks. A "borderline" depends on constant external approval, loves applause, cannot bear to be alone, and suffers "depressive, crashlike reactions" to rejection by others. A "borderline" tends to abuse alcohol and drugs, and to make suicide threats as gestures to obtain help.

This personality profile, made in 1984 on the basis of studies covering thousands of case histories, is chillingly recognizable in Marilyn Monroe. Marilyn's life was to be remorselessly faithful to the blueprint of her background, a scenario for brilliance and tragedy.

2

"MY ARRIVAL IN SCHOOL, with painted lips and darkened brows, started everybody buzzing. Why I was a siren, I hadn't the faintest idea. I didn't want to be kissed, and I didn't dream of being seduced by a duke or a movie star. The truth was that with all my lipstick and mascara and precocious curves I was as unresponsive as a fossil. But I seemed to affect people quite otherwise."

So spoke Marilyn Monroe in 1954, looking back on her teenage years. Thus at any rate, were her memories recorded by the writer Ben Hecht, to whom the newly successful star, at twenty-eight, told her "life story" that year.

Hecht hoped to ghost the young Marilyn's autobiography, which had been commissioned by a major New York publisher. It is an important record, for Marilyn gave no other interviews of comparable scope. It is also controversial.

After a long series of talks with Hecht, Marilyn got him to read her the entire 160 pages of manuscript out loud. Then, according to Hecht's widow, she "laughed and cried and expressed herself as 'thrilled.' She said she never imagined so wonderful a story could be written about her, and that Benny had captured every phase of her life."

Marilyn even helped correct the manuscript, but then relations soured. Marilyn's husband at the time, Joe DiMaggio, reportedly objected to publication, and she backed out of the deal. When the material appeared anyway, in the *British Empire News*, Marilyn threatened to sue, alleging misquotation.

If the ghostwriter erred, so did Marilyn, for the truths in her story were highly selective. Hecht reported to his editor during the interviews that he was sometimes sure Marilyn was fabricating. He explained, "When I say lying, I mean she isn't telling the truth. I don't think so much that she is trying to deceive me as that she is a fantasizer." Hecht found himself struggling to interpret Marilyn's "odd little physical

9

body language, to read when she was going into something fictional or when she was leveling.''

Many of Marilyn's statements on her early life, as reproduced in the Hecht manuscript, will be quoted in these pages. Where possible, they will be buttressed or countered by independent witnesses. We must treat what she tells us with informed skepticism, and that is no disadvantage. Marilyn, an international fantasy figure, constructed her image, both public and private, from a blend of fact and self-serving fantasy. She exercised to excess a common human license. Fantasy was part of this creature, and part of the challenge is to discover the woman who sheltered behind it.

What Marilyn did tell Ben Hecht was sad, strong stuff for the 1950s. What she did not tell might have finished her as an actress. At the time, indeed, it was nobody else's business.

At fifteen Marilyn was still ''Norma Jeane'' (or Norma Jean, when she felt like spelling it that way), the name her mother had given her at birth. It was early that year, 1942, that her legal guardian, a middle-aged woman named Grace McKee, abruptly decided to thrust her charge into the adult world.

Norma Jeane's future triumphs and calamities would be defiantly of her own making. Her first marriage, however, was arranged. Grace McKee had decided to move East with her new husband, and they did not find it convenient to take Norma Jeane along. The answer was to find her a husband.

McKee saw a likely candidate in Jim Dougherty, the son of a neighbor she knew well. His family had seen the worst of the Great Depression—today he recalls living, at one stage, in a tent beside their battered car. At twenty-one he was tough and hardheaded, a gifted football player who had turned down college in favor of a job embalming corpses at a funeral home, then work as a night-shift fitter at Lockheed Aviation.

Jim Dougherty knew Norma Jeane. They had had a couple of dates, and he had enjoyed the discovery that, when dancing, she ''would lean extra close, eyes tight shut.'' Norma Jeane ''laughed at the right moment and kept quiet when she was supposed to.'' Even so, Dougherty was running around with a number of other girls.

It came as a total surprise to Jim Dougherty when Norma Jeane's guardian suggested he marry Norma Jeane. His mother passed on the message. It was a thought that had never even occurred to Dougherty, but he agreed when told the alternative would be to send Norma Jeane back to the orphanage. That, he says, was the way decisions were made in his family.

A wedding date was set for June, to give Norma Jeane time to turn sixteen. In the weeks that remained the couple belatedly started courting. Dougherty's pride and joy was his car, a 1940 Ford coupe, and he would whisk Norma Jeane to a trysting spot in the hills called Pop's Willow Lake. They would rent a canoe, paddle under the trees at the water's edge, and kiss.

They were duly married, on June 19, 1942, when she was less than three weeks past her sixteenth birthday. There was no honeymoon. He went back to work at the aircraft factory on Monday morning.

Norma Jeane gave her account of the marriage in her first days of fame, in the interviews with Ben Hecht. Jim Dougherty finally told his full story in the seventies.

The couple seem to have been talking about entirely different relationships. She told Hecht, "It was like being retired to a zoo. Actually our marriage was a sort of friendship with sexual privileges. I found out later that marriages are often no more than that. I was a peculiar wife. I disliked grown-ups. . . . I liked boys and girls younger than me. I played games with them until my husband came out and started calling me to go to bed."

Jim Dougherty seems not to have noticed such coolness. "Our marriage," he has said, "may have been made in some place short of heaven, like in the minds of two older ladies, but there was no pretense in how Norma Jeane and I felt about each other once we'd formed that partnership."

At first the teenage wife was a hopeless housekeeper. She had no idea how to cook. Someone told her to put a pinch of salt in the coffee, so she made it a spoonful. Coffee came in handy to deal with a sparking short in the electrical wiring—she poured it over the carpet as well as the wiring, then locked herself in the bedroom. She served up raw fish.

Gradually, though, Norma Jeane learned. Dougherty says she cooked venison and rabbit very well, and cooked carrots and peas together "because she liked the color." All in all, the way Dougherty saw it, she had the makings of a good wife. Then, in the autumn of 1943, a year into their marriage, he joined the Merchant Marine.

The war was at first kind to Mr. and Mrs. Dougherty. He was merely posted to Catalina Island, just across the water

from Los Angeles County, and Norma Jeane joined him
there. The way it seemed to Dougherty, they spent an idyllic
year together. They fished, swam, and got fit. She took
weight-lifting lessons from a former Olympic champion. She
showed herself off a little too much to the hordes of uniformed males on the island, but Dougherty was not a worrier.
The couple went out a good deal, and one night Norma Jeane
spent most of the evening dancing with every man in the unit
except Dougherty. When he said, "Let's go home," Norma
Jeane wanted to dance some more. This caused their first real
row, but still Dougherty felt secure.

He continued to feel secure in 1944, after the call came to
go overseas. On arrival in New Guinea, he found a stack of
letters waiting for him. Norma Jeane, now living with Dougherty's mother, had written nearly every day. The letters
kept coming for months, while Dougherty sailed the Pacific
and his teenage wife took a job at Radio Plane, a plant
making aircraft used for target practice.

Norma Jeane inspected parachutes and sprayed fuselages.
She would say later, "I wore overalls in the factory. I was
surprised that they insisted on this. Putting a girl in overalls is
like having her work in tights, particularly if a girl knows
how to wear them. The men buzzed around me just as the
high-school boys had done. Maybe it was my fault that the
men in the factory tried to date me and buy me drinks. I
didn't feel like a married woman."

In her letters, Norma Jeane told Jim how much she missed
him. In one she quoted a song by Sammy Cahn and Jule
Styne, whom she would one day know in the movie business.
It was a song with a promise made by wartime sweethearts in
Allied countries around the world. "I'll walk alone," she
assured her sailor husband.

When Dougherty came home on his first leave, after several
months at sea, Norma Jeane was waiting at the railroad
station. He recalls, "We headed in my car for the most
luxurious motor lodge on Ventura Boulevard, the La Fonda,
and rarely left our room. Norma Jeane had bought a black net
nightgown for the occasion and we had most of our meals
brought to our room." He did notice, that week, that his wife
was drinking too much.

Shortly before he went back to sea, says Dougherty, "a
kind of dread took hold of her. She didn't want to talk about
or think of my leaving." But Jim Dougherty had no choice
about returning to the Pacific, and a few days later he did.

Norma Jeane went back to work at Radio Plane. At the end of 1944, with the war in its closing months, life changed. Or, more truthfully, Norma Jeane jumped at the chance to change it, when Private David Conover came to Radio Plane to take pictures of women doing war work.

Conover was an army photographer for an armed service motion picture unit. His commanding officer was Captain Ronald Reagan, the actor who was to become President of the United States. Conover's mission at Radio Plane was "to take morale-boosting shots of pretty girls" for *Yank* magazine. He later said he noticed at once that the eighteen-year-old Norma Jeane was different, that "her eyes held something that touched and intrigued me." Conover photographed her on the assembly line and then—changed at his request into a clinging red sweater—during the lunchbreak. He told Norma Jeane she belonged on a magazine cover, not in a factory.

Conover's new discovery was making $20 a week working ten hours a day at Radio Plane. He offered her $5 an hour as a free-lance model—unexpected pocket money which represented a bonanza to Norma Jeane. In the three weeks after meeting Conover there were several further picture sessions, and she joined him on a picture-taking safari through southern California. Some of the pictures ended up on the desk of the Blue Book Model Agency, and Norma Jeane was summoned for an interview. Her career as a cover girl had begun.

Success as a model came quickly. Soon photographs of Norma Jeane were appearing in girlie magazines with names like *Swank, Sir,* and *Peek.* Sometimes she would appear in a swimsuit, sometimes in shorts and halter top, but the pictures were perfectly respectable.

At nearly nineteen this model girl had a good figure—a thirty-five-inch bust which she used to the last centimeter*— and pale skin she liked to keep pale. She had shoulder-length California blonde hair, really fair only in summer, when the sun bleached it. Norma Jeane had no trouble getting work as a model.

When Jim Dougherty next came home, after a voyage round the world, his wife was not waiting at the station. She

---

* Marilyn's studio liked to say it was larger—37 inches was the official line in 1954. She herself once told a reporter she would like her epitaph to read "Here lies Marilyn Monroe—38-23-36." Dress designer and sometime lover Billy Travilla, who ought to know, says the true statistics—in Marilyn's prime—were 35-22-35. I have used his figure.

arrived an hour late, blaming the delay on a modeling assignment. She seemed cool toward Dougherty, was no longer living with his mother, and had left her job at the factory.

Norma Jeane now only wanted to talk about her success as a pinup girl, and Dougherty could only make a pretense at being impressed. She had spent their savings on new clothes, and spent a good part of the precious leave going out on modeling jobs. In the coming months Dougherty tried to stay nearer home, making short hauls up and down the western seaboard of the United States.

At Christmas 1945, Norma Jeane found it impossible to be at home—another modeling assignment. There was a showdown when she returned. Dougherty says, "I just told her she would have to choose between a modeling career and maybe the movies or a home life with me."

Norma Jeane failed to respond, and Dougherty went back to sea. He was in China, halfway up the Yangtze River, buying bracelets and nail polish for Norma Jeane, when he next had news of her. It came in the form of a lawyer's letter, enclosing divorce papers for signature. Dougherty decided not to sign till he had seen his wife.

Early one morning, on his return to California, he took a taxi straight from the dock to the house where Norma Jeane was living. She came to the door pulling a wrap around her shoulders, exhausted. She was sorry, she said, but could they meet tomorrow? The next day, and at several subsequent meetings, Norma Jeane told him of her new resolve. She was going to become a movie actress.

Dougherty had once won first place at a high school Shakespeare festival, for his delivery of Shylock's "revenge" speech in *The Merchant of Venice*. He said now, "I always thought I was the ham around here. How come you want to perform all of a sudden?" Norma Jeane took his mockery, but insisted the marriage was over.

"There was this secret in me—acting," she was to say years later. "It was like being in jail and looking at a door that said This Way Out."

Norma Jeane had acted in school plays, usually playing male parts, but otherwise she had no acting experience at all. Now, rattling in from the suburbs in the old car she had shared with Dougherty, she began exploring Hollywood.

"You sit alone," she remembered later. "It's night outside. Automobiles roll down Sunset Boulevard like an endless string of beetles. Their rubber tires make a purring high-class

noise. You're hungry, and you say, 'It's good for my waist-
line not to eat. There's nothing finer than a washboard belly.'

"I used to think as I looked out on the Hollywood night,
'There must be thousands of girls sitting alone like me,
dreaming of becoming a movie star. But I'm not going to
worry about them. I'm dreaming the hardest.' "

3

"THIS IS THE END of my story of Norma Jean. . . . I moved
into a room in Hollywood to live by myself. I wanted to find
out who I was. When I just wrote 'This is the end of Norma
Jean,' I blushed as if I had been caught out in a lie. Because
this sad, bitter child who grew up too fast is hardly ever out
of my heart. With success all around me, I can still feel her
frightened eyes looking out of mine. She keeps saying, 'I
never lived, I was never loved,' and often I get confused and
think it's I who am saying it."

This was Marilyn, by then a household name, talking in
1954, and the confusion was real. As her actual psychiatrists
would discover, and as armchair ones have insisted ever
since, Norma Jeane did not cease to exist when Mrs. Dougherty became an actress.

There was irony in the fact that the death certificate, in
1962, would refer only to the passing of a Hollywood invention called Marilyn Monroe. For it was Norma Jeane that
died, a Norma Jeane who had spent most of her life presenting herself to the world and—most troubling of all—to herself, through a filter of untruth. Norma Jeane had begun
weaving her web of delusion before the break with Jim
Dougherty, and along with the fantasies there was some
outright deceit. Only when that is dealt with can we move
along to the actress called Marilyn Monroe.

The former Mrs. Dougherty would tell Ben Hecht, "I was
completely faithful to my overseas husband." Jim Dougherty
could still maintain three decades later that "it never entered
my mind, and I don't believe to this day, that she was

deceiving me. In all the years I was seeing her, I never knew Norma Jeane to lie. If she was having dates, she would have told me.''

A spouse often closes the shutters of the mind to the possibility of infidelity. In the lonely wartime sailor husband there was the need to close out pain. In ex-husband Dougherty there is, not least when the wife was Marilyn Monroe, the muffler of simple pride. The record, though, says Norma Jeane was unfaithful.

In late 1960, less than two years before her death, Marilyn herself told another interviewer, "I didn't sleep around when I was married until my husband went into the service, and then it was just that I was so damn lonesome, and I had to have some kind of company, so once in a while I'd give in, mainly because I didn't want to be alone."

By her own account, then, the teenage bride began deceiving her husband about halfway through their four-year marriage. There can be little doubt what she was up to over the bleak Christmas of 1945, when she left Dougherty alone at home while she stayed away on a modeling assignment.

Norma Jeane had told Jim in December that she had to go away for nearly a month, to work with a photographer named André de Dienes. He wanted to take her hundreds of miles north, to Washington State. The fee would be two hundred dollars, exactly the amount needed to pay for repairs to the Dougherty's old Ford. She said she did not really want to go, but felt she should, not only for the money, but because de Dienes was a prominent photographer who would be good for her career. So she went.

Norma Jeane called long-distance, in tears, while Jim Dougherty was eating his Christmas dinner. She said she wished she could be home but now felt obliged to stay with de Dienes. "Most of his camera equipment was stolen because of me," she explained. "I left the car unlocked. . . ." When she did come home, says Dougherty, Norma Jeane refused to talk about the trip, except to say she never wanted to pose for de Dienes again.

André de Dienes, the immigrant son of a Hungarian banker, later told his side of what happened that Christmas. Aged thirty-two at the time, and a newcomer to California, he had been looking for a model who would pose outdoors in western settings, preferably nude. One day, in his bungalow at the Garden of Allah Hotel on Sunset Boulevard, the telephone rang. It was the Blue Book Agency, offering a new girl.

"There came this lovely little girl in a pink sweater and checkered slacks," de Dienes was to recall. "I fell right away in love with this young girl. In my subconscious I wanted to marry her. What was wrong with that? I was a nice young boy myself."

That afternoon de Dienes, who was indeed to become a successful photographer of the stars, told Norma Jeane he wanted her to pose nude. She was unsure. As he recalls it, "she told me she was married, but that her husband was at sea and she didn't love him."

De Dienes began courting Norma Jeane in Dougherty's absence, sent flowers, came to dinner at her home. It was against this background that he and Norma Jeane set off on their Christmas trip.

Norma Jeane did not go to bed with de Dienes immediately. He says he tried to seduce her for days, until one happy night when they failed to find a hotel with two vacant rooms. Norma Jeane agreed to share a room—and her favors. "She was lovely and very nice," the Hungarian was to recall. "But finally it was something she allowed me to do to her." In bed, de Dienes recalled, nineteen-year-old Norma Jeane discovered variations on sex untried with Jim Dougherty.

While working outdoors in the snow with Norma Jeane, de Dienes was moved. "She was sweet. Beautiful. Her smile. Her laughter. And she was frail—mentally and physically. As soon as she finished her work she would hop back in the car and fall asleep. This girl had no business in show business. She was a sensitive, sweet little girl."

Norma Jeane did leave the car unlocked, and de Dienes' equipment was stolen. He forgave her for that, and forgave her too when she still refused to pose in the nude. De Dienes was in love and soon, back in Los Angeles, he asked Norma Jeane to marry him. According to the photographer, she agreed. He then traveled on business to New York, where he papered his walls with her photographs.

Was de Dienes telling the truth? In this book there will be others, some more obscure than de Dienes, with claims to have bedded Marilyn. Were they her lovers, or are they braggarts and profiteers? The reader should know that those given this author's credence have either convinced me in personal interviews, or are supported by other witnesses.

One man I did not believe was David Conover, the Army private who indeed took the photographs that led to her first modeling job—the pictures are there to prove it. He then went on to write a book claiming that he became Marilyn's lover and lifelong friend. A visit to Conover in Canada satisfied me that his "documentation" was forged. He was either a confidence man or mentally ill, or both. Then there was Hans Jørgen Lembourn, a Dane who wrote a most literate account of what his publishers called "a forty-night affair with Marilyn Monroe." On analysis, his book has virtually no substance at all.

André de Dienes, on the other hand, has compelling backing. Jean-Louis, the fashion designer who served Marilyn in later years, knew de Dienes in the forties, and confirms that "he had a real relationship, a love affair, with Marilyn back then." Was de Dienes a lone folly in the dying days of her marriage to Jim Dougherty, and how was he treated in the end?

Still the ardent suitor, still assuming himself engaged to Norma Jeane, de Dienes sent her money to help pay for the divorce from Dougherty. "But when it came to get married," he was to recall wistfully, "she canceled it, on the phone, while I was driving to meet her in Vegas. Jealous, I drove to Los Angeles. And I surprised her, in her apartment, with a lover. . . . I knew then it was all over."

De Dienes bore no grudge. Till his death, in 1985, he treasured a copy of Mary Baker Eddy's book, *Science and Health,* given to Norma Jeane by her last foster parent, a Christian Scientist. On the flyleaf is the inscription in careful, childish handwriting:

> Dearest André,
> Lines 10 and 11 on page 494 of this book is my prayer for you always.
>
> Love, Norma Jeane

Lines 10 and 11 read:

> Divine love always has met and always will meet every human need . . . since to all mankind and in every hour, divine love supplies all good.

According to Norma Jeane herself, in her story of breaking into Hollywood, she firmly avoided giving herself to all mankind. Her sad tale went: "Now I was a sort of 'child widow.' I looked at the streets with lonely eyes. I had no relatives to visit or chums to go places with. . . . There were always men willing to help a girl be less lonely. They said 'Hi, baby,' when you passed. When you didn't turn to look at them they sneered, 'Stuck up, eh?' I never answered them.''

When she talked to Ben Hecht, Marilyn indicated that she lived a chaste life in 1946. She was broke that year, though, and there may have been some love that was less than divine. Later, while under the tutelage of drama teacher Lee Strasberg, she offered the private admission that in the early days in Hollywood she had been a call girl. Strasberg, who often sought out frank verbal biographies from would-be pupils, said this emerged during their first serious discussion.

According to Strasberg, talking years later to his biographer, "She told me she was the one summoned if anyone needed a beautiful girl for a convention." He said that later she felt "her call-girl background worked against her." Strasberg's biographer, Cindy Adams, has no doubt of his meaning. "He said it three times, on tape," she recalls. "And he meant exactly that—she was a call girl. It was exactly what he knew to be a fact from his pupil's own lips."

Lena Pepitone, Marilyn's New York maid from 1957 till her death, says the actress confided in her on many matters. She says Marilyn told her how, as Norma Jeane, she had once literally sold herself to a man shortly before the end of her marriage to Dougherty. The man, middle-aged, had persuaded a tipsy Norma Jeane, for fifteen dollars, to go to his hotel room. At first he merely asked to see her naked, then he demanded more. Norma Jeane wanted to run out, but changed her mind because, she supposedly told her maid, "Then I thought about it. It didn't really bother me that much. So what was the difference?" She did insist that the man use a contraceptive. According to Pepitone, there would be other visits to the same bar, other men, and more pocket money for the drifting Norma Jeane.

The real-life sexuality of the world's sex symbol can be glimpsed through a mass of recollection, sometimes droll, more often sad.

Philippe Halsman, the distinguished *Life* photographer, took many pictures of Marilyn over the years. The first session was in 1949, when she was twenty-three. Marilyn was one of eight girls selected to act out four situations: a confrontation with a frightening monster, the taste of a delicious drink, the hilarity of a really good joke, and being in the embrace of a wonderful lover. Marilyn, he recalled later, performed well only the part of the girl in the lover's embrace.

Halsman would say years later, "When she faced a man she didn't know, she felt safe and secure only when she knew the man desired her; so everything in her life was geared to provoke this feeling. Her talent in this respect was very great. I remember my experience in her tiny apartment with my assistant and the *Life* researcher. Each of us felt that if the other two would leave, something incredible would happen."

On one occasion Halsman had Marilyn jump repeatedly into the air for his camera. He said later, "I was greatly surprised to see the embodiment of sex appeal jump like a small, immature girl. I said to her, 'Will you jump again? I'm not sure you expressed your character the first time.' 'You mean you can read my character from my jump?' she asked. 'Of course,' I replied. She then looked at me with big, frightened eyes and trembled and wouldn't jump any more."

Halsman is the only man on record who asked Marilyn the question that may hold part of the explanation of Norma Jeane's perennial fear. "Tell me," he inquired, "how old were you when you first had sex?"

"Seven," Marilyn responded.

"Mon Dieu!" cried Halsman, lowering the camera. "How old was the man?"

The reply came in the famous whisper, with a catch of breath: "Younger."

This was Marilyn's only jest about childhood sex. Normally her theme was different—and grim. She claimed early on that she had been sexually molested as a child, and it was a theme she harped on obsessively throughout her life. Was it a real event?

The first firmly recorded reference to the violation of Norma Jeane seems to have been in 1947, when she offered it to Lloyd Shearer, a journalist who interviewed her at the request of the Twentieth Century-Fox publicity office. He listened to a horrific package story, and his reaction was this: "She confided to us over lunch that she had been assaulted by one of her guardians, raped by a policeman, and attacked by a sailor. She seemed to me then to live in a fantasy world, to be entangled in the process of invention, and to be completely absorbed in her own sexuality." Shearer was so skeptical that he decided to write nothing about Marilyn.

The childhood assault, as she told it herself in 1954, took this form: "I was almost nine, and I lived with a family that rented a room to a man named Kimmel. He was a stern-looking man, and everybody respected him and called him Mr. Kimmel. I was passing his room when his door opened and he said quietly, 'Please come in here, Norma. . . .' He smiled at me and turned the key in the lock. 'Now you can't get out,' he said, as if we were playing a game. I stood staring at him. I was frightened, but I didn't dare yell. . . . When he put his arms around me I kicked and fought as hard as I could, but I didn't make any sound. He was stronger than I was and wouldn't let me go. He kept whispering to me to be a good girl. When he unlocked the door and let me out, I ran to tell my 'aunt' what Mr. Kimmel had done. 'I want to tell you something,' I stammered, 'about Mr. Kimmel. He—he—' "

By Norma Jeane's account her current foster parent told her, "Don't you dare say anything against Mr. Kimmel. Mr. Kimmel's a fine man. He's my star boarder!" Kimmel later told Norma Jeane, she said, to go buy some ice cream.

Marilyn Monroe, the actress, told this story over and over again—to reporters, to lovers, to anyone who would listen. Peggy Feury, who today runs The Loft acting studio in Los Angeles, recalls meeting Marilyn at a New York party shortly before her death in 1962. She was still rambling on interminably about the assault.

Was the story true, or was it a perennial, self-serving fantasy designed to get sympathy? Not long before her death, during an interview with journalist Jaik Rosenstein, Marilyn said, "It did happen. But I didn't run out of the room crying or screaming. . . . I knew it was wrong, but to tell the truth I think I was more curious than anything else. . . . Nobody ever told me about sex, and frankly, I never did think it was all that important or that it was wrong."

Dr. Ralph Greenson, the Hollywood psychiatrist who treated and befriended Marilyn in her last years, accepted the fact that she had a "terrible, terrible background." However, he also referred to her "mistreatment fantasy." Delusions and hallucinations are a feature of schizophrenic disorders. Dr. Ruth Bruun, a New York psychiatrist who considered Marilyn's family history for this book, perceives indications of schizophrenia in the surviving information about her mother and grandmother.

Dr. Greenson was the only one of Marilyn's psychiatrists whose opinions have partially survived. In correspondence with a colleague, obtained exclusively for this book, he expressed his concern about Marilyn's "tendency to paranoid reactions." At first he thought perhaps, that rather than being schizophrenic, her paranoid tendencies were "more masochistic, and an acting out of the orphan-girl rejections . . . the tendency towards severe depressive reactions, and the impulsive defenses against this, seem to me to be central." In the end, after her death, Greenson would describe Marilyn as a woman with "extremely weak psychological structures. . . . ego weakness, and certain psychotic manifestations, including those of schizophrenia."

The story of sexual assault in childhood is not the only episode hinting at fantasy, or at least self-serving exaggeration. First husband Jim Dougherty recalls a night when, after a minor tiff during the evening, Norma Jeane woke him in the middle of the night. She said she had been for a walk, wearing only a nightgown. Dougherty remembers: "I felt her embracing me with tears streaming down her face as she cried, 'There's a man after me! There's a man after me!' I held her a few moments and then told her, 'Honey, you're having a nightmare.' 'No!' she insisted, 'I'm awake. I was going to leave home. And I walked down the street and a man chased me home.' "

Professional controversy still whirls around Sigmund Freud's so-called seduction theory, which proposed that the sexual abuse of children by adults was a primary cause of neurosis. Freud himself is said to have abandoned the theory later, shifting to the view that most patients' claims of sexual abuse are fantasy rather than fact. He wrote in 1900: "I must, after all, take an interest in *reality* in sexuality, which one learns about only with great difficulty."

Real or imagined, Norma Jeane would never put her childhood story behind her. Back in the world of the flesh, what of the less violent side of Norma Jeane's sex life?

She told a story of a happier episode that supposedly occurred at the age of eight, the same year as Mr. Kimmel's assault. "I fell in love with a boy named George. . . . We used to hide in the grass together until he got frightened and jumped up and ran away. What we did in the grass never frightened me. I knew it was wrong or I wouldn't have hidden, but I didn't know *what* was wrong. At night I lay awake and tried to figure out what sex was and what love was. I wanted to ask a thousand questions but there was no one to ask."

Norma Jeane said she fought off the boys till the age of

sixteen and marriage to Jim Dougherty. "There were," she said for publication in 1954, "no thoughts of sex in my head." Within two years of that statement, in a long private talk with her New York hostess and close friend Amy Greene, Norma Jeane asserted that she had first slept with a boy while she was in high school. Norma Jeane had gone to Emerson Junior High School when she was eleven, and to Van Nuys High School when she was just fifteen, dropping out in less than a year to marry Jim Dougherty. If Norma Jeane was telling the truth, she thus became one of the 3 percent of American females of the forties who, as Kinsey would shortly reveal to a startled nation, lost their virginity before the age of sixteen, and one of the 50 percent who did so before marriage.

All this would be news to Jim Dougherty, who asserts, "She began our married life knowing nothing, but absolutely nothing about sex. But Mom had cautioned me before our wedding day and I knew I had to be careful that first night. . . . That delicate threshold had never been crossed before . . . not ever."

Norma Jeane would say later, "The first effect marriage had on me was to increase my lack of interest in sex. My husband either didn't mind this or wasn't aware of it. We were both too young to discuss such an embarrassing topic openly."

Jim Dougherty's version: "Norma Jeane loved sex. It was as natural to her as breakfast in the morning. There were never any problems with it. . . . Getting undressed unfailingly set us both a-tingle, and almost before the light was out we were locked together. . . . Sometimes she would tease me just a little, wearing only two small red bandannas when I got home from Lockheed. . . ."

Dougherty also told an interviewer: "She was something else. I couldn't even put my lunch box down when I came from work before she'd drag me upstairs." One might dismiss Dougherty's version as the predictable boast of Marilyn Monroe's first husband, but he has a supporting witness. Working beside Dougherty at the factory was the then unknown Robert Mitchum, who a few years later would play opposite a new star called Marilyn Monroe. He found Dougherty perennially cheerful, not least the morning he turned up with a photograph of his "old lady." It showed the teenage Norma Jeane standing by the garden gate in the nude. She was posed, Dougherty told Mitchum, as if waiting for him to come home.

Of the men who followed Dougherty in Marilyn's life, those who have talked paint a starkly different picture of her sexuality. They, and Marilyn herself in comments to psychiatrist Dr. Greenson, suggest a woman who found little satisfaction in sex. The change may have been caused by the dismal personal experiences that followed the marriage to Dougherty. Somewhere in that same period also lies the genesis of perhaps the saddest preoccupation in the life of Marilyn Monroe—childbearing.

Year after year as the fifties unwound, a vast public would wait and watch as Marilyn tried to have babies. As marriage followed marriage the headlines would tell of repeated gynecological surgery or miscarriage after miscarriage. Time after time, Marilyn would speak of her longing for children, would make a point of favoring children's charities and funds for orphans. At her funeral, instead of flowers, donations were directed to children's hospitals. A bequest Marilyn made to one of her psychiatrists now goes to a children's clinic in London. Yet, in its origins, even this side of Marilyn was a sad confusion.

Looking back at the age of twenty-eight, the former Norma Jeane would say of her first husband: "He never hurt or upset me, except on one subject. He wanted a baby. The thought of having a baby stood my hair on end. I could see it only as myself, another Norma Jeane in an orphanage. Something would happen to me. I couldn't explain this to Jim. After he fell asleep, I would lie awake crying. I didn't quite know who it was that cried, Mrs. Dougherty or the child she might have. It was neither. It was Norma Jeane, still alive, still alone, still wishing she were dead."

Jim Dougherty again tells a different tale. He says Norma Jeane was eager to have a baby as soon as they got married, and he talked her out of it. He also tells a hilarious tale of Norma Jeane experimenting with a brand-new diaphragm purchased at his insistence. She got the device in, then had to summon her husband to help get it out.

Norma Jeane quickly demonstrated that she could cope with children, looking after Dougherty's nephews for weeks at a time. She reveled in doing so. When Dougherty joined the Merchant Marine, he says, his wife became frantic, "begging me to make her pregnant so that she could have a piece of me, in case something happened." Years later, as Marilyn, Norma Jeane would tell a friend, actress Jeanne Carmen, how much she had yearned for children by her first husband.

Yet during their four-year marriage, things turned around. In the final months it was Dougherty who was begging Norma Jeane to have children. She now refused, declaring that she dreaded the possibility of losing her figure. There had been a drastic change in Norma Jeane's mind, and two fragments of information—both sourced to Norma Jeane—may account for the turmoil.

Marilyn Monroe died childless, by every public account. In 1979 a book by her former maid, Lena Pepitone, contained an assertion that the teenage Norma Jeane had given birth to a child. Few noticed this claim and students of Marilyn suspected Pepitone was merely seeking headlines. Research for this book, however, turned up two other witnesses who said Marilyn spoke to them of having borne a child.

According to Pepitone, Marilyn told her story about being molested, but added that the man involved actually had intercourse with her. She became pregnant, but concealed the fact from her guardian for several months. When she did own up to the pregnancy, her guardian saw to it that she had medical attention and arranged for the child to be born in a hospital. Pepitone quotes Marilyn as saying, "I had the baby . . . my baby. I was so scared, but it was wonderful. It was a little boy. I hugged him and kissed him. I just kept touching him. I couldn't believe this was my baby. . . . But when it was time to leave, the doctor and a nurse came in with Grace [Grace McKee, her guardian]. They all looked real strange and said they'd be taking the baby. . . . I begged them, 'Don't take my baby. . . .' They took my baby from me . . . and I never saw him again."

In an interview in 1984 Pepitone said that Marilyn, on one occasion, said she had never learned what happened to the child; on another she said she did know and sent regular payments to the California couple who had reared the boy. Pepitone had the impression that the child had been born when Marilyn was about fourteen or fifteen.

Amy Greene, with whom Marilyn lived in 1955, also clearly recalls her saying she gave birth in her teens, let the baby go for adoption, and still felt guilty about it. Former actress Jeanne Carmen, who met Marilyn in the same period as Amy Greene, recalls a similar story with variation—the baby was born, Marilyn told Carmen, after the marriage to Dougherty and before the real Hollywood breakthrough, when Marilyn was about twenty-one. Carmen says, "Marilyn was enormously troubled over this. In one breath she would say,

'There's no God'; then, 'Am I going to be punished for giving the baby away?' Desperation was very near the surface."

"Marilyn," says Amy Greene, "used to fabricate a great deal, especially when she wanted to shock, to get a reaction." This may have been the fantasy of a woman who, by the time she was telling the story, feared she would never bear children.

Peter Leonardi, Marilyn's hairdresser and secretary in the mid-fifties, has said she had a "tube-tying" operation in her starlet days, on the advice of an agent who said pregnancy would spell professional failure. Robert Slatzer, who knew Marilyn for most of her adult life, says she later submitted to surgery to have the operation reversed. On top of that, persistent reports from friends suggest Marilyn had numerous abortions. Amy Greene, perhaps the most reliable of those sources, says Marilyn made the horrendous admission that she had had twelve abortions, some of them back-street butcheries dating back to her earliest days in Hollywood. "And then," says Amy Greene with a sigh, "she was surprised when she had trouble having babies. . . ."

Marilyn's poor battlefield of a womb had been a torment since adolescence, even before those surgical invasions. First husband Dougherty says, "Norma Jeane had so much trouble during her menstrual periods, the pain would just about knock her out."

Sometimes, in her earliest starlet days, period pain would cause Marilyn to stop her car with a screech of brakes, jump out, and crouch on the ground in agony. Maurice Zolotow, her early biographer, once penetrated her studio dressing room and noted no less than fourteen boxes of pills. Almost all were painkillers prescribed for menstrual cramps.

Henry Rosenfeld, the wealthy New York dress manufacturer, knew Marilyn from early in her career till her death. "She wanted a baby so much," Rosenfeld remembered, "that she'd convince herself of it every two or three months. She'd gain, maybe fourteen or fifteen pounds. She was forever having false pregnancies."

Marilyn was to tell writer Ben Hecht of her dream of having a daughter. "She won't be any Norma Jeane," she enthused. "And I know how I'll bring her up—without lies. No lies about there being a Santa Claus or about the world being full of noble and honorable people all eager to help each other and do good to each other."

There was something else Marilyn told Ben Hecht about

the world of Norma Jeane. Before she turned nineteen, Marilyn said, she had tried to commit suicide. She had done it twice—once by leaving the gas on, once by swallowing sleeping pills. When Ben Hecht came to write her story, he left out that detail.

On June 1, 1946, when she turned twenty, Norma Jeane had only her dreams. She spent her birthday in a rented room in Las Vegas, fulfilling residence qualifications for a quick divorce from Jim Dougherty. It was hot, and she was suffering from an unromantic case of trench mouth.

Two months later, in Los Angeles, Dougherty made one of his last visits to see Norma Jeane—to deliver his part of the divorce documents. In their last conversation she had shown no sign of a longing for children. On the contrary, she talked only of her urgent desire to become an actress, and no studio, she said, would spend money training a married woman who might get pregnant.

Now, when Norma Jeane opened the door to Dougherty, she looked radiant, and not because he had finally agreed to go along with the divorce. Earlier that week, without the help of divorce papers, she had obtained what she wanted most, the promise of a contract as a stock player at Twentieth Century-Fox.

When Norma Jeane told Dougherty about the contract she added a detail. The studio had given her a new name. What did Jim think of it? "Beautiful," he replied politely, "just beautiful." Then he left.*

The name was Marilyn Monroe.

---

* Dougherty remarried, and became a policeman. Years later he trained the police unit known as the SWAT team, which made headlines in the fiery finale to the kidnapping of Patty Hearst. Today he is a County Commissioner in Sabattus, Maine.

4

A MONTH BEFORE MARILYN got her big break, Robert Slatzer, a budding magazine writer from Ohio with a passion for show business, had been cooling his heels in the lobby of the old Twentieth Century-Fox studios on Pico Boulevard. He was reading a book of poems, Walt Whitman's *Leaves of Grass*, and waiting to interview some minor star of the day. Slatzer, then nineteen, remembers today that "this girl came pushing herself in through the big doors, carrying a big scrapbook. She caught her heel or something and the pictures fell all over the floor. I went to her rescue, and I'm glad to say there was only one place for her to sit down and wait—next to me. She said her name was Norma Jeane Mortensen. She was really interested in my poetry, and I said I might be able to write a story about her. We ended up making a date for that same evening."

That night Bob Slatzer borrowed a battered 1938 Studebaker and made his way to Nebraska Avenue to pick up Norma Jeane. They drove along the Pacific Coast Highway and ate dinner by the ocean. Malibu was still a lovely place in those days, not the clapboard and concrete jumble of 1985. Later they walked on the beach and paddled in the surf. Slatzer says he felt shy, shyer than Norma Jeane. He thinks, though he cannot swear to it, that they made love for the first time that very night. When they drove home, Norma Jeane asked him to leave her at the corner rather than take her to the front door.

"I think we had an instant affection towards each other," says Slatzer, as though a man need apologize for having slept with Marilyn Monroe. "For me there was something magic about her, different from the other girls the talent men at the studio would fix you up with. I don't know, I think I can say I loved her from the first time I saw her."

As the years passed and Marilyn became the love of other men and an international byword, Robert Slatzer would stay in love with the girl who dropped her modeling portfolio in the lobby of Twentieth Century-Fox.* In the summer of 1946 he had frequent dates with her, and so did other young men.

By 1984, sixty-year-old Tommy Zahn, a lieutenant in charge of a Los Angeles County rescue boat, had become a legendary figure on the beaches of California. In 1946, they say, he looked like Tab Hunter after a weight-lifting course. He was a lifeguard in those days, and he thought he might end up as an actor. The acting dream nearly came true, because he had met a teenager named Darrylin Zanuck on Muscle Beach. Darrylin fancied Tommy from afar, then introduced him to her father, Darryl Zanuck, chief of production at Twentieth Century-Fox. Zanuck signed Zahn as a contract player, and the beach boy went to the studio to learn to act, sing, and dance. So it was, in the late summer of 1946, that Tommy Zahn met an aspiring actress who became one of his modest stable of girls for the next year. His memories of Norma Jeane are fond, and perhaps unique.

"She was in prime condition," says Tommy Zahn, "tremendously fit. I used to take her surfing up at Malibu—tandem surfing, you know, two riders on the same surfboard. I'd take her later, in the dead of winter when it was cold, and it didn't faze her in the least; she'd lay in the cold water, waiting for the waves. She was really good in the water, very robust, so healthy, a really fine attitude towards life. I was twenty-two when I met her, and I guess she was twenty. Gosh, I really liked her."

While two men played on the beach with Norma Jeane, another lay injured in the hospital, ogling her photograph. Magazines like *Titter* and *Laff* were not the sort of thing you let your mother know you were reading, not that they showed much more than long legs in short shorts and pert breasts inside sweaters a size too small. By 1946 Howard Hughes, the actress collector, did not have to worry about his mother,

---

* Robert Slatzer is still in love with the memory of the girl on the beach. He has, indeed, become best known for a controversial book in which he not only claims a relationship with Marilyn that lasted till she died, but includes as well the assertion that he briefly married her six years after they met—a madcap three-day folly celebrated on the Mexican border. That claim, which will be dealt with later, aroused skepticism. Slatzer's story, however, remained consistent throughout a series of intensive interviews, and a number of compelling witnesses corroborate the closeness of his relationship with Marilyn.

and he was in the hospital following a serious flying accident. He sent out for girlie magazines by the score, partly because he enjoyed them and partly because he owned RKO Radio Pictures.

On July 29, 1946, the gossip column in the *Los Angeles Times* carried the following squib: "Howard Hughes is on the mend. Picking up a magazine, he was attracted by the cover girl and promptly instructed an aide to sign her for pictures. She is Norma Jeane Dougherty, a model." In those twelve months Norma Jeane had decorated the cover of *Laff* magazine no less than four times under three different names, two variations on her married name and as Jean Norman. It would have been hard for Hughes not to notice, but for once he was slow off the mark.*

A Hughes aide did indeed place a call to Norma Jeane's agent, who promptly used the opportunity to stoke up enthusiasm at another studio, Twentieth Century-Fox. Norma Jeane cut out the clipping from the *Los Angeles Times* and excitedly showed it to friends. By that time, though, she had already made the vital connection.

The casting director at Fox was Ben Lyon, himself a star of the thirties, and in Britain celebrated for his radio series "Life with the Lyons." Years earlier it had been Lyon who spotted the potential of Jean Harlow. Now it was he who agreed to see Norma Jeane. He recalled later that "she had a good face. You can tell with some faces—the way the flesh sits on the bones, the planes and angles—that they'll photograph well. . . . In addition, there was the way she moved."

Two days later a movie camera turned its glass eye on Norma Jeane for the first time. Dressed in a sequined gown, teetering on high heels, she obeyed instructions to "walk across the set. Sit down. Light a cigarette. Put it out. Go upstage. Cross. Look out a window. Sit down. Come downstage and exit."

The cameraman, Leon Shamroy, would one day photograph Marilyn in *There's No Business Like Show Business*. Now, as he looked at the rushes, he got a cold chill. "This girl," he was to say, "had something I hadn't seen since

---

* According to her acting coach, Natasha Lytess, Marilyn once mentioned that she was having a brief fling with Hughes. Actress Terry Moore, who married Hughes, says he gave Marilyn a piece of jewelry—a pin. Given that the donor was Howard Hughes, Marilyn was surprised to discover it was "only" worth $500, 1950's value.

silent pictures. She had a kind of fantastic beauty like Gloria Swanson . . . she got sex on a piece of film like Jean Harlow. . . . She was showing us she could sell emotions in pictures.''

Within a week Darryl Zanuck himself had seen the footage, enthused, and agreed that Norma Jeane Dougherty should be signed as a contract player, at seventy-five dollars a week, to be reviewed in six months. Her weekly pay would then probably go up to $100. Norma Jeane rushed home with the news, announcing, ''It's the finest studio in the world. . . . The people are wonderful, and I'm going to be in a movie. It'll be a small part. But once I'm on the screen. . . .''

Now Norma Jeane could shed not only her previous life, but also her name. Tommy Zahn, the sometime lifeguard she joined in the ranks of Fox contract hopefuls, reveals that the studio christening got off to a false start. ''Ben Lyon,'' says Zahn, ''could not abide her real name, so he changed it to Carole Lind. They tried that for a while, but it didn't sound right; it was a rather obvious composite of an opera singer and a dead actress.''

Ben Lyon and his actress wife, Bebe Daniels, who quickly became fond of Norma Jeane, decided they could do better. They invited Norma Jeane to their Malibu beachhouse to swap ideas. Lyon recalled, ''I finally said to her, 'I know who you are. You're Marilyn!' I told her that once there was a lovely actress named Marilyn Miller and that she reminded me of her. 'But what about the last name?' Marilyn said, 'My grandmother's name was Monroe and I'd like to keep that.' I said, 'Great! That's got a nice flow, and two M's should be lucky.' That's how she got her name.'' Marilyn was still doing modeling jobs, but her heart was at the studio. Tommy Zahn recalls that everyone worked hard, and nobody more so than her.

Zahn would pick up Marilyn early in the morning and the two of them would spend their weekdays learning to act, sing, and dance. The dancing did not come easy to either of them. On Saturdays all the stock players would meet at the studio. Some would do pantomime or charades, and others would guess exactly what they were portraying. Zahn would devise a pantomime, and he and a rather shy Marilyn would perform as a couple.

There were no real parts to play yet, but Marilyn busied herself paving the way. She made sure the publicity men knew who she was, and she courted the reporters permanently based at the studio. One of them, Ralph Casey Shawhan, remembers that often, when the artists' entrance was closed, Marilyn would whistle to the press men on the third floor to come down and let her in. Shawhan can still see her peering up at the window, dressed in "cut-off jeans frayed at the bottom, before anyone else was wearing them."

Marilyn, giggling in the cold, posed for still shots at the beach in mid-November. The journalists liked her, and the Press Club gave her a special award. None of this had anything to do with movies, but Marilyn understood early on the importance of a good press.

Sometime during the first year a diminutive figure, five feet tall, shoes scuffed and socks down round his ankles, was ambling through the Fox administration building. Sidney Skolsky, the legendary *New York Post* writer whose syndicated column on Hollywood could change careers, was headed for the water fountain. He was delayed, though less than irritated, by a shapely behind bent interminably over the fountain. He and the owner of the behind made jokes to each other about the capacity of camels, and ended up having a long conversation. Marilyn poured out the woeful tale of her childhood, and gained a new and influential friend. Except for an interruption during her New York years, Skolsky would remain Marilyn's confidant till she died.

Skolsky has observed, "It was clear that Marilyn was prepared to work hard to improve herself. She wanted to be an actress and a movie star. I knew nothing would stop her. The drive and determination and need inside Marilyn could not be halted."

"My illusions didn't have anything to do with being a fine actress," Marilyn would say a few years later. "I knew how third-rate I was. I could actually feel my lack of talent, as if it were cheap clothes I was wearing inside. But, my God, how I wanted to learn! To change, to improve! I didn't want anything else. Not men, not money, not love, but the ability to act."

In early 1947, Marilyn, at twenty-one, moved across a sound stage at last, as one of a dozen extras in *Scudda Hoo! Scudda Hay!*, a movie about a farmer and his team of mules. Much of Marilyn's part ended up on the cutting-room floor, but one spoken line—fittingly, the one word "Hello!"—survived, along with a brief long shot in which she was seen paddling a canoe.

Meanwhile the studio had been paying for Marilyn to

attend classes at the Actors' Lab, a drama school off Sunset Boulevard in Hollywood. "She came to classes on time and did all her assignments conscientiously," said Mrs. Morris Carnovsky, who ran the school with her husband, "but I never would have predicted she would be a success." To Mrs. Carnovsky, Marilyn seemed very young, self-conscious, and shy. It was at this point that Marilyn suffered a massive setback. A year into her contract, Fox decided to drop her.

The firing of Marilyn has never been explained. Ben Lyon, her first studio benefactor, was dumbfounded. Marilyn desperately wandered the studio corridors till she found the office of the great man himself, Darryl Zanuck. Whenever she tried to see him, Zanuck was "out of town." Tommy Zahn, Marilyn's lifeguard boyfriend, thinks he knows what happened, not least because he was fired at the same time. Zahn believes that he was only hired in the first place because Zanuck wished to groom him for marriage to one of his daughters. Zahn's dalliance with Marilyn was noted and disapproved from on high, and both were fired. Zahn shipped out to Honolulu. Marilyn was adrift, professionally and emotionally.

She did not give up. Living now in a succession of furnished rooms, apparently alone or sharing with other girls, Marilyn continued at the Actors' Lab. She tried to pay her way with the proceeds from new modeling assignments, and perhaps with the call-girl sideline she would later tell Lee Strasberg about.

One modeling job was arranged by Bill Burnside, a forty-three-year-old Scot who represented the J. Arthur Rank Organization in Hollywood. She was interested in him, not least because he knew her idol, Clark Gable, whose photograph accompanied her everywhere. Now that Marilyn was out of work, Burnside tried to help. He took her to pose for Paul Hesse, a top commercial photographer. Hesse said simply, "Darling, you're too fat," and Marilyn burst into tears. Burnside salvaged the moment by taking pictures himself, and the two became close.

The late Bill Burnside was to recall, "She was very aware of how she affected men. If I took her to a restaurant, however elegant, the waiters were ready to jump at her bidding. She had it there all right, the star quality, at the age of twenty-one. . . . Physically, she was wary of me for the first months of our knowing each other." In the end there was a sporadic affair, lasting for months. Burnside kept one of the photographs he took, inscribed, "Anything worth having is worth waiting for. Love, Marilyn."

"I think what she wanted from me was my education," said Burnside. "She was into Shelley and Keats, as well as some lighter stuff. She knew that she needed knowledge." During this workless period, Marilyn plunged into the acquisition of "Culture." In school, which she had quit when she was fifteen, her work habits had been generally graded as only "Acceptable"; but she had been rated "Good" in her English classes. Now, seeking to broaden her mind—partly to help in her career, partly because she was thirsty for information—she began to build up a considerable library.

Marilyn had a lifetime interest in the occult, and she often visited astrologers and psychics. She retained a sense of proportion, however, and dismissed one famous astrologer, Carroll Righter, in a way that demonstrated her priorities. Righter asked her, "Did you know you were born under the same sign [Gemini] as Rosalind Russell, Judy Garland, and Rosemary Clooney?" Marilyn looked him straight in the eye and replied, "I know nothing of these people. I was born under the same sign as Ralph Waldo Emerson, Queen Victoria, and Walt Whitman."

The sign of Gemini, Marilyn said, stood for intellect. Her search for knowledge was to become a lifetime preoccupation, one many would mock as pretentious posturing. It was not. Marilyn devoured Thomas Wolfe, James Joyce, poetry (mostly romantic), biographies, and history books.

Abraham Lincoln became Marilyn's special hero. (She would later strike up a friendship with Lincoln's biographer, Carl Sandburg.) Lincoln's portrait would follow her from home to home till the end of her life, and his Gettysburg Address usually hung nearby. It was her first love affair with a President of the United States.

From the Actors' Lab, Marilyn caught more than a whiff of left-wing politics; the Carnovskys, her teachers, would be labeled communists during congressional investigations into "Un-American Activity" in the fifties. Marilyn never threw herself into political activity, but she thought of herself as working class and paid homage to the common man. In her last interview, in 1962, she would say, "I want to say that the people—if I am a star—the people made me a star, no studio, no person, but the people did."

Meanwhile, as she continued to pose for pinup pictures, Marilyn sought to elevate even that. As early as 1947 photographer Earl Theisen noticed she owned a book called *De Humani Corporis Fabrica*, a learned study of the human anatomy by the sixteenth-century scholar, Andreas Vesalius. It was marked up in detail, and Marilyn explained that she was studying the bone structure of the body. Paintings from the book, by Jan Stephan van Kalkar, of the Titan School, would long decorate the walls of her poorly furnished rooms, and even near the end of her life when she was in the grip of drugs, Marilyn would instruct young friends with an encyclopedic knowledge of the human bone structure. The athletic Tommy Zahn had admired how she kept herself in shape, lifting weights and running in the mornings, thirty years before the jogging craze brought people out in the thousands to puff along the grass verges through the smog of Los Angeles.

Marilyn would never be poorer than she was at this time. She skimped on meals, when men were not buying them for her, to continue paying for acting lessons. She spent a good deal of time drinking coffee at Schwab's drugstore on Sunset Boulevard, which was the working headquarters of her journalist friend, Sidney Skolsky. Skolsky helped Marilyn open a charge account at a bookshop, and that helped finance the culture binge.

The affair with Bill Burnside withered when he went on an extended trip to Latin America. On his return she would give him a poem:

> I could have loved you once
> and even said it
> But you went away,
> A long way away.
> When you came back it was too late
> And love was a forgotten word.
> Remember?

It may have been one of the young men Marilyn met at Schwab's who made it hard to wait for Bill Burnside. The drugstore was full of out-of-work actors, and one of them was called Charlie Chaplin. To him, too, Marilyn gave a little of herself—for a while.

5

IN THE TWENTIES, *the* Charlie Chaplin had seduced and briefly married a fifteen-year-old girl named Lita Grey. She bore him two sons, a boy who was given no name for the first year of his life, and Sydney, born a year later. Lita, it is said, wanted to call her firstborn Charlie, but the great Charles was leery of having an actor son bearing the same name. After his parents' divorce, however, Charlie he became. In 1947 he was twenty-one, the same age as Marilyn. He was a would-be actor just as his father had feared, and struggling to make ends meet.

In spite of his father's immense wealth, young Charlie had been spurned, and he eked out a small allowance to keep himself and his grandmother while his mother toured the country as a nightclub singer. When she came home that year, Charlie brought his girl of the moment to lunch. It was Marilyn Monroe, whom Lita thought "really naive, not at all sophisticated, like a little country girl. She was way heavier then; she hadn't been thinned down and glamorized yet. Charlie was smitten with her, though."

Charlie stayed enamored for many months, and at Christmas he found the cash to buy Marilyn a number of stylish dresses. According to Arthur James, long a close friend of Chaplin, Marilyn would stay the night with Charlie. She would cram into a single bed with him, while brother Sydney slept in his bed in the same room. The romance ended one day when Charlie came home to find Marilyn in the wrong bunk—Sydney's. They remained good friends, though, and fifteen years later Marilyn would make some of her last despairing calls to Chaplin and James. Chaplin would not long survive her. He failed as an actor, was a lifelong heavy drinker, and was found dying in his bathroom in 1968.

There was a sad legacy of the affair with Chaplin. According to Arthur James, Marilyn became pregnant at some time in the winter of 1947 and had one of her many early abortions.

36

On and off, through this period of professional vacuum, Marilyn was still seeing Robert Slatzer, the young magazine writer from Ohio. Slatzer had a friend in town in Will Fowler, writer and newspaperman son of John Barrymore's biographer, Gene Fowler. Fowler's account of an evening at Marilyn's apartment suggests that, whatever her shyness in some situations, she was now using her body as a banner to amuse male friends.

"She was stoned," Fowler recalls. "She just took off her clothes. She liked to show her body off to men. She used to do anything that men would ask her, really just as a favor. She just walked around stoned and naked. It was her suggestion as much as ours, not even a sexual thing as far as that evening was concerned."

Compulsive nudity is too widely reported about Marilyn to be the boast of a chance acquaintance. Years later, in New York, she would give a naked interview to publicist Joe Wohlander. Mrs. Ben Bodne, wife of the owner of the Algonquin Hotel, confirms that she once met Marilyn on Fifth Avenue wearing a new mink coat. When she asked what Marilyn was wearing with it the actress replied, "Nothing," and snapped the coat open to prove it. From husband Jim Dougherty onward, innumerable witnesses confirm the legend that Marilyn disliked underwear, and loathed wearing panties.

Speaking of her childhood, Marilyn herself told an interviewer: "The wish for attention had something to do, I think, with my trouble in church on Sundays. No sooner was I in the pew with the organ playing and everybody singing a hymn than the impulse would come to me to take off all my clothes. I wanted desperately to stand up naked for God and everyone else to see. I had to clench my teeth and sit on my hands to keep myself from undressing. . . . I even had dreams about it. In the dreams I entered the church wearing a hoop skirt with nothing under it. The people would be lying on their backs in the church aisle, and I would step over them, and they would look up at me."

By 1947, when she was parading naked in front of Robert Slatzer and Will Fowler, the twenty-one-year-old Marilyn had begun dabbling in the writings of Sigmund Freud. His *Interpretation of Dreams* suggested that the "nakedness dream" is very common, and that the dream of being naked in public indicates a real-life fear of being unmasked. Perhaps, in Marilyn, life's irony was that the struggle to step away from her orphan childhood became a circular struggle, in which her most trusty weapon was to evoke sympathy for past mistreatment. In the summer of 1947 Marilyn added a fresh story to the catalogue of woes.

One midnight, while she was living at a house in Burbank, Marilyn rushed out into the street dressed in a skimpy nightgown and screaming blue murder. By her own account, and in the end there really is only her account, she had awakened to find a man clambering through her bedroom window. She challenged the man, then ran for her life. Neighbors were roused and the police called. According to Marilyn, the prowler reappeared, while the police were at the scene, and turned out to be a policeman himself. Marilyn claimed that the police pressured her not to file charges against their colleague, so the matter was dropped. This story has been treated as fact by previous biographers.

The reader must decide what to make of Marilyn's multiple stories of sexual assault. There is the perennial account of childhood molestation or, if we accept her maid's account, full rape leading to pregnancy. There is a separate account by Marilyn of a violent embrace by her guardian's husband, one which made her feel "violated." And in 1947, at a time when few people who mattered were noticing Marilyn, she claimed the sexual assault by a policeman.

Was Marilyn a freak case in assault statistics? For this writer, the key may be her first husband's account of the night, years earlier, when he was wakened by Marilyn screaming that she had been out in the street in her nightgown, running from a man. Jim Dougherty had no doubt this was a dream, and her loyal friend, Sidney Skolsky, never really believed her account of childhood rape.

The story served Marilyn well, however, as did the 1947 tale of the wicked policeman.

In late 1947 actor John Carroll met Marilyn at a drive-in restaurant. She was carrying a bag containing a few belongings, and said she was about to hitchhike to San Francisco. She told Carroll she was depressed—sick of Hollywood and her failure to get proper work. Carroll said he would try to help. They met again when Marilyn made an appearance as a "starlet caddy" at golf tournament, and this time Marilyn also met Carroll's wife, Metro-Goldwyn-Mayer casting director, Lucille Ryman. Carroll, hearing the story of the midnight prowler, and not having failed to see the lusciousness of the victim, suggested to his wife that they help "this little girl."

Soon the Carrolls were paying Marilyn's rent and providing

her with pocket money. Next she moved into an apartment the Carrolls owned but were not using, and there followed a now-familiar episode: Marilyn said she had seen a boy on a ladder peeping into her room. She then moved in with the Carrolls altogether.

Soon Carroll was giving Marilyn jewelry, which mysteriously vanished. For her part, Marilyn astounded Lucille one day by informing her, "You don't love John. . . . I think I'm in love with him. . . . Would you divorce him so we can marry?" Astonishingly, there was no lasting acrimony. The relationship brought Marilyn a personal management contract with the Carrolls, and Lucille would one day be instrumental in Marilyn's most important breakthrough in movies, her part in John Huston's *Asphalt Jungle*.

"Hollywood's a place where they'll pay you a thousand dollars for a kiss and fifty cents for your soul. I know, because I turned down the first offer often enough and my soul isn't for sale. Men who tried to proposition me made me sick. I didn't accept. . . ."

That was Marilyn's public line when she talked to writer Ben Hecht, in the first flush of success. She told a detailed story of how she foiled the advances of a casting-couch shark who lured her to his office at the Goldwyn studio. Tommy Zahn, Marilyn's old boyfriend, remembers that she could indeed be selective. Randolph Churchill, visiting California from England, had invited Marilyn to visit him in an otherwise empty beach house "to discuss a deal."

"I think she knew he had other things in mind," says Zahn, "and she asked me along as protection."

Cynics, however, have suggested that a real chance of advancement in movies would often buy Marilyn's body. The cynics, it seems, were right.

Two years before she died, in a conversation with writer Jaik Rosenstein, Marilyn said, "When I started modeling, it was like part of the job. All the girls did. They weren't shooting all those sexy pictures just to sell peanut butter in an ad, or get a layout in some picture magazine. They wanted to sample the merchandise, and if you didn't go along, there were twenty-five girls who would. It wasn't any big dramatic tragedy. Nobody ever got cancer from sex."

As for Hollywood, Marilyn told Rosenstein, "You know that when a producer calls an actress into his office to discuss a script that isn't all he has in mind. And a part in a picture, or any kind of a little stock contract is the most important thing in the world to the girl, more than eating. She can go hungry, and she might have to sleep in her car, but she doesn't mind that a bit—if she can only get the part. I know, because I've done both, lots of times. And I've slept with producers. I'd be a liar if I said I didn't. . . .''

By the time she said that, Marilyn had known Rosenstein for years. She trusted him not to write about it at the time, and he did not. Today, however, it is clear that Marilyn made judicious use of her favors. A key beneficiary, reportedly, was the man who got Marilyn that vital first contract at Fox—Ben Lyon. According to writer Sheilah Graham, Lyon had been sleeping with Marilyn and promising to further her career. When nothing materialized, and Marilyn began badgering him, Lyon called the casting director who worked for Sol Wurtzel, a B-movie producer of the time. According to the casting director, Wurtzel obliged by giving Marilyn a small part in *Dangerous Years,* a 1947 movie about juvenile delinquents which he was producing. Marilyn, playing a waitress in a café used by a teenage gang, had a couple of lines.

There has long been speculation about Marilyn's relations with Joseph Schenck, the seventy-year-old potentate of Twentieth Century-Fox. He was one of the founding fathers of the studio, which had been formed a dozen years earlier in a merger between Fox and Twentieth Century Pictures, the company he owned with his brother and Darryl Zanuck. He was a weathered bear of a man, aging but active, a *bon vivant* who rightly saw himself as one of Hollywood's grand old men.

Schenck had a shrewd eye for potential stars and a vast appreciation of beautiful women. He gathered them around him, to quote one writer, ''the way certain men prize fine stallions.'' By late 1947 the eye of this connoisseur had lit upon two such beauties, Marilyn Monroe and Marion Marshall, who would later become the wife of Robert Wagner.

Marion Wagner had met Marilyn when both were applying for a job modeling bathing suits. She recalls, ''Marilyn was the most spectacular girl I ever met, not particularly beautiful, but she radiated a special dynamism. I remember, when I first saw her, she arrived late as usual, after all the other girls. I'm sitting with all these very sophisticated models, dressed in silks, with the gloves and the hat and all that, and Marilyn came in a little scoop-necked gingham sundress, her hair unbleached and unstraightened. When she walked in, it was like the room stopped, and everyone in the room knew she was going to get the job, and she did.''

Marion Wagner's is one of the best observed and most compassionate views of the early Marilyn, and she well remembers the evenings they shared at Joe Schenck's house off Sunset Boulevard. A limousine would bring the girls, together or separately, to the elegant Mediterranean-style mansion. There would be cocktails, dinner, then perhaps a private showing of a movie in the old man's personal projection room. Joe had a passion for cards, and Wagner recalls that ''he used to get a kick out of backing us when we played gin rummy against his male pals, and if we won it pleased him. He liked both of us very much. . . . He was like a father figure to me, a father confessor, a very wise, lovely old man. When the evening was over, I would simply be taken home in the limousine, and so far as I know it was the same for Marilyn.''

In March 1948 Marilyn was given a six-month contract at Columbia Pictures. As at Fox, she was to be paid $75 a week. There are varying accounts of how it came about, but Jonie Taps, then executive assistant to Harry Cohn, head of Columbia, offers this personal recollection.

''I got a call from Joe Schenck. He said, 'I'm indebted to her, and if you can give her twenty-six weeks, I'd appreciate it.' I went to see Harry Cohn, and he said, 'Well if he needs it that bad, give it to him. Put the girl on.' ''

Marion Wagner says, ''Whatever she did, I don't think it was into bed every night. I think it was a tasteful relationship, that was my impression.'' Marilyn herself, asked straight out by a writer, flatly denied ever having had sex with Joseph Schenck.

Veteran Hollywood columnist James Bacon, however, has fueled the gossip in a highly specific way. He has written, and told me in 1983, an earthy account of the way he learned of services rendered to Schenck. Bacon says he met Marilyn in 1948, during her Columbia contract. They were introduced by press agent Milton Stein, and Bacon says his first thought was, ''Holy God! She's so exciting.'' He went on: ''There was something about this girl. The moment you met her you knew she was going to make it.''

As a male, Bacon had other reactions, and he made sure he saw Marilyn again. After a third meeting Bacon offered to drive her home to the Studio Club, a hotel for aspiring young actresses, where she had been living. According to Bacon,

Marilyn asked him to drive instead to Joe Schenck's property where, she explained, she was living in the guesthouse.

Bacon says Marilyn made it clear she was one of the girls who looked after Schenck's failing sexual needs. She had him in stitches, saying the old man could manage only an occasional brief erection, sometimes with medical assistance. By being in the guesthouse Marilyn was on hand should such a happy moment arise. She and Bacon merrily quaffed the great man's champagne, and ended up in bed themselves. Then, at 3:00 A.M., there came a knock at the door; it was Joe Schenck's butler, summoning Marilyn. She scrambled to oblige, only to return giggling that she had arrived "too late."

Bacon, as others confirm, did know Marilyn well. He has been a friend to many of the famous, and their press agents say he is an accurate reporter. He shrugs off criticism for having told his anecdote about Marilyn. He says, "I know she was promiscuous in those early days. She admitted it helped, and I had no illusions that Marilyn Monroe was after me for me. She liked me, sure, but she was also after all the newspapers my syndicated column appeared in."

Other stories seem to support what James Bacon says about Marilyn and Schenck. Two reporters for national magazines recall visiting Schenck at Palm Springs and becoming aware that Marilyn "looked after" the old man. One remembers Schenck affably suggesting that Marilyn could look after the reporter too. Perhaps the most compelling verdict comes from the venerable agent, George Chasin. What was going on between Marilyn and Schenck was, he said, a "physical thing."

The relationship with Schenck, however, was more than a passing convenience. Actor Nico Minardos, who was close to Marilyn in late 1952, recalls visiting her in the hospital when she was having a gynecological operation. He blundered into her room to find her locked in the arms of the elderly Schenck.

Joe Schenck lived on to the age of eighty-two. In 1960, when a massive heart attack began his final decline, the star Marilyn was filming Let's Make Love. At a dinner party given by producer David O. Selznick, there was an angry scene when a guest accused her of heartlessness, of failing to have the compassion to visit the dying Schenck.

Rupert Allan, her aide and friend in later years, says the opposite was true. He accompanied Marilyn to see the old man as he lay helpless in his mansion. Other visitors were banished from the sickroom, and Allan, waiting below, still remembers Marilyn's peals of laughter from the sickroom upstairs. Schenck's nurse, astounded, said the old man had rallied as soon as he heard Marilyn was coming. On the way home, Marilyn wept. She never saw Joe Schenck again.

Amy Greene, Marilyn's close friend in the mid-fifties, says, "She did give me the impression she slept her way to her start." Marilyn talked of this time, says Greene, using an obvious allusion: "I spent a great deal of time on my knees."

By 1948, at twenty-two, Marilyn was being regularly squired around the fashionable Hollywood restaurants and nightclubs. A favorite was Romanoff's, where Marilyn became close to the owner, "Prince" Mike Romanoff, and his wife, Gloria.

Gloria Romanoff knew Marilyn from the late forties until her death, and held her in great affection. She offers this opinion on how much Marilyn used sex to advance her career: "My view would not be a popular one. This was a girl who, early on, probably did whatever was necessary to get rolling in the business. As time passed, Marilyn, I think, became somewhat indifferent to sex. She didn't have any overwhelming need to be with men, and I think it had a lot to do with those early years."

The final word on this subject should be Marilyn's. When British writer W. J. Weatherby asked her whether the stories about the casting couch were true, she responded, "They can be. You can't sleep your way into being a star, though. It takes much, much more. But it helps. A lot of actresses get their first chance that way. Most of the men are such horrors, they deserve all they can get out of them!"

Marilyn would, on occasion, take younger lovers, but the men who mattered to her would from now on almost always be older.

"Insecurity is what bugs me," Marilyn was to say years later. "I have always been attracted to older men, because the younger men don't have any brains, and all they do is try to make a pass, and it isn't even me they are thinking about. They are horny just because I'm a movie star. Older men are kinder, and they know more, and the ones I've known were important in the business, and have tried to help me."

Marilyn told of having sat at the feet of Joe Schenck, "hearing him talk. He was full of wisdom like some great explorer. I also liked to look at his face. It was as much the face of a town as of a man. The whole history of Hollywood was in it." Now, in the real world of Hollywood, the men she seriously cultivated would be her seniors, and useful to her career.

Marilyn was looking for teachers. In 1948, when she was hired by Columbia, the first teacher to come her way happened to be a woman. Marilyn grasped the helping hand, and began an intense, strange relationship that would last seven years—longer than any liaison she would have with a man. That summer there was also a male teacher, and a passionate affair she was never able to forget.

6

"I HAVE A NEW girl for you," said the voice on the telephone. "Her name is—"

Natasha Lytess, head drama coach at Columbia, waited as the studio's talent chief fumbled through his papers to find the unfamiliar name.

"Marilyn Monroe," he said finally. "See what you can do with her."

It was spring of 1948.

Natasha Lytess, herself a former actress, was a scraggy, graying woman of Russian and French ancestry. Many years older than Marilyn, highly strung and sensitive, she had come to the United States as an artistic refugee from Nazi Germany, where she had trained with the Max Reinhardt theater company and been married to the left-wing novelist, Bruno Frank. She now lived alone with her three-year-old daughter in Hollywood, where she had been teaching acting for seven years. She was used to starlets without experience or talent, and at first Marilyn seemed just one more.

"I was not impressed," Lytess said years later. "She was inhibited and cramped; she could not say a word freely. Her habit of speaking without using her lips was unnatural, obviously superimposed. Her voice was a piping sort of whimper." Lytess, however, set to work on Marilyn, beginning a relationship that she would look back on with "pride and frustration, love and fear."

Marilyn came for her lessons regularly and fairly punctually, and worked with boundless enthusiasm. Lytess strove to get her "to let go, to say things freely, to walk freely, to know that relaxation brings authority. These new sensations, to a girl suffering from acute insecurity, were the difference between existing underwater and coming alive."

For a long time Marilyn told Lytess nothing about her background. Her teacher felt that "she was accustomed to hiding everything," and sometimes she did not know what to believe. One day, after coming to work for months in smart, expensive clothes, Marilyn arrived in tears. She explained that her last and kindest foster parent, her dear friend, Ana,* had died "of malnutrition." Lytess blinked, wondered, and decided it was none of her business. She was, by now, deeply attached to her young pupil.

There were those who would say that Natasha and Marilyn had a lesbian relationship. Marilyn's New York maid, Lena Pepitone, would report Marilyn as saying so herself. "Any warmth shown to her, by any person, regardless of sex," Pepitone wrote, "was welcomed and cherished." Marilyn needed to be loved—by anyone who was sincere. Florabel Muir, a veteran Hollywood reporter who knew Marilyn well, also said there was a lesbian relationship with Lytess. Sidney Skolsky, a really close friend, thought the same.

Years later Marilyn herself told W. J. Weatherby, "People tried to make me into a lesbian. I laughed. No sex is wrong if there's love in it." Earlier, speaking of her life in 1948, she said the sexual side of relations with men had so far been a disappointment.

"Then it dawned on me," she said, "that other people—other women—were different than me. They could feel things I couldn't. And when I started reading books I ran into the words 'frigid,' 'rejected,' and 'lesbian.' I wondered if I was all three of them. . . . There were times when I didn't feel human and times when all I could think of was dying. There was also the sinister fact that a well-made woman had always thrilled me to look at."

Marilyn decided she was not a lesbian, after all, she told writer Ben Hecht, after several months of studying with Natasha Lytess. The moment came as Marilyn landed the first movie role that gave her a chance to talk, sing, and dance, in a low-budget picture called *Ladies of the Chorus*. Marilyn

---

* Ana Lower.

played the part of a poor girl who rises from poverty to become a star, the first of many roles that would strike an echo of her own real-life experience. She had two songs to sing, "Every Baby Needs a Da Da Daddy," and "Anyone Can See I Love You."

It was while Marilyn was preparing to perform these songs, Lytess would recall, that "she opened up, and leaned on me like a child for comfort and advice. One day she told me she was in love." Marilyn did not at the time tell Lytess the name of her lover.

That summer of 1948 a young widow named Mary D'Aubrey, living with her mother on Harper Avenue in Hollywood, blundered into a bedroom to find her brother Fred in bed with his new girlfriend. "Hi! Can I have some juice?" was Marilyn's cheery greeting. Fred Karger was then thirty-two, ten years older than Marilyn, and shakily married to another woman. He was director of music at Columbia Pictures, and an accomplished composer best remembered today for the theme of *From Here to Eternity*. He was the son of Maxwell Karger, one of the founders of M-G-M, and Anne, a Boston Irishwoman of great warmth and vivacity. Max had died long since, and Anne—now sixty-two and universally known as Nana—ran a jolly household filled with children and grandchildren. Once, in her salad days, Nana had presided over a virtual *salon* of early Hollywood, and its gaiety still echoed through the life she lived, in reduced circumstances, at the house on Harper Avenue.

Marilyn had been sent to Fred for musical coaching by the producer of *Ladies of the Chorus*. Karger recognized a voice that was reedy and untrained, and its owner as someone drowning in insecurity and stage fright. He also saw that she was resolved to drill herself into performing successfully. He took her to his friends' homes to get Marilyn to sing for an audience, however small. Director Richard Quine recalls Karger playing the piano as Marilyn, screwing up her courage, stood by the mantel to sing "Baby, Won't You Please Come Home."

Lessons turned to love one day when Marilyn phoned to say she was sick. Karger dropped in to see her, and found her, forlorn and hungry, in a cramped one-room apartment. He invited her home to the maternal ministrations of Nana, and an affair began.

Fred's niece and nephew, Anne and Bennett, still remember their childhood awe at the strangely different creature their uncle had brought home. "There was an old closet where I used to keep my toys," says Bennett, "and one morning, not knowing she was there, I burst into Fred's room and she was sitting in front of the mirror nude, putting on her makeup. I hastily went to back out again, but she said to come on in and get my baseball bat and glove."

Bennett and his eight-year-old sister, Anne, shared a nearby room with bunk beds, and Anne recalls how one day "this vision walked in, a beautiful blonde lady. She was very, very fond of children, and she just sort of became part of our group of little friends. She gave me a birthday party, and sat there on the floor and played party games with us. We came to love her very much."

Marilyn, she of many names, took on a special one for her relationship with the Kargers. They always called her "Maril," and her generosity toward the children was boundless. At Christmas she arrived to find that Terry, Fred's daughter by a previous marriage, had more presents than Anne and Bennett. Marilyn quietly left, to return laden with extra gifts. The orphan was doing something that became characteristic, finding a new family and eagerly trying to make it her own. After the affair with Charlie Chaplin, Jr. had ended, Marilyn stayed close to his grandmother. Now she put her trust in Fred's mother. Nana cooked for her, mended her clothes, and got her off to the studio in the mornings. In years to come, Marilyn always remembered Nana's birthday, and sent her flowers on Mother's Day.

Marilyn had found a family, and for the first time she was dizzily in love. At Karger's urging she moved out of the depressing apartment to a better place, just down the street from the Kargers. The lovers also took a place they could use together, near the studio. Marilyn later told Ben Hecht, "A new life began for me . . . I had always thought of myself as someone unloved. Now I know there had been something worse than that in my life. It had been my own unloving heart. . . . I even forgot Norma Jeane. A new me appeared in my skin—not an actress, not somebody looking for a world of bright colors. When he said, 'I love you' to me, it was better than a thousand critics calling me a great star."

Marilyn worried about being an interloper in Karger's marriage, and wept when it finally broke up. At the same time she wanted him for herself, and the want went unfilled.

There was, as Marilyn put it, "one cloud in my paradise. I knew he liked me and was happy to be with me. But his love didn't seem anything like mine. Most of his talk to me was a form of criticism. He criticized my mind. He kept pointing out how little I knew and how unaware of life I was. . . . His cynicism hurt me, too. . . .''

Karger would ask, ''What's most important in life to you?''

''You are,'' Marilyn would say.

''After I'm gone,'' Karger would say with a smile.

When Marilyn wept he would tell her, ''You cry too easily. That's because your mind isn't developed. Compared to your figure, it's embryonic.''

Nana Karger hoped her son would marry Marilyn. He, meanwhile, was backing off. One night, according to Marilyn, he told her why. ''It would be all right for me, but I keep thinking of my son. If we were married and anything should happen to me—such as my dropping dead—it would be very bad for him.''

''Why?'' Marilyn asked.

Karger's answer was hard. ''It wouldn't be right for him to be brought up by a woman like you. It would be unfair to him.''

Marilyn, wounded in the part of her that needed children, tried to leave Karger. For a while they rode that saddest of roller coasters, the breakup that is inevitable, yet seemingly impossible. Marilyn recalled, ''There was a third and fourth good-bye. But it was like rushing to the edge of a roof to jump off. I stopped each time and didn't jump, and turned to him and begged him to hold me. It's hard to do something that hurts your heart.''

Marilyn could not forget Karger. At Christmas 1948 she went to a fashionable jeweler, and bought Karger a $500 watch on the installment plan. She was broke at the time, and would spend two years paying it off. Throughout her life Marilyn reveled in giving engraved gifts and signed photographs, but the watch was marked merely ''12.25.48.''

''You'll have some other girl to love,'' she told Karger. ''You wouldn't be able to use my present if my name was on it.''

A year or so later, after fending off Marilyn for months, Karger would marry actress Jane Wyman, former wife of President-to-be Ronald Reagan. He would later divorce Wyman, then remarry her in 1961, a year before Marilyn's death. Even then, Marilyn had not let go of the memory. Her friend, Sidney Skolsky, recalled, ''The only bitchy thing I ever saw Marilyn do occurred one night at Chasen's restaurant. As we approached the checkroom, there was an event taking place in the large private party room. . . . Marilyn and I were told that the Fred Karger and Jane Wyman wedding party was in the room. Marilyn said she had to go in and congratulate Fred. She knew this would burn up Jane Wyman. She boldly crashed the reception and congratulated Fred. As Marilyn and Jane were pretending they didn't know the other was in the same room, the tension in the atmosphere would have been as easy to cut as the wedding cake.''

Perhaps the best estimate of Marilyn's feeling for Fred Karger comes from Patti, the wife he was married to at the time of his affair with Marilyn. She says today, without bitterness, ''She deeply wanted him. I think her love was very profound.'' Vi Russell, who was best friend to Karger's sister and virtually a member of the family says, ''I don't think she ever got over Fred. After him, she could never believe a man could love her. But then she never believed in herself. How could anyone love her when she could not love herself?''

Fred Karger too, it seems, did not forget. In later years he was to call his former wife Patti, highly distraught, saying that Marilyn had just appeared to him in a dream. Karger died seventeen years after Marilyn, on the exact anniversary of her death.

In New York, in the mid-fifties, Marilyn would talk with remorse about her time with Fred Karger. The remorse was, not least, for the children she had not borne. In her months with Karger, Marilyn said, she had more than once made the now-familiar journey to the abortionist.

Natasha Lytess, the drama coach, told Marilyn that Karger was not worth her tears. She soon moved with her child into the apartment that Marilyn had taken to be near the Karger family. Neither of the women had much money, and the younger Kargers were bemused by the atmosphere of the place: two lonely women living in an apartment almost devoid of furniture, with Marilyn sleeping on a mattress on the floor. During the past months, Marilyn's acting hopes had collapsed again.

Jonie Taps, the executive assistant to Columbia Pictures chief Harry Cohn, took a call from Cohn the day his boss first saw rushes of Marilyn's scenes in *Ladies of the Chorus.* ''What did you put that fat pig in the picture for?'' yelled Cohn. ''What're you doing, fucking her?'' In September, when Marilyn's contract ended, Cohn failed to renew it. Old

Joe Schenck again tried to come to the rescue, but this time he was unsuccessful.

According to Marilyn she lost favor with Harry Cohn because she rebuffed his sexual advances. She claimed that Cohn enticed her into his office, promised her a cruise on his yacht, then tried to have sex with her on the spot. She refused, she said. When Cohn threatened her, saying, "This is your last chance," she walked out.

Fred Karger recalled accompanying Marilyn to Cohn's office in a last-ditch attempt to persuade the studio chief to extend her contract. Marilyn, whose mother and last foster parent were ardent Christian Scientists, had recently been going to church a good deal with Fred Karger's daughter. Now, on the way to see Cohn, she telephoned her Christian Science practitioner for guidance.

The guidance did not help. Cohn stuck to his decision, and Marilyn had been fired again.

In October of that year, 1948, Marilyn had some consolation. The film she had made at Columbia, *Ladies of the Chorus,* made its undistinguished debut. It was terrible, but Karger had worked well, and Marilyn received her first review. "One of the brightest spots is Miss Monroe's singing," said Tibor Krekes of the *Motion Picture Herald.* "She is pretty, and with her pleasing voice and style, shows promise."

That month, with members of the Karger family, Marilyn went to see herself in a public showing for the first time. *Ladies of the Chorus* was playing at the Carmel Theater on Santa Monica Boulevard—which in later years was to show only pornographic movies. Fred Karger's niece, Anne, recalls that "she was like a little child. She sat hunched in her seat so low that she could just see the screen. She came dressed in a big coat and wearing dark glasses."

There was nobody to recognize Marilyn that night. However, at Columbia, which had just dropped her, a little fan mail trickled in.

7

"SHE IS MOST DEFINITELY not a child," an embittered Natasha Lytess would say in the future. "A child is naive and open and trusting. But Marilyn is shrewd. I wish I had one tenth of her ability for business, of her clever knack of promoting what is right for her and discarding what is not." In early 1949 Marilyn was again broke, jobless, and losing Fred Karger, the first man to whom she had really given her heart. She was a bruised twenty-three, and the bruises served her well in a way. She wanted to act, and she had learned how to hustle.

Jimmy Starr, former columnist on the *Los Angeles Herald-Express*, claims to know the secret of the Marilyn Monroe walk. "She learned a trick of cutting a quarter of an inch off one heel, so that when she walked, that little fanny would wiggle. It worked."

It worked for Marilyn one spring day that year, when she was out of a job following abortive ventures as assistant to a magician and a trick golfer, and a session posing nude for a calendar series. By her own account, Marilyn was sitting in Schwab's drugstore when she heard that a sexy girl was needed for a walk-on part in a Marx Brothers film called *Love Happy*. Marilyn went to the set, met first the director, then Groucho and Harpo Marx. "Can you walk?" asked the cigar-chomping Groucho. "This role calls for a young lady who can walk by me in such a manner as to arouse my elderly libido and cause smoke to issue from my ears."

Marilyn walked—presumably on one cutoff heel. When she turned, the smoke was positively billowing from Groucho Marx. He called Marilyn "Mae West, Theda Bara, and Bo-peep all rolled into one," and the scene was shot next morning.

The producer of *Love Happy* decided to use Marilyn to promote the movie. He pumped up some publicity, portraying her as Hollywood's very own "orphan" trying to make good, and packed her off on a nationwide promotion tour. So it was

51

that Marilyn made her first trip to New York. Fred Karger
was not at the station to see her off.

A key assignment in New York State was an appearance in
front of *Photoplay* magazine's "Dream House," a publicity
caper that would simultaneously promote *Love Happy* and
household products. Adele Fletcher, then editor of *Photoplay,*
recalls a stuttering Marilyn asking her to accompany her to
the "p-p-powder room," to help rinse a coffee stain out of
her dress. There, as Fletcher worried about the time, her
charge stripped off all her clothes (her underwear had also
been stained). "What's she so cross about?" asked the nude
Marilyn as a shocked woman departed the restroom clucking
in outrage. Marilyn then emerged, dress over damp panties,
to push a vacuum cleaner around for the photographers.

New York had its consolations. Marilyn was interviewed
by Earl Wilson, the show business columnist who would
become her friend and a key East Coast press connection. At
the urging of studio publicity men, he introduced her as the
"Mmmmmm Girl." Marilyn also met her old lover, photographer André de Dienes, who carried her off for modeling
shots at the beach.

In Manhattan she was taken to El Morocco, then one of the
most exclusive nightclubs in the country. Marilyn, who arrived as a humble "tourist," found herself invited to the
"right" side of the club by Henry Rosenfeld, the thirty-eight-
year-old millionaire dress manufacturer.

Marilyn had made a long-term friend. She would join
Rosenfeld at his home in Atlantic Beach for trips in his
speedboat and for quiet evenings of talk and laughter. In
years to come the millionaire would offer sympathy in her
crises, find her doctors and psychiatrists, and sort out her
finances. In 1984, in his office in the Empire State Building,
seventy-three-year-old Rosenfeld merely wrinkled a still-boyish
face when asked whether he and Marilyn were lovers. He did
confide that "Marilyn thought sex got you closer, made you a
closer friend. She told me she hardly ever had an orgasm, but
she was very unselfish. She tried above all to please the
opposite sex. Ah, but it wasn't just sex. She could be so
happy and gay. How I remember that laughter!"

From New York, Marilyn was shunted off to the Midwest
to pose as "the hottest thing in bathing suits cooling off
again." Marilyn's enthusiasm for movie promotion also cooled.
She returned to Los Angeles, to a bit part in a western,
obtained for her by the man who had christened her, Ben

Lyon, and to the discovery that Fred Karger still did not want to marry her. It was now, at a house party in Palm Springs, that she met a man who did. He was also the man whose efforts assured the success of Marilyn Monroe.

Johnny Hyde, one of the most influential agents in the country, told Marilyn he could make her a star. He was fifty-three, thirty years older than she, and very wealthy. He was also seriously ill with heart trouble, and had less than eighteen months to live. Hyde devoted these months almost wholly to Marilyn.

Previously, Fred Karger had found a dentist to fix her uneven teeth. Now Hyde arranged cosmetic surgery to erase two tiny unwanted blemishes on Marilyn's chin.* He hired hairdressers who would from now on regularly bleach her hair, and was reportedly the agent who, according to the story Marilyn later told, persuaded her to have an operation to prevent conception.

Most important of all, Hyde had access to every potentate in Hollywood. By day he praised Marilyn's talents; by night he escorted her to the homes of the famous and powerful. By the time he died Hyde had secured Marilyn her first part in a major film and a new contract with the studio that had once spurned her, Twentieth Century-Fox. It ensured a salary of $500 a week for the first movie, and would develop into a deal covering the next seven years, with an eventual salary ceiling of $1,500 a week.

The major film arranged by Hyde was *Asphalt Jungle,* directed by John Huston. Three years earlier Huston had planned a screentest for Marilyn, then canceled it because he thought she was being set up, not for a role, but for sexual exploitation on the casting couch. Now she came to him, thanks to the machinations of three people—Johnny Hyde; her sometime lover Bill Burnside; and her forgiving former hostess, Lucille Ryman. Hyde brought her to a first meeting, then she went off to study a script.

Marilyn's coach, Natasha Lytess, said they worked together "for the better part of three days and nights" to prepare for the reading. She came back, again escorted by Hyde, extremely shy—and anxious in an unnecessary way. She arrived with padding stuffed into her already ample bosom, which Huston unceremoniously removed. Her acting,

* Contrary to rumor, there is no evidence that Marilyn ever had the shape of her nose altered.

however, easily carried the day. Huston says, "Marilyn didn't get the part because of Johnny. She got it because she was damned good."

Johnny Hyde now dismantled his marriage of twenty years and gave himself utterly to Marilyn. Accounts differ as to how she treated him. Scriptwriter Nunnally Johnson, who was close to Hyde, thought him "a dear and gentle man more stirred by female beauty than almost anyone I have ever known."

Johnson himself was unimpressed with Marilyn. "When I saw her at that time," he recalled, "I took it for granted that she fell into that category of eager young hustlers. It was usually at lunch at Romanoff's, and when I sat with them from time to time she took little part in the conversation, though both Johnny and I did what we could to include her in what was generally no more than casual gossip. She listened intently, her eyes never left us, as the eyes of most lunchers at Romanoff's did to see who was coming in, who was with whom. But I'm afraid I can't remember her ever uttering one word."

Gloria Romanoff, whose husband ran that restaurant and who knew Marilyn well, thought Marilyn somewhat indifferent to men, but she says, "Johnny Hyde was very important to her. She was very touched by his genuine concern. He didn't exploit her in any way, and normally she was a bit of a target."

When Hyde left his wife and bought a sumptuous new home, he had the dining room fitted with four white leather booths and a dance floor at the center. Marilyn called it "My own private little Romanoff's." Billy Wilder, who would one day direct her in two movies, recalls meeting Marilyn when he and Sam Spiegel would go to play cards with Johnny Hyde. "She just sat in the back of the room and read a novel," he remembers, "waiting for Johnny to finish his gin rummy."

Marilyn's silences may have been due to uncertainty about how to behave in exalted company, or just to the shrewd realization that she could trust Hyde to hustle for her. She told director Garson Kanin, "Look, I had plenty of friends and acquaintances—you know what I mean, acquaintances? But not one of them, not one of those big shots, ever did a damn thing for me, not one, except Johnny. Because he believed in me. . . ."

There was mockery in Hollywood about the affair, not least

about the sexual contradiction between Marilyn and the ailing Hyde. Writer James Bacon claims his own liaison with Marilyn continued while she knew Hyde, and that, between the sheets, she mocked the sick man's sexual abilities. Then there was a weekend when Marilyn abandoned Hyde in Palm Springs to visit Karger in Los Angeles. Marilyn, talking with Karger himself, said of Hyde, "He's so sweet. I love him dearly. But I don't feel the way he does."

Marilyn would say later that Hyde implored her to marry him, but she told him, "I don't love you Johnny. . . . It wouldn't be fair." Characteristically, Marilyn seemed uninfluenced by the fact that by marrying Hyde she could have reaped a major share of his fortune. Meanwhile, Hyde went on working feverishly to further her career, then suffered the first of a fatal series of heart attacks.

Roy Craft, a Fox publicity agent who worked closely with Marilyn, recalls a rather pathetic occasion when an anxious Hyde called from his hospital bed. Craft had organized a magazine photo session in which Marilyn and a young actor, Dale Robertson, would act out the correct etiquette for behavior in a nightclub. Hyde pleaded that the assignment be canceled, for fear it would create the impression that Marilyn was actually involved with Robertson. In deference to Hyde, the studio obliged.

Marilyn was still living, on and off, with her coach, Natasha Lytess. According to Lytess, Marilyn was dilatory in visiting this sick man who had given up everything for her. One night in December 1950, said Lytess, Hyde phoned to ask, "Where is Marilyn, Natasha? I've been waiting, waiting. Natasha, never in all my life have I known such cruelty, such selfishness."

A week later, after a deathwatch during which Marilyn was present, Johnny Hyde died in Cedars of Lebanon Hospital. In contrast to her earlier thoughtlessness, she now defied a Hyde family request that she stay away from the funeral, and threw herself sobbing on the coffin. Her New York friends, Amy Greene and Maureen Stapleton, say she was still mourning Johnny half a decade later, still miserable that his children had "hated her as a homewrecker."

Nunnally Johnson thought that "Johnny was the first man who had ever treated her with almost deferential respect, and was also the only person in the world who was seriously concerned about her at all. When Johnny was buried she was again alone in the world."

Days after the funeral, at Christmas 1950, Natasha Lytess drove home from work with the persistent feeling that something was wrong. She entered the apartment to find on her pillow a note from Marilyn reading: "I leave my car and fur stole to Natasha."

Another note, on Marilyn's bedroom door, asked the reader to make sure Lytess' daughter did not enter. Natasha burst in to find that "the room looked like hell on earth. Marilyn was in bed, undressed, her cheeks puffed out like an adder's."

Lytess said she shouted, "Marilyn! What have you done?" When there was no reply, "I jammed her mouth open and reached in and took out a handful of wet, greenish stuff she hadn't yet swallowed. On the night table was an empty bottle that had contained sleeping pills."

Nearly twelve years later the psychiatrists of the Los Angeles Suicide Prevention Center would say of the dead Marilyn: "On several occasions in the past, when she was disappointed or depressed, she had taken overdoses of barbiturates and summoned help."

If we accept her own account of two suicide attempts before she was nineteen, this was the third. Marilyn was still six months short of her twenty-fifth birthday.

8

"SHE WAS SUPPOSED TO be at the studio by seven o'clock in the morning, and she never made it. I lived just across the street, and I had to go and bang on her door. She'd open the door looking a mess, wanting a cigarette,* and I'd say, 'Come on, get your ass out of bed.' Sometimes I literally had to push her into the shower."

The man charged with getting Marilyn to work was French-born Alain Bernheim, who had come to Hollywood in the forties. Now a prominent producer, he was then working with Charles Feldman and Hugh French, who had taken over as

---

* She had stopped smoking by the mid-fifties.

Marilyn's agents on the death of Johnny Hyde. As he and others discovered, Marilyn was a mass of contradictions and a mistress of transformation.

German actress Hildegard Knef* first encountered Marilyn in a Twentieth Century-Fox dressing room, still only half-awake. She recalled this scene: "The sleepy-looking girl, with the transparent plastic shower cap over her white-blonde hair and a thick layer of cream on her pale face, sits down beside me. She digs around in a faded beach bag and takes out a sandwich, a pillbox, a book. She smiles at my reflection in the mirror. 'Hi, my name's Marilyn Monroe, what's yours?' "

Knef's first impression of Marilyn was of "a child with short legs and a fat bottom, scuffing over to the makeup room in old sandals." An hour and a half later, said Knef, "only the eyes are still recognizable. She seems to have grown with the makeup, the legs seem longer, the body more willowy, the face glows as if lit by candles. . . ."

The two appeared together the same evening at a dinner to announce awards and new discoveries. "Now," said Knef, "she's wearing a red dress that's too tight for her; I've seen it before in the Fox wardrobe—although it's too tight, it looks like one of Mum's old ones dug out of the wardrobe. Eyes half-closed, mouth half-open, hands trembling a little. One glass too many, a child's first go at the punch. The photographers hold their cameras up high, flash into her cleavage. She leans and stretches, turns and smiles, is willing, offers herself to the lenses. Someone bends forward and whispers into her ear. 'No, please,' she says, 'I can't.' The trembling hand knocks over a glass. Finally she stands up, the people snigger, the tight skirt presses her knees together, she trips to the microphone. The walk is absurd and she's got miles to go; they stare at the dress, wait for it to burst and liberate the bosom, the belly, the bottom. The master of ceremonies roars: 'Marilyn Monroe!' She steadies herself on the mike stand, closes her eyes, leaves a long pause in which one hears her amplified breathing—short, panting, obscene. 'Hi,' she whispers, and starts the trip back."

Asphalt Jungle, Marilyn's true break into pictures, appeared in June 1950. The tough story of a jewel robbery, of crime and punishment, and of what happens when thieves fall out, it still stands as one of the best of its kind ever made.

---

* Hollywood changed it to "Neff."

Marilyn played the young mistress of an aging criminal, a
relationship defined—to suit the morality of the day—as
"niece" and "uncle." She was noticed by the reviewers of
the *New York Post* and the *Herald Tribune*, and the *Times*
included Marilyn in its praise of "an unimpeachable performance."

In spite of that, Marilyn had little work that she wanted.
Her previous year had otherwise been a series of bit parts for
the Hollywood sausage machine. Johnny Hyde had arranged a
seven-year contract with Fox, but Darryl Zanuck, the man
who had once fired her, foisted her off with cameos in
forgettable movies. Marilyn, in response, campaigned adroitly
on two fronts—the flagrant advance of the sex symbol in
public and the creation of the cultured actress in private.

In 1951, now twenty-five, Marilyn signed on for an adult
extension course at the University of California at Los Angeles (UCLA). Her subject was literature and art appreciation,
with a focus on the Renaissance. She appeared for classes
quietly dressed, and hardly anyone knew she was a starlet. To
her literature teacher she "could have been some girl who had
just come from a convent."

When Marilyn had first met Hildegard Knef she had launched
into a barrage of questions about German literature, and
happened to be carrying a copy of Rainer Maria Rilke's
poetry under one arm. Jack Paar, later to become host of the
television show "Tonight," acted with Marilyn that year in
the film, *Love Nest*. When he met Marilyn she was reading
Marcel Proust, whom Paar had described as "a rather exotic
French author much in vogue among the intellectually pretentious of the time." Paar called this Marilyn's "act," and
commented, "I fear that beneath the facade of Marilyn there
was only a frightened waitress in a diner." Paar, himself not
best known for cultural devotion, was one of many who
underestimated her.

Quietly, as superficial roles followed one on another, Marilyn worked away at her acting. She made sure that her acting
coach, Natasha Lytess, followed her to Fox. Lytess would
recall, "Her habit of looking at me the second she finished a
scene was to become a joke in projection rooms. . . . The film
of the daily rushes was filled with scenes of Marilyn, finishing her dialogue and immediately shading her eyes to find
me, to see if she had done well."

Marilyn did not consult Lytess when she decided to take
separate lessons from Michael Chekhov, nephew of the play-

wright, who had studied under Stanislavsky. She played Cordelia to his King Lear in private acting sessions, and became mesmerized by his talent. Shortly before her death, she was still talking of him in interviews as her acting idol, the man "who showed me that I really had talent and that I needed to develop it."

Once, in the middle of a scene from *The Cherry Orchard*, Chekhov stopped to ask Marilyn whether she had not been preoccupied with sex while playing her part. Marilyn said no. Chekhov shrewdly replied, "I understand your problem with your studio now, Marilyn. You are a young woman who gives off sex vibrations, no matter what you are doing or thinking. And your studio bosses are only interested in your sex vibrations. I see now why they refuse to regard you as an actress. You are more valuable to them as a sex stimulant."

Marilyn told an interviewer that her reply to Chekhov was: "I want to be an artist, not an erotic freak. I don't want to be sold to the public as a celluloid aphrodisiac. It was all right for the first years. But now it's different."

Of course, Marilyn used the weapon of her sexuality when she chose, and not least to jolt studio chief Darryl Zanuck from his torpor. Writer Robert Cahn recorded the effect Marilyn achieved one night in 1951.

"The Café de Paris, more simply known as the Twentieth Century-Fox commissary, was crowded with a cheery assemblage of studio bigwigs and freshly manicured salesmen. The visitors were meeting, over highballs and hors d'oeuvres, such marquee names as Susan Hayward, Jeanne Crain, June Haver, Anne Baxter, Gregory Peck, and Tyrone Power. At the bar a weary press agent was asking for his fifth highball when he glanced toward the doorway where Marilyn Monroe, a recently acquired studio starlet, had just arrived. Amid a slowly gathering hush, she stood there, a blonde apparition in a strapless black cocktail gown, a little breathless as if she were Cinderella just stepped from the pumpkin coach. While the long-established female stars silently measured her, young Marilyn Monroe, who has logged less than fifty minutes' screen time, stole the show. . . . Finally, as the guests sat down for dinner, the blonde was installed at the head of the No. 1 table, at the right hand of company president, Spyros Skouras."

The public had already cast its verdict. Marilyn's minor screen appearances had brought a torrent of fan mail. Her pictures in pulp magazines had made her the nation's pinup—

"Miss Cheesecake of 1951" to the troops in Germany. Now, the morning after Marilyn took Spyros Skouras by storm, Darryl Zanuck bowed to the pressure. Marilyn's salary shot up to five hundred dollars a week, and Zanuck issued orders that Marilyn should be given more roles. Thanks to the intervention of her friend, Sidney Skolsky, she was loaned to another studio to make *Clash by Night,* a sophisticated movie from a play by Clifford Odets. Soon the *New York World-Telegram* would acclaim her as "a forceful actress, a gifted new star."

Marilyn had never ceased to cultivate her friends in the publicity office, and now it paid off. That year her picture appeared, with those of other starlets, in *Life* magazine. In the fall, Roy Craft placed calls to Rupert Allan, the West Coast editor of *Look,* and to Ted Strauss, his counterpart at *Collier's*.

Rupert Allan, a cultured product of England's Oxford University, was quickly won over. He waited, as men would almost always wait, as Marilyn finished dressing in her tiny apartment. He watched quizzically as she did exercises for the camera and expounded on her studies of the human anatomy as taught by Florentine doctors. He observed with educated eyes the inexpensive reproductions taped to the wall of Dürer, Fra Angelico, and da Vinci.

Allan's interest grew when he espied, beside the bed, a picture of a woman in black, not Sarah Bernhardt or Garbo, but the Italian actress, Eleanora Duse. Within days Allan was Marilyn's counsel on art. He was to become her future press agent and a lifetime friend. In immediate terms, *Look* granted Marilyn its accolade: her first cover in a nationally respected magazine. It informed the world that this Hollywood actress wished to use her brains.

The studio told *Collier's'* Ted Strauss what Marilyn was "terrified" of being interviewed for a major article, and urged that he take her to dinner. Strauss made the pilgrimage to the same apartment, waited, then took her to Romanoff's. Now he experienced Marilyn's effect on a roomful of people.

"She was an apparition," Strauss remembers. "She was in something red, semi-dressed and semi-undressed, with cleavage almost to her navel. We came in down a sort of Ziegfeld Follies staircase, and everything stopped. Everyone there looked—I remember how the lighting made death's-head sockets of their eyes—like a party in a cemetery. That was not all. I had expected a clichéd little girl on the make. I came away from that dinner so impressed. She was terribly bright and perceptive. She was doing what she thought people wanted her to do, but unsure—desperately trying to deal with where she came from. We talked about acting, but she talked as much about children, of having children who would be able to grow their own way."

In this year of her film breakthrough, 1951, Marilyn turned twenty-five. She moved out of the apartment she shared with her acting coach, and returned to the secretive personal life she had lived before the very public affair with Johnny Hyde. She usually lived alone, but for some months she had for a roommate a young actress she had met at a charity baseball game a few years earlier. The new friend was Shelley Winters, who shared with Marilyn a history of broken romances, unborn children, and a healthy disrespect for the show business establishment.

Winters noticed Marilyn's extreme insecurity. She craved attention so much that she pursued her friend everywhere, even into the bathroom. "When you went to the john," Winters had said, "she'd think you'd disappeared and she'd been left alone. She'd open up the door to see if you were still there. She was a little child."

On Sunday mornings the two young women would sit listening solemnly to classical music, promptly changing over to Sinatra or Nat King Cole as soon as the clock struck noon. One day, as they perused the photographs of single actors in the *Academy Players' Directory,* they bemoaned the frustrations of love. Shelley Winters recalls Marilyn musing, "Wouldn't it be nice to be like men and just get notches in your belt and sleep with the most attractive men and not get emotionally involved?"

The outcome was that each sat down to list the famous men they would like to have taken to bed. Marilyn's list, according to Winters, included Zero Mostel, Eli Wallach, Charles Boyer, Jean Renoir, Lee Strasberg, Nick Ray, John Huston, Elia Kazan, Harry Belafonte, Yves Montand, Charles Bickford, Ernest Hemingway, Charles Laughton, Clifford Odets, Dean Jagger, Arthur Miller, and Albert Einstein.

After Marilyn's death Shelley Winters would see among Marilyn's effects a framed photograph of Einstein inscribed. "To Marilyn, with respect and love and thanks, Albert Einstein." She drew what seemed the obvious conclusion. Another friend of Marilyn, a man who was on the original target list, puts this little matter in perspective.

Actor Eli Wallach later worked with Marilyn, but denies that he was ever a lucky victim. He gleefully takes responsibility, however, for the signed Einstein portrait. It was Wallach who gave it to Marilyn, as an ''in'' joke, after Marilyn gave him a book of Einstein's letters. Wallach wishes future historians well when they come to analyze the handwriting on the photograph.

Of the seventeen men on Marilyn's list, she would know nine, and three would be her authentic lovers. One, almost certainly, enjoyed her favors the year she made the list.

On a warm day in 1951 photographer Jean Howard, the former wife of Marilyn's agent, Charlie Feldman, came to Feldman's house in Coldwater Canyon. As she left, she recalls, ''I noticed this little blonde girl sitting by the pool. I didn't know who she was, but offered her some Coca-Cola, which she declined. Charlie was holding a meeting with Elia Kazan that day, and Marilyn was waiting for them.''

Elia Kazan—''Gadge'' to his friends—was already, at forty-one, a towering figure of the American stage and screen. He was both actor and director, and that year saw one of his great triumphs, *A Streetcar Named Desire*. Born in a suburb of the Turkish city of Istanbul, he was now an uncompromising New Yorker. He talked disparagingly of Hollywood, but had discovered it was a necessary evil for a leading film director. In 1951 he had long been married to playwright Molly Thatcher, and had four children. Today Kazan declines to discuss Marilyn Monroe, but others support the long-standing rumor of their affair.

Photographer Milton Greene learned of the relationship direct from Marilyn, and actor Eli Wallach knew about it. Alain Bernheim, then working for Marilyn's agent, was drawn into its secrets. He recalls that *''Streetcar* had been nominated for several Academy awards, but Marilyn could not go to the ceremony with him because he was married. So he parked her with me, and said he'd join us later in some little club in Beverly Hills. So I found myself spending hours in the dark in a little piano bar with Marilyn Monroe, waiting till Gadge was free.''

Another agent, Milt Ebbins, remembers a hilarious event at another stage of the affair. He went to a business meeting with Kazan at his room in the Beverly Hills Hotel, and was astounded when Marilyn walked in wearing only half of Kazan's pyjamas—the top half.

As he sat with Marilyn on the night of the Academy Awards, Alain Bernheim was startled in a very different way. "It was extraordinary," he says. "Marilyn was coming out with everything Kazan had told her, as though the ideas were her own. I knew Kazan well, and I knew it all came from him. She had swallowed whole, virtually memorized, everything he had to say about love, acting, and politics."

For Marilyn, the connection with Kazan no doubt meant a strong infusion of radical politics. Kazan had once been a member of the Communist Party. In 1952, within a year of meeting Marilyn, to the fury of friends and colleagues, he would testify about his past associates before Congress' Committee on Un-American Activities.

When Rupert Allan visited Marilyn at her home for his *Look* article, he had noticed a photograph beside her bed. It showed two men, one of whom he recognized at once as Elia Kazan. Asked to identify the other one, a tall fellow, Marilyn replied, "I'd rather not say, for the moment."

Allan had failed to recognize Arthur Miller.

Marilyn had met Miller in December 1950, in the company of Elia Kazan, just a few days after her suicide gesture over the death of Johnny Hyde. She was working on her part as a secretary in *As Young as You Feel* and feeling very low indeed. She would appear for scenes, then wander off to some corner to be alone with her thoughts.

Arthur Miller was then thirty-five, ten years older than Marilyn, a rumpled man with dark hair, toweringly tall. Newspapermen usually labeled him "gaunt," though on occasion his bespectacled face could seem rounded and quite gentle. The son of a garment manufacturer, he had been born into a comfortable New York family living on 112th Street, in what was then a pleasant part of Harlem. Then the Depression turned the Millers' world upside-down. The family was forced to move to a little frame house in Flatbush, and Miller's father never did recover his former affluence. "Art," as the family called him, grew up doing odd jobs. He was a flop as a coat salesman, then did a brief stint as a crooner on a small Brooklyn radio station. The jobs helped pay for his education, which eventually took him to the University of Michigan. An old football injury kept him out of active service in World War II, though he spent a year as a fitter in the Brooklyn Navy Yard.

When Miller met Marilyn he was married, with two chil-

dren, to a willowy brunette a year younger than himself. This
was Mary Slattery, his girlfriend from college days. They had
married in 1940, and Mary worked as a proofreader at a
publishing house—*Harper's*—while Miller was trying to get
his start as a freelance writer. During this period Miller
espoused radical causes and included Communists among his
friends, associations that would one day bring down on his
head the wrath of a congressional committee.

It was a conversation with his mother-in-law, about a
woman who had turned in her own father to the authorities for
supplying faulty parts to the government in wartime, that
gave Miller the spark for his first successful play. In 1947 *All
My Sons* won the New York Drama Critics' Circle Award,
and two years later *Death of a Salesman* brought him a
Pulitzer Prize and lasting fame. By Christmas 1950, when he
came to Hollywood with his friend, Elia Kazan, to discuss a
movie about labor racketeering, Arthur Miller was America's
most celebrated playwright.

From a variety of sources, including fragments provided by
both of them, these were the beginnings of Miller's romance
with Marilyn. According to Cameron Mitchell, a young actor
who had appeared in the Broadway production of *Death of a
Salesman*, he was walking to lunch with Marilyn one day
when she suddenly stopped short. A few yards away, leaning
against the wall of a sound stage, were two men—Kazan and
Miller. Miller, a gangling giant of a man, had caught her eye,
and she asked Mitchell who he was. Mitchell made perfunctory introductions.

The chance meeting, it seems, soon had Miller watching
Marilyn at work on the set of *As Young as You Feel*. Then,
with Kazan in tow, he sought her out in her dressing room.
She was not there, and the director of the movie, a friend of
Kazan's, warned Miller that she had withdrawn into herself
since the death of Johnny Hyde.

According to Miller, the two men eventually found Marilyn
in a nearby studio warehouse. Marilyn later recalled that she
was weeping when they found her.

Marilyn and Miller met again later the same week, at a
party given by Charlie Feldman, Marilyn's agent and Kazan's
neighbor. According to Natasha Lytess, Marilyn turned up
afterward at 4:00 AM, wanting to talk. "I'd seldom seen her
so contented," Lytess recalled, "She took off her shoe and
wiggled her big toe. 'I met a man, Natasha,' she said. 'It was

Bam! You see my toe? This toe? He sat and held my toe. I mean I sat on the davenport, and he sat on it too, and he held my toe. It was like running into a tree! You know, like a cool drink when you've got a fever.' ''

Miller wrote to Marilyn within days, with a reading proposal. "If you want someone to admire, why not Abraham Lincoln?" Marilyn, as the world could hardly fail to know, admired Lincoln already. Her idolatry had started, she said, in junior high school, when her essay on Lincoln was judged the best in the class. By happy coincidence, Arthur Miller had attended Abraham Lincoln High School. Five years later, before her marriage to Miller, Marilyn would enthuse to Joshua Logan, director of *Bus Stop,* "Doesn't Arthur look wonderfully like Abraham Lincoln? I'm mad for him!"

"He attracted me because he is brilliant," Marilyn would tell the queen of columnists, Louella Parsons. "His mind is better than that of any other man I've ever known. And he understands and approves my wanting to improve myself."

Natasha Lytess recalled that immediately after the first meeting with Miller, "I could tell Marilyn was in love with him. It wasn't anything big, but it showed in the way she acted." A year later a friend spotted the picture of Miller beside Marilyn's bed, the same one *Look*'s Rupert Allan had seen. This visitor recognized the photograph and reported afterward that "Marilyn squealed. She said other people who had been in the room had never recognized him. Marilyn gave the impression there was a great attraction between them. But she said he was married and she didn't think anything would come of it." Later, when reporters came visiting, Marilyn would hide the picture by turning it face down. This, of course, merely aroused curiosity—and prompt recognition when the picture was examined.

Actress Maureen Stapleton, who worked with Marilyn in New York five years later, said, "Marilyn told me she decided on Arthur long, long before they were married. She didn't come to New York and the Actors Studio just because she wanted to be a great artiste. That fellow didn't have a leg to stand on once she made up her mind. She'd decided on Arthur—and she got him."

In 1951, however, Miller stayed with his wife and children in New York. Marilyn, in Hollywood, continued to face the challenges she had made for herself. In his long first letter to her, Miller had written: "Bewitch them with this image they ask for, but I hope and almost pray you won't be hurt in this game, nor ever change. . . ."

On New Year's Eve, 1951, the telephone rang in the home of Associated Press writer Jim Bacon, who had now been seeing Marilyn sporadically for three years. She was calling with a plea: "I don't want to stay at home alone on New Year's Eve, Jim. Can I go to a party with you?" Bacon, who was married, said his wife would not appreciate it.

At the other end of the line, the small voice of that year's Miss Cheesecake said, "Oh, I understand," and hung up.

There would be many lonely holidays for the girl who had dreamed the hardest.

9

"I WANT YOU TO talk with this girl," said Fox publicity director, Harry Brand. "We're grooming her—or maybe I should say she's grooming herself—to be the sexiest thing in pictures since Jean Harlow." It was January 5, 1952, and Darryl Zanuck's fixer supreme was giving lunch to columnist Hy Gardner.

Brand had a tip for Gardner, the careful seeding of a major coup in spoof publicity. "There's only one thing we're a little worried about," he confided. "When things were real rough, Marilyn posed in the raw for a local photographer, and the pictures now adorn a calendar like *September Morn*'s torso, only more so. I'd show you the shots but our legal department has them stashed away in the vault."

On this tantalizing note Marilyn made her entrance, ready to hold court with the visiting columnist. Brand had laid the groundwork for the Calendar Caper, a story that would unfailingly win headlines for months, even years, to come.

The authorized version of the calendar story goes this way. In 1949, when she was twenty-three, Marilyn, broke and out of a job, had posed in the nude for photographer Tom Kelley. He eventually sold the pictures to the Western Lithograph Company for a calendar series, and three years later—to the supposed embarrassment of Marilyn, her studio, and the producer of the moment—someone happened to match the face of the new Fox star with the face and body hanging on garage and barbershop walls all over the United States.

In the early fifties nice girls did not pose nude, and soon the press was howling at the doors of Twentieth Century-Fox. Studio fingers were supposedly on the panic button. There was talk of canceling Marilyn's contract and withdrawing her current movie, *Clash by Night,* and Marilyn herself was reportedly in tears. Then Marilyn suggested she should admit having posed nude, but emphasize that she had done so only out of dire need, when she had no money to pay the rent. This pitiful tale should arouse public sympathy and turn shameful scandal into triumphant publicity.

It worked, of course, and Marilyn's calendar shots are still selling today. The truth about the breaking of the story, though, has never been told in full. It is a droll tale, and one that reveals a good deal about Marilyn as mistress of her own propaganda.

With the collusion of her friend, Sidney Skolsky, Marilyn stage-managed the newsbreak in her own mischievous way. She arranged to be interviewed by United Press International's female reporter, Aline Mosby. Mosby, whose agency serviced thousands of newspapers, magazines, and television and radio stations, was summoned to interview Marilyn and tipped off to ask her about the nude calendar. Sonia Wolfson and Johnny Campbell, studio publicity agents, sat in on the interview. They had been kept in the dark about the calendar ploy, and Marilyn found a way to give Mosby the impression she was truly getting a scoop.

"She asked Aline to follow her into the ladies' room," Campbell recalls, "making as though she was having some sort of menstrual mishap. I certainly would not follow them in there. Then, in the safety of the powder room, she proceeded to identify herself as the heroine of the calendar picture. We were all disturbed about it, but there was nothing we could do."

Mosby's sympathetic story broke a few days later, and Marilyn was all amazement. "I still don't know *how* I was recognized," she protested. As Campbell admits, "Marilyn understood the temperament of the country better than all of us. She understood that the times had changed."

The calendar story was one that would run and run. Soon the nude Marilyn Monroe was in living rooms across the nation, color-printed on cocktail trays and drinking glasses. Marilyn murmured that she did not want the picture to become "a national institution," but she said it very quietly.

Meanwhile, the defenders of American morals made certain the story did not die. In early 1953 a Los Angeles camera-shop owner was arrested after schoolboys had been observed peering at the calendar in his window display. The calendar was officially banned in Pennsylvania and Georgia. Marilyn graciously thanked the authorities, and the pictures reappeared draped in black lace. The calendar was still selling a full three years later, after the U.S. Post Office had ruled the picture was obscene.

In December 1953 one of the nude calendar shots, purchased for $500 by a young unknown named Hugh Hefner, was to grace the pages of the first edition of a new magazine, *Playboy*. Marilyn also appeared, clothed, on the cover. *Playboy* can therefore boast that its first Playmate—or Sweetheart of the Month, as the spread was then called—was Marilyn Monroe.

Marilyn therefore played a key role in this early offensive in the American sexual revolution. Contrary to a highly commercialized fiction, however, there is no substance to the notion that she once paid the rent by making pornographic movies. Recent years have seen the exploitation of two old stag films, one a crude portrayal of the sex act, and one a striptease act, rejoicing in the title of *Apple Knockers and the Coke Bottle*. Both have been sold on the basis that the woman involved is Marilyn, but in each case research has identified the actress as someone else.

The closest Marilyn is known to have come to making pornographic movies was when she was twenty-one, five years before the calendar episode—and that was tame stuff. Steffi Skolsky, daughter of Marilyn's friend Sidney, once accompanied her father to the studio on a Saturday. While waiting for him, she wandered into a viewing room, where the contract players were running sequences they had made "for fun and kicks, and because Zanuck liked to have something to run in the wee, small hours." Young Steffi saw Marilyn, fully dressed, in a "highly suggestive" embrace with the actor, Robert Karnes. The sequence, presumably, has long since been junked.

The nude calendar story broke on March 13, 1952. Meanwhile, one of Marilyn's less successful press operations was quietly brewing. She had never tired of telling people of the saga of deprivation her childhood had been. It had become another tree of sympathy, one that she would feed on and feed to others till the end of her life. One of its main branches was the mystery of her parentage.

At the age of eighteen, while married to Dougherty, Marilyn had suddenly announced that she was going to call her "father." She said she had identified him through people who had once worked with her mother. In front of Dougherty, she dialed a number, then quickly hung up. Her "father," she said, had refused to talk to her.

Marilyn always called her first husband "Daddy." After she died Inez Melson, her executrix, found an attaché case containing letters from another husband, Joe DiMaggio. Melson noticed that DiMaggio signed himself "Pa."

This need for a father figure seems to have become part of Marilyn's tapestry of fantasies. In 1950, as a young starlet, she asked Sidney Skolsky to take a drive with her, to "visit my father." Next day she drove him in the direction of Palm Springs, claiming the father lived on a dairy farm in the area. At a chosen spot Marilyn parked the car, then walked up the drive of a house that lay hidden behind trees. Skolsky could not see what happened next.

When she returned, Marilyn told Skolsky that her "father," a "sonofabitch," had told her, "Listen Marilyn, I'm married, I have children. I don't want you to start any trouble for me."

Skolsky did not write about the incident in his newspaper, though that may have been what Marilyn intended.

One wonders whether Marilyn really confronted anybody behind that screen of trees. Two weeks later, when Skolsky began telling the story to Natasha Lytess, she interrupted him. She explained, with most of the same details, that Marilyn had recently gone through the same performance with her.

Years later, again in two incidents separated by only a month or so, Marilyn rehearsed similar scenes with Ralph Roberts, her masseur, and with her press aide, Pat Newcomb. They occurred in 1961, not long after Marilyn had emerged from a psychiatric hospital.

Were these genuine contacts with the father who had abandoned her? Or were they manifestations of a complex fantasy, a long-running screenplay on a theme of sympathy for Marilyn? Stanley Gifford, one of Marilyn's possible fathers, did own a dairy near Palm Springs after World War II. Perhaps he was her father, and did reject her. What is certain is that after the odd double pilgrimage in 1950, Marilyn's mind became scrambled on the subject of paternity.

She was to tell her New York hostess, Amy Greene, that she had met her father. Yet Marilyn told Henry Rosenfeld, her longtime confidant, that she had discovered her father was "a farmer in the Midwest," and that she longed to meet him.

Once, at a New York party, Marilyn took part in a game in which she had to say what she wanted most in the world. Her reply, Rosenfeld says, was that she would like "to put on her black wig, pick up her father in a bar, and have him make love to her. Then she'd say, 'How do you feel now to have a daughter that you've made love to?' "

In early 1952, as the Marilyn legend began to take hold of the public imagination, she tried to capitalize on her family history. It happened when she went to meet reporter Jim Henaghan at his beachfront home in Malibu. Dusk fell and the drink flowed, Henaghan wrote later, and Marilyn began to expound. She said her father had been killed in a road accident, which had been the real fate of one of her putative fathers. Then she said, "I never had a house or a home that was mine. Or *anything* that was really mine alone. My mother died when I was a baby. . . ."

Whatever the truth about her father, Marilyn's mother certainly was not dead. Marilyn knew full well that she was in a mental asylum not far away. However, she had long told her public relations people that both her parents were dead, and now she was happily exploiting the myth.

This time, events boomeranged. Henaghan filed a story depicting Marilyn the orphan as "Hollywood's loneliest girl." Then another journalist, Erskine Johnson, discovered that Marilyn's mother was alive. His newspaper ran the story.

Somewhat to her surprise, Marilyn's world did not collapse. The newspaper thought it was just one more good Monroe story. Why would they do otherwise? Marilyn had become a public property, a national entertainment that nobody wanted to lose. Her life henceforth was to seesaw between sensation and sadness, with all the world watching.

In spring 1952, in the wake of the calendar affair, Marilyn received massive publicity. *Life* magazine bestowed its prestigious benediction, proclaiming that "the genuine article is here at last—a sensational glamor girl, guaranteed to entice people from all lands to the box office." Then, while Marilyn was making *Monkey Business* with Cary Grant, the world had perhaps its surest sign that a star was born—the newspapers began reporting Marilyn's illnesses.

On April 28 production of the movie ground to a halt, as Marilyn lay abed waiting to have her appendix removed. The operation was performed at Cedars of Lebanon Hospital, where her lover, Johnny Hyde, had died just over a year earlier.

In the operating room, a nurse wondered aloud whether Marilyn really was "blonde all over," as she had once joked to the press. (She was not, and in later years pubic-hair peroxiding would become one of her hairdresser's chores.) The jokes stopped abruptly when a nurse found this note, scrawled in pencil, taped to the patient's stomach:

> *Most important* to Read Before *operation.*
> Dear Doctor,
> *Cut as little as possible* I know it seems vain but that doesn't really enter into it—the fact that I'm a *woman* is important and means much to me. Save please (can't ask you enough) what you can—I'm in your hands. You have children and you must know what it means—*please Doctor*—I know somehow you will! thank you—thank you—for Gods sakes Dear Doctor No *ovaries* removed—please again do whatever you can to prevent large *scars*. Thanking you with all my *heart.*
> Marilyn Monroe

The surgeon, Dr. Marcus Rabwin, already knew of his patient's concern about being able to bear children. There was a small possibility of complications involving the pelvic area, and a gynecologist stood by. This was Dr. Leon Krohn, who would henceforth serve Marilyn through most of her long quest to bear children.

The operation went smoothly, and the star awoke with only the routine scar. "When I told Marilyn she could go home," Dr. Rabwin recalls, "she looked tearful and said, 'I can't because I don't have the money to pay the hospital bill.' I told her to call the studio; they would do all that. She said, 'Do you think they would?' She did call, and of course they had the bill paid and a limousine at the door within an hour."

Insecurities and all, Marilyn could now live like a star. The studio limousine swept her to the relatively modest Beverly Carlton Hotel, where she had been staying before the operation. Soon, though, she was ensconced in the luxurious privacy of a pool suite in the Bel-Air Hotel. She paid the $750-a-month bill, and she could now afford it.

On June 1, 1952, her twenty-sixth birthday, Marilyn received mountains of gifts and telegrams from Hollywood's elite. That night, it is said, the star dined alone; but she had a long telephone conversation with a man in New York. It was not Arthur Miller—he was not yet available. The man's name was DiMaggio.

Part II

THE DIMAGGIO
DISASTER

"It's no fun being married to an electric light."
JOE DIMAGGIO

10

THESE DAYS, WHEN THEY write the occasional feature story on the old man of baseball, newspapers tend to call him The Last Hero. Joe DiMaggio, who last swung a bat in earnest in 1951, has spent the thirty-four years since listening to the applause. He has played golf, made nostalgic appearances for the baseball faithful and, for those who watch television commercials, became "Mr. Coffee" and the Bowery Savings man. On thousands of sunny California mornings he held court in the taproom of the San Francisco restaurant that bore his name. Now seventy-one, without having done very much at all for thirty years, DiMaggio's laurels seem evergreen.

Year after year, in the publishing mills of New York City, editors have realized that the Last Hero has never written his autobiography. They have offered contracts, and he has refused. It is not that DiMaggio will not talk about his ancient heyday or the finer points of coffee commercials. "People aren't fooling me," said DiMaggio a couple of years ago. "They want to know about Marilyn, and that's something I'm not of a mind to talk about."

On paper, what DiMaggio will not talk about was a nine-month wonder, an embryonic marriage that flared and popped as briefly as the flashbulbs of the press that made it a public circus. In fact, it is a full decade that DiMaggio cannot bear to discuss, a time that began as glamor and ended in mystery and grief.

"There are two ways to look at it," DiMaggio has said. "One is, stories should be told as a point of history. The other is, guys have the right to go to the end in privacy." Without DiMaggio the story lacks a key witness. Other intimates, though, now provide a rounded picture for the first time. It is a sad saga in which the Last Hero often emerges as distinctly unheroic, and Marilyn, certainly, as no romantic heroine.

Suitably—since that was the way she made sure it continued—

Marilyn met Joe DiMaggio thanks to a publicity picture. In spring 1952, at the suggestion of press agent Roy Craft, Marilyn had posed at a training session with two players on the Chicago White Sox team. The picture had made the part of the newspaper that Joe DiMaggio read, and he studied it closely. Marilyn, looking refreshingly innocent in shorts and sweater stood teetering on stilt heels wielding a baseball bat. DiMaggio, who made something of a hobby of meeting young actresses, checked with Gus Zernial, one of the ballplayers who had posed with Marilyn.

It happened that DiMaggio knew a business agent named David March, and March had a different sort of interest in Marilyn—he wanted her to retain his services. DiMaggio had a word with March, who promised he would try to arrange a blind date. When he telephoned Marilyn, she was unenthusiastic.

"I don't care to meet him," Marilyn responded. "I don't like men in loud clothes, with checked suits and big muscles and pink ties. I get nervous."

Marilyn, who was vague as to the difference between baseball and football, admitted that she had heard the name DiMaggio. She ventured to say that he was, perhaps, an Italian actor. Finally, she agreed to make up a foursome for dinner with DiMaggio, March, and another young actress. The rendezvous was for 6:30 P.M. at an Italian restaurant—of course—called the Villa Nova.

Marilyn did not show up at the restaurant, and DiMaggio began to doubt whether his host really knew her after all. March telephoned Marilyn, who grumbled that she was too tired to come out. Finally, nearly two hours later, she floated into DiMaggio's vision for the first time. What Marilyn saw was a powerfully built, graying man, some twelve years her senior, wearing a conservative suit.

"He was different from what I'd expected," she would tell Sidney Skolsky. "I'd visualized him as having slick black hair, wearing flashy sports clothes, and with a New York line of patter." In fact, according to March, DiMaggio said hardly anything at all that evening.

The remainder of what took place at that first meeting is lost in a welter of imaginative reporting. By Marilyn's account, offered before the collapse of their marriage, she surprised herself by offering to drive DiMaggio home. Then, because there seemed to be a good deal to say after all, they drove around Beverly Hills for three hours. He ended up with her telephone number, and it dawned on Marilyn that DiMaggio was, as the rest of the nation already knew, a great celebrity in his world.

Next day at the studio, Marilyn promptly told her publicity man about the encounter. "She was giggling like a school-girl," recalls Roy Craft. "She'd met this marvelous man. At first she made a secret of who it was. You'd think she was a fifteen-year-old on her first date."

Craft's was the professional response—Marilyn must be photographed with America's favorite champion. When DiMaggio visited the set where Marilyn was making *Monkey Business,* he was persuaded to pose with Marilyn and Cary Grant. The photograph, with DiMaggio looking as if he wished he were somewhere else, was duly published around the country. Cary Grant's face had been carefully cropped out, and America had its new romance.

A few rumors aside, the love match would move from headline to inane headline for two years, and then to marriage. For Marilyn, and especially for DiMaggio, it was not so simple.

Joseph Paul DiMaggio is an Italian's Italian. He was the eighth of nine children born to a Sicilian couple who emigrated to the United States at the turn of the century. His father, Zio Pepe, was a fisherman, and after a false start in a fishing village to the north, he brought his children to San Francisco the year after Joseph was born. San Francisco was then an unspoiled place, but life in the port was tough. The business of catching fish aside, life on the piers was fiercely competitive and often dangerous. The brutal side of Sicilian custom had crossed the ocean with the immigrants, and violence was commonplace. Poverty, in those early days, was never far away.

Young DiMaggio was supposed to become a fisherman, but he disappointed his father. He did not much like boats; he got seasick, and his father and brothers made him feel less than a man. He would sneak off and practice baseball in the sand, using a broken oar for a bat. That was considered childish, and for years DiMaggio lost that vital Italian possession, the respect of his brothers.

Pride returned when Joe DiMaggio was nineteen. Playing for the San Francisco Seals, the boy established a Pacific Coast record by hitting safely in 61 games. The talent scouts started watching, and in 1936, at twenty-two, DiMaggio was in Yankee Stadium playing baseball for New York. For the

next fifteen years, with a break for Army Air Force service
during the last part of the war, his prowess mesmerized a vast
public. In 1941, six months before Pearl Harbor, DiMaggio
hit safely in 56 consecutive games—one of them with a
borrowed bat when his own had been stolen—and set a record
that has yet to be surpassed. The New York Yankees won the
pennant, and the World Series, and the nation's jukeboxes
blared out a song written specially for him:

> He'll live in baseball's Hall of Fame,
> He got there blow by blow.
> Our kids will tell their kids his name,
> Joltin' Joe DiMaggio.

After the war DiMaggio continued to play and to fascinate,
but was dogged by injury and illness. He had lived improbably hard through his years of glory, carousing more than his
stomach ulcers allowed and smoking two or three packs of
cigarettes a day. There had also been a marriage—to a blonde,
would-be film star. Dorothy Arnold was a singer in a New
York nightclub, and had a stock player's contract with Universal Studios. She and DiMaggio married in 1939, to joyous
accolades from thousands of San Franciscans waving Italian
flags. Four years later, after Dorothy sued him on the grounds
of cruelty, they were divorced.

By 1951, when Joe DiMaggio retired, there had been many
girls, but none that anyone remembers. He was known for his
male friends. There was Toots Shor, a Jewish entrepreneur
who had come up through Prohibition days, and through
friendship with racketeers, to running a celebrities' watering
hole in New York. There was George Solotaire, a would-be
songwriter who ended up as a wealthy ticket broker in New
York. DiMaggio lived on the fringe of show business, and it
was not unnatural. His own role had long been to entertain
America.

Now, at thirty-seven, DiMaggio was rich, retired, and very
obviously lonely. The king of the baseball field was out to
pasture and looking for a queen. He thought he had found her
in Marilyn Monroe. After the meeting at the Villa Nova,
DiMaggio launched immediate pursuit. There were more rendezvous, and probably physical conquest. At first DiMaggio,
not unaccustomed to horizontal triumph, was heard to brag a
little. For publication, Marilyn would later say she "had

dinner with him the next night, and every night until he had to leave for New York."

In less than two months the affair was more than just good copy for Marilyn's publicity office. Dr. Rabwin, who performed Marilyn's appendectomy, remembers streams of calls from DiMaggio in New York. Roses arrived by the dozen. By her twenty-sixth birthday, on June 1, 1952, the newspapers were starting to chatter about possible marriage. Marilyn refused to comment on that, but vouchsafed (exclusively), "I want to love and be loved more than anything else in the world." She also said, "Men are like wine—they improve with age. But I have nothing against younger men."

A year later columnist Dick Williams would quote Marilyn in these terms: " 'There are always rumors about other men going around about me,' she said, sipping a glass of water and watching me lazily with those bedroom eyes of hers. 'I honestly don't know what they're talking about. Besides, it makes Joe very angry. He'd like to punch some of these people.' "

Anger would have been a colossal understatement had DiMaggio known what was really going on. It appears that during their two-year courtship, and sometimes when DiMaggio was actually in Los Angeles, Marilyn had affairs with at least four other men. She seriously discussed marriage with one, and may even have been briefly—and secretly—married to another.

In spring 1952, on the set of her new movie *Monkey Business* Marilyn noticed a fledgling actor of twenty, some six years younger than herself. Nico Minardos was a burly, darkly handsome Greek recently arrived from Athens. He was studying acting at UCLA, a course which included production classes at Twentieth Century-Fox. Marilyn asked another Greek, then working at Fox, to introduce her to Minardos, and an affair began.

Minardos, now a successful producer and veteran actor, has never sought publicity in connection with Marilyn. He was interviewed for this book as the result of a chance remark by a doctor who also knew her. He said he had an affair with Marilyn from late spring 1952 for about seven months, and that they saw each other sporadically until her death ten years later. They were already involved when Marilyn met DiMaggio.

"I was a young buck," Minardos remembers, "and she was such a pretty girl. One of the most beautiful girls I've ever seen, waking up in the morning without makeup, absolutely gorgeous. She was bright—shrewd perhaps rather than profoundly intelligent—and such a sensitive kid. And yet she was a lousy lay. Oh, I used to love her. I was very young.''

"Lousy lay" notwithstanding, Minardos and Marilyn became close. They met either at her hotel or at his apartment on Wilshire Boulevard. Sometimes when she would arrive, driving her green Pontiac, he would be playing cards with a friend. The two young men would sit in their underwear in the summer heat, finishing the game, and Marilyn would have to wait. She did not seem to mind.

Clearly Marilyn was no longer the sexually fulfilled creature suggested by her first husband, Jim Dougherty. "She could never have a climax," Minardos says, "though she would try so hard. She had such severe psychological problems. She was very, very unhappy."

Marilyn told Minardos her story of childhood rape, and he was not sure what to believe. When she talked of wanting to have children, he somehow felt she was fantasizing. When she went to the hospital for the operation which the surgeon confirms was purely an appendectomy, she told Minardos she was "having an ovary removed." Looking back, Minardos feels that "the fascinating thing with Marilyn was that she was acting in her real life. She knew what the reality was, but she acted things out because she loved the drama. . . ."

Minardos ended up in no doubt that Marilyn had used sex, and was still using it, to get what she wanted. He names in particular Spyros Skouras, the Fox studio boss who had used his influence to advance Marilyn.

"One night at her hotel," says Minardos, "Marilyn said, 'Do you mind leaving for about an hour? I have a business appointment here between eight and nine.' I thought there was something odd about the way she said it. I was young and jealous and sort of dragged things out. There was a knock at the door and a voice saying, 'It's me, darling.' There was no way to get out. I put on my pants and opened the door, and it was Skouras. He was so angry he barred me from the studio then. And later, when I knew him, he never called me by my name—he would always call me 'Marilyn's boyfriend.' I criticized Marilyn for what she was doing, then and later. She was achieving success partly in a dishonorable way, by using people."

In November 1952, six months into the DiMaggio courtship, Marilyn would take Minardos to his first Thanksgiving

dinner—at the home of Fred Karger, the lover who had
rejected her four years earlier. The Karger family, one Marilyn adopted more than any other as her own, welcomed the
young Minardos. Months later, at Marilyn's request, Minardos
would take her to observe Greek custom—an Easter service at
the local Orthodox church. She was enthralled by the interminable ceremony, and to Minardos' chagrin insisted on staying
for the whole service.

By the fall of 1952, says Minardos, Marilyn was talking of
marriage. Things went so far as placing a long-distance call to
Athens to speak to his parents, whom Marilyn astonished by
announcing theatrically, "I want to have a child with your
son."

Young Minardos, however, had his own reasons for shying
away from marriage. He says now, "I was never going to let
myself become 'Mr. Monroe.' If I married a woman she was
going to be 'Mrs. Minardos.' "

Minardos recalls with a shudder that a year or so later
newspapers would be referring to Joe DiMaggio as "Marilyn's mate." Once while he was with Marilyn, Minardos
caught her laboriously writing a love letter to DiMaggio, with
a slim brown book open beside her. It turned out to be a
volume of letters by an English romantic poet, and Marilyn
was copying sections verbatim. In the end, the letter to
DiMaggio was a joint production by Minardos and Marilyn
together.

Early on, Minardos recalls, he realized that Joe DiMaggio
was "extremely jealous." This was something that did not
wholly escape mention even in the popular press, which
carried no news of Marilyn's dalliances on the side. The
newspapers had discovered that DiMaggio shunned publicity,
while Marilyn fed on it. At the Beverly Hills Hotel he would
stalk upstairs to wait for Marilyn, knowing full well she was
eating alone downstairs. The Italian from San Francisco was
not amused by Marilyn's flaunting of her body. She said she
was trying to moderate her style, but the exhibitionist in her
was stronger.

Billy Travilla, the designer who was now dressing Marilyn
for her films, tried in vain to stop her from wearing overtight
clothes. Once, when she had to wear a full skirt for the
roller-skating scene in *Monkey Business*, Travilla thought he
had her under control for once. He dressed her for the scene,
then watched helplessly as "she literally reached back, parted
her buttocks, and stuck one of the pleats in the crack to hold

them in place. 'Fooled you, Billy, didn't I?' she said as she
came off the set. 'You and your big silly skirt.' "

Marilyn had some trouble with nature when she tried another old trick. She told Travilla that Jean Harlow, one of her
idols, deliberately made her nipples prominent by rubbing
them with ice before going into a scene. "Mine," Marilyn
complained, "won't get hard. They're the wrong sort." The
problem was solved by artifice—a little round button inserted
in the brassiere at the relevant places. The *New York Daily
News* wrote of *Monkey Business*: "Marilyn Monroe can look
and act dumber than any of the screen's current blondes."
Marilyn reportedly took it as a compliment.

Offscreen, Marilyn's performance was guaranteed to grieve
Joe DiMaggio. On a visit to a U.S. Marine base, she teased
ten thousand men with "I don't know why you boys are
always getting so excited about sweater girls. Take away their
sweaters and what have they got?"

Later in the year, as Grand Marshal of the Miss America
Beauty Parade Pageant, she wore a ludicrous dress cut almost
to the navel. DiMaggio was said to be hurt and embarrassed.
If he knew what was going on behind the public cheesecake,
the hurt must have become torment. Away from Los Angeles,
on location, Marilyn had been toying with yet another man.

11

IT WAS NOW SIX years since Marilyn had enjoyed a summer
romance with Robert Slatzer, the young writer from Ohio
who met her in the lobby of Twentieth Century-Fox. He had
been dividing his time between his home in Columbus, where
he had regular work on local newspapers, and visits to Hollywood, where he hoped to break into the film industry. Meanwhile, as he grew into his twenties, Slatzer remained
mesmerized by the "girl without guile" who had given herself to him on a California beach. Marilyn, for her part,
encouraged him. He wrote letters from Ohio, and Marilyn
responded with streams of long-distance calls, a habit that

was to become a Monroe trademark. In the early days it resulted in unpaid bills and at least one lawsuit by the telephone company.

On and off, when Slatzer was in Hollywood, they shared furnished rooms. "It was out of necessity sometimes," says Slatzer. "If you didn't pay the rent, they could lock up and take all your possessions. It had happened to us both a couple of times, so we shared a place from time to time, to split the cost. You could say we lived together, but just for two weeks here, a month there. We were occasional lovers, but I think I had become one of her few lasting friends."

Today Slatzer, now fifty-nine and recovering from heart surgery, spends most of his time in his cramped crow's nest of a house high in the Hollywood hills. An American flag droops at the door, and the guest is ushered into rooms piled high with books which have long since overflowed their shelves. In his middle age, Slatzer enjoys the regular company of young and pretty women. Conversation is interrupted repeatedly by the squawks of a cage bird and the jangling of the telephone—often heralding another inquiry about Marilyn Monroe.

Since Marilyn's death Slatzer has gained the dubious reputation of being a Monroe obsessive. In 1974 his book, *The Life and Curious Death of Marilyn Monroe,* provided a platform for his persistent claim that Marilyn was murdered following an unhappy affair with Robert Kennedy. That, and Slatzer's rambling way of presenting his case, have invited scorn and the suggestion that he is a charlatan. Some doubt whether he ever knew Marilyn at all. The criticism, verging on ridicule, comes from reporters and editors who jump at the chance to run a Monroe headline, yet recoil from attempting serious research of their own.

Slatzer, to be sure, has none of the disciplines of the investigative reporter. His book on Marilyn, like his interviews, is muddled and virtually undocumented. In many ways I found it irritating and unconvincing. However, because of Slatzer's allegations about the last part of Marilyn's life—specifically, the very serious statements about President Kennedy and his brother Robert—it seemed essential to substantiate his claim to have known Marilyn or to knock it down. After intensive interviews with Slatzer himself covering a two-year period, and independent research, I had to accept that Slatzer was indeed close to Marilyn for her entire adult life.

This conviction is based on interviews with numerous

witnesses, most of them conducted without Slatzer's prior
knowledge. They include Allan "Whitey" Snyder, who made
up Marilyn for her first screen test, became her regular makeup
man, and finally prepared her, in death, for her funeral.
Snyder, everywhere accepted as one of Marilyn's closest
friends, says Slatzer indeed met Marilyn as early as 1946.
Snyder has written:

"Quite often while I was making her up she would tell me
that Bob sent me his best or mention that they had just talked
on the phone or even tell me about a date she had with him
that night. Bob Slatzer had the capacity for being a good
listener, which Marilyn so desperately needed through the
years that they were friends. . . . Marilyn used to tell me how
she could always call Bob in the middle of the night and he
would talk with her for hours. . . . In my opinion, she always
loved him very much."

The early days of the Slatzer affair with Marilyn are remembered by Noble "Kid" Chissell, a former Navy boxing
champion turned Hollywood stunt man and bit player. It was
his car that Slatzer borrowed the night of his first date with
Marilyn, and Chissell himself was with the couple when
Slatzer took Marilyn home. He recalls that Marilyn cooked
breakfast at Slatzer's home in those early days, and that their
romance survived innumerable separations. One Christmas,
late in the forties, Chissell accompanied Slatzer and Marilyn,
laden with small presents, to the orphanage where she had
once lived herself. It was Marilyn's idea to make a special
delivery of gifts for the children.

Half a dozen other witnesses, all of whom had known
Slatzer since the early fifties, confirm his connection with
Marilyn. They include Gordon Heaver, an Englishman who
arrived in Hollywood in 1952 as a story editor for Paramount
Studios. He met Marilyn in Slatzer's company that year.
Others, from Slatzer's hometown of Columbus, Ohio, recall
him talking about Marilyn as a close friend during the fifties.
They include playwright and longtime correspondent for the
Columbus Star, Doral Chenoweth; veteran *Scripps-Howard*
writer Ron Pataki; wealthy restaurateur Lee Henry; and Slatzer's
dentist, Dr. Sanford Firestone.

By the late fifties Dr. Firestone's interest was so piqued,
after hearing Slatzer talking on the telephone to a woman
identifying herself as Marilyn, that he went to great lengths to
discover whether his friend was pulling some elaborate hoax.
Using contacts of his own in Hollywood, Firestone managed

to speak to Marilyn himself. She confirmed that it had indeed been her voice on the recent call, and Firestone eventually met Marilyn, thanks to the Slatzer connection.

Slatzer's account of events in 1952, when Marilyn was already firmly labeled as Joe DiMaggio's girl, is startling.

In early June that year, with *Monkey Business* completed, Marilyn flew East to play the part of an unfaithful wife in *Niagara,* a film that would succeed not least because of its dramatic setting in the shadow of the falls. It became famous, however, for a sensual walking shot, then, and perhaps still, the longest walking shot in movie history.

While the cast and crew assembled at Buffalo, on the U.S. side of the Canadian border, Marilyn diverted to New York City for a brief interlude with DiMaggio. It was now, on a whirlwind round of Manhattan's night spots, that the champion showed off his prize to his friends.

The friends Marilyn met at Toots Shor's were men's men— boisterous sportsmen, gamblers, wrestlers, and habitual nightclubbers. A journalist who later interviewed her reported: "To Marilyn, valiantly fighting the battle of the descending eyelids for Joe's sake, it was sheer garbage. She had other interests she had devoutly hoped to indulge during her New York stay—an afternoon at the theater, a visit to the museums and the like, but Joe, who succeeded in calling the shots, would have none of that."

Meanwhile, presumably unbeknownst to DiMaggio, Marilyn was nurturing yet another interest—a tryst with Robert Slatzer.

Slatzer says Marilyn called him in Ohio before she left Hollywood, suggesting he meet her at the *Niagara* location. Now twenty-five, bored with his work in newspapers and still fascinated by Marilyn, Slatzer jumped at the chance. At the General Brock Hotel, on the Canadian side of the falls, he made contact with Frank Neill, a studio publicist. Neill, who saw Slatzer as a newspaperman and occasional reviewer, found him the perfect accommodation—a room adjacent to Marilyn's.

Slatzer says Marilyn greeted him with enthusiasm. She was drinking heavily and flaunting her nudity more than Slatzer remembered from his visits to California, a point corroborated by one of her hairdressers, who tells of Marilyn going naked to the window, then giggling when she saw a group of youths peering up at her.

Niagara Falls was a traditional honeymoon spot, and the

woman the press was touting as Joe DiMaggio's bride-to-be now astonished Slatzer. "Wouldn't this be a wonderful place to get married?" she said. "We wouldn't have to go to Niagara Falls because we're already here."

They had never considered marriage before, and Slatzer decided the drink was talking. Then, after another night of liquor and lovemaking, Slatzer found himself asking the question seriously. This time it was Marilyn who balked, saying she was not ready for marriage.

As shooting of *Niagara* continued, makeup man Whitey Snyder observed that Marilyn was again terrified of performing before the cameras. She was also extremely restless. The director appointed Snyder to the role that would soon become familiar, baby-sitting Marilyn. He spent hours gently talking her into appearing on the set, and escorted her to New York when she suddenly decided to visit DiMaggio again. Slatzer, meanwhile, had lost his job, as a result of dallying too long with Marilyn at Niagara. She called him, commiserated, and suggested he return to the location. Slatzer answered the summons and followed her to California when shooting ended.

Summer in Los Angeles appeared to be merely the next chapter in the DiMaggio romance. There were press reports about Marilyn, with DiMaggio and his ten-year-old son, Joe, Jr., lounging beside a Hollywood swimming pool, and DiMaggio's former wife noisily objected to her son being in such a place and in such company.

Then, curiously, the headlines began to fade. In early September 1952, Marilyn said she and DiMaggio had no wedding plans. On marriage in general, she ventured that a little male jealousy never hurt a wife. "It would be pretty dull without that occasionally," she said. "But it's like salt on a steak. All you need is a bit of it." DiMaggio, it seems, was certainly getting his share.

Robert Slatzer had come to California at Marilyn's bidding. For two months, he says, life was something of a French farce. "I saw her as much as DiMaggio did," Slatzer recalls. "I don't know if she made up excuses when he called her and she wanted to go out with me, and vice versa. DiMaggio had some deal with the network to broadcast during the World Series, and when he was out of town I saw her practically every night. I was at the house when he would phone. Sometimes I would call at midnight and DiMaggio would be there; then she might call me back at three o'clock in the morning saying, 'I can talk now.' "

Slatzer had one classic encounter with DiMaggio when both men turned up for a date on the same night. "I was there waiting for her," says Slatzer, "when DiMaggio drove up. We each knew who the other was, and there was a very quiet waiting period—there was not much we could say. Then Marilyn arrived and let us both into the house. He was a big guy, and I wasn't about to get into an argument. I poured myself a drink, and he was put out about the fact that I seemed to know the place pretty well. The two of them had an argument, and he asked me to leave. I wouldn't. And her temper just flared and she told us both to get out. About an hour later she called and apologized, and said she'd got her schedules mixed up."

In late August, Dorothy Kilgallen's column carried a three-line teaser that broke the stream of gossip about DiMaggio. It read: "A dark horse in the Marilyn Monroe romance derby is Bob Slatzer, former Columbus, Ohio, literary critic. He's been wooing her by phone and mail, and improving Her Mind with gifts of the world's greatest books."

Three weeks later Slatzer himself was in print, reporting that he had been supplying Marilyn with *The Rubyáiát of Omar Khayyám* and the works of Edgar Allan Poe. She in turn, he said, had given him *The Prophet*, by Kahlil Gibran. This was not, one can assume, reading that Marilyn could share with Joe DiMaggio.

One night in early October Marilyn talked at length about DiMaggio. According to Slatzer, "She told me she couldn't see any way she could be happy with him. Because he was so jealous, not only over me—he was jealous if they were sitting in a booth having dinner and somebody asked for an autograph. He'd be all knocked out of shape and start giving her hell. I would have bet at that time that she'd never marry DiMaggio, if she lived to be a hundred." Instead, if Slatzer is to be believed, Marilyn now married him instead, in a civil ceremony on the Mexican border.

Slatzer's account of marrying Marilyn has understandably aroused skepticism. It is not now formally documented, and sensible people recoil from the notion that Marilyn could have done anything so significant without making headlines. The doubters point out that Slatzer said nothing publicly about such a marriage until years after Marilyn was dead. However, several people interviewed for this book support the story.

Two sources seem especially significant, because they say Marilyn herself mentioned the episode. Dr. Firestone, Slatzer's dentist, remembers Marilyn talking years later of her "honeymoon in Mexico with Bob." At the time Firestone had heard nothing of the marriage from Slatzer, and assumed Marilyn was speaking loosely about a romantic visit.

Actress Terry Moore, former wife of Howard Hughes, says she knew Marilyn from her earliest Hollywood days; they were both under contract to Fox, and later to Columbia, at the same time. Moore says, "I remember very well her being excited about going out with Bob. She wanted so much to have culture, and she respected Bob because he was well-read. She did tell me she had married him, right after they did it. I remember, because I had been telling her about my own brief marriage to Glenn Davis."

Will Fowler, Slatzer's writer friend in Hollywood, says, "Bob told me he was going to slip away to Mexico and marry Marilyn. When they got back, I remember Bob showing me the marriage certificate. It looked like a fancy black-and-white high school diploma with a gold seal. . . ."

Slatzer says the marriage took place on October 4, 1952, after a long night of talk and alcohol, while DiMaggio was away in the East. They climbed into his prized possession, a 1948 Packard convertible, and headed for the Mexican border town of Tijuana. They had been to Mexico before on weekend trips, and Tijuana was famous for rubber-stamp marriages and divorces. A decade later, Marilyn would fly to another border town for her divorce from Arthur Miller.

"We weren't sure what the procedure was," says Slatzer. "I asked the assistant manager of the Foreign Club, whom I'd met before. He said to just go down the street to one of those real fast lawyers. Marilyn had been talking about a church, and she didn't think that was very romantic. Anyway, we found a lawyer behind a storefront right on the main street. I don't remember the name—it's going back so damn many years. He said he could take care of us in about an hour and we'd need two witnesses. His wife would be one, and we were going to find another one on the street."

It is the second witness who provides Slatzer's only first-hand corroboration of events on the wedding day. In 1982, without forewarning Slatzer, I contacted Kid Chissell, the old actor who first met Marilyn with Slatzer in the forties. Of the alleged marriage Chissell said, "It was pure chance. I was down in Tijuana looking up an old Navy buddy, and I suddenly saw Bob and Marilyn coming out of a shop. I gave him a shove and he swung round, looking mad. When they realized who I was, we all laughed, and they said, 'Would I be their witness?' I said, 'Yes,' I thought it was about time. . . . Then Marilyn said she'd feel better if she went into a church before she got married, and we went off to a Catholic church, which was the only sort they had there. Bob and I stayed near the door and Marilyn covered her head with her sweater and lit candles near the altar. When she was done we went to the lawyer, and his wife gave Marilyn a flower, and they filled out the forms, and he married them. Then we went to get Marilyn some Mexican sandals, because someone had taken the shoes she'd taken off at the lawyer's office. We did that, and then we went to the Foreign Club for a drink.''

If Chissell has fabricated his story, he has rehearsed it well. His account meshes with Slatzer's in all significant details. There was little likelihood that Marilyn would be recognized, says Slatzer. "She was not looking like the raving beauty, Marilyn Monroe," he said. "She had no makeup on, had her hair pulled back, looked just any little girl going to Tijuana for the weekend.''

That night, says Slatzer, he and Marilyn consummated the marriage in the bedroom of the Rosarita Beach Hotel, then an isolated old-fashioned place about twenty miles from Tijuana. "Next morning,'' he says, "I awoke to see her half sitting up in bed, kind of wiping her eyes. She was crying a little, but she wouldn't say why.''

The marriage lasted three days. "We got back to Los Angeles wondering what we were going to do about DiMaggio,'' says Slatzer, "but Darryl Zanuck got to us first. Late on Monday afternoon Marilyn called and said there were problems at the studio. She had told a couple of people on the qt and word had gotten around quickly. I ended up in a confrontation with Zanuck, and he was firm. He said, 'We've got a lot of money invested in this girl, and we're not going to be put on the hook with this marriage. Get it undone.' ''

According to Slatzer, he and Marilyn both bowed to the studio's will. His friend, Will Fowler, says this is what Slatzer also told him at the time; and actress Terry Moore says, "Marilyn told me the studio had put a stop on it in some way.''

Less readily, Slatzer admits that Marilyn thought better of the marriage as soon as she returned to Hollywood. There where phone calls from DiMaggio, and Slatzer's brief wife seemed confused and disoriented. Next day the couple were back in Tijuana, bribing the lawyer to destroy the marriage certificate, which had not yet been officially filed. It was done.

In the sprawling mess that is now Tijuana, the Slatzer marriage to Marilyn seems beyond further investigation. The saddest comment on the matter comes from Terry Moore. She says, "Marilyn wanted to be free, and yet she was so afraid of loneliness. I think she was in a muddle over DiMaggio, and she liked Bob. She just ran into it, and then ran out again."

In the last weeks of 1952 Marilyn started shooting *Gentlemen Prefer Blondes,* one of the major musicals of the fifties. It was also a mighty success for Marilyn, who shared top billing with Jane Russell. The two had attended the same high school, and Russell had once met Marilyn at a dance with her first husband, Jim Dougherty. Now, to the frustration of the gossips, Jane Russell and Marilyn Monroe became good friends.

Russell was married to a retired football player, Bob Waterfield, and Marilyn asked her advice about marrying a famous sportsman. Russell says, "I told her she must find time to go off with her own friends to talk about books and poetry and the arts. But apparently she wasn't able to go off and do that. Marilyn felt part of her was dying because she wasn't getting it expressed."

Joe DiMaggio showed no signs of going away. Marilyn's friend, Sidney Skolsky, told how 1952 ended. "She had attended the studio's annual Christmas party, appearing gay, seeming to be enjoying herself. Then she left, with nothing to do but to return home—at that time a single room at the Beverly Hills Hotel—and wait for a phone call from Joe, who was visiting his family in San Francisco. When Marilyn entered her room she found a miniature Christmas tree standing on the table, a pasteboard sign on which was hand printed 'Merry Christmas, Marilyn,' and Joe sitting in a chair in the corner."

Marilyn told Skolsky a few days later, "It's the first time in my life anyone ever gave me a Christmas tree. I was so happy I cried."

That same month, Marilyn's studio fed the press with stories that Marilyn Monroe was now, officially, a full-fledged star. According to the studio, she now had the curious double distinction of being "more publicized" than either Rita Hayworth or the Queen of England. She was receiving more than five thousand fan letters a week, and was now to occupy a luxurious dressing room once inhabited by Marlene Dietrich. The studio began calling her "*Miss* Monroe."

A few months earlier, a helicopter had clattered to earth beside the Hollywood swimming pool of bandleader Ray Anthony. The downdraft swept chairs and tables into the water, ruining the effect of thousands of floating gardenias. Marilyn descended from the helicopter in a flaming red dress that offended everyone except the photographers. She was there for a ceremony so tasteless that it appalled even the public relations man who had organized it—the unveiling of a song called "Marilyn." The words went:

> No gal, I believe,
> Beginning with Eve,
> Could weave a fascination like my MA-RI-LYN.
> I planned everything,
> The church and the ring,
> The one I haven't told it yet is MA-RI-LYN.
> She hasn't said yes,
> I have to confess,
> I haven't kissed or even met my MA-RI-LYN.
> But if luck is with me,
> She'll be my bride for evermore.

In fantasy, Marilyn was now wedded to all America. In the real world, she was a shipwreck in the arms of many, with a baseball champion for sheet anchor.

12

AT MIDSUMMER 1953, SHORTLY after her twenty-seventh birthday, Marilyn lay down on the sidewalk outside Grauman's Chinese Theater on Hollywood Boulevard. Beside her was Jane Russell, her co-star in *Gentlemen Prefer Blondes*. They placed their hands in wet cement, did the same with their feet, and then scrawled their names alongside the prints. A crowd roared approval, and Marilyn came up with her customary quips. She mischievously suggested that Russell, for whom Howard Hughes had once designed a special brassiere, should bend over into the cement. As for herself, celebrated since *Niagara* as being the one actress who could make an entrance by walking away from the camera, Marilyn proposed sitting in it. Her ideas were turned down, along with the suggestion that the *i* in her signature her dotted with a diamond to commemorate her song, "Diamonds Are a Girl's Best Friend." A rhinestone was used instead, and a thief stole it soon afterward.

The ceremony at Grauman's was corny but crucial, one more affirmation that Marilyn really was a star. Marilyn, says Jane Russell, was pleased and scared. Insecurity, those around her now saw, was ever-present in the world's most brazen actress.

On the day of the Grauman appearance, hairdresser Gladys Whitten, whom Marilyn called "Gladness," received a panic-stricken call from Marilyn. "I need your help," said the voice from miles across the city, "please come, Gladness, and bring your mom." It sounded like a real crisis, until Marilyn explained: "I can't decide which dress to wear."

Whitten obliged, as she always did. "She was like a little girl," says Whitten. "I couldn't help it. I just wanted to help her."

It was fortunate for Marilyn that her aides were long-suffering. "Sometimes," Whitten says, "she'd come in; we'd get her hair all done, and her makeup on, and she'd start to get dressed, and then she'd say, 'Oh, I forgot to take a shower.' And she'd go ahead and take the shower—and then we'd start all over again. . . ."

Marilyn could be as funny as she was frustrating. Once the helpless little voice called from just outside the studio. "Gladness," it begged, "would you come and pick me up? My car didn't arrive. I've had to walk all the way from Beverly Hills, and nobody would pick me up."

A puzzled Whitten hastened to the rescue, to find Marilyn waiting, her face thickly coated in vaseline. It would, she insisted, keep her skin young, though others advised that it would simply encourage the growth of unwanted hair.* Drivers that morning had scorned to pick up the "Fastest Rising

---

* As photographs taken in her thirties show, Marilyn did later grow facial hair on her cheeks.

Star of 1953," clad in jeans and sweater, with her face smothered in grease.

The once-punctual Marilyn now began to enrage directors with the lateness that would become legendary. Jane Russell remembers that "she would come in way before me, and she'd have rehearsed. She'd be all ready, but too nervous to go out on the set. So I'd arrange it with Whitey that when it was time to go I'd come and get her, and we'd walk out there together." The insecurity was now chronic.

On the set Marilyn was easily wounded by any sort of criticism. Actor Tommy Noonan was heard to say, after a stage kiss with Marilyn, "It was like being sucked into a vacuum." Marilyn's response to Noonan's comment was tearful collapse. "She was really distraught," says Jane Russell. "She said, 'How can people be so cruel? Nobody can be so cruel and not pay for it one day.' "

Behind the scenes Whitey Snyder had now become as much babysitter as makeup man. For some time now he had been assigned to sit with Marilyn, in hotel or dressing room, quietly coaxing her into facing the cameras. Snyder, now married to Marjorie Plecher, wardrobe assistant on several Monroe movies, says there never was a time when Marilyn did not feel "terror, pure terror" about acting. Plecher says, "She never felt secure in front of the cameras. She was so scared about looking right, acting right, that she was physically unable to leave the trailer. It was the ultimate stage fright. She had a great talent, but she never felt sure of herself, never could believe in herself."

Snyder, along with hairdresser Whitten and a handful of others, would now become Marilyn's loyal personal troops. These were the soldier ants of the industry, and Marilyn was more at ease with them than with most of the great and the famous. She knew their value, and tried to let them know it with gifts. It might be a gold-plated money clip for Snyder, a silver-tagged decanter for Whitten, or a signed photograph reading, "To Gladness, for making me look like this. I love you."

After *Gentlemen Prefer Blondes* Marilyn gave her car, a Pontiac she had owned only a few months, to drama coach Natasha Lytess. It was followed by a vicuña coat. For Lytess, gratitude was tempered with the reflection that Marilyn gave material things because "she was unable to give of herself." It was a character judgment to be echoed, in the end, by the next in Marilyn's succession of men. This was Billy Travilla, dress designer on *Gentlemen Prefer Blondes* and several other movies.

Travilla had first met Marilyn three years earlier in 1950. She was twenty-four, he twenty-five. "My introduction," he recalls, "was the sight of her in a black bathing suit. She opened the sliding doors of my fitting room, and a strap fell off, and her breast was exposed. She had a delightful quality, being so beautiful, of wanting to show herself. Some people were offended by it—and of course she did it on purpose. She was so childlike she could do anything, and you would forgive as you would forgive a seven-year-old. She was both a woman and a baby, and both men and women adored her. A man wouldn't know whether to sit her on his knee and pet her, or put his arms around her and get her in the sack. . . . I've dressed many women in my life, but never one like this lady. She was for me a dual personality. She was not well educated, but an extremely bright woman, and she had the whims of a child. She had a wonderful ability to woo. She'd come in the office, as people would, to complain about something; but Marilyn would always have a little tear, a real tear, in one eye, and her lips would tremble. Those lips! And a man can't fight it. You don't want that baby to cry."

"Billy Dear, Please Dress Me Forever. I love you, Marilyn," reads the inscription on the nude calendar Billy Travilla was given. After three years of knowing each other professionally, says Travilla, there was a brief affair during *Gentlemen Prefer Blondes*, "while my wife was in Florida and Joe DiMaggio was away." The liaison lasted only weeks, but Travilla provides an intimate glimpse of the woman with the ways of a child.

It had been hard to resist a dalliance with Marilyn. Once the designer's secretary came in while Marilyn was sitting on his knee. Marilyn stood up while Travilla—in a condition that discouraged getting up till he could adjust himself—remained seated. Delightedly, and in front of the secretary, Marilyn giggled and asked, "Billy, why can't you stand up?"

"I remember I was going to pick her up at seven-thirty," says Travilla. "I knocked at her hotel door, and she asked me to wait. Then came this handsome young actor, also carrying flowers. We knew each other casually, and we stood in line. He said he had a date, and I said I did. A good twenty minutes went by; then she opened the door. She took the flowers from the bellboy, told the other guy she had a date with me rather than him, and I went in. The place was obviously quickly made ready to receive a visitor, and done badly. Her barbells were sticking out from under the couch and she didn't know what to do with the flowers. I told her to call down to the office, and she said, 'No, I've got a better idea,' and put both the bouquets in the toilet. Then came the matter of whether she was too tall, in high heels, to go out with me. I had to prance to the mirror with her while we checked her height in high heels, and she was an inch taller than me. The high heels won anyway, after about twenty minutes.''

Another of Travilla's recollections is that ''one night we went to Tiffany's on Eighth Street. I went to the men's room, which was down past the club's office. I noticed Marilyn's nude calendar hanging in the office, and told Marilyn. She said, 'Oh, Billy, where? I want to see it.' We went back and the door was shut, so we knocked. A tall black man came and asked what we wanted, and Marilyn said she wanted to look at her calendar. As it turned out, Billie Holiday was using the office as a dressing room, and I guess she'd heard Marilyn Monroe was in the audience and thought Marilyn had come to say hello. When she learned different what we did see of Holiday was very fast—just a whirl of white sleeve with beads dangling from it, and a dark hand. She pulled the calendar off the wall, crumpled it, threw it in Marilyn's face, and called her a cunt. Dumbfounded, we went back to the table. The manager wanted us to stay and see the show, but we left.''

Looking back, Travilla tempers a lover's fondness with the keen perceptions of a lifetime spent working with female stars. ''I think she wanted to love, but could only love herself,'' he says. ''She was totally narcissistic. She adored her own face, constantly wanted to make it better and different. Everything she did in that regard, by the way, was right at the time. She once told me, 'I can make my face do anything, same as you can take a white board and build from that and make a painting.' But the only way she was highly sexed was the charge she got out of looking in the mirror and seeing that beautiful mouth that she'd painted with about five shades of lipstick, to get the right curves, the right shadows to bring out the lips, because her lips were really very flat.''

''If ever there was a prick-teaser,'' says Travilla, ''it was Marilyn, when she wanted to be. She did for real and for show. We'd be doing a still picture in the gallery, and I'd be standing right next to her, and she'd whisper, 'Say something dirty,' and I would. And you could read it in the pictures, you could see it, that mouth was saying, 'Fuck me' or 'Suck me.' It was a turn-on for her.''

"One time," Travilla recalls, "there was this little fuddy-duddy man from Eastman Kodak—we were using a new kind of film—and she comes out in this chiffon nightie, and she poses this way and that way, and the little guy gets uncomfortable. And she knew, and she came over and said, 'Is this okay for you, Mr. Eastman?' That was her sexual kick—to arouse.''

Like many others, colleagues as well as lovers, Travilla was amazed at his own tolerance of Marilyn. He says, "There was something about the girl you had to love. She would be late for a morning appointment, call at three to say she was on the way, and you'd wait till seven. She was the one woman I've known who could make a man feel tall, handsome, fascinating, with that unblinking look of hers, dead in the eyes. You were the king of the evening, if she so decided. She made you feel like the only one, even when you were not.''

Travilla had no illusions about being the only one. Another lover that year, for a month or so, was Edward G. Robinson, Jr. Robinson, son of the famous star, was a sad figure, the product of a broken home and a catastrophic relationship with his father. He never became more than an aspiring actor, and was to die an alcoholic at the age of forty, choking to death while watching one of his father's movies. In 1953 Robinson was nineteen, something of a hell-raiser, and chasing older women. Marilyn was one of them, according to Robinson's friend Arthur James and his last wife, Nan Morris.

James says Marilyn met Robinson through a mutual friendship with another son with a famous name—Charlie Chaplin, Jr., Marilyn's former lover. The acquaintance became an affair during *Gentlemen Prefer Blondes*. Robinson was looking for bit parts at Marilyn's studio, Twentieth Century-Fox, and Marilyn tried to help. He lived in an apartment in the same house as James' sister, and it was there that James would see them together.

Any passion in the Robinson affair was soon spent, and turned to friendship. James says, "We three men were a sort of trio, and Marilyn saw us all occasionally, together or separately, for the rest of her life. They were all depressives, Marilyn, Charlie, and Eddie, and they would hunt each other down when things were bad. She was very dear to both of them, and they would try to help. But Charlie and Eddie were suicidal, more so than Marilyn. They couldn't make it on their own, and they couldn't deal with their famous names. Sometimes it was Marilyn who literally kept them alive."

Arthur James, on the sidelines, became one of the many who put up with Marilyn's mindless late night calls. "She would call from somebody's place at three or four o'clock in the morning," he remembers, "asking me if I could come right over. I'd put something on over my pajamas, drive all the way there, and she'd be gone. . . ."

In Eddie Robinson, Marilyn had met not only a drinker, but a man experimenting with drugs, a "pill freak," as Arthur James puts it. It was probably now and in these circles, that Marilyn, the keep-fit girl with the barbells under the couch, crossed a grim new threshold into the Hollywood world of drugs.

Drug abuse has been the scourge of the movie colony since 1920. Only the fashion has changed. The earliest stars of silent pictures fell for marijuana or, worse, heroin. Pills came into their own in the forties and fifties, with the growth of the pharmaceutical industry. The postwar years were the heyday of "bennies," the various derivatives of Benzedrine. Bennies kept you awake, kept you slim by suppressing the appetite, and provided a vague euphoria.

Next came Dexedrine, son of Benzedrine, and then, with amytal sodium thrown in, Dexamyl. Dexamyl, went the Hollywood talk in the early fifties, gave the perfect high. After the highs, and the metabolic chaos, came the craving for sleep. Stars and failures alike reached for the new wave of barbiturates—Seconal and Nembutal—little tickets to oblivion on the jagged sea of insomnia. Add alcohol, which had been there all along, and the cocktail of peril was complete. One day, Nembutal would kill Marilyn.

In Hollywood the steady trickle of deaths had done nothing to stop the torrent of lethal prescriptions. Dr. Lee Siegel, a studio doctor for Twentieth Century-Fox, was physician to both Judy Garland, and for extended periods, to Marilyn Monroe. Still practicing on Wilshire Boulevard, Dr. Siegel now shakes his head, remembering how pill-taking was once positively encouraged by studio bosses. "In those days," he says, "pills were seen as another tool to keep stars working. The doctors were caught in the middle. If one doctor would not prescribe, there was always another who would. When I first treated Marilyn, back in the early fifties, everyone was using pills."

Since 1962, when Marilyn died of barbiturate poisoning, biographers have assumed she used only sleeping pills, and these only from the mid-fifties. Interviews today suggest an earlier entrapment. Amy Greene, who lived with Marilyn in 1955, says, "She told me she'd always used drugs. She was a baby when she started taking pills, just seventeen or eighteen years old." Milton Greene, Marilyn's partner when she broke away from Fox, says she had long been using Dexamyl, the fashionable "upper" of the period. This contained amphetamine, commonly known as "speed."

Bunny Gardel, who did Marilyn's body makeup on numerous pictures, knew her from her earliest days at Fox. By the early fifties, says Gardel, "She used to come to the dressing room and put down a plastic bag; and you never saw so many pills in one bag. There would be uppers, downers, vitamins, and God knows what in the bag."

In September 1953, Grace McKee, Marilyn's former guardian and the woman who had been the closest thing she ever had to a mother, committed suicide by taking an overdose of barbiturates. It may be that Marilyn never learned the precise cause, since the death certificate was only recently unearthed by a researcher, but she did know it was suicide. Meanwhile Marilyn herself careened onward into a life that would always, in varying degrees, be blurred by barbiturates.

In 1953 Marilyn's private confusions were matched by a growing professional dilemma. On the one hand, encouraged by a gleeful studio, she cemented her image as the national sex symbol. She caused an uproar by arriving at a *Photoplay* awards ceremony in dress that designer Billy Travilla had to sew into position on every famous curve. "When she wiggled through the audience to come up on the podium," wrote her former journalist-lover, James Bacon, "her derrière looked like two puppies fighting under a silk sheet."

Meanwhile, as the world sniggered, Marilyn was hanging on the words of director John Huston, who had once told her she could "turn into a very good actress." She now told the *New York Times*, "That is really what I want to be. I want to grow and develop and play serious dramatic parts. My dramatic coach, Natasha Lytess, tells everybody that I have a great soul, but so far nobody's interested in it."

Marilyn got her chance to act in *How to Marry a Millionaire*. She was to star with Betty Grable—the reigning queen of Hollywood—and Lauren Bacall, in a fairly sophisticated comedy about three New York models scheming to trap wealthy husbands. Brimming with doubts, Marilyn burst unannounced into the office of the director, Jean Negulesco. Her questions were self-conscious ones about "characterization" and "motivation," and an amused Negulesco soon learned that "she was concerned about how her role would transmit the sex image, which is what she believed she had to represent." He told her, "Marilyn, don't try to sell this sex. You *are* sex. You are the institution of sex. The only motivation you need for this part is the fact that in the movie you are as blind as a bat without glasses."

Marilyn understood, and plunged into her role. Nunnally Johnson, the producer and scriptwriter, believed that "the first time anybody genuinely liked Marilyn for herself in a picture, was in *How to Marry a Millionaire*. She herself diagnosed the reason for that very shrewdly. She said that this was the only picture she'd been in, in which she had a measure of modesty—not physical modesty, but modesty about her own attractiveness."

Marilyn's producers and fellow actors saw a troubled woman and a struggling actress. In one scene, involving a telephone call during breakfast in bed, she became "hopelessly confused, answering the phone before it rang, drinking out of the coffee cup before she filled it." After an entire afternoon of stalled production, Marilyn was oblivious to the producer's concern.

Lauren Bacall recalled, "Marilyn was frightened, insecure, trusted only her coach and was always late. During our scenes she'd look at my forehead instead of my eyes. . . . Not easy, often irritating. And yet I couldn't dislike Marilyn. She had no meanness in her, no bitchery. She just had to concentrate on herself and the people who were there only for her."

Soon scriptwriter Nunnally Johnson was writing to a friend, "Monroe is something of a zombie. Talking to her is like talking to somebody underwater. . . ." Johnson never forgot the image. Years later he placed her "ten feet under water. . . . You can't get through to her. She reminds me of a sloth. You stick a pin in a sloth's belly and eight days later it says, 'Ouch.' "

The sloth triumphed on the screen. Director Negulesco says, "In the end I adored her, because she was a pure child who had this 'something' that God had given her, that we still can't define or understand. It's the thing that made her a star. We did not know whether she'd been good or bad, and then when we put the picture together there was one person on that

screen who was a *great* actress—Marilyn.'' In the end, even
Nunnally Johnson was pleased.

On the night of the premiere of *How to Marry a Millionaire*,
Johnson and his wife included Marilyn in their party along
with Humphrey Bogart and Betty Grable. The evening proved
hilarious. ''Marilyn entered with a request for a drink, a stiff
one, bourbon and soda,'' Johnson recalled. ''Then, even
though it was to be a quick and early dinner, she asked for
another. She was on edge with excitement, nervous and
frightened too, terrified about the evening. I had no idea how
naive and youthful she was, how almost unbearably important
the evening was for her. Then, as we're about to get in the
car, a hired limousine with a driver, she asked for her third
drink, a really stiff one this time. Gentlemen to the last,
Bogey and I drank with her on the way to the theater. By the
time we made our entrance you couldn't have found three
more amiable people in the whole state of California.''

''In short,'' said Johnson, ''she was tight. She was tight
when she had to go to the ladies' room as the picture began.
Mrs. Johnson, not tight, accompanied her, for clearly she
needed company. She was tight in the ladies' room, and in a
tight dress, for she had been sewn into it. . . . It was a wild
and exhausting business (my wife told me afterward) getting
Marilyn in condition for the john and then properly dressed
again to return to her seat. Women who have been sewn into
their clothes should never drink to excess. . . .''

The critics judged *How to Marry a Millionaire* an unquali-
fied success. An actress was emerging from the chrysalis of
flagrant sexuality. And now, behind the ballyhoo about celluloid husbands, Marilyn was on the brink of a new marriage of
her own.

Lauren Bacall remembers how Marilyn ''came into my
dressing room one day and said what she really wanted was to
be in San Francisco with Joe DiMaggio in some spaghetti
joint. She wanted to know about my children, my home
life—was I happy? She seemed envious of that aspect of my
life, wistful, hoping to have it herself. . . .''

Marilyn had asked to join the Johnson party at the premiere
because she did not want to be seen at the theater with any
man other than Joe DiMaggio. The lover who had seemed
dull a year ago was now her safe landfall. By November
1953, marriage to an American hero was only two months
away. It had not been an easy passage.

13

THERE HAD COME A moment, during the summer of 1953, when the trials of being Marilyn's suitor defeated even Joe DiMaggio. They had conducted a public courtship of more than a year, and the press was still parroting stories of the couple's devotion. Marilyn had taken an apartment on Doheny Drive, on the unfashionable side of Sunset Boulevard, a modest three-room place which Jane Russell helped her to organize.

The apartment on Doheny would be a perennial retreat for years to come—and so far as the press was concerned, it was a love nest for Marilyn and DiMaggio. Marilyn made sure the public knew Joe had moved in some of his clothes. She would tell her reporter friend, Sidney Skolsky, that she was rushing home to cook dinner for her man. Skolsky dutifully regaled his readers with the details: Joe had taught Marilyn how to prepare Italian spaghetti, they drank Italian wine, and Marilyn had learned a few words of Italian. Joe liked to watch television, said Skolsky, breaking off occasionally to offer his actress lady a word of advice, such as "Never mind the publicity, baby. Get the money."

In late spring 1953 DiMaggio's brother Mike had been found dead in the water near his fishing boat in Bodega Bay, north of San Francisco. Marilyn traveled north with DiMaggio to the very Italian family gathering that followed. The word in Hollywood, when she came home, was that the sight of DiMaggio's grief had finally opened Marilyn's heart. She was ready to marry him—but not quite yet.

On the heels of the marriage rumor came conflicting news. The couple were at bitter odds, virtually splitting up. For the proud DiMaggio, Marilyn brought as much humiliation as bliss. He hated the foolish publicity, detested the way Marilyn flaunted her body in public. He had refused to attend the *Photoplay* awards ceremonies, where she made an exhibition of herself; it was not the way an Italian's woman behaved. Instead he was spotted lurking outside, waiting to whisk her away afterward. We now know that, worse than all this, these had been months in which Marilyn had a succession of lovers. If DiMaggio heard even a whisper of this, it was remarkable that he contained himself at all. He was possessive, and jealous of Marilyn's Hollywood intimates, regardless of sex.

Natasha Lytess, Marilyn's drama coach, was to say, "I first met him when I went to her apartment on Doheny one evening. He opened the door, and I disliked him instinctively—a man with a closed, vapid look. She introduced us, and only two weeks later when I phoned her, he answered and said, 'I think if you want to talk to Miss Monroe, you'd better call her agent. . . .' She hadn't the courage to stand up to him about it."

There was more than a touch of jealousy on Lytess' part, too. George Masters, Marilyn's hairdresser in later years, knew both women well. Natasha, he says, once told Marilyn, "You're wonderful. I love you." To which Marilyn reportedly replied, "Don't love me, Natasha. Just teach me."

Henry Rosenfeld, Marilyn's New York confidant, suggests Natasha's love for her pupil was unrequited. He quoted Marilyn as saying harshly, "God! If I had a cock, Natasha would never leave me."

Natasha Lytess provides the first hint that the private DiMaggio could be different from the strong, silent hero of American imagination. Lytess was to say, "All during those months of 1952 and 1953 she would phone me day and night, sometimes in tears, complaining about the way he misused her."

In late summer 1953 Marilyn stepped off a train at Jasper, in the Canadian Rockies. She was arriving to make *River of No Return*, with Robert Mitchum, a movie that overran its schedule so seriously that Mitchum dubbed it Picture of No Return. Marilyn, unhappy in love and resentful at being packed off to such a remote location, at first seemed a withdrawn, reclusive figure. Jim Bacon, sent to interview her before she left Los Angeles, had been shocked. "Her hair was in tangles," he wrote. "She had cold cream all over her face, and her eyebrows were smeared. She was the same old Marilyn in spirit, but on the outside she was Dracula's daughter. I couldn't get out of there fast enough."

Now, out in the wilderness, Marilyn hid behind the mask of grease, even on trips into the nearest town. Whitey Snyder, the trusty makeup man, finally told her, "Get that crap off your face. You scare people."

One person not scared was Robert Mitchum. He had first heard about Marilyn from Jim Dougherty, her first husband, on a factory line during World War II. On the set Mitchum was now playing the tough-guy lover to Marilyn's barroom singer. Off the set Mitchum introduced her to his roistering hard-drinking style, and brought her out of herself. The result was a string of bawdy anecdotes, still making the rounds today.

Mitchum recalls finding Marilyn poring over a dictionary of terms used in psychoanalysis, and asking for enlightenment. She listened wide-eyed, at the age of twenty-seven, as he attempted an explanation of "anal eroticism."

This was not the only hilarity over definitions. One day, says Mitchum, "My stand-in went up to her and said, 'Hey blondie, let's have a round robin this afternoon.' 'What's that?' she says. 'Well, what about my friend and me giving you a little bob?' She said, 'Both at the same time?' He says, 'Why not?' 'Why,' she said, 'that would kill me.' He said, 'Well, I never heard of anybody dying of it yet.' She said, 'Oh, but they do. Only that's not what they put in the papers; they call it natural causes.' " Mitchum, telling the story in 1982, added that Marilyn was joking. He was not so sure about his stand-in.

The shooting of *River of No Return* was a genuinely rugged affair. There were hair-raising scenes on a raft careening down a turbulent river, scenes which director Otto Preminger insisted could not be performed by stuntmen. The result was a chapter of accidents, both genuine and spurious.

First Marilyn slipped into the water while wearing high waders. The boots filled with water and she was hauled out by members of the crew, with Mitchum helping. Headlines across the country read: MARILYN MONROE NEARLY DROWNED. Another time, stuntman Norman Bishop recalls, "Marilyn and Mitchum went out on a raft, and the goddam thing got stuck on a rock. It was bounding and setting to turn over any second." Bishop and a colleague reached the raft with a lifeboat, and the day was saved once more.

A third incident, on August 20, would also make headlines, this time reading: MISS MONROE INJURES LEG IN CANADA. The report gave no details of any accident, because there were none. Marilyn had repeatedly clashed with director Otto Preminger, and it seems that she now took crafty revenge. Actress Shelley Winters, who had once shared an apartment with Marilyn, recently revealed the deception.

Winters, who was working on another movie nearby, had come to visit Marilyn on the set. She watched, along with hundreds of tourists, as Marilyn stood on a raft tethered to a pier, making a scene that had taken all day. "Marilyn," Winters recalls, "did what she always did when she was confused. She just opened her mouth and smiled at anything in sight. Preminger began to use dreadful language, implying that she was so untalented that she should stick to her original 'profession.' Marilyn never looked up; her smile just became more frozen."

When shooting finished, Winters helped Marilyn come ashore and noticed that she slipped a little. "Watch your step," she warned her, "you can break a leg on this slippery pier." This inspired Marilyn. When the limousine reached the hotel she told Winters, "I can't get out. I've broken my leg." Strong men were summoned, doctors called. Winters fed Marilyn Percodan, a pain reliever, and a double vodka, then listened as the star talked long-distance with studio chief Darryl Zanuck. She expected, she said generously, to be able to finish the film, in spite of "considerable pain."

Winters recalls, "She didn't seem to be in any pain to me." Marilyn, Mitchum, and Winters then enjoyed a vast lobster dinner, washed down with copious alcohol.

Next morning a posse of doctors arrived by private plane from Los Angeles. X rays revealed no damage, and the experts politely suggested there was "perhaps" a sprain. Marilyn insisted on being fitted with a plaster cast and crutches. Shooting resumed after an expensive delay, with Marilyn rigged out as a cripple, and Preminger oozing studied courtesy.

"Dumb? Like a fox, was my young friend Marilyn," says Shelley Winters. "That night we celebrated at a nightclub, and at one point she was sort of doing a rumba with Mitch. 'For God's sake, Marilyn, sit down!' I told her. 'You're supposed to be crippled!' 'Oh, yes, I forgot,' she said, giggling, and sat down on Mitch's lap."

The caper not only tamed Otto Preminger, it brought Joe DiMaggio running. According to Maurice Zolotow, who interviewed Marilyn a year or so later, he called her the night she began the injury charade. She wept, and DiMaggio arrived next day accompanied by yet another doctor. DiMaggio also brought along his habitual shadow, New York ticket broker George Solotaire. They made a curious pair in the Canadian wilderness: DiMaggio in sports clothes, toting fishing gear; Solotaire tagging along behind in suit, dark glasses, and Homburg.

DiMaggio was more at home in the outdoors than he could ever be in the surreal atmosphere of Hollywood. He loped around, cigarette drooping, helping the crew and snapping pictures of Marilyn. The couple went fishing, taking with them ten-year-old Tommy Rettig, the child actor who played Mitchum's son in the movie. Earlier the boy had confided to Marilyn that, according to his priest, it was all right to work with "a woman like you," but not to see her socially. Shocked by the implication, Marilyn now tried hard to win his confidence. Children, it seems, were now increasingly on her mind.

One evening, on the train chartered to carry the cast, makeup man Whitey Snyder asked Marilyn, "Why don't you marry that dago and raise a dozen kids?"

"Maybe I will," she replied.

During the DiMaggio visit the couple vanished for a weekend, sparking rumors of a secret wedding. Soon there were visits to DiMaggio's home on Beach Street in San Francisco, the house he had bought for $14,000 in the early days of his success and where his sister Marie played hostess. Sometimes the couple would rise before dawn to go fishing, Marilyn bundled up in leather jacket, jeans, and scarf. They were rarely recognized, and the times when they were spotted DiMaggio angrily told reporters to "beat it." On his home turf, DiMaggio offered a tranquility rarely experienced by Marilyn.

On Halloween that year, writer Lee Belser spent the evening with a new and calmer Marilyn. She lounged around the Doheny apartment, worried about a kitten crying outside, and took apples and cookies to young trick-or-treaters who came ringing the doorbell. The cookies had been made by Joe's sister, and Joe was the focus of conversation.

"The later it got," Belser noticed, "the older the guys got that came to the door. Marilyn asked me to start answering the bell, and it got really funny. There I was opening Marilyn Monroe's door, turning away all these grown men in Halloween regalia."

In the last weeks of 1953, Marilyn effectively vanished, beginning a new game with the press and her studio. She was due to start shooting a movie called *Pink Tights*, and Frank Sinatra was to be her co-star, a detail which was not enough to bring her back to work. After Christmas, when DiMaggio gave her a mink coat, Marilyn surfaced by telephone to say she had no plans to get married. A DiMaggio emissary arrived in Las Vegas, made plans for a marriage ceremony at a local hotel, then canceled.

The next day, in Los Angeles, Twentieth Century-Fox announced Marilyn's suspension for failing to appear for work. Marilyn, at last fully aware of her power, did nothing at all. She had decided that *Pink Tights* was not good enough for her.

A year later Marilyn was to offer a winningly prosaic scenario of what happened next: "After much talk Joe and I decided that since we couldn't give each other up, marriage was the only solution . . . . One day Joe said to me, 'You're having all this trouble with the studio and not working, so why don't we get married now? I've got to go to Japan on some baseball business, and we could make a honeymoon out of the trip.'

"And so we were married."

14

ON JANUARY 14, 1954, San Francisco Judge Charles Peery was disturbed at a Bar Association lunch by a phone call from Reno Barsochinni, manager of Joe DiMaggio's restaurant on Fisherman's Wharf, asking if the judge could perform a civil marriage ceremony at once. Peery arrived at City Hall just moments before DiMaggio and his bride. Marilyn was demurely dressed in a brown suit with an ermine collar. The bridegroom was accompanied by Barsochinni, his best man; and Frank "Lefty" O'Doul, the old baseball star who gave DiMaggio his start in baseball before the war. No friends of Marilyn were at the wedding. Marilyn would say later that the decision to marry had been made only two days earlier.

The secrecy about the wedding had its drawbacks. There was an embarrassing delay on the third floor of City Hall when the Chief Clerk had to send out for a typewriter to fill out the marriage license. This was useful to Marilyn, who made a series of phone calls she considered vital.

Before leaving for the ceremony she had telephoned the publicity director at Fox, briskly announcing what she was about to do. Now, ignoring romance in her last unmarried minutes, she looked after her key press contacts. She tried to call Sidney Skolsky and got no reply. She was able to leave a message for the immensely powerful columnist, Louella Parsons. Then she personally reached Los Angeles journalist Kendis Rochlen, couching her news in terms Rochlen has never forgotten.

There was hubbub around Marilyn in City Hall as Rochlen asked Marilyn how she felt about getting married. "Kendis," she whispered, in the familiar fluttery voice, "I have sucked my last cock. . . ."

Journalistic legend has Marilyn making this announcement on a number of occasions. Perhaps she did, but Rochlen, a veteran professional, insists she did say it minutes before she took her vows with DiMaggio. At the time, as Marilyn well knew, the remark was unprintable.

By now five hundred people were gathered in the plaza outside City Hall. When the judge opened a window to let in the breeze, the baying of the crowd drowned out all conversation. Reporters peered over a partition. Finally DiMaggio cried, "Okay, let's get this marriage going," and the judge appealed to the crowd for quiet. An obedient "sh-h-h" drifted up from the plaza.

Marilyn signed the marriage certificate as Norma Jeane Mortenson Dougherty, and falsely gave her age as twenty-five; she was nearly twenty-eight. DiMaggio produced the ring—white gold with a circle of diamonds.* The press observed that Marilyn pledged only to "love, honor, and cherish" DiMaggio, and did not promise to obey him. This was already a fashionable omission by 1954, but it may not have sat easily with the son of a Sicilian immigrant. That afternoon a spokesman for the archbishop declared DiMaggio, whose previous marriage had been in the Catholic church, "automatically excommunicated" by his civil wedding to Monroe.

In the melee after the ceremony DiMaggio was asked what

---

*As her wedding gift, Marilyn gave DiMaggio nude photographs of herself, pictures from the famous calendar series that had been considered too suggestive for publication. This was not revealed until years later.

he and the bride were going to do next. "What'cha think?"
he replied with an emphatic wink. Asked whether they would
have children, he said, "We expect to have one. I can
guarantee that." Marilyn added, "I'd like to have six."
Finally DiMaggio exploded. "I've had enough of this mob.
Let's call the reception off," and the couple drove away.

Marilyn and DiMaggio sped south two hundred miles to the
town of Paso Robles, where they ate steak by candlelight with
the curious peering round the door. They then said they were
leaving for Hollywood, but doubled back to the Clifton Motel. There, after DiMaggio had been assured there was a
television set, the couple took a four-dollar room, hung out a
Do Not Disturb sign, and stayed inside for fifteen hours. In
days to come the room would be adorned with a brass plaque
reading, Joe and Marilyn Slept Here. After leaving the motel,
Mr. and Mrs. DiMaggio vanished for more than two weeks, a
rare event in the life of Marilyn Monroe.

In the last week of January, however, when DiMaggio flew
to New York on business, Marilyn could not resist calling a
journalist. Soon she was closeted with Sidney Skolsky in a
car parked on a quiet street. Marilyn, who said she had been
"told she shouldn't be seen," poured out the story of her
honeymoon.

She and DiMaggio had holed up at a friend's cabin in the
mountains near Palm Springs. "There weren't any other
guests," she said. "Joe and I took long walks in the snow.
There wasn't a television set. We really got to know each
other. And we played billiards. Joe taught me how to play."
Skolsky had a national exclusive and Marilyn prepared for the
next stage of the honeymoon, which would be an international
spectacle. The DiMaggios were to go to Japan.

For the baseball champion the trip to the Far East was
routine business on familiar territory. Two years earlier in
Tokyo, to shouts of "Banzai DiMaggio!", Joe had played his
last competitive game. General MacArthur and Joe DiMaggio
were rated the two most popular Americans in Japan, and
baseball was now big business there. The DiMaggios' honeymoon was, in fact, a long-planned promotional trip, funded
by the newspaper *Yomiuri Shimbun* to launch the opening of
the Japanese baseball season.

At San Francisco the couple were ushered aboard their
Pan-American Clipper flight by Kay Patterson, the *Shimbun*'s
representative in California. She says, "Joe looked very
comfortable—he was Mr. Big in San Francisco—and Marilyn

seemed charming, so in love, ogling him, playing the second-ary role, of course."

The airplane made a refueling stop at Hawaii, where the truly explosive nature of their union may have dawned on the couple for the first time. A crowd thousands strong swarmed on to the tarmac screaming Marilyn's name. Frenzied hands ripped out strands of Marilyn's hair on the way to the transit lounge. She recovered herself enough to murmur to the press, "Marriage is my main career from now on."

Hawaii was a foretaste of the utter hysteria in Tokyo. The couple had to be smuggled out of the aircraft through a baggage hatch. The scream now was "Mon-chan! Mon-chan," which means, roughly, "sweet little girl." Later, at the Impe-rial Hotel, two hundred police struggled with a throng that would not be satisfied until Marilyn appeared on the balcony. She thanked them for the "the wonderful reception," but again she was frightened. "I felt," she told Sidney Skolsky later, "like some dictator in a wartime newsreel."

Marilyn tried to muzzle the monster of her own image. She emerged with dignity from a press conference at which two hundred Japanese reporters bombarded her with inanities. To the question, "Do you wear underwear?" Marilyn replied, "I'm buying a kimono." Photographs reveal that she was, for once, wearing underwear on the occasion—DiMaggio's influ-ence perhaps.

As the days passed the Japanese themselves calmed down a little. "The Japanese will probably not discard their under-wear as a result of the visit of the Honorable Buttocks-Swinging Actress," one pundit observed, "because it is much too cold . . . but I'm sure they will soon start swinging their buttocks."

For ten days in Japan, and especially after they escaped from Tokyo, Marilyn did seem to play the "secondary role" to DiMaggio's baseball hero. Modestly dressed, quietly made up, she traipsed behind as her husband played golf, and sat unobtrusively in the car while DiMaggio held court for sports fans. In the evenings she watched as DiMaggio played snooker with his friend and colleague, Lefty O'Doul. Then, after two weeks, Marilyn stepped back into her own myth. She went off to entertain the American troops in Korea—without her husband.

Weeks earlier Marilyn had talked of "a Marine who came to the door of my home after having been in Korea. He told me how much pictures had meant to the men in the service and while he talked he started to cry. . . ." Now, behind the canvas curtain of a makeshift dressing room, in freezing cold, she was changing into her Marilyn Monroe costume for the men of the First Marine Division. Thirteen thousand of them roared approval as she sang in a reedy voice unaided by amplifiers, "Diamonds Are a Girl's Best Friend," "Bye, Bye Baby," and "Do It Again."

Marilyn had trouble with "Do It Again," when an interfering officer claimed the song was too suggestive. She appealed in vain that it was written by the illustrious George Gershwin, then changed the chorus line to "kiss me again."

Marilyn did not allow censorship to percolate to her audience. In whirling snow, gowned in lowcut purple, she was the soldiers' angel of lust for three hectic days. Film of the concerts shows a Marilyn high on her own gyrations, visibly reveling in the excitement of a uniformed multitude.

Marilyn was later to tell her friend, Amy Greene, that after this, crowds no longer scared her. She was to say, "I never felt like a star before, in my heart. It was so wonderful to look down and see a fellow smiling at me." Joe DiMaggio, waiting in Japan, had seen the newsreels, and did not think them very wonderful.

There had been tense phone calls between the couple during her Korea trip; one of them, thanks to the expertise of the Signal Corps, was broadcast over loudspeakers to a dinner party Marilyn was attending. The military audience had heard her ask, "Do you still love me, Joe? Miss me?" DiMaggio's response had been distinctly muted.

A few weeks later, in front of Sidney Skolsky, Marilyn bubbled on for a while about her visit to sing for the troops, then turned to DiMaggio. "Joe," she said, "do you have any idea what that's like? Did you ever have ten thousand people stand up and applaud you?"

Skolsky recalled later: "Joe's voice was as unemotional as a pair of discarded spikes, underplaying his reply just as he had always underplayed his incredible feats in Yankee Stadium. 'Seventy-five thousand,' he answered quietly. Marilyn looked as embarrassed as a pinch runner picked off first base in the World Series."

Marilyn came back to Tokyo to a mild case of pneumonia and an uneasy reunion with her husband. Accounts conflict as to how Marilyn originally decided to interrupt her honeymoon for the benefit of the U.S. Armed Forces. By her account an American general approached her with the idea during the flight from Hawaii to Tokyo. DiMaggio, she claimed, did not object at all. According to Sidney Skolsky, however, Marilyn planned the visit even before leaving the United States. Joe DiMaggio did not approve, but Marilyn went ahead against his wishes.

There had been one odd detail among the crass honeymoon headlines. The *Los Angeles Times* reported that Marilyn left for Tokyo "with her right thumb in a sling, hidden most of the time under her mink coat. 'I just bumped it,' she said. 'I have a witness. Joe was there. He heard it crack.' She declined to go into details about the injured thumb." The thumb was shown in its splint in an accompanying photograph.

Marilyn's story in private—and like all her stories it must be treated with great caution—was that the thumb was injured by Joe DiMaggio in a moment of irritation. She told this to several friends, including Amy Greene. As Greene recalls the story, "Marilyn went to put her arms around him. He was talking to George Solotaire, and it annoyed him. Joe had such huge hands. All he did was fling her arms away, and the impact of the flinging of her arm injured her thumb in mid-air. . . ."

Amy Greene's account suggests the injury was the accidental result of DiMaggio not knowing his own strength. It prefaces, however, a series of reports that later in the brief marriage DiMaggio physically mistreated his wife.

Lois Weber, Marilyn's press agent in the mid-fifties, has said, "I'm sure Marilyn was afraid of him, physically afraid. She said Joe had a bad temper. He was obviously rigid in his beliefs." Sources agree that DiMaggio was possessive and jealous.

Henry Rosenfeld, Marilyn's New York confidant, quoted her as saying that even on the honeymoon "he started accusing her of going to bed with everybody." Marilyn told hairdresser Gladys Whitten, for whom she had brought a gift from the Far East, that DiMaggio was enraged by the hoopla over her visit to Korea. "She went over so big," says Whitten, "that he got angry. Marilyn said, 'He threatened to divorce me on our honeymoon!' "

After the marriage was over, Marilyn sat looking through old photographs with actress Maureen Stapleton. She held up a picture and said, "Look, this was right after the wedding. And see my hands—I was really pushing him away. Really, deep down, I didn't want to marry him."

Astonishingly, even when the ink on the marriage certifi-

cate was barely dry, Marilyn was already talking about marrying someone else. Immediately after the honeymoon, Sidney
Skolsky was invited to visit the DiMaggios in their suite at
the Beverly Hills Hotel. After a while Joe DiMaggio left the
room and then, as Skolsky recalled years late, Marilyn "dropped
a bombshell."

"Sidney?" she said.

"Yes."

"Do you know who I'm going to marry?"

"Marry? What're you talking about?"

"I'm going to marry Arthur Miller," Marilyn said.

Skolsky, dumbfounded, told Marilyn he did not understand.

"You wait," said Marilyn. "You'll see."

Little more than a year after Marilyn's remarks to Skolsky,
she and the playwright would begin courting in earnest. The
year after that, she would fulfil her prophecy and marry
Miller.

The marriage to Joe DiMaggio, launched in discord, would
last less than nine months.

15

AFTER THE DEBACLE IN Asia, DiMaggio brought his wife home
to his quiet house in San Francisco. There, for a month or so
in early 1954, the couple were away from the intrusions of
the press.

The world did get glimpses of them: Mr. and Mrs. DiMaggio
boarding Joe's boat, the *Yankee Clipper*, with Marilyn, in
jeans and mocassins, toting a paper bag containing the day's
lunch. In San Francisco she could venture out more easily.
She went shopping at Magnin's, and once startled bystanders
by helping a brakeman turn one of the cable cars at the
bottom of a hill.

The gossip columns burbled about a possible pregnancy,
but neighbors and fishermen on the wharf saw more than any
reporter. They wondered when they saw Marilyn standing
alone on the back patio in the late evening, a coat thrown

over her shoulders. One night she was seen running along the road away from the pier, weeping hysterically, with DiMaggio in pursuit. The fishermen looked away.

Hollywood was waiting. In March 1954 Marilyn was back in Los Angeles, signing in at her hotel with a wry joke about leaving blank the space in the register for children. She was in Hollywood to receive an award as "Most Popular Actress," a ceremony that turned into a tumultuous welcome home, one from which DiMaggio was absent. He said he would accompany Marilyn only when she won an Oscar—and that honor never would be hers.

Behind the scenes, and calling the contractual tune more than ever before, Marilyn now patched up her differences with Twentieth Century-Fox. She agreed to make *There's No Business Like Show Business,* a frothy musical tribute to composer Irving Berlin. For Marilyn the challenge was in the song-and-dance routines, one of them called, perhaps aptly, "After You Get What You Want You Don't Want It." DiMaggio, certainly did not want the instant change caused by Marilyn's return to Hollywood.

Earlier in the year Marilyn had cooed, "Joe's the head of our household, and I'll live wherever he decides." Now DiMaggio was press-ganged into living for a while in Los Angeles, the town he most despised. The couple moved into a rented house on North Palm Drive in Beverly Hills. It had eight rooms—one for Joe's young son to use on visits—and a swimming pool. Twin black Cadillacs stood parked outside. It was also one of the least secluded houses in town, for its front door virtually opened to the sidewalk.

Writer Sidney Skolsky, sitting in on one of Marilyn's music rehearsals at the studio, noticed the phone calls coming in from Joe DiMaggio, and assumed all was well. Marilyn seemed genuinely concerned that Joe, not she, was doing most of the moving in. She hurried home, with Skolsky in tow as the trusted chronicler, to observe the domestic scene.

Soon an avid public learned that Marilyn had placed the television set next to the fireplace so that her husband could watch sports events from his favorite armchair. She confided that he was addicted to baseball, big-time boxing, and sometimes western movies, and that she served him his dinner in his chair.

"Joe doesn't have to move a muscle," she told the press. "Treat a husband this way and he'll enjoy you twice as much. I like to iron Joe's shirts, but often I haven't the time.

I like to look at Joe in a shirt I ironed. A man should never have to think about his clothes. A wife should see to it that his shoes and suits are sent out to be cleaned." All this, of course, was made easier by the trio of servants Marilyn had hired.

Sidney Skolsky duly published her cozy chatter, and allowed one fragment of reality to see the light of day. "Joe and I have our quarrels," he quoted Marilyn as saying. "You can't outlaw human nature. Marriage is something you learn more about while you live it." In fact the couple had quickly discovered they were hopeless at living together.

Marilyn's discourse on housekeeping was fantasy. Writer Sheilah Graham, who talked to Marilyn once the marriage was over, reports, "They were equal in fame but not in habits. Joe was obsessively neat. Everything on his dressing table was arranged in alphabetical order: A, aspirin; B, brush; C, comb, etc. You could find Marilyn by following the trail of her stockings, her bra, her handkerchief, and her handbag, all dropped as she went. He was always trying to train her. And he could not. They reached a point where they could not speak without screaming."

Sex was not the problem. By most accounts, including her own comments to friends and doctors, the world's sex symbol found little satisfaction in the many beds she shared. With her baseball champion, that at least was different. "Joe's biggest bat," Marilyn delighted in telling Jet Fore, a friend at the studio, "is not the one he uses on the field." She would later tell Truman Capote, "If that's all it takes, we'd still be married."

In a more serious vein, Marilyn had praise for DiMaggio's bedroom prowess when she went to live with her New York friend, Amy Greene, a few months later. "She said nobody in her life was as good in bed as Joe," Greene says, "but at some point you had to get out of bed and start talking. And they couldn't do it."

One night that year the phone rang in the home of Brad Dexter, an actor who had met Marilyn much earlier, during the shooting of *Asphalt Jungle*. They had not spoken since, and Dexter could hardly believe the caller was Marilyn Monroe. "I'd like you to meet Joe," she said. "Can you come over to dinner? And come a little early, before Joe gets home, so we can talk."

Dexter arrived at the appointed time, and Marilyn at once poured out her troubles. "I have a very serious problem in my marriage," she said. "Joe has isolated me; he doesn't want me to associate with anybody in the movie industry. He has a terrible insecurity. He has estranged me even from my actress friends, and I don't know who to turn to. I thought maybe you could be a bridge between us. You're a tough guy, you play poker, and you like sports, and I thought you and Joe could become friends. Then, when we're together, you and I could talk about what we did at the studio all day."

Somewhat appehensively, Dexter said he would try to help. When DiMaggio arrived, though, the effort seemed pointless. "Boy, was he stiff and unbending!" Dexter recalls. "Joe just sat there and I could see all these things going through his mind—like, had I been to bed with her? Why was I there? We could all see it wasn't going to work. I pretended to have another appointment, and I didn't stay to dinner."

When things finally fell apart, Marilyn was to tell the divorce judge: "Your honor, my husband would get in moods where he wouldn't speak to me for five to seven days at a time. Sometimes longer. I would ask him what was wrong. He wouldn't answer . . . . I was permitted to have no visitors, no more than three times in the nine months we were married. . . . The relationship was mostly one of coldness and indifference."

DiMaggio's duodenal ulcer, an old torment, started bleeding again. At the studio, still working on *There's No Business Like Show Business*, Marilyn began to break. Billy Travilla, her dress designer, remembers a day when, for technical reasons, it was essential to shoot three pages of script without cutting. "Marilyn had just one line on the third page," Travilla says, "and she kept fluffing it. They told her they had to wrap the scene, and she started crying. She ran to her dressing room, then apologized like a little girl. Afterwards she told me, 'You know, I'm losing a piece of my mind each day. My brains are leaving me. I think I'm going crazy, and I don't want to be seen this way. If I go crazy, please take me away and hide me.'

"She was talking herself into the idea that she was going mad," Travilla says. Marilyn's fear of inheriting mental illness, prompted by her family history, was now a perennial worry.

DiMaggio, the traditional Italian husband, was more than ever affronted by his wife's display of her body, not only in her work but—against his wishes—at home. Marriage had tempered Marilyn the exhibitionist to the extent that she wandered around the house nude only in front of females.

One woman guest, sitting with DiMaggio on such an occasion, jokingly suggested that Marilyn was trying to lure him to the bedroom. DiMaggio was not amused.

When Marilyn had married DiMaggio, her bosses at Fox dreamed that their publicity cup would now overflow, with regular appearances by a tame baseball hero. One executive boasted, "We haven't lost a star; we've gained a center fielder." DiMaggio disappointed them. He showed up on the set only once during the filming of *There's No Business Like Show Business,* and then objected to posing for pictures with his wife dressed in a revealing costume.

In August 1954, without even one day off, Marilyn moved from the *Show Business* set into production of *The Seven Year Itch,* directed by Billy Wilder. For her this movie was the payoff for having done *Show Business* at all, a chance to play a sustained role opposite one other lead actor. The distinction must have been lost on DiMaggio. *Itch* was the story of a fortyish married man, Tom Ewell, tempted by the girl upstairs, Marilyn, while his wife and children are away. It was an exercise in titillation and sexual double-entendre.

Wilder still chuckles about the shooting of a scene in which Marilyn had to sneak down a back staircase to see the married man living below. "She was wearing a nightdress," he says, "and I could see she was wearing a bra. 'People don't wear bras under nightclothes,' I told her, 'and they will notice your breasts simply because you *are* wearing one.' Marilyn replied 'What bra?' and put my hand on her breast. She was not wearing a bra. Her bosom was a miracle of shape, density, and an apparent lack of gravity."

Marilyn seemed to be nude in another scene, in which she leaned over a balcony, in the New York summer heat, to inform a male neighbor that she kept her underwear in the refrigerator. This was strong meat for the early fifties, but Wilder had to disabuse Marilyn of the idea that she could play one of her love scenes in the nude. No persuasion would be needed to get her to do the famous "skirt" scene, which the press would call "the most interesting dramatic display since Lady Godiva," and which would leave DiMaggio beside himself with rage.

Late that summer Marilyn visited Marlon Brando, then playing Napoleon on the set of *Désirée.* He noticed, as had others that day, that Marilyn's right arm was black and blue. When he asked why, Marilyn replied that she had bitten herself in her sleep. A few weeks later, after the skirt scene, friends would see other bruises, and she would claim DiMaggio had beaten her.

Marilyn flew into New York for the *Itch* location shooting on September 9, 1954. The scenes that followed were such that Roy Craft, Marilyn's publicity man, recalls, "The Russians could have invaded Manhattan, and nobody would have taken any notice." When Marilyn had left Hollywood, the town was awash with rumors that her marriage to DiMaggio was ending. She arrived in New York without him, but assured the press, "Everything's fine with us. A happy marriage comes before anything."

Five nights later, outside the Trans-Lux Threater, she arrived to shoot a sequence with her co-star, Tom Ewell. The scene called for Marilyn to stand with a grinning Ewell as the draft from a subway grating blew her skirt high in the air.

Studio publicity men did not fail to inform the press exactly where the scene would be shot—at 52nd Street and Lexington Avenue—and that Marilyn's revealing costume would "stop the traffic." It was after midnight, but thousands of people stood ogling behind wooden police barriers as huge wind machines sent Marilyn's skirt billowing to her shoulders. Ironically, Wilder says, the shots of the lower half of Marilyn's body would eventually be shot in the studio—quite modestly. What New Yorkers saw that night, in take after take, was a bottom encased in panties thin enough to show a blur of pubic hair. Then Marilyn's husband arrived.

Joe DiMaggio, who had followed his wife to New York, had not intended to watch the filming. He remained a few blocks away, drinking with Broadway ticket broker George Solotaire. Then persuaded by columnist Walter Winchell, an old acquaintance, he made his way through the police lines to watch the filming. DiMaggio stood briefly beside Camera 1, watching as his wife teetered on the grating, listening as the roar of the mob rose and fell in time with her skirt. Winchell heard him mutter, "What the hell's going on here?" then, "I told you I never did this. Let's get out of here."

When filming was over Winchell went with DiMaggio to Marilyn's dressing room. He watched the forced gaiety of Marilyn's "Hi, Giuseppe!"—one of her pet names for her husband—as she slumped exhausted in a chair. He listened as they quarreled about DiMaggio's baseball commitments and then bickered their way through dinner. Embarrassed, in spite of his profession, Winchell left them to it.

That night at the St. Regis Hotel, crew members in rooms

near the DiMaggio suite got little sleep. The cameraman on *Itch,* Milton Krasner, heard shouts of anger through the wall. Though one must ever be alert for fantasizing on Marilyn's part, the accounts that follow are hard to dismiss.

Hairdresser Gladys Whitten and the unit wardrobe mistress did not hear the rumpus during the night, but Marilyn came to them in the morning. ''She said she had screamed and yelled for us,'' Whitten recalls.''. . . Her husband had got very, very mad with her, and he beat her up a little bit. . . . It was on her shoulders, but we covered it up, you know . . . a little makeup, and she went ahead and worked.''

Amy Greene, Marilyn's New York friend, also saw bruises. She was in the suite at the St. Regis to fulfil the fantasy of trying on a mink coat. ''I was sitting on the bed with her mink around me,'' Greene says, ''and Marilyn started to get undressed. She forgot I was sitting there and that she was taking off her blouse. . . . Her back was black and blue—I couldn't believe it. . . . She didn't know what to say, and she wasn't a liar, so she just said, 'Yes. . . .' ''

Amy Greene adds: ''Marilyn could be a smartass, and when she drank champagne she'd goad him. And they weren't intellectuals, they couldn't discuss their pain, so they lashed out at each other. . . .'' Greene saw only this one example of mistreatment.

Makeup man Whitey Snyder, one of the few Hollywood people who got on with DiMaggio, says, ''They loved one another, but they couldn't be married to one another. . . . Sometimes he gave her a bad time—he'd hit her up a bit.''

In September 1954, after the skirt sensation in New York, Marilyn showed a brave face to the world. ''I'm just a pretty girl who's soon forgotten,'' she told a group of sportswriters. ''But not Joe. He's an all-time great.''

In private the pretty girl was in pieces. Tom Ewell, her co-star in *Itch,* noticed she was physically sick, ''shaking like hell'' and guzzling medicine. Milton Greene, visiting her at the St. Regis, found Marilyn in a haze of drugs—sedatives, he guessed—and incapable of sensible conversation.

Marilyn and DiMaggio flew back to California together, and went to ground for ten days. Marilyn spent a good deal of time talking to Mary, Fred Karger's sister. Neighbors spotted her a couple of times walking the streets after midnight, apparently weeping. Within days she had taken to her bed, where she gave Sidney Skolsky an interview full of trivia about the visit to New York. Skolsky also observed a quarrel between the couple, but published nothing.

On the morning of Monday, October 4, Marilyn telephoned Billy Wilder, director of *Itch*. Distraught and stammering, she said she would not be coming to work because "J-Joe and I are going to get a d-d-divorce."

The Twentieth Century-Fox publicity office promptly began a response masterminded by its director, Harry Brand. Everything was carefully stage-managed, and Brand conferred with Jerry Giesler, the colorful lawyer who habitually disentangled Hollywood follies. (It emerged later that Marilyn had been in touch with Giesler for the past ten days). On Monday afternoon lawyer and publicity director emerged together to say that "conflict of careers" had caused the breakup. Giesler said he would file a divorce suit the next day on Marilyn's behalf, "the usual mental cruelty," he explained. He said the star herself was sick of an illness variously reported as a virus or a nervous disorder. One newspaper reported his only other comment—that Marilyn was not pregnant.

A horde of newsmen descended on the house on Palm Drive. Bus companies changed itineraries so that tourists could gawk at the DiMaggios under siege. Marilyn and DiMaggio stayed in the house for two days while the studio orchestrated a final spectacle. "The Monroe divorce," former Fox publicity officer Roy Crafts recalls, "was quite a production."

Early on the morning of October 6, as the press gathered outside by appointment, Twentieth Century-Fox delivered Marilyn's usual team of beauticians. Hairdresser Gladys Whitten remembers, "Somebody sneaked us in by the back alley. And all the time we were preparing Marilyn, she kept saying, 'I don't want to do this,' and holding her head and crying."

Dress designer Billy Travilla was there, drinking wine with Marilyn in spite of the early hour. He says, "She was crying, saying 'I wish I had been different. If only I could have given more love.' She was cursing herself, without saying exactly why." Their work done, the cosmetics crew were smuggled out again, and went round to the front of the house to watch.

Joe DiMaggio, offered the escape route through the alley, declined. At 10:00 A.M. he opened the door and ran the gauntlet of the reporters down the rose-lined walk to his car.

"Where are you going?" the newspapermen asked.

DiMaggio, briefly trapped in the crush, shouted above the din, "I'm going to San Francisco."

"Are you coming home again?"

"San Francisco's my home," DiMaggio said, running for his car. "It's always been my home. I'll never be coming back to this house." The car, driven by his friend Reno Barsochinni, took off, and DiMaggio vanished with a perfunctory wave.

Gladys Whitten remembers what happened next as "horrible." *New York Herald Tribune* correspondent, Joe Hyams, said years later that he still could see "as clearly as I had seen it then, her [Marilyn's] tear-stained face as she came out of the front door, the half-a-hundred newsmen crowded in on her like animals at the kill. Only little Sidney Skolsky tried to protect her. Something about the scene and my profession of journalism sickened me."

The Associated Press correspondent had no such qualms. He merely wrote, "Marilyn Monroe today made an exit worthy of an Academy Award . . . ."

She appeared fifty minutes after her husband had driven off. Though her face was caked with theatrical makeup, it was not enough to hide what appeared to be a bruise on her forehead. She was dressed in black, clinging to the arms of her lawyer and the Fox publicity boss. The reporters, promised a press conference, bombarded Marilyn with questions. She sobbed, "There is nothing I can add," and said repeatedly, "I'm sorry. . . ." She started stuttering and rocking on her heels as though about to faint.

There was an immediate reason to sob. Billy Travilla says. "On Marilyn's way to the car someone gave her an envelope with a piece of toilet paper inside. The word *whore* was written on it in fecal matter. The public was so cruel with her. The ordinary people in front of the house were his fans, not hers."

Early next morning Marilyn reported for work, confiding to her makeup man that she "felt alive for the first time in days." In San Francisco DiMaggio slept till noon, posed gamely for pictures, then played golf. So far as the outside world was concerned the drama was over. The press had little left to do but wait for the formal divorce hearing, due in three weeks. Behind the scenes, the dirty business had hardly begun.

As his marriage was collapsing, an utterly frustrated Joe DiMaggio, jealous of shadows, tried to buy confidence. He turned to private detectives, those Raymond Chandler characters of the fifties, gumshoes whose reports could bring a spouse comfort—or heartbreak.

Meanwhile, at Twentieth Century-Fox, other men had the same idea, but for different reasons. Uneasy Fox executives feared their investment in Marilyn could explode in scandal, a catastrophe they might be able to prevent. They too called out their retinue of paid investigators. Now, and not for the last time, Marilyn was being watched.

One night in that year of the DiMaggio marriage Marilyn came, as she would till she died, to visit Anne, mother of the man she had once loved and lost, Fred Karger. She had known the family since she was dirt poor, and they gathered round delightedly to admire the clothes, the mink, and the Cadillac convertible. "When she came to leave that night," says Patti Karger, "there were two guys out there, waiting to follow her. Everybody at the house picked up on it, and we tried to help her. Marilyn didn't know what to do."

Marilyn had taken to phoning Sidney Skolsky at all hours. Once, his daughter Steffi recalls, she called again and again, starting in the early hours. "I finally woke up my father," the daughter recalls, "and Marilyn came over at seven o'clock in the morning, with no makeup, her hair all over the place, and her fur coat just slung on. . . . My father said later Marilyn just had to get out, to get away. She thought 'they' were trying to drug her."

Within days of the DiMaggio separation, actor Brad Dexter bumped into DiMaggio in Los Angeles at the Villa Capri restaurant. He was in a huddle with Frank Sinatra and a private detective named Barney Ruditsky.

Ruditsky was a former New York City detective who had emigrated to California and become part owner of Sherry's, on the Sunset Strip, then a known rendezvous for gangsters. As a sideline he ran the City Detective and Guard service, which specialized in bodyguard work and the sleazier sort of divorce investigation.

Frank Sinatra, who listed his profession in *Who's Who* as "baritone," had, at thirty-nine, just struggled back from a slump in his fortunes. He had won an Academy Award for his role as Private Maggio in *From Here to Eternity,* and was established as "the first great bedroom singer of modern times." Within a few months *Time* magazine would be calling him, in a remarkable cover story, "one of the most delightful, violent, dramatic, sad, and sometimes downright terrifying personalities now on public view."

Time also said of Sinatra: "The man looks, in fact, like the popular conception of a gangster, model 1929. He has bright, wild eyes, and his movements suggest spring steel; he talks out of the corner of his mouth. He dresses with a glaring, George Raft kind of snazziness—rich, dark shirts and white-figured ties . . . he had, at last count, roughly $30,000 worth of cuff links. . . . He hates to be photographed or seen in public without a hat or hairpiece to cover his retreating hairline."

Sinatra had once written: "If it hadn't been for my interest in music, I'd probably have ended in a life of crime." *Time* noted: "He is an admitted friend of Joe Fischetti, who is prominent in what is left of the Capone mob, and he once made himself a lot of trouble by buddying up to Lucky Luciano in Havana—all of which is not to say that he mixes his pleasure with their business; Frankie is too smart for that. . . ."

Frank Sinatra and Joe DiMaggio, both first-generation Americans, were then the most celebrated Italians in the world. They patronized the same watering holes, such as Toots Shor's in New York City, and in 1954 it could be said they shared the same misfortune. Sinatra was having his own problems in the disastrous marriage with actress Ava Gardner. In Reno, even before they married, he had taken an overdose of sleeping pills. Two years into the marriage he was admitted to a New York hospital with "several scratches on his lower arm." At the time of DiMaggio's break with Marilyn Monroe, this tumultuous relationship with Ava Gardner remained unresolved.

So it was, in the fall of 1954, when Brad Dexter found the baritone, the baseball player, and the private detective huddled together in the Villa Capri. Dexter had seen neither Marilyn nor DiMaggio since the awkward encounter at North Palm Drive, when Marilyn vainly tried to use him as a bridge to her husband. Now, in the shadows of the Villa Capri, DiMaggio vouchsafed, "Jesus Christ, I'm sorry about the other night. I didn't know who you were, or what sort of guy you were. Can you help me now?"

According to Dexter, Marilyn was hiding out in her dressing room at Twentieth Century-Fox, refusing to see DiMaggio as the days ticked by to the divorce. DiMaggio was now desperate to get her back. Fox chief Darryl Zanuck had given orders that nothing should interfere with Marilyn's work, and had barred DiMaggio from the studio. The scheme now proposed was that Dexter, an actor known to the security guards, should smuggle DiMaggio into the studio in his car, hidden under a blanket.

"They tried to pressure me," Dexter recalls, "so I said 'I'll call Marilyn and ask if she wants to see you.' I spoke to her, and she said, 'Brad, please, I don't want to see Joe, I don't want to talk to him; it's over.' So I went back, and I told them, and I refused to do it."

On the morning of October 27, Marilyn appeared at the courthouse in Santa Monica. After a perfunctory hearing, she was granted a divorce on the grounds of "mental cruelty." Joe DiMaggio was not in court and did not contest the hearing. Formalities aside, however, he was still desperately trying to retrieve the situation. Seen in Los Angeles the day before the divorce, DiMaggio claimed he was only there "to see my son."

Then, on the day of the divorce itself, DiMaggio took the uncharacteristic step of contacting the press about his private life. He let it be known that he hoped for a reconciliation. "I hope she'll see the light," he was quoted as saying.

Marilyn, meanwhile, was sending strange and contradictory signals. On the eve of her court appearance she gave her first interview since the rift, to emphasize that there was no involvement with another man. Then, as she prepared to persuade a judge of DiMaggio's mental cruelty, she sought solace—with DiMaggio. She reportedly spent the night before the hearing, and the night of the divorce itself, closeted with her husband. Their hiding place was Frank Sinatra's apartment.

Skeptics in Los Angeles did not accept the reasons given publicly for the DiMaggio divorce. The courtroom script about DiMaggio's "coldness and indifference" did not ring quite true. Nor did people accept that Marilyn's occupational displays of sexuality had triggered the separation. Fox spokesman Roy Craft bluntly rejected that explanation. "Marilyn had a flamboyant reputation when they got married," he said. "If you build a home behind a slaughter house, you don't complain when you hear the pigs squealing."

Eight years later, when Marilyn died, DiMaggio's friend, Walter Winchell, would write: "After the divorce Joe told me the 'real' reason she filed. It has never been published and it won't be here. He wept telling it to me as the Cub Room crowd stared and wondered why he cried."

With Marilyn dead and Joe DiMaggio silent, the smoke of

mystery still eddies around the end of their marriage. Today, though, thanks to new information, a new scenario is emerging. It reveals an extraordinary pursuit of Marilyn, and the harassment of a man she was seeing.

Thirty years later, the man still recoils at the very mention of the name DiMaggio.

16

A FEW DAYS AFTER the divorce hearing, in early November 1954, Joe DiMaggio telephoned Marilyn's journalist friend Sidney Skolsky, asking for an urgent meeting. Skolsky suggested lunch, but DiMaggio insisted they talk in the privacy of his bedroom at the Hollywood Knickerbocker Hotel. What happened at the meeting made Skolsky squirm. He felt himself "confronted by an idol on his knees, begging to have his clay feet examined."

As Skolsky later recalled, DiMaggio "pointed toward the bed and asked me to sit down on the edge of it. He drew his chair up close to me. 'You know everything. There's one thing I must know,' he said, as softly as a torch singer squeezing the pathos out of every note. 'Is there another man? Why did Marilyn divorce me?' "

Skolsky, deeply embarrassed, talked around the subject and ended the meeting as speedily as possible. He had been aware for some time of DiMaggio's obsessive jealousy. There had been Marilyn's frenzied calls, saying that she was being watched and trailed. In recent months, Skolsky believed, DiMaggio had picked up the widespread rumor that Marilyn was homosexually involved with her drama coach, Natasha Lytess. The watching and the trailing, however, had been focused above all on a man—Marilyn's twenty-nine-year-old voice coach, Hal Schaefer.

Schaefer, a brilliant composer and pianist who had started as a protégé of Duke Ellington, would one day count among his pupils Peggy Lee, Judy Garland, and Barbra Streisand. He had won Marilyn's confidence the previous year during the shooting of *Gentlemen Prefer Blondes* and, two films later, they had become close friends. Marilyn had specifically requested his services, at the start of her marriage to DiMaggio, while she was doing *There's No Business Like Show Business*, and by April 1954 she and Schaefer were working flat out in Bungalow 4, at the back of the Fox lot.

The heads of the music department did notice the mutual devotion of the star and the voice coach. They also noted gratefully that Marilyn's singing skills were improving by the day. Nobody made much of the fact that they worked till all hours of the night in Bungalow 4, or that they slipped out together for meals. As work progressed, though, Marilyn showed herself violently protective of Hal Schaefer.

The present head of the Fox Music Department, Lionel Newman, recalls an incident when Irving Berlin himself descended on the studio to hear some of the new arrangements of his songs. "He raved about how good it was, and how well Marilyn was performing," Newman remembers. "Then next day Marilyn came to my office in a rage, asking why Hal was not getting the credit he deserved. She said that if Irving Berlin didn't go over and personally tell Hal how wonderful he was, she wasn't going to finish the picture. Eventually Berlin did sort it out, but she was ranting about it, screaming."

For thirty years Hal Schaefer has kept silent about his relationship with Marilyn Monroe, not least because of the appalling price he paid. In 1984, traced at his home in another state, the musician talked quietly of a period that he recalls as the most painful year of his life. When he first met Marilyn, Schaefer says, "She struck me as kind of fey, as not being altogether in this world, not all there. She was quiet, didn't open up much. At first she had no confidence, but she reacted to my teaching and she got better. I made her go out and buy a bunch of Ella Fitzgerald albums, and that was the strongest influence on her—she really became quite good. . . . Professionally, she was fine to work with. There came a time when she started to show up late, but I told her it wouldn't work with me. . . . I had my reputation established. I told her she didn't impress me just because she was Marilyn Monroe, and she stopped being late."

For many months, says Schaefer, the relationship with Marilyn remained strictly professional. "It was during *No Business Like Show Business*," he remembers, "that I started to know her more personally. Marilyn seemed to feel that I was the kindest, most gentle man she'd been involved with. And she loved the way I played the piano, thought I ought to be world-famous. I wasn't the world's greatest lover, I wasn't Tyrone Power, but I did give what she needed most—help. I didn't use her. I was supportive—I cared about her.''

There came a time when Schaefer and Marilyn became lovers, though he makes it clear that sex was not at the core of their affair. He echoes the irony other lovers report, that "Marilyn must have been frustrated almost all of the time. I think she regarded it as her function, being this great attractive female, that she was *supposed* to have sex with a man, because that was something she could do, that she could give. She wasn't very successful at it, in terms of her own fulfillment.''

Schaefer insists, "I was not the cause of the breakup with DiMaggio. It was already broken up, and not because of me. She would have left him no matter what. It had nothing to do with me. It was not to do with anyone else. But DiMaggio couldn't believe that. His ego was such that he couldn't believe that.''

In midsummer of 1954 Marilyn had told Schaefer of her troubles with Joe DiMaggio. She was to claim to him, as she did to others, that her husband sometimes physically mistreated her, that he was hugely possessive. Quite soon, Schaefer says, he found that out for himself. He soon became convinced that DiMaggio's detectives had Marilyn's car wired for sound.

"She had this big, black, Cadillac convertible," Schaefer remembers, "and sometimes she'd say, 'Let's just get in the car and go for a ride.' I took her once to that Jewish section on Fairfax Avenue—it wasn't late—and she put on a black wig and no makeup. But finally somebody recognized her as we were leaving, and we got in the car and left. We were talking in the car, and talking about where we were going, and suddenly somebody shows up there. Either we were bugged or we had been followed. I told her I thought we were bugged.''

After a while Schaefer and Marilyn had no doubt they were under surveillance. "The whole thing became a nightmare," he says. "She was terrified, and also furious, because she felt she couldn't live her life. She was completely frustrated.''

After weeks of this, Schaefer says he decided to have it out with DiMaggio. He called the house on North Palm Drive and spoke to Marilyn's husband, who told him to come over in about an hour. At the last moment, Marilyn, fearing violence, persuaded Schaefer not to go.

On the night of July 27, 1954, three months before the divorce, Schaefer failed to turn up for an appointment with friends. They finally found him at four o'clock in the morning, lying unconscious on the floor of his room at the studio. At the time it was said Schaefer had collapsed from overwork, but close friends knew he had tried to kill himself. Today Schaefer shudders as he remembers. ''I drank typewriter cleaning fluid, I drank carbon tetrachloride [a cleaning fluid], I drank about a quart of brandy, and I took about a hundred pills—anything that was there. . . .''

Schaefer barely survived. ''I just didn't want to go on any more,'' he says. ''A great deal of the focus was on Marilyn, but it wasn't totally that. It was the way I was in my life. I was despondent, depressed, drinking too much.'' Schaefer's liver and kidneys were seriously damaged, and he suffered several relapses. Once released from the hospital he hired two male nurses and took a house on the coast north of Los Angeles, there to begin a long and painful recovery.

Marilyn had visited Schaefer in the hospital immediately after his suicide attempt, and now she began visiting him at the beach.''Marilyn came up there,'' Schaefer says. ''I think she may have stayed on a Friday or Saturday night, but not all the time. I don't think Marilyn and I had any sex at that point. . . . I was still as sick as could be, and the male nurses were there.'' Now, says Schaefer, the harassment began once more.

''Again, on one of the occasions Mairlyn came,'' Schaefer recalls, ''they followed her. I can't remember it well because I was so sick. I can only remember them screaming through the window, and the threatening. And they said they were going to come in. We said we'd call the police. They said they'd cut the phone lines. I remember one night it was about dawn. And neither of us had slept, and Marilyn was standing in the corner. And after the threats they'd said, 'We'll come in, and we'll just take her out and we'll leave you alone. We won't harm you. We know she's there and we want to get her out.' Marilyn was terrified. Eventually, she slipped out, reached her car, and got away. There never was any actual violence.''

The ordeal drew Schaefer and Marilyn closer to each other. ''Marilyn came up to help nurse me. She was very sweet, and quite practical. I got well there, and Marilyn enjoyed it. She looked well, went swimming, got some sun—it was a very isolated spot. We thought, we really did think, we could build something for the future.''

As summer turned to fall Schaefer recovered sufficiently to return to Los Angeles. He and Marilyn met rarely and in secret, hoping to avoid the publicity surrounding the DiMaggio divorce. They did not entirely succeed.

On the day of the separation one major newspaper carried reports that DiMaggio had ''disapproved'' of Marilyn's visits to see Schaefer in the hospital the previous July. Columnist Louella Parsons, who knew Marilyn well, used this as the basis for a powerful lead. She wrote: ''I believe that it was jealousy that reared its ugly head when Marilyn Monroe and Joe DiMaggio had their final battle. . . . Joe is Italian and of a jealous nature.''

After the divorce had been formalized, the press began blathering about a possible reconciliation. Marilyn and DiMaggio were indeed engaged in a series of meetings, but they did not end happily. Things came to a head on November 5, a day that neither of them would ever forget.

On the morning of that day Marilyn offered a firm comment for publication: ''There isn't a word of truth that we are reconciling.'' DiMaggio, already divorced and therefore without conjugal rights of any kind, was now at his most desperate. Meanwhile, staked out on street corners and in parked cars, his private detectives were still on the prowl. That night, accompanied by his friend Frank Sinatra, DiMaggio set in motion a great folly.

What happened that Friday night was to boomerang on DiMaggio and Sinatra in an unpredictable way. Two years later a report in *Confidential,* a scandal magazine, would stir enough uproar to warrant probes by a California State Senate committee and a Los Angeles grand jury. The reconstruction that follows is drawn from evidence heard by those official bodies, a mass of conflicting eye-witness and press accounts, and new information gathered for this book.

On the evening of November 5, James Bacon, the ubiquitous journalist who had himself once enjoyed Marilyn's favors, took himself off to the Villa Capri restaurant. It was by no means the most star-studded watering hole in Los Angeles; it was more a cozy rendezvous serving spaghetti and meatballs, but it was patronized, even subsidized, by some famous Italians. These included Frank Sinatra and Joe DiMaggio, and both men were there when Bacon arrived.

''Over at a nearby table,'' Bacon recalled later, ''it looked like a Sons of Italy meeting—Sinatra, DiMaggio, and a few other *paisanos*. Hank Sanicola, Sinatra's manager and a close friend in those days, was among the group. I didn't join the table, although I have always been a friend of Frank's, because I could see that DiMaggio was in a terrible mood.''

Meanwhile, across the city, a quiet evening was ending for the inhabitants of an apartment building on the corner of Kilkea Drive and Waring Avenue in West Hollywood. In her tiny downstairs apartment, fifty-year-old Florence Kotz was having an early night. Mrs. Virginia Blasgen, the landlady, was preparing for bed, and her teenage son was already asleep. Upstairs, on the only other floor, an actress called Sheila Stewart was giving late dinner to Marilyn Monroe. Stewart, aged thirty-seven, had been friendly with Marilyn for some time, and they shared a common interest in singing. That evening, Marilyn was studying a movie script.

Out in the darkness, a young private detective, twenty-four-year-old Philip Irwin, was cruising around in his car. He was employed by Barney Ruditsky, the detective hired by DiMaggio to watch Marilyn, and he had been involved in the surveillance for months.

Now, on a run past the Kilkea Drive apartment, Irwin spotted Marilyn's parked car. He hurriedly telephoned his boss. Ruditsky arrived, staked out the house for a while, then went off to call Frank Sinatra at the Villa Capri.

In the restaurant reporter Jim Bacon watched as Sinatra and Joe DiMaggio argued, then bustled out. DiMaggio was first to arrive at the apartment building. He circled the block twice, then parked behind his ex-wife's car.

"He was very upset. He was proceeding toward the apartment," Irwin later testified. "I stopped him and tried to calm him down." Frank Sinatra drove up shortly afterward.

It was now that the landlady, Virginia Blasgen, looked out of the window. She said she saw two men, "a tall one and a short one . . . the tall one was mad, and was walking up and down . . . the little one was jumping up and down and grinning at me. . . ." Mrs. Blasgen recognized the large man as Joe DiMaggio, the small one as Frank Sinatra. About an hour later, at 11:15 P.M., mayhem came to Kilkea Drive.

The greatest shock was for Florence Kotz, asleep and oblivious to the strange comings and goings outside. She awoke to a crashing and splintering as men broke down her door, then to the glare of white light as the intruders began taking photographs. Mrs. Kotz screamed. Then the men fled as quickly as they had come, tumbling over each other in haste.

The DiMaggio war party, searching for Marilyn, had blundered into the wrong apartment. The idiotic adventure was to be known henceforth as the "Wrong Door Raid."

At the time, in 1954, the assault at Kilkea Drive was written off by the local police as attempted burglary. The frightened victim, Florence Kotz, was left with a broken door and a bad case of nerves. Not until 1957, when the California State Senate looked into the doings of unethical private detectives, was there any public accounting. The hearings then turned into a tussle for credibility between Philip Irwin, the detective who had spotted Monroe's car in the first place, and Frank Sinatra.

Ironically, it had been another dawn raid, with himself as the target, that forced Sinatra to answer the senators' questions: he had been served with a subpoena by two Los Angeles policemen who had marched into his Palm Springs bedroom at four o'clock in the morning. Then, under oath, Sinatra flatly denied that he was one of the men who broke into the Kotz apartment. He claimed he was sitting outside in his car when Joe DiMaggio, Barney Ruditsky, and Philip Irwin broke down the door. Irwin insisted that Sinatra had been one of the participants, and contested much of the detail in Sinatra's story. State Senator Edwin Regan, having listened to both statements, said drily, "There is perjury apparent here." The matter was referred to a grand jury.

Sinatra's lawyers, hunting for information to counter Irwin's claims, now hired another flamboyant Hollywood detective, Fred Otash. Otash sought to show that Irwin was a liar, and that nobody could have recognized Sinatra on the dark night of November 5, 1954. The matter was never fully resolved. The Grand Jury proceedings fizzled out, with jurors referring the case to the Chief of Police for "other possible testimony."

Joe DiMaggio never gave his version of the "Wrong Door Raid." Two years later, when the California State Senate and the Grand Jury wanted to question him, he sent messages saying he was unable to attend. He did so from the safety of the East Coast, where he was beyond the reach of a California subpoena.

The official airing of the case did bring some small comfort to the aggrieved Florence Kotz. She sued Sinatra and DiMaggio, along with various friends and the detectives, and accepted an out-of-court settlement of $7,500.

In all the verbiage expended on the "Wrong Door Raid," one name is glaringly absent—that of the real intended target, Marilyn's lover, Hal Schaefer. Marilyn's hostess that night, Sheila Stewart, now reveals that "Hal Schaefer was there with Marilyn that evening, and I made dinner for them. They were sitting in the dining room, and I had taken the dishes into the kitchen when we heard the crash."

Schaefer, who admits he was there, still recalls the shock. "It was like somebody set off a bomb," Schaefer recalls. "The whole house shook. It was terrifying. . . ." Asked whether he and Marilyn were in bed at the time, Schaefer says, "Not at that moment, no . . . but we were two grown, consenting adults, and she was already separated. . . ." He adds, "It was so lucky they got the wrong door. I think they would have done me terrible injury."

Sheila Stewart says Marilyn understood at once what was going on. She and Schaefer left the apartment in separate cars, and made their way to their separate homes. For Marilyn there was to be a confrontation with Joe DiMaggio that night. Yet another private detective, one of the large team assigned to the operation, was watching from the shadows two hours after the raid, when DiMaggio turned up on his ex-wife's doorstep. She let him in, and DiMaggio was still there when the detective finally left in the early hours of the morning.

Marilyn's avalanche of trouble was not yet over. She had been described, at the time of separation, as "emotionally and physically ill." Her lawyer said she had a virus, and denied she was pregnant. He did say, however, that she was being attended by Dr. Leon Krohn.

Dr. Krohn, "Red" to his friends, was a prominent Hollywood gynecologist for several decades. His rare male patients, who he served as a general physician, included his friend Frank Sinatra. Krohn mixed his profession with his social life, and played a special role following the collapse of the DiMaggio marriage. Joe DiMaggio became his houseguest, and he fielded dawn telephone calls from Marilyn, who checked regularly "to see if Joe was okay."

Dr. Krohn had been looking after Marilyn for two years now, ever since her demand that a gynecologist be present at her appendix operation. On the morning after the "Wrong Door Raid," an event that would remain hidden from the press for a long time, it was announced that Marilyn would enter the hospital within twenty-four hours for "an operation of a corrective nature," to be performed by Dr. Krohn.

Next day, Marilyn, feeling "sick to her stomach," appeared at the studio to pose for publicity photographs. Then, driven by Joe DiMaggio, she checked into the Cedars of Lebanon Hospital, by now a familiar port of call, for the operation. Dr. Krohn told the press that the procedure was to correct a gynecological problem from which Marilyn had suffered "for years." Joe DiMaggio spent the night at the hospital, catnapping in the doctors' lounge or pacing the corridors outside Marilyn's room.

Marilyn was released after four days, ungroomed and haggard, and without speaking to reporters. That night she and DiMaggio were seen dining at the Villa Capri, the restaurant where he had embarked on the "Wrong Door Raid" just a week earlier. There would be more such meetings in the next month, and the press would again prattle about reconciliation. Marilyn, however, had decided otherwise.

Within weeks Joe DiMaggio would find himself truly alone. Soon he would become a frequent visitor to the office of Marilyn's business manager on Sunset Boulevard, a sad hulking figure begging to know whether Marilyn had mentioned his name. He would see Marilyn many times in the future, would become famous as the man who carried a torch for her till her death and beyond. Marilyn would humor his obsession, would be grateful for his help, but she would never give him her heart.

In December 1954, as the newspapers watched DiMaggio's struggle to turn back the clock, nobody paid attention to the other man who waited. Hal Schaefer, now deeply in love with Marilyn, was soon discarded. He received a phone call from her in which she said, "Perhaps, one day, we'll meet again," and he knew he had lost her.

Schaefer still speaks of DiMaggio with a fear that three decades have done little to erase. He remembers Marilyn with sadness. "She told me that she loved me," he says quietly, "but I don't think she really knew what that meant."

Within twenty-four hours of the "Wrong Door Raid," and on the eve of her gynecological operation, Marilyn had danced till 3:00 A.M. at a party in her honor at Romanoff's to celebrate the completion of *The Seven Year Itch*. She had looked in wonderment at the guests and whispered to Sidney Skolsky, "I feel like Cinderella. I didn't think they'd all show up. Honest."

Marilyn had arrived an hour late because her car had run out of gas. Those lining up to sign a huge "Marilyn" souvenir portrait included Humphrey Bogart and Lauren Bacall, Claudette Colbert, William Holden, Jimmy Stewart, Susan Hayward, Gary Cooper, and Doris Day. For the first time Marilyn met her childhood idol, Clark Gable, and they discussed making a movie together.

Also at the party, showering Marilyn with praise, were the moguls of Hollywood: Sam Goldwyn, Jack Warner, and Marilyn's old adversary, Darryl Zanuck. "This party," wrote Skolsky a few days later, "was a big deal to Marilyn because it signified in its peculiar Hollywoodian manner that the elite of the town had finally accepted her."

The elite of the town were about to get a nasty shock. While they were accepting her, at the age of twenty-eight, as a full-fledged star, Marilyn had already decided to reject them. She had in fact resolved to turn her back on Hollywood altogether—husband, lovers, moguls, and all. Just before Christmas 1954 Marilyn put on her black wig and dark glasses, and drove to the Los Angeles airport carrying a ticket in the name of Zelda Zonk.

Cinderella, alias Zonk, was about to disappear.

Part III

BROKEN MARRIAGE—
BROKEN MIND

"How can I capsulize Marilyn? The more you know about people the more complex they are to you. If she were simple, it would have been easy to help her."

ARTHUR MILLER

17

IN THE FROZEN DARK before dawn, as Marilyn's plane flew east, a diminutive young woman steered a station wagon along the wooded roads near Weston, Connecticut. Amy Greene was on her way to LaGuardia Airport to pick up Marilyn and her traveling companion. Amy's thirty-three-year-old husband, Milton, was Marilyn's accomplice in her flight from Hollywood. For the next two years he was to be her close friend and champion, and her business partner.

Greene's wooing of Hollywood's most valued asset had not happened overnight. His meeting with Marilyn, eighteen months earlier, is recorded in Monroe lore rather like Stanley's with Livingstone. One look at the baby-faced Greene prompted her to say, "Why, you're just a boy!" He replied, "You're just a girl," and they immediately took a liking to one another. Greene, photographer of distinction, had been in Los Angeles to take pictures for *Look* magazine, and his approach had won over not only Marilyn, but even Joe DiMaggio. He photographed her in bulky clothes and modest poses, depictions that departed from the sexpot cliché but kept all the Monroe allure.

The plan that would outrage Hollywood took its initial vague shape at their first dinner together. Over the wine Greene enthused about his personal dream of independent filmmaking. Marilyn said she would like to be in one of his future movies. She was unhappy at Fox for two reasons.

On the one hand, Marilyn felt that the studio was taking advantage of her. In spite of her huge success she was still tied to a contract that paid her a maximum of $1,500 a week. On that basis, *Gentlemen Prefer Blondes,* five successful films ago, had brought her only $18,000. That did not amount to much, by Hollywood standards, after she had paid taxes, agent fees, acting coach Natasha Lytess, and beauticians. By contrast, Marilyn's co-star Jane Russell, not bound by a long-term contract, had been paid $100,000.

Milton Greene agreed with Marilyn that this was unfair. He assured her she could earn much more, were she to break away from Fox.

Marilyn also complained about her studio's insistence on casting her in stultifying roles. That troubled her at least as much as the poor pay. For a long time now she had been telling reporters that she was "really eager to do something else, roles such as Julie in *Bury the Dead,* Gretchen in *Faust,* and Teresa in *Cradle Song.*" She wanted to work opposite "serious" actors like Marlon Brando and Richard Burton. She wanted to *act*—and nobody at Fox was listening.

Greene could not help listening. "I thought I'd seen them all," he said in 1983. "Being in the business I'd seen so many models and actresses. But I'd never seen anyone with that tone of voice, that kindness, that real softness. If she saw a dead dog in the road, she'd cry. She was so supersensitive you had to watch your tone of voice all the time. Later I was to find out that she was schizoid—that she could be absolutely brilliant or absolutely kind, then the total opposite." In the early days, though, Marilyn seemed to Greene to be a prize without blemish.

The conspiracy began at once. Greene asked to see Marilyn's contract, got legal advice, and was soon telling her that her contract was void, that she could and should leave Twentieth Century-Fox. Marilyn was infected by the heresy of the notion. When Greene left for New York she drove him to the airport, and surprised him with the fervor of her kiss.

In the months to come there were more meetings. They talked at a cocktail party attended by the Bogarts, Frank Sinatra, and Judy Garland, and huddled together during an evening of charades at Gene Kelly's home, a regular haven for visitors from the east.

Greene and his wife, Amy, were on hand when Marilyn came to New York to shoot the skirt scene for *The Seven Year Itch.* Amy watched as an ashen-faced DiMaggio stalked away, and she was at the St. Regis Hotel the next day to sympathize over the bruises. When Marilyn returned to Los Angeles, Milton stayed in touch by telephone, talking her through the fine details of her contractual commitments. In the coming weeks, miserable and confused during the collapse of her marriage, Marilyn simply did not know what to do about the contract. She was wooed, in the end, as much by the promise of tranquility as by the hope for a better professional future: Milton and Amy Greene were offering to take the famous foster child into their home.

So it was, in the dying days of 1954, that Marilyn came in secret to the Greene home in Connecticut. An old farmhouse, dating from the early eighteenth century, it stood on twenty-five acres of woodland, with its own trout stream and a little lake. The living room was a cavernous place, the full two-story height of the old stable, warmed by an enormous log fire. Marilyn was given the studio, a home within a home, with its own balcony overlooking the water. For her, this house in the woods was wonderland.

Marilyn had rarely seen snow before or watched the seasons change. In the coming months, when spring came, she would greet it with the naive astonishment of a child. Here nobody bothered her. She could bundle up in Greene's warm clothes and go walking in the woods. She could wander off to lunch on sandwiches and homemade chocolate eclairs at The Little Corner, a nearby restaurant run by Greene's brother.

Amy recalls, "She liked to drive. We'd take the convertible and go sailing along the highway with the top down. We both liked to feel the wind on our faces and the warmth of the heater on our legs."

At home, Marilyn quickly became "Auntie" to the Greene's year-old son, Josh. She helped feed and bathe him, and surprised the Greenes by staying home to baby-sit him, so that they could go out on New Year's Eve. Marilyn would tell an interviewer that year that the Greenes were "the only real family I have ever known."

That, of course, was untrue. Marilyn had said the same of the DiMaggio family in San Francisco and, years before, of Fred Karger's family. She made a habit of grafting herself onto other people. As Amy Greene noticed with prescience, though, Marilyn also had a way of "shedding" people when they were no longer useful.

"Never forget," says Amy Greene, "that Marilyn wanted above all to become a *great* movie star. She would do anything, give up anyone, to move on up."

It was now that Hal Schaefer, back in Los Angeles, was unceremoniously dumped with one phone call. Marilyn's friend, Sidney Skolsky, who had loyally resisted the temptation to publish what he knew about the DiMaggio marriage, was put on ice until further required—several years hence. The curious intimacy with her dramatic coach, Natasha Lytess, now came to an end.

Lytess, realizing that her pupil was drawing away, pressured Marilyn for financial help. She later wrote: "I had been her private director for long years, working with her day and night. Yet when she was asked to do something for me, she had the feeling that she was being used." There were others, Marilyn aside, who felt Lytess did expect too much. At all events, she was soon to be discarded as redundant.

In her newfound world Marilyn needed new friends. The Greenes were soul mates who could show her Eastern sophistication and culture. Amy Greene, a former fashion model with looks that reflected her Latin ancestry, was lovely in her own right. She told Marilyn, six years her senior, that looking good in ordinary life did not demand the overtight skirts and sweaters that had made Marilyn's name on the screen.

"It dawned on me what pitiful clothes she had," Amy recalls. "She had to rummage through my drawers every time we wanted to go out. We brought Norman Norell to dinner, one of the top dress designers of the day, and had him design an elegant wardrobe for her." Marilyn welcomed the change. She and Amy went off on shopping sprees in Manhattan—at Milton Greene's expense.

Marilyn rarely had a close woman friend of her own age. In this sudden intimacy with Amy Greene she revealed a good deal of herself. Some of it was trivia. Amy learned, not least when Marilyn scandalized dressing-room attendants at Bonwit Teller on Fifth Avenue, the truth of the legend about Marilyn's reluctance to wear panties. She was, however, fanatical about wearing a brassiere. "Somebody, somewhere, had told her that if she always wore a bra her boobs wouldn't sag," Amy Greene says, "and she insisted on it. She slept with a bra on. She told me she'd finish making love with someone and then, zoom, on with the bra." At Bonwit Teller she wore the brassiere and a sanitary belt.

Much about Marilyn was irritating, certainly for the meticulously tidy Amy Greene. She observed that Marilyn lived in a chaos of clothes cascading from suitcase and closet, of cosmetics and toiletries scattered across her room. She was oblivious to the tedious responsibilities of her own life, such as a pending trial in Los Angeles for driving without a license. Her friends would sort it out.

The Greenes watched bemused as Marilyn plunged into their library. She started reading about Napoleon, discovered Josephine, and scooped up every book she could find about her. Supper conversation in the Greene household was dominated for a while by Marilyn enthusing about Josephine and her entourage.

"She was fascinated," says Amy Greene, "by women who had made it." Marilyn expecially enjoyed learning how Josephine's friend, Juliette Récamier, who was renowned for her figure, treated a specially commissioned nude statue of herself. As she aged, and her breasts started to droop, she had the marble breasts smashed.

Marilyn would sit on the stairs with Amy contemplating a cameo portrait of Emma, Lady Hamilton, Lord Nelson's mistress. She could hardly bring herself to believe that this imposing woman had begun life as a servant girl, and she made a personal celebration of the way Emma improved herself. "She was like a child about stories," Amy Greene recalls. "She said nobody had told her stories in her childhood, so when anybody told her a story, she was hooked."

Milton Greene had a motorcycle with a sidecar, and took Marilyn riding in it. One day, as they prepared to set off, Amy noticed Marilyn was wearing a long white scarf. She made a crack about Isadora Duncan, the eccentric American dance pioneer who died of strangulation when her scarf caught in the wheel spokes of a friend's sportscar. "Who's Isadora Duncan?" Marilyn asked, and was enthralled by the explanation. "It was," Amy Greene recalls, "Isadora Duncan Week in Connecticut."

To record her new experiences Marilyn bought a small leather-covered diary, one with a clasp and tiny key. She would carry it around the house, making notes on conversations or magazine articles that caught her interest. At night the Greenes would hear the radio playing in Marilyn's room till all hours, as she fed her unquenchable appetite for reading. They became aware of the torment that would now never leave Marilyn—insomnia. Sleep, when it did come, was ushered in by barbiturates; the pills, Seconal in those days, were never far from Marilyn's bedside.

It was now that Marilyn told Amy of the misery in her past as a female, of the child she claimed to have had in her teenage years, the endless string of abortions. Marilyn still suffered excruciating period pain. Amy would find her screaming in agony that no pills could quell, and took her to see a gynecologist friend.

Marilyn's longtime Los Angeles physician, Dr. Lee Siegel, has identified her ailment as endometriosis, a condition in which womb-lining tissue forms in places other than the womb, such as the ovaries or Fallopian tubes. Extreme pain during menstruation, and pain in the reproductive organs, is a usual symptom. Women who have endometriosis and want to have children are urged not to wait too long before becoming pregnant, for the disease is progressive and worsens with time.

Marilyn was now nearly twenty-nine. With her history of myriad abortions, some of the early ones perhaps performed inefficiently, she had courted additional disaster. As Amy Greene puts it, "Her whole womb was weeping." Marilyn now feared gynecologists, and insisted that Amy Greene stay in the room during the doctor's examination. The abortions had indeed caused damage, making it unlikely that Marilyn would ever bear children.

The doctor suggested that, with so much pain so often, Marilyn should consider a hysterectomy. She rejected the idea out of hand. "Marilyn was emphatic," says Amy Greene. "She said, 'I can't do that. I want to have a child. I'm going to have a son.' She always talked of having a son."

In the coming months Marilyn would hear from the actress Jane Russell, her friend from *Gentlemen Prefer Blondes*, asking her to help WAIF, an organization that found homes for unwanted children. This marked the beginning of Marilyn's active interest in children's causes, one she would maintain till she died. Soon the world's press would be chronicling her own frantic efforts to bear children.

During Christmas 1954, Marilyn and the Greenes delighted in the sheer naughtiness of Marilyn's escape from Hollywood. Amy answered the phone with lofty innocence to the stream of famous callers. Frank Sinatra, still holding Joe DiMaggio's hand back in Los Angeles, was fobbed off with a tall story. So was Billy Wilder, Marilyn's director on *Itch*. Bob Hope, who wanted Marilyn for his Christmas show in Korea, called in person. With the others sitting around giggling, Amy Greene struggled to sound serious as she inquired, "Tell me, Mr. Hope, is Miss Monroe lost?" Afterward, she and Marilyn rolled about on the floor, hooting with laughter.

Marilyn did not remain wholly hidden for long. In early January 1955, Milton Greene called a press cocktail party in New York, limited to a select audience of eighty. Dripping ermine, Marilyn announced that she had formed her own corporation, Marilyn Monroe Productions, with herself as president, holding 51 percent of the shares; and Milton Greene, as vice president, holding 49 percent. She said she did not intend to renew her contract with Twentieth Century-Fox. It was all very startling for her Fox bosses, who were under the impression that her existing agreement had yet to expire.

Marilyn was, she said "a new woman." She told the press she was making the break "so I can play the better kind of roles I want to play. I didn't like a lot of my pictures. I'm tired of sex roles. I'm going to broaden my scope. People have scope, you know . . . they really do." Asked what sort of roles she now wished to play, Marilyn mentioned "one of the parts in *The Brothers Karamazov,* by Dostoyevsky." Asked by a tittering reporter how those names were spelled, Marilyn replied, "Honey, I couldn't spell any of the names I told you."

Milton Greene tried to explain his grand plan, which was to form a group of actors and directors who would conceive their own films freed from the production-line tyranny of the big studios. The press took little notice. For them the focus remained Marilyn, and Greene would soon discover that running Marilyn Monroe Productions was a full-time occupation—and a crushing financial burden.

Marilyn had told Greene she was underpaid—and that her only present asset was fame. She was broke, and—because her contract with Fox was still enforced—she could not legally take other paid work. Using his earnings as a photographer, Grene paid all her expenses during 1955.

For a year Greene was to gamble all on his conviction that, whatever the legal niceties, Hollywood could not afford to pass up the box-office bonanza that came with the name Monroe. Twentieth Century-Fox would have to come to terms, however much it objected to Marilyn going independent. Greene would be proved right, but meanwhile he mortgaged himself to the hilt to keep Marilyn in luxurious, and visible, limbo.

Greene believed Marilyn must maintain a star's standard of living, not slip into dowdy obscurity. Marilyn did not demur, and was soon installed in grand style at the Waldorf Astoria Towers. Her working base was now a vastly expensive three-room luxury apartment, her first home in Manhattan. Greene paid for everything—clothes, beautician expenses of five hundred dollars a week (in 1955 prices), and the cost of keeping Marilyn's mother under care. He also bought Marilyn a black Thunderbird sportscar; Marilyn had become a fast driver who fancied herself an expert behind the wheel.

Under the stipulations of the Fox contract, Marilyn could make unpaid public appearances. Greene saw to it that the public saw a nice mix of the new Marilyn and the old. First, he made sure that the rogue glamour girl did not disappear. In March 1955, scantily costumed, Marilyn rode a pink elephant into Madison Square Garden, as her contribution to an extravaganza in aid of the Arthritis and Rheumatism Foundation. She and the elephant made their entrance to the commands of a ringmaster in the person of comedian Milton Berle, who has also claimed he was once Marilyn's lover.* Twenty-five thousand people roared approval at her entrance, and Marilyn stole the show.

At breakfast time on Good Friday, 1955, the Greene home in Connecticut was invaded by television crews. Milton Greene had arranged for an appearance on "Person to Person," a live interview program conducted by Edward R. Murrow. The show was supposedly "informal" visit with Mr. and Mrs. Milton Greene and their celebrated houseguest. Marilyn, who had been dousing a worse menstrual period than usual with painkillers and sleeping pills, wished she had never agreed to take part. She was not used to television, was petrified at the idea of talking directly to fifty million viewers. Her voice quavering, the seasoned star seemed amateurish compared to her coolly articulate hostess, Amy Greene.

Murrow hastily started asking the Greenes about their guest. Did she cook? Did she help clean the house and make her own bed? The Greenes lied obligingly. Marilyn herself offered a few worthy thoughts about the importance of working with the right film director, then fell back on a trusty old theme. She had really enjoyed riding the pink elephant, she said, "because I hadn't been to a circus as a kid."

Away from the Greenes' country home, which she now used more as a weekend retreat, Marilyn spent most of her time in New York City. She was exploring, seeking the pulse of that seething town, avidly striving to become a New Yorker herself. In the process she made myriad acquaintances and a few real friends. One of them, improbably, turned out to be one of her own fans—a sixteen-year-old boy.

Late the previous year, when Marilyn was in New York to shoot the skirt-blowing scene for *Seven Year Itch,* a crowd of

---

*In his memoirs, published in 1974, Berle claimed to have had an affair with Marilyn in 1948, during the making of *Ladies of the Chorus.*

hundreds had gathered each night to see her emerge from the St. Regis Hotel. One evening the crowd included Jim Haspiel, a youngster who had left home at the age of fifteen and who was now living from hand to mouth, moving from furnished room to furnished room. He idled away a good deal of his time at the movies and, as he puts it, he was expecting to see the Marilyn of the screen, "the oversized, over-everything lady from *Niagara*." When the flesh-and-blood Marilyn emerged, Haspiel was surprised that she seemed so small— she was five foot six according to her passport application— and by the fact that she had big ears. The youth knew at once that he wanted to meet her, and he was there when Marilyn returned two hours later.

When Marilyn emerged from her car she was surrounded by fans taking pictures or begging for her autograph. Then Haspiel, who had neither camera nor paper, asked for a kiss. "The word 'No' was all over her face," Haspiel remembers, "and I said, 'C'mon, just here on the cheek,' and a couple of people in the crowd went 'Oh-h-h,' and she gave in, and she did kiss me." The next night Marilyn refused a kiss even to an eight-year-old boy, muttering that "Joe" would not like it. For Haspiel it meant that something had drawn her to *him*, and events proved him right.

In those days Marilyn was followed everywhere in New York by a gaggle of persistent fans known as the Monroe Six, whose ages ranged from fourteen to thirty. They at first kept lonely, individual vigils outside apartments and office buildings, waiting for their heroine. Then, as they grew to know each other, they joined forces. Haspiel sometimes tagged along with the Six, but never became one of them. He was a loner, and believes Marilyn liked him for it.

After Marilyn's death a brown manila envelope would be found in her room, containing pictures of her "children." The photographs inside were those of Joe DiMaggio's son, Arthur Miller's children—and Jim Haspiel. In life, she had singled him out for a singular intimacy.

Marilyn quickly gave the sixteen-year-old her trust. He was welcomed to her New York apartments and accepted as a backseat companion as she zoomed around New York by cab. For many months, though, Marilyn did not even know his name. She never asked him, and he forgot to introduce himself until so long afterward that it seemed superfluous. It was not till a year later, in the middle of a conversation, that Marilyn suddenly called him "Jimmy." He concluded that

she had finally asked members of the Monroe Six to brief her
on the youngster who had never bothered to tell her his name.
In hindsight, Haspiel thinks she liked him for his audacity,
and because she saw in the solitary, obstinate adolescent the
orphan that was her image of herself.

Haspiel's friendship with Marilyn was conducted on the
run, and many of his anecdotes are based on taxi journeys.
Marilyn, he discovered, was impatient with a certain kind of
New York pushiness. When she waited after handing a cab
driver the fare, he said, "You're Marilyn Monroe, and you
expect change?" she made a point of extracting every last
dime. Having made her point, she then gave a large tip.

Young Haspiel's feeling for Marilyn verged on infatuation.
Once she rebuffed him as he started to follow her into a cab.
She wanted to travel alone, and thrust a twenty-dollar bill at
him to pay for his own taxi. He rejected the money and, in
pique, slammed the door in her face.

"I was quite wrong, of course," Haspiel says. "But I
think what separated me from the others for her was that, in
her world of sycophants, I sometimes answered back."

Marilyn's correspondence files, located in 1986, contain
letters between the star and her young friend. Haspiel's story
is undoubtedly truthful. Today, in middle age, married, and
with two teenage sons, Haspiel is probably the world's most
erudite student of Marilyn, the owner of a massive collection
of photographs, many of them taken with a five-dollar camera
he acquired thirty years ago.

Haspiel's Marilyn is one that few saw, a woman who
hardly ever wore makeup, who hated dressing up in normal
life, who "ran around the streets of New York in bobby-
sox." He watched as Marilyn wobbled off on her brand-new
English bicycle for rides in Central Park, or on excursions to
Nathan's hot-dog emporium in Coney Island. He helped as
she did her shopping at Whelan's, a favorite drugstore at 93rd
Street and Lexington Avenue. In this real world, Haspiel
thought, Marilyn was most at ease.

Haspiel also saw that Marilyn was more than an apprentice
New Yorker. She was on the mission of self-improvement
that Hollywood had debased and delayed. When Haspiel
offered her the *New York Post*, a tabloid, to read some columnist's tidbit about herself, Marilyn turned it down in disdain.
She devoured instead the *New York Times*, even the *Wall
Street Journal*. That summer, another visitor to Marilyn's
apartment observed the coffee table strewn with books: Emer-

son's *Essays*, Edith Hamilton's *Greek Mythology*, the letters
of George Sand, Joyce's *Ulysses*, and Michael Gorchakov's
How Stanislavsky Directs. The last title reflected the goal that
Marilyn held in deadly earnest—her determination to become
a serious actress.

18

IN LATE APRIL 1955, three weeks after her appearance on
television with Milton and Amy Greene, Marilyn slipped
quietly into the chapel of the Universal Funeral Home on
New York's Lexington Avenue. She was there for the funeral
of the British actress, Constance Collier, who had died at the
age of seventy-seven. Marilyn sat next to the writer, Truman
Capote, whom she had met a few weeks earlier at the El
Morocco nightclub. Capote remembered her dressed all in
black, "gnawing an already chewed-to-the-nub thumbnail . . .
periodically removing her spectacles to scoop up tears bubbling from her blue-grey eyes." She told Capote, "I hate
funerals. I don't want a funeral—just my ashes cast on waves
by one of my kids, if I ever have any. . . ."

Marilyn had been introduced to Constance Collier by Truman Capote, and had taken acting lessons from the legendary
actress in the weeks before she died. Collier, who spent her
last years training American actors, offered this snap verdict
on Marilyn: "Oh, yes, there is something there. She is a
beautiful child. I don't think she's an actress at all, not in any
traditional sense. What she has—this presence, this luminos-
ity, this flickering intelligence—could never surface on the
stage. It's so fragile and subtle, it can only be caught by the
camera. It's like a hummingbird in flight; only a camera can
freeze the poetry of it. But anyone who thinks this girl is
simply another Harlow or harlot or whatever, is mad. I hope,
I really pray, that she survives long enough to free the strange
lovely talent that's wandering through her like a jailed
spirit. . . ."

*   *   *

Even as Collier died, Marilyn was seeking a liberator for her talent. She found him in Lee Strasberg, founder of the Actors Studio, the New York theater workshop that had become the most influential institution of its kind in the world. Its alumni of the fifties included Marlon Brando, James Dean, Eli Wallach and Anne Jackson, Paul Newman, Montgomery Clift, Steve McQueen, Shelley Winters, Maureen Stapleton, and Tom Ewell, Marilyn's co-star in *Seven Year Itch*. Their teacher, Strasberg's recent biographer notes, has been called rabbi by some, pope by others, guru, god or genius, fake, charlatan, or the Ultimate Shrink.

Strasberg, aged fifty-three when Marilyn came to New York, had been born into poverty in a Jewish ghetto in Poland. He came to America with his family as a boy and was deeply involved in theater by the time he turned twenty-one. His revelation, and the guiding light he would show to generations of American actors, was the Stanislavsky Method, the science of acting that has been called the "total immersion system." It held that actors must break away from the banal through intense exploration of their scenes and themselves. They must seek "motivation" in every act and phrase, draw on their own personal experience, their own past pain and joy, to communicate with the audience. Self-analysis was thus obligatory, and Strasberg, an ardent student of psychology, encouraged his students to undergo psychoanalysis.

In the muddle that was Marilyn, Strasberg was to discover a creature of dangerous potency. She would find a teacher, a priest for her personality, and a new dependency.

Marilyn had met Strasberg's wife and daughter on a set in Hollywood, and had talked longingly of one day studying at the feet of the master. Now, in March 1955, Marilyn found herself seated opposite producer Cheryl Crawford, one of the co-founders of the Actors Studio. She talked of her interest in becoming a serious actress, and Crawford promised to help. The very next day Marilyn was sitting opposite Strasberg in his cluttered, book-lined apartment at Broadway and 86th Street. After a brief conversation he agreed to take her on as a private pupil; full membership in the Studio was reserved for those who had already had stage experience. The first lessons would be at home because, as Strasberg saw at once, Marilyn was "the kind who had emotional problems."

As Marilyn described her past (it was now that she told Strasberg she had once been a call girl), he noticed that she was very nervous. She was literally stammering in her fright. Nevertheless, the new teacher enthused.

Strasberg would recall, "I saw that what she looked like was not what she really was, and what was going on inside was not what was going on outside, and that always means there may be something there to be worked with. It was almost as if she had been waiting for a button to be pushed, and when it was pushed a door opened and you saw a treasure of gold and jewels."

In the end, no hyperbole was too much for Strasberg to use in describing Marilyn. He said of her presence: "She was engulfed in a mystic-like flame, like when you see Jesus at the Last Supper and there's a halo around him. There was this great white light surrounding Marilyn."

In 1955, though, Strasberg did not flatter Marilyn with overblown phrases. He offered instead months of grueling exercises and hard work. In the mecca of American acting, all were equal and none were stars. Marilyn would appear in baggy sweater and jeans, without makeup, and seek out the most obscure place in the room. Actor Kevin McCarthy hardly noticed her at first, as they sat side by side watching a badly acted scene from Chekhov's *Three Sisters*. When he did recognize her, he observed Marilyn's disconcerting ability to switch her Monroe persona from "off" to "on," from obscurity to the white light of Strasberg's perception.

"This tousled piece of humanity was sitting on my right," McCarthy remembers, "looking like nothing. Then, fifteen minutes later, after I'd interrupted the scene with some fairly rude comments, I looked again. I realized that a breathing, palpitating Marilyn Monroe had developed out of that nothing. . . . I remember looking and thinking, 'My God, it's her'—she'd just come to life."

Marilyn was quickly befriended by Eli Wallach, then just back from London and acting in *Teahouse of the August Moon*. Wallach, who like McCarthy would one day act with her in *The Misfits*, was also struck by the phenomenon of Marilyn's instant metamorphosis. In the street heads would turn to stare or ogle whereas a moment before everyone had passed her by. "I just felt like being Marilyn for a moment," Marilyn would murmur.

Wallach was bemused by the contradictions in her. In the summer of 1955, when *Seven Year Itch* was about to open in New York, he sat watching with Marilyn as workmen erected a forty-foot-high poster of the famous skirt scene. Only the bottom half, showing her legs and upper thighs, was in place. As a huge crane lowered the cutout image of her torso into position, Marilyn mused, "That's the way they think of me, with my skirt over my head."

Wallach says, "She didn't seem to mind. She accepted it."

Sometimes the Strasberg acting sessions seemed intellectually beyond Marilyn. One of her colleagues, Frank Corsaro, came to call himself "Marilyn's translator." He says, "She didn't know what Lee was talking about half the damn time."

Peggy Feury, who now runs an acting workshop in Los Angeles, disagrees. She says, "Marilyn was so bright about acting. Her trouble was only that she'd get so scared she wasn't going to be able to do it, and so tied up in knots, that then everyone thought she was dumb."

Some work came more naturally to Marilyn than to others. Asked in improvisation class to make believe she was a kitten, she excelled. Marilyn had borrowed a kitten, watched it for hours, then undulated to perfection. The challenge for Marilyn was to overcome the terror, the abject stage fright, that accompanied that actual speaking of dialogue in front of an audience.

Outside the Studio, Marilyn's thirst for security was now accommodated by Lee and Paula Strasberg. As she spent more and more time in the city, and less with the Greenes in Connecticut, the orphan by vocation allowed herself to be taken to the bosom of yet another family. She was permitted total freedom of access to the Strasberg home. In a bustling New York Jewish household, Marilyn became Paula Strasberg's third child. She spent holidays at the family's weekend place on Fire Island.

Strasberg's daughter, Susan, herself an actress at the age of seventeen, sometimes shared a room with Marilyn. From her bed, Susan would watch in awe as the famous body, soon to be thirty years old, was prepared for the day. At night Susan would watch as Marilyn "would kick off her shoes and dance in the middle of the room alone, if no one was willing to dance with her."

Once, when the guest said she envied people who could draw, Susan lent her a sketchpad and pen. Marilyn's facility in drawing came as a surprise. "I saved two of her sketches," Susan says. "In one, with quick, round lines depicting a feline sensual grace and movement, she had done a self-portrait. The other was of a little Negro girl in a sad-looking dress, one sock falling down around her ankles." Marilyn called this drawing "Lonely." A number of her drawings have survived, amateurish in execution, but showing wit and sensitivity. One, of an elegant woman holding a glass of champagne, she called, "Oh, What the Hell!"

Over the years Marilyn repaid the Strasberg hospitality with her own whimsical generosity. She paid Lee Strasberg's traveling expenses for a trip to the Soviet Union. She gave her Thunderbird car to Strasberg's son, John, on his eighteenth birthday. At fund-raising events for the Studio, Marilyn's very presence raised many thousands of dollars.

In her last will, Marilyn bequeathed all her personal effects to Strasberg. Dresses, furs, film awards, books, letters, even her underwear, would one day be delivered to the Strasberg home in New York. As an unexpected windfall, Strasberg was later to inherit the rights to one of Marilyn's films, *The Prince and the Showgirl*. Many of her personal belongings today remain, jealously guarded, in the care of Strasberg's second wife, Anna.

There is no doubt Marilyn brought greater renown to the Studio and greater wealth to Strasberg personally. His occasional habit of bringing to the Studio people who were famous personalities, qualified by fame as much as by acting skill, paid off handsomely. Critics have assailed Strasberg as an opportunist, and his own son says, "The greatest tragedy was that people, even my father in a way, took advantage of her. They glommed on to her special sort of life, her special characteristics, when what she needed was love. My parents did give her some love, but it was inextricably linked with the acting."

Also mentioned in Marilyn's will would be a New York couple who could never be accused of taking advantage of her. The poet Norman Rosten and his wife, Hedda, gave Marilyn uncomplicated privacy and companionship, and perhaps the longest association of pure friendship in her entire life. It began, utterly by chance, on a rainy day in the spring of 1955.

Norman Rosten was seated at his desk at home in Brooklyn Heights, when a friend, photographer Sam Shaw, called to ask if he could drop in. He and a companion had been caught in a downpour in nearby Prospect Park. Minutes later Rosten was watching Shaw tramp up the stairs followed by a drenched figure in a camel's-hair coat. Shaw mumbled an introduction, and Rosten thought he caught the name "Marion." The girl picked up a volume of poems Rosten had written for his

daughter Patricia, and sat silently reading. It was later, when
Hedda Rosten asked what she did for a living, that she
timidly offered her name, Marilyn Monroe.

Rosten and his wife, almost alone among Marilyn's Eastern
friends, had no concern with anyone but the private Marilyn.
"We really didn't give a damn who she was," Rosten says,
"and she did step out of her stereotype in real life. With us
she was thoroughly enchanting, such an odd human being. . . ."

Throughout the summer of 1955, and sporadically for the
next seven years, Marilyn enjoyed privacy with the Rostens.
They kept a few of her notes and letters, rare windfalls, since
they were from a woman who did not often correspond. After
that first meeting Marilyn wrote from the Waldorf-Astoria:

Dear Norman,
It feels a little funny to be writing the name "Norman"
since my own name is Norma and it feels like I'm writing my
own name almost, however—
    First, thanks for letting Sam and me visit you and Hedda on
Saturday—it was nice. I enjoyed meeting your wife she was
very warm to me—However again—
    Thanks the most for your book of poetry—which I spent all
Sunday morning in bed with. It touched me very much—I
used to think that if I had ever had a child I would have
wanted only a son—but after "Songs for Patricia"—I know I
would have loved a little girl as much—but maybe the former
feeling was only Freudian anyway or something—
    I used to write poetry sometimes but usually I was de-
pressed at those times. The few I showed it to—(in fact about
two people)—said that it depressed them—one of them cried
but it was an old friend I'd known for a long time.
    I hope to see you again.
    So anyway thanks.
    And my best to Hedda and Patricia and you—
                                                Marilyn M.

"She liked poetry," Rosten recalls. "It was a shortcut for
her. She understood, with the instinct of a poet, that it led
directly into the heart of experience."

In 1952, drunk on whisky with Robert Slatzer in the hotel
at Niagara Falls, Marilyn had sat scribbling what Slatzer
called "herniated sonnets." Now, in the upholstered hush of
her room at the Waldorf-Astoria, she was trying her hand at
poetry again.

The experiments grew from her evenings with the Rostens, who often held informal poetry readings. Two favorites were Walt Whitman, whose work Marilyn had long liked, and W. B. Yeats, a new discovery for her. At the Rosten readings, each person in turn would take a book of verse and read aloud the poem on whatever page fell open. Marilyn came to read, of all things, Yeats' "Never Give All the Heart." Rosten says, "She read rather slowly, softly, as if in class, low but breathless":

> Never give all the heart, for love
> Will hardly seem worth thinking of
> To passionate women if it seem
> Certain, and they never dream
> That it fades out from kiss to kiss;
> For everything that's lovely is
> But a brief, dreamy, kind delight.
> Oh, never give the heart outright,
> For they, for all smooth lips can say,
> Have given their hearts up to the play.
> And who could play it well enough
> If deaf and dumb and blind with love?
> He that made this knows all the cost,
> For he gave all his heart and lost.

There was a silence when Marilyn finished. Rosten says, "She had thought poets were mystical, somehow separate and apart from ordinary people. I tried to disabuse her of that idea. . . ." Soon, Marilyn was tentatively sending Rosten her own efforts, including these lines:

> Life—I am of both your directions
> Existing more with the cold frost
> Strong as a cobweb in the wind
> Hanging downward the most
> Somehow remaining
> those beaded rays have the colors
> I've seen in paintings—ah life
> they have cheated you. . . .
> thinner than a cobweb's thread
> sheerer than any—
> but it did attach itself
> and held fast in strong winds
> and sin(d)ged by (?) leaping hot fires

('Better if done with an sir. Olivian accent)

For Norman

From time to time
I make it ~~Ryme~~ rhyme
but don't hold that kind
of thing
against
me.

Oh well what the hell
so it went so
what I want to tell —
—Is whats on my mind   →(intendendal to rymewith)

taint Dishes
taint Wishes
its thoughts
flinging
by
before I
die. (and to Think | in ink

Scrawled lines given by Marilyn to poet Norman Rosten in the mid-fifties. She was still capable of poking fun at herself.

life—of which at singular times
I am both of your directions—
~~somehow I remain hanging downward~~
the most
as both of your directions pull me.

For Marilyn 1955 was a year of exploration—of herself, of acting, and of arts she had never had time for in the past. Sometimes she would "borrow" Rosten from his wife to escort her to a play or concert. Once, at Carnegie Hall, they were invited to meet the Russian pianist, Emil Gilels. He kissed Marilyn's hand and said she should visit the Soviet Union. Marilyn told him, as she had been telling all and sundry for some time now, that she was currently reading Dostoyevsky.

When the press spotted Rosten as Marilyn's companion, gossip columns soon hinted at an affair. Rosten, who was happily married, says the idea never seriously occurred to him. "With Marilyn, you're not talking about going to bed with a woman, you're talking about going to bed with an institution. Who can handle that? And how awful to be one!"

The Rostens saw a Marilyn who liked to be domestic, so long as hosehold work was occasional entertainment rather than necessity. She would boast of her skill at doing the dishes, the legacy, she said, of childhood slavery in foster homes. Marilyn the cook used her new friends as guinea pigs. Rosten recalls good stews and bouillabaisse, and disastrous salads drowned in vinegar. He said "her color schemes" (peas and carrots), if not striking, managed to be consistent. She once offered to "tone down" a spicy dish by using a hair dryer!

The Rostens' daughter, Patricia, who was then eight, has a child's-eye memory of a new acquaintance who "was fun to be with because she broke the rules, and children love being around grown-ups who can get away with that. When Marilyn touched me or hugged me I felt a warmth and softness (dare I use the word 'maternal' in relation to her?) that was very reassuring. It was not unlike falling into that champagne-colored quilt that graced her bed."

Once Marilyn surprised Patricia in her bedroom, her nose in the enormous makeup box. "She plunked me down at her vanity mirror," Patricia remembers, "and said she would show me how to do the job right. I watched her skillful hands transform my kid's face into something that even I might have called glamorous. She made my eyelids glimmer, my cheekbones appear accentuated, and my mouth rosy with color. She also arranged my hair, lifting it off my shoulders into an elegant French twist. 'Why,' I thought, 'I could pass for seventeen.' Then, proud of her handiwork, she happily took me by the hand back to the living room to show me off to the grown-ups.''

Sometimes the Rostens invited Marilyn to their rented summer place on Long Island. An excursion in her company could be anything but peaceful. Rosten tells of one weekend, when Marilyn had spent a while sitting demurely on the beach, in bathing suit, straw hat and sunglasses, shaded by an umbrella.

''Slowly, imperceptibly,'' says Rosten, ''as though the news had spread by some sort of telepathy, a group of young people appeared in swim attire and, before we were aware of it, closed us in a circle. They stared at Marilyn, unbelieving, as at a mirage. They came up to her, uttering little cries of joy, reaching out to touch her. They began crowding, their enthusiasm getting out of control as she moved back, a reflex of fear now in her eyes.

''I was struck by this double effect: love of the crowd and the need of their adulation, and at the same time a nameless fear. She laughed nervously, abruptly broke from the circle, and ran toward the water about fifty yards away. The youthful admirers cheered and chased after her into the water. She began swimming out, calling for me to follow. I was a little scared, especially when the noisy kids surrounded her while I tried to push them away. . . .''

Suddenly, Marilyn began to splutter and swallow water. ''I'm not a good swimmer even when I'm good,'' she gasped, her aquatic prowess with Tommy Zahn, the surfing champion of a decade earlier, apparently a thing of the past. She and Rosten were rescued by the crew of a passing speedboat. Its driver, a boy in his teens, then drove round and round in circles, staring transfixed at the exhausted female in his boat, until Rosten told him to snap out of it.

In other situations Marilyn had compassion for those who recognized her. Once, disguised in a bandanna and dark glasses, she and a male companion stopped at a gas station on the East Side Drive. The station attendant conferred with his mate, then announced, ''I just bet my friend here ten dollars that you're Marilyn Monroe.''

Marilyn's companion replied, "No, she's not, though she's often mistaken for her."

They were about to drive off when Marilyn cried, "My God, he's paying his friend the ten dollars." She called the attendants back, took off her glasses, and said, "Give him back the money. I am Monroe."

Jim Haspiel, the fan turned friend, went Christmas shopping at Saks Fifth Avenue with Marilyn at the end of that first year in New York. She had "disguised" herself with a silk kerchief tied under the chin, an Ivy League cap, dark glasses, and hormone cream, instead of makeup, all over her face. It fooled no one, for when Haspiel left for a few minutes, after arranging with Marilyn to rejoin her at the men's tie counter, he returned to find that "eight" salesmen were waiting on her, and "about two hundred and fifty" customers were thronging around. The rest of the store was virtually empty.

Marilyn made her way through the crowd to Haspiel and whispered, "Please don't say my name, I don't want anyone to know it's me." Haspiel decided she had lived so long in the crowd she didn't see it anymore. Others might suspect Marilyn thrived on the recognition—when it was convenient.

Norman Rosten concluded that Marilyn reveled in being female, accepted it for the power it gave her. "She sensed the difference in sexual psychology between men and women," Rosten believes, "and would never censure a man for beating the woman to the draw, so to speak. We could lust after her, dream of possessing her, but no one would be hurt. She could be alluring and warm, and yet had the courage to battle alone against male-dominated Hollywood power—and win."

Months after they first met, toward the end of 1955, Marilyn asked Rosten to take her to the Rodin exhibition at the Metropolitan Museum of Art. "Two pieces fascinated her," says Rosten, *Pygmalion and Galatea* and *The Hand of God*.

The Hand of God, in white marble, depicts a great curving hand holding a man and a woman locked in passionate embrace. "They are together and apart," the poet remembers. "The woman's hair streams from the stone. Marilyn walked around and around that small white miracle, her eyes wide as she removed her dark glasses."

In her year of limbo in New York, Marilyn began telling friends that she had found her love. She was, certainly, close to achieving another ambition: she had America's foremost playwright on the hook, and soon it would be just a matter of reeling him in.

19

ARTHUR MILLER RARELY TALKED willingly about Marilyn Monroe during her lifetime, and in the twenty years since he has remained silent. He corresponded courteously during the writing of this book, but said, "When I have something to say about Marilyn I will do it on my own typewriter."

Considering that he lived in a glare of banal publicity for half a decade, Miller's position is to be respected, even in this age of intrusion. However, thanks partly to his and Marilyn's own statements in 1956, when their romance was at full flood, we can now reconstruct the courtship that led to one of the most ballyhooed marriages of its time.

When Marilyn settled in New York, Arthur Miller was about to turn forty. She was twenty-nine. He still lived in Brooklyn, where he had been raised, with Mary, his wife of fifteen years, and two children not yet into their teens.

Although America knew Miller only as a playwright, he believed fervently in the value of hard physical work, not least as vital grounding for his plays about the common man. At one point of his life Miller made a point of working a few weeks each year in a factory. He has said, "Anyone who doesn't know what it means to stand in one place, eight hours a day, doesn't know what it's all about. It's the only way you can learn what makes men go into a gin mill after work and start fighting. You don't learn about those things in Sardi's."

Miller had little time for such after-theater night spots or for the fashions of New York City. When he absolutely had to buy a new suit he delighted in announcing that he had found it on sale. He was partial to stout shoes with thick leather soles, and liked to say that he bought just one pair for each play he wrote. His favorite uniform, when not in town, was a windbreaker and khaki pants.

Not being in town was, by 1955, becoming a preoccupation with him. After his first success, with *All My Sons*,

Miller had bought four acres, cheap, in Connecticut. He worked steadily for six weeks building himself a work shack, then sat in it during the next six weeks fashioning the play that won a Pulitzer Prize, *Death of a Salesman*.

Since 1950, when he had first met Marilyn in Hollywood, Miller had produced three more plays. *The Crucible*, based on the Salem witch trials of two hundred and fifty years ago, came in 1953, when Senator Joseph McCarthy's investigation of imagined communism was at its most pernicious. *A View from the Bridge*, about a man who betrays the illegal immigrant suitor of his daughter, appeared in 1955, the year Marilyn came East.

Arthur Miller was a man who for some time had been able to say, "I have the name. They have to listen when I talk." He was not enormously rich but he had money. He would say, "You live fruitfully in tension. To create, and I don't only mean writing, is to be under tension. Paradise is a state of inertia where nothing happens. It is a form of death. The tension is necessary. Once it's over, you drop dead in six months."

Marilyn arrived in New York when the vital tension had gone from Miller's personal life. His marriage was in the doldrums. The wife who had worked to keep him in the early days, who had borne his children, and corrected his manuscripts, was no longer enough. They were headed for divorce, he was to say a year later, "Marilyn or no."

Miller told a *Time* reporter in 1956, "I didn't know a thing about Marilyn coming to New York until I read about it in the papers." There had been no contact between them since their encounter in late 1950, but neither had forgotten.

Miller's memory was of a young woman at a Hollywood cocktail party, "so terrified she couldn't speak a word, just stood there mute but refusing to engage in the vacuous small talk." He said he had gained Marilyn's confidence, then seen her for about eight hours over three days. She had told him of her "smothering feeling of inferiority, her inability to make any real friends, the fact that people thought of her only in terms of an inviting body and nothing else."

Miller was struck by Marilyn's "sensitivity and feeling and grasp of reality," and he told her he thought she should come to New York and learn how to act. When he left California, she poured out her troubles in letters, and he responded—for a while. Then, as he plunged into writing his next play, the letters stopped.

Author and critic Maurice Zolotow, who knew both Miller and Marilyn, believes the encounter in Hollywood haunted Miller and influenced his work from then on. In both *The Crucible* and *View from the Bridge*, Zolotow noted the themes of the eternal triangle, of unfaithfulness in marriage, and of an older man's love for a young girl. Miller himself, though not till years later, would write that *View from the Bridge* "was expressing a very personal preoccupation . . . not at all apart from my own psychological life. . . ."

Fellow playwright, Clifford Odets, said after reading *The Crucible*, which Miller wrote following his first meeting with Marilyn, "No man would write this play unless his marriage was going to pieces."

At all events, sometime in April 1955, when Marilyn had ridden her pink elephant, appeared on national television, and discovered Lee Strasberg, Miller reached out for the girl from Hollywood.

According to Marilyn the reunion occurred at another party, for theater people in New York. She was drinking vodka and orange, and Miller made the approach. They talked for a while and parted at the end of the evening. Miller held out for two weeks, then called Paula Strasberg of the Actors Studio, to ask for Marilyn's phone number. They met at the home of a mutual friend, poet Norman Rosten, who had been to the University of Michigan with Miller, and the affair began.

The couple managed a remarkable feat. They met for the best part of a year without being discovered by the press. Miller, who had been borrowing his son's bicycle for a long time, went out and bought a new one for himself. It was English, with gears, as Marilyn's was, and the two of them would pedal unnoticed around Brooklyn's Sheepshead Bay or Coney Island, places where no gossip columnist lay in wait. They ate in corners of obscure restaurants.

Peter Leonardi, Marilyn's assistant that year, said later, "I was with her morning, noon, and night for weeks, and I never even heard the name 'Miller.' "

In the summer of 1955 Marilyn gave a dinner party for friends who were in on the secret. Miller recalled that "she did nothing else for two days. I never saw anyone so worried about a simple meal. Actually the whole thing was overdone, too formal, too meticulous, too manicured. She worked herself into a frazzle about the whole affair."

On another occasion Marilyn was more true to her usual chaotic form. Maureen Stapleton, her colleague at the Actors

Studio, remembers an evening when Marilyn, hurrying home from rehearsal, announced that she had to prepare a roast for Miller and some friends. Unfortunately, she had forgotten that the meat would take hours to cook, so dinner was served at an hour when most people were going to bed.

Miller, whose presence had long been nurtured, but only as a photograph at Marilyn's bedside, was now a day-to-day reality. He indeed looked, as journalists had long chorused, like a whiskerless version of the man in the other picture that accompanied her everywhere—Abraham Lincoln. Years later, asked what one thing she was most grateful to Miller for, Marilyn would say, "He introduced me to the importance of political freedom in our society." Miller was a man who liked to talk social theory for hours, a pipe gripped between his teeth or, when pipeless, swiveling a cigarette from tooth to tooth, like a gun. Marilyn listened.

A close friend of the couple said, "Aside from personal attraction—and that's the biggest aside in history—a lot of what interested her in Arthur was this: here was a man with a whole structure of social ideas clarified by a great deal of reading."

It was only twelve months since Marilyn had tried in vain to persuade Joe DiMaggio to read "everything from Mickey Spillane to Jules Verne." On DiMaggio's birthday Marilyn had given him a gold medal for his watch chain, inscribed with a quotation from *The Little Prince* by Antoine de Saint-Exupéry: "True love is visible not to the eyes, but to the heart, for eyes may be deceived." Perplexed, DiMaggio had asked, "What the hell does that mean?" With Arthur Miller the roles were neatly reversed; Marilyn was asking the questions.

She did admire Miller's intellect, as she had years earlier, but soon she would also insist, "I'm in love with the man, not his mind. The Arthur Miller who attracted me was a man of warmth and friendliness. Arthur has helped me adjust myself. I've always been unsure of myself. Arthur has helped me overcome this feeling."

Marilyn, for her part, wrought a transformation in Arthur Miller. "Miller was in love, completely, seriously," Norman Rosten would say. "It was wonderful to behold."

Miller told *Time* reporter Robert Ajemian, "She is the most womanly woman I can imagine. Being with her, people want to die. This girl sets up a challenge in every man. Most men become more of what they are natively when they are around her: a phoney becomes more phoney, a confused man becomes more confused, a retiring man more retiring. She's kind of a lodestone that draws out of the male animal his essential qualities.''

Miller was persuaded that Marilyn's reputation for promiscuity was vastly exaggerated. "Sure, she had her men," he said, "but not from couch to couch, man to man. Any relation she ever had was meaningful to her, built on a thread of hope, however mistaken. I've known social workers who have had a more checkered history than she has.''

The playwright in Miller admired the honesty in Marilyn, thought her "literally incapable of saying anything unless it was the truth.'' He said that as an actress, "she'll either do the truth or go on strike. There's something in her that's looking for the basic reality of a given situation. In acting, of course, this is a terrific thing. It enables you to get to the core.''

Miller talked of Marilyn's obsessive worry about her lack of education. "She'll come to me and say, 'I heard a new word the other day, what does it mean?' The other day she asked me about the word 'impermeable.' She often mispronounces a word—perhaps she will say 'intraveniously' instead of 'intravenously.' But she wants to learn.''

Miller said Marilyn had recently been reading a book on the art of Goya. "When I talked to her on the phone she said to me, 'I haven't got to the good part yet.' Next time I called her she said, 'I'm two-thirds through and I still haven't hit the good part.' The truth was, of course, that the book was mostly surmise, not positive fact. When Marilyn reached the end of the book she said to me, 'Well, I finished it and there's still nothing. Why did they write it?' It was a good question. That's the way a book ought to be read.''

Miller told *Time*, "Instead of becoming a disbeliever in life, which she had every reason to become, she kept her ability to feel and search for a genuine relationship. She has stopped wanting to throw herself away. She was preached to so much that she was a bad girl, not worth anything, that she developed an enormous self-destructiveness. She's coming out of it now.''

Miller was utterly smitten. So, thought their mutual friends, was Marilyn. She, however, was pursued by familiar ghosts—and new temptation.

*   *   *

In the early months of 1955 Joe DiMaggio had still not given up his pursuit of Marilyn, and she had not yet cut herself entirely free of him. Ironically, he reached her most through the family of the most important lover in Marilyn's youth, Fred Karger. Fred's sister, Mary, had by now moved to New Jersey with her children, and Marilyn, sometimes accompanied by DiMaggio, visited often.

To the Kargers, Marilyn and DiMaggio now seemed to be on good terms. DiMaggio played golf with Mary, and Marilyn delighted the children with her eccentric diets and sense of fun.

Mary's daughter Anne recalls an afternoon when the neighbors, knowing Marilyn was next door, pulled an effective practical joke.

"Their son was in the Fire Department," Anne recalls, "and he called in a false fire alarm. Maybe ten trucks appeared in front of our house—someone told the firemen Marilyn was there, and they all insisted on meeting her. And she went out and talked to them; she was very sweet about it."

In New York City, however, DiMaggio continued to show his jealous streak. He cast around pathetically, begging help and counsel from outsiders, even journalists. He asked columnist Earl Wilson and his wife for advice on how to get Marilyn back. Marilyn told her long-time New York friend, Henry Rosenfeld, that one night DiMaggio "came into the Waldorf and almost broke the door down. Police had to be called to calm him down. He was very, very jealous."

On June 1, 1955, Marilyn's twenty-ninth birthday, Marilyn arrived on DiMaggio's arm for the premiere of *Seven Year Itch*. He gave a party for her afterward at Toots Shor's, but the mood quickly soured. The couple had a row at the supper table, and Marilyn left with her photographer friend, Sam Shaw.

Jim Haspiel tells the saddest story of Joe DiMaggio's tormented persistence. Haspiel himself kept vigil for Marilyn at all hours of the day and night, and more than once he spotted DiMaggio "literally standing in a doorway near her apartment, in the late evening, just as any fan might stand on the street waiting to catch a glimpse of her. That was the extent of his need."

The Seven Year Itch also gave Marilyn the opportunity to mount a somewhat devilish practical joke against the lover she had so much wanted to marry in 1948, Fred Karger. He was by now embroiled in marital problems with his second

wife, actress Jane Wyman, and Marilyn delighted in remind-
ing Wyman that she had once enjoyed Karger's love.

When *Seven Year Itch* was playing in Los Angeles Marilyn
and two friends—one of them Karger's first wife, Patti—
ventured out in the dead of night to Grauman's Theater to
steal a cardboard blow-up of Marilyn in the famous skirt-
blowing scene. They took the life-size likeness to Holmby
Hills, and planted it on Jane Wyman's lawn. She failed to see
the joke.

In the summer of 1955 Fred Karger found himself staying
at the Waldorf-Astoria in New York. Marilyn was living on
one of the upper floors, and he called to invite her down for a
drink. When she failed to appear, Karger called again, and
this time Marilyn sounded drunk. Later, when he went up to
her apartment, she was lost in a haze of alcohol and—an
ominous new factor in her life—sleeping pills.

Marilyn did not see only Arthur Miller in the early months
of their relationship. Dress manufacturer Henry Rosenfeld
had been instrumental in arranging for her suite at the Waldorf,
and loaned her a good deal of money. From then on, Marilyn
consulted him about her financial affairs, and would one day
propose that he take all the proceeds from one of her movies
in exchange for paying her a guaranteed thousand dollars a
week for life. Rosenfeld gently declined, explaining that he
would make far more on the capital than was fair. He himself
became deeply involved with Marilyn and, Marilyn told one
close friend, even proposed marriage.

The year 1955 also saw an embryonic scheme to marry
Marilyn off to the head of a European royal family—an idea
supported by Aristotle Onassis. The millionaire was concerned because one of his favorite watering holes, the princi-
pality of Monaco, was going through a slump. The fashionable
set had started going elsewhere. Onassis thought they might
return if Prince Rainier married a suitably glamorous for-
eigner, and asked a friend, George Schlee, to cast around for
brides in the United States. Schlee consulted Gardner Cowles,
publisher of *Look* magazine, who happened to be a neighbor
of Milton Greene in Connecticut.

"I suggested to Schlee that it might be a good thing to
marry off Rainier to a movie actress," Cowles told me. "He
asked if I had anybody in particular in mind. I said, 'Well,
Marilyn Monroe is at the peak of her fame, and she's staying
nearby. Let's put the idea to her.' "

So it was that Marilyn and the Greenes were invited to

meet Schlee at the Cowles' country home. Cowles said, ''We didn't beat about the bush. When I told Marilyn, she said the idea appealed to her, but she didn't even know where Monaco was. She said she'd be glad to meet the prince.''

Princess Marilyn of Monaco? That night, as the Greenes and Marilyn drove home, the atmosphere was one of huge hilarity tinged with the realization that the proposition was serious. For a while there was much chatter about Prince Rainier, who was quickly dubbed ''Reindeer.''

The idea fizzled altogether when Monaco's royal household announced that the prince was going to marry another actress, Grace Kelly. Marilyn added her own postscript. She telephoned Kelly with congratulations, adding, ''I'm so glad you've found a way out of this business.''

Arthur Miller may have thought Marilyn was not promiscuous, that she was now less insecure. However, just as she had been during the DiMaggio courtship, Marilyn was a less than constant lover. During 1955 she drew close to Marlon Brando.

Brando was Hollywood's most celebrated product of the Actors Studio, and Marilyn had long admired him. The previous year, after his triumph in *On the Waterfront,* she pressed Sam Goldwyn for a part in Brando's next film, *Guys and Dolls.* In New York, Marilyn hoped that one of her first independent projects would star Brando and Charlie Chaplin.

Asked to define sex appeal, Marilyn said, ''There are people to whom other people react and other people who do nothing for people. I react to men, too . . . personally, I react to Marlon Brando.'' Marilyn never did achieve her ambition to work with Brando, but in 1955 they had an affair.

Amy and Milton Greene, who still saw Marilyn regularly, became aware by the summer that she was involved with Brando. Other friends and colleagues confirm the relationship. Brando, famous on screen and off for arrogance and a tendency to violence, is also loved by intimates for his gentleness and loyalty. Marilyn spoke of him to Amy Greene as ''sweet, tender.'' She referred to him by the code-name ''Carlo,'' and relished the fact that most people had no idea whom she was talking about. A photograph taken of them together in December 1955, at an actors' benefit, shows Marilyn and Brando looking dreamily happy together.*

The Brando affair, which had remained secret, faded as Marilyn prepared for a public involvement with Arthur Miller.

---

* Not the photograph shown in the picture section.

The friendship, however, endured. In 1962, in the last days before her death, Marilyn would spend hours talking on the telephone with Brando. Contacted in connection with this book, Brando responded with a rare personal call. Speaking with evident emotion, he said, "I did know her, and out of that sentiment for her, I could never talk about her for publication. I think you can understand that."

Throughout 1955 Marilyn contrived, for once, to keep her private life, if not entirely hidden from the press, at least indecipherable. Toward the end of the year, in a long interview with columnist Earl Wilson, she danced around cunningly baited questions. Asked who her favorite actor was, Marilyn named Brando—then quickly added a few others. Who was her favorite playwright? Marilyn said Arthur Miller—and Tennessee Williams. Asked if she had any love interests, her answer was classic Monroe: "No serious interests, but I'm always interested."

In January 1956, Earl Wilson broke the story that Arthur Miller and his wife were planning to divorce. In private, Miller and Marilyn were now talking about marriage. In public they stonewalled for five more months, but Marilyn had effectively fulfilled the wish callously expressed to Sidney Skolsky at the end of her honeymoon with DiMaggio— the hand of Arthur Miller in marriage. The New Year, it seemed, was awash with success, and not only in love.

After nearly a year Lee Strasberg had decided Marilyn was ready to perform before an audience of her peers at the Actors Studio. She and Maureen Stapleton worked for a while on a scene from Noel Coward's *Fallen Angels*, gave up, then settled on the opening scene from Eugene O'Neill's *Anna Christie*, which Marilyn had once done as an exercise with Natasha Lytess. Marilyn played Anna.

Maureen Stapleton remembers that "she had terrible trouble remembering lines. I said, 'Look, it's not as though it's some damn opening night. We'll just put the book in front of us on the table—lots of people do it.' Marilyn refused to do that, and we never did get through it in rehearsal with her knowing the lines. Then when we did the scene she was fine, didn't forget a line in fifteen minutes. That exceedingly wispy voice of hers seemed to carry all right, for all her worrying about it. Afterwards we went out to a bar on Tenth Avenue, and celebrated having cheated death one more time."

Some of the skeptics' voices were now stilled. "She *was*

wonderful," says actress Kim Stanley. "We were taught never to clap at the Actors Studio—it was like we were in church—and it was the first time I'd ever heard applause there."

Others retained their doubts. The triumph, some felt, was that Marilyn had managed the scene at all. Lee Strasberg's success was that he had got her to do it competently, not that she had done it brilliantly. Marilyn herself sensed this reaction, and played down the praise.

In early 1956, however, Lee Strasberg offered this accolade: "I have worked with hundreds and hundreds of actors and actresses," he told director Joshua Logan, "and there are only two that stand out way above the rest. Number one is Marlon Brando, and the second is Marilyn Monroe. . . ."

Meanwhile, on top of such acclamation and her engagement to Arthur Miller, Marilyn had won her battle with Twentieth Century-Fox.

For a year now, ever since Marilyn's flight to New York, the studio had kept her Hollywood dressing room undisturbed. The cleaners still walked around a mountain of unanswered fan mail to dust the jumble of makeup, the false eyelashes, the bottles and boxes of pills, the discarded book of love poems—and a photograph of Joe DiMaggio. Now Milton Greene's gamble paid off. In the absence of any replacement for Marilyn, the studio struck a deal.

On New Year's Eve 1955 Marilyn signed a new contract with Fox, giving her uniquely favorable terms. She was required to make only four films for the studio over the next seven years, and would be free to make one film a year for a different studio. Marilyn Monroe Productions would receive $100,000 in salary for each film made for Fox, plus a percentage of the profits. It was an excellent deal by 1955 standards, and promised a potential income of some $8,000,000 over the full contract period.

A special clause, really important to Marilyn, gave her the right to reject any film she deemed not to be "Class A," and to reject directors or cameramen who did not meet with her approval. She submitted a list, largely concocted for her by Milton and Amy Greene, of sixteen directors with whom she was prepared to work. Twentieth Century-Fox did not argue.

In the flush of victory, Marilyn greeted 1956 with a barrage of plans. She would return to Hollywood to make *Bus Stop* with one of her chosen directors, Joshua Logan. She stood side by side with Sir Laurence Olivier to announce that they

would soon work together on a film version of Terence
Rattigan's play, *The Sleeping Prince*.

The world's most distinguished actor pronounced a benediction. Marilyn was, Sir Laurence told the press, "a brilliant
comedienne and therefore an extremely good actress." He
watched in astonishment as 150 newsmen jostled for photographs, then became frenzied when the shoulder strap broke
on Marilyn's dress.

Something about Marilyn bothered Sir Laurence. Away
from the microphone, in the limousine that bore him away, he
said to producer Saul Colin, "Saul, I wonder if I've made a
mistake?" Sir Laurence would find out later that year.

Meeting Marilyn now was a confusing experience. Writer
Dorothy Manning at first had the impression the "gone was
the shy, tense, little-girl voice, the slow groping for just the
right word. . . . In its place was a poised woman. Gay,
relaxed, less self-conscious, she came up in a few minutes
with sprightlier conversation than most stars can manage in
hours."

The same day, meeting Marilyn a second time, Manning
was startled by the abrupt change in her. She wrote: "In the
air was the feeling that Marilyn was again troubled, shrinking
back into the shadows, anxious, still unsure. Now she was a
strange, bewildering girl, one whose defenselessness caught
at your heart."

Manning was finding a kind way to express what Sir
Laurence Olivier had glimpsed. Later, recalling their first
meeting, Sir Laurence was to write, "You would not be far
out if you described her as schizoid."

Even before she left Hollywood, Marilyn was no stranger
to the psychiatrist's office. It was the heyday of the couch
psychiatrist, especially in California. As one doctor who knew
Marilyn puts it: "At that time out here, you could get psychoanalysis and a high colonic under the same neon sign. It was
a time of fraudulence. A lot of questionable doctors had come
here and succeeded just because they were glib and good at
promoting themselves. They had a ready market—a lot of
highly neurotic actors and actresses."

The first record of Marilyn seeing a psychiatrist is in 1954,
during her marriage to DiMaggio. She saw an analyst, identity unknown, for some six months.

Marilyn's medical doctors had no doubt she needed
psychiatric help. Dr. Milton Gottlieb, who gave Marilyn

gynecological care, says, "She was insecure, frightened of the reality of life. A very disturbed young woman."

Dr. Elliot Corday, Marilyn's physician from 1948 till the mid-fifties, says, "I eventually withdrew from the case *because* she would not employ a decent psychiatrist. People would understand her death better had they been listening to her in my office back then. There had been many suicide attempts, more than were known. And by 1954 she was using drugs—I think the hard stuff as well as the sleeping pills. In the end I told her I was not going to be around to witness what was going to happen."

Evidence of hard drug use by Marilyn is meager. Joe DiMaggio's detectives, appointed to investigate Marilyn's personal life, had reported finding "hypodermic syringes, two or three vials containing some kind of powder, and other paraphernalia," in Marilyn's apartment. Whatever their significance, the woman who fled Hollywood for New York needed help.

Marilyn told Milton Greene she had stopped having psychiatric treatment. Greene said she should continue, and promised to find her a top-flight analyst. Greene, who himself gradually came to consider Marilyn "schizo," sent her to see Dr. Hohenberg, a female psychiatrist practicing on New York's East Side. Marilyn saw this doctor five times a week during much of 1955.

At the Actors Studio, Lee Strasberg thought Marilyn's sessions with the psychiatrist "freed" her for the rigors of his "total immersion" acting technique. Arthur Miller was to say, after she had undergone a year of treatment, that psychiatry had helped Marilyn a good deal. "She is seeing the issues more clearly now," he said, "discovering that in so many situations in her life she was not the one who was wrong. She feels psychiatry has made a big difference to her."

In time Miller was to wonder how much real use the analysis had been. Others were vocal in their scorn. Billy Wilder, Marilyn's director on *Seven Year Itch*, offered a coldly professional point of view: "There are certain wonderful rascals in this world, like Monroe, and one day they lie down on an analyst's couch and out comes a clenched, dreary thing. It is better for Monroe not to be straightened out. The charm of her is her two left feet."

By any normal standards Marilyn was still an emotional mess. Henry Rosenfeld saw a Marilyn who "came out in red blotches at the idea of meeting a new acquaintance, such was her fear."

Writer Adele Fletcher waited to have lunch with Marilyn one day in Elsa Maxwell's suite at the Waldorf Towers. "She arrived at Elsa's suite three hours late, at precisely the hour when she was supposed to be at the Cecil Beaton studio. I later learned that she had had her hair shampooed and set three times before leaving. She was continually apprehensive that she would not look her best and people would start saying her looks were fading."

Marilyn' aide in 1955, Peter Leonardi, said, "She sits and sits and *projects* before every interview or public appearance. Sometimes she stares out of the window for hours, thinking and pulling at a lock of her hair. She often worries so much she becomes nauseated."

While working, Marilyn often scribbled her thoughts and acting notes in a notebook. "What am I afraid of?" one prying crew member read in the book. "I know I can act. But I'm afraid. I am afraid and I should not be and I must not be. Shit!"

Milton Greene witnessed Marilyn gradually losing herself in addiction to barbiturates. She would take sleeping pills for insomnia at 3:00 A.M., knowing she had to be up to drive into the City at six. On the way to the appointment there would be more pills, often the stimulant Dexamyl, to shatter the stupor. Marilyn was drinking more, too, and in conjunction with the pills.

In 1955, Marilyn told Amy Greene and Henry Rosenfeld, she had had yet another abortion. It brought the total to thirteen at this point in her life—at twenty-nine years old—if Marilyn's own account to Amy Greene is correct, and it was surely yet another blow to her reeling psyche. Amy Greene does not know the father's identity, and Rosenfeld prefers not to identify him.

In spite of the security offered by the relationship with Arthur Miller, Marilyn still acted as though she were desperately lonely. More than before, she indulged her habit of telephoning people in the early hours of the morning. Compliant friends would accept her suggestion that they go for a drive anywhere, around Manhattan or into the darkened suburbs, till dawn. Marilyn was now afraid to be alone at night.

Lee Strasberg tried to help by inviting her to sleep at his home. "She was emotionally upset," he recalled. "She wanted a family. She wanted to be held. Not to be made love to but just to be supported, because when she'd taken the pills they'd somehow react on her so that she would want more. We wouldn't give them to her. That's why she got in the habit of coming over and staying over. I'd hold her a little and she'd go to sleep.''

In May 1956, *Time* magazine was to give Marilyn the accolade of a cover. Reporters worked for months on the research, doing interviews in places as far-flung as Tokyo, Paris, and London. Ezra Goodman, who had known Marilyn through Sidney Skolsky, spent weeks in Los Angeles unearthing facts about her. He sieved the myth she had spun about her past, talked to teachers from her schooldays, colleagues, doctors, and psychiatrists, and filed a massive report to *Time*.

Goodman concluded: ''It may be, as has been psychiatrically observed about her, that she has such contempt for herself that she is really trying to make peace with the world, not by adjusting to reality, but by reconstructing herself and the world around her . . . there is in her some sort of enigmatic, almost magical, quotient, which no one has really been able to define, that has gotten her where she is today in spite of a background that might normally have found her ending up a schizophrenic in a state mental hospital or an alcoholic in the gutter. Perhaps the quality that many people find attractive in her is her very insecurity, her unhappiness, her sleepwalking through life. But the riddle that is Marilyn Monroe has not been solved. It is doubtful whether a year of ambulance chasing, flagpole climbing, and flatfooting would do the trick. That is probably one for the analyst's couch.''

According to Goodman, *Time* magazine ignored most of his report and printed a reassuring story about an actress on the road to an even more glorious future. The public, perhaps, would not have had it otherwise.

Norman Rosten, perhaps the most compassionate of Marilyn's New York friends, was not blind to her deep trouble. He hoped it could be balanced by the other side of her, the woman ''wise in the ways of the survivor.''

Surviving, for Marilyn, meant going on—and ''on'' meant more films. There was no one, it seems, to tell her otherwise. Had there been, she would probably not have listened. Marilyn had made twenty-four films in the first seven years of her career. In the seven years from 1955 to her death she would complete only five. The very first of them, as she promised *Time* magazine, proved that she was indeed ''a real actress.''

20

IN FEBRUARY 1956, ENDING a year of self-imposed exile, Marilyn flew back to Hollywood to a tumultuous reception. Hundreds of photographers mobbed the plane, and a crowd churned around for two hours before she could leave the airport.

Marilyn was back, and on her own terms, to make the movie of the recent Broadway success *Bus Stop,* with a director tailor-made for the Monroe fresh from the Actors Studio. On Milton Greene's advice Marilyn had asked Fox for Joshua Logan, the only American director to have studied in the Soviet Union under Stanislavsky. Initially Logan balked at the notion of working with Marilyn, but Lee Strasberg's lavish praise of her persuaded him. Today, more than any other director, he still bubbles with enthusiasm about Marilyn.

"I had no idea she had this incandescent talent," Logan says today. "She made directing worthwhile. She had such fascinating things happen to her face and skin and hair and body as she read lines, that she was—it's a cliché, but she was inspiring. She got me all hot and bothered just with her acting. Sexually it went way beyond that, *ça va sans dire.* She was gorgeous to look at, to get close to, to smell, and feel—that, with her talent too. I was a goner for her. I still am."

Bus Stop was the story of Cherie, a weary girl singer with too many men in her past, and Bo, the naive young cowboy who falls in love with her. Many in Hollywood sneered, saying the result would merely be a variation on the theme of Marilyn the sexpot. They were proved wrong, partly because of the disciplines she had learned from Strasberg, and thanks to Logan's infinite indulgence.

Milton Greene had warned the director, "Watch the tone of your voice with Marilyn, because if you scare her, you'll lose her." Although time has softened the memory, there were times Logan had to invoke patience worthy of Buddha.

For the first time Marilyn was included in key script discussions. Logan appreciated Marilyn's contribution until she took exception to the way somebody *else's* role was being planned. She called Buddy Adler, the new chief at Fox, and Adler called Logan. As any director would be, Logan was furious that an actor had gone over his head to a studio executive.

Marilyn now had no further use for her original acting coach, Natasha Lytess. Lytess had gone to see Marilyn on her return to Hollywood, only to be turned away from the door by an aide. Her last sight of her most successful pupil was of a lone figure watching stonily through the window. The replacement for Lytess was Lee Strasberg's wife, Paula, a figure who now became indispensable.

Paula Strasberg was a lump of a woman in her mid-forties, described by her daughter Susan as "a combination delicatessen, pharmacist, Jewish mother." She dressed almost exclusively in flowing black robes, like a postcard Greek widow. She was never without a huge handbag crammed with food, medicines, flashlight, and magnifying glass. On hot locations— and many of Marilyn's locations were swelteringly hot—Paula was to be seen cooling herself with one of a vast selection of fans.

Although emotionally estranged from her husband, Paula had turned herself into the indispensable *doyenne* of the Strasberg household. She had long stage-managed life for Lee, promoting him as a genius, and she never tired of extolling the virtues of her children.

Now Marilyn had become virtually the third Strasberg child, one who thought she needed the master's help on all her acting endeavors. Lee Strasberg was tied to his work at the Studio. So Paula, who herself had experience both as actress and teacher, was now appointed to hold Marilyn's hand. She offered genuine devotion to Marilyn, and vast irritation to film directors.

Joshua Logan was appalled when he heard Marilyn intended not only to use Paula as coach, but to have her on the set during filming. He appealed to Milton Greene, who was now diplomat and trouble-shooter. Greene negotiated with Lee Strasberg, and it was agreed that Paula could be present, but only in the dressing room.

In many ways Paula Strasberg was beginning a thankless task. She received an excellent salary—as much as $2,000 a week—but she was to become the butt of derision, and sometimes hatred, from film crews, and the target of Marilyn's increasingly arrogant whims. On *Bus Stop,* though, Greene's peace formula worked partly because the language of the Actors Studio was compatible with Logan's style of directing.

Logan was on the Studio wavelength when he advised Marilyn to slip into a coat "as though you were slipping into a bubble bath." On future films, though, the Strasberg system was ridiculed. On *Let's Make Love,* Paula exhorted Marilyn to kiss Yves Montand "as if it were cold water going over an iron fence." Script supervisor Rosie Steinberg is still chuckling over that one.

On at least one occasion, Marilyn took method acting a step too far. A scene required her to slap co-star Don Murray with a piece of torn costume. Marilyn had not got on well with Murray, and now struck him viciously enough to slash his face. Marilyn may have been emulating her recent lover, Marlon Brando, who was known for carrying acted violence to extremes, but this incident caused a crisis. Despite Logan's pleas, Marilyn could not bring herself to apologize, and screamed at her colleagues in helpless fury. The Miller relationship seemed to be supplying neither stability nor peace of mind. During *Bus Stop* Paula Strasberg made sure that Marilyn's friends in a bottle—her tranquilizers—were always within reach.

Marilyn was also to rely on Paula Strasberg for functions far removed from acting. On social occasions, it would be Paula who went in first to vet the other guests. If she disapproved of them, Marilyn would sit waiting in the limousine, while Paula did the courtesies inside. Paula became a sounding board for Marilyn's problems in love, a nurse when she was sick. On *Bus Stop,* as almost always from now on, she was needed as a nurse.

In April 1956 came the now-familiar headline, MARILYN MONROE IN HOSPITAL. The doctor's diagnosis was "virus infection, exhaustion, overwork, and acute bronchitis." In a more relaxed comment the doctor said Marilyn was just "tied in knots."

Director Logan says his star was sick, "but not two weeks' worth." Since the company had to be paid anyway, Logan whiled away the time shooting and reshooting a scene that did not require Marilyn's presence. The company spent fifteen days, at $40,000 a day, filming a fight that lasted half a minute in the movie.

Once, when Marilyn was working, Logan realized she was

going to be late for a key scene in which she had to run through the streets at sundown. She had had three hours to get ready. He ran to the dressing room and found "the poor darling still looking at herself in the mirror." Logan wasted no words. He physically lugged Marilyn to her camera position, shouting "Run!" to her and "Roll 'em!" to the cameraman.

Logan was able to forgive Marilyn for everything. He remembers with admiration her total involvement in her part, her ability to weep real tears when other actors would reach for the glycerine. He shared with her a determination to sneak risqué shots past the censor, a gleeful delight in sexual innuendo that was ahead of its time in the fifties.

Logan indulged Marilyn's hesitant performances by letting her do a speech over and over while the camera consumed a vast amount of film. He tolerated her on the days when she failed to deliver one usable take, and when, with Paula Strasberg's support, she walked wordlessly away "to work out the motivation." Others were not so patient.

The press, which Marilyn had courted to her advantage for so long, was kept away from her during *Bus Stop*. She was whisked to the door of her trailer in a limousine, then hustled in through specially constructed entranceways. No facilities were provided for the photographers, who were there in force. The press fell back on guerrilla tactics. They sat in ambush in neighboring hotel rooms, then lured Marilyn and her entourage to her balcony by abruptly switching on high-powered strobe lights.

Bill Woodfield, then a photographer for *This Week* magazine, found himself snatching pictures of Marilyn during the rodeo location in Arizona. Woodfield says, "It got so bad that we were all hiding out and taking pictures under the stands at the stadium. I got some pictures of Marilyn throwing up under the bleachers, damn near on top of me. She'd be playing a scene and she'd lean over and throw up, or dry heave, and I was underneath. I had the pictures printed, threw them down in front of Milton Greene and said, 'This is what we have to go with unless you give us some pictures.' Finally he broke her loose, and I got my shots."

When *Time* magazine mounted its first cover story on Marilyn, during the shooting of *Bus Stop*, its researchers began uncovering a good deal about Marilyn's parentage. This was a vulnerable area because of her various deceptions.

As a result, one of *Time*'s youngest reporters, Brad Darrach, was granted a personal interview, in bizarre circumstances.

Darrach collected Marilyn at Fox at 11:00 A.M., and drove her to her hotel, the Chateau Marmont. Marilyn, herself a fast driver, asked the reporter to drive slowly. She seemed to him to be afraid, not of his driving, but "generally frightened." Once in her suite Marilyn soon declared she was tired, and asked if they could do the interview in the bedroom.

So it was that Darrach ended up, as he now jokes, "spending ten hours in bed with Marilyn Monroe." She lay down with her head at one end of the bed. He settled at the foot, and there they talked until long after dark.

"She was Marilyn, and reasonably pretty," Darrach remembers. "And of course there were those extraordinary jutting breasts and jutting behind. I've never seen a behind like hers; it was really remarkable, it was a very subtly composed ass. Yet I never felt for a moment any sexual temptation. There was nothing about her skin that made me want to touch it. She looked strained and a little unhealthy, as though there was some nervous inner heat that dried the skin. But there was no sexual feeling emanating from her. I am sure that was something that she put on for the camera."

For a while during *Bus Stop*, Marilyn's press was handled by Pat Newcomb, who worked for Arthur Jacobs, owner of one of Hollywood's top public relations firms. Newcomb, a very young woman from the East Coast, was new to the job. Her father was a judge, her mother a psychiatric social worker, and she herself had majored in psychology. Even this background, however, was insufficient for the handling of Marilyn Monroe.

"We had this terrible falling out almost immediately," Newcomb says. "I didn't know why for years, but it turned out to be over some guy that Marilyn thought I liked, someone I didn't have any interest in at all. I didn't know how to cope with it, and Arthur Jacobs told me I'd better get out of there at once."

Newcomb had to leave the location. Ironically, years later she would become Marilyn's key press adviser and confidante, and was one of the last people to see Marilyn on the day she died. Even then, at the very end, they would be quarreling.

Rivalry, or jealousy, was not limited to her press assistant. Marilyn had a tussle with her director over Hope Lange, who was playing the part of a young girl in *Bus Stop*. Lange's

hair, Marilyn insisted, was too fair; she feared it would
detract attention from herself. Logan had to surrender and
have Lange's hair darkened. (In the last months of her life,
during *Something's Got to Give*, Marilyn was to go into a
similar irrational panic over her co-star, Cyd Charisse.) On
Bus Stop, for the first time, Marilyn's New York psychiatrist
was flown to attend her at the location.

Out of the folly and misery came an excellent film and a
brilliant performance by Marilyn. *New York Times* critic,
Bosley Crowther, said flatly that Marilyn had "finally proved
herself an actress." He went on: "Fortunately for her and for
the tradition of diligence leading to success, she gives a
performance in this picture that marks her as a genuine acting
star, not just a plushy personality and a sex symbol, as she
has previously been."

This was the accolade Marilyn had yearned for, even though,
to her own dismay and that of many others, *Bus Stop* was not
rewarded with an Oscar nomination. The tragedy, however,
was that the woman was disintegrating even as the actress
grasped her dream. In the midst of her success Joshua Logan
sounded a warning. "She can become one of the greatest stars
we've ever had," he said, "if she can control her emotions
and her health."

Logan knew the depth of Marilyn's problems earlier than
most. "I almost choke up when I really think of her," he
says now. "I don't think she ever really had two days of
happiness or contentment in her life, unless it was when she
was working."

As she approached her thirtieth birthday, Marilyn at last
appeared to have found happiness in love.

21

EVERY DAY FOR EIGHT weeks, in the spring of 1956, the telephone rang in the office of the Pyramid Lake Guest Ranch,
fifty miles northeast of Reno, Nevada. The caller, who identified herself as Mrs. Leslie, would ask to speak to Mr. Leslie.

A genuine Red Indian would hasten to a small cabin with the message, and Mr. Leslie, pipe in had, hurried to take his call.

"Mrs. Leslie" was Marilyn Monroe, busy making *Bus Stop*. "Mr. Leslie" was Arthur Miller, holed up in the desert waiting out his residency to qualify for a Nevada divorce. They had taken their code names from Vina Delmar's novel, *About Mrs. Leslie,* the story of a nightclub singer and a married man who live together as man and wife for six weeks each year. In real life, Marilyn and Miller would soon be able to dispense with such deceptions.

Miller was cautious, as a man in the middle of divorce was bound to be. When he talked to *Time* magazine, huddled with the reporter in a parked car, he avoided saying whether he wished to marry Marilyn. "I can't afford to get married for a long time," he said. "Where will I get the money to support two families? My play, *View from the Bridge,* just closed on Broadway. I got thirty-five thousand dollars, and that will have to last me for two years until I can write another one. And she is not ready to be married either. She's fanatic about the projects ahead of her."

Marilyn, for her part, could not resist a few confidences. Just as she had done before marrying Joe DiMaggio, she made sure that her favorite reporters knew her plans. May Mann, of the New York *Herald Tribune,* was surprised to receive a telegram from Marilyn, setting up a call for a specific hour. Marilyn phoned right on time, to confide that she and Miller would be married "at midsummer—but don't print it yet."

On June 2, with *Bus Stop* completed, Marilyn hurried back to New York. As Miller prepared to follow, disaster loomed. Still in Nevada, he was served with a subpoena by Congress' Committee on Un-American Activities. The congressmen intended to question the nation's leading playwright about his supposed Communist affiliations. As Miller well knew, this was an ordeal that had ruined dozens of his colleagues in the past decade.

The House Un-American Activities Committee had leapt to prominence in 1947, when it gained access to the Attorney General's list, a catalogue of organizations that held allegedly totalitarian, Fascist, Communist, or "any other subversive views." Its function was to interrogate and expose, and its sights were leveled above all at Communists, real or imagined.

From 1950 on, the witch-hunters gained a figurehead in the shape of Senator Joseph McCarthy, the demagogue whose

name has become synonymous with the repressive policies of
the time. The Committee's friends included two future presidents, Richard Nixon and minor actor Ronald Reagan.

The Hollywood film community, which included many
idealistic left-wingers of thirties' and forties' vintage, was a
prime target. Arthur Miller had watched appalled as the
victimization of writers and directors took its toll. Some, their
careers ended, committed suicide or became human flotsam.
Screenwriter Alvah Bessie, whose career had held great promise, ended up as a technician in a nightclub. Mystery writer
Dashiell Hammett went to prison rather than inform on left-
wingers he had known. His career never recovered.

Until 1956 the Committee had never found a reason to call
Arthur Miller, though he had long been assailed by the vocal
right. A protest over his early play, *All My Sons*, led to it
being banned in occupied Germany, because of its "twisted"
scenario of crooked military suppliers and lax military inspec-
tors. In 1949 the film version of *Death of a Salesman* was
picketed by right-wingers. It was at the height of the campaign, four years later, that Miller produced *The Crucible*, his
powerful evocation of witch-hunting hysteria in the seven-
teenth century. Few missed the modern message in the play,
yet Miller remained unscathed. On Broadway, the blacklist
circulating in Hollywood—which prevented alleged left-wingers
from working—had never taken hold. Now, in 1956, the
House Un-American Activities Committee found an excuse to
summon Miller.

It was quickly apparent that the decision had as much to do
with Marilyn Monroe as it did with Miller. The press was
alive with rumors of her impending marriage to Miller, and
the Committee's Chairman, Congressman Francis Walter, saw
an opportunity to get into the newspapers. The Committee
had not been front-page news recently. Secretly, Miller was
offered an easy ride if he would arrange for Marilyn to pose
for photographs beside Congressman Walter. Miller refused.

His confrontation with the Committee came on June 21,
1956, in the vast Caucus Room of the Old House Office
Building. Miller, in blue suit and horn-rimmed spectacles,
admitted having "signed some form or another" at a Marxist
study course in about 1939. He said he had "no knowledge"
of having applied for Communist Party membership.

Miller's real clash with the Committee came when he
refused, time and again, to name others he had met at Communist gatherings. "I could not use the name of another

person and bring trouble on him," he told the congressmen. "These were writers, poets, as far as I could see, and the life of a writer, despite what it sometimes seems, is pretty tough. I wouldn't make it any tougher on anybody. I ask you not to ask me that question."

Miller's refusal to name names placed him in legal jeopardy. A month after his appearance the House of Representatives voted him in contempt of Congress, a charge which could have put the playwright in prison for a year. He was first convicted, appealed, and was finally acquitted two years later. From the start, it was a fight conducted with the support of Marilyn Monroe.

Asked at the time to comment on Miller's congressional testimony, Marilyn played the good little woman. "I don't know much about politics," she said. "I'll have to have a talk with him and I think he's very tired." Two years later, when the case was finally resolved in Miller's favor, she said she never doubted the outcome, "because I have been studying Thomas Jefferson for years and, according to Thomas Jefferson, this case had to turn out this way. . . ."

Marilyn played the ingenue, but she was fiercely loyal to Miller, and learning to apply her shrewdness to political affairs. At brief press appearances during Miller's ordeal before the House Committee, she was a model of dignity and quiet support. The very aura of Marilyn protected Miller from adverse public opinion in a way that none of the committee's other victims enjoyed. Instead of being regarded as a left-wing writer under attack, Miller was transformed by the headlines into the harassed lover of the nation's sex symbol. Later Marilyn helped in a material way. It was her money, according to her financial adviser, Henry Rosenfeld, that eventually paid many of the daunting legal fees.

Marilyn also proved, if it still needed proving, that she could be brave. In 1960 she told British writer W. J. Weatherby, "Some of those bastards in Hollywod wanted me to drop Arthur, said it would ruin my career. They're born cowards and want you to be like them. One reason I want to see Kennedy win is that Nixon's associated with that whole scene."

According to Marilyn, it was she who put the steel into Arthur Miller's resolve not to name names. A year before her death, Danny Greenson, the student son of Marilyn's psychiatrist, talked to her about the Committee hearings. "The way Marilyn told it," Greenson says, "was that Miller was afraid and might even capitulate. And she would tell him, 'No, you can't let those bastards push you around. You've got to stand up to them.' She really was unsophisticated politically, but her instincts were always with the underdog and—to me—on the side of right. There was more to Marilyn than met the eye.''

Miller aside, some of Marilyn's closest associates were now, in fifties' terms, of the Far Left. The House Committee on Un-American Activities had records on both Lee and Paula Strasberg, linking them with what the Committee called ''Communist fronts.'' Paula, a former member of the Communist Party, was now Marilyn's coach. The FBI had not failed to notice such associations.

Repeated applications under the Freedom of Information Act have prised a clutch of documents on Marilyn out of the FBI. The earliest, dated August 19, 1955, when Marilyn was several months into her new friendships in New York, has been almost entirely blanked out by the censor before release, under the B-1 exemption. The B-1 category is meant to cover matters of national security, though it is frequently used to withhold anything dealing with foreign affairs. This report on Marilyn was also routed to the Deputy Director of Plans, at the Central Intelligence Agency.

Other documents on Monroe for the period are withheld altogether, many of them under the national security classification. Those irritated by the FBI's procedures may find light relief in a revelation about its director. J. Edgar Hoover, whose only close friend in forty years was a male colleague, proudly displayed in his home an original copy of Marilyn's nude calendar.

On June 21, 1956, in the middle of his congressional testimony, Arthur Miller broke his own security. Asked why he currently wanted a passport to go to England, Miller replied, ''The objective is double. I have a production, which is in the talking stage in England, of a *View from the Bridge*, and I will be there with the woman who will then be my wife. That is my aim.'' Afterward, talking to reporters in Washington, Miller ensured that any adverse publicity was totally defused. He said flatly that he would marry Marilyn Monroe ''very shortly.''

That same day, at lunchtime in New York, Marilyn called Norman Rosten. She sounded almost hysterical. ''Have you heard?'' she asked, ''He told the whole world he was marrying Marilyn Monroe. Me! Can you believe it? You know he never really asked me. You've got to come down right away.

I need moral support. I mean, 'Help!' I'm surrounded here, locked in my apartment. There are newspapermen trying to get in, crawling all over the place, in the foyer, in the halls.''

As the reporters milled around outside, Marilyn chatted with a repairman fixing the air-conditioner. It was he who finally emerged to announce triumphantly, "She told me: 'Sure I'm going to be married.' " The journalists raced for their telephones, and the wedding circus began.

Soon the apartment building in New York's exclusive Sutton Place was besieged by a crowd three hundred strong. Marilyn and Miller climbed into an old station wagon and fled to the country retreat at Roxbury, Connecticut. The newsmen followed, and enraged Miller by camping on the doorstep. He finally persuaded them to go away by promising a press conference at the end of the week.

In their few days of relative peace, the couple juggled with wedding plans and waited to know whether Miller would be granted a passport to travel to England. With them at the house were Miller's seventy-two-year-old father, Isadore, and his mother, Augusta. Marilyn had told them in tears: "For the first time in my life, I have somebody I can call Father and Mother." The Millers were Jews, devout though not over-zealous, and Marilyn announced that she wished to marry in the Jewish faith.

For the past year Miller's bride had been surrounded by Jewish friends—the Rostens and the Strasbergs—and had latched on to their traditions. She had celebrated Passover with Milton Greene during *Bus Stop*, and had eaten bagels and gefilte fish with Eli Wallach. Friends had explained the *mezuzahs*, cylindrical containers bearing the Ten Commandments on Jewish front doors.

Things reached the point where Marilyn was more enthusiastic about Jewish customs than Miller. At the Roxbury house, she bustled about learning Jewish recipes from Miller's mother. That week, at Marilyn's insistence, a phone call was placed to a rabbi of the Reformed branch of Judaism. He agreed to give Marilyn instruction and to perform the marriage ceremony.

Arthur Miller was happy. Marilyn behaved as if she were happy, but there was something frenetic about her. She was, the press learned, "under doctor's orders to rest." Miller's father, who was to become one of Marilyn's loyal friends, wondered, "Have they weighed this step carefully?"

The reporters, meanwhile, were never far away. They discovered the couple had taken blood tests, as required under local marriage laws, and Miller's cousin, Morton, had rushed the vials of blood to the laboratory in his car. There were rumors the couple had obtained a wedding license, but the journalists checked fifty registry offices in vain.

The next day, June 29, was the day Miller had promised a press conference. The reporters returned in a horde, four hundred of them swarming around the intersection of Old Tophet and Goldmine roads. Soon they were wandering all over the Miller property, trampling the grass and dangling from the trees. There was no sign of the quarry.

At about one o'clock, from the near distance, came the sound of a crash and rending metal. Minutes later a car abruptly pulled up short of the crowd, and disgorged Marilyn and Miller, who ran wordlessly for the house.

Minutes later, fighting back tears, Miller's cousin explained that there had been a tragedy. He had been taking Marilyn and Miller home, driving fast along the country road to evade a pursuing press car. The driver behind, who did not know the road, had lost control of the wheel and cannoned into a tree. His passenger, Mara Sherbatoff, a White Russian aristocrat and New York bureau chief for *Paris-Match*, had been hurled through the windshield. She was bleeding profusely from a severed neck artery, and would die later on the operating table.

Inside the Roxbury house Marilyn alternated between hysteria over the accident, and rage at her press assistant because television sound cameras were being set up outside. Marilyn hated television. She finally appeared with Miller and his parents for a travesty of a press conference.

Milton Greene ran about issuing instructions and trying to keep the peace. The actress in Marilyn offered seeming serenity. Miller, a cigarette dangling unlit at his lip, almost snarled at the newsmen. He still refused to say where or when they would be married.

That afternoon Marilyn called Milton Greene into the bedroom and asked for advice on a matter Greene thought long settled. "Arthur wants me to marry him," she said, "now—tonight. Tell me if I'm making a mistake. What do you think?" Shaken, Greene walked to the window and back again. Then he said lamely, "Marilyn, you must do what you think best."

That evening, after a flurry of phone calls to lawyers and local authorities, Miller and Marilyn drove across the state line to White Plains, New York. For the second time in less than three years, a Marilyn Monroe wedding interrupted a judge's dinner appointment.

Judge Seymour Robinowitz, postponing his own anniversary celebration, hurried to the courthouse. Marilyn, in sweater and skirt, once again filled out a marriage license. She said her father had been Edward Mortenson, made no mention of any marriage to Robert Slatzer, and this time told the truth about her age. Marilyn had turned thirty at the beginning of the month. Miller, now nearly forty-one, wore a blue linen suit and no tie. He produced a borrowed ring.

The couple were married at 7:21 P.M., in the steamy heat of a New York summer evening. The press knew nothing till afterward.

Two days later, again in secret, Marilyn got the Jewish wedding she wanted. She had taken brief instructions from Rabbi Robert Goldburg, who explained the basic tenets of Judaism. Marilyn satisfied him that any children of the marriage would be brought up in the Jewish faith.

This second ceremony took place in front of a marble mantelpiece at the home of Miller's literary agent, in Waccabuc, New York. This time Marilyn looked like a bride in gown and veil, and Miller managed a tie and a flower in his buttonhole. The couple drank wine, exchanged rings, and the bridegroom crushed a goblet in memory of the destruction of Jerusalem by its ancient foes.

The weeks of tension now ended in a bucolic scene. Twenty-five wedding guests went outdoors to lunch on lobster, turkey, and champagne. Marilyn and her husband cut the wedding cake, made overnight by a New York baker after eight others had refused to bake one on twenty-four hours' notice. Bride and groom kissed and cuddled without restraint, with Miller exhibiting the physical abandon that had transformed him in recent months.

"It was a fairy tale come true," Norman Rosten later recalled. "The Prince had appeared, the Princess was saved."

By now Miller had purchased a gold wedding band. It was inscribed "A. to M., June 1956. Now Is Forever." Marilyn, for her part, wrote three words on the back of a wedding photograph: "Hope, Hope, Hope."

22

TWO WEEKS AFTER THEIR wedding, in an elegant English country house, Mr. and Mrs. Miller were dancing cheek to cheek to the tune of Gershwin's "Embraceable You." Miller's passport had been issued after all, and they had arrived in Britain to make *The Prince and the Showgirl* with Sir Laurence Olivier.

Terence Rattigan, author of the original stage play, had invited a glittering assemblage to welcome the honeymooners. Joining them on the dance floor were Sir John Gielgud, Douglas Fairbanks, Jr., Dame Sybil Thorndike and Sir Lewis Casson, Dames Peggy Ashcroft, Edith Evans and Margot Fonteyn, assorted dukes, duchesses, and knights, and the American ambassador.

At a more plebeian level, Britain had been excited about Marilyn for weeks. The national newspapers now rushed to outdo each other in fatuous headlines and overblown trivia about Marilyn. The story of her arrival dominated the front pages, eclipsing Prime Minister Anthony Eden's speech warning that the nation faced economic disaster. One newspaper presented Marilyn with a bicycle to ride around the English countryside, then complained when her servants were seen riding it instead. Little old ladies crocheted Marilyn's image in gold and silver thread. Marilyn was invited to attend cricket matches, shoot grouse in Scotland, and eat fish and chips with Teddy Boys. A band of students sang bawdy songs—and the 23rd Psalm—beneath the Millers' window.

None of the approaches, even more sensible ones, met with any response. Gone was the Marilyn who once courted and indulged the press. In her place was a withdrawn woman and a shy husband, hiding behind the gates of Parkside House, the country mansion rented from Lord Moore.

The staff had been warned in advance that "Miss Monroe must have complete darkness when she sleeps," and special window blinds had been installed. The bedroom had been fitted out in white—white bed, white curtains and furnishings, white carpet—to match Marilyn's Manhattan apartment. (The butler and cook, who dared mention such secrets to the press, were soon fired.) Marilyn was accompanied everywhere by a hulking ex-Scotland Yard police superintendent. She appeared, people noticed, to have lost her sense of humor. She was now a star in all the worst senses.

Months earlier, when he had heard of Olivier's plans, Noel Coward had written in his diary: "Larry is going to make a movie of the Sleeping Prince with Marilyn Monroe, which might conceivably drive him round the bend."

Marilyn had met Olivier a couple of times years before, when she was a nobody and he was already Sir Laurence, the leading actor in the English-speaking world. Now he was to be director and leading man to her leading lady, in a frothy tale about an American showgirl who falls in love with a reluctant Ruritanian prince.

Olivier had heard stories about the perils of working with Marilyn, but thought he could cope.

He had talked to three of her previous directors, John Huston, Billy Wilder, and Joshua Logan. Logan, who was emerging bloodied but triumphant from *Bus Stop*, wrote repeatedly, warning Olivier. "Please don't tell her what to do," he told him. "She probably knows more about acting in films than anyone in the world. Don't order her about, because it'll throw her and you won't get anything out of her." That aside, Logan had said cheerily, "It's the best combination since black and white."

Olivier was irritated that Marilyn brought along her coach, Paula Strasberg. Then, remembering how "schizoid" Marilyn had seemed to him in New York, he hoped that Strasberg "would bring out the better of those two halves." When Marilyn proved disappointing at rehearsals, Olivier tried to get through by cultivating Strasberg instead. Soon he concluded that "Paula knew nothing; she was no actress, no director, no teacher, no adviser, except in Marilyn's eyes. For she had one talent: she could butter Marilyn up."

This realization come to Olivier one day as he, riding in the front of a limousine, listened to Marilyn and Strasberg talking in the back. "My dear," Paula Strasberg was saying, "You haven't yet any idea of the importance of your position in the world. You are the greatest woman of your time, the greatest human being of your time, of any time—you name it. You can't think of anybody, I mean—no, not even Jesus—except you're more popular.''

Olivier swears his account is no exaggeration, that the flattery went on for a full hour, and that Marilyn lapped it up. During the filming Olivier was to exile Paula Strasberg to New York, and Marilyn was to make sure she came back again. Olivier was in for four months of professional hell.

Olivier tried to help Marilyn with her problems of drying up in front of the camera. He suggested she sit still, count up to three, then speak the line. When this failed, he burst out, "Can't you count either?" Logan had warned that being authoritative, not to mention losing one's temper, was to lose Monroe, and Olivier swifly lost touch with her altogether. He despaired even when Marilyn's system worked.

It was hard for an Olivier to watch Marilyn capture a mood only after Paula Strasberg told her, "Honey, just think of Coca-Cola and Frankie Sinatra!" He concluded she was "a glorious amateur in show business, an untrained, probably untrainable, artist of instinct."

"I saw the difference between Larry and Marilyn grow as they became more tired and tense," cameraman Jack Cardiff recalled. "She began asking herself whether he was really the genius she had at first imagined." Marilyn herself said years later, "Sir Olivier [sic] tried to be friendly, but he came on like someone slumming. . . . I started being bad with him, being late, and he hated it. But if you don't respect your artists, they can't work well. Respect is what you have to fight for."

It was Marilyn who failed to give respect, to Olivier and everyone else, in big and little things. She failed to thank Olivier and his wife for their kindnesses, for the roses sent to welcome her, for the exquisite, engraved watch presented to her at the end of filming.

One day Marilyn managed to break even her record for unpunctuality, by arriving for an appointment more than nine hours late. She made Dame Sybil Thorndike, who was elderly and also acting in a stage play at night, wait all morning for her. Marilyn's columnist friend, Louella Parsons, visiting from the United States, thought she was "testing to see if she was really the co-star. She behaved like a child asking to be spanked."

Arthur Miller, too, bore the brunt of Marilyn the child. Two weeks into the filming, traveling under the name "Mr. Stevenson" to avoid reporters, he flew back to the United

States. His purpose was to see his daughter by his previous marriage, who was ill, but Marilyn saw it as desertion. She stayed at home for a week, claiming a "severe attack of colitis." Production ground to a halt until Miller cut short his visit and returned.

The other partner in Marilyn Monroe Productions, photographer Milton Greene, who had bought an English Jaguar car, shuttled around from Marilyn's home to the studio, from the studio to London, trying to mend fences between Marilyn and Olivier, and between both of them and the British press.

It was in part thanks to Greene that the film was finished at all, yet *Prince and the Showgirl* was the beginning of the end of his connection with Marilyn. Word filtered back from England that Arthur Miller wanted Greene removed. Miller retorted, "I have no more than the normal family interest in my wife's business affairs. Rumors of conflict between myself and Milton Greene are space fillers for unimaginative columnists."

Greene said, "Miller and I have had no trouble. Sell my stock in Marilyn Monroe Productions? Never."

It was all a smokescreen. Miller, supposedly busy finishing his next play, was being drawn inexorably into his wife's professional life. Greene saw the writing on the wall when he found Miller selecting Marilyn's publicity photographs and organizing her scrapbook. Soon Miller was flying into rages over Greene's press releases. Greene told me, "Miller would scream at me. He wanted her for himself, to do a movie and a play—for him."

A year later Greene was to be driven out as vice-president of Marilyn Monroe Productions, and paid off with $100,000. The new board of directors included Miller's brother-in-law and one of his friends. It was small thanks to Greene, who wryly recalled that the two films he was involved with, *Bus Stop* and *Prince and the Showgirl*, were the only major Monroe films to be finished within their budgets.

Against all odds *The Prince and the Showgirl* was not a disaster. When it appeared, most critics would be kinder than Noel Coward, and even he noted in his diary: "Larry is superb. Marilyn Monroe looks very pretty and is charming at moments, but too much emphasis on tits and bottom. It is to me a charming picture." The miracle Olivier had been promised by previous directors had occurred. In the finished product, Marilyn was magically effective. Olivier would write wearily in his memoirs that people thought "I was as good as could be, and Marilyn! Marilyn was quite wonderful, the best of all. So. What do you know?''

Before leaving England, Marilyn managed a courteous exchange with Queen Elizabeth, at the Royal Command film performance. She had the guts to apologize, at Olivier's insistence, to the assembled company of *Prince and the Showgirl*. She said, ''I hope you will all forgive me, as it wasn't altogether my fault. I have been ill.''

Marilyn would shortly be immortalized in wax at Madame Tussaud's in London. Her effigy stood glamorously gowned, holding a glass of champagne; but for Marilyn and her husband, after four and a half months of marriage, there was little to celebrate.

A year before marrying Miller, Marilyn had been asked how she defined love. She replied that love was trust, that to love a man she had to trust him completely. Trust took a beating during the Miller honeymoon. The first blow came early on in the making of *Prince and the Showgirl*.

It was an incident that Marilyn would refer to time and again in years to come, though not always with quite the same details. The core of the story is that, after a party, she happened upon some of Miller's notes lying on a table. They included comments about herself that Marilyn found deeply hurtful. Lee and Paula Strasberg, both in England at the time, were the first to hear what had happened.

''It was something about how disappointed he was in me,'' Marilyn told the Strasbergs. ''How he thought I was some kind of angel but now he guessed he was wrong. That his first wife had let him down, but I had done something worse. Olivier was beginning to think I was a troublesome bitch and that he, Arthur, no longer had a decent answer to that one.''

Marilyn told Bob Josephy, a Connecticut friend of the Millers, that the sense of Miller's note was, ''My God, I've married the same woman''—meaning that he saw in Marilyn some flaw identical with a trait in his first wife, Mary Slattery. The discovery plunged Marilyn into misery because, she told Josephy, Miller had ''hated'' his first wife. Years later, Marilyn was to claim that Miller's note described her as ''a whore.''

There seems no doubt a note did exist; according to one source, it remained in the possession of Paula Strasberg for many years. Miller has not commented in full on the incident. Less than two years after Marilyn's death, however, his controversial play, *After the Fall,* appeared, drawing heavily on the playwright's experiences with Marilyn. While it is dangerous to make too much of fiction, Miller did include a scene in which the female protagonist finds an upsetting note.

In *After the Fall* the Marilyn character, "Maggie," angrily tells her husband not to mix her up with his former wife. Her husband replies, "That's just it. That I could have brought two women so different to the same accusation—it closed a circle for me. And I wanted to face the worst thing I could imagine—that I could not love. And I wrote it down, like a letter from hell."

During *Prince and the Showgirl* Miller may have realized, as he certainly would in the future, that he could not count on Marilyn's fidelity. There had long since been a public question mark over Marilyn's true relationship with her partner, Milton Greene. The rumors evaporated in the excitement over the marriage of Miller, but they may have been founded on truth.

In 1980, in his autobiography, entertainer Sammy Davis, Jr., wrote of Marilyn: "While she was making *The Prince and the Showgirl* with Laurence Olivier, she was going through one of the most difficult periods of her life. She was having an affair with a close friend of mine. He was a photographer. . . . They met clandestinely, often at my house. She was always being followed there, and we had to get up all sorts of intrigues to keep the affair secret. I used to pretend we were having a party, and Marilyn would arrive and leave at different times from my pal."

Milton Greene was, of course, a photographer, and he did count Sammy Davis among his friends. It was Greene, indeed, who introduced Davis to Marilyn. In 1984, asked about Davis' story, Greene laughed hugely and asked, "Did he really say that? You may be right, but I'm not saying anything. I think the best way to keep it, is that we were close friends and associates, and we loved each other. Period."

In *After the Fall* the scene over the husband's notes occurs as he struggles to prevent his wife from suicidally swallowing a combination of alcohol and sleeping pills. That, certainly, reflected a real situation during the making of *Prince and the Showgirl.*

On Marilyn's arrival the press, all unknowing of the true situation, had asked fatuous questions about her sleeping habits. Marilyn replied, "Well, let's say that now I am in England I like sleeping in just Yardley's Lavender."

The truth was less romantic. Marilyn was sick from lack of sleep, and from the remedies she used to try to induce it. Author Fred Guiles, who talked to Miller, wrote: "Before, she had been troubled by insomnia partially relieved by pills. Now even they didn't work. As the night deepened, she became hysterical. He was unwilling to risk the amount of barbiturates that could drop her into a sodden slumber. Nightly vigils began."

Milton Greene, who dealt with the wreckage of Marilyn in the mornings, adds frightening detail. "She wanted gin with her tea at 9:00 A.M. before going on the set. I would cut it, and cut it again, to weaken it, and she would get angry. I would have to feed her the uppers she wanted. They came in a different color in London, and she'd think I was faking, changing the pills."

On the set Paula Strasberg acted as keeper of the pills, and doled them out during breaks in filming. Greene put it bluntly: "She was going out of her mind." As on *Bus Stop,* Marilyn's New York psychiatrist was flown to London to calm her down.

While in England Marilyn once again met the poetess Edith Sitwell, whom she had first encountered three years earlier in Hollywood. Sitwell declined to tell the press what they discussed, but she was to say when Marilyn died, "If anyone had asked me to compile a list of people who I thought might commit suicide, I would have put her name on it."

Arthur Miller and Sir Laurence Olivier found common ground in the ordeal of dealing with their women. Olivier's wife, Vivien Leigh, had long been subject to breakdowns and uncontrollable violent rages. During the shooting of *Prince and the Showgirl,* Leigh suffered a miscarriage. Marilyn began vomiting, was attended by the Queen's obstetrician, and rumors flew around that she too was pregnant. Sources conflict as to whether she too lost a baby.

In the course of all the dramas Olivier and Miller began to confide in each other. The British critic Kenneth Tynan learned something of what passed between them.

"Larry identified with Miller," Tynan recalled. "He saw the troubles Miller was going through in his marriage to Monroe, who was not far from being a madwoman with all her psychoneurotic idiosyncrasies—whereas Miller was a stable, sober character, much like Larry. He and Miller talked about it—about the trials of being married to huge stars who, in one way or another, were round the bend.

"Miller was very defensive. He went on and on trying to justify his sufferance of Marilyn. But Larry soon came to realize that it was just rationalizing. He could see Miller being consumed by the relationship with Marilyn. Miller himself was confused, paralyzed, and he couldn't work, he couldn't do the things he needed to do, he couldn't concentrate."

Miller had said he would be using the stay in England to finish his next play. Ther servants at Parkside House heard the clatter of the typewriter, but there would be no major work from Miller till the screenplay of *The Misfits*, four years later.

In mid-November 1956 a subdued Marilyn, wearing black under her mink, flew back to the United States with her husband. There would be no more filming for nearly two years. In that oasis of leisure, perhaps, the wounded marriage would have a chance to heal.

23

MARILYN'S UNION WITH ARTHUR Miller was to last four and a half years, the longest full-time relationship of her life. She would one day say ruefully, "I was never used to being happy, so that wasn't something I ever took for granted. I did sort of think, you know, marriage did that." If ever Marilyn hoped for happiness, and worked at it, it was now. As for Miller, he gave more of his life and love to Marilyn than did any other man.

After the false start in England the couple embarked on their first real honeymoon, in Jamaica. For a week or so, undisturbed by the press, they relaxed at Moot Point, the luxurious villa of a British aristocrat. Then it was back to New York, and a new apartment at East 57th Street.

This was to be known as "Marilyn's apartment," just as the home in Connecticut would become "Arthur's farm." The phone number, curiously enough, was in the telephone directory, for those who knew where to look. It was listed under "Marilyn, Monroe," as opposed to "Monroe, Marilyn." Here, once again, the color scheme was white—white walls, white curtains, pale furniture, and white piano.

The piano, which had followed Marilyn from California, was virtually the only physical object to survive her childhood. It had once belonged to the actor Fredric March, and Marilyn's mother had bought it, "a bit banged up," when Marilyn was eight. She could pick out a few tunes on it, light classics such as "To a Wild Rose," "The Spinning Wheel," and "Für Elise."

The apartment overflowed with books and records, and another familiar resident, Marilyn's lithograph of Abraham Lincoln, stared down from the wall. On a chess table in the library, ivory kings and queens usually stood suspended in mid-play. Beyond Marilyn's traditional Alaska of a living area was a well-appointed study for her husband.

That year, in two of the rare interviews she would now offer on her private life, Marilyn made her priorities clear. If ever it became an issue, she said, she would have no hesitation in giving up her career to preserve her marriage. "Movies are my business," she said, "but Arthur is my life. Wherever he is, I want to be. When we're in New York Arthur is the boss." Marilyn said later that at the start of their marriage she had a "pupil-teacher relationship" with Miller.

Marilyn made other declarations of intent. She insisted, just as she had in the DiMaggio marriage, "I need to be here to get my husband's breakfast and to make him a cheerful mid-morning cup of coffee occasionally. Writing's such a lonely kind of work." Now, more than in the DiMaggio marriage, Marilyn actually did some of these things. "Marriage," she told one interviewer, "makes me feel more womanly, more proud of myself. It also makes me feel less frantic. For the first time I have a feeling of being sheltered. It's as if I have come in out of the cold."

Miller, whom Marilyn called "Art," "Poppy," or "Pa," called her "Penny Dreadful," "Sugar Finney," and "Gramercy 5." When his collected plays were published that year, he dedicated them to Marilyn. He said he had come to terms with being recognized wherever he went with Marilyn, and he vigorously defended her taste for revealing clothes. Miller's enthusiasm for Marilyn matched hers for him, in his serious way.

"Marilyn is a perfectionist," he said, "and she makes impossible demands of herself. I do, too. You can never reach what you're after. I try to help Marilyn accept this truth, and she helps me.''

On the wall of his study Miller kept a photograph of a blonde, the face almost lost in shadow, not instantly recognizable. "That's Marilyn," he would say. "I like the tenderness in it, the dreaming quality, and I like it because she's relaxed. Not many people ever see her that way." That year Miller would proclaim himself "a new man at forty-one. I've learned about living from her."

Jim Proctor, a close friend of Miller, has said of that spring and summer, "I don't think I ever saw two people so dizzy with love for each other. . . ." The ugly experience of England seemed to have been a false portent. Away from filming, Marilyn seemed to be getting herself under control.

Marilyn and her husband went rowing on the lake in Central Park. Disguised in Miller's horn-rimmed glasses, she walked Hugo, the basset hound. Marilyn sang what was by now her party piece, "Diamonds Are a Girl's Best Friend," at a Miller family gathering. She sat at the feet of Miller's father, Isadore, and the old man pretended to be annoyed when she pampered him.

Marilyn entered eagerly into the role of stepmother to Jane, Miller's teenage daughter by his first marriage, and Robert, his nine-year-old son. Soon Marilyn would puzzle Hollywood visitors to the Manhattan apartment by abruptly vanishing during an important meeting. She would return to explain that she "had to get the kids off to school."

Years later she said of Miller's children and DiMaggio's son, "I take a lot of pride in them, because they're from broken homes. I think I understand about them. I think I love them more than anyone. I wanted to be their friend. Only time could prove that to them and they had to give me time." Marilyn kept in touch with "her children" long after the Miller marriage was over, and their pictures would be found in her room after her death.

Marilyn, with the aid of a maid and a cook, achieved a degree of domesticity in the first year of the Miller marriage. She could still be two and half hours late for her own dinner party, but Miller would explain with a grimace, "Ah, she's still in the tub."

Actor Kevin McCarthy remembers Marilyn at the East 57th Street apartment, "in high heels, without stockings, wobbling about in a short black dress. She had gashes in her legs because she'd made a mess of shaving them. She had a strange manner—sweet, poignant, a little distrait."

Norman Rosten recalls happy champagne parties. "Marilyn loved to dance," he says, "and Miller too—with a few drinks—would attempt an eerie, loping fox-trot, perilously off-balance." Rosten, himself, dancing with Marilyn with more than a drink or two in him, promised to write a poem in praise of her breasts.

Miller had said, "Life will go on the only way I know how to make it go—with a lot of work, a couple of laughs, and a lot of worry." The spring of 1957 had its worries.

All was not joy when, in the first stage of the contempt-of-Congress case, Miller was found guilty. There was embarrassment when the "Wrong Door Raid" inquiry brought national headlines, and the threat that Marilyn would have to testify. She begged off, claiming "a virus infection."

The collapse of Marilyn's partnership with Milton Greene brought heartache and divided loyalties. A scandal magazine raked up a story about Marilyn's infidelities to Joe DiMaggio in 1952, with Bob Slatzer. The article, complete with pictures of Marilyn and Slatzer together, had been leaked by Marilyn's former Hollywood maid. Marilyn placed panicky calls to Slatzer, reporting that her new husband was very annoyed.

These were mere irritations. "It's no fun being married to an electric light," Joe DiMaggio had said. "Mr. Miller seems to be faring better. But then he knows how to switch off."

Switching off, for Arthur Miller, had always meant escaping to the countryside. In the summer of 1957 he and Marilyn spent little time in Manhattan. Norman Rosten, invited to use the apartment in their absence, would find a scrawled note of welcome from Marilyn. One read:

Dear Norman,
There is a homemade strawberry shortcake in the Fridge, Also milk—help yourself. Also, however long you need to be here—1 wk—2 wks etc. feel free to come and go as you please . . .
    You are not imposing. We're glad you're aboard—even if we go down—sinking—the more ther merrier!
    I'm leaving you with this stanza (from an unchildlike childhood)—

Here goes—
Good nite
Sleep
and Sweet repose
Where ever you lay your Head—
I hope you find your nose—

Marilyn

In June 1957 the Millers climbed into a white Lincoln convertible and drove out of New York to the eastern tip of Long Island. Here, at Amagansett, they found their summer idyll. They rented a weatherbeaten wooden house, Stony Hill Farm, and dropped out of public view for several months. The locals saw Marilyn, dressed in tattered shorts and one of her husband's shirts, shopping at the village store. Posterity can record that the couple ate a great deal of angel food cake and ice cream, and that Arthur Miller liked his steaks thick.

Miller brought his typewriter to Amagansett, and wrote in the mornings. He was still unable to finish his next stage play, but he did complete some short stories. They included *The Misfits*, which was to grow into a screenplay for the last film Marilyn would ever make.

At Amagansett, though, work took second place to wife. The couple were seen every day on the beach, walking or just quietly sitting. One photograph, taken by a friend, shows Marilyn clasping Miller adoringly around the waist as he fishes in the surf. Miller admitted to having gained twenty-five pounds since marrying Marilyn, and the picture shows it.

There were some excursions to the city. Miller was persuaded to get into a tuxedo, his wife into a gown, for the New York premiere of *Prince and the Showgirl*. Marilyn, mysteriously, had agreed to open a Sidewalk Superintendents' Club at the site of the new Time and Life Building. Her husband declined to be dragged out for that one, and Marilyn agreed only if she could be whisked back and forth by helicopter. She arrived more than two hours late for a meeting with Laurance Rockefeller, and Rockefeller departed, grumbling that he had "never waited that long for anyone."

For Marilyn-watchers these excursions offered related clues. The premiere was in aid of a children's charity, and Marilyn visited the Sidewalk Superintendents' Club feeling "woozy in the stomach."

Marilyn was pregnant. In June, in an interview suppressed in her lifetime because the publicity people judged it out of tune with her image, she had said, "A man and a woman need something of their own. A baby makes a marriage. It makes a marriage perfect." Within weeks of her thirty-first birthday, and on the eve of her first wedding anniversary, she conceived.

After all the talking about childbearing, Marilyn was delighted, awed, also confused. One evening, at a party on Long Island, Norman Rosten found her out on the porch alone, sobbing. Marilyn would keep a photograph of herself taken that month, and told a friend years later, "It was the happiest point of my entire life."

Miller was pleased too. "To understand Marilyn best," he was to say, "you have to see her around children. They love her; her whole approach to life has their kind of simplicity and directness." Not entirely in jest, for Miller was a handsome fellow, a wit among their friends had reversed Shaw's famous reply to Isadora Duncan. "How wonderful it would be," he exclaimed, "if their first child had his looks and her brains!"

The pregnancy did not last two months. On the first day of August, as Miller worked indoors at Amagansett, he heard Marilyn scream. She was in the garden, doubled up in pain. An ambulance rushed her to her own gynecologist at Doctors Hospital in New York City. His efforts were in vain, for this was a tubular pregnancy. Marilyn awoke from surgery to learn that the embryo had been surgically removed.

Marilyn's friend Jim Haspiel visited her at the hospital. She was lying in near darkness, Miller at her side, with classical music playing on a bedside radio. She told Haspiel that, according to the doctors, the child she had lost would have been a son. Marilyn was to die, five years later, on the anniversary of this miscarriage.

At the time Marilyn seemed to rally well. She made a point of reviving an appointment for a champagne party that had been canceled on the day of the miscarriage. The doctors said she could yet bear a child, and Miller declared "she wants as many babies as she can have, and I feel the same way. She has more courage than anyone I've met."

Back at Amagansett, Marilyn rested and tried. It was a sad ordeal. She would write to the Rostens:

I think I've been pregnant for about three weeks or may be two. My breasts(s) have been too sore to even touch—I've never had that in my life before also they ache—also I've been having cramps and slight staining since Monday—now the staining is increasing and pain is increasing by the minute. I did not eat all day yesterday—also last night I took 4 whole amutal sleeping pills—which was by actual count really 8 little amutal sleeping pills.

Could I have killed it by taking all the amutal on an empty stomach? (except I took some sherry wine also)

What shall I do? if it is still alive I want to keep it.

Marilyn was not pregnant that month, nor would she be for many months to come. In the last days of the summer of 1957 the couple returned to the Manhattan apartment.

A new personal maid hired that fall, Lena Pepitone, paints a picture of a disturbed Marilyn, unhealed by the quiet months in the sun. Her mistress, Pepitone says, lounged around in bed till all hours, and wandered around the apartment naked. She frequently called for a drink, usually vodka, as soon as she woke up. Miller seemed stoical, and kept mostly to himself. Fortunately for both of them, winter brought a new preoccupation: "Arthur's farm."

Miller, who was and is addicted to the country life, had been prospecting for some time for a new home in Connecticut. He had sold the house he had shared with his first wife, and in 1957 he and Marilyn searched for a new estate. Bob Josephy, their friend who lived in the area, remembers Marilyn arriving "completely unequipped as far as clothing was concerned, tripping around a rough field in her high heels." Late in the year, largely with Marilyn's funds, they bought a three-hundred-acre farm. It was near Miller's old property, and not far from the colonial town of Roxbury.

As Marilyn described it, the eighteenth-century farmhouse was "a kind of old saltbox with a kitchen extension." The couple ignored advice to tear it down and build anew, and started a refurbishing operation that Marilyn never considered really finished. Original beams and ceilings were left intact, and a studio was built for Miller's use when writing. They also built a new wing, which Marilyn, in renewed hope, christened the Nursery. Miller said, "It's the place where we hope to live until we die."

The Roxbury area of Connecticut is peopled by gentlemen farmers and families who built their country retreats generations ago. There were some show business folk—including Richard Widmark, who had co-starred with Marilyn in *Don't Bother to Knock*—but no one pestered them here.

Marilyn assimilated easily, as a somewhat exotic addition

to an established country clique. The immediate neighbors, the Diebolds, took a shine to her after meeting at a cocktail party. They treated her like one of their children, not as a movie actress, and Marilyn seemed happy.

To these American country squires, Marilyn seemed a Marie Antoinette figure playing at being a country girl. Here, more than ever, she could indulge her compulsive affection for all living things. Hugo, the basset hound, was admitted, rain-soaked and muddy, to the newly decorated living room. Marilyn adopted Cindy, a half-starved mongrel of uncertain breed who had stumbled into the backyard. She fixed a feeding station for birds in a maple tree, and worried about how birds eat during their migration. She acquired two talking parakeets, which henceforth made innumerable flights to and from Hollywood. Butch, her favorite, was smuggled aboard his first flight to New York, only to awaken en route, squawking his new chorus: "I'm Marilyn's bird, Marilyn's bird."

The concern for animals and nature was obsessive, and psychiatrists would make much of it. Inez Melson, Marilyn's former business manager in California, was once wakened to take an urgent call from Connecticut. It was four o'clock in the morning on the East Coast, and Marilyn was calling to say that Butch, the parakeet, was frightened by a thunderstorm.

Arthur Miller discovered how fraught life could be with a mate who became frantic about the death of any living thing. He based a short story, "Please Don't Kill Anything," on what had happened the evening he and Marilyn watched fishermen hauling in their catch. Marilyn ran about throwing back the living rejects from the catch, worrying about their chances of survival.

"She looked up," he wrote, "like a little girl, with that naked wonder in her face, even as she was smiling in the way of a grown woman, and she said, 'But some of them might live now till they're old . . . and see their children grow up!' "

In New York, on a walk to the little park at East 58th Street, Marilyn once came upon two boys trapping pigeons. When they explained the birds would fetch fifty cents each at the market, she paid the boys to release their catch. For a long time after that, she returned to the park every week to pay the ransom.

Another episode was truly pathetic. Once, arriving home at Roxbury, Marilyn noticed that the grass borders had been mown while she was out. The myriad nasturtiums that had covered the grass now lay in orange and yellow ruin. Marilyn, "crying as if she were wounded," made Miller stop the car. Then she rushed about picking up the fallen flowers, sticking the stalks back into the ground, to see if they might recover.

Arthur Miller watched and listened, and worried. In *Please Don't Kill Anything* he wrote that "while part of his heart worshipped her fierce tenderness toward all that lived, another part knew that she must come to understand that she did not die with the moths and the spiders and the fledgling birds."

At Amagansett, after the loss of the baby, there had been an evening when Miller noticed his wife slumped in the chair, breathing stertorously. He counted her sleeping pills, or rather the lack of them, and realized Marilyn was going into a barbiturate coma. Her life was saved only because of the prompt action of an emergency medical crew from a nearby clinic.

One night at 3:00 A.M. in New York, Norman and Hedda Rosten were summoned urgently to the apartment on East 57th Street. There had been another overdose, and Marilyn's stomach had been pumped. When he arrived, Marilyn was weeping quietly in her bed. It had been close; her fingers were still blue. Rosten leaned over in the half-light, and asked, "How are you, dear?"

"Alive. Bad luck," came the slurred reply. "Cruel, all of them, all those bastards. Oh, Jesus. . . ."

At a party in Brooklyn Heights in 1958, Norman Rosten watched Marilyn sitting on a windowsill, glass in hand. She looked moody, "in her personal daydream, gripped by thoughts that could not be pleasant." Rosten walked to her and said, "Hey, psst, come back."

Marilyn talked of her sleepless nights, then pointed out the window. "It's a quick way down from here. Who'd know the difference if I went?"

"I would," said Rosten, "and all the people in this room would care. They'd hear the crash."

Marilyn laughed.

Jokingly, yet not entirely so, Rosten got Marilyn to agree to a pact. If either came close to committing suicide, he or she would call the other, to be talked out of it. Rosten thought then that, one day, Marilyn would call. He still keeps a fragment of a poem she wrote in 1958. It reads:

Help Help
Help I feel life coming closer
When all I want to do is to die.

In New York that year, in the divided self behind the famous eyes, Marilyn had begun to die.

24

"THIS, THEN," MUSED BRITISH photographer Cecil Beaton, "is the wonder of the age—a dreaming somnambule, a composite of Alice in Wonderland, Trilby, and Minsky artist. Perhaps she was born the postwar day we had need of her. . . . Lke Giraudoux's *Ondine*, she is only fifteen years old; but what will happen with the years, only time can tell."

Of the millions of words disgorged on Marilyn, Beaton's three pages are among the most articulate and shrewd. He saw a creature "as spectacular as the silvery shower of a Vesuvius fountain, an incredible display of inspired, narcissistic moods." Marilyn's performance, for Beaton, was "pure charade."

In 1958 Marilyn posed for photographer Richard Avedon for a brilliant series of still pictures portraying film stars of the past. Across the pages of *Life* magazine Marilyn became Jean Harlow, Clara Bow, Lillian Russell, Theda Bara, and Marlene Dietrich. It was, as Arthur Miller commented, "a kind of history of our mass fantasy, so far as seductresses are concerned."

That year, as she performed fantasy to perfection, Marilyn really began her slide to defeat in the real world. The child was a woman of thirty-two, drinking real alcohol and too much of it, and she knew she was breaking apart. Marilyn now met one of her film idols—and a future co-star on *The Misfits*—Montgomery Clift. At their first encounter, a specially arranged dinner, both got drunk, he on Scotch and Marilyn on rum cocktails.

Later, during an evening with Marilyn and her husband,

Clift disintegrated as he regularly did, falling about, failing to complete his sentences. Marilyn commented, "He's the only person I know who's in worse shape than I am."

Marilyn had arrived back in Los Angeles in early July, to make *Some Like It Hot*. She had not filmed in Hollywood since *Bus Stop*, and the press turned out in force at the airport. At first there was confusion as to whether she had arrived at all. Then, thirty minutes after the last passenger had left the aircraft, Marilyn appeared.

"An apparition in white materialized in the doorway," wrote the *Los Angeles Times'* reporter, "white hair aswirl in the propwash of another plane; white silk shirt open at the powdered white throat; white, tight silk skirt; white shoes; white gloves. Marilyn Monroe blinked big, sleepy eyes at the world . . . began descending—slowly and wickedly—down the steps. 'I'm so sorry,' she cooed. 'I was asleep.' "

Reporters observed three books under Marilyn's arm: *The Importance of Living* by Lin Yutang, Shirley Jackson's *Life Among the Savages*, and *To the Actor* by Michael Chekhov. It was later reported that Marilyn's suite at the Bel-Air Hotel was decorated largely in white, to duplicate the New York apartment, and that she had purchased another parakeet because she was lonely for her dog, left on the East Coast.

Marilyn's behavior during the shooting of *Some Like It Hot* outdid all previous delinquencies. Director Billy Wilder, who four years earlier had survived *Seven Year Itch* with Marilyn, now began a five-month ordeal. Marilyn appeared for a lunchtime call at six in the evening. One day, while sitting in her dressing room reading Thomas Paine's *The Rights of Man*, she responded to an assistant director's call with "Go fuck yourself."

Marilyn, not generally known for foul language, apparently fell into it now. She responded to early rushes with "I'm not going back into the fucking film until Wilder reshoots my opening. When Marilyn Monroe comes into a room, nobody's going to be looking at Tony Curtis playing Joan Crawford. They're going to be looking at Marilyn Monroe."

Some Like It Hot is the comic tale of two men on the run from gangsters, who don female clothing to join a touring dance band made up entirely of women. One of them, played by Tony Curtis, falls for the girl played by Marilyn, a ukulele player with a taste for whisky and millionaires. Advertisements for the film would describe Curtis and his co-star, Jack

Lemmon, as Marilyn's "bosom companions." On the set, things were otherwise.

It is now film legend how Marilyn drove Curtis and Lemmon to distraction with her interminable delays and inability to remember even the simplest dialogue. One three-word line required no less than sixty-five takes. Curtis, whom she once doused with a glass of champagne, was to speak later of Marilyn's "vicious arrogance" and "vindictive selfishness." It was also Curtis, in an off-the-cuff remark while watching rushes, who inadvertently recorded for posterity his feelings about the world's sex symbol. Kissing Marilyn, he vouchsafed, was "like kissing Hitler."

Marilyn's preparations for performing astonished onlookers and infuriated colleagues. "Before each take," wrote Lloyd Shearer, "Marilyn would close her eyes and enter a deep trance. She would pull down on her creeping-up bathing suit, style 1927, then suddenly start to flail her hands violently, up and down, up and down, as if she were desperately intent upon separating her hands from her wrists." This was part of the technique Marilyn had picked up at the Actors Studio. Paula Strasberg, garbed in black robe, black hood, and dark glasses, was never far away.

Director Billy Wilder was ill during the making of *Some Like It Hot*. When it was over, he said, "I am eating better. I have been able to sleep for the first time in months. I can look at my wife without wanting to hit her because she's a woman." Later, comparing the ordeal to a journey by air, Wilder said, "We were in mid-flight—and there was a nut on the plane."

"When you are a director," Wilder says today, "you try to be a psychologist to some extent. You must establish communication with your people. Normally I learn quickly how to size them up. Marilyn was so difficult because she was totally unpredictable. I never knew what kind of a day we were going to have. I used to worry: What character is she going to be today? Will she be cooperative or obstructive? Will she explode, and we won't get one single shot? That was the problem. I can cope with anything, but I need to know what is in store. I never knew with Marilyn."

In hindsight, like most other directors, Wilder had no regrets. In her uncanny way, Marilyn had once again worked celluloid sorcery. The film received a chorus of critical praise and made a fortune at the box office. It is the Monroe film most frequently shown on television today.

Even before the film appeared, Wilder was saying, "She

has a certain indefinable magic that comes across which no actress in the business has. . . . I have an aunt in Vienna, also an actress. Her name, I think, is Mildred Lachenfarber. She always comes to the set on time. She knows her lines perfectly. She never gives anyone the slightest trouble. At the box office she is worth fourteen cents. Do you get my point?''

Today Wilder says, ''She was an absolute genius as a comic actress, with an extraordinary sense for comic dialogue. It was a God-given gift. Believe me, in the last fifteen years there were ten projects that came to me, and I'd start working on them and I'd think, 'It's not going to work, it needs Marilyn Monroe.' Nobody else is in that orbit; everyone else is earthbound by comparison.''

On September 11, 1958, Marilyn wrote to Norman Rosten from location at Coronado, California. The hotel notepaper was decorated with a beach scene, to which Marilyn added a little female stick figure in the water, waving its arms and shouting ''Help.'' The letter read (see facing page):

> Dear Norman,
>   Don't give up the ship while we're sinking. I have a feeling this boat is *never* going to dock. We are going through the Straits of Dire. It's rough and choppy but why should I worry I have no phallic symbol to lose.
>
>   Marilyn
>
> P.S. ''Love me for my yellow hair alone''*
>
> I would have written this
> by hand but its trembling

Once again during this film Marilyn was attended by a psychiatrist and a medical doctor flown in from the East. Now, four days after writing to Rosten, she was admitted to Cedars of Lebanon Hospital suffering from ''nervous exhaustion.'' This time there was reason for concern about Marilyn's physical health. She was pregnant again.

As the weeks slipped by Arthur Miller became increasingly

---

*Marilyn was misquoting a Yeats poem in her postscript. The actual lines read:

. . . only God, my dear,
Could love you for yourself alone
And not your yellow hair.

HOTEL DEL CORONADO
Coronado California

September 11, 1958

Dear Norman,

Don't give up the ship while we're sinking. I have a feeling this boat is never going to dock. We are going through the Straits of Dire. It's rough and choppy but why should I worry I have no phallic symbol to lose.

"S "Love me for my yellow hair alone"

I would have written this by hand but its trembling

San Diego—ACROSS THE BAY
Old Mexico—18 MILES AWAY

Marilyn's note to Norman Rosten from the set of *Some Like It Hot*. Her stick figure is shouting "help" at top right.

worried. He asked Wilder to start letting Marilyn go home early in the afternoon.

Wilder retorted, "But Arthur, I don't get my first shot until three o'clock. What does she do in the mornings?"

A puzzled Miller replied that, to his certain knowledge, Marilyn left their room for the set each morning at 7:00 A.M. The mystery of the lost mornings never was resolved.

On October 27, Marilyn wrote to Rosten:

Dear Norman,
Thank you for your Halloween wishes. It's too bad we can't be together. I might scare you.

I haven't been writing anyone, let alone poems—it's so spooky here! Arthur looks well though weaker—from holding me up. . . . I need something to hold on to. . . .

Marilyn signed her note with the name of "e.e. cummings," whose poetry she had been reading.

The last scenes of *Some Like It Hot*, completed in early November, involved strenuous physical effort in high temperatures. Marilyn returned to the hospital, then took to her bed at her hotel, "so as not to jar the baby." She then traveled by ambulance to the airport, and flew back to New York. There, shortly before Christmas, she lost the baby.

Before she had started *Some Like It Hot*, Marilyn asked Rosten, "Should I do my next picture or stay home and try to have a baby again? That's what I want most of all, the baby, I guess, but maybe God is trying to tell me something, I mean with my pregnancy. I'd probably make a kooky mother; I'd love my child to death. I want it, yet I'm scared. Arthur says he wants it, but he's losing his enthusiasm. He thinks I should do the picture. After all, I'm a movie star, right?"

The movie star had made her film and lost another baby. Marilyn submitted to more surgery to improve the chances of bearing a child, but 1959 brought no new pregnancy. Close friends now have the clear impression that the marriage to Miller was foundering. Rosten, watching the couple, thought they were playing out "a facade of marital harmony."

Susan Strasberg and her parents, visiting the couple at Roxbury, felt "there was a heavy feeling in the house. We thought perhaps they were having a fight. We sat in the living room for well over an hour. Arthur neglected to offer us anything to eat or drink."

The Strasbergs had been invited to lunch, yet when Marilyn

did appear, it turned out there was no food. Marilyn got drunk, Miller sat around moodily, and the guests ended up by going out to lunch.

Marilyn was continuing to attend the Actors Studio. In the summer of 1959, driving to the country with Susan Strasberg, Marilyn exclaimed, "You know, if it weren't for the work [at the Actors Studio] I'd jump out of the car." Miller, on the other hand, was increasingly disenchanted with the Strasbergs.

Actress Maureen Stapleton, Marilyn's friend from the Studio, was appalled by the imbalance she now saw in the couple. "Arthur was becoming a lackey. He was carrying her makeup case and her purse, just doing too much for her, and I had the feeling things had gone hopelessly wrong." The director Martin Ritt had the same feeling when he dined with the Millers. "It was a disastrous evening," says Ritt. "He was at her beck and call, running around after her all evening, and it disturbed me."

At the same time, as Norman Rosten saw it, Miller was drawing away from Marilyn emotionally, becoming an observer of his own marriage rather than a participant.

In his New York workroom Miller sat among a pile of scribbled notes, a new *Encyclopaedia Britannica*—a gift from Marilyn—at his elbow. Miller kept two photographs of her above the desk. Three years earlier he had been "finishing" a new play, yet none had been forthcoming. None would be completed till after Marilyn's death. In the fall of 1959 *Esquire* published a profile of the playwright, and called it "The Creative Agony of Arthur Miller."

For public consumption Marilyn continued to make cheerful statements, but they sounded more and more like rehashed versions of an analyst's advice. That summer she told a British interviewer, "I've been scared all my life, really, until now. Scared about so many things, even picking up the phone to make a call. That is the sort of thing I'm getting over at last. My philosophy now is 'Enjoy the day.' I don't fear the future any more."

The immediate future included a visit to Hollywood. In September 1959, Soviet leader Nikita Khrushchev came to Hollywood during a visit to the United States. Various stars, including Marilyn, Elizabeth Taylor, and Debbie Reynolds, were asked to attend a welcome luncheon at Twentieth Century-Fox. Miller, wary after his battles with the House Un-American Activities Committee, did not go.

Marilyn flew to California alone, spent five hours beautify-

ing herself, and actually arrived early for the lunch. Khru-
schev stopped to speak to her, and she offered him greetings
from Arthur Miller. Marilyn would later pound her chest with
pride, recalling with delight how "Khrushchev looked at me
like a man looks at a woman."

That episode probably added one more report to the FBI
file on Marilyn.

There had reportedly been CIA interest in making use of
Marilyn's acquaintance with another visiting political leader.
During the shooting of *Bus Stop*, in 1956, Marilyn had met
the Indonesian president, Achmed Sukarno. At first she had
no idea who he was—she called him "Prince" Sukarno—but
she turned up for a diplomats' party at the Beverly Hills
Hotel.

Marilyn and the Indonesian took a shine to one another.
"They kept disappearing to the edges of the party," *Bus Stop*
director Joshua Logan recalls. "The atmosphere was all
S-E-X. I think they made a date to meet afterwards."

Years later Sukarno told his biographer that Marilyn, who
was also staying at the Beverly Hills Hotel, telephoned to
suggest a private meeting. A man who loved bragging about
his conquests, he uncharacteristically failed to do so about
Marilyn.

Marilyn, for her part, was to react with remarkable passion, a year or so after the Hollywood meeting, to news of an
attempted coup against Sukarno. She amazed Arthur Miller
by announcing her desire to "rescue" the Indonesian by
offering him a home in the United States. She would tell her
friend Robert Slatzer that she and Sukarno had "spent an
evening together."

Whatever occurred at the original meeting, it had not gone
unnoticed at the Central Intelligence Agency. In those years
Indonesia loomed as large as Vietnam in Washington's view
of Asian priorities. In 1957 and 1958, the record shows, the
CIA had engaged in all sorts of skullduggery aimed at dis-
lodging Sukarno, who was seen as responsible for his country's drift toward communism.

Part of the CIA effort involved a scheme to produce a
phoney pornographic film, supposedly showing a blonde Soviet agent in bed with Sukarno. The intention was to use the
film to discredit the Indonesian president, but the project was
aborted. Later, however, when the United States needed to
curry favor with Sukarno, the CIA dreamed of using sex—in

the shape of Marilyn Monroe—to make the dictator feel honored.

According to Joseph Smith, a former CIA career officer in Asia, "There was an attempt to get Sukarno together with Monroe. In mid-1958 I heard of a plan to get them in bed together. I remember someone from Washington coming through and talking about 'some crazy business with Marilyn Monroe that didn't work out right.' "

There is no knowing how far the CIA went in its foolishness involving Marilyn. Applications for relevant documents have produced nothing, and the episode remains secret.

There was little secrecy, however, about the marital folly that Marilyn committed in 1960. At nearly thirty-four, after an unhappy, idle year, she began to tear apart the faltering marriage to Arthur Miller. The final phase began when she returned to Hollywood for the filming of *Let's Make Love*, opposite the French actor Yves Montand.

25

IN SEPTEMBER 1959, MR. and Mrs. Arthur Miller, M. and Mme. Montand, and Mr. and Mrs. Rosten stood in a Broadway dressing room, laughing uproariously about M. Montand's fly buttons. It was the Frenchman's American debut, and his theater audience had been laughing at improbable moments. The guffaws, Montand learned from his New York friends, were because his fly buttons gleamed in the spotlight whenever he put his hands in his pockets. Thus began, in jollity, a relationship that would end in national scandal and private misery.

Improbable though it seemed at the time, Twentieth Century-Fox had to struggle to find a leading man for Marilyn's next film, *Let's Make Love*. For one reason or another Yul Brynner, Cary Grant, Rock Hudson, Charlton Heston, and Gregory Peck all sent regrets. In the moment of crisis George Cukor saw Yves Montand doing his song-and-dance routine on television, and suggested his name to Marilyn. The call came just weeks after the meeting in New York. Marilyn's opinion, soon to be written in headlines, was that "Next to my husband, and along with Brando, Yves is the most attractive man I've met." Montand was hired.

Let's Make Love is the story of a billionaire (Yves Montand), the target of a satirical revue, who finds himself falling in love with one of its girl singers (Marilyn). The film was to prove disappointing, inane, an exception to the run of fine films that ended Marilyn's career. She distinguished herself, nevertheless, with her song-and-dance routines, not least in a sensual rendering of Cole Porter's "My Heart Belongs to Daddy." Long before the film was finished, however, Marilyn's heart belonged to Yves Montand.

Arthur Miller knew and liked Montand. Montand had starred in the French production of *The Crucible*, and he shared some of Miller's political convictions. With his wife, Simone Signoret, who had received an Oscar for her performance in *Room at the Top*, Montand had long avoided the United States rather than sign a declaration that he had never been a member of the Communist Party. He and Signoret regularly lent their names to liberal causes in France.

Montand was one inhabitant of the universe who had never seen a Monroe movie, and he spoke little English. Yet Miller's judgment was that "He fits the role splendidly. He and Marilyn are both very vital people. They possess internal engines which emit indescribable rays of energy. Yves will be one of the big stars of the American screen."

So it was, in January 1960, that the Montands and the Millers moved into Bungalows 20 and 21 at the Beverly Hills Hotel. It was a cozy arrangement. The two couples joined each other for home-cooked meals, and sat around talking into the night.

Simone Signoret befriended Marilyn and humored her eccentricities. She was amused by the ritual each Saturday, when a little old lady arrived to peroxide Marilyn's hair. The old lady had been Jean Harlow's hairdresser, and Marilyn had her specially flown to Los Angeles every weekend.

Signoret thought Marilyn looked like "the most beautiful peasant girl imaginable from the Île-de-France, as the type has been celebrated for centuries." Late at night Signoret told Marilyn acting anecdotes, and felt like a mother telling bedtime stories. As a woman, Marilyn did not seem to be any sort of threat.

As for Montand, he was soon bemoaning the irritations of

working with Marilyn. Sometimes, without warning, she would leave the studio for an entire afternoon, and filming would grind to a halt. Montand would pace up and down mumbling, "Where is she? I cannot wait and wait. I am not an automobile."

Within weeks Miller had to go to Europe on business, and Marilyn promptly went into a decline. She told her doctors she could not continue working on the film because, according to her, one of the camera crew was homosexual.

One morning Montand telephoned his wife from the studio to say Marilyn had failed to arrive and did not answer her telephone. Simone Signoret hammered on Marilyn's door in vain. Then the switchboard operator revealed that, though Marilyn was failing to answer the phone, she had recently made an outgoing call. The actress was simply malingering.

A furious Montand came storming back to the hotel. He wrote a note reading, in essence:

> Next time you decide to hang around too late listening to my wife tell you stories instead of going to bed, because you've already decided not to get up the next morning and go to the studio, please tell me. I'm not the enemy. I'm your pal. And capricious little girls have never amused me.
>
> Best,
> Yves

Montand and his wife slipped the note under Marilyn's door, leaving one end protruding into the corridor, then watched as it was slowly pulled inside. Marilyn had the message, but still she did nothing. Montand then shouted through the door that the day's work was canceled "because of absentees," and went out till evening.

At eleven that night there was still no word from Marilyn. Then Miller called the Montands long-distance from Europe to say Marilyn had telephoned him. He asked the Montands to go to her room.

"Suddenly," Signoret recalled later, "I had in my arms a weeping girl, who kept saying, 'I'm bad, I'm bad, I'm bad. I won't do it again, I promise.' " Montand patted her on the head, and told her to be on time the next day.

Let's Make Love was not all gloom and dissension, and Marilyn's sense of humor had not deserted her. She was told the censor would object to a kissing scene if it was performed lying down, on the grounds that she and Montand would appear to be actually making love. "Well," Marilyn responded, "we could equally well do *that* standing up!"

Sometime that spring, for all their professional differences, Marilyn and the Frenchman began an affair. According to a close friend of the Millers who prefers not to be named, Marilyn had for some time ceased to be wholly faithful. "She had this terrible neediness," says the friend, "she went with other men simply for something to hold on to, however short-lived." One such brief infidelity had been with Nico Minardos, her lover of nearly a decade earlier. Now Marilyn turned to Yves Montand.

Marilyn had earmarked Montand long ago, when she and roommate Shelley Winters compiled lists of longed-for lovers. Now she began telling friends, including her psychiatrist, that the Frenchman looked like Joe DiMaggio, that he excited her physically. On the set, it was obvious that they enjoyed playing at being in love. Not for the first time for a pair of screen lovers, the borderline between the theater and reality became blurred.

Simone Signoret sensed danger, but had to leave to honor a contract in Europe. Arthur Miller was in and out of Los Angeles and, immediate peril aside, seemed increasingly resigned to the collapse of his marriage. Marilyn and Montand were now frequently alone in their adjoining bungalows.

One reporter, drawing on a later interview with Montand, says Marilyn, nude under her mink—an old Marilyn game—simply knocked on the Frenchman's door one night and took him by storm.

Arthur Miller, by another account, once surprised the couple in bed together when he returned to the bungalow to fetch his pipe. Soon a room-service waiter was blabbing bedroom stories to a journalist patron. The affair, or the heavy hint of it, became public knowledge.

That summer, when filming finished, Montand flew back to Paris via New York. Marilyn, already on the East coast, planned an elaborate interception. She reserved a room at a hotel, and turned up at the airport laden with champagne. The short stopover turned into a five-hour delay, and Marilyn and Montand were observed huddled together in the back of her limousine. The Frenchman, vastly embarrassed, then departed for Paris—and a reunion with the long-suffering Simone Signoret.

More than a month later Marilyn, now working on *The Misfits* in Nevada, brought production to a halt with another of her breakdowns, and was flown to Los Angeles for detoxification. She was there when Montand made a brief return visit to California. Marilyn bombarded the Frenchman with telephone calls from her hospital bed, but now he refused to speak to her.

Montand told columnist Hedda Hopper, who was with him when Marilyn called, "I think she is an enchanting child, and I would like to see her to say good-bye, but I won't talk to her on the telephone; somebody might be listening. I've never met anyone quite like Marilyn Monroe, but she is still a child. I'm sorry, but nothing will break up my marriage."

In the midst of denying there had been an affair, Montand was evidently a very confused man. "The trouble was," he told Art Buchwald, "that Marilyn and I were a big contact together. . . ." He told another reporter, "If I were not married, and if Marilyn were not married, I would not object to marrying her."

Marilyn, for her part, would not let go. For months to come, as her own marriage finally crumbled, she would fall back pathetically on the hope of luring Montand to her side. But they did not meet again.

Simone Signoret, although deeply upset, handled the matter impeccably. "If Marilyn is in love with my husband," she said in a rare comment, "it proves she has good taste. For I am in love with him too."

Recently, in a poignant passage of her biography, Montand's wife said of Marilyn: "She never knew to what degree I never detested her, and how thoroughly I had understood. . . . She's gone without ever knowing that I never stopped wearing the champagne-colored silk scarf she'd lent me one day. It's a bit frayed now, but if I fold it carefully, the fray doesn't show."

26

DURING ONE OF MARILYN'S "collapses" while making *Let's Make Love*, a new doctor began attending her in Bungalow 21 at the Beverly Hills Hotel. Dr. Ralph Greenson, a prominent California psychiatrist, had been asked by Marilyn's New York analyst to look after the actress while she was in California.

So began a most unusual relationship between doctor and patient. Ralph Greenson, with his wife and children, would in the end find themselves acting as yet another surrogate family for Marilyn. Two years later, Greenson would be one of the last people to speak to Marilyn alive, the first known to have seen her in death.

Marilyn's new psychiatrist was internationally respected. Of Russian extraction, trained in Vienna and Switzerland, he brought to his practice a firm grounding in the teachings of Freud. He was, indeed, close to Sigmund Freud's family and associates. During the war Greenson had been chief of the Combat Fatigue Section of the Army Air Corps. He was author of dozens of learned publications, and by 1970 had long been Clinical Professor of Psychiatry at the University of California at Los Angeles. In the words of a colleague, the doctor was "the backbone of psychoanalysis in the western United States."

Greenson was no stranger to Hollywood; he had had numerous show business clients, among them Frank Sinatra. The psychiatrist was forty-nine when he first met Marilyn, an intense, slender man, known for his sensitivity and deep personal concern for his patients.

Quite properly, Dr. Greenson generally refrained from discussing his most famous client. However, after her death, he did give long briefings to psychiatrists of the Los Angeles Suicide Prevention Center, which had been asked to look into the case by the Coroner. Greenson, now dead, also gave guarded interviews to two writers, who kept their notes.

This author also discovered a source who had preserved a good deal of the doctor's professional correspondence on Marilyn, dating from their first encounter. The material throws a stark new light on the gravity of Marilyn's condition two years before her death.

Marilyn's first visit to Dr. Greenson was after a day's work on the set of *Let's Make Love*. He noticed at once that she seemed heavily sedated, slurred her words, and had poor reactions. She seemed remote, failed to understand simple conversational sallies, and rambled on incoherently. She wanted to go straight on to the couch for a session of Freudian therapy. Greenson, alarmed by her condition, decided instead on "supportive therapy" rather than deep psychoanalysis. He explored first the facts of her day-to-day life.

Marilyn poured out a string of complaints. She said she disliked her part in the film, although she had earlier declared *Let's Make Love* the best screenplay she had ever read. She now said her acting coach, Paula Strasberg, was of little use, because she paid too much attention to her own daughter, Susan. Psychiatrist Greenson found himself taking the role of "supportive acting coach."

Marilyn told of her chronic insomnia, and used that to justify a use of drugs that Greenson considered hugely excessive. The new patient moaned about her medical doctors, revealing in the process that she was flitting from doctor to doctor to obtain the drugs she wanted. As Greenson discovered, Marilyn would play one doctor off against another, secretly calling one behind another's back. She amazed Greenson with her knowledge of drugs, and appalled him with the dangerous jumble of medicines she had been able to obtain.

Greenson discovered that Marilyn was accustomed to taking Demerol, a narcotic analgesic similar to morphine. She also used the barbiturate phenobarbital HMC; sodium pentothol, a depressant of the nervous system, primarily used in anesthesia; and Amytal, another barbiturate. She habitually took several of these drugs intravenously.

Privately, an angry Greenson railed against the "stupid doctors" who had caved in to Marilyn's past blandishments. He tried to make sure she henceforth used only one medical doctor, insisted on an end to drugs by injection, and especially objected to further use of Demerol, which can be highly dangerous if abused.

From doctors who had attended Marilyn, Greenson concluded that "although she resembled an addict, she did not seem to be the usual addict." She seemed able to give up her drugs on occasion, without withdrawal symptoms. Both doctors, however, feared she was on the way to becoming an addict.

As Greenson strove to wean Marilyn from drugs he tried to teach her the art of sleeping. It was an uphill struggle. One day, called to her hotel room, he found Marilyn "begging for intravenous sodium pentothol or Amytal—this despite some fourteen hours of sleep the day immediately preceding."

"I told her," the doctor wrote, "that she'd already received so much medication that it would put five other people to sleep, but the reason she wasn't sleeping was because she was afraid of sleeping. I promised she would sleep with less medication if she would recognize she is fighting sleep as well as searching for some obvious oblivion which is not sleep."

Dr. Greenson also listened to Marilyn's "venomous resentment" toward Arthur Miller. She claimed her husband was "cold and unresponsive" to her problems, attracted to other women, and dominated by his mother. She accused Miller of neglecting his father and not being "nice" to his children. She said Miller would tell Greenson a different story, but not to believe him.

Greenson did meet Miller, and found him "very interested in helping his wife and sincerely concerned about her, but from time to time gets angry and rejecting." The psychiatrist felt Miller had "the attitude of a father who has done more than most fathers would do, and is rapidly coming to the end of his rope." He advised Miller that what Marilyn needed was love and devotion without conditions. Anything less was unbearable to her.

Much later, after Marilyn's death, Greenson told colleagues that he thought the Miller marriage had collapsed "to a considerable degree" on sexual grounds. Marilyn, he observed, felt that she was frigid. She "found it difficult to sustain a series of orgasms with the same individual."

Greenson would also report that, pathetically, this sexually dissatisfied woman "gloried and revelled in her personal appearance, feeling that she was an extremely beautiful woman, perhaps the most beautiful woman in the world. She always took great pains to be attractive and to give a very good appearance when she was out in public, although when she was at home and nobody could see her she might not be able to put herself together very well. She felt at times that she was unimportant and insignificant. The main mechanism she used to bring some feeling of stability and significance to her life was the attractiveness of her body.''

In 1960, as Greenson first listened to Marilyn's complaints about other people, he wrote, ''As she becomes more anxious, she begins to act like an orphan, a waif, and she masochistically provokes them to mistreat her and to take advantage of her. As fragments of her past history came out, she began to talk more and more about the traumatic experiences of an orphan child.'' Dr. Greenson perceived that the thirty-four-year-old woman still fed on the idea of herself as a ''fragile waif.''

Over the months, though he never voiced a firm diagnosis, Dr. Greenson would move from noting symptoms of paranoia and ''depressive reaction'' to observing signs of schizophrenia. He knew, above all, that he was dealing with a psyche so fragile that it could crumble into crisis at any time.

For the time being, in 1960, Greenson hoped mainly to bring a deteriorating situation under control, not least by enforcing a drastic cut in Marilyn's use of drugs. He told her flatly he ''would not help her kill herself, or spite her husband, or rush into oblivion. . . .'' It was a fine strategy, but a vain hope.

''The most serious complication of a major depressive episode,'' says the *Manual of Mental Disorders*, the book used by psychiatrists in the United States for formal diagnosis, ''is suicide.''

27

THREE YEARS EARLIER IN New York, as his wife lay recovering from one of her miscarriages, Arthur Miller had stepped out for a stroll in the little park in front of Doctors Hospital. He told a companion, photographer Sam Shaw, of a short story he had written, called ''The Misfits.''

The idea had come to Miller before marrying Marilyn— when he was living in a cabin in Nevada establishing residence for a divorce. There, at the Stix Ranch in Quail Canyon, Miller had met three cowboys who made their living hunting wild horses. They were wanderers, determinedly living their lives outside the conventional structure of American society, and they struck Miller as the last of a vanishing type of American. The horses they caught, which would be sold as dog food for six cents a pound, were also rarities, the harried survivors of a decimated breed. A story of the wilds could hardly be a play, Miller's usual medium, so he wrote it as a rather long short story for *Esquire* magazine.

Then, in the park outside Doctors Hospital, it occurred to Miller that he could expand "The Misfits" into a screenplay, with a major role for his wife. It was his first screenplay, and it was, as a close friend put it, a valentine for Marilyn.

Miller's relationship with Marilyn had changed a great deal by July 1960, when a unique gathering of talent assembled at the Mapes Hotel in Reno, Nevada, to make what the producer described to *Time* magazine as "an attempt at the ultimate motion picture." It was to star Clark Gable and Marilyn Monroe, Montgomery Clift and Eli Wallach, and a number of noted actors playing minor roles just for the privilege of taking part. The director was to be John Huston, lured back to make a film on American soil for the first time in years.

Marilyn was to play Roslyn, a lonely, troubled woman from the East, who comes to Reno seeking a divorce. She falls in love with Gay, an older man and rugged individualist, portrayed by Clark Gable, who teams up with two other fellows to round up horses.

Roslyn, like Marilyn in real life, schemes and struggles to prevent the slaughter of the animals. Her fight for the horses becomes an epic struggle between man and woman, and from that—we are permitted to hope—love may survive.

Arthur Miller arrived in Nevada before Marilyn. He knew the marriage was disintegrating, and he was aware, though perhaps not fully, of his wife's treachery with Yves Montand. A few months earlier, when Miller was in Europe working on the *Misfits* script with John Huston, Huston had told a story about a couple who separated after each told the other of their infidelities. Miller had nodded and replied, "Truth destroyed them."

Brad Dexter, the actor whom Marilyn had asked to intervene when the DiMaggio marriage was crumbling, now found himself playing marriage counselor again. Marilyn said of Miller, "He's accusing me of going to bed with every guy I ever met. It's terrible. Would you talk to him?'' Dexter dined with Miller at La Scala restaurant in Beverly Hills, but got nowhere.

The Montand affair did not destroy Miller's marriage to Marilyn. It seems to have been at this time, though, that Miller ceased the endless effort to rescue his wife from her own turmoil. It was time to think of self-preservation.

On the set of *The Misfits*, shooting still photographs in company with Henri Cartier-Bresson, was a distinguished female photographer, Inge Morath. In her, Miller would eventually find his third wife, and a happy marriage that has lasted. The last painful act of marriage to Marilyn was to be played out during the making of *The Misfits*.

In New York, in the third week of July, Jim Haspiel went to the airport to see Marilyn off to the West Coast. He saw at once that she looked ravaged and unkempt, with "bags under the eyes and a period stain across the back of her skirt. I didn't want to see her like that, and I turned away.'' When Marilyn arrived three days later at Reno, Nevada, she kept everyone waiting—as usual—while she changed in the lavatory of the aircraft. Among those waiting was the wife of the governor of Nevada, who had been sent by her husband to welcome Marilyn with a bouquet.

Next day, as the desert heat crept up to over a hundred degrees, Marilyn began filming. On the set, she could still look wonderful. Photographer Cartier-Bresson saw in her beauty and intelligence combining to make "a certain myth of what we call in France *la femme éternelle*.''

Alice McIntyre of *Esquire* thought her "like nothing human you have ever seen or dreamed. She is astonishingly white, so radically pale that in her presence you can look at others about as easily as you explore the darkness around the moon. Indeed, there seems the awful possibility in the various phases of her person that MM is a manifestation of the White Goddess herself: disdaining all lingerie and dressed in tight, white silk emblazoned with countless red cherries, she becomes at once the symbol of impartial and eternal availability, who yet remains forever pure—and a potentially terrible goddess whose instinct could also deal death and whose smile, when she directs it clearly at you, is exquisitely, heartbreakingly sweet.''

The White Goddess exulted that she was working with the King. Clark Gable was the idol who so resembled the picture her mother had once told her was a photograph of her father.

He was the man who, in occasional fantasies, she had some-times suggested really was her father.

"All these years," she told an interviewer, "and now, Rhett Butler! Doesn't he look marvelous? We were rehearsing a very long scene, and he started to tremble, just the slightest bit. I can't tell you how endearing that was to me. To find somebody—my idol—to be, well, *human*."

Clark Gable himself, the quintessential professional, real-ized Marilyn's worth as an actress. He would live long enough to tell his agent, George Chasin, that working with Marilyn on *The Misfits* resulted in one of the very best of his seventy films. It was also Gable's turn to ask, "What the hell is that girl's problem? Goddamn it, I like her, but she's so damn unprofessional. I damn near went nuts up there in Reno waiting for her to show."

Soon the question each morning on the set of *The Misfits* was, "Is Marilyn working today?" Away from the control-ling influence of Dr. Greenson, she was drowning once more in drink and pills. At one point John Huston reckoned she took up to twenty Nembutal sleeping pills a day, swilled down with vodka or champagne. Often, in the coma of the morning, her old friend Whitey Snyder made her up while she was still lying flat in bed.

"Marilyn would come to the set," Huston recalls, "and she'd be in her dressing room, and sometimes we'd wait the whole morning. Occasionally she'd be practically *non compos mentis*. I remember saying to Miller, 'If she goes on at the rate she's going she'll be in an institution in two or three years, or dead. Anyone who allows her to take narcotics ought to be shot.' It was in the way of being an indictment against Miller, and then I discovered that he had no power whatsoever over her."

On John Huston's birthday, August 5, Marilyn and Miller had a violent row in front of the *Misfits* company. It was even mentioned in the newspapers.

The immediate cause of the conflict was almost certainly guilt. Marilyn had been making weekend dashes to Los Ange-les to see—or try to see—Yves Montand, now returned from Europe. Back on the set, she spread a false rumor that Miller was having an affair with John Huston's script assistant, Angela Allen. Her motive, Allen assumes, was to "work out her own guilt over Montand. She could never allow herself to feel guilty, so attack became her means of defense."

As Miller slaved away on the script, which required constant rewriting, Marilyn distanced herself from him in a physical way. One night she arrived in the makeup man's room and announced her intention of sleeping there to avoid being with Miller. It was Miller who resolved the problem by lugging his typewriter off to another room. Paula Strasberg moved in with Marilyn.

"I found myself on Miller's side," John Huston says. "He had done everything in the world to make that marriage survive. During the picture she embarrassed him in front of people. One time she left him on the set, by which I mean in the middle of the fucking desert. We were riding away and I saw Miller standing there. There were no other cars, and she hadn't let him in her car. It was sheer malice, vindictiveness. It was shameful."

Two weeks later a monstrous cloud of black smoke masked the sun over Reno, as forest fires raged across the sierras. Electric power failed, and the only lights that night shone out from the major casinos, the hospital, and one window on the ninth floor of the Mapes Hotel, where Arthur Miller toiled over the script, his desk lit by *The Misfits* company generator.

As Miller worked, Marilyn stood in the darkness with Rupert Allan, her press aide and friend, gazing out over the Truckee River. Allan told her about the life cycle of fish, how salmon go upriver to spawn, and how many thousands then die—or, as Allan put it, "just give up the struggle, to be eaten by other fish or by the raccoons."

"That's terrible," said Marilyn. "I can understand the salmon. I've felt like them."

Marilyn told Allan of yet another occasion when she had considered suicide. In New York, she said, she had climbed out on to the ledge of her thirteenth-floor apartment in her nightgown, determined to jump. "I saw a woman in a brown tweed suit," said Marilyn, "and I thought if I jumped I would do her in too. I waited out there for about five or ten minutes, but she did not move and I got so cold, so I climbed back in. But I would've done it."

Allan felt Marilyn was serious. He said he too had sometimes considered killing himself, and—like Norman Rosten before him—he suggested they made a pact. "If you ever think of suicide again, and if I ever do," he said, "the one of us will call the other." They agreed that if ever they had to make such a call, but had to leave a message, their code word would be "Truckee River."

Making suicide pacts, for Marilyn, was becoming a habit.

After those with Norman Rosten and Rupert Allan, there would be one with Lee Strasberg, her acting teacher. Strasberg would recall that sometimes in the next two years, "I extracted a promise from her that if she got in that sort of mood she would call me first. . . ."

On August 26, 1960, seated with Marilyn in a station wagon, Gable had a speech that went: "Honey, we all got to go sometime, reason or no reason. Dyin's as natural as livin'; man who's afraid to die is too afraid to live, far as I've ever seen. So there's nothing to do but forget it, that's all. Seems to me."

The next day, amid reports that she had been saved from death only after having her stomach pumped, Marilyn was evacuated to Los Angeles. In the broiling heat, she was carried to a plane wrapped in a wet sheet. Behind her at the airport, as the rest of the company dispersed, girls waved placards reading Come Back Soon, Marilyn and The Misfits Need You.

Marilyn languished in Westside Hospital for ten days, under the care of psychiatrist Ralph Greenson and an internist, Dr. Hyman Engelberg. It was now that she tried desperately, and without success, to reach Yves Montand on the telephone. She did receive solicitous calls from her friend, Marlon Brando, and from Frank Sinatra.

By the time Marilyn returned to work, an air of unreality and restrained hysteria had taken over the company of *The Misfits*. During Marilyn's hospital stay, Louella Parsons had published a column saying flatly that Marilyn was "a very sick girl, much sicker than at first believed," and that she was under psychiatric care. The condition of the star on whom *The Misfits* depended was now public knowledge, and her colleagues persevered in a mood of fond hope fortified by black humor.

Once, at 4:30 A.M., a New York wire service telephoned to check a report that Marilyn had committed suicide. "Why, that's impossible!" responded a *Misfits* press officer. "She has to be on the set at seven-thirty! Besides, Paula Strasberg would never stand for it."

In an early scene of *The Misfits*, Marilyn, as the woman in the throes of getting a divorce, is advised to toss her ring into the Truckee River. Local folklore, she learns, says this will keep her safe from divorce for the rest of her days. The scene left Marilyn morose, for her own next divorce was closer than anyone knew. During her stay in the hospital she had begged reporter Earl Wilson not to publish details of her drug-taking. There would soon be a bigger story, she said, about herself and Arthur Miller.

At the end of September, W. J. Weatherby, feature writer for England's *Manchester Guardian*, arrived on the set of *The Misfits*. His first impression "was that it was like standing in a minefield among all those manic-depressive people."

The reporter interviewed both Marilyn and Miller and found Miller protective and concerned about his wife. Perhaps, thought Weatherby, the rumors of a breakup were wrong? Then, on October 10, after he and Miller had watched one of the Kennedy–Nixon debates on television, Marilyn came banging into the room. "Thank goodness, you've brought someone home," she said coldly to Miller. "You never bring any company. It's so dull." She then vanished into the bedroom.

"Miller," Weatherby noticed, "looked as if he'd been struck."

A week later the company celebrated Arthur Miller's forty-fifth birthday with a dinner at the Christmas Tree Inn. It was a rowdy affair, for the next day would see the end of the location shooting. Marilyn, for once, deigned to attend. In the midst of the merriment the unit's resident jester, cameraman Russell Metty, clambered to his feet. He aimed a few barbs at the famous males in the company, then turned to Marilyn. "Marilyn, please do us a favor," Metty said. "Stand up and say Happy Birthday to Arthur." There was a silence, in which Marilyn shook her head.

The dinner broke up quickly, and Marilyn joined John Huston at one of the crap tables. She knew nothing about gambling, and asked Huston, "What should I ask the dice for, John?"

"Don't think, honey, just throw," Huston told her. "That's the story of your life. Don't think, do it."

Huston recalls now that "She had a lucky roll, but she didn't know what to do with it."

When the shooting of *The Misfits* was finally over, Marilyn and Miller returned to New York on separate flights. On November 11—Armistice Day, 1960—Marilyn kept her promise to give Earl Wilson an exclusive. "The marriage of Marilyn Monroe and Arthur Miller is over," Wilson wrote in his story, "and there will soon be a friendly divorce."

Marilyn, once again besieged by newsmen, emerged pale and tearful to confirm the truth of the story. In the melee, one reporter shoved his microphone right into her mouth, chipping a tooth.

Less than a week later, at four o'clock in the morning, Marilyn was wakened to the news that Clark Gable had died of a heart attack. Speaking on a house phone to a journalist in the lobby, Marilyn sobbed, "Oh, God, what a tragedy! Knowing him and working with him was a great personal joy. I send all my love and my deepest sympathy to his wife, Kay."

Kay Gable, then pregnant with the child her husband would never see, held equivocal feelings for Marilyn. She had privately suspected Marilyn of pursuing her husband. She certainly felt, Mrs. Gable told her friend Kendis Rochlen, that "the strain of working with Marilyn had contributed to Clark's death." The following year, however, Marilyn was invited to the christening party, where she held the Gables' newborn son so long and so fervently that other guests felt uncomfortable.

Marilyn did indeed feel guilty about Gable's death. Admitting she had treated him shabbily during the making of *The Misfits*, she asked Sidney Skolsky, "Was I punishing my father? Getting even for all the years *he's* kept me waiting?"

She was, Skolsky recalled, "in a dark pit of despair."

John Huston and Arthur Miller had worked doggedly to complete *The Misfits*, yet the film was not received as "the ultimate motion picture." Few reviewers thought the movie worked, though many praised the acting by Gable and Marilyn.

Today, accurately, John Huston reflects that Marilyn had not been acting at all, in the usual sense of the word. "She went right down into her own personal experience for everything, reached down and pulled something out of herself that was unique and extraordinary. She had no techniques. It was all the truth, it was only Marilyn. But it was Marilyn, plus. She found things, found things about womankind in herself."

Arthur Miller said years later, "In *The Misfits*, her performance as a dramatic actress was extraordinary, but I'm not sure if all that torture was worth the result, all that agony. It's not worth anything."

At the time, a week after the divorce announcement, Miller had sat in a viewing room, stunned. "I still don't understand it," he said. "We got through it. I made a present of this to her, and I left it without her."

When *The Misfits* company disbanded, Marilyn sat on a desk drinking straight bourbon, and said, "Mostly I am thinking ahead, hoping I will give a better performance next time." Then she sighed. "I am trying to find myself as a person. Millions of people live their entire lives without finding themselves. The best way for me to find myself as a person is to prove to myself I am an actress.''

For Marilyn, the actress, the hope would not be realized. She would never complete another film. As a person, Marilyn was flailing around for solace. Weeks earlier, at her lowest ebb during the filming, she had renewed contact with her friend Robert Slatzer. She gave him a photograph inscribed:

> To Bob, with many unforgettable memories of Reno—and other places—from one ''Misfit'' to another,
>
>   All my love,
>
>   <u>Always</u>
>
>   September 8, 1960   Marilyn

In November, from New York, Marilyn called Nico Minardos, another old lover. He was in Greece, filming with Jayne Mansfield, and Marilyn seemed pathetically concerned to know whether he and Mansfield were having an affair. Marilyn also tried to reach Milton Greene but, for reasons he cannot now recall, he didn't call back. Above all, though, Marilyn still clung to a straw of hope that she could retrieve Yves Montand.

News of Marilyn's divorce plans had led to a new surge of speculation about the Frenchman. Reports from France suggested there was a real crisis between Montand and his wife, Simone Signoret. Such rumors, apparently, were not unfounded. In the week before Christmas 1960, Pat Newcomb, the press aide who would henceforth be one of Marilyn's closest intimates, was present in Marilyn's apartment as the marital drama was being played out. Montand was due in New York any day, and Marilyn expected to see him again. Then Simone Signoret, swallowing her pride, telephoned Marilyn out of the blue. Marilyn asked Newcomb to listen in on the extension.

''Simone begged Marilyn not to see Montand, to please leave him alone,'' Newcomb recalls. ''I felt so awful. Here was this wonderful woman, such a fine person, pleading with Marilyn.''

Montand did not come to New York. He canceled his trip

at the last minute, and Marilyn, says Newcomb, was "devastated."

That Christmas, according to her maid, Lena Pepitone, Marilyn again came close to suicide. Pepitone found her standing by her bedroom window, "clutching the outside molding." When the maid grabbed her around the waist Marilyn cried, "Lena, no. Let me die. I want to die. I deserve to die. What have I done with my life? Who do I have? It's Christmas."

The rescuer, at Christmas 1960, was Joe DiMaggio. He had always been available, and now, in the knowledge of the breakup with Miller, he came running. By one account, he arrived on Marilyn's doorstep on Christmas morning bearing a massive poinsettia plant.

Pepitone says DiMaggio began to appear regularly at dinner time, dressed in his sober city suit, entering discreetly by the service elevator. He would depart early in the morning, before other callers arrived.

In the first days of 1961 Marilyn's deterioration was evident. She had disturbed her lawyer over Christmas to ask about making a new will. She made no secret of her drug abuse. Friends watched her taking her barbiturates in the morning, like a ritual, pricking the capsules with a pin to speed the effect.

Some nights, during this desperate time, Marilyn sought comfort and shelter at the apartment of Paula and Lee Strasberg. She would use the bedroom of their son, John, and he would camp on the couch in the living room. John Strasberg vividly remembers the night he awoke to find Marilyn standing beside him dressed in a nightgown. John, then nineteen, did not know how to cope with a woman in her thirties, muttering vaguely about being "kind of lonely . . . needing to talk. . . ."

John's sister, Susan, tells of Marilyn, groggy on pills and alcohol, crawling "on her hands and knees to my parents' doorway, scratching at it with her fingernails. . . ."

On January 20, 1961, at eight o'clock in the evening, a judge once again opened his office as a special favor to Marilyn Monroe. This time the scene was Ciudad Juárez, Mexico, the task the dissolution of the four-and-a-half-year marriage between Marilyn and Arthur Miller. Marilyn, accompanied by Pat Newcomb and a Mexican lawyer, requested the divorce on the grounds of "incompatibility of character." A lawyer representing Miller said the desire to separate was mutual.

Dressed in black, Marilyn signed the papers without reading them, then fought her way out through the paparazzi. In an effort to dodge publicity, Marilyn had chosen the day of President Kennedy's inauguration to fly to Mexico. She was back in New York by lunchtime the next day.

In the loneliness after the divorce, Marilyn was back in touch with Jim Haspiel, now a constant friend, who had kept his distance during the Miller years. She was to shock him with the gift of a photograph inscribed, "For the one and only Jimmy, my friend. Love you, Marilyn." "Only Jimmy" was heavily underlined, and Haspiel, by now a grown man, reflected sadly on Marilyn's implication that she had no real friends.

Early February saw the first reviews of *The Misfits*, many of them highly critical. One said of Marilyn's role, "It really expresses no more than a neurotic individuality and symbolizes little." Even Haspiel, who was always frank with Marilyn, phoned to say he disliked the film.

The next day John Huston's prediction came true earlier than he had foreseen. Marilyn entered a mental hospital.

28

THE PAYNE WHITNEY PSYCHIATRIC Clinic lay at the heart of New York Hospital–Cornell Medical Center, a white-brick skyscraper overlooking Manhattan's East River. It had been recommended to Marilyn by her regular New York psychiatrist, Dr. Marianne Kris. She had been visited by her patient no less than forty-seven times in the previous two months. Now she persuaded Marilyn that she needed specialized treatment to avoid the slide into drugged oblivion.

Hospital, for Marilyn, had usually meant a pampered rest cure. In those terms, her reception at Payne Whitney came as a sharp shock.

Marilyn arrived at the Clinic enveloped in a huge fur coat. She registered as "Faye Miller," and was ushered to a room on a floor reserved for "moderately disturbed" patients. By her own account, she at once felt more prisoner than patient. The door was locked from the outside, her clothes were taken away, there was no door on the bathroom, and phone calls were strictly limited.

Marilyn later told Susan Strasberg, "I was always afraid I was crazy like my mother, but when I got in that psycho ward I realized *they* were really insane—I just had a lot of problems."

A Payne Whitney nurse, interviewed years later by *Life* magazine, recalled how Marilyn stood behind her door shouting again and again, "Open that door! I won't make any trouble, just let me out! Please! Open the door!" The door stayed closed.

What happened next, Marilyn would later insist, occurred because she decided: "Okay, if you're going to treat me like a nut, I'm going to act like one."

According to another member of the staff, Marilyn stripped off her clothing and stood naked at the window. She was then taken to a security ward on the ninth floor, where she threw a chair through a glass door.

The hospital nurse told *Life*: "We felt so protective toward her. She made us all feel like we wanted to hold her in our laps. We wanted to soothe her, wanted to say, 'It's all right now.' It was the feeling lonely, small children give you. You know, sort of dry their tears and pat them on the head and hold their hands."

Months later, in California, Marilyn offered her lurid version of the experience to her friend, Gloria Romanoff. "It was like a nightmare," she said. "They had me in a re-strainer. They had me sedated, but not so sedated that I didn't know what was going on. You'll find this hard to believe, but at night there was a steady procession of hospital personnel, doctors and nurses, coming to look at me. There I was, with my arms bound. I was not able to defend myself. I was a curiosity piece, with no one who had my interests at heart."

The press soon discovered Marilyn had been admitted to the Clinic, but spokesmen would say only that she suffered from "an illness of undetermined origin." One doctor denied the illness was schizophrenia, but said Marilyn was "psychiatri-cally disconnected in an acute way because she works too hard."

Marilyn, meanwhile, fought to be released. Here, complete with misspellings, is the note she dashed off to the Strasbergs:

Dear Lee and Paula,
    Dr. Kris has had me put into the New York Hospital—

pstikiatric division under the care of two <u>idiot</u> doctors. they <u>both</u> <u>should not be my doctors</u>.

You haven't heard from me because Im locked up with all these poor nutty people. I'm <u>sure</u> to end up a nut if I stay in this nightmare. please help me Lee, this is the <u>last</u> place I should be—maybe if you called Dr. Kris and assured her of my sensitivity and that I must get back to class . . . Lee, I try to remember what you said once in class "that art goes far beyond science"

And the science memories around here I'd like to forget—like screeming women etc.

please help me—if Dr. Kris assures you I am all right you can assure her <u>I am not</u>. I do not belong here!

I love you both
Marilyn

P.S. forgive the spelling—and theres nothing to write on here. I'm on the dangerous floor its like a cell. can you imagine—cement blocks they put me in her because they <u>lied</u> to me about calling my doctor and Joe and they had the bathroom door locked so I broke the glass and out side of that I havn't done anything that is uncooperative.

It was Joe DiMaggio, not the Strasbergs, who arranged for Marilyn's discharge from the Clinic. She had used one of her ration of calls to telephone him in Florida, and he flew to New York at once. In the evening of her fourth day at the Clinic Marilyn was smuggled out through a basement passageway. She spent the next three weeks in the neurological department of Columbia–Presbyterian Medical Center. There were no more stories of hysteria and high drama.

News film of Marilyn's departure from this second hospital shows a mob of reporters disgracing themselves in a way unprecedented in all the years of covering her personal miseries. Marilyn was propelled into a waiting limousine by a flying wedge of sixteen policemen and hospital security staff.

The *New York Journal-American* outdid all rivals with an utterly tasteless story. The report quoted Marilyn as saying, "I feel wonderful." Then it added:

All's well with the world, men, so fear not, fear not. Marilyn's face still has the ethereal rose-petal texture, the smile's as delicately soft as ever, the figure—ah, yes, the figure—and best of all they've untied the knots in her nerves.

Norman Rosten, who visited Marilyn several times in the

hospital, had a different verdict. "She was ill," he wrote later, "not only of the body and mind, but of the soul, the innermost engine of desire. That light was missing from her eyes."

For many weeks that spring Marilyn was propped up by Joe DiMaggio, the husband who had been unable to forget. No other woman had replaced Marilyn in his life and, when she permitted it, he offered some stability. Marilyn flew to see him in Florida, where he had been training his old team, the New York Yankees. Later, in New York, Marilyn's staff were again aware that DiMaggio sometimes stayed overnight. Rumors buzzed that they were thinking of remarrying. Marilyn, however, was in no condition to commit herself to anything at all.

Months earlier, plans had been made for Marilyn to play the part of Sadie Thompson in a television dramatization of *Rain*, the Somerset Maugham short story. The plans were shelved.

There had also been talk of her playing in *Freud*, which John Huston was about to make from a screenplay by philosopher Jean-Paul Sartre. Sartre thought Marilyn "one of the greatest actresses alive," and Marilyn was first choice to play the part of Cecily, one of Freud's psychotic patients. Dr. Greenson, her California psychiatrist, advised against it—in part because Freud's daughter, whom Greenson knew, did not want the film made. Privately, Greenson must have balked at the upset such a role would have meant for Marilyn.

Marilyn did not work at all in 1961. Twice that summer she found herself back in hospital beds, this time for physical ailments. In May, in Los Angeles, there was yet another gynecological operation. Doctors now determined that her Fallopian tubes were blocked, apparently as a result of inept surgery following some earlier abortion.

A month later, in New York, Marilyn was carried on a stretcher into the Polyclinic Hospital, clutching a sheet over her face. The problem this time was an acutely inflamed gall bladder. Dr. Richard Cottrell, who handled the case, was appalled to find that behind the glamorous exterior was a creature plagued with physical problems.

Gall bladder aside, Marilyn suffered frequent abnormal bleeding from the uterus, and also had an ulcerated colon. Dr. Cottrell thought this last complaint was the result of "a chronic fear neurosis," and he found his patient "highly nervous, frightened, and confused." In pain after the operation, Marilyn once again had to be restrained.

The last scene of *The Misfits*, one of hope, had Gable and Marilyn driving into the night, following a star that would guide them home. Now, in the hospital, Marilyn stepped onto her balcony with Dr. Cottrell and gazed up at the sky. "Look at the stars," she murmured. "They are all up there shining so brightly, but each one must be so very much alone." Later she muttered despondently, "It's a make-believe world, isn't it?"

Dr. Cottrell was not quite sure what to make of Marilyn. He did notice that, perhaps thinking of her origins, she had registered at the hospital under the name Norma Jean Baker.* It was a name she had not used for years.

Reality, in 1961, was harsh. Her New York secretary, Marjorie Stengel, whose employers have included Montgomery Clift and Faye Dunaway, remembers Marilyn, at thirty-five, as "the emptiest human being I have ever encountered." Stengel told her hairdresser, who was pleading for insights into the life of the world's most celebrated star, "My dear, in twenty-four hours your life is more busy and more glamorous than Marilyn Monroe's is in two weeks."

Stengel found that Marilyn's apartment was now "filthy, dirty, and depressing, with dog stains all over the carpets." She says, "Really, her life was nothing. She did not see friends, she didn't go out, I never saw her really read anything—except once, Harold Robbins—she didn't do anything. There were phone calls, long secretive phone calls conducted in another room, often with her analyst in California. It was creepy."

The Marilyn Stengel remembers had become habitually foul-mouthed, a woman who more and more talked in harsh tones, nothing like the breathless baby voice of legend.

For all the psychiatrists' efforts, drugs were still a permanent feature. Stengel says, "Her apartment was littered with half-empty pill bottles, made out to my name, her name, friends' names. Some doctors will do that for you, if you're rich and famous."

On her visits to California, a young hairdresser named George Masters had begun to work for Marilyn. He remembers seeing her soon after the gall bladder operation "wearing a ripped terry-cloth robe. She said she was living on caviar, champagne, and hard-boiled eggs. She could let herself look like an old bag for two weeks. She'd smell sometimes, and

---

*Baker was the name of Marilyn's mother's first husband, gone before she was born.

never comb her hair for weeks. That's why it would take nine hours to get her ready and recreate Marilyn Monroe.''

Once Marilyn summoned Masters from California to New York to do her hair, then met him at the door to say she was sorry, she was too tired to see him. By way of consolation, she handed him a check for two thousand dollars.

Masters, too, observed Marilyn's drug-taking. ''I remember one time,'' he says, ''when she offered me a pill, a Nembutal, like other people offer you a drink. I kept it under my lip, and spat it out afterwards. I think she popped the pills early in the morning. She'd keep me waiting for two hours while she was in the bathroom, supposedly washing her face. For two hours! I mean, that's very strange.''

''When I was working on her,'' Masters says ''she would start transforming, almost like a chameleon. Her voice would begin to change, and her actions. I would get goose bumps as she started changing into Marilyn Monroe.''

Masters had the impression that Marilyn had become ''asexual. I think if she had any drive at all by then it was to *conquer* men. That was the challenge, and I think that turned her on. I think she was two people, maybe even three—herself, Marilyn Monroe, and the asexual, calculating person only concerned with herself.''

In autumn of 1961 a malodorous smell drifted into the Los Angeles apartment occupied by Jeanne Carmen—in a small building three blocks south of Sunset Strip. It came, Carmen discovered, from the garbage pail in which Marilyn Monroe was jettisoning used wound dressings, necessary for a while in the aftermath of her gall bladder operation.

Marilyn had returned to the same apartment on Doheny that she had used in the early fifties, and in Jeanne Carmen she rediscovered an old friend. The two had met years earlier at the Actors Studio in New York, and now, as neighbors, became close.

The place on Doheny was a low, nondescript corner building. Marilyn's mailbox bore not her name, but that of her East Coast secretary, Marjorie Stengel. Marilyn's apartment was one of a number clustered around a courtyard. A dark hallway led into a large and even darker bedroom, a room of almost Stygian gloom thanks to heavy blackout curtains over the windows. Originally designed as the living room, it was now dominated by an enormous double bed. The apartment had become, as one friend puts it, ''a shrine to sleeping.'' It contained no pictures and few personal possessions.

Here at Doheny, Marilyn and Jeanne Carmen whiled away the time, and especially the night hours, talking and drinking. Carmen, at twenty-seven some eight years younger than Marilyn, was a would-be actress who sometimes used the name Saber Dareaux. She had begun her career like Marilyn, as a cover girl for girlie magazines, then graduated to parts in minor movies.

Carmen had a brilliant talent for golf, and worked it up into a trick golf act that brought her television appearances all over the country. She shared doctors with Marilyn—both visited Dr. Lee Siegel and gynecologist Leon Krohn—and they held fervent discussions on injections to enlarge the bust, and surgery to narrow the vagina.

To Carmen, Marilyn's drinking capacity seemed "Olympic standard." On the subject of drugs, though, the two had much in common. "I had gotten addicted to sleeping pills while I was living in Vegas," says Carmen, "and we became sleeping-pill buddies. We were both using Seconal and Nembutal, and we'd borrow each other's prescriptions. But I was knocked out on two or three a night; Marilyn was using a tremendous amount when I met her. . . ."

The two talked about men and sex. Marilyn talked about the baby she claimed she had had as a teenager, and of her fear that God would "punish" her for not keeping it. "From what she told me," Carmen says, "Marilyn got nothing out of sex at all. She'd never had an orgasm—she used to fake it."

"She was so insecure," Carmen recalls. "She was sure that she'd lose even her best friends if she ever got old and ugly and down and out. . . ."

Marilyn was still talking about suicide. "There's no way out for me except death," she would say when in her cups. "I'd want to go out in white, in a white satin nightgown and with white satin pillows. And I'd have someone come in and close my eyes and make me look beautiful. How about you doing it for me?"

In May that year, after her experience at the Payne Whitney Psychiatric Clinic, Marilyn had turned to Dr. Ralph Greenson for her full-time psychiatric care. Greenson, distressed at Marilyn's "terrible loneliness," now made a decision—a highly unusual one in his tradition of psychiatry—to open his own home to Marilyn.

Greenson was to be criticized for this decision by some of his psychiatrist colleagues. At the time, says his widow, he felt he was providing a little of what Marilyn most lacked, security and a sense of family. He was also genuinely touched by this thirty-five-year-old waif. From now, until she died, Greenson's wife and two children acted as a virtual foster family for Marilyn.

The Greensons lived in a fine Mexican-style house at the summit of the only hill in Santa Monica, and to spare Marilyn needless exposure at his office, Dr. Greenson usually received her there. Uncharacteristically, perhaps because Greenson said unpunctuality was a sign of disliking someone, Marilyn started arriving early. Greenson's daughter Joan, a twenty-one-year-old art student, would greet Marilyn when the doctor was not ready for her, and the two would amble along by the nearby reservoir, gazing out over the city and the Pacific Ocean.

For Joan Greenson the experience was unnerving but fascinating. Soon she was visiting the great star at her apartment, driving her around town, and beginning an unusual friendship. Marilyn offered advice about boyfriends, helped with makeup—she showed Joan how to bleach the hair shadowing her upper lip—and the two of them swapped clothes.

"The Twist craze was just starting," Joan recalls, "so she taught me her version of the Twist, and how to do a bump-and-grind—one you could see on TV, not anything lewd. Marilyn treated me in a sense as a younger sister. She never let me see pictures of her nude, would never allude to the fact that she slept with anybody. She presented herself to *me* as a very virginal creature."

Danny Greenson, Joan's twenty-four-year-old brother, had not expected to get on with Marilyn. He was a student, politically radical by contemporary standards, and he expected "a rich Hollywood bitch." Instead he found himself drawn to a woman who was "in no way put on or artificial, with a real warmth." Marilyn, in her black wig, went along with Danny when he was apartment hunting. They talked politics, and he found her sympathetic to his leftist opinions.

Marilyn was seeing Dr. Greenson six, even seven, times a week. Because her appointments were at the doctor's home, and he had to return from his office, she was usually the last patient of the day. She sat upright in a chair facing Greenson across his study, pouring out her troubles for the allotted hour. Then she and the psychiatrist would emerge to join the family, as often as not, for a drink. Marilyn's personal bottle of Dom Perignon champagne, perhaps a bit flat if she had

WESTERN UNION
TELEGRAM

CLASS OF SERVICE
This is a fast message
unless its deferred character is indicated by the proper symbol.

W. P. MARSHALL, PRESIDENT

SYMBOLS
DL = Day Letter
NL = Night Letter
LT = International Letter Telegram

1201 (4-60)

The filing time shown in the date line on domestic telegrams is LOCAL TIME at point of origin. Time of receipt is LOCAL TIME at point of destination

SRA369 SSB410

1961 JUN 1   PM 2 31

Ḷ BHA160 PD=BEVERLY HILLS CALIF 204P PDT=

=DR RALPH GREENSON=

DEAR DR GREENSON: IN THIS WORLD OF PEOPLE I'M GLAD
THERES YOU. I HAVE A FEELING OF HOPE THOUGH TODAY
I'M THREE FIVE=

MARILYN:

THE COMPANY WILL APPRECIATE SUGGESTIONS FROM ITS PATRONS CONCERNING ITS SERVICE

Marilyn's telegram to her psychiatrist, on her thirty-fifth birthday, June 1, 1961.

brought it along on a previous occasion, would be produced from the refrigerator. Sometimes Marilyn would stay to dinner and join in the washing up, often throwing in the evergreen story of how she had once done kitchen chores at the orphanage.

Greenson wrote hopefully in May 1961, before Marilyn's gall bladder operation and the decline that followed, that she was "doing quite well." He added: "I am appalled at the emptiness of her life in terms of object relations. Essentially, it is such a narcissistic way of life. . . . All in all, there's been some improvement, but I do not vouch for how deep it is, or how lasting."

Three weeks later, on her thirty-fifth birthday, Marilyn sent Dr. Greenson a telegram, reading (see previous page):

DEAR DR GREENSON IN THIS WORLD OF PEOPLE I'M GLAD THERE'S YOU. I HAVE A FEELING OF HOPE ALTHOUGH TODAY I AM THREE FIVE. MARILYN.

Meanwhile, at the beginning of 1961, Marilyn had uttered a momentous confidence to Gordon Heaver, an Englishman she had known for many years. Heaver had lived in Hollywood throughout the fifties, was a story editor at Paramount Pictures, worked on several Hitchcock films, and married into money. He prides himself for his recall of facts—Hitchcock had dubbed him "Mr. Memory," after a character in *The Thirty-nine Steps*.

In early January 1961, Heaver says, Marilyn told him she had recently had "a date with the next President of the United States." From the way she said it, Heaver did not doubt that Marilyn meant she had been to bed with John Kennedy. The conversation took place just weeks before the President's inauguration. Kennedy's inauguration and Marilyn's divorce made news at the same time.

The affair with the President, and the ramifications that connect with Robert Kennedy, Frank Sinatra, and his friends, has become the cornerstone of the legend of the last days of Marilyn Monroe. Within less than two years, in the aura of those involvements, Marilyn would die.

Part IV

MARILYN AND THE
KENNEDY BROTHERS

"Marilyn Monroe never told anybody everything."
    PAT NEWCOMB, **Marilyn's Press Assistant**
            and close friend of the Kennedys

"There is danger for the man who snatches a delusion from a woman."

                    PERSIAN SAYING, **quoted by**
                    Sir Arthur Conan Doyle

29

ON A WARM SUMMER night in the second week of July 1960, just before the filming of *The Misfits*, two men in a car had cruised along the Pacific shoreline north of Santa Monica, California. They drove past a group of grand beachfront homes, weaved around a muddle of double-parked cars, and quietly drew into the curb. Then they took off their shoes, padded down to the edge of the surf, and began walking back the way they had come.

The figures in the darkness were plainclothes officers of the Bureau of Investigation of the Los Angeles District Attorney's office. The mansion they were watching was the home of Peter Lawford, actor, and his wife Patricia Kennedy Lawford, sister of the Democratic presidential candidate. This was the week of Kennedy's nomination by the Democratic party convention, and—as the noise from the house made obvious—the Lawfords were throwing a party.

Frank Hronek, the senior of the two officers, had gone from a wartime career in intelligence to become a legendary figure in California law enforcement. Now a top investigator for the Los Angeles District Attorney, he was a walking encyclopedia on all matters that concerned his profession—and some that did not—from organized crime and political corruption to the seamier side of show business. Hronek had asked his superior for clearance to observe the Lawford party for the possible presence of guests linked to the mob. When his superior, a Democrat, told him to stay away, Hronek went along anyway.

That night, as the two officers drew closer to peer over the fence, they were intercepted by private security guards armed with shotguns. Hronek kept the guards talking for a while, then walked away. There had been time enough to observe a wild party going on around the Lawfords' pool, one that included a bevy of women, some familiar to the officers as call girls supplied by a known madame. Several of the girls

were, as one of the officers put it, "stark-ass naked." Also
present was John Kennedy.

The man shortly to be President departed soon afterward,
according to a spokesman, because "the candidate needs
some rest." The rest, an informant told the DA's officers
later, was in the company of Marilyn Monroe.

True or false? The revelry at the Lawford house was described to the author by Investigator Hronek's colleague, and
there is no good reason to doubt him. What, though, to make
of the allegation about Kennedy and Marilyn? Was the informant in 1960 just passing on gossip, the sort to file and
forget? Was there really a Kennedy in Marilyn's love life?
Finding the answers, two decades later, has involved a major
investigation.

Stories of an affair between Marilyn and President Kennedy, or with his brother Robert, or with both, have circulated ever since her death. They have been so numerous, so
often the farfetched fodder for supermarket scandal sheets,
that thinking people may reasonably have written them off as
legend. Fresh research now establishes that the stories have a
basis in truth.

This book is not the place to rehearse the full sexual history
of the Kennedys. Some attempts to do so have established a
mythology that throws dust in the eyes of the public as much
as on the legend of Marilyn herself. Nevertheless, there has
been sufficient responsible reporting, and firsthand recollection by contemporaries, to allow a measure of balanced
judgment.

It is evident that the Kennedys, from their fortress of a
family, with their vast wealth and power and with the arrogance that such a heritage endows, led sex lives that were, in
ordinary mortals' terms, outside the ordinary. To comprehend
the Kennedys' dealings with Marilyn we must glimpse, at
least, the sexual tradition in which they thrived.

It began, for the children of John Kennedy's generation, in
the attitudes of their father. Joseph Kennedy, a growing body
of literature confirms, was a man who, like some feudal Lord
of the Manor, pursued anything in skirts, as though by right.
He did this in front of his children, daughters as well as sons,
and enlisted their help in arranging infidelities.

John Kennedy once confided to Clare Boothe Luce, former
United States Ambassador and wife of the publisher of *Time*,
"Dad told all the boys to get laid as often as possible." John,

A model girl, aged about nineteen. Hollywood was only a dream.

Marilyn's mother, Gladys, in 1963, aged sixty-two, and *(inset)* as a young woman. She has survived her famous daughter.

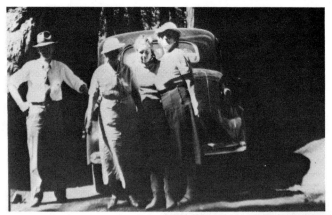

Above: An early developer. Marilyn, the foster child, aged twelve, with one of her "families."

Below: With her first husband, Jim Dougherty, on Catalina Island, 1944. She was seventeen, and her eyes were already wandering to other men.

Somebody else's baby—during the Dougherty marriage. The idea of having a child "stood my hair on end," Marilyn was to say. Dougherty says the opposite was true. Abortions would follow, then fruitless efforts to bear children.

A starlet with a library. Marilyn immersed herself in art and culture. She admired the Italian actress Eleanora Duse *(in photograph at upper left)*. The half-obscured picture *(center right)* shows Arthur Miller, who met Marilyn in 1950, six years before they married.

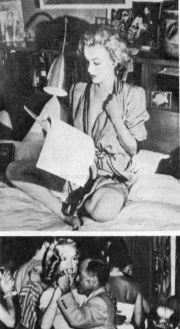

The jogger. In about 1952, twenty years ahead of her time. Marilyn used to run through the Hollywood alleyways before breakfast.

A little man with mighty influence. Lover and agent Johnny Hyde, dying of heart disease, set Marilyn firmly on the road to fame.

SOME OF THE LOVERS

Top left: The photographer. André de Dienes, in northern Arizona, 1946. Marilyn took the picture.

Bottom left: The voice coach. Fred Karger, to whom Marilyn gave her heart in 1948. He did not want to marry her.

Top right: The lifeguard. Tommy Zahn, 1946.

Bottom right: The second husband? Robert Slatzer at Niagara Falls with Marilyn in 1952. He knew her all her adult life.

Right: At home with "Nana" Karger *(left)*, mother of a former lover, 1960. The "orphan" attached herself to a number of families, and to Mrs. Karger above all.

The acting lesson. With Natasha Lytess, her first acting coach, in the early 1950s. They lived together for a while.

The courtship of the Last American Hero. With Joe DiMaggio, shortly before their 1954 marriage. The honeymoon was hardly over before she was talking of one day marrying Arthur Miller.

Announcing separation from DiMaggio—their marriage lasted nine months.

"Co-conspirators." Marilyn with photographer Milton Greene, who engineered her flight from Hollywood in 1955.

The fan who became a friend. James Haspiel started by cadging a kiss from Marilyn at the age of sixteen and—in the New York period—became a regular companion.

A brief affair. With Marlon Brando, 1955.

A final fling. Mexican screenwriter José Bolaños with a drunken Marilyn in 1962.

Above: Table companions. With another Hollywood personality, Ronald Reagan, in 1953.

Left: The man who lasted longest. With playwright Arthur Miller in 1959. Their marriage survived more than four years.

The French lover. The 1960 affair with Yves Montand coincided with the collapse of the Miller marriage but did not cause it. Marilyn's mental health was deteriorating rapidly.

Below: Actress at work. On the set of *The Seven Year Itch,* 1954.

Above: A mistress of The Method, Paula Strasberg *(left),* eccentric wife of the Actors Studio founder, was Marilyn's acting coach from 1956 on. Arthur Miller, seated *(right),* during the shooting of *Some Like It Hot,* had his doubts about the Strasbergs' influence.

Lovelier without makeup, 1955.

Vodka at the casino. Carousing with friend and later brief lover Frank Sinatra, at the Cal-Neva Lodge, Lake Tahoe. Marilyn's visits to the Lodge exposed her dangerously—it was a watering hole for the Mafia.

The Attorney General and the singer. The man presumed to be Marilyn's last lover, Robert Kennedy, with Sinatra in 1961. Kennedy is the central figure in the mysteries surrounding Marilyn's death.

Trysting place. Marilyn met both Kennedy brothers at Peter Lawford's California beach house. This rare photograph, showing the President *(seated center)*, was taken by a neighbor in 1962.

The President at midnight—returning to his New York base, the Carlyle Hotel. Marilyn, reportedly, was one of his female visitors there.

Above: "Happy Birthday, Mr. President..." Madison Square Garden, May 1962.

Left: The psychiatrist. Dr. Ralph Greenson, in whom Marilyn confided about her Kennedy affairs. He and his family befriended her in her final months of distress.

Sunglasses, at right: Giancana, Mafia chieftain. "I know all about the Kennedys ... and one of these days we are going to tell all."

Below: Jimmy Hoffa, Teamsters' leader. "I already had a tape on Bobby Kennedy and Jack Kennedy..."

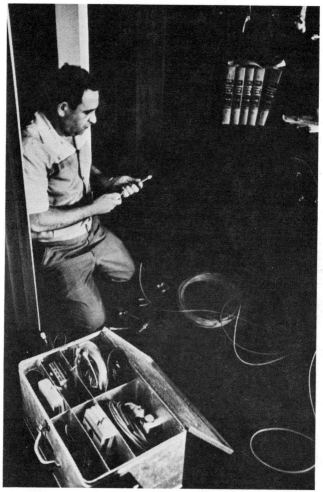

The bugging expert. Bernard Spindel, Hoffa's wireman. "A confidential file containing tapes and evidence concerning circumstances surrounding causes of death of Marilyn Monroe…"

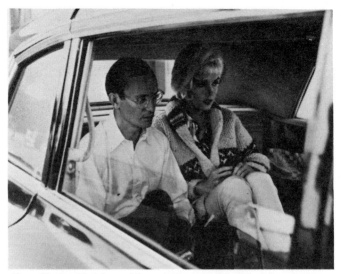

Above: The last birthday and the end of a career. Marilyn, thirty-six that day, leaves Twentieth Century-Fox for the last time on June 1, 1962. Her companion is comedian Wally Cox.

Right: Drinks with the President's brother-in-law. Marilyn with Peter Lawford at the Cal-Neva Lodge, scene of the last drug overdose before the one that killed her. Lawford was the go-between for the Kennedy brothers, and—according to one of his wives—destroyed evidence on the night that she died.

Three months before the end. Marilyn had once said, "Gravity catches up with all of us."

A place to die. The house in Brentwood, the morning of August 5, 1962. The room where Marilyn died lies behind the tree on the left. Twenty-four hours earlier she had sunk into deep depression after a messenger had delivered a toy tiger—perhaps the stuffed animal here seen abandoned on the grass.

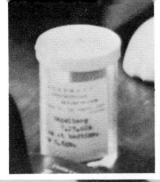

Death in a bottle. The Coroner's office never received some of the pills that littered Marilyn's room. The bottle above bears the name of her internist, Dr. Hyman Engelberg, and is dated 7.25.62., eleven days before the end. It probably contained chloral hydrate, which helped kill Marilyn.

The floor is heaped with scripts and a Western Union telegram offering fresh work. The glass object beside the bed may or may not be a water container. In an incomplete investigation, it was never properly identified.

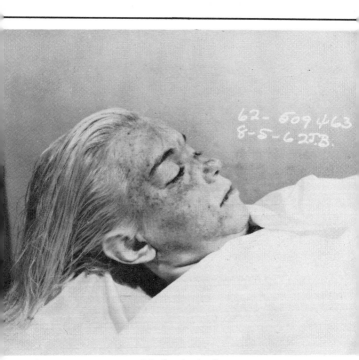

Marilyn in death.

The photograph, taken after autopsy, bears a police file number. The facial discoloration occurred after death, and it is the surgeons work that caused her face to sag. Before the procedure, say those present, the lifeless Marilyn remained beautiful.

as has been well documented, more than followed the paternal advice. From his days in the Navy, when he was known to his pals as "Shafty," to his years in the White House, the future President never ceased womanizing.

Nancy Dickerson, a reporter who dated Kennedy, has said, "You couldn't help but be swept over by him. But sex to Jack Kennedy was like another cup of coffee, or maybe dessert." For this Kennedy, evidently, sex was not to be confused with love.

In contrast, the wheels of the rumor mill have been virtually still when it comes to Robert Kennedy—except where Marilyn is concerned. His brother John spoke of Robert's "high moral standards . . . a puritan, absolutely incorruptible." By 1960, when Robert turned thirty-five, he had been married ten years and had seven children. He had just been named America's "Father of the Year."

All this is fact, but it need not force the conclusion that Robert Kennedy was a saint in sexual matters. Historian Arthur Schlesinger, his biographer and a Kennedy loyalist, gave me a frank answer when we lunched together in 1983. "Bobby was human," he said. "He liked a drink and he liked young women. He indulged that liking when he traveled— and he had to travel a great deal."

All the Kennedys were fascinated by the world of the movies. Joe, the father, had moved to California in the twenties to make films, and additional fortune, in Hollywood. Joe's most highly publicized affair was with the actress, Gloria Swanson.

John Kennedy, on the West Coast in the forties and fifties, more than followed suit, so far as Hollywood women were concerned. His targets over the years were names that now read like faded photographs: Gene Tierney, Sonja Henie, Angela Greene, Kim Novak, Janet Leigh, and Rhonda Fleming. During the presidency, Angie Dickinson was at least a close friend.

Judy Garland was befriended by Robert Kennedy. Greta Garbo was an honored guest at a White House dinner attended only by the President, his wife, and Kennedy's friend, Lem Billings.

Film director Joshua Logan quotes Marlene Dietrich as telling him, "Jack Kennedy got me to the White House and tried a little hanky-panky. Then, as I was getting into the elevator, he asked with great concern, 'Just one thing—did you ever sleep with my Dad?'"

The Kennedy brothers needed a base of operations in California, and by 1960 they had one—the beachfront home of their brother-in-law, Peter Lawford. In every scenario involving Marilyn and the Kennedys, Lawford is cast as the connection.

In the halcyon years of the Kennedy ascendancy, Peter and Pat Lawford lived the high life in the palatial mansion, complete with fifty-foot heated swimming pool and a movie projection room, that had originally been built for Louis B. Mayer, chief of Metro-Goldwyn-Mayer.

Lawford was thirty-seven in 1960, the British-born son of a World War I general who had fallen on hard times after emigrating to Florida in the thirties. Lawford had departed for Hollywood a few years later, and his good looks whisked him from a job as an usher in a movie theater to starring roles in B-movies.

By the mid-fifties, Lawford's acting career seemed to have peaked. His celebrity was based mostly on an incessant social whirl and an addiction to surfing. Then, in spring 1954, he married Patricia "Pat" Kennedy, the sixth of Joseph Kennedy's brood and the loveliest of his daughters. By 1960, on the eve of the Kennedy presidency, they had settled at Santa Monica with their three children.

As a couple the Lawfords seemed a rare and enviable combination, one of California's Beautiful Beach People married into a great Eastern dynasty. One writer described Lawford as "sun-tanned, unruffled, with that peculiar impersonal friendliness of the overprivileged." Another wrote: "The problem with the Lawfords is that they seem to have no problems."

In private the Lawfords were on the way to problems a-plenty. The marriage would not last, and both, according to neighbors, were already heavy drinkers. Lawford, who was to die of liver disease in 1984, liked to drink till dawn in his own private bar. Friends and associates say he was an indiscriminate user of prohibited drugs.

Lawford liked bizarre sex. His mother, Lady Lawford, once confided to the press, somewhat opaquely, that her son had been spanked a good deal in his youth. She said, "I still insist, and Peter agrees, that the spankings did more than anything else to fit him for his present role."

That curious judgment aside, two former female intimates say Lawford had outlandish tastes in sex. One recalls that, rather than making love, "he wanted me to bite his nipples till they bled." Another left him because he demanded that she take part in group sex.

It was this sad Sybarite who played host to the Kennedy brothers when they sought relaxation in California. Even today, few will discuss what went on during those visits. In 1984, however, I spoke at length with Jeanne Martin, former wife of singer Dean Martin. She and her husband were frequent guests at the Lawford home, and were there when both John and Robert Kennedy were present. Her memories are unromantic.

"I saw Peter in the role of pimp for Jack Kennedy," says Jeanne Martin. "It was a nasty business—they were just too gleeful about it, not discreet at all. Of course there was nothing discreet about either of the Kennedys, Bob or Jack. It was like high-school time, very sophomoric. The things that went on in that beach house were just mind-boggling."

Martin continues, "Ethel* could be in one room and Bobby could be in another with this or that woman. Yes, Bobby was a grabber, but not in the terms that Jack was. Jack really was instinctive, you know, straight for the jugular—'Come upstairs, come in the bathroom, anything.' Bobby didn't have eyes for me, but I do know this. I have a friend that was in the library with him, and before she knew it the door was locked and he threw her on the couch—amazing. . . ! It was so blatant. Here was the President of the United States and the Attorney General."

Jeanne Martin was sometimes present when Marilyn Monroe came to the Lawford beach house. She became "quite sure" Marilyn was involved sexually with both Kennedy brothers but says, "Unless you're in the bedroom, it's unfair to presume."

The story of Marilyn's sexual connection with the Kennedys is told by other witnesses. On the basis of the assembled information it must now be considered beyond presumption.

*Wife of Robert Kennedy.

30

IN THE FALL OF 1954 John Kennedy, then a thirty-seven-year-old senator, had undergone major surgery in a New York hospital. He was suffering from spinal trouble complicated by Addison's disease, a progressive malfunction of the adrenal glands. As he recovered, he amused himself playing checkers and firing a popgun at floating balloons.

A reporter who visited Kennedy, Priscilla McMillan, thought the atmosphere was "like that of a college dorm." She noticed a tank of tropical fish, a Howdy Doody doll on the bed, and—on the wall—a poster of Marilyn Monroe. The picture showed Marilyn in blue shorts standing with her legs spread apart. It had been fixed upside down so that her feet stuck up in the air.

It was, by then, two years since Marilyn's nude calendar had become the talk of the nation, and thousands of males had her picture on the wall. The ailing Kennedy, though, may have gazed at his poster more knowingly than most. For nearly a decade his regular host on trips to Hollywood had been the prominent agent, Charles Feldman. Feldman had represented Marilyn in the early fifties, and two witnesses suggest that Kennedy met Marilyn through him as early as 1951.

Feldman's longtime secretary, Grace Dobish, believes there was such a meeting. Alain Bernheim, who worked with Feldman and knew Marilyn well, thinks she was present at a dinner Feldman gave for Kennedy. Bernheim drove Kennedy home, however, and recalls that he left with another girl that night.

Two friends of Marilyn also refer to meetings with Kennedy in the fifties. Robert Slatzer, who knew her all her adult life, says she mentioned encountering Kennedy during the DiMaggio marriage—again at Charles Feldman's home—and later, during the Miller marriage, in New York. Arthur James, who knew Marilyn from her liaison with Charlie Chaplin,

Jr., in the late forties, offers specific memories of the earliest phase of her relationship with the Kennedys.

In the mid-fifties James was a prosperous real-estate agent spending most of his time in Malibu, where he still lives. He says an affair of sorts with John Kennedy occurred as early as 1954, in the declining months of the DiMaggio marriage. James says Marilyn told him she saw Kennedy when he visited California, and James himself once observed them together.

"Although Jack Kennedy was a Senator," says James, "he was unknown here, relatively speaking. He and Marilyn could get away with a great deal. They sometimes drank at the Malibu Cottage, which was the raunchiest place you've seen in your life. It was just a bar, with maybe eight stools, and sawdust on the floor, but in those days it was a hangout for some of the most famous names in Hollywood."

James, who still shakes his head over the fact that it was "all so damn open in a way," says he saw John Kennedy, then Senator, walking on the shore with Marilyn near the Malibu pier. Marilyn told James that she and Kennedy had quietly used rooms at the Holiday House Motel in Malibu, and at another hotel located where Sunset Boulevard meets the Pacific Coast Highway—one regularly used for illicit lovers' rendezvous. (Its name has since changed.)

"I don't think it was ever really important to Jack Kennedy," James says, "but Marilyn never got over it, least of all when he became President. In the end, though, their headquarters was Peter Lawford's place, back at Santa Monica."

Peter Lawford, whom I interviewed not long before his death in 1984, knew Marilyn as early as 1950, when she was twenty-four. They met first at the William Morris agency, then at a party, and Lawford took a shine to her.

"I'll never forget going to pick her up on our first date," Lawford said. "When I walked into the apartment I had to step around the dogshit. Marilyn just looked and said, 'Oh, he's done it again.' She just clammed up over dinner, but I saw her some more. We went down to Malibu in the jeep, to go surfboarding. I remember her shielding her skin under a big sun hat. We had a couple of dates, I guess."

Lawford glosses over the fact that he fell for Marilyn in a big way and she failed to respond. She complained about him to Anne, mother of her former lover, Fred Karger. "Lawford was chasing her and calling her," recalls Anne's close friend

Vi Russell, "and she'd come over to our house at three in the morning to get away from him and try to get some sleep. I don't think she had much love for Peter Lawford; she always talked about him giving her a hard time."

Lawford and Marilyn continued to bump into each other as the years went by, though at a safe distance. Both were weekend guests at the home of Gene Kelly, who exhausted his famous friends with volleyball parties that tended to start *after* the party, when the sun was coming up. By that time Lawford was involved with Pat Kennedy, who became his wife.

Pat Lawford liked Marilyn and felt she needed help. It was her idea—according to Lawford—to start inviting Marilyn to the beach house in the months before John Kennedy's presidency. (Mrs. Lawford did not respond to an interview request for this book.)

Lawford, whose lasting devotion to Kennedy was little short of idolatry, flatly denied there was ever any affair between Marilyn and either of the Kennedy brothers. He told a Los Angeles District Attorney's investigator, during a fresh inquiry into Marilyn's death in 1982, that Marilyn did not meet John Kennedy until 1961, when he was already President. That occasion, said Lawford, was a party at which Marilyn happened to be a guest. "The whole thing about an affair is balls," Lawford told me. One who knew him most intimately, however, tells a different story.

In 1976 Peter Lawford entered into his third marriage with a young would-be actress named Deborah Gould. He was fifty-two and she twenty-five, and the union lasted only a matter of months. Gould found she had married a man who was, as she saw it, "destroying himself." As well as alcohol, he was using drugs, especially cocaine and "angel dust," or PCP, a highly dangerous chemical often sold as LSD.

I interviewed Gould in 1983, and told her of Lawford's denials concerning Marilyn and the Kennedy brothers. With her, in private one night when he was "kind of high," Lawford was more forthright. Gould recalled Lawford broke down. As she held him in her lap, he talked at length about the Kennedys and Marilyn.

"Peter told me," said his former wife, "that Jack—he always called him Jack—had always wanted to meet Marilyn Monroe; it was one of his fantasies. Could Peter arrange for that? He did—he would do anything he was asked to do."

Quoting Lawford, Gould says an affair with John Kennedy

began before the presidency, and lasted during it. What Gould says is corroborated, in an interview conducted as this book went to press, by Lawford's second wife, Mary Rowan. Both former wives quote Lawford as telling of Marilyn's affairs with both John and Robert Kennedy. Gould's account covers the end of the affair with the President, and tells how Robert Kennedy became involved. That will be covered later.

Lawford, says Gould, was consumed with worry the morning after he poured out his story. He could not remember exactly what he had revealed. He had to fly to New York that day, and later telephoned, still in a panic about what he might have said. "He told me," says Gould, "that I should forget everything he had said."

In early 1960, as the Kennedy campaign went into high gear, the Lawford house at Santa Monica became a meeting place for the candidate's advisers. One was Pete Summers, a Kennedy political strategist with the key job of handling relations with the television networks. Summers met Marilyn in Kennedy's company several times, always at the Lawford house, and as one of a group of perhaps a dozen people.

"They were very close friends," Summers recalls. "I would say she was a very special guest—the President was really very, very fond of Marilyn. She was delightful, a little bit nervous perhaps, but I think the nervousness was because she was in a new territory with people who were political animals. She wasn't totally at ease. I did feel that she was so impressed by Kennedy's charm and charisma that she was almost starry-eyed. . . . But she was totally able to hold her own conversationally; she was very bright."

Given Marilyn's psychological problems, and her abuse of alcohol and sleeping pills, one might wonder what attraction she held for a Kennedy. It is clear, however, that she never lost the ability to hide her miseries under a mask of dazzling beauty. That aside, she was by now more politically sophisticated than has ever been acknowledged.

For years, and especially during the Miller marriage, Marilyn had been mixing with people who talked politics a great deal. In New York she had cultivated a lasting friendship with the eminent journalist, Lester Markel.

Markel had been Assistant Managing Editor of the *Herald Tribune* at the age of twenty-five, and was Sunday Editor of the *New York Times* for nearly half a century. Marilyn had written to him in the mid-fifties, in one of her bursts of eagerness to widen her intellectual horizon. They had lunched at Sardi's, and afterward the sixty-year-old Markel, himself a star in his own professional world, amazed his colleagues by giving Marilyn a guided tour of the *Times* newsroom.

After Markel's death in the seventies, at the age of eighty-four, his daughter discovered—stuffed in the back of a desk drawer—a letter Markel had received from Marilyn in March 1960, while she was making *Let's Make Love*. It provides a remarkable insight into Marilyn's intelligence and political savvy. Marilyn wrote:

Lester dear,
Here I am still in bed. I've been lying here thinking—even of you. . . . About our political conversation the other day: I take it back that there isn't *anybody*. What about Rockefeller? First of all he is a Republican like the New York Times, and secondly, and most interesting, he's more liberal than many of the Democrats. Maybe he could be developed? At this time, however, Humphrey might be the only one. But who knows since it's rather hard to find out anything about him. (I have no particular paper in mind!) Of course, Stevenson might have made it if he had been able to talk to people instead of professors. Of course, there hasn't been anyone like Nixon before because the rest of them at least had souls! Ideally, Justice William Douglas would be the best President, but he has been divorced so he couldn't make it—but I've got an idea—how about Douglas for President and Kennedy for Vice-President, then the Catholics who wouldn't have voted for Douglas would vote because of Kennedy so it wouldn't matter if he *is* so divorced! Then Stevenson could be Secretary of State!
    . . . .It's true I am in your building quite frequently to see my wonderful doctor* as your spies have already reported. I didn't want you to get a glimpse of me though until I was wearing my Somali leopard. I want you to think of me as a predatory animal.

Love and kisses,

Marilyn

P.S. Slogans for late '60:
    "Nix on Nixon"
    "Over the hump with Humphrey(?)"
    "Stymied with Symington"
    "Back to Boston by Xmas—Kennedy"

---

*The Markels lived in the same building as the Strasbergs and Marilyn's current New York psychiatrist, Dr. Marianne Kris.

The New York Times
Times Square
May 23, 1960

Dear (I think) Marilyn:

I write to the President of the United States and I get a prompt reply.

I write to the Vice President of the United States and I get a prompt reply.

I write to Sir Laurence Olivier and I get a prompt reply.

I write to Jayne Mansfield and I get a prompt reply.

I write to you and three weeks go by without even an acknowledgment of an important enclosure.

Who do you think you are -- Marilyn Monroe?

In any case, would you please return the script of that speech? I need it.

Yours, in sorrow and bewilderment,

LM:ls

Mrs. Arthur Miller
Beverly Hills Hotel
Beverly Hills, California

A letter from Lester Markel, Sunday editor of *The New York Times*. His worry was unfounded—correspondence shows that Marilyn stayed in touch with the legendary journalist.

Obviously this was the letter of someone who either knew their politics, or—as was likely the case with Marilyn—someone who had been giving themselves a crash course in current affairs.

Marilyn by now talked regularly with the Greensons, whose politics were quietly liberal. They thought Marilyn quite radical. "Marilyn was passionate about equal rights, rights for blacks, rights for the poor," recalls Joan Greenson. "She identified strongly with the workers, and she always felt they were her people."

Years earlier, when she had first plunged into her self-education through reading, Marilyn expressed admiration for India's leader, Nehru. She felt Cuba's Fidel Castro should be given a chance to show whether he really intended to permit democracy.

In the spring of 1960, her name headed a list of Hollywood figures, including Marlon Brando, Gene Kelly, Shirley MacLaine, and Peter Lawford, sponsoring SANE, the National Committee for a Sane Nuclear Policy. Asked by an interviewer what dreams or nightmares she had, Marilyn responded, "My nightmare is the H-bomb. What's yours?"

Marilyn had a healthy skepticism, which might not have seemed so healthy to right-wingers of the time, about U.S. foreign policy. In the summer of 1960 she telephoned long-distance to Rupert Allan, one of her press aides, to discuss the morning's newspaper headlines. She was irritated that more prominence had not been given to a story about an American naval aircraft trespassing in Soviet airspace. Moscow claimed the plane was spying, while Washington said it was merely conducting an oceanic survey. This assertion of innocence came just weeks after a far greater furor, over the downing by the Russians of a CIA U-2 plane piloted by Gary Powers. The U.S. government had at first claimed, falsely, that the U-2 had only been engaged in weather research.

Marilyn wanted to know why this fresh story was being treated as minor news. Allan, a Navy veteran, replied that this time, perhaps, the U.S. government was telling the truth. "I don't know, Rupert," Marilyn said. "I don't trust us." On the other hand, says Allan, Marilyn "loved being an American. She was very pro-America, naively sometimes."

Marilyn was a registered Democrat. In April 1960, with the primaries under way, the Democratic town committee in Roxbury, Connecticut, where she and Arthur Miller were residents, named her as an alternate delegate.

"Wouldn't it be nice," said a committee spokesman, "if Marilyn could be a delegate to the convention?" The gesture was not entirely serious, but on the eve of the convention a Los Angeles newspaper reported that "Marilyn Monroe's own Democratic friends are urging her to attend."

31

IN THE SECOND WEEK of July 1960, meeting in Los Angeles for the first time in forty years, the Democrats gathered to choose their candidate. The Kennedys, of course, were there in force—brothers John and Robert, and their father, Joseph, the latter ensconced in the Beverly Hills mansion loaned to him by one of the great movie stars of his own era, Marion Davies.

Of Marilyn Monroe there was not a sign, nor was she mentioned, except behind the scenes at the Beverly Hilton Hotel. Fred Karger, the musician Marilyn had wanted to marry twelve years earlier, refused to play at a ball attended by John Kennedy. He withdrew his entire band, says Karger's first wife, Patti, because he "had heard of Kennedy's fooling with Marilyn, and it appalled him." The Democrats made do with Frank Sinatra and Judy Garland instead.

Marilyn was not to be seen for a good reason: she was in New York during the brief hiatus between finishing *Let's Make Love* and starting *The Misfits*. Ralph Roberts, the actor who at this time became her masseur and friend, was giving her a massage at the 57th Street apartment when news came through that Kennedy had won the nomination.

Two days later, as the sun began to set, a weary Kennedy stood in the Los Angeles Coliseum to declare: "We stand today on the edge of a New Frontier—the frontier of the 1960s—a frontier of unknown opportunities and perils. . . . I am asking each of you to be new pioneers on that New Frontier."

By now, the evidence suggests, Marilyn had flown to Los Angeles and was with Kennedy on his night of triumph.

That night Peter Lawford threw a party for Kennedy, and borrowed the head bartender from Romanoff's, the Beverly Hills restaurant owned by one of Marilyn's closest friends. The bartender, Ross Acuna, was a man used to watching the famous at play, and he has a long memory.

Acuna says of the party on the night of the Coliseum speech, "I saw Sammy Davis coming in with Marilyn Monroe. I couldn't get the drift, but I was a bartender; you see a lot of things, you keep your mouth shut. But pretty soon here comes the Kennedy boy, from making that speech at the Coliseum. In fact when he ordered his drink he never told me what he wanted—he wrote it down because his voice was gone from making so many speeches. He used to drink daiquiris. Soon I saw that Monroe and the Kennedy boy were pretty close together. Sammy Davis? I think they just asked him to bring Monroe in."

Jeanne Carmen, then Marilyn's neighbor and confidante at the Doheny apartment, also says Marilyn met Kennedy that night. Her source is Marilyn, who mentioned it months later. Taking together Acuna's statement, and Carmen's, it seems the information given to the District Attorney's investigators may have been well-founded.

Peter Summers, the Kennedy campaign official who had seen Marilyn with Kennedy earlier in the year, now saw them again. He noticed that Marilyn's lack of confidence around Kennedy had evaporated. "I think that the next couple of times I saw them together, right after the nomination, she seemed so much more comfortable."

If Marilyn did indeed see Kennedy at the Convention, she did so in the midst of her turmoil over Yves Montand and the collapse of her marriage to Miller.

Later, on the set of *The Misfits*, Marilyn asked British correspondent W. J. Weatherby what he thought of Kennedy. Weatherby replied cautiously that he preferred Kennedy to Nixon. Marilyn, who struck Weatherby as "mischievous . . . excited," said how fine it would be to have a President who was so young and good-looking.

"You mean he has a Hollywood image?" asked Weatherby.

"You must admit," Marilyn replied, "it's better than having old uglies who have no brains *or* beauty."

Marilyn now told Weatherby she wanted Kennedy to win in November. He did, of course, and just a day later Art Buchwald wrote:

Let's Be Firm on Monroe Doctrine
Who will be the next ambassador to Monroe? This is one of
the many problems which President-elect Kennedy will have
to work on in January. Obviously you can't leave Monroe
adrift. There are too many greedy people eyeing her, and now
that Ambassador Miller has left she could flounder around
without any direction.

Few, except her psychiatrists and closest friends, knew
how desperately Marilyn was floundering. She was now in
that solitary three-month period before the ordeal at Payne
Whitney Psychiatric Clinic. Miller was gone, Montand was
finally rejecting her, and Marilyn was in a narcotic nose
dive. She found some solace in occasional visits to the Actors
Studio, and it was there she bumped into reporter W. J.
Weatherby again. The Englishman suggested a drink, and
thus began a series of conversations any journalist would have
envied.*

Weatherby and Marilyn met several times in the coming
weeks in a nondescript, now defunct, bar on New York's
Eighth Avenue. Over the first drink, Marilyn eyed Weatherby's
notebook warily, then decided to trust him. "Put me in the
notebook if you like," she said, "but don't write about it now.
Do it when I retire!" Weatherby duly scribbled a record of
their conversations in two shorthand notebooks, and honored
Marilyn's embargo till long after her death. In context, her
comments on the Kennedys are revealing.

A month after the election Weatherby got a curt response
from Marilyn when he ventured that even John Kennedy did
not talk sense all the time. "Oh, he does," came Marilyn's
quick riposte.

Joan Greenson, daughter of Marilyn's psychiatrist, recalls
that Marilyn "liked to have everything black or white, right
or wrong, good or bad. Her intensity of feelings made it, at
times, difficult to have discussions." This was something
Weatherby now discovered.

In January 1961 Marilyn arrived for their meeting in a state
that had Weatherby worried. She said she had been on pills,
and her mood veered wildly from bright to irascible, from
articulate to long, depressed silences. They talked of civil
rights; Marilyn had mentioned once having had an affair with

*Weatherby's contact with Marilyn is confirmed by the discovery of his
name in Marilyn's address book, located in 1986.

a young black, and Weatherby himself was involved with a black girl. He now dared to suggest that Kennedy would give only limited help to the black cause. "The President will go all the way. . . . ," Marilyn insisted. "The Kennedys know all about the situation already. . . . You just wait and see. You're in for some surprises."

Two decades later, when I talked to him, Weatherby still remembered vividly that "Marilyn would not have me say a word against Kennedy. She talked in a knowing way, as though she had some sort of inside track."

At their next rendezvous, the last in 1961, Marilyn was again dopey, fading in and out of the conversation. She enthused about establishing a memorial to her late drama teacher, Michael Chekhov, and seemed serious at the notion that the President himself might help. "She seemed like a star-struck girl at the mention of the President's name," Weatherby recalls. It struck him as odd, and he hastily steered her away from the subject of the Kennedys.

When in New York, before and after the election, John Kennedy favored the Carlyle Hotel as his base. There he had a suite with spectacular views of Manhattan, a management who catered to his every whim, and total respect for his privacy. The press might be on watch downstairs, but during the presidency Secret Service men would accompany the President on his private escape route, a series of tunnels that connected the Carlyle with the nearby apartment houses and hotels. The hotel was eighteen blocks from Marilyn's apartment.

Reports that Marilyn visited Kennedy at the Carlyle are supported by Jane Shalam, a member of a New York family prominent in political circles. The windows of her apartment looked down on the side, or back, entrance of the Carlyle. "I saw Marilyn coming and going at that time," says Shalam, "and she was certainly in and out enough to notice her. Most times people wouldn't know who she was—when she took her makeup off, and had her hair back, you wouldn't know it was Marilyn Monroe. I saw her going there when the Kennedys were at the Carlyle. There seemed no other reason that she would be there."

The President, like other mortals, once had to wait for Marilyn when he invited her to an intimate dinner at the Carlyle, according to reporter Earl Wilson, quoting the "beard" of the evening—the front man used to escort Marilyn to the rendezvous. Wilson will not identify his source, but Peter Lawford's agent, Milt Ebbins, once played a similar role.

Ebbins, by now a man on friendly terms with the President, recalls Marilyn asking him to take her to a party on Park Avenue. He finally got her there two hours late, whisked her, unrecognized, past a group of newsmen in the lobby (Marilyn was wearing wig, bandanna, and dark glasses), and was then promptly abandoned. The President was at the party, and Marilyn was with him when Ebbins slipped away.

Marilyn herself told several people about her relationship with John Kennedy. Paula Strasberg, now dead, said privately that Marilyn told her of the affair. She added that she was in possession of related correspondence, which she had "placed in a safe deposit box, to remain unopened for fifty years, so that people should not be hurt by it."

Marilyn also talked about John Kennedy with Sidney Skolsky, the veteran Hollywood reporter who had advised her since the start of her career. In 1983, weeks before he died, Skolsky said, "She told me she was having an affair with the President, and I did not doubt her." Skolsky wrote nothing about Marilyn's confidence until years after her death, and, when he did refer to it, reflected, "I confess I still find it grim to speculate on what might have happened to me if I had tried to write about this romance in my column when it first came to my attention."

Skolsky said Marilyn always referred to Kennedy as "the President," never by his first name. "She did complain to me," Skolsky recalled, "about the difficulties involved in being alone with the President. And even when Marilyn and the President were alone in Peter Lawford's beach house in Santa Monica, they had to leave a light on. If anything happened, if the light went out, the Secret Service would break down the door and burst in. I don't think that ever actually happened!"

Two other West Coast reporters claim they learned from prime sources of Marilyn's affair with the President. James Bacon, who had known Marilyn for years, says, "She was drinking heavily at the time—I think it was less than a year before her death—and she said she was sleeping with Jack Kennedy. She said he wouldn't indulge in foreplay, because he was on the run all the time."

Jimmy Starr, also a Los Angeles columnist at the time, learned of Marilyn's involvement with Kennedy from actress Angie Dickinson, then a younger and less tight-lipped lady than she is today. Like Skolsky and Bacon, he published nothing at the time.

"When he became President," recalled Marilyn's New York confidant, Henry Rosenfeld, "she became very excited. Her opinion was that this was the most important person in the world, and she was seeing him. She was so excited, you'd have thought she was a teenager."

Rosenfeld, as did Skolsky, thought Marilyn gloried in the secrecy of the whole business, even as she was being indiscreet. Sometimes, on the telephone, she would refer to the President as "You know who."

As Rosenfeld understood it, "In New York I believe they met occasionally at a place on Fifty-third Street, near Third Avenue. And Marilyn went to Washington to see him once or twice, though I'm almost sure she never went to the White House."

In 1984, in Los Angeles, I talked to Pat Newcomb, Marilyn's last press aide and the woman most in her company at the end of her life. She knew John Kennedy before the election, and grew close to the Kennedy family. Asked about Marilyn and the President, Newcomb said, "No comment." Asked about Marilyn and Robert Kennedy, she replied, "I did not know about it."

Almost everyone close to the Kennedys has stayed silent on the subject of Marilyn, but I did find one distinguished exception. Senator George Smathers of Florida was a freshman Congressman with John Kennedy in 1947, and preceded him to the Senate. Smathers himself was known as "Gorgeous George" or "Smooch." He was the only politician to act as an usher at Kennedy's wedding, and by the time of the presidency had become an old and trusted friend, invited to private dinners at the White House. Today, in his seventies, he continues to run his law practice in Florida.

Senator Smathers says he heard about Marilyn Monroe from John Kennedy himself, and then in the context of his brother, Robert. "I never did believe that Jack Kennedy had a big deal going with Marilyn Monroe until after Bobby," he says. "He took her away from Bobby, something like that—Jack would take a girl away from his brothers, or a friend, for a short relationship, at any time."

Smathers added that he also heard about Marilyn "around the White House and in family circles." He says he asked the Kennedy's brother-in-law, Stephen Smith, about it, and that Smith, too, said, "I thought Bobby was the first one to get involved with Marilyn Monroe."

An accumulation of compelling evidence suggests that Marilyn was indeed involved with both Kennedy brothers. For the President she may have been another female diversion. For Robert, the "puritan," as his elder brother called him, the commitment may have been greater.

Robert Kennedy was hardly ever seen in public in Marilyn's company. They were observed once, though, by a man who knew the Kennedys well: Stanley Tretick, the *Look* magazine photographer who took some of the most memorable pictures of intimate moments in the life of the First Family. He had access to the White House, visited the Kennedy compound at Hyannisport, and frequently traveled with Robert Kennedy.

Tretick saw the Attorney General with Marilyn at a social occasion "for invited guests only,"—he believes it was during a stop in San Francisco, and during the last nine months of Marilyn's life. According to him, "They were dancing together. It was in a hotel, at a posh, semi-private affair, a fund-raiser sort of thing. They were dancing very closely, with their bodies very close together, and it looked rather romantic. It just struck me at the time, 'My, they really look like a nice couple together,' but then I just dismissed it out of my mind."

Tretick did not photograph the couple. He recalls, "There were certain times when you couldn't photograph, or when something was not relevant to the story I was doing. I am not even sure I had my cameras with me. The reason I remembered the incident is that they looked very good together, looked like they were very friendly. . . ."

Another witness has no doubt about the nature of Marilyn's relationship with Robert Kennedy: Jeanne Carmen, Marilyn's neighbor at the Doheny apartment in Los Angeles, remembers an astonishing episode, which probably occurred in the spring of 1962. "I was at Marilyn's place one evening when the doorbell rang. She was in the tub, and she called to me to get it. I opened the door, and there was Bobby." Carmen says she recognized the Attorney General at once, but was completely nonplussed. So was Robert Kennedy. "He had that expression of not knowing whether to run, or walk, or stay," says Carmen. "I was stunned, and I kept saying, 'Come in,' but went on standing in his way. Finally I got out of the way, and Marilyn came flying out of the bathroom, and jumped into his arms . . . she kissed him openly, which was out of character for her. . . ."

That night, says Carmen, she shared a glass of wine with Marilyn and Robert Kennedy—in a somewhat awkward atmosphere—then left them alone. She says Marilyn had told her some time earlier that she had seen John Kennedy, but never said much about the elder brother.

There was another occasion, says Carmen, when John and Robert arrived together with a couple of companions, then left almost at once with Marilyn. There was, she says, one further encounter with Robert Kennedy. She talks about it with some reluctance, and understandably so. If true, it was a remarkable episode, with a bizarre background.

Carmen discovered early on Marilyn's mischievous delight in nudity. They once went to the movies together, each of them naked under a mink coat. (Given Marilyn's history of such antics, this seems plausible.) Carmen says they were both friends with comedian Jack Benny; Marilyn had known him since 1953, and witnesses confirm they were friends. Benny's home number appears in Marilyn's address book.

Benny, says Carmen, would accompany Marilyn and herself to a massage parlor on Sunset, where they would all have facials. Once, for a lark, and to tease Benny, the two women walked out of the building and "flashed" their mink coats open at Benny, who was waiting outside in the car. Both were naked under the coats.

Carmen says nudity became something of a running joke for the trio—she makes it clear there was no sexual aspect so far as Benny was concerned—and they occasionally ventured forth to a "nude beach." In the early sixties there was a beach where nude swimming was permitted, well to the north of Santa Monica, near the present Pepperdine University. As a sort of mutual dare, Carmen says, Jack Benny and Marilyn would accompany her to this beach in disguise—Marilyn in her black wig, Benny in a false beard acquired specially for the purpose. It worked; nobody recognized them. The false beard remained lying around Marilyn's apartment and—in 1962—that was how Robert Kennedy came into the story.

"The beard was lying there," Carmen says, "when Bobby came to see Marilyn, and I think he asked us what it was for. We explained, and told him about the Benny thing, and he said, 'You could recognize Benny if he had ten beards on.' And Marilyn said, 'Oh, no, you couldn't. Nobody'd recognize you if we fixed you up.' And she put the beard on him, I put sunglasses on him, and we put a hat on him like a baseball cap sort of thing. And he looked in the mirror and said something like 'I could probably get away with this.' And we said, 'Okay, we dare you! Let's go.' "

Carmen is aware her story sounds preposterous, but she says Robert Kennedy simply seemed unable to resist a dare. That, certainly, is in character. They went off to the nudist beach in Carmen's convertible—Kennedy in his getup and Marilyn in her wig. It was late, she says, and not many people were around. "We walked up and down, and sat on a blanket we brought from the car," Carmen recalls. "Once we got out there and found nobody cared. Here were two famous people that nobody recognized—we just sort of lounged around. On the way back, we really laughed a lot."

Checks of her background, and her own voluminous file on her show business career, indicate that Carmen was what she says she was and had many of the friends she claims she had in that period, including Peter Lawford and Frank Sinatra. She correctly named the landlady of the Doheny apartments at the relevant time, and was clearly familiar with the building when we visited it together in 1983. Marilyn did not give up the apartment at once when she moved to her new house in spring 1962.

Carmen says the first encounter with Robert Kennedy was "after Marilyn telling me about being at a party at the Lawfords', and what a blast it was seeing RFK." New research dates the party as having been held in February 1962.

The evidence is that Marilyn also saw Robert Kennedy's elder brother in the fall of 1961. In mid-November, a year into his presidency, John Kennedy returned to Los Angeles for the first time since his election. He had come to make speeches, and to fire the enthusiasm of key supporters in California. At the Beverly Hilton Hotel, where he stayed, there was a reception for about two hundred guests drawn from the ranks of local politics and administration.

One of the guests was Philip Watson, then beginning his campaign to become Los Angeles County Assessor, a post he would win and hold till 1977. Watson was a Republican, but the Assessor's office was a nonpartisan appointment, and he was courting support from both parties. An introduction to the President could open many doors, and Mark Boyar, Kennedy's finance chief in California during the presidential campaign, fixed Watson's invitation. First, upstairs in the Hilton's Escoffier Room, Watson, one of a long line, shook the President's hand. Later, to get him closer to Kennedy, Boyar took Watson to a smaller gathering in a suite on a lower floor. This time, he found the President was accompanied by Marilyn Monroe.

"She was there in the room with him," Watson recalls, "along with a couple of dozen other people. I had heard stories about them, and it came as no particular surprise. I was introduced to them both, I spoke to her too, and thought her a beauty—she was in a skin-tight white dress—but empty-headed was how I thought of her that evening. There was nothing obvious. They weren't holding hands or anything."*

Whatever the precise nature of the Kennedy brothers' overlapping contacts with Marilyn, they were playing with fire. Robert Kennedy's former press secretary, Edwin Guthman, recalls that Marilyn was present at two or three parties attended by Robert Kennedy at the Lawford house, although he knew of no sexual relationship between them. "After one of the parties," Guthman remembers, "she had too much to drink to drive home, and we both drove her to her place. Bob asked me to come along too. He didn't say why, but his reason was pretty obvious. He didn't want to be seen to be going off alone in a car at night with Marilyn Monroe."

The Attorney General was aware of the risk that came with philandering, or even the appearance of philandering in an innocent situation. Perhaps, however, he was neither sufficiently worried nor soon enough. By the time Marilyn died, the danger would be extreme. Only today can we piece together the extent to which the Kennedys' bedroom secrets were uncovered at the time by their bitter enemies—the leaders of organized crime.

Former FBI Assistant Director Courtney Evans, J. Edgar Hoover's liaison with Robert Kennedy, is famous among reporters for his elliptical way of parrying questions. In 1984, however, discussing the vulnerability of President Kennedy to sexual blackmail, Evans told me, "There was, I know, an effort to bring pressure on the presidency—by organized crime. . . . That's my recollection." He had said little, but more than any official source before him.

Pleading a poor memory, Evans will not be lured into providing detail, but points the reporter towards two key

---

*The day after the Hilton reception the President visited the Lawfords at Santa Monica. Whitey Snyder, Marilyn's makeup man, drove her to meet the President at the Lawfords' beach house, almost certainly on that day November 19, 1961.

Kennedy enemies—Sam Giancana, one of the most powerful Mafia bosses in history, and Jimmy Hoffa, criminal head of the Teamsters' Union. Evans indicates that at least some of the pressure involved Marilyn Monroe.

I asked the former Assistant Director whether at any stage he was aware of "any sort of a flap about Monroe . . . or of organized crime attempting to use involvement with Monroe as pressure on the President or his brother."

Evans replied, "I certainly heard such stories, because they were rampant both in Washington and Los Angeles, well before she died. Whether they were true or not I had no way of knowing. I had my own suspicions. . . ."

Evans points out, almost with relief, that his unenviable role as liaison between Hoover and Robert Kennedy, two men who deeply disliked each other, meant that neither necessarily gave him all the facts.

Some of the facts about Marilyn and the Kennedys may still be locked in FBI files. In a telltale footnote to correspondence, a Bureau official has revealed that the Bureau's "references pertaining to the late Marilyn Monroe are voluminous." The word "voluminous," one of a number of stock descriptions used to describe file holdings, in no way describes the few dozen documents that the FBI has produced in response to repeated requests under the Freedom of Information Act. The researcher, driven back to his jigsaw puzzle, must take a hard look at another of Marilyn's lovers, one with whom she was having an affair at the same time she was involved with the Kennedys. He was, and is, a singer named Frank Sinatra.

32

SHORTLY BEFORE HER DEATH a reporter asked Sinatra how well he knew Marilyn Monroe.

"Who?" Sinatra replied sarcastically. "Miss Monroe," he observed, "reminds me of a saintly young girl I went to high school with, who later became a nun. This is a recording."

Marilyn, told of his exchange, responded tartly, "Tell him to look in *Who's Who*."

Marilyn had first met Sinatra, according to photographer Milton Greene, at a dinner at Romanoffs in 1954, when the DiMaggio marriage was collapsing. The "Wrong Door Raid," in which Sinatra helped his friend DiMaggio in his pursuit of the unfaithful Marilyn, followed within weeks.

Six years later, in 1960—when the Miller marriage was falling apart, and just after John Kennedy's nomination as President—Sinatra made contact with Marilyn again. In August of that year he invited the entire company of *The Misfits* to see him perform at the Cal-Neva Lodge, not far from the Nevada location where the movie was being made. Marilyn went, accompanied by an Arthur Miller who looked rather out of his element.

Sinatra was in the process of buying the Cal-Neva Lodge, a casino and resort complex on the wooded shores of Lake Tahoe. It sat on the heights overlooking the lake, with a swimming pool and a cluster of luxury bungalows. Advertisements called it "Heaven in the High Sierras," but it was a paradise custom-built for gangsters.

The Lodge's gimmick was that the state line dividing California and Nevada bisected its public rooms and swimming pool. Casino activity could take place only on the Nevada side of the line, because of the laws banning gambling in California. Sinatra expanded the casino facilities, and brought in new managers. One was Paul "Skinny" D'Amato of Atlantic City, one day to be described by the Chief Counsel of Congress' Assassinations Committee as "a New Jersey gangster." His role in the Lodge, according to the same authority, was to protect the interests of Chicago Mafia chieftain, Sam Giancana.

Giancana was the "boss of bosses" of the Chicago syndicate, the ruler on the throne once occupied by Al Capone. By 1960 he was master of an organized crime network reaching across huge swathes of the United States, including casinos and show-business rackets on the West Coast. With the advent of the Kennedy administration Giancana would become a prime target for prosecution. As Attorney General, Robert Kennedy took on no less a task than the destruction of the Mafia in the United States. Giancana, if cornered, would be desperate.

In 1981, in a sworn testimony to the Nevada Gaming Control Board, Sinatra was to say that, as of 1960, he knew

Giancana only slightly, and did not realize he was a mobster. He said he never invited Giancana to the Cal-Neva Lodge, and—when he did learn he was there—issued instructions that he was to leave.

Giancana's daughter, however, says she was present at several meetings between the two from as early as 1954, and that Sinatra always greeted Giancana "with an embrace of respect and friendship." According to Peter Lawford, Sinatra "almost took a pleasure in flaunting his friendship with Giancana," and "Giancana often stayed at Frank's house in Palm Springs."

The Cal-Neva Lodge was to bring Sinatra his greatest public embarrassment, arising from his reported association with Giancana. The Mafia boss, overheard on FBI surveillance microphones, said he owned part of the Cal-Neva. In 1963, the official discovery of Giancana's presence at the Lodge would lead to Sinatra's withdrawal from the business, and a decision by the Gaming Board to revoke his gambling license.

The Kennedy family also had links with Cal-Neva. President Kennedy's father often visited the place before the Sinatra takeover, and the Cal-Neva maintenance manager used to ship two ten-foot Tahoe Christmas trees to the Kennedy family each December.

The President's brother-in-law, Peter Lawford, was a regular, and would accompany Marilyn to the Cal-Neva during the last weeks of her life. Marilyn's comings and goings at the Lodge were to loom large in the mysteries surrounding the end of her life.

At the end of 1960, as soon as Marilyn separated permanently from Arthur Miller, Sinatra became solicitous. He presented her with a replacement for Hugo, the basset hound, which stayed with Miller. The new dog was a white poodle, and Marilyn swiftly dreamed up a name for it. In the light of the talk about Sinatra's friendships with mobsters, she christened it "Maf," for Mafia. She thought the idea was hilarious.

In 1961, when Marilyn flew back to California after her spell in the Payne Whitney Psychiatric Clinic in New York, Sinatra, who was away at the time, gave her the use of his house. According to George Masters, Marilyn's hairdresser at this time, Sinatra sometimes used an apartment in the Doheny building where Marilyn settled that year.

Masters says, "I had never met Sinatra, though I felt as if I knew him intimately from my association with Marilyn. . . .

Marilyn would take me with her to his home in the Bel-Air hills—when I was driven there, I never knew where I was going, it was a big secret—or to his openings in Las Vegas. So far as I was concerned he remained as invisible as Howard Hughes.''

In May, Marilyn's psychiatrist, Dr. Greenson, wrote to a colleague: "Above all, I try to help her not to be so lonely, and therefore to escape into the drugs or get involved with very destructive people, who will engage in some sort of sado-masochistic relationship with her. . . . This is the kind of planning you do with an adolescent girl who needs guidance, friendliness, and firmness, and she seems to take it very well. . . . She said, for the first time, she looked forward to coming to Los Angeles, because she could speak to me. Of course, this does not prevent her from canceling several hours to go to Palm Springs with Mr. F. S. She is unfaithful to me as one is to a parent. . . .''

Early the next month, when Sinatra performed at the Sands Hotel, Las Vegas, Marilyn was there. Also present were two of President Kennedy's sisters, Pat Lawford and Jean, wife of Stephen Smith.

Singer Eddie Fisher, who was there with his then wife, Elizabeth Taylor, recalls, "Elizabeth and I sat in the audience with Dean and Jeanne Martin and Marilyn Monroe, who was having an affair with Sinatra, to watch his act. But all eyes were on Marilyn as she swayed back and forth to the music and pounded her hands on the stage, her breasts falling out of her low-cut dress. She was so beautiful—and so drunk. She came to the party later that evening, but Sinatra made no secret of his displeasure at her behavior and she vanished almost immediately.''

In July, when Marilyn was back in Los Angeles after her gall bladder operation, Dr. Greenson saw her constantly. He now thought, as he later wrote to a colleague, that "she was terribly, terribly lonely,'' and expressing a "feeling of mistreatment, which had paranoid undertones.'' Greenson said he felt Marilyn was reacting to her current involvement with "people who only hurt her.'' He did not name the people concerned.

The next month, August 1961, Marilyn spent a weekend with Sinatra on his yacht. Dean Martin's wife, Jeanne, and Gloria Romanoff, who were also aboard, make it clear that Marilyn was present as Sinatra's woman of the moment—she shared his cabin.

Marilyn put up a show of socializing, but she seemed disorientated and was using drugs heavily. Jeanne Martin says, "I remember going up to Frank's house before we got on the boat. And he said, 'Will you please go in and get Marilyn dressed, so we can get in the limo and go.' She couldn't get herself organized."

"She was taking sleeping pills," Gloria Romanoff recalls, "so she'd disappear at ten o'clock at night and not be awake till eleven or twelve the next day. We kidded Frank, saying, 'Some romance this is!' " Jeanne Martin remembers Marilyn "wandering around the dock, pitifully trying to find more pills. She'd be unable to sleep, and go lurching about half-dressed, trying to find someone who could give her 'reds' at three o'clock in the morning."

At the end of the trip, as everyone else was planning a get-together ashore, Marilyn simply walked off and vanished, without saying a word to anybody.

A month later Marilyn summoned her maid, Lena Pepitone, from New York, to bring out a dress she wanted for an evening with Sinatra. Pepitone was present when Sinatra came to pick up Marilyn. "He pulled a box out of his pocket," Pepitone says, "and clipped two gorgeous emerald earrings on Marilyn's ears. They kissed so passionately that I was embarrassed to be standing by."

Hairdresser George Masters, who also remembers the earrings, says Marilyn wore them only once. She then gave them away to Pat Newcomb, her press assistant.

In the summer of 1961, according to Pepitone, Marilyn had started talking about marrying Sinatra. She became upset when he saw other women. In a few months Sinatra would announce his brief engagement—it lasted only six weeks—to actress Juliet Prowse. There is no evidence that he was ever passionately involved with Marilyn, yet he continued to see her till her death. By that time Marilyn had her reservations about Sinatra. She told a companion, as she glanced through photographs of the yacht cruise, "I don't think I'll give him copies. I think I've already given him enough."

The troubling question mark over Marilyn's relationship with Sinatra concerns not so much the singer himself as the potential opportunity it gave to others to hurt the Kennedys. The Sinatra association brought Marilyn into a milieu peopled by some of the Kennedys' worst foes at a time when she was also seeing both Kennedy brothers. The question is—How much did the Mafia know?

33

NEW RESEARCH REVEALS THAT mobsters in California had taken an interest in Marilyn Monroe some time before the Kennedy presidency. It was a predatory interest, probably directed by Los Angeles gangster Mickey Cohen.

Cohen, a New Yorker by birth, cut a strange figure in the history of American organized crime. He was not a member of the Sicilian Mafia, and his proud boast was that he had triumphed in the gang warfare of the forties over who would run the Los Angeles rackets. The truth was more complex, but Cohen—the survivor of innumerable assassination attempts—murdered his way to an uneasy coexistence with the national crime families.

By 1959, after a spell in prison that weakened his power, Cohen was reasserting his strength. Publicly, he was a flamboyant figure, a man who had made it his business to hobnob with big Hollywood names, including Sinatra and those around him. Cohen had put up the money for Dean Martin and Jerry Lewis to bring their show to California from the East Coast early in their careers. In 1951, asked by a Senate Committee on organized crime to explain how he came to have Sinatra's private telephone number, Cohen replied, "Why, he's a friend of mine." With his pet bulldog, which had a penchant for lasagna, Cohen liked to patronize the Villa Capri restaurant, where Sinatra and DiMaggio once discussed the "Wrong Door Raid" against Marilyn Monroe.

In late 1959, as her marriage to Miller began to crumble, Marilyn was in Hollywood more than she had been for years. These were the months of the protracted filming of *Let's Make Love*. It was also the time Marilyn featured, to the surprise of the investigators, in the investigation of Mickey Cohen.

All that year the Bureau of Investigation of the Los Angeles District Attorney kept permanent surveillance on Cohen and the Italians who were his closest henchmen. Cohen was out of jail, and the intention was to put him inside again as soon as possible. The DA's men were taking a special interest in Cohen's involvement in narcotics, and in his efforts to compromise film stars sexually for blackmail or commercial exploitation.

The method was old-fashioned and ruthless. One of Cohen's men would work calculatedly on the seduction of a female star, then arrange for their lovemaking to be filmed and recorded. This was done, reportedly, during the affair between Lana Turner and Cohen's accomplice, Johnny Stompanato, which ended in Stompanato's killing at the hands of Turner's teenage daughter. Recordings of Turner and Stompanato making love were peddled for hundreds of dollars each.

One night in late 1959, along with his colleague Frank Hronek, DA's investigator Gary Wean was observing a restaurant—he believes it was the Plymouth House—on Sunset Boulevard. They saw Marilyn Monroe enter the restaurant, accompanied by a female companion and two men. Her escort, says Wean, was one of Cohen's "good-looking Italian boys," twenty-eight-year-old George Piscitelle.

"We sat out there till about two o'clock in the morning," Wean recalls, "then Piscitelle came out with Monroe. We followed their car over Coldwater Canyon to a motel on Van Nuys Boulevard. We saw them go in, but Frank and I split soon afterwards. We didn't see them come out."

According to former investigator Wean, Marilyn was trailed on other occasions, with less titillating results. Intelligence, however, revealed that Marilyn occasionally associated with both Piscitelle and Sam LoCigno, another Cohen henchman. Wean says he actually heard a bedroom recording of Marilyn, and assumes the purpose was extortion.

Frank Hronek, Wean's colleague, is dead. The story, however, receives some corroboration from Jack Tobin, former crack reporter on organized crime for the *Los Angeles Times*. He recalls Hronek telling him about the episode.

In addition, a senior law-enforcement source confirms that the Cohen group were investigated for a "shakedown" operation against leading stars. Piscitelle was involved, and Marilyn Monroe was identified as one of the Mafia's targets.*

---

*Reports in files of the Los Angeles DA's Bureau of Investigation, covering 1961, refer to Peter Lawford raising funds to aid Cohen's associate, Candy Barr, then in jail on narcotics charges. Lawford was "desperately attempting" to obtain compromising sound tapes of "parties" he had attended in Barr's dressing room.

Cohen and his relevant associates are dead, and cannot be questioned. The silence they leave behind them, though, concerning their purpose with Marilyn, is heavy with potential evil. Authorities on organized crime say that, long before the Kennedy era, Mickey Cohen had links with Sam Giancana. He also met with, and by 1960 probably toed the line for, Giancana's Hollywood representative, Johnny Roselli. Roselli, in turn, knew Marilyn.

Before Marilyn set foot in Hollywood, Roselli was criminally close to two men who figured large in her career. Harry Cohn, who gave her one of her first contracts, had used mob money, procured by Roselli, to gain control of Columbia Pictures. He remained indebted to Roselli, and very close. The two men wore identical ruby rings, provided by Roselli, who said it was the nearest a mafioso could come to making a non-Italian into a "blood brother."

Joe Schenck, the old Twentieth Century-Fox mogul, had served time in prison for perjury before the young Marilyn became his protégée and intimate guest at his dinner parties. He had been convicted because of his involvement in making payoffs to the Mafia—he had personally delivered the first cash payments, wrapped in brown paper. One of the mobsters convicted in that extortion racket was Johnny Roselli.

Roselli may have met Marilyn when he emerged from prison after the Schenck affair. Patti Karger, first wife of Marilyn's lover Fred Karger, says Roselli was a familiar face at the Karger home. He used to come to pick up his girlfriend and her mother, who came to the Kargers to play poker.

Two other sources say Roselli knew Marilyn. One is Joseph Shimon, former police inspector in Washington, D.C., who sat in with a CIA representative on the Castro assassination plotting with Giancana and Roselli. Shimon was Roselli's close confidant until he died. He says, "Roselli met Monroe. He met her socially, he knew a lot of her friends, and he knew her close business associates."

In 1984 a senior former Treasury Department official recommended that I interview Harry Hall, who was long a "highly reliable" informant for law enforcement authorities, especially on organized crime. He was also, incidentally, a trusted friend of Joe DiMaggio. Shortly after Marilyn's death, Hall bumped into Roselli in the drugstore of the Beverly Wilshire Hotel. The two men discussed Marilyn and, says Hall, "Roselli made it clear that he knew Marilyn personally.

He said he had liked her. . . . What personal things he had going with her, I don't know. . . .''

As Giancana's man in California, Roselli had had considerable contact with another woman now known to have been the mistress of President Kennedy—Judith Campbell. Campbell, as was revealed by the Senate Intelligence Committee a decade ago, had a sporadic affair with John Kennedy from early 1960 till at least spring 1962. Within about six weeks of beginning that relationship, Campbell met Mafia boss Sam Giancana. He stayed in close touch with her during the affair with Kennedy.

There are striking points in common between the Campbell story and Marilyn's. Though insignificant compared to Marilyn, the twenty-six-year-old Campbell was a creature of Hollywood. She was a starlet who had contracts with Warner Brothers, M-G-M, and Universal. She too had an affair with Frank Sinatra, who subsequently introduced her to John Kennedy. In that context, she encountered others who were involved in Marilyn's life.

Campbell met Gloria Lovell, Sinatra's secretary, who became one of Marilyn's few neighbors at the small Doheny apartment complex. Dr. Red Krohn, a close friend of Sinatra, was to become Campbell's gynecologist. He had long been Marilyn's too, and a frantic Marilyn would call him a few days before she died.

Nobody has ever established Giancana's motive in carrying on a liaison with Judith Campbell. He was murdered in 1975 before the Senate Intelligence Committee could question him. His henchman, Johnny Roselli, was killed in 1976. The Committee failed to press Judith Campbell on detail, and did not call Frank Sinatra to testify.

William Safire, of the *New York Times*, has listed a number of Questions Frank Sinatra should have been asked had he been summoned to testify. Did the mobsters discuss with Sinatra Judith Campbell's affair with the President? Were any recordings made, or pictures taken, of Kennedy and Campbell that could have been used by organized crime for blackmail purposes? Did the mobsters ask Sinatra to introduce her or anyone else to the Kennedys?

Some of these same questions could usefully be put to Sinatra and others regarding Marilyn Monroe and at least one other woman.* There are disturbing indications that the lead-

---

*Sinatra was approached for an interview in connection with this book but declined—as is his usual custom.

ers of organized crime were indeed watching the Kennedys with predatory interest.

In early 1961 comedian Jerry Lewis was advised that he was going to be named as co-respondent in a divorce suit brought by the husband of a starlet named Judy Meredith. Lewis asked Judith Campbell, who was working for him at Paramount Studios, to get Mafia boss Sam Giancana to intervene with the detective handling the divorce investigation. Giancana obliged, according to Campbell, and the evidence of adultery was destroyed.

The detective in the Meredith case was the celebrated Hollywood private eye, Fred Otash. He confirms the story, but adds that a number of other men were due to be named in the Meredith divorce. An FBI document, scrutinized recently by congressional investigators looking into another matter, notes they included "Dean Martin, Jerry Lewis, Frank Sinatra, *etc., etc., etc.*."

One of the *"et ceteras,"* Otash says, was John Kennedy. The detective says Kennedy's name was removed from the divorce evidence, thanks to the intervention of the Mafia. It happened, Otash says, in spring 1961. He received a call from Johnny Roselli, Giancana's lieutenant, requesting a meeting at the Brown Derby restaurant "at the request of the Attorney General." Otash says Roselli virtually ordered him to remove the President's name from the divorce evidence. After a meeting at which Giancana was present, Otash obeyed.

Judy Meredith, questioned today, denies having slept with John Kennedy. The man who commissioned the divorce investigation on behalf of Meredith's husband, Peter Fairchild, maintains that it did produce evidence of her adultery with Kennedy.

The issue, within this shabby subplot, is Roselli's claim that he intervened in the Meredith case "at the request of the Attorney General." Of course nobody close to the President, let alone Robert Kennedy, personally asked a top mobster to hush up a sexual indiscretion. The Kennedy administration, under Robert's impassioned leadership at the Justice Department, was committed as no other administration to fighting organized crime. Yet the Meredith case was fraught with the risks John Kennedy ran by associating with Sinatra and his friends.

If John Kennedy was about to be named in a divorce suit, along with Sinatra and friends, and if Sinatra and his group knew it, it could be that one of them mentioned the problem to Roselli. What Hollywood's top mafioso had done for Jerry Lewis he would do for Kennedy, for his own reasons.

Sandy Smith, the veteran investigative reporter for *Life* and the *Chicago Sun-Times*, is an authority on the Justice Department and organized crime during the Kennedy era. Told about the Meredith case, he says of the Sinatra group, "They were very close to Jack Kennedy at the time, and it would be very easy for them to do a favor for the President and whisper into Roselli's ear. And Roselli would be very eager to do a favor for the President."

Sinatra was close to the President at this time. A man of catholic political tastes (he has since emerged as a staunch champion of Ronald Reagan), he and his "Clan" had been a great boost to the Kennedy campaign. Sinatra's songs, "All the Way" and "High Hopes," were rerecorded as campaign jingles. He helped catapult Kennedy into the presidency, masterminded the inaugural gala, and was publicly seen as the President's friend.

As for the mob, reporter Sandy Smith says, "It's entirely in character for those guys to leap at the opportunity to do something for the government, or someone in a position in the government, just to have a marker or an IOU that they can call in at some future time. For Roselli it would be entirely in character."

Thanks to the CIA, it was not surprising Roselli saw himself as a man who could notch up an IOU with those in government. It was just before Kennedy's election, over drinks in the same Brown Derby where he later arranged the hushing up of the Judy Meredith divorce, that Roselli had been recruited by the CIA for the infamous series of plots to assassinate Fidel Castro. The Agency would not break off contact with the Mafia, and with Roselli and Giancana in particular, until 1963.

Early in the evening of July 12, 1961, many months after the beginning of the Kennedy connection with Marilyn, Giancana walked into a waiting room at Chicago's O'Hare Airport, on a routine stopover en route to New York. He was accompanied by Phyllis McGuire, the tallest and loveliest of the three McGuire Sisters, then one of the most popular female singing groups in the United States. The Mafia boss was head over heels in love with McGuire, who was by now his constant companion.

Waiting for the couple as they arrived at O'Hare was a team of FBI agents, acting on the orders of Robert Kennedy's

Justice Department. They were working full-time on the pursuit of Giancana, and this was an opportunity to get at him through his lover, Phyllis McGuire. Two of the agents offered McGuire the choice of accepting a subpoena or submitting to an interview then and there. She opted for the interview, and was whisked away from Giancana into a private room.

Giancana fumed impotently for a while, reboarded the plane, then walked back into the waiting room carrying McGuire's handbag and hat. The FBI men hooted with laughter at the sight of the mafioso toting a woman's handbag, and Giancana lost his temper. Today, knowing what we now do about the President's sex life, part of his tirade seems to have been fraught with danger for the Kennedys. According to the FBI report:

> Giancana then indicated that he was aware that the Agents intended to report the results of this interview of him to their "boss," who in turn would report the results to their "super boss" and "super super boss," and he said 'You know who I mean, I mean the Kennedys.' He then said, *'I know all about the Kennedys, and Phyllis knows a lot more about the Kennedys and one of these days we are going to tell all.'* [author's italics]. . . . You lit a fire tonight that will never go out. You'll rue the day. . . .''

What was the "all" that the mafioso knew about the Kennedys? When the agents asked what he meant, Giancana refused to comment.

Did Giancana only know about the President's affair with Judith Campbell? Or about the President and Judy Meredith? What was the "lot more" that Phyllis McGuire knew?

I spoke to McGuire in 1983, and she refused to discuss Sam Giancana. She was voluble, however—at first—about Marilyn Monroe. It turns out that McGuire knew Marilyn quite well. They had met in New York when Marilyn was married to Arthur Miller, and McGuire lived only four buildings away on East 57th Street. They did meet during the Kennedy presidency, though McGuire will not say exactly when or where. Joe DiMaggio, McGuire said, is still "a very dear friend of mine."

When I asked McGuire about Marilyn and the Kennedys, she said at once, "The initial relationship was with John. And there definitely was a relationship with Bob. . . . They were seen together at their little hideaways. And, you know, that's very like the Kennedys, just to pass it down from one to the other—Joe Kennedy to John, Jack to Bobby, Bobby to Ted. That's just the way they did things.''

Of Robert Kennedy, McGuire recalled, apparently with firsthand knowledge, that Marilyn ''was mysterious about it a lot. But when she had a few drinks, mainly when she was depressed, she would talk about it. At first it was really kept under the lid. Then she was pushing him to make a decision because she wanted to marry him. . . .''

At this point, in a telephone conversation with me, McGuire became nervous. Asked what Giancana had said about Marilyn, she replied, ''I wouldn't want to say anything. . . .'' She made an appointment to meet me, then failed to respond further to calls or letters.

What Phyllis McGuire has revealed is hugely troubling, for what she knew, Sam Giancana surely knew too.

''As in Greek tragedy,'' writes Robert Blakey, former Chief Counsel of the congressional committee that recently investigated John Kennedy's murder, ''there was in the President's character a fatal flaw, a *hamartia,* one that left him vulnerable to assassination by organized crime. . . .''

The fatal flaw in question was the President's womanizing. In 1961 and the next year, the year of Marilyn's death, womanizing—and their connection with Marilyn Monroe— left the Kennedys vulnerable to a different sort of assassination. They were wide open to pressure from the Mafia. The Kennedy brothers, it seems, did not take the threat seriously enough.

Senator Smathers, the President's friend, does not think he worried much about the risks that came with his voracious sexual appetite. ''He felt that he could walk on water so far as women were concerned,'' the Senator told me in 1983. ''He did not hold back.''

During the Kennedy presidency, William Kane, now a security consultant in New York, was an FBI supervisor working on organized crime cases. He remembers Robert Kennedy with admiration, and treasures the cigarette case the Attorney General gave him. He still recalls, in a bemused sort of way, a remarkable episode that took place just before the Labor Day weekend in early September 1961.

The FBI, says Kane, had been told by informants that the Attorney General had spent an afternoon ''out in the desert near Las Vegas, with not one, but two girls, on a blanket. Somebody—in organized crime—had taken telephoto pictures . . . and the word we got from our informants was that they were going to use them to blackmail the Attorney General of the United States. And this was confirmed several times over from several different sources. . . .''

According to Kane it fell to Courtney Evans, Hoover's liaison with the Justice Department, to warn Robert Kennedy. The Attorney General, says Kane, listened in a characteristic pose, sleeves rolled up and feet on the desk. Then he simply asked what Evans was doing for the holiday weekend, and ended the meeting. "He couldn't have given a shit less," Kane thinks. "There was as much of a chance of shaking him down, or embarrassing him, as of flying to the moon.''

Former Assistant Director Evans does not recall this particular incident, but explains, "It probably did happen as described. There were many times I had to go in with that sort of information. That was a typical Bobby Kennedy response.''

He adds, "When I would take an allegation to the Attorney General concerning the President, he never said yes or no. He was just noncommittal. If it concerned himself he was inclined to say, 'I can't be responsible for what other people say about me.' I was there to give information, not to get it.''

Evans, who regularly traveled with Robert Kennedy, says, "The only place he ever went out alone at the end of the day was when we were in Los Angeles. I had my own suspicions at the time that he was seeing Marilyn Monroe. What I guessed, others may have known.''

The Kennedy brothers' insouciance was foolhardy, for little escaped the notice of their enemies. Involvement with Marilyn was folly, for she was by now unreliable. By the end of 1961, she was disintegrating.

34

FOR ABOUT A WEEK, in September 1961, the same female voice kept coming up on the call-in line of radio station KDAY in Los Angeles. Tom Clay, then as now a well-known disc jockey, handled the calls. "I asked for the woman's name," Clay says, "because that's the only way you put anyone on the air," and she said she'd give it to me only if I promised *not* to say it on the air. She sounded really frightened, and I promised, and she said, 'I'm Marilyn Monroe.' I said, 'Oh, okay, and I'm Frank Sinatra,' and I hung up on her. She called back, really mad. And three or four days later she asked me if I'd ever like to come and have a cup of coffee with her."

Tom Clay still did not really believe it, but he went to the address the voice provided. He cannot recall the exact address, but the description fits that of the Doheny apartment. The woman he found there was indeed Marilyn.

She welcomed Clay to her home, about 9:30 in the morning, wearing a bathrobe and drinking champagne. There was no question, he says, of a seduction routine—only the outpourings of a lonely, disorientated woman.

"For about three weeks," Clay recalls, "I'd go over about every other day and stay about an hour. The thing she was most interested in was my family life, my wife, and my children. She wanted to hear just every word she could about my kids. She would ask me about my littlest baby, whom I called 'Rebel' because she was such a devil. I asked her once, 'How can you be so lonely?' Marilyn said, 'Have you ever been in a house with forty rooms? Well, multiply my loneliness by forty."

Marilyn's life in Los Angeles was now a dangerous vacuum, more dangerous than has ever been understood. Gloria Romanoff, who saw a good deal of Marilyn during her Sinatra summer in 1961, says, "There were several incidents when she had been mixing drink and sleeping pills, and had to be revived—very close calls.''

After one such scare, a sleeping-pill overdose, Twentieth Century-Fox chiefs hired security consultants to make sure the matter was hushed up. For the studio, Marilyn's self-destructive tendencies meant a risk of ''wrong'' Monroe publicity and higher insurance when she came to make her next film.

In the same period, the consultants were also used to smooth over a bizarre matter involving a Hollywood woman who claimed to have had a lesbian encounter with Marilyn and who seemed likely to brag about it. The woman was silenced with a cash payment, though the facts of the matter were never resolved.

Homosexuality was again a factor in Marilyn's psychiatric treatment that summer. Dr. Greenson was seeing Marilyn seven days a week, ''mainly because she was lonely and had no one to see her, and nothing to do if I didn't see her.'' He identified two clear problem areas: Marilyn's obsessive fear of homosexuality and her inability to cope with any sort of hurt.

''She couldn't bear the slightest hint of anything homosexual,'' Dr. Greenson wrote. ''She had an outright phobia of homosexuality, and yet unwillingly fell into situations which had homosexual coloring, which she then recognized and projected on to the other, who then became her enemy.'' An example, Greenson said, was the occasion one of Marilyn's female friends dyed her hair with a streak roughly the same color as Marilyn's hair. ''Marilyn instantly jumped to the conclusion that the girl was 'trying to take possession of her, that identification means homosexual possessiveness.' She turned with a fury against this girl.''

Dr. Greenson identifies the girl as ''Pat'' in his correspondence. Apart from Pat Lawford, the ''Pat'' Marilyn was close to in her last years was her press aide, Pat Newcomb. She indeed remembers incidents like the pathetic fuss over hair coloring, and vividly recalls Marilyn's ''frequent rages.'' It comes as news to Newcomb, though, that Marilyn had an anxiety concerning homosexuality.

As for his patient's attitude toward men, Dr. Greenson was to note Marilyn's increasing trend toward random promiscuity. In her last months she was to tell him she was having sex with one of the workmen remodeling her house. Once she invited in a taxi driver who brought her home late at night.

An undercover investigator for the Los Angeles District Attorney, engaged on another case, told of stumbling on Marilyn having sex with a man in a darkened hallway during a Hollywood party.

By late 1961, for Dr. Greenson, Marilyn was both patient and ever-present family friend. It was difficult to maintain the vital separation of the doctor-patient relationship. Marilyn, he found, took great offense at the slightest irritation on his part, could not abide the notion of any imperfection in "certain ideal figures in her life."

"Marilyn could not rest until peace had been reestablished," Greenson wrote. But the psychiatrist feared that only one conclusion could bring the perfect peace Marilyn sought. Her inability to handle anything she perceived as hurtfulness, along with her abnormal fear of homosexuality—Greenson was to write—"were ultimately the decisive factors that led to her death."

In December 1961, Greenson wrote, "She went through a severe depressive and paranoid reaction. She talked about retiring from the movie industry, killing herself, etc. I had to place nurses in her apartment day and night and keep strict control over the medication, since I felt she was potentially suicidal. Marilyn fought with these nurses, so that after a few weeks it was impossible to keep any of them."

Marilyn's address book for this period, located by the author in 1986, lists no less than thirty-six doctors and several nurses. Few can have been necessary, and all—for Marilyn—represented optional sources of unnecessary drugs.

That last Christmas was not wholly desolate for Marilyn. Joe DiMaggio, who had made the holiday bearable the previous year, again came to the rescue—almost certainly in response to an initiative by Dr. Greenson. Marilyn bought a tiny Christmas tree and lights, and tried to make her apartment look cheerful. She and DiMaggio spent the afternoon of Christmas Day at the Greensons' home, where—to Marilyn's delight and everyone's amusement—DiMaggio, the baseball hero, was the center of attention.

On New Year's Eve, after midnight, Dr. Greenson's daughter Joan, with a boyfriend, dropped in at the apartment to see Marilyn and DiMaggio. They drank champagne and roasted chestnuts on the open fire.

DiMaggio seemed "doting, caring, like family," Joan recalls. "As for Marilyn, it seemed to plase her to be doing things for him. It was like visiting an old married couple."

Long after the holidays were over, and DiMaggio gone, Marilyn kept the lights burning on the minuscule Christmas tree. It stayed till the decorations were drooping and the tree dead.

As 1962 began, at Greenson's suggestion, Marilyn began to look for a house of her own. She had never owned her own home, and Greenson hoped it would give her security, encourage her to stop thinking of herself as a homeless orphan.

Marilyn began house-hunting, helped by Eunice Murray, a sixty-year-old woman with some experience in looking after psychiatric patients. She had been brought in by Dr. Greenson before Christmas, when trained nurses refused to tolerate Marilyn's behavior.

From now on, Mrs. Murray was to act as general factotum and helpmate; she herself prefers the tag "devoted assistant."

House-hunting had its difficulties. At one potential house a woman shrilled, "Get off my property!" when she saw the would-be purchaser was Marilyn Monroe. At the end of January, though, a house was found—a modest, single-story home in the residential district of Brentwood. The style was Mexican, like Dr. Greenson's house, with wood-beamed ceilings, a large, central living area, and small bedrooms.

The house was a far cry from the ostentatious homes expected of Hollywood stars, but it was what Marilyn wanted. It was at the closed end of a cul-de-sac, and therefore private. It was also close to homes where Marilyn sought a very different kind of solace. Dr. Greenson lived a few minutes' drive away, and so did Peter Lawford, at whose home Marilyn sometimes saw the Kennedy brothers.

The house was quickly purchased, using the lawyer Marilyn shared with Frank Sinatra, and some borrowed funds. She had not made a film for a year now, and her percentage of profits from previous movies would not come in for a long time. Much of that money, indeed, would come in only after Marilyn's death. She had little ready cash when she bought her new home, and was to die with a mere $5,000 in her current account.

Marilyn burst into tears when she signed the contract for the Brentwood house, and explained later, "I felt badly because I was buying a home all alone."

By early 1962, Dr. Greenson felt the drug problem was under control, and hoped Marilyn was at last going to make real progress. Nobody, it seems, took note of the odd little coat of arms emblazoned on tiles outside the front door of the house. The motto read, in Latin, *Cursum Perficio*. This means, in English, "I am finishing my journey."

Marilyn was nearly thirty-six. She had six months to live.

35

"GODDAMMIT," MARILYN SAID, SITTING with Dr. Greenson's son, Danny, in the dining room of the Greenson home, "I'm going to dinner at the Lawfords' place, and Bobby's going to be there. Kim Novak will be talking about her new house near Big Sur, and I want to have something serious to talk to him about."

It was late January 1962. Marilyn was indeed about to dine with Robert Kennedy—and it would be no secret. Marilyn was one of several guests invited to be at the Lawford home on February 1, when the Attorney General and his wife would pass through Los Angeles at the start of a world tour.

That much was reported at the time in the newspapers, and the occasion is nowadays used, depending on one's loyalties, either to pinpoint the start of an affair or as evidence that Marilyn and the Attorney General were meeting for the first time.

In her talk with Danny Greenson, Marilyn was looking for political issues that would make talking points. "She ended up writing them down," recalls the younger Greenson. "They were left-of-center criticisms—way back then I was worried about our support of the Diem regime in Vietnam—and there were questions about the House Un-American Activities Committee, and civil rights and so on. . . . She wanted to impress him. . . ."

Robert Kennedy was at first impressed. Then he caught Marilyn peering into her purse at the list of questions, and was much amused. The story has been used to mock Marilyn's intelligence. In fact, ever eager to make a good showing, Marilyn for years made a habit of planning dinner-table conversation in advance. In this case, her homework seems to have paid off.

A few weeks later, on a trip to Mexico City, Marilyn talked about the dinner to Fred Vanderbilt Field, an American expatriate. Field recalls Marilyn telling him that "sometime in the evening, she and Kennedy retired to what she called the den. She said they had a very long talk, a very political talk. She told me she had asked Kennedy whether they were going to fire J. Edgar Hoover—she was very outspoken against him—and Kennedy replied that he and the President didn't feel strong enough to do so, though they wanted to."

Gloria Romanoff, one of the guests at the dinner, remembers Marilyn dancing with Kennedy that evening, in all propriety. She adds a merry detail: "Kennedy called his father long-distance to say he was seated with Marilyn Monroe, and would his father like to say hello to her?"

Six months later, when Marilyn died, many of her personal papers were destroyed. Her executrix, Inez Melson, simply threw them out while clearing the house. She did, however, keep a handwritten letter she found in a drawer, because it shocked her. It had apparently been sent to Marilyn by Jean, one of the Kennedy sisters.

Under the letterhead bearing the address "North Ocean Boulevard, Palm Beach, Florida"—the Kennedy vacation home—the note reads (see following page):

Dear Marilyn—
Mother asked me to write and thank you for your sweet note to Daddy— He really enjoyed it and you were very cute to send it—
    Understand that you and Bobby are the new item! We all think you should come with him when he comes back East!
    Again, thanks for the note—

                                        Love,
                                        Jean Smith

The John F. Kennedy Library, the repository of vast quantities of family correspondence, says it is "unable" to find a specimen of Jean Kennedy's handwriting for the relevant period.

In 1984, I took the letter to Jean's husband, Stephen Smith, who today manages the finances of the Kennedy family, to ask whether the letter seemed authentic. Smith said, "It could

NORTH OCEAN BOULEVARD
PALM BEACH, FLORIDA

Dear Marilyn —

Mother asked me to
write and thank you
for your sweet note
to Daddy. He really
enjoyed it and you
were very cute to send
it —

Understand that you
and Bobby are the
news item! We all think
you should come with him
when he comes back
East.!

Again thanks for
the note —

Love,
Jean Smith

The letter, supposedly written by Jean Kennedy Smith to Marilyn, found after the actress's death. The reference to "Bobby" has yet to be explained. Jean Kennedy Smith's name, however, appears in Marilyn's address book. The two were undoubtedly in touch with each other.

be, could be, it's a possibility, let's say. The script is not
entirely dissimilar. If Jean wrote the letter, she might or
might not remember if she did. She would certainly remember her own hand. I'll have to ask Jean.''

The Kennedy brother-in-law became irritated as he reread
the letter, but said he would indeed consult his wife. Smith
later wrote to me to say that she ''has no recollection of ever
writing such a letter and cannot identify the document. . . .''

Assuming the note is genuine, what does it mean? It is
undated, but there may be a clue in the reference to Marilyn's
''sweet note to Daddy.'' ''Daddy,'' seventy-three-year-old
Joseph Kennedy, had suffered a serious stroke on December
19, 1961, at Palm Beach. He would remain chronically ill for
many months, and incapacitated till the end of his life.

As for ''Bobby'' returning to the East Coast, this could
refer to his return from the global trip he was starting at the
time of the Lawford dinner party.

On the other hand, the Attorney General's sister may have
been replying to a note of sympathy sent to Joseph Kennedy
anytime after Christmas, or—if Gloria Romanoff correctly
recalls Marilyn speaking to the elder Kennedy on the phone
from the party—just after the dinner. Either way, that would
place the date of the letter as January or February 1962.

Timing aside, what does one make of the provocative
sentence, ''Understand that you and Bobby are the new item!''
Was this a wry jest, uttered in light of some public gossip
linking Marilyn and Robert Kennedy? Hardly. There was no
such gossip at this stage. Did this then mean exactly what it
said, in the vernacular of the period? Was Jean Kennedy
cheerfully acknowledging an affair, a dalliance of some sort,
between Marilyn and her brother? If so, it had clearly begun
some time earlier, which tends to support the statements of
Marilyn's neighbor, Jeanne Carmen, referring to meetings in
1961.

Until now, allegations about Marilyn and Robert Kennedy
have been made of fragile stuff, mostly malicious whispers.
Both are dead and cannot defend themselves. Not least because Kennedy figures so prominently in the mysteries surrounding Marilyn's death, their relationship demands exhaustive
investigation.

Robert Kennedy's personal secretary, Angie Novello, responds circumspectly but frankly to questions about Marilyn
and her former boss. She remembers meeting Marilyn at the
Lawford house in spring 1962, when both Kennedy and Pat

Newcomb were present. Dating from about then, she recalls—
and Marilyn's available phone records confirm—Marilyn made
numerous calls to Kennedy at the Justice Department.

Angie Novello says Kennedy always accepted a call from
Marilyn, or would return it soon afterward. "He was such a
sympathetic kind of person; he never turned away from anyone who needed help, and I'm sure he was well aware of her
problems. He was a good listener and that, I think, is what
she needed more than anything." Novello points out that
Kennedy was also a good friend to singer Judy Garland, and
nobody hints at an affair with her.

Kennedy's press secretary, Ed Guthman, says the Attorney
General "may have met Marilyn a total of four or five
times." Other Kennedy associates have different memories.
One, who preferred not to be named, told the *Manchester
Guardian* reporter, W. J. Weatherby, that he "accepted a
Monroe affair as a fact, but that it had been Bobby's only
one."

Tongues were apparently loosed in 1968, on the night of
Robert Kennedy's murder. Two of his friends, writer John
Marquand and Freddy Epsy, the present wife of George
Plimpton, sat reminiscing. The conversation, says a participant, included the matter-of-fact recollection that "there was
a good deal of flying about and flirtation, and that Miss
Monroe was very much in love with Bobby Kennedy." This
witness, a former member of Professionals for Kennedy, also
prefers to remain anonymous. Others are more forthcoming.

Peter Lawford's third wife, Deborah Gould, who says
Lawford broke down one night and told her about the Kennedys and Marilyn, reports finding a photograph among papers
her husband kept tucked away in a closet. It "showed Peter
Lawford, Marilyn Monroe, and Bobby Kennedy," Gould
recalls, "They were all arm in arm. As I recall Marilyn had
on a robe, and was holding a bottle of Dom Perignon champagne. It looked like they were all having a wonderful time;
they were at the beach."

Gould's understanding, quoting Lawford, is that Robert's
involvement started when he went to Marilyn, as his brother's
"messenger boy," to say that the relationship with the President could not continue. "Marilyn took it quite bad," says
Gould, "and Bobby went away with a feeling of wanting to
get to know her better. At the beginning it was just to help
and console, but then it led into an affair between Marilyn

and Bobby. From what Peter told me, he fell head over heels.''

The best evidence on Marilyn's relations with Robert Kennedy comes from firsthand contemporary witnesses. Dr. Greenson's daughter, Joan, who was very friendly with Marilyn in her last months, recalls sharing ''girlie talk'' with her. Most of it concerned Joan's love life, but in early 1962 Marilyn was bubbling with excitement about a ''new man in her life.''

''She told me,'' says Joan Greenson, ''that she was seeing somebody, but she didn't want to burden me with the responsibility of knowing who it was, because he was well known. So she said she was going to call him 'the General.' We both laughed. It wasn't so abstract that one couldn't figure it out, or have a good idea what was happening.''

Joan Greenson knew nothing of the actual use of the title. ''General,'' and her guess was that Marilyn was referring to the President. A *Life* magazine profile, published at this exact period, shows that, in the Justice Department, Attorney General Robert Kennedy was addressed as just that—''General.''

Dr. Greenson himself struggled for years to stick to the letter of professional ethics regarding what he had learned of Marilyn's love life. The psychiatrist did so in the face of much scandalmongering, and usually fended off reporters altogether. In 1973, however, outraged by unsupported innuendo in the book on Marilyn by Norman Mailer, Greenson talked to writer Maurice Zolotow. ''Marilyn,'' Dr. Greenson now said, ''did not have any important emotional involvement with Robert Kennedy or any other man at this time.''

Perhaps Greenson, a liberal who kept a Kennedy silver dollar on his desk, was simply trying to bury the rumors. Immediately after Marilyn's death, in private interviews with psychiatrists of the Los Angeles Suicide Prevention Center, Dr. Greenson said something quite different.

In 1984 I talked to Dr. Robert Litman, one of two Suicide Prevention Team members who questioned Greenson. He recalls that Greenson was terribly upset, to the extent that Litman felt as much a bereavement counselor as a formal questioner. He had studied under Greenson, respected him greatly, and ''felt it right not to talk about this until after Dr. Greenson's death.''

Marilyn's psychiatrist died in 1979, and I have an access to Dr. Litman's reports and original notes. Referring to early 1962, Litman wrote:

Around this time, Marilyn started to date some "very important men." Greenson had very considerable concern that she was being used in these relationships. . . . However, it seemed so gratifying to her to be associated with such powerful and important men, that he could not declare himself to be against it. . . . He told her to be sure she was doing it for something that she felt was valuable and not just because she felt she had to do it.

Dr. Litman says today that Greenson spoke to him of a "close relationship with extremely important men in government," that the relationship was "sexual," and that the men concerned were "at the highest level." Dr. Litman says that while Dr. Greenson did not actually name the Kennedys, he had "no real doubt" whom he meant by "important men in government." Litman also felt Dr. Greenson had not been "totally candid," even with him.

Greenson also told another member of the Suicide Prevention Team, Dr. Norman Tabachnick, about "two important men" in Marilyn's life, and Tabachnick had no doubt the reference was to the Kennedy brothers. The Suicide Prevention Team was commissioned by Los Angeles Coroner Theodore Curphey, who declared that it would question "all persons with whom Marilyn had recently been associated." The head of the Team, Dr. Norman Farberow, says neither Kennedy brother was questioned. He adds: "I'm sure discretion entered into it."

There were others Marilyn had talked to, apart from her psychiatrist. Henry Rosenfeld, her friend in New York, learned that she and Robert had become close, although he was convinced that, for Marilyn, the important affair was with John Kennedy. Ralph Roberts, Marilyn's masseur, had the same impression.

From the evidence, it does appear that the affairs with the brothers overlapped at certain stages. This is a bewildering notion, but not incompatible with Kennedy legend. According to family lore, it was not unheard of for the males in the dynasty to compete for the same woman. In the case of Marilyn, it may have been not so much a matter of brothers competing as of an unbalanced woman imagining she could play one Kennedy off against another.

In her last months Marilyn told Anne Karger, mother of Fred, Marilyn's great love of years earlier, that she was having an affair with Robert. Joe DiMaggio does not talk about Marilyn, but told his friend Harry Hall, who spent the days after Marilyn's death with DiMaggio, that he knew of an affair with Robert Kennedy. DiMaggio, says Hall, was "angry about it, very angry."

The Lawford home at Santa Monica was one of a string of beachfront houses owned by wealthy people. The neighbors were fascinated by the comings and goings at the Lawfords during the presidency, and some had special knowledge. Lynn Sherman, daughter of Harry, a well-known maker of Western movies, lived next door to the Lawfords. She became aware that Marilyn was a regular visitor from watching volleyball games on the beach.

Sherman recalls, "She would go out to join in, and just drop. It happened more than once. The combination of sun and pills was just too much, and they'd have to carry her into the house."

Lynn Sherman believes there was an affair with Robert Kennedy. "Only fools draw conclusions when they don't really know what was going on," she says now, "but there were many, many rendezvous there. The official car used to drive up, and you knew Robert Kennedy was in town, and then the help would come in and say, 'Marilyn's arrived.' She'd be wearing, maybe, a scarf over her head, and pants. Sometimes I'd notice Bobby and Marilyn go out through the patio to the beach to walk. From my balcony, it was pretty obvious they were there together on many occasions—there was no doubt in my mind."

Sherman says her belief in an affair was confirmed after Marilyn's death by Robert's sister Pat, who would drop in for a drink. "It was casual," says Sherman. "She was complaining about Peter, and said, 'But we all go through it—look what Ethel's been going through.' "

Another neighbor, then Mrs. Sherry James, talked to Peter Lawford about Marilyn's death. His version was that "Marilyn had been passed from him to Jack, and from Jack to Bobby." Lawford was probably gilding the lily—all evidence is that he pursued Marilyn, but she always turned him down.

Of the people at the beach, the Lawfords were perhaps closest to Mr. and Mrs. Peter Dye. Marjorie Dye, an heiress to the Merriweather Post fortune, does not respond to interview requests. Her former husband, however, now a teacher, did talk to me.

Peter Dye met Marilyn at the beach, and remembers her as a sad figure, "half-doped a lot of the time." Once, as she lounged on the cushions at the beach house, Dye noticed blood spreading across Marilyn's white pants. As in the past, she seemed oblivious to it. One night at dinner, when a guest picked on Marilyn for some mistake in grammar, she left the table in tears.

Dye came to know the Kennedys well, and saw Marilyn with Robert Kennedy on several occasions at the Lawford house. He thinks "there was certainly an affair. She was star-struck over him, staring at him half the time with her eyes fluttering. I hate the word 'macho,' but Kennedy was playing a sort of macho role. He was never animated, never cracked a smile. She was all over him. I think she was turned on by the idea of mental genius. She liked that type, instead of being pushed around like a piece of meat. She was trying to get away from that."

Marilyn's studio maid, Hazel Washington, remembers calls from Robert Kennedy. So does the New York maid, Lena Pepitone. "I know Bobby used to phone her many times," says Pepitone, "but they were very secretive. He would only say, 'May I speak to Marilyn'; then she would close the bedroom door and speak for maybe one hour. I knew it was him because she told me once, and after that I knew the voice."

Where did the couple meet during the last months, other than the Lawford house? Eunice Murray, Marilyn's frequent companion at the new house in Brentwood, usually speaks of only one Kennedy visit to Marilyn at home, a fleeting afternoon visit to "see her kitchen." In one interview, she raised the figure to "maybe two or three times," but said there was nothing furtive about the visits.

Murray's son-in-law, Norman Jeffries, was employed by Marilyn in 1962 to help with the remodeling of her house. Murray proved oddly reluctant to assist me in reaching Jeffries, but a researcher located him. There was indeed secrecy about the Robert Kennedy visit that he witnessed.

"It was funny," says Norman Jeffries, "because Eunice and I were there with Marilyn, and we were to leave. She and I were to clear out before he came, and that's what we did." In fact, Jeffries was still outside the house when Robert Kennedy arrived alone, driving a convertible.

On the West Coast, Marilyn and Kennedy may sometimes have been prudent enough to meet at a secret location. Police sources, and interviews with security officers of General Telephone, suggest Marilyn used an apartment in Culver City, in the southwest section of Los Angeles. Three officers recall investigations in the area after Marilyn's death.

On the East Coast, the maid, Lena Pepitone, says there were no Kennedy visits to the Manhattan apartment. She does remember that Marilyn quietly visited Washington during 1961, and that the trip involved the Kennedys.

Far too many people for safety knew about Marilyn's secret relations with the Kennedys, but the meetings continued. Meanwhile, perhaps to fill the lonely gaps that so worried her psychiatrist, Marilyn embarked on a flurry of activity.

36

IN FEBRUARY 1962, ON vacation in Florida, Arthur Miller's father, Isadore, received a telegram:

ARRIVING EASTERN AIRLINES FLIGHT 605 AT 9:05 TONIGHT.
HAVE RESERVATIONS AT FONTAINBLEAU. LOVE YOU. MARILYN.

That night the old man and the actress dined at the Club Gigi, watched a bad floor show, and walked back to the hotel together. There Marilyn broke the news that Arthur was getting married again, to Inge Morath.

The playwright's father was taken aback. He said later, "Marilyn wanted to make me feel right. She wanted me to protect her, but she also protected me." Later that night Miller found $200 in his coat pocket. Marilyn, who had always tried to look after him, had been hiding her own pain.

In January she had been jolted by the news of Frank Sinatra's engagement to Juliet Prowse. Now Arthur Miller's impending remarriage reduced her to virtual collapse. She shut herself away from the world, and refused to answer the telephone. Seven months later the new Mrs. Miller would bear a child, a joy that had eluded Marilyn. Perhaps she knew the birth was coming, and was all the more upset.

Marilyn was now involved in preparations for *Something's Got to Give*, the last film Twentieth Century-Fox was demanding under her existing contract, and one she would not complete. Henry Weinstein, producer of the film and a friend of the Greenson family, had a frightening glimpse into Marilyn's true condition.

One morning, about the time she learned of the new Miller marriage, Marilyn failed to turn up for an 8:00 A.M. costume conference. Weinstein telephoned her, heard a thick-tongued, rambling voice, and said he would come over at once. Marilyn had murmured vaguely, "There's only one bed. Where will you sleep?" She was flat out in a barbiturate coma by the time Weinstein arrived. A doctor was called, the often-pumped stomach was pumped once more, and Marilyn recovered.

There was a conference at Twentieth Century-Fox. One executive said the film should be called off, because Marilyn was clearly in no condition to work. "If she'd had a heart attack," he said, "we'd cancel. What's the difference if she's liable to kill herself any day with an overdose?"

"Ah," a colleague replied, "if she'd had a heart attack we'd never get insurance for the production. We don't have that problem. Medically, she's perfectly fit."

This ruthless view prevailed. *Something's Got to Give*, aptly named, was to continue. First, though, on Dr. Greenson's recommendation, Marilyn had time for a break. She went to Florida, saw Arthur Miller's father and Joe DiMaggio, and then, on February 20, sped off to Mexico.

Hairdresser George Masters found himself sitting in an airplane toilet with the world's most famous star on his knee. Marilyn had insisted on retreating there to have her hair and makeup fixed for the arrival in Mexico City. The trip had been intended as a private visit, but the secret was out.

At the Hilton Hotel, where Frank Sinatra had arranged accommodations, a quiet expedition turned into a state of siege. Armed guards prowled the corridors, and the press bayed for interviews. They got their way a couple of days later at a riotous press conference. Photographers fell over themselves for angles that would measure up to their readers' fantasies. One picture, not used at the time, came as close to pornography as any known photograph of Marilyn. It proved once and for all that Marilyn preferred not to wear panties. Marilyn, looking gaunt, drank champagne throughout the press conference.

Tribute once paid, the reporters allowed Marilyn a few

days of peace. She traveled outside Mexico City to the Toluca market and the mountain resort of Taxco. Accompanied by Eunice Murray, her Los Angeles companion, Marilyn bought things for the new house: a table, silver-framed mirrors, and paintings. She also made new friends.

Old Connecticut neighbors had given Marilyn an introduction to a couple who could show her around Mexico—Fred Vanderbilt Field and his Mexican wife. Field, born into the hugely wealthy Vanderbilt family, has been called "America's foremost silver-spoon Communist." He and his wife, part of a colony of left-wingers living in virtual exile in Mexico, took to Marilyn at once. They found her "beautiful beyond measure—warm, attractive, bright, and witty; curious about things, people, and ideas—also incredibly complicated."

By Fred Field's lights, Marilyn's politics were "excellent—she told us of her strong feelings about civil rights, for black equality, as well as her admiration for what was being done in China, her anger at red-baiting and McCarthyism and her hatred of J. Edgar Hoover."

Marilyn confided in the Fields a good deal. She spoke of the excitement of knowing Robert Kennedy and of her trust in Frank Sinatra. Most of all, though, she spoke of past failures and hopes for the future.

"She talked a great deal about her marriage with Arthur Miller," says Field, "in terms of the things she'd lost, the marriage that had not worked, and the loss of her babies. She said she wanted to quit Hollywood and find some guy—a combination of Miller and Joe DiMaggio, as far as I could make out—someone who would be decent to her but also her intellectual leader and stimulant. She wanted to live in the country and change her life completely. She spoke a lot of her intellectual shortcomings, her inability to keep up with people she admired. She talked of her age, the fact that she would soon be thirty-six, and of the need to get going."

Field saw that Marilyn drank heavily. He recalls, "My impression was that, sexually, Marilyn did a fair amount of one-night stands, and apparently got some release from that sort of thing."

Field noted, with alarm, Marilyn's speedy involvement with one man in particular. This was José Bolaños, a Mexican scriptwriter ten years her junior.

Bolaños, a slim young man with obvious good looks, a little too obvious, began a courtship that was more a bombardment. He started by sending flowers on a silver platter (he said it was the family plate) to Pat Newcomb, Marilyn's press assistant. Newcomb, mildly impressed, introduced Bolaños to Marilyn, so that she could "go out and have a good time."

Fred Field, arriving the next morning, saw at once that the Mexican had stayed the night. Later, when Marilyn traveled to Taxco, Bolaños followed. He arrived in the middle of the night, recruited not one, but several, mariachi bands, and mounted an almighty serenade outside Marilyn's hotel. In spite of being warned off by Field, Marilyn was to see more of him.

Bolaños, son of a middle-class family, was known in the film world. He counted himself a friend of the great director, Luis Buñuel, and had written the script for the highly praised *La Cucaracha*, when barely into his twenties. His career, though, was now in the doldrums.

Interviewed in 1983, Bolaños was still rhapsodizing about Marilyn. He says he had an affair with her that lasted till her death, five months after their meeting, and that he gave her a sexual satisfaction she had rarely known in previous relationships. He also claims that at the time she died Marilyn was planning to marry him. His lawyer and friend, Jorge Barragan, says the same—and said so in 1962 within days of Marilyn's death. Those close to Marilyn paint a contradictory picture.

According to the New York maid, Lena Pepitone, Marilyn talked about Bolaños and said that he did want to marry her. Photographs taken shortly after the Mexico visit show Bolaños dancing with Marilyn. She looks ecstatic, but witnesses say she was very drunk that night. Others, including Pat Newcomb, Eunice Murray, and hairdresser George Masters, confirm that Bolaños came to Los Angeles.

Was the Bolaños relationship just Marilyn's swan song? As we shall see, it may have had sinister overtones. Whatever his motives, though, Marilyn's mind was now a jumble of confusion and regret.

Before leaving Mexico, Marilyn visited the National Institute for the Protection of Children, which provided for thousands of orphans and deprived youngsters. She had intended to make a donation of $1,000, but then, on impulse, tore up the check and wrote a new one for $10,000.

Some reports indicate Marilyn made an application to adopt a Mexican child during her visit. Certainly she would now keep harking back to her own yearning for motherhood, a factor that will shortly take on a grim significance.

At mid-morning on March 2, when Marilyn was due to fly home, she could not be roused. Her hairdresser, George Masters, recalls, "I had to carry her. I remember lifting her up out of the bed, and carrying her out of the room. I think she had taken too many pills again." She appeared at the airport in dark glasses and with her hair awry, stumbling. One newspaper reported tartly that her breath smelled of alcohol, that the visit to Mexico had ended up as a drinking marathon.

Marilyn managed an *"Adios, muchachos"* for the newsmen, then walked unsteadily to the plane that would take her back to Los Angeles. She was now on the last lap.

37

IT WAS MARCH WHEN Marilyn returned from Mexico, and it was in March that President Kennedy was confronted with the peril his womanizing had brought. The storm warnings had been sounding for months.

Nearly a year had passed since Mafia boss Giancana's threat to "tell all" about the Kennedys. As Attorney General, Robert Kennedy should have been fully briefed on the outburst. If he was not—and that would have been a dire omission—he certainly learned of the ominous developments during 1961.

Giancana was only one of the Kennedys' dangerous foes. Jimmy Hoffa, President of the Teamsters' Union, was also by now locked in a bitter personal struggle with Robert Kennedy. Kennedy's work on Senate committees had persuaded him that the Union, as run by Hoffa, was "a conspiracy of evil." He had linked Hoffa indisputably to organized crime, and specifically to the Chicago syndicate led by Giancana.

Like Giancana, Hoffa was being remorselessly investigated. He struggled by every means, including jury tampering and intimidation of witnesses, to avoid going to jail. It was Robert Kennedy's origial initiative that would eventually—years later— put him there. Meanwhile, during Marilyn's last year alive,

Hoffa was fighting a battle against the Attorney General that involved her studio, Twentieth Century-Fox.

During 1961, Fox had announced plans for a movie based on Kennedy's book *The Enemy Within*—the exposé of Hoffa and the mob that had been published during election year. The producer was Jerry Wald, who had produced two of Marilyn's earlier films.

Within days of the announcement Wald was listening to an anonymous caller asking, "Are you the SOB who is going to photograph *The Enemy Within*?" It was the first of many calls and letters menacing Wald and the studio. The film project would founder in the end, after blatant intimidation by one of Hoffa's attorneys.

In 1962, though, the film was very much alive. Paul Newman was named as the star, and Robert Kennedy continued to attend script conferences. Meanwhile, Warner Brothers was pressing ahead with a movie about John Kennedy's war exploits while in comand of PT 109. Like Wald, Jack Warner also received anonymous mail. It contained the assertion that the President was "a sex pervert, with many mistresses," and the promise that "the scandals soon coming up for air will kill your picture and you."

In November 1961 the FBI received a letter offering proof that the President was an adulterer, "including photographs." It would not have been hard to obtain pictures that were at least embarrassing. Within days of that letter being sent, President Kennedy had allowed himself to be seen, with Marilyn at his side, at a reception in the Beverly Hilton Hotel.

Robert Kennedy had also continued to take risks. Wald, the producer of *Enemy Within*, once arrived to meet Kennedy at a house in Malibu, and found him accompanied by Marilyn.

Then danger signals began literally pouring in. On December 11, 1961, J. Edgar Hoover advised Robert Kennedy that FBI surveillance had picked up information that Sam Giancana hoped to use Sinatra to intercede on his behalf with the Kennedys. According to the information, there had been three contacts between Sinatra and the President's father.

Justice Department lawyers were now complaining that they did not see how the administration could fight the Mafia while the Kennedys continued a friendship with Frank Sinatra, a man who reportedly had criminal associates. On the initiative of a young lawyer, Dougald McMillan, department staff began preparing a series of reports on Sinatra.

Just before Christmas 1961, FBI bugs overheard Johnny Roselli talking with Giancana on the telephone. He had just been at Romanoff's restaurant with Marilyn's friend, Peter Lawford—one of the Sinatra "Clan"—and the two mafiosi now spoke of Sinatra with scorn. He had been useless to them as a hot line to the Kennedys. Roselli offered Giancana the politics of desperation: "You've got the right idea, Mo, go the other way. Fuck everybody. . . . Let them see the other side of you."

In February 1962, while Marilyn was in Mexico, surveillance of Roselli had revealed the fact that another of the President's mistresses, Judith Campbell, was simultaneously in touch with both the President and Giancana. One of the time bombs ticking away under the presidency had been detected, and the Director of the FBI moved to defuse it.

Hoover had lunch with the President within weeks, and it is assumed they discussed Judith Campbell. According to the White House phone log, there were no further contacts with Campbell. She, however, says the President continued to see her for months to come. John Kennedy, it seems, did not take Hoover's warnings seriously. Kenneth O'Donnell, the Kennedy aide present when the FBI Director met the President, later quoted Kennedy as saying, "Get rid of that bastard. He's the biggest bore."

On March 23, the day after the Hoover lunch, both Kennedys were due to fly to California. John Kennedy had planned to stay with Frank Sinatra in Palm Springs, but switched at the last minute to Bing Crosby's home in the same area. Peter Lawford later said the President asked him to organize the change because, "it was virtually a case of the President going to sleep in the same bed that Giancana, a man whom his brother is investigating, vacated only weeks before. How could anyone blame the President?" Sinatra, mightily offended, expressed his wrath partly by breaking off relations with Peter Lawford.

Marilyn herself provides the only other insider's version of the worry over Sinatra. She told Sidney Skolsky that she had been present at a gathering in the Lawford house attended by at least one of the Kennedy brothers and Sinatra himself.

Robert Kennedy, said Marilyn, held forth on why the President could no longer be seen with Sinatra. According to Marilyn the Attorney General spoke with great emphasis, and even talked of resigning if the president continued to see Sinatra. The party broke up in an icy silence.

Danger did not deter John Kennedy from seeing Marilyn again. They met within three days of the lunch with Hoover, during the presidential trip to California.

On Saturday, March 24, 1962, as Kennedy awoke in the Crosby home near Palm springs, Marilyn—now in her new home—rose early. The plumbing was temporarily disconnected during the remodeling, so she sped over to Dr. Greenson's house to wash her hair. Then she returned, had her hair done, and spent hours dressing, turning the aging Norma Jeane into "Marilyn."

Peter Lawford, who came to drive her to the desert, paced up and down in the hall, waiting. "When Marilyn came out of the bedroom," says Eunice Murray, "she was wearing a black wig over the new hairdo."

That weekend the President openly entertained famous show business guests, but Marilyn had a role not recorded in the newspapers. Two witnesses offer a glimpse of the weekend and an apparent presidential excursion from Bing Crosby's home, where he was officially staying.

Former Los Angeles County Assessor Philip Watson, who had seen Marilyn with the president at the Hilton four months earlier, was now astonished to meet them together again. At the Hilton there had been no overt intimacy, but Watson now had no doubts about the relationship.

"I was staying at a private home in Rancho Mirage," says Watson, "and I was invited to go to a party at a place that was represented to be the Sinatra compound. It was a cold desert evening, and there were, in a sense, two parties. There were a lot of people at poolside, and some people were wandering in and out of a rambling Spanish-style house. I did not see Sinatra, but Marilyn was there and the President was there, and they were obviously together. There was no question in my mind that they were there having a good time, doing what comes naturally."

Watson says the President was with Marilyn at a cottage in the grounds, and was receiving a selected few guests. Watson was taken in, as he had been at the Hilton, by a friend keen to help his campaign to become Assessor. He spoke briefly to the President, who remembered him from their last meeting. "There were only two or three other people present," Watson says. "The President was wearing a turtleneck sweater, and she was dressed in a kind of robe thing. She had obviously had a lot to drink. It was obvious they were intimate, that they were staying there together for the night."

The second witness corroborates Watson's eyewitness impression of what was going on that weekend at Palm Springs. In her last months Marilyn often confided in Ralph Roberts, the actor and masseur she had first met at the Strasberg home in New York. In her darkened room, as Roberts tried to ease her insomnia with a long, relaxing massage, Marilyn would discuss the mechanics of the human anatomy, a subject on which she was herself well informed.

Marilyn had mentioned to Roberts that she expected to see the President shortly, and asked him to explain how, as the old song has it, the thigh bone connects to the hip bone. During the Palm Springs weekend, Roberts received a call from Marilyn. She sounded mischievous.

"I've been arguing with my friend," she said, knowing that Roberts would know who she was talking about, "and he thinks I'm wrong about those muscles we discussed. I'm going to put him on the phone, and you can tell him."

"A moment later," Roberts recalls, "I was listening to those familiar Boston accents. I told him about the muscles, and he thanked me. Of course, I didn't reveal that I knew who he was, and he didn't say."

Marilyn later told Roberts that she and Kennedy had started discussing the muscle system while she was massaging the President's bad back. "I told him he should get a massage from you, Ralph," Marilyn said, "but he said that wouldn't really be the same. I think I made his back feel better."

Clearly, Marilyn was dangerously talkative. She had by now discussed her relations with the Kennedy brothers with a whole string of friends. The President and the Attorney General, for their part, had behaved as though they were untouchable. In secret, others had been eavesdropping. Some were the Kennedys' sworn enemies, and their activity placed the presidency itself in jeopardy.

38

SHORTLY AFTER MARILYN'S RETURN from Mexico the phone rang in the home of Art James, the real-estate agent who had known Marilyn for years, ever since her affairs with Charlie Chaplin, Jr., and Edward G. Robinson, Jr. James, Chaplin, and Robinson, long close friends, often saw Marilyn now that she was living in Los Angeles. People knew about James' friendship with her, and that was why he received the troubling telephone call in March 1962.

The caller was a go-between, passing on a message from Carmine DeSapio, the corrupt Tammany Hall politician with links to the Mafia, and especially to Teamsters' boss Jimmy Hoffa. "The request," says James, "was that I should get Marilyn away from her house for a while, perhaps for a weekend at my place in Laguna Beach. They wanted her place empty so they could install bugging equipment. I knew about Marilyn's relations with Robert Kennedy—she had told me—and that was evidently the reason for wanting to bug her."

"I told them I wouldn't do it," James says today, "and I didn't. To my great relief I never heard any more about it. But I did not warn Marilyn. I figured she worried about things enough, anyway. And if they wanted to bug the house, they would find a way."

Marilyn's new California home was indeed wide open to eavesdroppers. With the extensive remodeling going on throughout 1962, workmen were constantly coming and going. As for her New York apartment, it was empty a good deal of the time—an easy target.

Research for this book has turned up a mass of information indicating that Marilyn and the Kennedy brothers were indeed the target of electronic eavesdropping, and that it began as early as 1961. Ironically, according to one source, it may have been commissioned initially, not by criminals at all, but by Marilyn's former husband, Joe DiMaggio.

Whatever happened to Marilyn mattered to DiMaggio. He had hired private detectives to watch her years earlier, at the time of the "Wrong Door Raid." Now, in his role as Marilyn's protector, he allegedly did so again.

I tracked down John Danhoff, a policeman at a Department of Defense facility who had once worked for Fred Otash, the private detective who had helped extricate Frank Sinatra from the embarrassments of the "Wrong Door Raid." Danoff had been involved in many surveillance operations for Otash and claims Marilyn was the target of several.

Danoff says Joe DiMaggio would often telephone Otash's office, and sometimes came in for discussions. "I got the impression," he recalls, "that DiMaggio remained intensely interested in Marilyn, and wanted to be kept informed of all her movements."

In 1961, according to Danoff, the Otash team succeeded in wiring the rooms and telephone lines at both Marilyn's apartment and the Lawford beach house. They were also "hooked into" Marilyn's answering service.

Danoff's main part in the operation, he says, was to sit in a vehicle monitoring receiver equipment. The bug at the Lawford house, he claims, transmitted desultory conversation between the President and Marilyn, and the unmistakable sounds of lovemaking. Danoff's recollection is that this occurred "around Thanksgiving" in 1961. As we have seen, the President was in Los Angeles that November, and did meet Marilyn.

Danoff is described as "an honest informant" by a Treasury Department intelligence agent who used him in the sixties. His former employer, Fred Otash, denies any personal involvement in bugging Marilyn and the President, but adds, "You're right, there was surveillance." Otash says, and a colleague confirms, that government agents forced him to hand over files on both Kennedy brothers at mid-term in the Kennedy presidency.

John Dolan, the former boss of an East Coast detective agency, recalls visiting Los Angeles, shortly after Marilyn's death, for a meeting of the Council of International Investigators. There, along with others, Dolan met Fred Otash. "Otash said," Dolan recalls, "that he had had a tap on Monroe's phone, and supposedly did this tap for Joe DiMaggio." Victor Piscitello, a former president of the World Association of Detectives, was present at the same Los Angeles meeting. He too remembered the conversation with Otash.

If DiMaggio did commission a surveillance operation, however innocently, there was serious risk of a leak. Danoff, for example, says that he met mobsters Mickey Cohen and Johnny Roselli while working for Otash. DiMaggio himself, while doubtless interested in Marilyn for purely personal reasons, sometimes circulated in places and with people with disturbing associations.

Judith Campbell, who consorted with the President and Mafia boss Giancana at the same time, has told how she once complained to Giancana that she could not get a reservation at the Plaza Hotel in New York. "Don't worry," Giancana said. "When you get there, call Joe DiMaggio . . . he'll get you into the Plaza."

Marilyn's former husband spent a good deal of time at Lake Tahoe, where he had an old friend in the gangster Skinny D'Amato, the manager of the Cal-Neva Lodge. D'Amato, interviewed in 1984, said he and DiMaggio had been close since the forties. He proudly pointed to numerous photographs of himself posing with DiMaggio.

Whatever their source, mobsters did learn at the time about the Kennedy's and Marilyn. Phyllis McGuire, who was seeing Giancana all the time, says she knew about the affairs as they progressed. Skinny D'Amato told me, "I knew—we knew— about Monroe and the Kennedys, and about Robert especially, but I'm not going to be quoted on it. Imagine it, a friend of Frank Sinatra being quoted as saying what we knew about Marilyn." D'Amato, clearly a very sick man when he talked to me, died soon afterward.

Arthur Balletti, a Florida wireman involved in another bugging operation commissioned by Giancana, says he learned in 1961 that Marilyn had met with the President at a house in Virginia, just outside Washington.

Teamsters' leader Jimmy Hoffa is at the center of the most specific allegation that criminals obtained compromising information on Marilyn and Robert Kennedy. At the core of the story is Hoffa's personal wireman, Bernard Spindel.

Spindel was a pioneer in the field of electronic eavesdropping. He saw war service with the U.S. Army Signal Corps, where his technical brilliance brought postings to intelligence agencies. After the war Spindel turned his skills to all the tricks involved in divorce and fraud cases. Then, in the mid-fifties, he was hired by Jimmy Hoffa to bug his own Teamsters' colleagues and to advise him on defense against other eavesdroppers. From then on he worked regularly for Hoffa.

Spindel was a problem for Robert Kennedy. He was effective in protecting Hoffa, and expert at avoiding conviction himself. Kennedy had once tried to "turn" Spindel, to get him to testify against Hoffa. The plan misfired, and from then on the two men detested each other.

Spindel is dead, but during research for this book I located Earl Jaycox, who was his assistant in 1962. A bluff man, who displayed no partisan feelings during extensive interviews, he appears to have been strictly a technician. "Some months before Marilyn Monroe died," Jaycox recalls, "Spindel showed me some tapes. I was in the dining room of his house at Holmes, New York. I remember he held up two tapes, and said, 'I've got to give you copies of these, so you can keep a set.' He said they were tapes of conversations between Marilyn Monroe and Bobby Kennedy. There were two seven-inch reels, fifteen hundred feet of tape, which could contain twelve hours of conversation. . . . He said the tapes included conversations with both Kennedys."

"Spindel made it clear," says Jaycox, "that there had been a relationship with John Kennedy, and that there was a current one with Robert Kennedy."

After Marilyn's death, says Jaycox, he was working in New York on security inspections for Fabergé, the perfume company, which had premises not far from Marilyn's old apartment on East 57th Street. He says, "Bernie made mention to me rather gleefully that he'd just received all the toll receipts for calls going from Marilyn's apartment. . . ." Jaycox says Spindel had originals of the toll receipts, and that they showed calls to Robert Kennedy in Washington. Though the toll receipts involved only Bobby Kennedy, Spindel's tapes, as Jaycox understood it, covered conversations with the President as well.

Spindel told Jaycox that some of the information on Marilyn and Robert Kennedy came from a bug installed at the Justice Department in Washington. Spindel described the bug as transmitting through conductive paint from a device hidden in the baseboard of the Attorney General's office. The "product" was then collected by Spindel's contact in the Justice Department.

Preposterous though this sounds, newly obtained FBI documents show that, from summer 1961 till the spring of the year Marilyn died, there was serious concern that Hoffa had "two contacts in the Criminal Division of the Department." One Hoffa infiltrator was identified and investigated; the second source of the leaks remains a mystery. Was this Spindel's hidden bug, rather than a human being?

We know Marilyn did make frequent calls to the Justice Department, from interviews with Kennedy's own secretary and from what remains of Marilyn's California telephone records. The most distinguished corroboration for Spindel's claims, though, comes from a man who spent much of his career working for Robert Kennedy.

James Kelly, a former police detective, worked closely with Robert Kennedy on Senator McClellan's Committee on Investigations, Kennedy's original forum for the pursuit of Hoffa. He went on to become Chief Investigator for another congressional committee, and director of a law enforcement training project for the Justice Department. Kelly also worked for the CBS News' Fact-finding Unit, and became director of a Boston television channel. He was universally respected for his integrity as a congressional investigator. His investigative skills had been praised by Kennedy personally, in *The Enemy Within*.

Kelly knew Spindel from 1955, when the electronics expert was acting as a consultant to the New York City Anti-Crime Committee. Although on opposing sides of the law enforcement fence, the two men developed a professional respect for each other. Kelly was sometimes an overnight guest at Spindel's country home.

In 1979, shortly before his death, Kelly had lunch in Washington with Dan Moldea, the author of a major book on Jimmy Hoffa. One Kennedy loyalist was confiding in another, and Moldea was shocked to hear what Kelly said when the talk turned to wiretapping and Bernard Spindel. Kelly said Spindel had not only told him about his "Monroe tapes," but had allowed him to hear one of them. It was purportedly a record of "pillow talk" between Marilyn and one of the Kennedys. The sound quality was poor and somewhat garbled, as are many surveillance tapes. Kelly, however, who knew both brothers, believed the tape was genuine.

Joseph Shimon, the former Washington police inspector, knew both Spindel and Hoffa well. "Jimmy Hoffa hired Spindel," says Shimon. "He was trying to get something on Bobby to blackmail him. . . . The rumor was that Bobby was playing around with Marilyn Monroe, and Spindel was to bug Marilyn—and I knew Bernie was out on the West Coast that year."

Hoffa himself was asked directly, in the seventies, what he

had known about the Kennedy brothers' sex lives. He reacted with a series of violent denials when asked if he had Marilyn bugged, adding, "I already had a tape on Bobby Kennedy and Jack Kennedy, which was so filthy and nasty—given to me by a girl—that though my people encouraged me to do it, I wouldn't do it. I put it away and said the hell with it. Forget about it. . . ." Asked whether he might have wanted to use such a tape against Robert Kennedy, Hoffa declared, "I would not embarrass his wife and family."

Few would believe that protestation. Two of those closest to Hoffa say he did obtain smear information on Robert Kennedy. Chuck O'Brien, Hoffa's foster son and once-trusted aide, still with the Teamsters, says, "Spindel told me he was in California working on this thing. He was working on the Monroe thing for the old man and for some political people. He did obtain tapes."

Laurence Burns, who was then a Teamsters' attorney, says he was "well aware" that Hoffa got compromising material on Kennedy, but declines to discuss the matter further. "It's a touchy subject," Burns says. "Hoffa was closemouthed."

Hoffa disappeared, presumed murdered, in 1975, and his wiretapper, Spindel, is also dead. As we shall see, it seems Hoffa did scheme to use the Monroe affair against Robert Kennedy, and was still toying with the idea of using the information after her death. It is clear enough that he commissioned electronic eavesdropping, with evil intent, in the months before she died.

In the light of all the new information on the bugging of Marilyn, I went back to Fred Otash, the Hollywood detective alleged to have been commissioned by Joe DiMaggio. At this second interview Otash revealed, "I was contacted by Bernard Spindel on behalf of Jimmy Hoffa. I said I would have nothing to do with it. Spindel did come out to the Coast and hit the phones. There was a room bug too—it wasn't just the phone. Barney Ruditsky had been covering Monroe already. He worked with me, and he had files on Monroe and the Kennedys."

Barney Ruditsky, the former New York policeman who organized the "Wrong Door Raid" for Joe DiMaggio, is dead. DiMaggio remains as inaccessible as he has always been on everything concerning Marilyn.

Despite all the loose ends, there is now enough testimony to indicate that there was a bugging operation against Marilyn and the Kennedys' and that tapes were obtained. It is fair to theorize that an operation that began with no evil intent—if first commissioned by Joe DiMaggio—ended up as the focus of malign interest by Jimmy Hoffa, one of the Kennedys' most dangerous foes.

If Marilyn had even an inkling of what was going on in 1962, she had good reason to be frightened. There are signs that she was indeed nervous. According to her companion, Eunice Murray, she "had her neighbors checked out" and did not have her private number printed on her telephone.

Mrs. Murray interpreted all this as a great star's natural obsession about privacy, and that may have been part of her concern. The worry, though, went deeper. In New York and California, Marilyn now made many of her calls from public telephones. Two West Coast friends, in particular, noticed this.

Robert Slatzer, who had known Marilyn since the forties, says, "She said she thought her phone lines might be tapped, and she started carrying a heavy purse of coins around—she tried to go out to a public phone when she had to make a call of any importance. She seemed very paranoid."

Arthur James, whom she saw a good deal in her last months, says, "Marilyn would call up every few weeks from a booth in Barrington Park, and say 'Please, can we meet?' She'd say she'd been standing in the booth watching the children play—it was very sad. She called from public phones, as I understood her, because she was obsessed with the idea that the secret life she was leading would leak. I couldn't blame her, when I myself had been asked a few months earlier to help bug her home. But I still didn't tell her that."

Even if Marilyn had been warned of the dangers, it is doubtful if she would have been able to fully understand and assess them. She was now highly volatile, less in control of herself than ever before.

In the spring of 1962 another friend, poet Norman Rosten, was in Hollywood. He and his wife visited Marilyn at her new home in Brentwood. They listened to her eager chatter about the house, made appreciative noises about the tin masks from Mexico and the Aztec calendar. Yet, standing in the half-furnished rooms, their windows temporarily curtained with white sheets, Rosten felt a deep unease. Listening to Marilyn, he heard only "controlled desperation."

By chance, Rosten met both DiMaggio and Sinatra. "DiMaggio," Marilyn said, "keeps an eye on me, sort of. If I have any trouble, I just call on Joe." With Sinatra, who came to take her to dinner, Marilyn seemed "giddy, a bit nervous." Next morning she called at 7:30 A.M. to talk about Sinatra. "He's nice, isn't he?" Marilyn asked.

"The tone in her voice," Rosten thought later, "was not eagerness, but panic."

One evening Rosten sat with Marilyn as they listened to a tape of him reading his poetry. She said she had "taken a little pill" before he arrived, and she got into bed. Rosten left as she lay there drowsing, with the tape recorder still turning. He felt, increasingly, that she was drifting beyond the help of friends.

On Rosten's last day in California he and Marilyn clambered into a limousine and went to look at art galleries. Marilyn's eye was caught by a Rodin, as it had been seven years earlier—again with Rosten—in New York's Metropolitan Museum of Art. This Rodin, one of a set of bronze copies, showed a man and woman embracing—the man predatory, the woman submitting. "Look at them both," said Marilyn, "how beautiful. He's hurting her, but he wants to love her, too." She promptly bought the statue—for more than a thousand 1962 dollars—and insisted on rushing off to show her purchase to Dr. Greenson. What followed was troubling to both Rosten and the psychiatrist.

Greenson said he found the statue striking. Marilyn, not satisfied, kept touching it. "What does it mean?" she wanted to know. "Is he screwing her, or is it a fake? I'd like to know. What's this? It looks like a penis." Her voice was oddly on edge. Examination suggested it was not a penis, but Marilyn kept asking, "What do you think, Doctor? What does it *mean*?"

Rosten felt Marilyn wanted answers to the unanswerable—how could she feel, recognize, be protected against, love's tenderness or brutality? "The truth was," he decided, "she was falling apart."

Rosten knew nothing of Marilyn's tangled involvement with the Kennedy brothers, had no inkling of electronic eavesdroppers or of the sinister forces swirling around her. Sidney Skolsky, her reporter friend, did know by now—from Marilyn—about the connection with the President. She called Skolsky regularly each weekend, in an atmosphere of intrigue so palpable that Skolsky got his daughter to listen on an extension to witness what was said.

"She was lost," Skolsky reflected later, "a climber. A child of nature. The higher she climbed the more lost she became. Like Hemingway's leopard on Mount Kilimanjaro."

39

IN THE MIDST OF Marilyn's turmoil, there was a film to be made. A few months earlier, Marilyn had sat down in the Polo Lounge of the Beverly Hills Hotel and guzzled three bottles of champagne. She drank them with the paternal assistance of Nunnally Johnson, the scriptwriter of two previous Monroe screenplays. Now they were talking about *Something's Got to Give*, the film which Twentieth Century-Fox insisted that Marilyn make and which Dr. Greenson hoped would get her out of herself.

Marilyn had little confidence in the movie, a rehash of a 1939 comedy called *My Favorite Wife*—the story of a woman, presumed dead for years, who comes home the day her husband remarries. The studio hoped to convince her, with the appointment of Henry Weinstein—a friend of Dr. Greenson— as producer and Johnson as scriptwriter, that it could be a success. Marilyn was agonizing over Arthur Miller's real-life remarriage, but Johnson—and the champagne—won her over.

"She had slipped during the last two years," Johnson recalled, "and she was convinced that this was the one that would bring her back." When he left California, the script complete, Marilyn rose uncharacteristically early to see him off. She got herself up to Johnson's hotel room by telling the desk she was a prostitute, then drove him to the airport "soaring with happiness." Once he was gone, things quickly fell apart.

Marilyn had confidence in her director, the great George Cukor, with whom she had made *Let's Make Love*. That trust, though, was soon dissipated in arguments about the script. Cukor felt it was still not right, and in early April, two weeks before shooting was due to start, a new scriptwriter was asked to produce another rewrite. The changes threw Marilyn into panic, and her friend Nunnally Johnson was not there to hold her hand.

Something's Got to Give was doomed, caught up in a disaster greater than the fears and foibles of its star. Twentieth Century-Fox was being bled dry by the financial hemorrhage caused by another star and another movie half a world away, in Rome: Elizabeth Taylor and her *Cleopatra*. The studio had lost $22 million the previous year, and the new Monroe film was seen as a relatively low-budget moneymaker. The star came cheap—she was to be paid a mere $100,000, under the old 1955 contract with Fox made by Milton Greene. For Marilyn it was a way to work out her commitment. Nobody got what they wanted.

Producer Weinstein had feared the worst weeks earlier, when he personally rescued Marilyn from a barbiturate overdose. Now he discovered that this was indeed "one very ill, very paranoid lady." Marilyn was sent script pages with the suggestion that she put one cross by a line she felt uncertain about, and a double cross—XX—by one she really disliked. To Weinstein's consternation, Marilyn read this as meaning that, somehow, she was going to be double-crossed. Only Dr. Greenson's intervention resolved the upset.

The new scriptwriter, Walter Bernstein, found Marilyn "at once tentative, apologetic and intransigent."

"Remember you've got Marilyn Monroe," she told him once, when she insisted on wearing a bikini in a scene. "You've got to use her."

This Monroe, however, outdid her own legendary insecurity. She convinced herself that fellow actress Cyd Charisse wanted to have blonde hair like herself. Assured that Charisse's hair would be light brown, Marilyn replied knowingly, "Her *unconscious* wants it blonde."

Just to be on the safe side, the studio darkened the hair of even the fifty-year-old actress playing the part of a housekeeper. Scriptwriter Bernstein was ordered to remove any and all lines suggesting that Marilyn's screen husband, Dean Martin, could be attracted to any other woman.

The studio could fall over itself to please, but it had no way to counter Marilyn's absenteeism. In thirty-five days' shooting, Marilyn graced the studio with her presence only twelve times. When she did appear, the guard at the studio gate would shout to subsequent arrivals, "She's back! She's back!"

The excuse was illness. Marilyn had been suffering from a virus, ever since the Mexico visit that gave her sinusitis and sporadic high temperatures. The study of her temperature now became everyone's daily preoccupation. It was agreed that the star would work unless the thermometer registered higher than 98.8 degrees, and executives hovered in the corridors as the studio doctors made the crucial readings.

Marilyn was by now cooperative only when it suited her. Hairdresser George Masters, attending her at home, recalls maddening delaying tactics. "She tried to keep me 'accidentally on purpose,' by smearing cream in her hair, just so I wouldn't make a plane. When I was getting her ready to go out she would take nine hours. Not that I worked on her all that time—she just wanted me to be there."

At the studio, Marilyn was infuriating. One day she swept out on learning that Dean Martin had a cold, deaf to medical assurances that he was no longer contagious. Virus or no virus, she procrastinated. Billy Travilla, her designer friend, was walking toward the studio exit one afternoon when a limousine stopped beside him. The window rolled down, and a figure in dark glasses called excitedly, "Billy! Billy!" Then, after chatting normally for a minute, Marilyn clapped a hand to her mouth. "Oh, Billy," she whispered hoarsely, "I forgot. I've lost my voice today."

When she did arrive at the studio in the mornings, Marilyn was sometimes seen standing near the entrance gate, retching. Producer Weinstein, a kind man, put it down to sheer dread of performing. "Very few people experience terror," he says today. "We all experience anxiety, unhappiness, heartbreaks, but that was sheer, primal terror."

Marilyn's anchor, to the extent that she had one at all, was Dr. Greenson. She saw him almost every day. As crisis followed crisis, and as Marilyn threatened to fall back wholly on drugs, his sessions with her would last four or five hours. "I had become a prisoner of a form of treatment that I thought was correct for her, but almost impossible for me," Greenson later wrote. "At times I felt I couldn't go on with this."

Greenson's wife was unwell, and the doctor had repeatedly postponed a vacation in order to see Marilyn through the movie. On May 10, leaving her in the care of a colleague, he departed with his wife for Europe. That very day, Marilyn's "virus" stopped production. A week later she absconded to

the East Coast to make her last memorable public appearance—
for President Kennedy.

Earlier, in an atmosphere of great intrigue, Marilyn had
summoned designer Jean-Louis to create a dress that was
extraordinary even for her. He says, "It was nude, very thin
material, embroidered with rhinestones, so she would shine in
the spotlight. She wore nothing, absolutely nothing, underneath. It cost about $5,000. It didn't look very pretty from
the back, but. . . ."

As Jean-Louis struggled with pins and zippers, a maid told
Marilyn, "You have a call from Hyannisport." Jean-Louis
knew that was the Kennedy home in Massachusetts, and
Marilyn's excitement told him what the dress was for. She
started singing, "Happy Birthday, Mr. Presi—" and then
said with a giggle, "Oops, I'm not supposed to say that."

The Birthday Salute at Madison Square Garden on May 19
had some of the flavor of a British Royal Birthday—it was
not held on the President's actual birthdate. Fifteen thousand
Democrats were gathering to cheer on their leader, and pour a
million dollars into party coffers. Jack Benny, Henry Fonda,
Ella Fitzgerald, Peggy Lee, and Maria Callas were going to
perform, and Peter Lawford said, "Wouldn't it be fun if
Marilyn Monroe could sing 'Happy Birthday' to the President."

The idea had been mentioned to the producers of *Something's Got to Give*, before the production turned into a
debacle. Now they protested vociferously, but Marilyn tricked
Weinstein. She pleaded a heavy period as a reason for missing yet more work. By the time Weinstein had asked himself,
"Why didn't she have a period *last* month?" it was too late.
Weakly, the producer waved good-bye as Peter Lawford
whisked Marilyn away from the studio aboard Frank Sinatra's
helicopter.

The terror was on Marilyn again. With Joan Greenson
listening, she had sat in the bathtub to rehearse, turning
"Happy Birthday" into a seduction serenade. She would
falter, muttering that she would never be able to pull it off.
Joan Greenson had then lent her a children's book, *The Little
Engine That Could*, about a broken-down train that tried and
tried, and finally made it over the mountains. Marilyn took it
with her to New York, for reassurance.

In her Manhattan apartment, Marilyn practiced her special
lyrics hour upon hour, singing along to a rehearsal record.
The gala organizers instructed her to drop in a couple of extra
lines of her own, sly little political digs concocted with the

help of Danny Greenson. She was still bungling even the well-known birthday refrain, and the President was forewarned by telephone. He laughed heartily. As the moment approached, heavy shots of liquor were added to the comfort of *The Little Engine That Could.* By the time Marilyn was waiting in the wings at the Garden, she was drunk. Sewn, literally, into her dress, she could hardly move.

Out in the vast auditorium sat the Kennedy brothers. Robert was with his wife, but the President had come alone. In spite of the glamour of the occasion, the First Lady was in Virginia—horseback riding.

John Kennedy sat in the presidential box, feet up on the rail, chomping contentedly on a cigar. With the show in full swing, Peter Lawford took the microphone to start a running gag.

"Mr. President," he announced, "on this occasion of your birthday, this lovely lady is not only pulchritudious but punctual. Mr. President—Marilyn Monroe!" The audience cheered, but no Marilyn appeared.

Later, after acts by other stars, the brother-in-law coughed, looked over his shoulder, and again announced: "A woman of whom it may truly be said—she needs no introduction." On a drum roll, nothing happened.

Marilyn was to be the finale. At last Lawford said, "Mr. President, because, in the history of show business, perhaps there has been no one female who has meant so much, who has done more—" (here the audience tittered) "Mr. President—"(a heavy emphasis now) "the *late* Marilyn Monroe!"

In the wings, Lawford's agent, Milt Ebbins, virtually propelled Marilyn onto the stage. For a long thirty seconds she collected herself. Then, soft and hesitant, she began:

> Happy—birthday—to you,
> Happy birthday to you,
> Happy birthday Mr. Pres—id—ent,
> Happy birthday to you.

After applause, Marilyn went on—with no mistakes—into the special verse written by Richard Adler to the tune of "Thanks for the Memory":

> Thanks, Mr. President,
> For all the things you've done,
> The battles that you've won,

> The way you deal with U.S. Steel,
> And our problems by the ton,
> We thank you—so much.

Marilyn led the throng in a birthday chorus, and stepped away from the microphone. Then the President said, "Thank you. I can now retire from politics after having had, ah, 'Happy Birthday' sung to me in such a sweet, wholesome way."

After the gala, at a backstage gathering, Marilyn introduced the President to her former father-in-law, Isadore Miller, whom she had invited along that evening. Later she appeared at a smaller party given by Arthur Krim, President of United Artists. Arthur Schlesinger, then Special Assistant at the White House, observed her there. He was "enchanted by her manner and her wit, at once so masked, so ingenuous and so penetrating. But one felt a terrible unreality about her—as if talking to someone under water."

Adlai Stevenson, the American representative at the United Nations, recalled getting to Marilyn "only after breaking through the strong defenses established by Robert Kennedy, who was dodging around her like a moth around the flame."

Schlesinger, who included himself among the moths, wrote in his journal: "Bobby and I engaged in mock competition for her; she was most agreeable to him and pleasant to me—but then she receded into her own glittering mist."

Marilyn was back in Hollywood for work on Monday morning. The next day, a special hush descended over Stage 14 at Twentieth Century-Fox. Marilyn, back from the East Coast in apparently high spirits, was about to do a swimming scene for *Something's Got to Give*. It was scripted as a nude midnight dip, and she first entered the water in a flesh-colored bikini. The cameraman complained that it was obvious she was wearing a bathing suit. Marilyn consulted with director George Cukor, then vanished into her dressing room.

Minutes later she was back, as an electrician called to a colleague that one of the overhead lights was not bright enough. "Bobby," he called to the lighting operator, "will you make 10-K a little hotter?"

Below, by the pool, Marilyn giggled. "I hope Bobby is a girl," she said. Then she shrugged off her blue robe and slipped naked into the water.

Cukor had cleared the set of all casual bystanders, but had not said why. So it was that three still photographers, on routine call for the studio, found themselves snapping away, oblivious at first they they were taking the first nude pictures of Marilyn Monroe since the famous calendar pictures of a dozen years earlier.

William Woodfield, one of the still photographers, recalls, "We didn't have any idea what was going to happen. We couldn't really see much while she was in the water. Then, as she came out of the pool, it was suddenly very apparent that she was wearing nothing. The motor drives on our Nikons were whirring, we were taking picture as fast as we could— and then she was gone."

The fact that Marilyn had performed naked promptly made news. It brought welcome publicity for the studio, and generous comments about Marilyn's fine state of physical preservation. Her figure, the world was informed, was still a miraculous 37-22-35. The next month, *Life* magazine printed a series of pictures revealing enough to show that Marilyn was naked but fairly decorous all the same.

Meanwhile, as they rushed their films to processing, Woodfield and his colleagues realized they were sitting on a gold mine. "Some of the pictures showed nipples and her behind," Woodfield remembers, "and we couldn't release them without Marilyn's personal permission. So we went to see her. She said, in effect, 'Look, fellas, what I want is to push Liz Taylor off the magazine covers around the world. Let me look through the photographs, and take out what I want—and you get me on the covers.' "

The photographers mounted a slick marketing operation. After Marilyn had checked the pictures (she deleted very few), they created an air of drama by placing the originals in a bank vault. Then they sent a set of copies to Hugh Hefner, publisher of *Playboy*, which, in 1962, was the only possible American market for such pictures. Hefner made a deal for a record price of $25,000, and global sales brought the total to more than $150,000.

Woodfield says with feeling, "It had been a good morning's work. . . ." In 1949, when Norma Jeane had posed for the nude calendar, she had been paid $50, and the photographer made $200. *Playboy*, as it turned out, published its pictures of the nude swim after a delay of more than a year, a decent interval after Marilyn's death.

On June 1, Marilyn was thirty-six. That evening, a mink beret perched on her head, she stood misty-eyed behind a cake adorned with crackling sparklers. It was her turn to listen to "Happy Birthday," raggedly sung by the crew of *Something's Got to Give*. Her stand-in, Evelyn Moriarty, had arranged for the cake, which was decorated with two replicas of Marilyn in scenes from the movie, one in a négligée and one in a bikini. The inscription on the cake read: "Happy Birthday (Suit)."

Later that evening at Dodger Stadium, Marilyn threw out the first ball in a baseball game for the benefit of the Muscular Dystrophy Association. Studio executives, fearing more illness, had begged her not to go. She went anyway, partly because she had promised to take Dean Martin's young son. Then she dined with a friend, and went home to drink champagne with Danny and Joan Greenson, sitting on cardboard boxes in the half-furnished house.

The Greensons gave her a champagne glass with her name engraved inside. "Now," Marilyn said, "I'll know who I am when I'm drinking."

Her birthday had been on a Friday. Within forty-eight hours Marilyn called Dr. Greenson's son and daughter at home. She sounded heavily drugged, said she was unhappy, and they hurried over.

"She was in bed naked, with just a sheet over her," Danny Greenson remembers, "and she was wearing a black sleeping mask, like the Lone Ranger wore. It was the least erotic sight you could imagine. This woman was desperate. She couldn't sleep—it was the middle of the afternoon—and she said how terrible she felt about herself, how worthless she felt. She talked about being a waif, that she was ugly, that people were only nice to her for what they could get from her. She said she had no one, that nobody loved her. She mentioned not having children. It was a whole litany of depressive thoughts. She said it wasn't worth living any more."

Nothing the younger Greensons said could reassure Marilyn. With their father on vacation out of the country, they called in one of his psychiatrist colleagues. He saw the array of pill bottles by the bed, and promptly swept them into his bag. There was nothing more the Greensons could do, so they left.

The crisis continued all the next week. Paula Strasberg, her acting coach, called the studio to say Marilyn was sick. The next day, unable to use the phone herself, Marilyn got Eunice Murray to call Dr. Greenson in Europe with a list of questions that seemed urgent to her.'' Mrs. Murray says she cannot remember what the questions were.

On Thursday that week, her black wig crammed on her head, Marilyn went for a nose X ray. She also consulted Dr. Michael Gurdin, a plastic surgeon, complaining of a nose injury. Gurdin remembers being told she had ''slipped in the shower.'' Mrs. Murray says she cannot remember either the injury or the medical visits.

Meanwhile, at Fox, the curtain was falling on the famous career. The producers, viewing the rushes of *Something's Got to Give,* saw a Marilyn who was acting ''in a kind of slow motion that was hypnotic.'' Director George Cukor was shaken by what he saw, and top executives were talking about finding a replacement for her.

Dr. Greenson called Henry Weinstein, the producer, to say he was on his way home. He would, he promised, have Marilyn back on the set by Monday. Greenson flew to Los Angeles at once, arriving late at night, and drove straight to his patient's house. He was too late. On Friday, Marilyn had been fired. Then the movie was canceled altogether.

''The star system has got way out of hand,'' said Fox Executive Vice-President Peter Levathes. ''We've let the inmates run the asylum and they've practically destroyed it.'' He was speaking three days after Marilyn's dismissal, as *Something's Got to Give* collapsed in a tempest of recriminations and lawsuits. The studio sued Marilyn for half a million dollars. When Dean Martin refused to work with any other actress, they sued him too.

Marilyn, for her part, rushed off telegrams to all and sundry. Members of the *Give* crew had placed a sardonic announcement in *Variety,* ''thanking'' her for putting them out of work. She responded with a message to each of them saying, ''Please believe me. It was not my doing. I so looked forward to working with you.'' She reached Frank Sinatra, then in Monte Carlo, and he asked the attorney they shared, Milton Rudin, to intercede with the studio.

Less than two months later, on Marilyn's death, it would be said she died in a state of depression following professional disgrace. Yet Marilyn did not weep long over the dismissal. Indeed, as the studio realized, nobody could replace Monroe, and negotiations soon began to reinstate her. Meanwhile, Marilyn embarked on a remarkable series of advertisements for herself.

Within two weeks of being fired, she was engaged in

lengthy interviews and photographic sessions with three major magazines, *Life*, *Vogue*, and *Cosmopolitan*.

"Thirty-six," Marilyn told one interviewer, "is just great when kids twelve to seventeen still whistle." Susan Strasberg, daughter of her coach, told her she was looking good. "You know," Marilyn responded, "I am in better shape than I've ever been in. My body looks better now than when I was a young girl." To prove it, she pulled up her blouse to show off her breasts.

In the few weeks that remained to her, Marilyn sought to show that her body could graduate through sixteen years, from *Laff* and *Peek* to the glossies of the sixties, without losing allure. For *Life*, she swung from the rafters in sweater and pants. At Peter Lawford's beach house, for *Cosmopolitan*, she posed champagne glass in hand, and stood windswept, in a Mexican sweater, at the ocean's edge.

In extraordinary night sessions for *Vogue*, at the Bel-Air Hotel, Marilyn indulged her exhibitionism one last time. Alone with the photographer and the bottles of champagne she posed in furs, and was nude behind a diaphanous scarf. Finally she was photographed completely naked. The camera saw the weariness, the slash in the belly—a legacy of the gall bladder operation—but the cameraman saw some sort of immortality.

"Marilyn had the power," photographer Bert Stern wrote two decades later. "She was the wind, that comet shape that Blake draws blowing around a sacred figure. She was the light, and the goddess, and the moon. The space and the dream, the mystery and the danger. But everything else all together too, including Hollywood, and the girl next door that every guy wants to marry. I could have hung up the camera, run off with her, lived happily ever after. . . ."

Another observer was not so overwhelmed:

Life, which had been negotiating with Marilyn since the weekend of the President's birthday gala, sent reporter Richard Meryman to Los Angeles. He was thirty-six, Marilyn's own age, fresh from the position of Religion Editor in *Life*'s "Manners and Morals" department. The magazine was preparing a series on Fame, and Marilyn's aide, Pat Newcomb, had suggested her client as a subject. Meryman rented a tape-recorder, which he did not know how to operate, and made his way to the house in Brentwood. His interview, which Marilyn saw in print a couple of days before she died, stands as her last public testament.

Meryman was sitting in the living room, tinkering with the recorder, when a voice said, "Can I help?" The reporter's eyes moved up a pair of bright yellow pants to the famous face.

"I was struck," he says today, "by how pasty her skin was—pasty and lifeless-looking. There was not much health in that skin. It wasn't white and it wasn't gray. It was a little bit coarse, lifeless. It looked like skin that had had makeup on it for a long, long time. She looked terrific, but when you really studied that face, it was kind of cardboardy. Her hair was lifeless, had no body to it, like hair that had been primped and heated and blown a thousand times."

Meryman and Marilyn got on well. He had been asked to supply questions in advance, and at their first encounter Marilyn offered rehearsed answers. After all the years in the business, she was still preparing, just as she had for the Robert Kennedy dinner party. Gradually she relaxed, and Meryman listened as she chattered to a friend on the telephone, her high, squeaky laughter echoing through the bare rooms. The laughter was somehow troubling; it went on too long, did not seem normal.

Pat Newcomb was ever-present. Later, Meryman would remember her as "obsessively loyal, totally devoted. She had made herself Marilyn's last friend." Covertly, Marilyn apologized for Newcomb, shrugging her shoulders as if to say, "What can I do?" Newcomb, today, says she only attended the interview at Marilyn's insistence.

Marilyn told Meryman she wanted no pictures taken of her house. "I don't want *everybody* to see exactly where I live," she explained. She talked—eloquently but as she had always talked—of her deprived childhood. She talked of acting, of her allegiance to the ordinary people who made up her audiences rather than to the studio. "An actor," she said, "is not a machine."

"I've always felt," said Marilyn, "that the people ought to get their money's worth, and that this is an obligation. I do have feelings some days when there are some scenes with a lot of responsibility towards the meaning and I'll wish, gee, if only I could have been a cleaning woman. I think all actors go through this. We not only want to be good; we have to be. . . ."

"Fame has a special burden," Marilyn told the *Life* reporter. "I don't mind being burdened with being glamorous and sexual. We are all born sexual creatures, thank God, but it's a pity so many people despise and crush this natural gift. Art, real art, comes from it—everything."

Marilyn talked with yearning of the stepchildren she had found and lost in the DiMaggio and Miller marriages. Again and again, she came back to "kids, and older people, and workingmen," the people who were no threat, who understood her. When Meryman left, late that first night, he said he would bring a transcript the next day. Marilyn was glad. "I don't sleep very well," she said. "It'll give me something to read at night."

Meryman went back to the Hilton thinking that he had interviewed a woman he liked, a woman who was "very smart." "I felt very keenly," he recalls, "that Marilyn knew what she was doing every minute I was there. She was sculpting herself for me, for *Life*, for the situation, whatever it really was."

He returned several times. Marilyn read his transcript carefully, tinkered with it little. She seemed particularly concerned to make sure she had said nothing that would hurt her stepchildren, and emended those paragraphs with skill and honesty. Once, when Meryman came by appointment, he rang the doorbell in vain, although it was obvious there were people in the house. Another time, when he did get in, Marilyn went out to the kitchen and returned holding up a little ampule. "No kidding," she said, "they're making me take liver shots."

"The last time I came," Meryman recalls, "she came to the door, and talked about the flowers in the garden. I walked down the drive and she stood at the door and watched me, and called to me, and said, 'Hey, thanks!' I felt sad for her. It was very touching, that little girl thing was very strong."

There was another feeling. Meryman says, "I was glad to leave. I didn't like the atmosphere in that house—there was something creepy, something sick about it. I felt that it was an island. There was a fortress feeling, a feeling of us against the world, of being embattled."

Marilyn had given Meryman a line to fit *Life*'s theme. "Fame will go by," she had said into his microphone, "and, so long, I've had you, Fame. If it goes by, I've always known it was fickle. So at least it's something I've experienced, but that's not where I live."

They sounded like last lines, and have been treated so ever since, though Meryman had no such thought as he flew back to New York, the interview transcripts in a briefcase at his feet. At the same point on the tape Marilyn had said something else: "I now live in my work," said the nervous, rapid-fire voice. "and in a few relationships with the few people I can really count on."

There was no more work, and Marilyn was left to agonize about her friends.

40

DURING THE PHOTO SESSION for *Vogue*, the photographer noticed Marilyn looking pensive, when he wanted her laughing, alive. He asked Pat Newcomb to lighten her mood, and Newcomb said, "What about those two loves in your life?" Marilyn giggled. The photographer had no idea who the lovers were, but he got his shot.

Something's Got to Give had portrayed Marilyn as a shipwreck survivor who has been out of the world for years. She was to ask her rescuers, "Who's President now?" Told it is Kennedy, she would respond, "Which Kennedy?" In real life, Marilyn's friends could be forgiven for asking the same question, as they picked up stories linking her first to one brother, then to the other, then again to the first.

New York had been abuzz with gossip when Marilyn sang at the President's birthday concert. Legend has since placed Marilyn in bed with one or the other brother that night. Susan Strasberg, who attended the party afterward, recalls that both the President and Marilyn left early—separately.

The *New York Times*, in its normal coverage, said the President returned to his hotel, the Carlyle, at 2:00 A.M. His recent biographer, Ralph Martin, quotes an unnamed eyewitness as saying that Marilyn joined him there. If she did, she and the President had a fairly brief meeting.

Jim Haspiel, Marilyn's young friend, was waiting outside her apartment that night. He had been to Madison Square Garden earlier, and hoped to catch Marilyn for a word when she came home. She arrived alone soon after four o'clock, stepping out of a limousine, carrying her shoes.

"Her hair," says Haspiel, "was no longer groomed as it had been for the show. It now looked like cotton candy, as though she had combed it out."

Marilyn needed company and attention after she got home. Ralph Roberts, the masseur, remembers her calling him to request a massage. He shook himself awake, and hurried to her apartment to oblige.

Whatever occurred that night, the presidential follies were continuing. Once again they touch Marilyn's life, and there are allegations that add another factor to the dangerous scenario—drug-taking.

From early 1962 till his death, according to a number of sources, the President carried on a Washington liaison with a woman named Mary Meyer. Meyer, nearer to Kennedy's own age than his other mistresses, had known him since university days. In the late fifties, after a failed marriage to a senior CIA officer, she had moved to a home in Virginia, where she had Robert Kennedy and his family as next-door neighbors. During the presidency she pursued a somewhat dilettante life as a painter and friend of the famous. One friend was Jackie Kennedy, and Meyer on occasion visited the White House.

In the seventies, during a welter of controversy about her relations with the President, one of Meyer's intimates made news with the allegation that she had introduced the President to marijuana. James Truitt, a friend and former *Washington Post* executive, said Meyer took six marijuana cigarettes to the White House on one of her trysts with Kennedy. They smoked together, and the President joked about a forthcoming conference on narcotics. He also showed an interest in drug use in general, according to Truitt, and mentioned that he was familiar with cocaine.

The President also discussed drug use with Marilyn, according to a statement made by Peter Lawford in 1982, when law-enforcement officials were reviewing the circumstances of Marilyn's death. Lawford said that when Kennedy and Marilyn met at his home in 1961 "they spent a portion of the evening discussing pills."

Mary Meyer did not long survive Marilyn—she was shot dead in 1964, in circumstances that were never satisfactorily resolved. Her name came up again two years ago, with publication of an autobiography of Dr. Timothy Leary, the psychologist best known for his experiments and advocacy of mind-altering drugs, LSD in particular.

Leary, who in 1962 was conducting research at Harvard University, says Meyer came to see him in the spring of that year. She talked of a mysterious lover, "a very important man . . . a public figure." She said the lover was impressed by what he had heard of LSD, and wanted to try it himself.

Meyer had come to Dr. Leary, as a sort of academic fountainhead, to find out all she could about the drug. Intrigued, Leary obliged, and the two met several times in the coming months. Then, a few weeks later, Leary met Marilyn Monroe.

The encounter occurred in May, during Marilyn's hopeless weeks on *Something's Got to Give,* and probably just before she sang for the President. In California, just starting to take on its image as the fulcrum of the sixties' drug culture, Dr. Leary was bemused to find himself feted as the guru of psychedelia, the role that would eventually make him a household name. On the East Coast his research had been largely academic; here he found a host of people, most of them in show business, who had already been experimenting with mind-altering drugs. Some of them were doing so with the support and approval of prominent psychiatrists.

The meeting with Marilyn came at the end of a party in the Hollywood Hills attended by a mix of doctors and celebrities, including Jennifer Jones and Dennis Hopper. "I was exhausted," Leary says. "I had been rushed around town, taken to one of the big studios, and then bombarded all evening with questions about drugs. I went to a bedroom and lay down, and after a while Marilyn came in and roused me. I had not seen her earlier at the party, but guess she'd arrived after I'd gone to bed. She wanted to meet me, and she wanted me to introduce her to LSD."

Leary tried to explain that LSD was not a drug one took nonchalantly. None was taken that night—indeed it was Marilyn who pressed a drug on Leary. She gave him two pills she called "Randy-Mandys." That is the street name for Mandrax, a sedative popular among drug users in the early sixties because it gives a sense of euphoria when combined with alcohol. Marilyn said she had got hers "from a Mexican boyfriend," and joked that they were aspirin. The pills sent Dr. Leary off into a deep sleep.

Marilyn called Leary's hostess in the morning and they lunched at a restaurant on Sunset Boulevard, today called The Source. Leary, now awake and interested, found Marilyn "full of contradictions. Funny and playful, but very shrewd.

We talked about drugs, and I told Marilyn about a project I was setting up in Mexico that summer. She said she wanted to come on down and join us. But she also wanted to try LSD then and there.'' Leary says Marilyn seemed "wobbly," but he had no idea that she was under constant psychiatric care, nor how disturbed she was.

That night Leary did introduce Marilyn to LSD—"a very small dose." They drove together to the wide beach at Venice, and walked by the sea in the dark. "It was joyous," says Leary.

Dr. Oscar Janiger, now Associate Clinical Professor of Psychology at the California School of Medicine, was a central figure in West Coast drug experimentation in the early sixties. He confirms details of Leary's visit to Los Angeles that summer, and remembers that Leary's hostess, Virginia Dennison, gave Marilyn yoga lessons. Dr. Janiger says, "People I was working with knew Marilyn well."

Leary's account indicates that two of the President's women—Meyer and Marilyn—were seeking out LSD at the same period. The image of Marilyn playing with LSD, in her mental condition and at that point in her life, is horrifying.

Early in the week after her dismissal by Twentieth Century-Fox, Marilyn flew to New York. That week also, or soon after, she met for the last time with W.J. Weatherby, the British reporter she had been seeing occasionally since *The Misfits*. They had not met since the previous year. "I could see the change in her as I walked toward her," Weatherby recalls. "There was a delicate, worn air about her now . . . I couldn't believe that the woman I saw had changed so much."

Weatherby and Marilyn talked about Arthur Miller's remarriage, and then Marilyn said mysteriously, "Maybe I'll get married again myself." She seemed serious, then vouchsafed, "Only problem is, he's married right now. And he's famous, so we have to meet in secret." She added that her lover was in politics in Washington. Then, minutes later, she was singing the President's praises. She thought he was "going to be another Lincoln." Later, in Central Park, Weatherby dared to ask whether Marilyn knew the President personally. She did not reply, and went on throwing potato chips to the squirrels.

Henry Weinstein, producer of *Something's Got to Give*, dates the beginning of Marilyn's slide to death, not as her firing on June 8, but to the previous weekend, when—as we now know from the Greenson children—she was plunged in black despair.

"Something happened that weekend," Weinstein says, "and what it was nobody really knows. I mean, people *do* know. I think the only one who really knew what happened is Pat Newcomb."

Newcomb, the press aide, spent a great deal of time with Marilyn when she collapsed. According to Mrs. Murray, she brought Marilyn sedatives to replace those taken by Dr. Greenson's stand-in. It even occurred to Norman Jeffries, Mrs. Murray's son-in-law, that Marilyn "seemed to be a prisoner in her bedroom."

Pat Newcomb, for her part, vigorously denies ever supplying medication and rejects the notion that Marilyn was a "prisoner." Although a personal friend of the Kennedys' since before her time with the actress, she throws no light on what caused the sudden crisis. Yet Marilyn's total collapses during her life can generally be linked to some specific disaster: the loss of a baby or the failure of a relationship. Had Marilyn's relationship with the Kennedy brothers started to collapse?

On June 13, Marilyn sent an odd, wordy telegram. It went to Robert Kennedy's home in Virginia, and read (see following page):

> DEAR ATTORNEY GENERAL AND MRS. ROBERT KENNEDY: I WOULD HAVE BEEN DELIGHTED TO HAVE ACCEPTED YOUR INVITATION HONORING PAT AND PETER LAWFORD. UNFORTUNATELY I AM INVOLVED IN A FREEDOM RIDE PROTESTING THE LOSS OF THE MINORITY RIGHTS BELONGING TO THE FEW REMAINING EARTHBOUND STARS. AFTER ALL, ALL WE DEMANDED WAS OUR RIGHT TO TWINKLE.
>
> MARILYN MONROE

Somewhat improbably, Marilyn was refusing a Kennedy invitation. Two weeks later, though, she did meet Robert Kennedy. He flew into Los Angeles on the evening of June 26, as part of a cross-country journey to discuss organized crime. FBI documents do not mention his wife, Ethel, as being with him.

Marilyn now met the Attorney General over dinnar at the Lawford house, arriving two and a half hours late. The next day, according to Mrs. Murray and one of the neighbors, he visited Marilyn at home.

WESTERN UNION
TELEGRAM
W. P. MARSHALL, President

SYMBOLS
DL = Day Letter
NL = Night Letter
LT = International Letter Telegram

The filing time shown in the date line on domestic telegrams is LOCAL TIME at point of origin. Time of receipt is LOCAL TIME at point of destination

RA455 OA461 LE625

SSP090 SSB606 L BHA239 PD FAX BEVERLY HILLS CALIF 13 536P PDT

1962 JUN 13 PM 10 15

ATTY GENERAL AND MRS ROBERT F KENNEDY

HICKORY HILL MCLEANVIR

DEAR ATTORNEY GENERAL AND MRS ROBERT KENNEDY I WOULD HAVE
BEEN DELIGHTED TO HAVE ACCEPTED YOUR INVITATION HONORING PAT
AND PETER LAWFORD. UNFORTUNATELY I AM INVOLVED IN A FREEDOM
RIDE PROTESTING THE LOSS OF THE MINORITY RIGHTS BELONGING TO
THE FEW REMAINING EARTHBOUND STARS. AFTER ALL, ALL WE DEMANDED
WAS OUR RIGHT TO TWINKLE.

MARILYN MONROE.

JF 940A BROWN

6/14 LB 929A CC

DA1030PMCF—

DA1111PM/CF—

The rambling telegram to Robert and Ethel Kennedy, less than two
months before Marilyn's death.

Eunice Murray says Kennedy arrived alone, driving himself in an open Cadillac convertible. "He was casually dressed," she recalls, "looking almost boyish in slacks and open shirt." It was on this occasion, according to Normal Jeffries, that he was supposed "to clear out before Kennedy came." But he happened to be leaving just as the distinguished visitor arrived. According to Mrs. Murray, Kennedy stayed about an hour. She says Marilyn "did not seem bubbly or excited by his visit."

In the five weeks that remained, Marilyn would not be seen again with either Kennedy brother. By most accounts, she was now deeply dejected whenever she was out of the public eye. According to Peter Lawford, his wife, Pat, the Kennedys' sister, did her best to cheer Marilyn up. On several occasions the Lawfords invited her to stay overnight at the beach house, and once they were made acutely aware of her misery.

"I'm a light sleeper," Lawford told me, "and one night I woke up for some reason. It was dawn, and I looked out of the window and saw a figure standing on the balcony. It was Marilyn with a robe on, and it seemed like she was drunk, and I went out and said, 'Are you okay?' There were tears streaming down her face. Pat by then had woken too, and we brought her in and talked to her."

Peter Lawford claimed he did not know why Marilyn was so unhappy.

From early July, Marilyn turned to her doctors in a way that suggests utter desperation or hypochondria or both. She saw psychiatrist Greenson on twenty-seven of thirty-five days, and her physician, Dr. Engelberg, on thirteen. Assuming the doctors' records are correct, Marilyn was therefore in Los Angeles almost all that time. We know, though, from a number of witnesses, that she made at least three trips out of town—two of them to Cal-Neva Lodge at Lake Tahoe, the casino resort reportedly owned jointly by Frank Sinatra and Sam Giancana.

Peter Lawford says he and his wife took Marilyn to the Cal-Neva three weeks before she died, when Sinatra was performing there. She stayed in Chalet 52, one of the cluster of cabins used by Sinatra and his guests. The staff, from the housekeeper to the bellboys, remember a sad, withdrawn figure.

Mae Shoopman, then a cashier at the Lodge, recalls, "She wasn't well. She kept herself disguised pretty much, kept herself covered with a black scarf, and stayed in her room a good deal of the time. In fact, everyone became alarmed about it, because she would go to sleep with the telephone at her ear open to the switchboard. I think she was frightened, and it was a way of not being alone.''

It was thanks to the telephone operator, perhaps, that Marilyn did not die that weekend. Sitting up in the casino office, as the music blared and the late-shift croupiers hovered over the tables, the operator heard strange sounds and stertorous breathing on the line from Chalet 52. She called the manager, who raised the alarm, and Marilyn made it through another overdose.

Peter Lawford told me he knew nothing about the crisis till morning. In one statement to the police he said his wife, Pat, was in Marilyn's room that night, and realized the danger when Marilyn fell out of bed. Gloria Romanoff, who was also there that weekend, says, ''I think some of this gets a bit hazy because they were all drinking a good deal.''

As Romanoff recalls it, ''Marilyn drank champagne, and some vodka, and would take sleeping pills. The Lawfords walked her about, after midnight, trying to keep her awake, and I think they called Frank in, too. I remember Marilyn telling me one of her problems was that she'd taken pills so long, they didn't work for her the way they did for other people. So she'd begin about nine in the evening, and build up that lethal combination of booze and pills.''

In this pathetic state, Marilyn was whisked over the mountains to the airport at Reno, onto Frank Sinatra's private plane—which was making news that year as a sort of flying pleasure-dome—and back to the care of her doctors and her companion, Eunice Murray.

Today Murray says she recalls no trips to Tahoe. Nor does she have any recall at all on another vital issue—the possible real trigger for this week of Marilyn's despair. She may have been pregnant again.

''I'd like to be a complete woman, and have a child,'' Marilyn had said early in the year, during her trip to Mexico. She was still hoping, after all the miscarriages and all the damaging abortions. She went on talking about babies throughout her last months, and seemed to dwell on it in one of her last interviews.

In late June she told photo-journalist George Barris, ''A woman must have to love a man with all her heart to have his child. I mean, especially when she's not married to him. And when a man leaves a woman when she tells him she's going to have his baby, when he doesn't marry her, that must hurt a woman very much, deep down inside.''

Marilyn was talking less than a month after her abrupt collapse into a haze of drugs. Several people, interviewed during research for this book, believe Marilyn had been pregnant a few weeks earlier.

Arthur James, mutual friend of Marilyn with Charlie Chaplin, Jr., and Edward G. Robinson, Jr., says Marilyn came to his house at Laguna Beach for a weekend ''about a month, maybe six weeks'' before her death. Chaplin and Robinson, both now also dead, were present.

''It was obvious the poor girl was in trouble,'' says James, ''even by her standards. She had told us about the Kennedy thing previously, and now she was sick. Marilyn said she had lost a baby, and I thought there had been a miscarriage.''

A word was going around at the time that Marilyn had had an abortion. Bill Woodfield, one of the photographers on call for *Something's Got to Give,* recalls one of Marilyn's dressing-room team—he thinks it was hairdresser Agnes Flanagan—telling him that Marilyn was ''looking so poorly'' because she had just had an abortion. He was told it had been performed in Mexico.

The same suggestion is made by Fred Otash, the private investigator who was allegedly engaged in surveillance of Marilyn at this period. He says he learned from a police source at the time that there had been an abortion. ''An American doctor went down to Tijuana to do it,'' Otash asserts, ''which made Marilyn safe medically, and made the doctor safe from U.S. law.''

Bordertown abortions were commonplace in 1962, when the operation was still illegal in the United States. Ironically, on the day Marilyn died, an American woman would make international news by traveling for an abortion to Sweden, where the operation was legal.

There is no medical evidence to support the theory that Marilyn had been pregnant. Her autopsy, on August 5, offered no information one way or the other, but neither a miscarriage nor a properly performed abortion would necessarily leave traces after some weeks had passed. Marilyn's phone records do show that she was placing calls to Cedars–Sinai Hospital during June, which may or may not be significant.

The sources so far quoted on the alleged pregnancy all say they were told the father was one of the Kennedy brothers, but differ on whether he was John or Robert. Arthur James, who learned of a "miscarriage" from Marilyn herself, understood that Robert was responsible.

Two other sources, who were well placed to know what was happening to Marilyn, become relevant here. Michael Selsman, now a Hollywood producer, in 1962 worked for Arthur Jacobs, a close friend of Marilyn's who ran her press relations. He was thus a colleague of Pat Newcomb, who personally handled Marilyn. Selsman says he had heard Newcomb and his employer, Jacobs, discussing Marilyn's affairs with the President, and subsequently with Robert. They were concerned, he says, that exposure of the relationships would damage the Kennedys politically. Selsman says he too heard that Marilyn had an abortion in her last months.

Arthur Jacobs, who was also a prominent Hollywood producer, is dead. His widow, Natalie, however, is an important source on Marilyn's last year. "Everyone that knew her," says Natalie Jacobs, "knew about her and the Kennedys. It was so pathetic in those last months. Sometimes Arthur and I would stay at her house till five or six in the morning talking to her, to try to stop her drinking or taking pills."

According to Natalie Jacobs, "Arthur absolutely knew about the affair with the President. John Kennedy used to come here—Arthur told me this—very often not in Air Force I, but incognito. Don't ask me how he managed to be incognito— God knows how he did it. He always stayed at Peter Lawford's house on the beach."

She continues, "Marilyn was madly pursuing the President. I think he was enamored of her, but it was a passing thing. There's a children's book called *A Wrinkle in Time*, and I think that's what she was for him, a wrinkle in time. I am not clear what the relationship was with Bobby, but he too came to see here here."

Natalie Jacobs also heard about Marilyn's supposed pregnancy shortly before she died. "Marilyn said she had had a miscarriage. Arthur did not know whether to believe her, or whether she had fantasized it."

Marilyn's friend Arthur James, the only person who claims to have heard about the pregnancy direct from Marilyn, is still not sure what to make of it. He knew she had serious gynecological problems, and knew she would sometimes go for months without having a period.

Doctors consulted for this project say that people using drugs and alcohol lose touch with reality. Marilyn was in any case prone to fantasizing, and—not least because she appears to be the main source—the pregnancy story must be treated with caution. Truth or fantasy, it made the danger of potential scandal over Marilyn even greater. Now at last, almost certainly, the Kennedys tried to distance themselves from her.

Natalie Jacobs says that in her last weeks Marilyn desperately tried to get through to the brothers, but found herself fobbed off. ''I believe that was the cause of her final despair,'' says Mrs. Jacobs, ''and so did my husband.''

During the weekend at Laguna, some six weeks before her death, Marilyn's friend Arthur James had the same impression. ''She spoke quite openly,'' he says, ''with nothing but love and admiration for the Kennedys. But she was terribly hurt when she was told never to call or contact them—either John or Robert—again.''

Marilyn may now have seen a bitter irony in the fact that she had sung to President Kennedy, at his birthday gala, to the tune of ''Thanks for the Memory.'' For her Kennedy connection, it appears, was now severed.

41

MARILYN HAD BEEN CALLING Robert Kennedy at the Justice Department using an assumed name, according to the Attorney General's biographer, Arthur Schlesinger. Kennedy had given her a ''special number'' to call, says Marilyn's companion, Eunice Murray.

The phone records for Marilyn's home numbers have long been missing, but research for this book recovered a large part of them, covering June to early August 1962. They consist of a list of calls, compiled by police during a visit to the General Telephone Company after Marilyn's death. They show that, as of June 25, Marilyn was no longer calling a special number but the main Washington switchboard number of the Justice Department—RE7-8200 (see page 331).

The call listed on June 25 lasted only a minute, and presumably contained no significant conversation. As she was
probably told, Robert Kennedy was already in the air headed
for the West Coast by way of Chicago. She would see him
the next night for dinner at the Lawford house, and the day
after that, during the Kennedy visit to Marilyn's home witnessed by Eunice Murray and her son-in-law.

There were two more calls to the Justice Department, both
very brief, on July 2, when Kennedy had just returned to
Washington. Another occurred on July 16, when the Attorney
General was about to leave for Las Vegas, and two more the
next day.

During this month Marilyn was in repeated contact with
Robert Slatzer, the lover of years earlier who had always kept
in touch. As noted earlier,* I have traced a number of witnesses
who confirm the Slatzer relationship existed, and who were
on occasion present when Marilyn called him. In 1974, in his
controversial book about Marilyn, Slatzer said Marilyn told
him in her last weeks about her affairs with the Kennedy
brothers, and how the liaison with Robert was collapsing.‡

Slatzer's book was received with some skepticism, not
least because he used the dubious technique of wholesale
reconstructions of long conversations he could not possibly
have remembered verbatim. Now, in the context of the new
information gathered for this book, his claims seem far more
credible.

Slatzer quotes Marilyn as saying of Robert Kennedy, "He's
been ignoring me. I've been trying to reach him on the
telephone, and I just can't get to him." Slatzer said Marilyn
was cut off from Kennedy after he had the number of his
private line changed. He told me he heard this from Marilyn
in the first two weeks of July 1962, the very period that the

---

* See chapter 11, p. 84.

‡ In 1972, when he was first ready to publish his Monroe book, which
dealt at length with the Kennedy aspects of her story, Slatzer received a
specific threat that his life would be in danger if publication went ahead.
His then publisher, a minor California company, also received a frightening warning. Two men came to the home of Slatzer's editor, Thom
Montgomery, and beat up the man who answered his door in the belief
that they were attacking Montgomery. Montgomery, who confirms this
incident and other threats, says the company almost simultaneously went
out of business, summarily bought out in a way that executives believed
was part of an operation to suppress the Monroe book. The book was
published two years later, without incident, by Pinnacle House.

phone records show Marilyn started making repeated calls to the main Justice Department number. In judging Slatzer's veracity, it goes in his favor that he made his allegations years before the discovery of the telephone logs.

In the course of intensive interviews, Slatzer estimated dates of his contacts with Marilyn in a way that fits wholly with the phone records and other details, none of which Slatzer knew. Indeed, as this book goes to press, he is still unaware that the telephone logs exist.

In the summer of 1962, Slatzer produced a television wildlife series, dividing his time between Hollywood and a cutting room in Columbus, Ohio. In mid-June, he says, he visited Marilyn at home. Like others, he had heard rumors about Marilyn and the Kennedys, and asked her about it.

Marilyn startled Slatzer by admitting that she was having an affair with the younger Kennedy, and even seemed to be deluding herself that she might one day marry him—shades of her hints to British reporter Weatherby. Slatzer was appalled. He told her it was ludicrous to imagine the Attorney General would wreck his political career, and gravely endanger the President's, by doing any such thing. Monroe, however, was in no mood to listen to common sense. Slatzer says he simply warned her some more, and assumed the affair was headed for disaster.

Several weeks later—Slatzer reckons it was about ten days after the Independence Day holiday, and thus just before or after her miseries at the Cal-Neva Lodge—Marilyn called him from a pay phone to arrange a meeting, around the corner from her house. That evening they drove up the coast to the beach at Point Dume, which they had visited in the past. Marilyn, says Slatzer, seemed weary and tense. When she blurted out that Robert Kennedy had been refusing to take her phone calls, Slatzer again advised her to put the whole thing behind her.

Marilyn alternated between tears and anger. Slatzer says she suddenly fished in an outsize shopping bag and produced—from a clutter of pill bottles and makeup paraphernalia—some papers held together with a rubber band. They were handwritten, on Justice Department stationery, and Marilyn said they were notes to her from Robert Kennedy. She allowed Slatzer only a glimpse, but she also showed him "a small red book."

Marilyn let Slatzer peruse the book, which she called her "diary." He says it contained notes of conversations with Kennedy, including references to Cuba, the Bay of Pigs

June 20	Brooklyn, N.Y.	875-1367
June 20	Brooklyn, N.Y.	Mrs. Rosten - Collect
June 25	Washington	RE 7-8200
July 2	Washington	RE 7-8200
July 2	Washington	RE 7-8200
July 6	San Diego	GR 6-1890
July 6	San Diego	DiMaggio - Collect
July 9	New York City	EL 5-2288
July 9	New York	MU 3-6522
July 16	Washington	RE 7-8200
July 16	New York City	OR 3-7792
July 17	Fullerton	TR 1-3190
July 17	Washington	RE 7-8200
July 17	Washington	RE 7-8200

LONG DISTANCE

MUNROE PHONE CALLS — PO Box 6473
FROM TWO PHONES 6400 Sunset
4761890 × 472 4830 Hollywood

7/18	NYC	BR 91175	3 "	
7/23	WASH (D.C.)	RE 78200	1 "	
7/28	NYC	PL 92497	10 "	Ninichi?
4830 7/30	NYC	LA 41600	1 "	
7/30	WASH (D.C.)	RE 78200	8 "	
7/30	BKLN	TR 51367	13 "	
7/31	NYC	TR 72212	11 "	
8/3	BKLN	TR 51367	32 "	
8/4	ANANE	GR 61890	5 "	

Parts of Marilyn's phone records, missing since her death and retrieved by the author. Each of the lists cover one of the actress's two telephones. Note the eight calls to Washington RE 7-8200, a 1962 number of the Justice Department. ''Kennedy'' (in the right-hand margin) has been written in by a detective.

invasion of the previous year, and to Kennedy's determination to put Teamsters' leader Jimmy Hoffa in jail.

Incredulous, Slatzer asked Marilyn why she had made the notes. "Because," Marilyn replied, "Bobby liked to talk about political things. He got mad at me one day because he said I didn't remember anything he told me."

Many have scorned Slatzer's entire story because of the diary anecdote. Marilyn, they claim, was not organized enough to keep any sort of record. They are wrong. For years Marilyn kept scribbled notes precisely because she was disorganized. Slatzer says the book he saw was "not a day-to-day log but a record of highlights of Marilyn's activities,"—and that was in character.

Marilyn bought herself a "daily diary and memo book" as early as 1951, according to *Time* correspondent Ezra Goodman. Reporter James Bacon was amused to see her using it to write down something witty he had said. In 1955, Amy Greene noticed Marilyn carrying around "a leather-covered diary with a little key," and Susan Strasberg remembers her as "a great note-taker." As late as 1960, the writer Richard Gehman observed her jotting in a notebook. Marilyn was still scribbling during her acquaintance with Rober Kennedy, and it seems he knew it.

According to Jeanne Carmen, Marilyn's neighbor at the Doheny apartment, "She did keep some sort of diary. She would say, 'Oh, wait, I want to write that down before I forget it,' and she'd take it out and write a few lines. It could be trivial things. On one of the occasions I saw her with Bobby, he told some joke about the difference between a wife and a secretary. Marilyn reached for her book, and Bobby took a look at it and said, 'Ah, get rid of that.' At the time I thought it was purely dismissive. Now, I don't know, maybe he was really concerned."

It may be that Kennedy did tell Marilyn more than jokes and, without giving away state secrets, said things that were better left unsaid. Slatzer and the diary references aside, two people Marilyn met in Mexico say she was full of her latest conversation with the Attorney General at the Lawford house. The man who introduced her to Mexico, Fred Vanderbilt Field, tells of Kennedy's confidences about his attitude to J. Edgar Hoover. José Balaños, her Mexican lover, quotes Marilyn as saying she and Kennedy discussed Castro's Cuba. As we shall see, Marilyn's loose lips may have made her a security risk.

Less than a month before Marilyn's death, Marilyn's last agent, George Chasin, realized how close his client was to Robert Kennedy. On July 13 the government brought an anti-trust suit against his company, the Music Corporation of America, because of MCA's takeovers in the empire of show business. Chasin had been aware of a government investigation, but did not expect the suit. Six months earlier, over dinner in Romanoff's, Marilyn had warned him there would be one. When he failed to take her seriously, she hinted that her source was the Attorney General. That is not the way government is supposed to operate.

Harris Wofford, former Special Assistant to the President, says, when writing of Judith Campbell, Sam Giancana, and the CIA plots to kill Castro: "Aside from moral issues, the morass of potential blackmail in which the Attorney General found himself must have appalled him. . . . How could the CIA and John Kennedy have been so stupid? . . . . What could they or the Attorney General do to extricate themselves and minimize the risk of exposure?"

Perhaps by July the Kennedy brothers finally realized the folly of associating with Marilyn, not to mention the other women the President had been seeing. It was none too soon.

In May, after months of shilly-shallying, the CIA had told Robert Kennedy of its involvement with Mafia leaders—and with Sam Giancana and Johnny Roselli specifically—in the plots to assassinate Castro. Only two months had passed since Kennedy had been told the FBI knew that the President was seeing Judith Campbell while she was also consorting with Giancana.

Also in May, the day before the President's birthday jamboree, teamsters' leader Jimmy Hoffa had been indicted for extortion, the latest blow in a judicial assault that was now occupying all his time. In June, although investigators did not know it till later, Hoffa went so far as to discuss one solution to the problem—Robert Kennedy's murder. Sitting in his Washington office, Hoffa said of the Attorney General, "Kennedy has got to go. . . . Somebody needs to bump that sonofabitch off. . . . You know I've got a rundown on him. He drives about in a convertible and swims by himself. I've got a .270 rifle with a high-power scope on it that shoots a long way without dropping any. It would be easy to get him with that. But I'm leery of it; it's too obvious. . . ."

Hoffa said this at the end of June or in the first days of July. It was on June 27, in exactly that period, that Kennedy had visited Marilyn at home, driving alone in a convertible. It seems that Hoffa, the man said to have been requesting surveillance of Marilyn and Kennedy, indeed had "a rundown" on the Attorney General.

In the same week, in a conversation with a woman identified only as Jeanne, New York mobster Eddie McGrath had been wiretapped by the FBI. He was overheard saying, "Since when is fucking a federal offense? . . . . And if it is . . . I want the President of the United States indicted because I know he was whacking all those broads Sinatra brought him out. . . ."

Less than two weeks later, Justice Department attorneys produced the first of their reports on Frank Sinatra. Two more would follow that summer. they went into detail about the Cal-Neva Lodge and its criminal manager, Skinny D'Amato. They referred flatly to Sinatra's "friendship" with Sam Giancana, the man who had threatened to "tell all" about the Kennedys.

The man who compiled the Sinatra reports, Dougald McMillan, shies away when asked whether he knew at the time of Marilyn's simultaneous connection with the Kennedy brothers and Sinatra. "You know," he says, "I don't think I should get into that."

In May, in light of Giancana's involvement with the CIA, Robert Kennedy agreed not to prosecute the Mafia chieftain in a wiretapping case. He met FBI Director Hoover two days later, and Hoover noted that Kennedy "well knew the 'gutter gossip' was that the reason nothing had been done against Giancana was because of Giancana's close relationship with Frank Sinatra who, in turn, claimed to be a close friend of the Kennedy family. The Attorney General stated he realized this and it was for that reason he was quite concerned. . . ."

On June 27, the day Robert Kennedy visited Marilyn at home in Los Angeles, he showed uncharacteristic hesitation with regard to Jimmy Hoffa. An FBI report, partially censored for release to the public, reveals that the Attorney General conferred that day with Jerry Wald, the would-be producer of Kennedy's own exposé of the Teamsters, *The Enemy Within*. "There seems to be some question in the Attorney General's mind," said the report, "as to whether this picture should be produced until after prosecutions in which James Hoffa is involved are completed."

Robert Kennedy was aware that this was a time of extraordinary peril. There had to be an end to the Kennedys' escapades with Marilyn Monroe.

On July 19, Joan Greenson's birthday, Marilyn put on a brave show. She helped arrange a surprise party, then made a point of doing the Twist with a black girl who had no dancing partner. She and Joan were to talk on the telephone a few more times, but Marilyn's mind seemed elsewhere. Four days later she tried calling the Justice Department again, but again hung up within a minute.

Jeanne Carmen saw Marilyn briefly, and thought "she looked like death." In the midsummer nights, sleep came harder than ever. She called on Ralph Roberts for late-night massages. Once she saw Dr. Greenson twice in one day, as well as her internist, Dr. Engelberg. She also telephoned Engelberg at two o'clock in the morning.

Marilyn now indulged her taste for intrigue and the ugly side of her temper. When studio bosses came to discuss a possible revival of *Something's Got to Give,* she had Pat Newcomb hide in the next-door room to witness what was said. Paula Strasberg, summoned back from Europe to help in the negotiations, found herself spurned. Marilyn abused her for doing nothing, and Strasberg flew back to New York.

Eunice Murray was not immune to Marilyn's rage. One day her son-in-law, Norman Jeffries, arrived to find Murray with her bags packed, ready to leave. Then she stayed on, after all.

The nights began to merge with the days. While Strasberg had been there, she had awakened to see Marilyn pacing the hall in the small hours. In happier days, Marilyn had sometimes donned a wig and dark glasses to watch the merry-go-round on the Santa Monica pier. Now she was seen loitering on the pier, just a few hundred yards from the Lawford house, in the dark of the night.

At the end of the week before her death, Marilyn returned to the most dangerous territory of all—the mob-infested Cal-Neva Lodge at Lake Tahoe. Eunice Murray says she "just cannot remember" the trip, and Peter Lawford never mentioned it.

This was a trip shrouded in mystery, unmentioned in the press except by Marilyn's friend, Sidney Skolsky. Members of the Cal-Neva staff, who remember it well, tell of a miserable episode.

Joe Langford, who worked under the Bell Captain, his

brother Ray, recalls picking up Marilyn at the airport. "I'd say it was a week before she died," he says. "She came on Sinatra's plane, and I remember the pilot saying, 'God, am I glad to get rid of her.' I guess she'd been drinking heavily, she drank a lot that weekend."

Ray Langford, the Bell Captain, saw Marilyn in her chalet that weekend, after Sinatra called for room service. He places the visit "just a few days before she died." When he saw her, Marilyn had "a kerchief round her face, and dark, dark glasses. She looked very sad." Other employees tell a similar story.

When Marilyn left, says Joe Langford, it was "in an awful hurry. I think she was giving them some problems." Two witnesses—the widow of Sinatra's pilot, and the co-pilot— tell a haunting tale of the return to Los Angeles.*

Sinatra's aircraft, a twin-engined Martin named after the singer's daughter Christina, was a $6 million investment, a flying palace with wood paneling, wall-to-wall carpeting, bar, luxurious bathroom—and a piano. According to the pilot's widow, Barbara Lieto, her husband was ordered to Lake Tahoe on short notice. He came home in the early hours, uncharacteristically furious.

According to Mrs. Lieto, Marilyn boarded the plane drunk. It seems the flight first took Marilyn, Peter and Pat Lawford, and one of Marilyn's hairdressers to San Francisco. The crew waited while the passengers went into the city, then Mrs. Lawford took a commercial flight to the East Coast.

It was late when the Sinatra plane left for Los Angeles and, according to Mrs. Lieto, Peter Lawford, also now drunk, got into a violent argument with the pilot about where it should land. Lawford insisted they should land at Santa Monica, even when the pilot pointed out that the airport there was closed during the hours of darkness.

When the plane finally landed at Los Angeles, after midnight, Marilyn was "out of it, a mess." She emerged from the airplane barefoot, and the pilot had to help her put on her shoes. She then left for home in a limousine, while the crew gave Lawford a ride to Santa Monica in their car. The pilot

---

* Witnesses are somewhat confused about the timing of Marilyn's departure. At least two suggest it was the day before her death. The passing of time has presumably led them to concertina events in their minds, for other data place Marilyn fairly firmly in Los Angeles in the very last days of her life.

became further angered when Lawford insisted on stopping a few blocks from his home to make a half-hour telephone call from a public booth. Why, they wondered, could he not wait a mere five minutes, till he got to the beach house?

With hindsight, one must wonder whether Lawford, too, was now worried about security.

There had clearly been great tension during the visit to the Cal-Neva Lodge. One of Marilyn's East Coast friends, Dr. Sandy Firestone, remembers a call from Marilyn in the weeks before she died, complaining that "she was being pressured to go to parties, that she didn't particularly like Peter Lawford because he was having big orgies."

A film processor, who wishes to remain anonymous, says he developed pictures of Marilyn, taken by Frank Sinatra that last weekend. "I suggested he burn them," says the witness, "and he did—in front of me." The pictures, according to the processor, showed Marilyn in utter disarray.

During the final nightmare, Joe DiMaggio, still trying to help Marilyn, came to Lake Tahoe. The Cal-Neva Bell Captain, Ray Langford, recalls getting him a room at the nearby Silver Crest Motel. DiMaggio wanted to know where Marilyn was, and Langford, not yet aware that she had arrived—said he did not know. Langford's brother, Joe, says DiMaggio wanted to get in touch, but did not actually enter the Cal-Neva "because there was a feud between him and Sinatra at the time."

Another witness, who arrived at the Cal-Neva within a week of Marilyn's death, was told an eerie story by an employee. He recalled looking down from the casino, near dawn, to see Marilyn "at the edge of the pool, barefoot, swaying back and forth. She was staring up the hill." Concerned, the Cal-Neva man went to Marilyn, and found her still standing there, still looking upward. He followed her gaze, and there was DiMaggio standing in the driveway, "staring back."

Before she died Marilyn talked about the Cal-Neva visit to her masseur, Ralph Roberts. "She told me it was a nightmare, a dreadful weekend," Roberts recalls. "She didn't want to go particularly, and when she got there she found Joe there. She couldn't go out of her room without the conflict of Sinatra. Joe was terribly jealous of Sinatra."

Earlier in the year, when Marilyn had just moved into the new house, DiMaggio had gone to see her with Harry Hall, his old friend from sports-promotion days. "He knocked at the door,'' Hall recalls, ''and she opened it, saw Joe, and slammed the door. Joe said, 'Well, one of these days.' '' They went back again later, Hall says, and this time Marilyn let them in. He believes DiMaggio still had hopes of remarrying Marilyn, and others confirm that they had met on friendly terms in the last months.

Sometimes even DiMaggio lost patience. During *Something's Got to Give,* scriptwriter Nunnally Johnson tried to get him to go to California to help Marilyn. ''He promised to call her on the phone,'' Johnson recalled, ''but was adamant against trying anything further. . . . So far as he was concerned, she was a lost lady, and while there might be someone to save her, he wasn't the one. In short, he'd had it.''

In the last months, though, DiMaggio returned to his obsession. The goings-on at Lake Tahoe enraged him. ''He was very upset,'' says Harry Hall. ''She went up there, they gave her pills, they had sex parties, and Joe thought—because at that time he was a friend of Sinatra—it should never have happened. . . . I don't think he's ever talked to him again. He felt he should've had enough respect for Joe; he should've left her alone.''

In 1962, DiMaggio had a lucrative job, at a salary of $100,000 a year, as a representative of V. H. Monette, an East Coast company supplying American military post exchanges. He had told the company president, Valmore Monette, that he was ''still very much in love with Marilyn.'' On August 1, 1962, the week Marilyn was to die, DiMaggio quit the company. According to Monette, ''He told me he had talked to Marilyn and thought she had finally agreed to leave the movies and remarry him.''

In her final months Marilyn had acknowledged DiMaggio's devotion. She wrote her former husband:

> Dear Joe,
> If I can only succeed in making you happy—I will have succeeded in the biggest [sic] and most difficult thing there is—that is to make *one person completely happy [Marilyn's italics]*. Your happiness means my happiness.

The letter, never sent, was found after Marilyn's death.

DiMaggio was not only furious with Sinatra, he was furious with the Kennedys. In the spring of the year he had visited Marilyn along with his son Joe, Jr., and the son's fiancée, Pamela Ries. Ries remembers that Marilyn talked with DiMaggio about Robert Kennedy, and a row followed.

Marilyn was now twisting and turning in her bitterness about Kennedy. In late July, during a massage session with Ralph Roberts, she suddenly asked, "Ralph, have you heard any stories about me and Bobby?"

Roberts replied, "All Hollywood is talking about it!" To which Marilyn retorted, "Well, it isn't true. He's not my sort. He's too puny."

That same week, just before the last Cal-Neva visit, Robert Slatzer was about to leave for the East Coast. During a farewell drive with Marilyn she veered from enthusiasm to despondency, from talking about "starting a whole new life" to complaining about Robert Kennedy. She wondered gloomily whether he had abandoned her because she was not sufficiently educated. Finally she burst into tears, sobbing that men wanted her "only as a plaything." Kennedy, she supposed, "had got what he wanted."

Marilyn had said of Kennedy, as she and Slatzer looked at her diary together, "Maybe his wife would like to know some of the things he told me. It's all in here, and I'm glad I made notes."

Former private detective John Dolan, one of the sources on the wiretapping of Marilyn, says the wiretappers discovered she had been desperate enough to call the Attorney General at home in Virginia. He had been enraged.

"Robert Kennedy became incommunicado," Robert Slatzer says, "and she wasn't going to settle for that."

Paul D'Amato, the man said to have represented Giancana's interests at the Cal-Neva Lodge, confirmed to me in 1984 that Marilyn had been there just before she died. Chain-smoking Marlboros, while sitting in pyjamas in what would prove to be his deathbed, D'Amato spoke of the visit and the flight that took Marilyn away for the last time.

Then, pursing his thin lips, D'Amato murmured, "Of course, I didn't say that." He added, "There was more to what happened than anyone has told. It would've been the big fall for Bobby Kennedy, wouldn't it?"

Marilyn was now thinking about death. She consulted the lawyer she shared with Sinatra, Milton Rudin, about making a new will. She reportedly wished to cut the Strasbergs out of it because they had "taken advantage" of her. The will never was changed. Rudin, who thought "she was obviously deeply ill," kept putting Marilyn off.

Dr. Greenson, the psychiatrist, had been seeing Marilyn almost every day, except when she went to Lake Tahoe. In other circumstances, he would write to a friend within days of her death, ''I should have played it safe and put her in a sanitarium, but that would only have been safe for me and deadly for her. . . .''

Weeks earlier, talking about her career to *Life* magazine, Marilyn had said, ''It might be kind of a relief to be finished. It's sort of like I don't know what kind of a yard dash you're running, but then you're at the finish line and you sort of sigh—you've made it! But you never have, you have to start all over again.''

On July 26, Robert Kennedy came to Los Angeles once more, and made a speech to the National Insurance Association. At midday, as he was on his way to the engagement, the Los Angeles office of the FBI received an anonymous call, warning of a plan to kill him. The caller said ''gangland characters'' were plotting the murder.

On July 30, 1962, Marilyn made her final call to the Justice Department, as logged in the surviving telephone records. The call lasted eight minutes, and she made it on the Monday of her last week alive.

Part V

THE CANDLE
BURNS DOWN

"Who killed Marilyn Monroe?—that's a question. . . . That was a tragedy."

SEAN O'CASEY

42

"DO YOU KNOW WHO I've always depended on?" Marilyn had asked reporter W. J. Weatherby. "Not strangers, not friends. The telephone! That's my best friend. I love calling friends, especially late at night when I can't sleep. I have this dream we all get up and go out to a drugstore."

Marilyn worked her mechanical friend hard in her last days. Ensconced at home, she rattled off calls to friends on the East Coast. She told Henry Rosenfeld, the fashion tycoon, that she would be coming to New York soon, and wanted him to escort her to the first night of *Mr. President,* a new show opening in Washington. She called Lena Pepitone, her New York maid, and talked about plans to give a party in September.

Marilyn was in a whirl of discussions about future projects. She talked to Gene Kelly about a musical with a World War I setting, to Sidney Skolsky about a film on Jean Harlow, with herself playing the lead. She made outings to a screening room to see the films of director Lee Thompson, who was keen to use her in the film that would later be made as *What a Way to Go.* She spoke to composer Jule Styne about plans for a musical version of *A Tree Grows in Brooklyn,* starring herself and Frank Sinatra.

Firm arrangements came out of the calls. On Sunday Marilyn was due to meet with Skolsky and Kelly, then dine with Sinatra and the Romanoffs. She was scheduled to see Lee Thompson on Monday, then fly to New York to meet with Styne.

None of the people Marilyn spoke to thought she sounded depressed that last week. Two old friends from the studio, makeup man Whitey Snyder and wardrobe assistant Marjorie Plecher, came round for drinks. Today they recall, "She never looked better; she was in great spirits."

There were glimpses of another mood. Marilyn called the California psychic, Kenny Kingston, whom she had consulted in the past. On this occasion her theme was love. Kingston, who gets carried away remembering it, quotes Marilyn as saying, "Love is the one immortal thing about us. Without it, what can life mean?"

On Wednesday that week, gynecologist Dr. Leon Krohn played a round of golf at the Hillcrest Golf Course. It was his day off, and he was irritated when summoned to the club-house for an urgent call. It came from Marilyn, whom he had last treated years earlier, shortly before her miscarriage at the end of *Some Like It Hot*.

At that time Marilyn had stamped off in a temper over his warnings that she stay away from drugs and alcohol, and to take it easy if she wanted to have her baby. Now, calling out of the blue, Marilyn asked, "Are you still angry with me—about the baby?" Nonplussed, the doctor assured her he was not.

Marilyn wanted to see Krohn as soon as possible. They agreed to have dinner, but Marilyn was to die before they could meet. Was Marilyn mourning her unborn children? That last week was the fifth anniversary of the loss of her first child by Arthur Miller. Or did she want to talk to Krohn about a more recent female disaster, the reported abortion of a few weeks earlier?

Marilyn was reaching out to old friends. A day or two before she died, as masseur Ralph Roberts kneaded away the tension, she told him whom to take calls from, and whom to refuse. One caller she wanted to talk to was Marlon Brando, by now an intimate of seven years' standing. They chatted for a long time when he returned her messages. According to Roberts, Brando made her laugh a lot. The actor himself prefers not to comment on their last conversations.

Marilyn talked to at least three people about the Kennedys, in a way that suggests great confusion. From the Barrington Park phone booth, where she stood watching children for the last time, she telephoned Arthur James.

"What can I do about 'He'?" she asked, apparently refer-ring to the President. She went on to complain, as she had to Slatzer, that Robert Kennedy had "cut her off cold," but it was "Jack" she could not get out of her mind.

Marilyn called James again on the last Wednesday, but reached only his answering service. She left word that she needed his help. "I tried to call back," James says, "but another female answered the phone, and hung up."

On Friday afternoon, August 3, according to the phone records, Marilyn telephoned Norman Rosten in New York.

She wanted to know what he and his wife thought of the *Life* interview, and talked about new job offers and of coming East soon. "We'll have a great time," she said. "Let's all start to live before we get old. . . ."

Marilyn's voice seemed to Rosten frenetic, racing on unnaturally from one thing to another. He was worried enough by the call to write a follow-up letter, but she was to die before it arrived.

Marilyn was flailing around for solace. On Friday she also called Anne Karger, mother of her old lover Fred and a loyal friend. "It was the day before she died," says Elizabeth Karger, Fred's last wife. "She said she was very much in love, and was going to marry Bobby Kennedy. But she sounded depressed." Anne Karger, says her daughter-in-law, told Marilyn she was deluding herself. She merely replied, "If he loves me, he will."

That same day—Friday—Marilyn went to a phone booth to call Robert Slatzer, now at his home in Columbus, Ohio. Four friends were with him at the time, and the three still alive confirm the call occurred. Two of them spoke to her themselves. Marilyn had been looking at a script by Doral Chenoweth, a writer friend of Slatzer, and she told him she liked it. He was impressed by the fact that she had clearly read his work carefully. The play, *This God Bu$ine$$*, was later successfully produced.

Slatzer's restaurateur friend, Lee Henry, also talked to Marilyn for a few moments. He recalls recognizing the famous voice, but says, "You could tell she was either on booze or drugs."

Slatzer himself talked to Marilyn at length, not for the first time that week. The previous day, he says, he had called her to tell her Robert Kennedy was going to California that weekend and that—if Marilyn must—it would be a good chance to talk to him.

Now, on Friday, Marilyn was saying she had continued to try to reach Kennedy in Washington, but in vain. Was Slatzer sure Kennedy was coming to California? Slatzer told her to look in the papers. Marilyn said she would telephone her friend, and Kennedy's sister, Pat Lawford. Pat was at the Kennedy compound in Massachusetts, but Marilyn would call Peter Lawford to get the number. Pat Lawford, in turn, would tell her how to reach Robert Kennedy.

Peter Lawford later confirmed that Marilyn did call to ask for Pat's number. He gave it to her. We do not know whether

Marilyn then obtained a number for Robert Kennedy, and actually reached him. We do know Robert Kennedy was in California that weekend.

Press coverage and FBI documents show that Kennedy flew into San Francisco on Friday afternoon, accompanied by his wife and four of their children. The Attorney General was combining business with pleasure: an address to the American Bar Association would be followed by a vacation in the mountains of Washington State. The San Francisco *Chronicle* reported that he arrived "without his usual flashing smile" and shook hands "woodenly" with those who welcomed him.

A special FBI report, submitted to headquarters two weeks later, said the Attorney General and his family "spent the weekend at the Bates ranch located about sixty miles south of San Francisco. This was strictly a personal affair." The ranch was owned by John Bates, a wealthy lawyer who was acting as Kennedy's host on behalf of the Bar Association.

Bates says there were no calls from Marilyn that weekend at the ranch. One of the few contemporary reporters who did any serious research, however, found traces of Marilyn's despair. Florabel Muir, then Hollywood columnist for the *New York Daily News*, spent several weeks trying to reconstruct Marilyn's last days. Although Kennedy chose to spend the weekend at the Bates ranch, outside San Francisco, the Bar Association had provided accommodations in the city, at the St. Francis Hotel. That is where Marilyn would have expected to find him.

According to her former assistant, Elizabeth Fancher, reporter Muir paid a telephone operator at the St. Francis for information about calls made that weekend. "She discovered Marilyn had called the hotel several times, leaving messages for Kennedy," says Fancher, "and the calls were not returned."

As Robert Kennedy flew West that day newspapers published a White House announcement that his brother would be going to California in two weeks' time. Marilyn had already advised reporter Sidney Skolsky, whom she had told only about her relationship with John Kennedy, that the President was coming. She said she expected to "be with him" during the visit.

If either Kennedy brother read the *New York Journal-American* that Friday, they saw all the more reason to shrink from contact with Marilyn. Columnist Dorothy Kilgallen wrote a teaser, saying that Marilyn had recently "proved vastly alluring to a handsome gentleman who is a bigger name than Joe DiMaggio in his heyday. So don't write off Marilyn as finished.''

Friday, August 3, was the day before Marilyn was to die. She spent part of it normally enough, visiting Frank's Nursery in Santa Monica and picking out plants for her garden. She also saw her doctor and her psychiatrist, which for her was routine. What she did that evening, however, presumably after the abortive effort to reach Robert Kennedy in San Francisco, remains mysterious.

Some information, albeit vestigial, suggests she made a frantic flying visit northward, to seek out Robert Kennedy for herself. Pat Newcomb, Marilyn's press aide and a friend of the Kennedys, says she and Marilyn dined out that night at a Santa Monica restaurant. It was a favorite of theirs, she says, but she can no longer remember its name or where it was located.

The District Attorney's investigators, who talked to Newcomb during a review of the case in 1982, were not happy with Newcomb's account of the evening. There are some other, though inconclusive, clues. During the day Marilyn ordered food and liquor worth forty-nine dollars—a major purchase when translated into today's prices—from the Briggs Delicatessen. That night, according to Jean Leon of the fashionable La Scala restaurant, she ordered food to be brought to her home.

Leon, a Frenchman, had risen from being a waiter at the Villa Capri—haunt of Frank Sinatra and Joe DiMaggio—to becoming proprietor of La Scala. He had known Marilyn for years. In a recent interview, he went as far as saying he had taken food to Marilyn's house the night before she died, but then backed off from saying anything more. He indicated that somebody else was at Marilyn's home that night, someone he refused to name. "I have a vivid memory," said Leon, "but you have to go into a lot of things, big personalities, and they are not here now.''

For reasons that remain mysterious, events that Friday evening demand secrecy. For Marilyn, it was to be a sleepless night.

43

ON SATURDAY, August 4, Jeanne Carmen, in bed at her Doheny apartment, was awakened by the telephone at first light. Still half-asleep, she listened as Marilyn poured out a story of a night disturbed by more than the usual demons.

Carmen recalls that "she said some woman had been calling all night, harassing her and calling her names, then hanging up. Then she would call and not say anything, and hang up. Marilyn said the voice sounded familiar, but she couldn't put a name on it."

In the first calls, according to Carmen, the anonymous woman said words to the effect, "Leave Bobby alone, you tramp. Leave Bobby alone." The calls had gone on till 5:30 A.M., and Marilyn was now exhausted. "She wanted me to come over. She said, 'Bring a bag of pills'—we were sleeping-pill buddies, and we always referred to them that way—'and we'll drink some wine.' "

Carmen, who had appointments that day, said she could not come around. They agreed to talk again later. It was Carmen's birthday and, when she opened her mail, she found Marilyn had remembered to send her a card. As others confirm, Marilyn was good about remembering birthdays.

At three that morning, presumably during the spate of anonymous calls, Marilyn had tried to reach Arthur James. He was out of town, and did not get the message until after her death.

It was going to be another hot day, with the temperature up in the eighties. Eunice Murray, who had stayed at her own apartment the previous night, came to work about eight o'clock. She says Marilyn wandered into the kitchen about an hour later, then chatted a little over a spartan breakfast of grapefruit juice. She said Pat Newcomb had stayed overnight, and was still asleep. She was to stay asleep till noon, a state of bliss which irritated Marilyn.

Arthur Miller's father, Isadore, called that morning. He

was told that Marilyn was dressing and would call back. She did not, which he found out of character. Marilyn was devoted to him, and usually interrupted even urgent business to return his calls.

During the morning Norman Jeffries, working on the kitchen floor, found himself looking at a pair of bare female feet. He looked up to see Marilyn wrapped in a huge bath towel, and was appalled.

"I will never forget the sight of her," Jeffries says. "She looked sick, desperately sick—not only in the physical sense—and I thought there must be something terribly wrong. She must have taken a lot of dope or something, or maybe she was scared out of her mind. I had never seen her look that way before."

Marilyn had two telephones: one pink, with a number provided to ordinary callers; one white, with a number given only to the specially privileged. Both were on long extension leads, so Marilyn could wander about the house as she talked.

The surviving phone records, for ominous reasons that will emerge later, throw no light on Marilyn's calls during her last twenty-four hours. However, closeted in her room—probably with the white phone—Marilyn had several conversations that last morning.

Ralph Roberts, the masseur, says Marilyn called to get him to do a chore: she wanted him to get hold of an unreleased record by a singer she hoped to help. She also talked of having dinner with Roberts that evening—a cookout on the patio—and they agreed to talk more about it later. By late afternoon, Marilyn said, she should know what she was doing.

From his home across the city, reporter Sidney Skolsky made his regular weekend call to Marilyn. He had been alarmed by her confidences about the Kennedy family and, as on other recent occasions, had his daughter Steffi listen in on an extension. He felt he wanted a witness.

"What are you doing tonight?" Skolsky asked cheerily. By now Marilyn appeared to have a plan for the evening. She replied, "Maybe I'll go down to the beach. Everyone's going to be there." As Skolsky's daughter remembers it, Marilyn said she expected to be seeing one of the Kennedys at the Lawford house.

That Saturday, probably in the late morning, Marilyn received a visit from Agnes Flanagan, one of her hairdressers and a longtime friend. Something very odd occurred while

Flanagan was at the house, one of the most bizarre incidents of a mysterious weekend.

Soon after she arrived, said Flanagan, a messenger arrived with a package. Marilyn opened it and walked out to the pool carrying its contents—a stuffed toy tiger. She then sat down by the pool, holding the tiger and saying nothing. Flanagan thought she was "terribly, terribly depressed," but did not say why. Flanagan, wholly at a loss, got up and left.

Photographs of the back of Marilyn's house, taken the next day, showed two stuffed animals lying by the pool. One of them could be a tiger. Had some devastating note arrived with the tiger or—curious thought—was the tiger itself the message? Marilyn, at all events, now lost control.

The events of her remaining hours hang largely on the accounts of Peter Lawford, Pat Newcomb, Eunice Murray, and Dr. Greenson. The first two witnesses are controversial, not least because of their close relations with the Kennedy brothers. Mrs. Murray's statements about the evening hours, as will be seen, are dubious.

Research for this book, including interviews with Dr. Greenson's family and colleagues, and his contemporary correspondence, satisfies this author that Marilyn's psychiatrist was honest about that weekend. It is he who takes up the story of that Saturday afternoon.

"I received a call from Marilyn about 4:30 in the afternoon," Greenson was to write. "She seemed somewhat depressed and somewhat drugged. I went over to her place. She was still angry with her girlfriend who had slept fifteen hours that night, and Marilyn was furious because she had had such a poor sleep . . . but after I had spent about two and a half hours with her she seemed to quiet down."

Dr. Greenson's letters, and his statements to fellow psychiatrists on the Los Angeles Suicide Prevention Team, offer information on two key factors in Marilyn's last hours. They show that as early as Friday, when he had also seen her, Marilyn had been "angry and resentful towards her friend Pat"—clearly, in this context—Pat Newcomb. On Friday night, according to Greenson, they continued bickering, and Marilyn was still in a rage against Newcomb as late as Saturday afternoon.

Why such rage against Pat Newcomb? The press aide agrees "it made Marilyn crazy that she was not able to sleep. She was furious, it's true. But I think that she also was furious about something else, and I was there and became the focus of it, the eye of the storm. But I think there was a lot more, not related to me, and that I don't even know about.''

Clearly referring to Newcomb, Susan Strasberg recalls that Marilyn nicknamed her publicity aide—as early as *The Misfits*—''Sybil,'' for sibling rivalry. Steffi Skolsky says the same. Marilyn had been jealous of Newcomb in the past, as on *Bus Stop* years earlier, when she believed Newcomb—a woman a dozen years younger than herself—was pursuing a man Marilyn liked.

Now Steffi Skolsky, listening in on one of Marilyn's last conversations with her father, heard Marilyn say the tables were turned. ''Pat's jealous of me,'' she said. Marilyn's quarrel with Newcomb, at the end, may have been about Robert Kennedy.

Dean Martin's former wife, Jeanne, who is still close to Newcomb, remembers how involved she got with her clients, how they became ''literally, her whole life. She always got overly involved.'' Another deep commitment, apparently, was with Robert Kennedy.

Martin says, ''Pat got far too involved; she was deeply in love with Bobby Kennedy. She's only just got over that. If you want to know who knew more about Marilyn than anyone, it's Pat Newcomb. But you could never get anything out of her.'' To this day, Newcomb clams up when asked about the Kennedys.

Of the squabbles with Marilyn that fatal Saturday, Newcomb will say only, ''Marilyn had calls that morning, and by the time I saw her she was in a rage.'' Psychiatrist Dr. Greenson, in his talks with the Suicide Prevention Team after Marilyn died, dropped heavy hints as to why she was so upset.

Along with saying that Marilyn had recently had sexual relationships with ''extremely important men in government . . . at the highest level,'' Dr. Greenson revealed that on Saturday afternoon she ''expressed considerable dissatisfaction with the fact that here she was, the most beautiful woman in the world, and she did not have a date for Saturday night.''

According to one Suicide Team doctor, Norman Tabachnick, Greenson said Marilyn had been expecting to see one of the ''very important people'' that night. She had called Greenson when she learned the meeting was off. Marilyn died, Greenson said, feeling ''rejected by some of the people she had been close to.''

Sometime before she called Greenson that day—over the telephone or conceivably in a message accompanying the mysterious tiger—Marilyn had learned she would not be seeing Robert Kennedy in the evening. That, on the evidence, triggered her final despair.

After seeing Marilyn virtually every day for weeks, Greenson had hoped to keep that weekend free. He had a dinner appointment on Saturday night, and his afternoon visit to Marilyn seems to have been a holding operation.

Marilyn wanted Pat Newcomb to leave, and Greenson asked her to go. Newcomb says today that she left of her own accord. Eunice Murray says Newcomb sprang up and left without saying good-bye.

At 6:30 P.M. Ralph Roberts called as planned, to ask Marilyn whether he was to come round to dinner. Greenson answered the phone and said Marilyn was out. Then, his dinner appointment in mind, the psychiatrist prepared to leave.

"Marilyn wanted to go for a walk on the pier at Santa Monica," Dr. Greenson recalled later, "and I said she was too groggy for that, and if she drank a lot of fluid, I would allow the housekeeper to drive her to the beach." Greenson thought, "She seemed somewhat depressed, but I had seen her many, many times in a much worse condition." As a precaution, he asked Eunice Murray to stay overnight. Then Greenson dashed home to dress for dinner. It was 7:15 P.M.

One of Marilyn's stepchildren, Jo DiMaggio, Jr., had twice tried to call her that afternoon. DiMaggio, a young marine serving at Camp Pendleton, California, telephoned collect, only to hear Mrs. Murray say that Marilyn was out. Now, soon after Greenson had left, Joe, Jr., got through.

At 7:40 P.M. Marilyn called Dr. Greenson, now busy shaving. He was glad to hear her sounding more cheerful: Joe, Jr.'s news had been that he had broken off his engagement, and that pleased Marilyn. Dr. Greenson told her to get a good night's sleep and to call in the morning.

According to Eunice Murray, Marilyn now announced that she would not be going for a drive after all. Then she went into her bedroom and closed the door. Mrs. Murray heard the sound of music from the record player—Frank Sinatra songs.

According to Mrs. Murray, she never saw Marilyn alive again. It was about eight o'clock, and dusk began to fall along the Pacific shore. In Marilyn's room, the music played on and on.

In her last call to Dr. Greenson, Marilyn had asked, "Did you take away my bottle of Nembutal?" He had not, and he was caught off-balance because he thought Marilyn had recently cut down on barbiturates. Nor was Greenson especially worried—if his patient had no sleeping pills.

The psychiatrist would have been more concerned had he known then what he learned later. An empty bottle, with a label indicating it had contained twenty-five Nembutal pills, would be among the medicines retrieved from Marilyn's room after her death. The label showed it had been prescribed on Friday, the day before her death. There would also be an almost empty bottle that had contained fifty capsules of chloral hydrate, a less dangerous sleeping aid, which had been prescribed on July 31.

Dr. Hyman Engelberg, Marilyn's internist, has rarely given interviews. However, his contemporary bill shows that he visited Marilyn at home on Friday, the day of the Nembutal prescription, and a document in the Coroner's file says he prescribed Nembutal that day.

The Suicide Prevention Team would conclude that Marilyn had been receiving Nembutal prescriptions from both Dr. Engelberg and from a Dr. Lou Siegel, and that neither doctor knew of her visits to the other. Dr. Lou Siegel, a gynecologist who has since died, vehemently denied in 1982 that he had ever treated Marilyn. Dr. *Lee* Siegel, the studio doctor who did frequently treat Marilyn, says he did not see her for many weeks prior to her death.

Dr. Greenson would later say he had brought in Dr. Engelberg to try to wean Marilyn away from sleeping pills. The two doctors agreed to keep in touch concerning the drugs they prescribed for her, but the system may have broken down.

Marilyn had made an odd inquiry earlier that day, according to Eunice Murray. "Mrs. Murray," she supposedly said, "do we have any oxygen?" Marilyn let the subject drop, but Murray says it bothered her enough to telephone Dr. Greenson. Greenson never mentioned such a call. Oxygen, of course, is used by medical teams as an aid to resuscitation.

Certainly Greenson knew nothing of Marilyn's dawn call to Jeanne Carmen, asking her to come over with "a bag of sleeping pills." According to Carmen, she called again later, pressing the request. Carmen still pleaded other engagements.

Marilyn's wealthy New York friend, Henry Rosenfeld, telephoned her—probably between eight and nine, California time—and she answered the phone herself. He said she sounded "groggy," but that was not unusual.

At about 9:30 P.M. Marilyn called Sidney Guilaroff, a prom-

inent Hollywood hairdresser who knew her well—he has not
featured in these pages because he never discusses his clients.
Marilyn told Guilaroff, "I'm very depressed," and she rang
off without saying good-bye. Guilaroff was used to Marilyn,
and saw no cause for alarm. He refuses to elaborate on what
else she had said.

José Bolaños, the lover who followed Marilyn from Mexico, says he telephoned Marilyn from the Ships Restaurant,
not far from her home, between nine-thirty and ten o'clock.
He will not reveal what they discussed. He does say Marilyn
ended the conversation by simply laying down the phone—
she did not hang up while he was on the line. Like Guilaroff,
Bolaños thought it was typical Marilyn behavior. He thinks he
was the last person to speak to Marilyn—but perhaps not.

At about ten, says Jeanne Carmen, Marilyn telephoned yet
again. "Are you sure you can't come over?" she said. Marilyn sounded nervous and said she was afraid there would be a
repetition of the previous night's calls, telling her to leave
Robert Kennedy alone. Otherwise she sounded all right, and
Carmen begged off one last time. Later the telephone rang
again, but Carmen did not answer it.

Also at about ten o'clock, Ralph Roberts learned next day,
a woman with a "slurred voice" called his answering service.
Told Roberts was out, the caller hung up.

Roberts, who was staying at a temporary address, had
given his number to only two people apart from Marilyn, and
they were business contacts. He believes the caller was Marilyn.

There were no more known calls. At about 3:30 A.M., at the
Greenson home in Santa Monica, the psychiatrist's daughter,
Joan, heard the telephone ring in her parents' bedroom. There
were muffled voices, the sound of her parents going downstairs, then the car starting. Feeling hungry, Joan went to the
kitchen to raid the refrigerator.

"I asked Mom what happened," Joan recalls. "She said
there was a problem over at Marilyn's, and I said, 'Oh'—and
went back to bed."

It was just a mile and a half from the Greenson house to
Marilyn's home. As he drove, the psychiatrist already feared
the worst. The caller had been Eunice Murray, saying that she
had noticed a light in Marilyn's room at midnight. Then, after
three, she had wakened to see the light still on. This was most
unusual. Afraid to anger Marilyn by waking her unnecessar-
ily, Murray said, she had called Greenson instead.

"I told her to bang on the door," Greenson wrote to a

friend that month. "She did, and there was no answer. And she went to the front of the house and looked into the window and could see Marilyn lying very quietly on the bed. I told her I was coming right over, and for her to call Dr. Engelberg."

Greenson reached Marilyn's house in five minutes. He too found the bedroom door locked. He too went outside to peer through the window. Some have questioned whether this was possible, because Marilyn's windows were masked with heavy blackout drapes brought from the old apartment.

In fact, according to Murray and Greenson, a barred window at the front of the house was ajar that hot summer night. An examination of contemporary photographs, and the window today, shows it was possible to reach in, part the drapes, and look straight at Marilyn's bed.

There was no way, however, of getting into the room, because of the bars. Greenson said he took a poker, broke an unbarred window at the side of the house—the smashed pane appeared later in press photographs—and then reached in to turn the handle. It was then easy to climb over the low sill.

"I could see from many feet away," Greenson was to write, "that Marilyn was no longer living. There she was, lying face down on the bed, bare shoulders exposed, and as I got closer I could see the phone clutched fiercely in her right hand. I suppose she was trying to make a phone call before she was overwhelmed. It was just unbelievable, so simple and final and over."

Police pictures, taken a few hours later, show Marilyn stretched out, more or less covered with rumpled bedclothes. Her head lies on the pillow, right cheek down, eyes closed and face in repose as though serenely asleep.

Dr. Greenson opened the door and told Eunice Murray, "We've lost her." Dr. Engelberg arrived fifteen minutes later and agreed, in Greenson's words, that "she was hopelessly gone."

At 4:25 A.M., less than an hour after Eunice Murray had raised the alarm, the Central Los Angeles police switchboard took a call from Dr. Engelberg. It was transferred to the West Los Angeles desk, which covered Marilyn's neighborhood. The watch commander, Sergeant Jack Clemmons, picked up the phone himself. When the doctor said, "I am calling from the home of Marilyn Monroe. She's dead," Clemmons suspected a practical joke. He decided to go to the scene himself.

At the house, now alive with light, Eunice Murray showed

the sergeant straight into Marilyn's room, where the two
doctors were sitting with the body.

Dr. Greenson, who did most of the talking, pointed out one
pill bottle among the many that littered the bedside table. It
seemed to tell its own story: the bottle was empty, with the
top on, and the label read "Nembutal." There was no sign of
a suicide note. The telephone was back on its rest, replaced by
Dr. Greenson.

Everything seemed in order—indeed, Mrs. Murray was
tidying up in the kitchen and even doing the laundry. Yet
something bothered Clemmons. "It's not evidence," he says,
"but I left with this uneasy feeling there was something I did
not understand."

44

AT ABOUT FIVE O'CLOCK IN THE MORNING, on Sunday, August 5,
a young reporter named Joe Ramirez got a world scoop. The
great actor, Charles Laughton, was dying, and Ramirez had
asked a contact in the Coroner's office to call him as soon as
it happened. The contact called instead to say Marilyn Monroe was dead. Ramirez, who worked for a minor agency
called City News, rushed to his office and put the news on the
wire.

The story came too late for the Sunday newspapers, but it
flashed around the world, startling early-morning radio listen-
ers and sending news editors scrambling for the telephones.

Over in Studio City, photographer Bill Woodfield was
rousted out of bed by reporter Joe Hyams. Both men knew
Marilyn—Woodfield was still in the midst of negotiations
over the nude swim pictures; Hyams, the respected correspondent of the New York *Herald Tribune,* had written a story on
her only weeks earlier, after a chance encounter in a store.
Hyams and Woodfield piled into Hyams' black Mercedes,
which had once belonged to Humphrey Bogart, and headed
for Marilyn's house in the first thin light of dawn.

Associated Press columnist James Bacon, a sometime lover

from Marilyn's starlet days, had been tipped off about the death by a friend with a radio tuned to the police network. He too drove to the scene. There were a couple of police cars there now, and a small cluster of neighbors standing in the street in dressing gowns. "I pulled an old trick," Bacon says. "I went up to a cop and said I was from the Coroner's office, and got into the house. I didn't stay long, just long enough to see her lying there on the bed. . . . I noticed that her finger-nails were unkempt. The Coroner's staff did arrive a few minutes later, and I got out of there right away."

The Coroner's man, Guy Hockett, saw at once, as Dr. Greenson had also observed, that Marilyn had been dead for "several hours." *Rigor mortis* was advanced, and "it took about five minutes to straighten her out. . . . She was not lying quite straight, sort of in a semifetal position. Her hair was all burnt up, in terrible condition from all those treatments, you know. She didn't look good, not like Marilyn Monroe. She looked just like a poor little girl that had died, no makeup, fuzzy unmade hair, a tired body. To some degree or other, we all come to that. . . ."

The Coroner's men wheeled out Marilyn's body, covered by a blue blanket, and loaded it into a battered station wagon. They took their burden first to Westwood Village Mortuary, next to the cemetery where her maternal grandmother was buried. The remains of the most famous star on earth were lodged for a while in a broom closet cluttered with brushes, coats, and specimen bottles.

A couple of hours later the body was moved to Crypt 33 at the County Morgue, in the Los Angeles Hall of Justice. Marilyn had become a statistic—Coroner's Case No. 81128.

Two photographers got into the morgue that day. One, Bud Gray of the *Herald-Examiner*, snatched a picture of the shrouded corpse while a colleague covered the click of his camera shutter by flicking his cigarette lighter. Leigh Wiener, a freelance photographer who sent his pictures to *Life* magazine, arrived carrying a camera case in one hand and bottles of whisky in the other. Offered a drink, one of the attendants opened a stainless-steel door and pulled out the sliding shelf carrying Marilyn's remains. Wiener took pictures of the body, covered and uncovered. One, which has been published, shows a toe sticking out of the crypt, with an identification tag attached. The press had photographed the famous body for the last time.

Across the country, the living were asked for their reactions. The husbands said little. Reached on the beat by police radio, James Dougherty managed only, "I'm sorry." Arthur Miller, for all his skills as a wordsmith, could hardly speak at all. Through a family member, he was quoted as saying, "It had to happen. I don't know when or how, but it was inevitable." Miller said he would not be going to the funeral, because "she's not really there any more."

The day before, in San Francisco, Joe DiMaggio played in an exhibition game, then met friends at Bimbo's club. He heard the news very early in the morning, probably relayed to him through friends of Frank Sinatra. He took the first available flight to Los Angeles, contacted his son Joe, Jr., at Camp Pendleton, and retreated with two close friends behind the door of Suite 1035 at the Miramar Hotel, not far from Marilyn's house.

DiMaggio quietly did what somebody had to do. Marilyn's body was at first unclaimed. Her mother was incompetent, in a home, and Marilyn's half sister agreed that DiMaggio should arrange the funeral. He insisted it must be a small, restrained affair. DiMaggio said nothing at all to the press. In private, his friend Harry Hall remembers, he sat weeping in his room, unopened telegrams scattered on a table beside him. When he did talk, he fulminated about Sinatra, those in his circle, and about the Kennedys. "He held Bobby Kennedy responsible for her death," Hall remembers. "He said that right there in the Miramar."

Between fits of weeping, Paula Strasberg said Marilyn had "a quality second to no actress in the world." She added, incredibly, "Marilyn had no worries at all." Her daughter, Susan, later offered the compassionate reflection, "An iron butterfly, some people had called her. Butterflies are very beautiful, give great pleasure, and have very short life-spans."

Milton and Amy Greene heard the news over the telephone in their hotel bedroom in Paris. They were especially shaken because Amy had had a premonition that Marilyn was in serious trouble, and had made Milton call her before leaving New York. She had said she was fine, and everyone had laughed.

Directors, bosses, and stars were badgered for opinions. Billy Wilder, getting off a plane in Paris without knowing the news, was asked what he thought of Marilyn. "I said whatever I said, probably not all that kind," Wilder recalls ruefully. "Then in the cab on the way to the hotel I suddenly saw the placards through the cab window. They never told me, those SOB's. . . .''

Later Wilder made his tribute to Marilyn's acting ability, as did John Huston. During *The Misfits*, Huston recalled, he had feared ''it would only be a few short years before she died or went into an institution.'' Joshua Logan declared Marilyn ''one of the most unappreciated people in the world.''

Darryl Zanuck, President of Twentieth Century-Fox and a man who had taken a long time to appreciate Marilyn, was generous. ''Nobody discovered her,'' he said, ''she earned her own way to stardom.''

Sir Laurence Olivier thought, ''Popular opinion is a horribly unsteady conveyance for life, and she was exploited beyond anyone's means.''

''I heard the flash over the radio at seven A.M.,'' said Clark Gable's widow, Kay, whose husband had died after *The Misfits*, ''and I went to Mass and prayed for her.''

The Greenson family was grief-stricken. Dr. Greenson had telephoned the news from Marilyn's home during the night, and came home exhausted. He kept repeating that he was sure it had been an accident. Long afterward, still punishing himself, he would say, ''She was a poor creature, whom I tried to help and ended up hurting.'' In the immediate aftermath, he met Joe DiMaggio; each found himself consoling the other.

Frank Sinatra said he was ''deeply saddened . . . I'll miss her very much.'' His valet, George Jacobs, recalls, ''It was a bad time, that August. Strange things had been happening. Frank was in shock for weeks after Marilyn died, distraught. He called me and said, 'Let's get out of here,' and we went down to Palm Springs.''

Pat Newcomb, who reached Marilyn's home early that morning, caused a scene as she left. ''Keep shooting, vultures!'' the press aide shrieked at photographers. She was quoted as saying—though she denies it today—''When your best friend kills herself, how do you feel, what do you do?'' In total contradiction of all we now know, Newcomb said Marilyn had been ''feeling great,'' had been in high spirits the previous evening.

In public, Peter Lawford said ''Pat [Kennedy] and I loved her dearly. She was probably one of the most marvelous and warm human beings I have ever met. Anything else I could say would be superfluous.''

On the telephone to a friend that morning, Lawford had been incoherent. He had found a pair of Marilyn's sandals at the beach house, and ordered his butler to have them bronzed. He wandered into the home of a neighbor, Sherry Houser, "in a complete state of shock, devastated, weeping. He kept saying he had been the last person to talk to her." That detail, far from superfluous, lies at the core of the mystery surrounding Marilyn's death.

In New York that day, Marilyn's biographer, Maurice Zolotow, found himself at a party crowded with people in politics, some of them close to the Kennedys. Already, Zolotow recalls, the name of Robert Kennedy was woven into the conversation about Marilyn's tragedy.

In the afternoon, East Coast time, at the Kennedy compound at Hyannis Port, the elderly Joseph Kennedy, still recovering from his stroke, was doing convalescent exercises in the swimming pool. Relatives and members of the entourage were close by. Old Kennedy's chauffeur and Man Friday, Frank Saunders, was in the water with him. "His niece, Ann Gargan, came up and said Marilyn Monroe was dead," Saunders recalls. "The old man began saying 'No . . . no . . .,' and we left the pool. A strange silence came over everybody who was there. It was such a curious reaction, I thought, and it stuck in my mind. Years later, when the rumors came out about Marilyn Monroe and John Kennedy and then Robert Kennedy, I remembered the silence that August afternoon. It was like attending a wake, but there wasn't one. . . ."

In California, at the Bates ranch south of San Francisco, Robert Kennedy went to church that morning. Afterward he relaxed with his hosts, horseback riding and playing touch football. John Bates says Marilyn's name had come up several times since the Attorney General's arrival on Friday, but only in the general context of her problems. "We were all aware," he adds, "that she had some acquaintance with Jack."

Bates thinks the fact that Marilyn had died came up only on Sunday evening, when the party returned to the city. Asked whether Kennedy showed any reaction, Bates says, "No. It was really taken rather lightly. . . ." As if it was just another Hollywood tragedy? "That's right. It was discussed," says Bates, "in sort of an amusing way."

On Monday, Robert Kennedy addressed a meeting of the American Bar Association. Then he dined privately with the Director of the CIA, before setting off on vacation with his family.

In Washington, President Kennedy made a scheduled announcement. He called on Congress for laws to enforce stricter control over the use of dangerous drugs.

Early on Sunday morning, in Los Angeles, a young Deputy Medical Examiner, Dr. Thomas Noguchi, had reported for the weekend shift. He found a note on his desk from his chief, Coroner Theodore Curphey, asking him to perform the autopsy on Marilyn Monroe. A Deputy District Attorney with forensic experience, John Miner, would attend as observer for the DA.

The Los Angeles Chief of Detectives, Deputy Police Chief Thad Brown, was a legendary figure, a man given to working around the clock. When he did relax he would escape to a hideaway at Malibu, a trailer with no telephone. That Sunday morning a police dispatch rider arrived with an urgent message. Marilyn Monroe had died, and there was a problem. Would the Chief of Detectives please come to headquarters at once?

The man ultimately responsible for the inquiry was Police Chief William Parker, a nationally respected officer. He shared a good deal of his worries with his wife, Helen, and she remembers that "he wanted special attention paid to this particular case by the investigators, and he tried to send the best men out there, including detectives from the downtown office, because there was so much talk that she was very close to John or Robert Kennedy. And Mr. Parker was very fond of Robert, thought he was very intelligent, thought he would've been a better President than John."

"Robert and John Kennedy were supposed to be Catholics, I think," says the Chief's widow, "and Mr. Parker was a Catholic. And maybe he thought undue pressure would be brought, that possibly the Republicans would jump on it. And so he said, 'The thing has to be straightened out in more ways than one.' Mr. Parker was very, very strict, and he would lay the law down to get to the bottom of this. He would say, 'Save no one.' "

Chief Parker is indeed remembered as a man of integrity. Yet weeks later, when his wife asked how the Monroe case was going, Parker was uncharacteristically vague. "It seemed to be a big question mark," Helen Parker recalls. "I remember him just doing this"—and she draws a big question mark in the air.

There was a Coroner's investigation, and it was flawed. There was a police investigation, and there was a cover-up.

45

BY 10:30 A.M. on August 5, within six hours of the first official knowledge that Marilyn was dead, the most highly advertised, overpromoted body on earth lay, covered by a plastic sheet, in a long, windowless room under the Hall of Justice. Eddy Day, the autopsy assistant, had prepared Marilyn on Table 1, a stainless-steel slab equipped with a water hose and drainage system, and a scale for weighing human organs.

Since that day Dr. Noguchi, the autopsy surgeon, has become a controversial figure. Recently, long after rising to the post of Chief Medical Examiner, he was demoted for allegedly mismanaging his office and for sensationalizing celebrity deaths, a charge he is still fighting. In the storm of controversy that followed, his colleagues elected him Chairman of the Board of the National Association of Medical Examiners.

Noguchi's subjects have included Sharon Tate, William Holden, Natalie Wood, and John Belushi. In 1968 he probed the ruined head of Senator Robert Kennedy.

Noguchi and John Miner, the observer from the District Attorney's office, were profoundly affected when the sheet was drawn back on Marilyn Monroe. Miner says, "Tom and I had looked at thousands of bodies, but we were both very touched. We had a sense of real sadness, and the feeling that this young, young woman could stand up and get off the table any minute."

Noguchi labored over Marilyn for hours, his scalpel slicing into the body that had graced so many pinups, his surgeon's saw carving a way to remove the brain that had made millions lust and laugh. We learn from his notes that Marilyn was a "36-year-old, well-developed, well-nourished Caucasian female weighing 117 pounds and measuring 65½ inches in length. The scalp is covered with bleached blonde hair. The eyes are blue." We are told that "distribution of the pubic hair is of female pattern. The uterus is of usual size.'' We learn of the scars the photographer's airbrush had hidden so efficiently, of the appendectomy, of the gall-bladder removal. We learn that, for all the storied excess, the living Monroe had been in fairly good shape.

When Marilyn was wheeled away, the beauty was gone. A picture retrieved from police files—the only known surviving postmortem photograph—shows a sagging, bloated face, hair hanging limp and straight over the edge of the table. The facial muscles had been severed during the removal of the brain, and the remains sluiced with water once the doctor's work was done.

The surgical part of the autopsy, Noguchi knew by now, did not hold the medical explanation of Marilyn's death. Apart from a couple of bruises, which could have been caused by blundering into furniture, there was no evidence of physical violence. Knowing pill bottles had been found on the bedside table, Noguchi says, he guessed already that the vital answers would come from the toxicologist—the poisons specialist.

Early on Monday morning, while Los Angeles commuters were still on their way to work, Head Toxicologist Ralph Abernethy considered a range of specimens waiting in his laboratory. They included eight pill containers—one of them the empty Nembutal bottle—vials of blood and urine, and specimens from Marilyn's stomach, intestines, liver, and kidneys. Dr. Noguchi was requesting a test for alcohol and for barbiturates.

Within hours Noguchi knew Marilyn's blood contained 4.5 milligrams percent barbiturates, and no alcohol at all; she had not drunk any quantity of her favorite tipple, champagne, for several hours before expiring. Contrary to repeated assumption down the years, Marilyn did not die from the classic combination of alcohol and pills.

The drugs, however, were the key. Further tests showed 13 milligrams percent pentobarbital in the liver, and 8 milligrams percent chloral hydrate in the blood. Pentobarbital is the chemical identified in the sleeping pill, Nembutal, and chloral hydrate was one of the less dangerous sedatives found at Marilyn's house.

A pathologist at St. Bartholomew's Hospital in London, Dr. Christopher Foster, points out that it is notoriously difficult to say precisely how much of a drug has been consumed. He calculates, however, that Marilyn's Nembutal intake was some ten times the normal therapeutic dose. The chloral hydrate level itself indicates "a fairly stunning intake," up to twenty times the amount usually recommended for sleep. Either of the drugs, taken in such quantities, could individually have proved fatal. Taken together, they were even more likely to kill.

Noguchi's internal examination had shown congestion and hemorrhaging of the stomach lining, a typical result of the irritation caused by barbiturates taken in excess. This, together with the laboratory analysis and the bottles found in Marilyn's room, was all too familiar to men who saw overdose victims every day.

On August 10, five days after the death, Dr. Noguchi submitted his final autopsy report, giving the cause of death as "acute barbiturate poisoning due to ingestion of overdose." Under the heading "Mode of Death," he circled "Suicide," adding the word "probable" in his own hand. This was the verdict the Coroner would announce to the press a week later.

The suicide finding has not satisfied a number of critics, and they dispute, above all, Noguchi's conclusion that Marilyn swallowed the overdose, or—in Coroner Curphey's phrase—that it was "self-administered."

The critics raise several objections. They say it is usual to find traces of pills in the stomach—fragments of gelatin capsules and sometimes intact undigested pills. They say barbiturate capsules leave a telltale trail of colored dye in the system. They suggest that barbiturate victims usually vomit before expiring.

Skeptics also note that no drinking glass was found in Marilyn's bedroom, and no water—she would surely have needed water to wash down all those pills. In short, they suspect that somebody else administered Marilyn's fatal dose—that she was murdered.

The absence of a drinking glass is curious. A District Attorney's review in 1982 tried to resolve the problem by referring to a published photograph of the death scene, which "appears to show a drinking vessel." The relevant picture shows an object by the bedside table that could conceivably be a flask.

Marilyn's bathroom, which opened off her bedroom, had no functioning plumbing that night because of the remodeling operations. If she went to another room for water, Mrs. Murray did not notice.

Good police work at the start should have documented the

presence or absence of a glass. Yet none of three relevant police reports mention the subject. The meager record only creates further confusion. The Death Report states that fifteen medicine bottles were found on the bedside table. Only eight are listed in the toxicology reports.

Press reports noted that Marilyn's house was formally sealed by 8:30 A.M. on the morning of her death. Inez Melson, as her mother's guardian, was authorized to deal with Marilyn's effects. She was allowed in with her husband a day later, and recalled that the bedside table was still littered with pill bottles. "We found bottle after bottle after bottle," Melson told me. "There were sleeping pills, including Nembutal and Seconal. Whoever had been there before us did not take them away."

Mrs. Melson, thinking impetuously of Marilyn's reputation, destroyed the drugs. "We threw them all down the toilet, and I think I took the bottles away and put them in the garbage," she recalled. "There've been many times since that I've wished I'd saved them." Melson cannot be blamed; it was immensely inefficient that each and all of the bottles were not delivered to the Coroner long before.*

Inefficiencies aside, the critics' further objections have generally been rebuffed by leading forensic pathologists. Medical Examiners from six American cities, two British pathologists, two toxicologists, and a gastroenterologist were consulted during research for this book, in some cases without knowing that the subject was Marilyn Monroe.

On the minor issues raised, the doctors agree with the opinions offered to the Los Angeles District Attorney, during his 1982 review, by Dr. Boyd Stephens, Chief Medical Examiner for San Francisco.

As to the absence of vomit, pathologists unanimously reject the notion that most barbiturate victims throw up before dying. Sometimes they do; more often, especially when Nembutal is taken over several hours, they simply go peacefully to sleep.

Nembutal capsules do contain a coloring agent, but it rarely

---

* Press coverage shows that, ludicrously, photographers were able to trample through the house before it was sealed. One unpublished picture, traced by the author, clearly shows a bottle bearing the words; "Engelberg . . . 7.25.62 . . . 0.5 gms . . . at bedtime." The name of the drug is indecipherable, but this was probably the chloral hydrate, which did reach the Coroner's office.

leaves a trail, unlike Seconal, which often does. The coloring, when it is found, comes from the capsule rather than the Nembutal itself. There would be no stain at all if the capsules had been broken open and swallowed as liquid, and this is something Marilyn sometimes did do.

These details dealt with, there is a considerable difference of opinion over the matter on which the critics have been most vociferous—the fact that no residue of the capsules was discovered in Marilyn's stomach. This indicates, say the critics, that she did not swallow the fatal dose, that it was administered some other way—perhaps by injection. This, they say, points to murder.

Dr. Stephens, reporting to the Los Angeles DA in 1982, was not troubled by the absence of capsule residue. It is, he points out, again a question of "sometimes, and sometimes not." Remnants of capsules are often found in the stomach, but whether they are found depends on several factors: when the victim last ate, or drank liquid, and how much; the victim's individual metabolism; whether the victim was a habitual drug user with a high tolerance; and whether the drug was taken in one dose or over a period of several hours.

In Marilyn's case there is conflicting evidence on food intake. Eunice Murray says Marilyn did not eat all day, while Pat Newcomb recalls eating a hamburger lunch with her. By evening, in either case, her stomach would have been virtually empty and prone to rapid absorption of barbiturates. After years of drug abuse, Marilyn almost certainly had a high tolerance for barbiturates; friends recall her taking astonishingly high dosages without serious effect.

None of the doctors consulted have been prepared to commit themselves on the number of capsules consumed. Dr. Noguchi has ventured a figure of between thirty and forty, and other doctors' estimates hover between fifteen and forty.

In 1962, at his press conference, Los Angeles Coroner Curphey expressed the opinion that Marilyn ingested a large amount of the drugs "within a short period of time." He was quoted as estimating she swallowed the pills in "one gulp within—let's say—a period of seconds."

None of the doctors commenting today, including Dr. Noguchi, agree with this notion. Absorption of a drug by the liver, as in Marilyn's case, means the digestive process has been underway for some time. The liver evidence suggests that Marilyn had taken some drugs several hours before dying.

It is here that the experts start to differ. Dr. Stephens, of

San Francisco, reporting to the Los Angeles District Attorney in 1982, said that, on the basis of the autopsy record, he too would have concluded that Marilyn died "of acute barbiturate poisoning from the ingestion of an overdose." Other eminent doctors find that conclusion too sweeping, and it is the empty stomach that bothers them.

Dr. Keith Simpson was Professor Emeritus in Forensic Medicine at London University and senior pathologist to the Home Office, the top government forensic expert in Britain. In 1985, shortly before his untimely death, he studied all the available information on Marilyn's death, at my request. He commented: "Had I been doing that autopsy I would not have been happy to write it off promptly as suicide due to ingestion. The barbiturate levels in the blood and liver are high enough, in my experience, to make it likely that you would find a residue of the capsules in the stomach. Yet nothing was found."

Professor Simpson said, "It should have been routine to look further on in the digestive process, in the duodenum and the rest of the small bowel. An examination of those organs would probably have located at least some small residue if the overdose was indeed a result of swallowing Nembutal capsules."

In Los Angeles, Dr. Noguchi admits ruefully that no such examination was ever made. He sent specimens of the relevant organs to the laboratory, but they were not tested. The tests were not done, Noguchi assumes, because the toxicologist felt the evidence in blood and liver was sufficient proof of the cause of death.

Noguchi says he did in fact try belatedly to have the specimens tested. "For some reason I felt uncomfortable," he says, "and shortly after the case was formally closed I called Toxicology and requested the check. . . . Abernethy told me the organ specimens had been destroyed."

Toxicologist Abernethy refuses to comment on the destruction of the medical evidence. Former Deputy DA John Miner, who was at the autopsy, says the slides from the specimens, which are listed in the official record, should have been preserved to this day. In 1984, though, efforts to find them turned up nothing. Nor do any medical photographs survive, though many were taken.

Dr. Noguchi says he wishes he had demanded checks on the intestines·in the first place. "I should have insisted that all the organs be analyzed," he says. "But I didn't follow through as I should have. As a junior member of the staff, I didn't feel I could challenge the department heads on procedures. . . ."

A fuller examination of the small intestine might have revealed the capsule residue that was absent in the stomach, and a great deal of controversy would have been avoided. As it is, the field is left clear for murder theories.

Was Marilyn given the fatal barbiturate dose by injection? All the doctors interviewed say this method—by introducing the drug straight into the bloodstream through a vein, into a muscle, or subcutaneously—would cause very rapid death, and that goes against the fact that a large quantity of barbiturates had been in the system long enough to be absorbed by the liver. All three people present at the autopsy say that Dr. Noguchi used a magnifying glass to look for injection marks, not omitting to study the vagina and under the tongue. He found nothing.

There is one other way the fatal dose could have been administered. It is possible to insert drugs colonically—in layman's terms, by enema—and this is a possibility that has not been raised before.

John Miner, the Deputy District Attorney who attended the autopsy—and who has lectured as an Associate Clinical Professor at the medical school of the University of Southern California—does not discount the enema option.

Amy Greene, Marilyn's friend in New York, says Marilyn took frequent enemas, as early as the mid-fifties. Marilyn's former Los Angeles neighbor, Jeanne Carmen, remembers her complaining about chronic constipation. Enemas are used to relieve that complaint. Their use was also a common fad, particularly among show business people in those days, as an aid to instant weight loss.

Peter Lawford's former wife, Deborah Gould, who says her husband confided in her about Marilyn, has attributed a strange remark to him. She said she asked Lawford whether he knew anything about how Marilyn had died. His only response, Gould told me—during an interview in which enemas had not been mentioned—was, "Marilyn took her last big enema."

This was indeed a bizarre comment, but Peter Lawford died in 1984. He cannot now be asked to explain it.

"The colon shows marked congestion and purplish discoloration," says the autopsy record. This could have been a clue, except that it does not say where on the colon the damage was. Former Deputy DA Miner recalls noticing the state of the organ, and suggesting to Dr. Noguchi that an anal smear be taken. That was not done. Miner indicates that, during subsequent work on the case, he learned that Marilyn indeed received enemas in her last days. Because this was a professional confidence, he declines to comment further.

Professor Simpson summed up: "The absence of capsule residue, somewhat surprising in view of the barbiturate level in the blood and liver, would suggest to me one of three things. The first possibility is that Marilyn Monroe took a gradual intake of barbiturates during the course of the day—and Dr. Greenson did think she was somewhat drugged when he visited her in the afternoon. This earlier Nembutal intake would have stayed in the blood for up to eight to twelve hours. She may then have taken a sudden dose of perhaps fifteen pills together—not necessarily more—and this, coupled with the previous doses, may have proved fatal. Monroe is known to have abused sleeping pills, and may have survived such a dose in the past. She may have believed she could do so again, not realizing the cumulative effect of the pills taken earlier. In that case, her death may have been not suicide, but a tragic mistake."

Before hearing Professor Simpson's second possibility, it is important to reconsider Marilyn's series of telephone calls to her friend, Jeanne Carmen, on that fatal Saturday. She had called early in the morning, asking Carmen to bring over some sleeping pills. She had made the same request later, and then called again about 10:00 P.M.—though Carmen cannot now remember whether she was still asking for pills.

If Marilyn was begging for pills, what does that mean? Did she want to be sure of having enough drugs to commit suicide? Had she already consumed the bulk of the twenty-five capsules prescribed on the previous day? Was that why, as Eunice Murray's son-in-law observed, she looked so ravaged on Saturday morning? The questions are unanswerable, but they bring us to Professor Simpson's next option. It is as sad to contemplate as the first.

"I would also want to know," said the Professor, "whether, on top of the pills taken during the day, there was a separate dose administered by another route. On the evidence, the possibility of another mode of entry should be seriously considered. The fatal dose—the one that pushed her over the edge—could have been administered rectally. It could easily have been put in along with a washout."

Such a final dose, Professor Simpson pointed out, could have been given by somebody who was unaware of the dangerously high drug level that had accumulated in Marilyn's system during the preceding hours. Again, her death would have been an accident, inadvertently caused by a second person.

The third possibility, and it is just that—a possibility—is that the fatal dose, by "another mode of entry," was delivered with malice aforethought. That, of course, would have been murder.

Evidence aside, what reason was there to kill Marilyn? Did anyone have a motive? Three main theories have been offered.

Some have hinted darkly that Marilyn knew too much, that she and her diary had become too explosive, that the Kennedys—or some shadowy agency on their behalf—did away with her. Others speculate that Marilyn, already linked to the Kennedys by gossip, was killed by the brothers' enemies to insure an explosion of scandal that would destroy the presidency. Which enemies?

One right-wing tract, noting that many of those around Marilyn had leftist connections, suggested a Communist murder plot designed to protect Robert Kennedy—portrayed by the Right as a rabid left-winger—from scandal.

Norman Mailer, in his 1973 book on Marilyn, took the murder option seriously. He considered "there was much motive for the right wing of the FBI or the CIA to implicate Bobby Kennedy in a scandal."

Hank Messick is an award-winning writer on organized crime and a former consultant to New York's Joint Legislative Committee on Crime. He believes that the Mafia—aware of the Kennedy affairs, and inspired by Marilyn's recent close call with death at Lake Tahoe—manipulated a drugged Marilyn, calling out for help, to lure Robert Kennedy into a trap.

Messick points out that in 1961 mobsters used chloral hydrate, one of the drugs found in Marilyn's system, in a scheme to discredit a man running for local office by drugging him, putting him in bed with a young woman, then having photographs taken. In Marilyn's case, Messick suggests, the plan was to have Robert Kennedy come to Marilyn's rescue. Then, compromised by being at Marilyn's home in the dead of night, he would be forced to ease up on organized crime or be destroyed by exposure.

The plot failed, Messick says, when Kennedy hardened his

heart and failed to rise to the bait. He refused to respond to Marilyn's pleas, and she died. Messick says his thesis is based on unattributable interviews with sources at the Justice Department and in organized crime.

Those who scorn murder theories point to the fact that Marilyn had tried suicide before, and was plainly on the way to destroying herself. Her life story certainly demonstrates that. Still, murder theorists would retort, what safer way to murder a test pilot than by sabotaging his aircraft? What easier way to murder Marilyn than by simulating suicide?

Norman Mailer wrote: "For anyone who wished to embarrass the Kennedys profoundly, and begin perhaps a whispering campaign which would destroy them by '64, how perfect a move to kill Marilyn in just such a way as to make it look like suicide in the first reports. As a suicide, however, it is so clumsily staged that by the second week every newspaper would be hinting at murder. That could do the Kennedys an unholy damage. Given the force of underground gossip . . . who would believe they had nothing to do with it? Even loyal Democrats might begin to wonder."

As he admits with regret, Mailer wrote on the basis of little research. It was a gamble for a great writer, and one for which he was rightly attacked. Now that the research is done, however, Mailer looks far from foolish.

In a real sense, outside the requirements of justice, it does not matter whether Marilyn was murdered, whether she died by her own hand, or—as is just possible—overestimated her capacity for Nembutal. The key to the events surrounding her end lies in the word "scandal."

It has been said that President Kennedy's womanizing, and the mob's knowledge of it, ultimately may have led to his assasination in Dallas in November 1963. The womanizing in the summer of 1962—and the loving and leaving of Marilyn— left the Kennedy brothers open to a different sort of assassination. Failing proof, jurists have said, we must sometimes assemble the evidence in piles, then consider their comparative size. For the historian, that is a legitimate exercise.

The piles of information in this book leave no doubt that the Kennedys took a perilously cavalier attitude toward sex, perilous because the evidence shows that their enemies knew, watched, listened, and waited for an opportunity to expose them. Murder or not, Marilyn's death was such an opportunity.

It was wonderfully lucky for the Kennedys that the press failed to investigate Marilyn's passing in 1962, that the job was left to right-wing scandalmongers with a limited audience. Luck, though, is perhaps an ill-chosen word. The circumstances of Marilyn's death, which very much involved the Kennedys, were deliberately covered up.

46

IN THE WEEKS AFTER MARILYN'S DEATH, autopsy surgeon Thomas Noguchi was troubled by things other than forensic detail. From his chair in the Hall of Justice, he says, he "had the strong feeling that the case was being delayed, and that the scene of death had been disturbed."

In 1962, before Coroners' investigators were introduced, a forensic pathologist had to rely on law-enforcement sources for relevant evidence other than the dead body itself. Noguchi says, "It seemed to me, from all I observed, that it's very likely the Police Department did close things down. I've encountered this often in my experience, in deaths involving important people. . . ." The facts support his hunch.

On the morning Marilyn died, and before her house was sealed, experienced reporters saw the familiar beginnings of a police inquiry into an unnatural death. "It was a typical police scene," recalls James Bacon of the Associated Press, "with the cops checking things, making chalk marks, measuring, and so on." Many photographs were taken, the Los Angeles District Attorney determined during his 1982 review. According to a retired police officer, who wishes not to be named, fingerprints were lifted. Joe Hyams, for the New York *Herald Tribune,* saw detectives covering Marilyn's bedroom "with large, canvas, evidence-preserving cloth."

At this earliest stage, it seems, the inquiry was being conducted by detectives of the West Los Angeles Division, because the death occurred in their jurisdiction. Meanwhile, just as Police Chief Parker had told his wife he intended, headquarters began its own investigation. Although never publicly revealed, it lasted for weeks.

Thad Brown, the Chief of Detectives summoned from his

weekend retreat when Marilyn died, was a man who insisted on staying in personal touch with his men and the cases they were investigating. ''Thad involved himself personally in the Monroe case,'' recalls one of Brown's senior staff, former Inspector Kenneth McCauley. ''He was particularly interested in it. The boys did their homework.'' Brown's brother and son, both former policemen themselves, confirm this.

Brown's adjutant, ''Pete'' Stenderup, handled the Chief of Detectives' paperwork. ''Thad followed through considerably on that one,'' he remembers. ''If any guys that were working on it wanted to see him, I was to make sure they got in to see him. If there was anything written came in, I made sure he got it. I remember anything from three to eight pages a day for weeks and weeks. These were notes, what we called ''fifteen/sevens,'' officers' memoranda. They were confidential, not part of the package that can be subpoenaed into court—the informal suspicions as to what might have happened. Robert Kennedy was mentioned frequently in those reports. . . .''

Brown was not personally running the Monroe inquiry. His responsibility was Homicide, and—perhaps thanks to the early forensic indications—his men never got the case. It was sent instead to another legendary figure, Captain James Hamilton, head of the Intelligence Division. He handled the matter in an atmosphere of secrecy that cut off his most trusted employees.

Hamilton's top aide, Lieutenant Marion Phillips, says, ''We knew about the inquiry, but we didn't get in on it at all. It was too damned hot. Captain Hamilton and Chief Parker were conferring on it. It went on and on, and weeks later the file went to the Chief.''

Today virtually nothing remains of the blizzard of paperwork that went across police desks. In 1974, after a new surge of public interest in the case, Kenneth McCauley, by then Commander, requested a search for the Monroe records. Homicide Special Section informed him that:

RHD (*Robbery and Homicide Division*) has no such records. Investigators contacted West Los Angeles Division and were informed that had no crime reports in their files pertaining to Miss Monroe's death. . . .

The report concluded that the vacuum was the innocent result of routine file destruction every ten years. A year later, after press allegations that Chief Parker had blocked the

Monroe inquiry to curry favor with the Kennedys, the then Police Chief asked Organized Crime Intelligence to make a fresh search. They found that even the routine Death Report, the most basic record of an unnatural death, was missing from the files. Officers began a somewhat humiliating paper chase across the city.

The Death Report, along with a handful of other documents, was finally located in a suburban garage. Chief of Detectives Thad Brown, never satisfied with the outcome of the case, had squirreled away a few documents from the early stages of the investigation. His son now handed them back to the Intelligence team, who duly collated them and reported to the Office of Operations.

In 1979, in an apparent follow-up to the 1975 inquiry, a note went to Captain Finch of OCID (Organized Crime Intelligence Division). It reads:

> The case folder prepared for Chief Gates is on file in OSS, the case folder in OSS contains all the reports in this folder, plus additional information and photographs.

OSS (Office of Special Service) was used for oddball jobs that did not fit normal categories. Since the Police Department has found it so hard to keep track of things, it seems sensible to record where the surviving Monroe file was last sighted. It would, of course, be interesting to examine the file, along with its "additional information and photographs," but the Police Department does not welcome research on Monroe.

The man who supervised the 1975 review of the case was Daryl Gates, then Director of Operations. In 1984, as Police Chief, he refused to release the police file on Marilyn's death. It was, he said, "retained in a confidential file." Subsequently, as this book was being published, he did release what appears to be part of the original dossier.

Lieutenant Marion Phillips, the former senior desk man in Police Intelligence, does not know what happened to the original files. He was told in 1962 that Chief Parker "had taken the file to show someone in Washington. That was the last we heard of it."

After Parker's death, in 1966, the Republican Mayor of Los Angeles, Sam Yorty, asked the Police Department to send over the Monroe file; he had heard the Kennedy rumors and was curious. The police told him simply, "It isn't here. . . ."

It would be wrong to imply that Chief Parker broke his tradition of iron integrity over the Monroe case. On the evidence, it seems more likely that—presumably satisfied murder was not involved—he passed the file on to a higher authority, thus washing his hands of the matter. That would account for the Chief's weary gesture to his wife weeks later, when he simply drew a question mark in the air.

The Police Department was not the only authority to investigate Marilyn's death. In 1982, after a fresh burst of public controversy, the Los Angeles Board of Supervisors asked the District Attorney's office to review the case.

The specific cause of this review was a public statement by a former Coroner's aide, Lionel Grandison. He had claimed publicly that he had been pressured into signing Marilyn's death certificate when he worked in the Coroner's office in 1962. Because he had been a County employee, the Board of Supervisors felt his allegations should be examined.

Assistant District Attorney Ronald Carroll investigated Grandison's claims, and some other aspects of the case. He did not find Grandison credible, and disposed of some red herrings that had been raised over the years. He then concluded— and has been at pains to point out his careful qualification— that "based on the information available, no further criminal investigation appears required into Miss Monroe's death."

The Carroll enquiry, however, did discover that the District Attorney's office was actively involved after Marilyn died. The Deputy DA then assigned to the case, John Dickey, today steadfastly avoids discussing the matter. Specifically, he will not say whether he tried to interview Peter Lawford or Robert Kennedy. No trace of his inquiry can be located in existing files.

New research, however, reveals that a number of reports were made in 1962 by the DA's Investigator, Frank Hronek, who—as we noted earlier—had earlier observed both Marilyn's contacts with mobsters and the nocturnal goings-on at the Lawford house. Today there is no trace of Hronek's reports in the DA's files.

According to his family, Hronek died suspecting that organized criminals were involved in the events surrounding Marilyn's death, and that there was indeed linkage to the Kennedy affairs. He specifically mentioned mobsters Sam

Giancana and Johnny Roselli, and said the Central Intelligence Agency intervened at some stage. Hronek suspected Marilyn had been murdered.

Another former Deputy District Attorney is sure there should be at least one document on file. This is John Miner, the DA's observer at Marilyn's autopsy. He says he was asked by Dr. Curphey, the Coroner in 1962, to secure an interview with Dr. Greenson. He assumes he was picked because he had taught at the Institute of Psychiatry and knew Greenson personally.

According to Miner he and Greenson met for about four hours at the psychiatrist's office, within days of Marilyn's death. Dr. Greenson was grief-stricken. He spoke freely and frankly to a man he was bound to talk to, but who would not publicly betray his trust. Miner, a lawyer of admirable, but frustrating, old-fashioned ethical standards, will reveal no details. What he does divulge, however, is vital information.

Greenson not only discussed Marilyn's confidences, but allowed Miner to listen to a forty-minute tape of Marilyn talking. This was evidently not a recording of a therapy session (Greenson did not record his patients), and Greenson's voice was not on the tape. Marilyn, however, who purchased a tape recorder a few weeks before she died, may have offered her private outpourings to her psychiatrist. Miner says Greenson subsequently destroyed the recording.

The Deputy District Attorney came away from Dr. Greenson's office in professional confusion. What he learned, he says, persuaded him it was "highly improbable" Marilyn deliberately killed herself. "Among other things," says Miner, "it was clear that she had plans and expectations for her immediate future." He will neither confirm nor deny that these plans involved one of the Kennedys.

Asked if Dr. Greenson thought Marilyn was murdered, Miner says, "That is something on which I cannot respond."

In August 1962, as a Deputy District Attorney, Miner had to report on the Greenson interview. What he did was to write a memorandum, which he recalls roughly as follows:

> As requested by you I have been to see Dr. Greenson to discuss the death of his late patient Marilyn Monroe. We discussed this matter for a period of hours, and as a result of what Dr Greenson told me, and from what I heard on tape recordings, I believe I can say definitely that it was not suicide.

This message went to Coroner Curphey, with a courtesy copy to the Chief Deputy DA, Manley Bowler. Miner waited in some trepidation for the response. He thought that, on all the evidence, that the District Attorney would convene a grand jury, and that he would be asked to testify. Miner says now, "I would have had to refuse, on ethical grounds, and I might well have been cited for contempt."

Miner need not have worried. The report went wholly unanswered, and cannot now be found. Asked why there was no reaction, Miner shrugs. Now in private legal practice he says, "Look, Bowler, my boss, was a bureaucrat. He saw the Coroner's Report—why rock the boat? That's the way things operate."

At first, in 1962, officials made fine statements. Within thirty-six hours of Marilyn's death, Coroner curphey asked that "all available information" be passed to the Los Angeles Suicide Prevention Center. Next day the Center's founder, Dr. Norman Farberow, said, "We are interviewing anybody and everybody. We will go as far back as is necessary." Two days later, as he was saying that his inquiries had no limitations, the *Los Angeles Times* reported: INQUEST POSSIBILITY LOOMS. Next day the New York *Herald Tribune* headline was WHAT KILLED MARILYN? PROBE WIDENS.

Quite suddenly, the investigation died. On August 12, exactly a week after Marilyn's death, the headline in the San Francisco and New York press—but not in Los Angeles—read BARE MYSTERY "PRESSURES" IN MARILYN PROBE. Florabel Muir, a veteran police reporter, wrote that "strange pressures are being put on Los Angeles police . . . sources close to the probers said tonight. . . . The purported pressures are mysterious. They apparently are coming from persons who had been closely in touch with Marilyn the past few weeks."

Five days later Coroner Curphey closed down the case. Seventy newsmen were summoned to hear him and the Suicide Prevention Team announce the verdict of "probable suicide." There was plenty to say about pills, and past history, and probable time of death. Newsmen went away satisfied, and that was that.

Dr. Greenson, struggling with his ethical conscience, had tried to tell the truth. He had assisted the authorities when they came to him, and nothing had happened. Now he was left to be the target of malicious gossip. Two years later, caught on the run by a reporter, Greenson would say,

"I can't explain myself or defend myself without revealing
things that I don't want to reveal. It's a terrible position
to be in, to say I can't talk about it. I just can't tell the
whole story."

47

THE KEY TO the "whole story" may have been the silent
witness grasped in Marilyn's stiff fingers when Dr. Greenson
stepped in to find her dead—the telephone. It was a dramatic
angle, and the press pounced on it. So, before the abrupt end
to their investigation, did the Suicide Team.

The Team's chief, Dr. Farberow, wanted to ask Greenson
whether, before he hung up the phone, he heard a dial tone or
silence, indicating a broken connection. Had Marilyn died
talking to someone, and who? By the second day there were
banner headlines about the "Mystery Phone Call," and the
star of the show—for a while—was Eunice Murray.

In her personal press interview Murray said she "thought
Marilyn might have been phoning someone when she saw that
the light was on in Marilyn's bedroom as she went to bed at
midnight."

As early as 8:00 A.M. the next morning, Mrs. Murray was
being quoted on radio broadcasts as saying she "saw a light
shining under Miss Monroe's door." Just how Murray knew
the light was on, since she agrees the pile of the new carpet
allowed no light to shine through, has been a bone of conten-
tion. To see the light, she would have had to go out into the
yard and look at the windows.

Today Murray maintains that it was not the light, but the
sight of the telephone extension cord, snaking across the hall
and under the door, that drew her attention. Whatever she
saw, the telephone mystery became a major news item.

Murray was quoted as saying of the call, "I don't remember what time it was and I don't know who called her, but
Marilyn seemed disturbed about it. . . ." How Murray knew
the call *disturbed* Marilyn, when she says she last saw her

around eight o'clock, is another moot point. Today she says she cannot remember the call at all.

As the banner newspaper headline became HUNT MYSTERY FRIEND, one of Marilyn's friends came out of the woodwork. The Kennedy brother-in-law, Peter Lawford, issued a statement through his agent, Milt Ebbins. "At approximately 7:00 P.M.," said Ebbins, Lawford "called to invite her and her friend, Pat Newcomb, to attend a small dinner party at his home." He says Miss Monroe told him she would like to come but that she was tired and was going to bed early. In a personal interview, Lawford said, "There didn't seem to be anything at all wrong with Marilyn. She sounded fine."

Whatever the truth of the Lawford tale—and he was to change it as time went by—it was certainly not, as one newspaper claimed, "the end of the mystery." If he called at seven, whose call "disturbed" Marilyn much later that evening?

In 1962 the authorities successfully snuffed out further speculation about the telephone. "There was no mystery call," said a member of the Suicide Team at Coroner Curphey's final press conference. The police, for their part, had blandly announced that Marilyn "received no telephone calls at a time which might have been related to her death." Sergeant Byron, the detective who had initiated the inquiries at Marilyn's house, said flatly that Lawford's call was the last Marilyn received.

This conclusion, reportedly made "after an extensive investigation," suggests supernatural sleuthing ability—there is no way to determine what calls have been received at a number; only outgoing calls are registered at the telephone company, for billing purposes. Marilyn's outgoing calls were potentially vital information. The police did check them, on the very first morning, but thereby hangs a really troubling tale.

One of the surviving fragments of the police file was written in the late afternoon of the day after Marilyn's death. Inspired by information given to Sergeant Byron by his boss, Lieutenant Armstrong, it states,

Miss Monroe's phone, GR6–1890, has been checked and no toll calls were made during the hours of this occurrence. Phone number 472–4830 is being checked at the present time.

Exhaustive interviews with employees of General Telephone (GTE), the company that supplied Marilyn's service, suggest this report was nonsense. In 1962 toll calls were recorded by hand, on cardboard slips, by the operator handling the call at the local traffic center. They were filed in boxes, which were then picked up at about midnight, seven days a week, and taken to company headquarters. Calls that could be dialed, Measured Message Unit calls, were recorded on a yellow tape roll, and that also ended up at headquarters. The toll calls were sorted first thing in the morning, then vanished into the accounting system for at least a week, usually longer.

"There was just that brief time in limbo, in the very early morning, when you could theoretically get to them," says a former company security officer. "After that, they were irretrievable for days, even if J. Edgar Hoover himself wanted them. With the formalities we had then, no ordinary cop could have got to Marilyn's records till nearly two weeks after her death."

Sergeant Byron himself refuses all comment on the Monroe case, but GTE officials assume his "check" on one of Marilyn's lines added up to no more than a comment from the security department that the only record immediately available had been that of Marilyn's collated bill, which was probably made up till the end of July, four days *before* the crucial night.

Routine practice, if a police check was required, was for the Police Chief personally to sign a request to the telephone company. Then, when the call slips came back to roost, an officer would go in person to General Telephone and make handwritten notes. Marilyn's surviving phone records reflect exactly this procedure—done some weeks after her death. They, in turn, offer up remarkable information of their own.

The records for Marilyn's two phones, as processed for billing up to late July, show a stream of toll calls, including the ones to the Justice Department. The police list of calls covering her last days, August 1 to 4, show only three calls. One, on Friday, was to Norman Rosten in New York, and the other two were to places near Los Angeles. This is odd indeed, for we know Marilyn spent a good deal of time talking long-distance in her last two days. What happened, in the ten days before the police made their notes, to the missing calls?

On August 12, in her article reporting "strange pressures"

on the police inquiry, reporter Florabel Muir said flatly of Marilyn's phone records: "The police have impounded the telephone company's taped record of those outgoing calls." Muir was an old hand on the police beat, with excellent contacts.

Joe Hyams of the *Herald Tribune*, meanwhile, who, with Muir, was one of the very few reporters who did any serious digging, was also using his contacts. He stumbled on something sensational.

"The morning after her death," says Hyams, "I contacted a telephone company employee and asked him to copy for me the list of numbers on her tape—a service he was willing to provide for a fee. Within the hour my contact called me back from a pay phone. 'All hell has broken loose down here,' he told me. 'Apparently you're not the only one interested in Marilyn's calls. But the tape's disappeared. I'm told it was impounded by the Secret Service—I've never before heard of the government getting in on the act. Obviously somebody high up ordered it.' "

Checks on how Hyams and Muir got their information support their stories, and indicate that the phone records had already been removed by mid-morning on Sunday, within hours of Marilyn's death being known publicly. It seems, moreover, that it was in fact the FBI that took the records, rather than the Secret Service.

It is significant that the records had already been removed by early Sunday morning, because that was the one time they could be scooped up, before vanishing for weeks in the accounting system. Obviously, such prompt and sweeping action required the intervention of someone with great authority and clout, someone who could roust a top General Telephone executive from his bed early on a Sunday, then pressure him into immediate action.

One of General Telephone's 1962 security team, Bob Warner, is still with the company today. He says that he "does not recall" the removal of Marilyn's phone records. Another man, however, has very specific recollections. Dean Funk, former publisher of the Santa Monica *Evening Outlook*, was a close friend of the Division Manager for General Telephone, the late Robert Tiarks.

Funk clearly recalls sitting with Tiarks before a board meeting, not long after Marilyn's death, discussing the affair. "He told me that the FBI came in and got the records, the next day."

In a partially censored FBI document, written in 1973, a former senior FBI Los Angeles agent recorded that he had responded to a press inquiry on the subject by saying that he too "had no recollection of any such event." "No recollection" is a time-honored official formula for providing a negative while reserving the right to "remember," if facts are later exposed.

As this book went to press the truth was exposed. I traced another former FBI agent, who has asked to remain anonymous. He was a senior figure, who in 1962 was in charge of organized crime investigations in a major West Coast city.

"I am convinced," he says, "that the FBI did remove certain Monroe phone records. I was on a visit to California when Monroe died, and there were some people there, Bureau personnel, who normally wouldn't have been there— agents from out of town. They were on the scene immediately, as soon as she died, before anyone realized what had happened. I subsequently learned that agents had removed the records. It had to be on the instructions of somebody high up, higher even than Hoover."

Higher than Hoover? The former agent understood at the time that the orders came from "either the Attorney General or the President. I know that from my knowledge of the structure of the FBI, the way things were handled in those days. I knew this had come from someone via telephone and not through any trackable communication." So that it would not appear on the record? "That's right," the agent replied.

Dean Funk, the Santa Monica newspaper publisher, remembers one final detail from his conversations with former telephone company executive, Robert Tiarks. "He was hesitant in talking about it," Funk recalls, "but he said he knew there had been a call to Washington on the night Monroe died."

Before his enquiry was closed down, Dr. Litman, of the Los Angeles Suicide Prevention Team, also learned that Marilyn had called the East Coast at about 9:00 P.M., as the last minutes of her life ticked away.

The most significant testimony on the removal of the telephone records is clearly that of the retired West Coast FBI agent. His certainty that the orders came "higher even than Hoover"—from Robert Kennedy or the President himself— not only indicates the brothers' awareness of the incalculable damage they could suffer were the phone records made public. To contain the damage, they were forced to turn for help to the one man in office who most detested Robert Kennedy, Hoover. It was more than humiliating—it meant that the brothers would forever be indebted to the FBI Director. They had to rely on him, of all people, to keep the Marilyn connection secret.

Robert Kennedy, meanwhile, was still threatened by the record of earlier calls which—by the night of Marilyn's death—had progressed so far into the accounting system that they could not be removed by FBI intervention at General Telephone. The string of calls Marilyn made to the Justice Department in June and July, obtained by this author from Los Angeles police records, could only be obtained in the formal way, by a police visit to General Telephone's office a couple of weeks after the actress' death. Once again, somebody saw to it that normal routine was bypassed.

In 1962 one police secretary, Shirley Brough, was responsible for typing all applications to see telephone records. She specifically recalls that, quite exceptionally, she was not given the Monroe paperwork. Brough, who then worked in the Intelligence Division, remembers that "it was all handled by the Captain's secretary. This was done for confidentiality. This was something very extraordinary, because of the people Marilyn Monroe was known to have associated with. So they figured they would not take any chances at all."

The Captain, and head of the Intelligence Division, was James Hamilton, who personally directed the Monroe work for Chief Parker. Some time after the event he lunched with a crime reporter he had come to know and trust, Jack Tobin of the *Los Angeles Times*. Tobin says, "Hamilton told me he had the telephone history of the last day or two of Marilyn Monroe's life. When I expressed interest, he said, 'I will tell you nothing more.' But it was obvious he knew much more."

Robert Kennedy knew Captain Hamilton very well indeed. He mentioned him several times in his book, *The Enemy Within*, and referred to him in the foreword as "my friend." Kennedy admired Hamilton's intelligence-gathering system, and used his advice during his work in the Senate and at the Justice Department.

A year after Marilyn's death, on his retirement from the police force, Hamilton became Chief Security Officer for the National Football League. Robert Kennedy was one of those who recommended him for the job. Hamilton's son says, "He had a relationship with the Kennedys independent of his professional function."

On the morning of Marilyn's death, when Chief of Detectives Thad Brown was summoned to headquarters because of a "problem," he was about to spend the day with the Assistant Chief of the regional Intelligence Division of the Treasury Department, Virgil Crabtree. The problem, Brown told Crabtree, was that a piece of crumpled paper had been found in Marilyn's bedclothes. It bore a White House telephone number.

Police Chief Parker's successor was Tom Reddin, who in 1962 was a Deputy Chief. He says, "Where Hamilton and his Intelligence Division were concerned, nobody knew a bloody thing about what was going on. Hamilton talked to only two people, God and Chief Parker. I was aware of the fact that there was a Hamilton investigation on the Monroe case, but I never knew what it was. I was also aware that there was supposed to be an internal document that never became public."

Former Chief Reddin adds: "The Kennedy connection was a matter of common knowledge at the Police Department level I was at. The Kennedy—I should say Kennedys'—relationship with Marilyn Monroe was pretty generally accepted. We heard that one of her last calls was to Bobby."

Lawrence Schiller, one of the photographers who had covered the nude swim in *Something's Got to Give*, was out of town when he heard the news of Marilyn's death. He hurried back to Los Angeles, and that evening found himself sitting in the office of Arthur Jacobs, Marilyn's public relations consultant.

As he sat in the office, Schiller says, he overheard Jacobs talking with Pat Newcomb. Their great concern at the time, he says, was "what would be revealed by the telephone records."

They need not have worried. That embarrassment, it seems, had been well looked after.

48

WHAT REALLY HAPPENED the night Marilyn died? Who did what in the vital hours? The answers are there, but they are elusive. Witnesses talk reluctantly, and some will now talk no more.

In 1983, in a fashionable Los Angeles restaurant, Peter Lawford looked like a frail old man. He was only sixty, but worn out by a lifetime of excess. As conversation turned to the fatal night, the slouched figure stiffened, a shaking hand crawled across the table to the ashtray. The drawling voice started to tell the story. Then Lawford said, half-sobbing, "To this day I cannot forgive myself; there is no excuse for the fact I did not go. . . ." He burst into tears, and the subject had to be dropped. Lawford died as this book was going to press.

Also in 1983, Eunice Murray, as sharp as a pin at eighty-two, sat in a rundown house in Santa Monica, taking the questions and answering carefully. A memory that seemed clear on irrelevant minutiae suddenly became fogged on key issues concerning the night of the tragedy. The reporter departed feeling that, very courteously, Murray had been playing with him.

Lawford and Murray have always been prime witnesses to Marilyn's last hours, but they were never heard under oath. Police questioned Murray within hours of Marilyn's death, then again a few days later. The second time, Lieutenant Armstrong, Commander of the West Los Angeles Detective Division, was present. The report of the interview, revealed here for the first time, reads (see next page):

It is officers opinion that Mrs. Murray was vague and possibly evasive in answering questions pertaining to the activities of Miss Monroe during this time. It is not known whether this is, or is not, intentional. . . .

385

Form 15.1
Rev. July 1953   EMPLOYEE'S REPORT   62-509-463

Subject RE-INTERVIEW OF PERSONS KNOWN TO MARILYN MONROE

Date & Time Occurred August 6, 1962	Location of Occurrence Various	Division of Occurrence

Zone, Zone, Assignment, Division   Date & Time Reported
G. H. ARMSTRONG, COMMANDER, WEST L.A. DETECTIVE DIVISION 8-10-62 8:30A

DETAILS

The following is a resume of the interview conducted in an effort to
obtain the times of various phone calls received by Miss Monroe on
the evening of her death. All of the below times are estimations of
the persons interviewed. None are able to state definite times as
none checked the time of these calls.

MRS. EUNICE MURRAY -

Mrs. Murray stated that she had worked for Marilyn Monroe since
November, 1961, that on the evening of 8-4-62 Miss Monroe had received
a collect call from a Joe DiMaggio, Jr. at about 7:30P. Mrs. Murray
said that at the time of this call coming in, Miss Monroe was in bed
and possibly had been asleep. She took the call and after talking to
Joe DiMaggio, Jr., she then made a call to Dr. Greenson and Mrs. Murray
overheard her say, "Joe Jr. is not getting married, I'm so happy about
this." Mrs. Murray states that from the tone of Miss Monroe's voice,
she believed her to be in very good spirits. At about 9P, Mrs. Murray
received a call from Mr. Rudin who inquired about Miss Monroe.
Mr. Rudin did not talk to Miss Monroe. Mrs. Murray states that these
are the only phone calls that she recalls receiving on this date.
Note: It is officers opinion that Mrs. Murray was vague and possibly
evasive in answering questions pertaining to the activities of
Miss Monroe during this time. It is not known whether this is, or is
not intentional. During the interrogation of Joe DiMaggio, Jr., he
indicated he had made three phone calls to the Monroe home, only one
of which Mrs. Murray mentioned.

JOE DiMAGGIO - Miramar Hotel, Room 1035, Santa Monica

Mr. DiMaggio was informed of the rumor which quoted him as saying that

Date & Time Typed 8-10-62 9A WLA	Div. Rpt. 	Clerk jg	Employee(s) Reporting R. E. BYRON	Ser.No. 2730	Div. WL
Supervisor Approving			Serial No. 59	LT. G. H. ARMSTRONG, CMDR 59 WL	

Part of the police file on Marilyn's death, released in 1985 only after it
had been obtained privately by the author. It shows that investigating
officers were less than satisfied with the evidence of housekeeper Mrs.
Murray, a key witness.

If Mrs. Murray left the police feeling uneasy, Peter Lawford left them empty-handed. A 1962 police report reads: "An attempt was made to contact Mr. Lawford, but officers were informed by his secretary that Mr. Lawford had taken an airplane at 1:00 P.M." It was August 8, three days after Marilyn's death, and Lawford had sought refuge in Robert Kennedy's house in Hyannis Port.

He was joined there, at Robert Kennedy's invitation, by Pat Newcomb. According to Dr. Farberow, chief of the Suicide Prevention Team, Newcomb had declined to be interviewed before leaving. "She stone-walled me," Farberow recalls, "was uncommunicative."

It took thirteen years before Peter Lawford was finally interviewed by the police, during the police review of the case in 1975. He also talked to the District Attorney in 1982. Investigators have found it hard to evaluate Lawford's statements. "He was intense," says one interrogator. "He was not iffy about it, he was real sure about what he was saying."

Lawford's story changed as the years passed, and from one police interview to another. Happily, comparing the key players' statements with those of others never before interviewed, we cna make a stab at reconstructing the last hours.

Several people were invited to Lawford's home on that fatal Saturday evening. They included a television producer, Joe Naar, and his wife, Dolores. The Naars lived two miles from the Lawford beachhouse, and just four blocks away from Marilyn. They were friendly with the Lawfords, and had met both Marilyn and Robert Kennedy at their home. According to the Naars, Peter Lawford telephoned sometime on Saturday to ask them over for supper. Since Mariyn was also invited, Lawford asked if they would bring her in their car.

Joe Naar says that later, before they set out that evening, "Peter called to say Marilyn would not be coming after all. She was tired and felt like staying at home."

It may be, however, that Marilyn did make a brief appearance at the Lawford house, early in the evening—perhaps going ahead with her intention, as expressed to Dr. Greenson in the afternoon, of driving to the beach.

In 1979, in a conversation after Darryl Zanuck's funeral, actress Natalie Wood, who had been a friend of Marilyn for years, said she and actor Warren Beatty had been at the Lawford house a few hours before Marilyn died.

Following up on this, I contacted Beatty in 1983. He said,

very hesitantly, "I, ah, I did see her the night before she died. But, ah, I don't think I would see any particular thing to be gained by expounding on it, er . . . I don't really want to be quoted. I don't think I'll speak about it. . . ."

By "the night before she died," is Beatty referring to Friday or the fatal Saturday? Mystery surrounds Marilyn's activity on both evenings. Beatty refuses to say any more on the subject.

If Marilyn did go to the Lawford house on Saturday evening—or indeed if Beatty and Wood were there—it was an extremely brief visit, and before the other supper guests arrived. None of them were there when Joe and Dolores Naar arrived, at around eight-thirty.

With the Naars at the supper party was producer George "Bullets" Durgom. He had been at the Lawfords in the past, he says, when Marilyn "would come in with Bobby and then leave." That night, Durgom recalls, Lawford had ordered a Chinese dinner to be sent in, and there was talk of Marilyn having been invited. It is at this point that the stories start to diverge.

Lawford, in his original statement to the press, spoke of only one call to Marilyn, at 7:00 P.M., in which she begged off, claiming weariness. This meshes with the Naars' version, which has Marilyn canceling before they arrived at the party. Lawford, however, when finally interviewed by the police in 1975, introduced a whole new series of phone calls to Marilyn and an ensuing drama.

Lawford told the police he had first telephoned Marilyn about 5:00 P.M., which was around the time Marilyn, distraught, had called in Dr. Greenson. Lawford said she "sounded despondent" over the dismissal from *Something's Got to Give* and "some other personal matters." He urged her to come over for the evening, and she said she would think about it.

At 7:30 P.M. or a little later, according to this Lawford version, he called Marilyn again because she had failed to turn up. She still sounded depressed, and "her manner of speech was slurred. She stated she was tired and would not be coming. Her voice became less and less audible and Lawford began to yell at her in an attempt to revive her. [He described it as a verbal slap in the face.] Then she stated, 'Say goodbye to Jack [John Kennedy], and say good-bye to yourself, because you're a nice guy.' "

The phone then went dead, Lawford told the police in 1975.

He assumed Marilyn had hung up, tried several times to call her back, and found the number consistently busy.

In 1982 Lawford told a similar story to the District Attorney's investigators, with variations. He now said there was no second conversation, that the number was busy when he tried to call back. It stayed busy for half an hour, so he called the operator. Told the phone was off the hook, he became seriously concerned. By this time, according to one of his servants, Lawford was also very drunk.

A member of the Suicide Prevention Team, Dr. Litman, says he learned that, after the last call from Marilyn, Lawford placed a call to Washington.

Lawford says he wanted to go himself to check on Marilyn, but first turned to his agent, Milton Ebbins, for advice. Ebbins confirms that this conversation occurred, though accounts differ as to whether Ebbins was present at supper or whether Lawford called him at home. He says he told Lawford it would be a mistake to go, and promised instead to call the attorney Marilyn shared with Frank Sinatra, Milton Rudin, who also happened to be Dr. Greenson's brother-in-law.

Ebbins says he reached Rudin at another party, and Rudin, who was interviewed by police in 1962, said he received the call at about 8:45 P.M.. He said Ebbins told him of the cause for concern and he agreed to call Marilyn's house. About fifteen minutes later he did call, and the phone was answered by Mrs. Murray.

Rudin turned down an interview request in 1983, so we must make do with what he told the police three days after Marilyn died. According to the police report, he said he had asked Mrs. Murray "as to the physical well-being of Miss Monroe, and was assured by Mrs. Murray that Miss Monroe was all right. Believing that Miss Monroe was suffering from one of her despondent moments, Mr. Rudin dismissed the possibility of anything further being wrong."

Eunice Murray agrees that Rudin called, but insists the lawyer said nothing about the troubling call Marilyn had supposedly had with Lawford. She assumed it was merely a casual inquiry and, without checking on Marilyn, said all was well. According to this version, that was effectively that. Mrs. Murray would then doze till about 3:30 A.M., then awake, find the door locked, and call Dr. Greenson in alarm.

The rest would be history, except that this scenario presents some major problems. First, consider two questions, two weak points in the public account. They concern motivation.

Twenty-three years later, we still do not know *why* Murray became concerned about Marilyn in the middle of the night. Given that, according to her, Rudin had said nothing to arouse concern about Marilyn, is it really likely that the mere sight of a telephone extension cord under Marilyn's door would have sent Murray rushing to the telephone to wake Dr. Greenson in the early hours of the morning?

More recently, in a memoir ghosted by a relative, Rose Shade, we are told merely that "some sixth sense warned Eunice of danger." That is not easy to accept.

With Mrs. Murray the question is "Why?" In the case of Peter Lawford, it is "Why not?" Why, after his worrying telephone conversation with Marilyn, did Lawford not simply get in his car and make the short trip to her house?

Lawford's answer was that he called his agent, Milt Ebbins, and that Ebbins told him, "You can't go over there! You're the brother-in-law of the President of the United States. Your wife's away. Let me get in touch with her lawyer or doctor. They should be the ones to go over."

Ebbins has backed up the gist of this story, but does it ring true? If, as Lawford always maintained, there was no Marilyn involvement with the Kennedys, why did he feel it necessary to start a complicated chain of phone calls? Why did Ebbins feel the matter was so sensitive? There really was no reason not to respond naturally, and simply go to see Marilyn.

The next snag is the problem of timing—both of Mrs. Murray's actions and of the activity at the Lawford house. Here the stories collapse in a mess of inconsistencies, which, once unraveled, help resolve the bigger questions.

Mr. and Mrs. Naar, who offer the most cogent account of the evening, say they left the Lawfords' supper party fairly early, "well before eleven." They were home, and getting undressed for bed, when they got an unexpected call from Lawford. He said he was worried because "Marilyn had called to say she had taken pills, perhaps too many. She herself had expressed concern that perhaps she had overdone it."

Lawford asked Joe Naar to stand by to go to check on Marilyn, and Naar agreed. Then, say the Naars, Lawford called again to say there was, after all, no cause for alarm. The Naars went to bed.

The Naars' evidence is vital, because it shifts the whole drama to a much later point in the evening. Both Mr. and Mrs. Naar are adamant that, during the supper party, between eight and soon after ten, there was no talk of concern for Marilyn, not a word about "good-bye" phone calls. Had this drama started already, they insist, they could not have failed to hear about it. It was an intimate gathering, and they knew Lawford and Marilyn well. Yet, until the Naars left the Lawford house, all was calm.

The evidence of Bullets Durgom, the other known guest, is consistent with the Naars over the vital question of timing. He says it was late that evening, when he and Lawford were sitting around drinking, that Lawford declared his serious concern about Marilyn. It was then, Durgom says, that inquiries were started.

Here we must turn back to Mrs. Murray. Immediately after the death, Dr. Greenson wrote to friends saying Mrs. Murray had first noticed a light on in Marilyn's room at *midnight*. She had then, as Greenson understood her, dozed off again till her "sixth sense" woke her again about 3:30 A.M.

In the very first press quotation attributed to her, Murray spoke of first seeing the light on "at midnight." The first officer on the scene, Sergeant Clemmons, says Murray told him she had first become alarmed "at midnight."

In a long initial interview with this author, she told me—three times—that she had wakened to discover the body "about midnight." Pressed on the point, Murray backtracked, saying the events of that unhappy night may now be jumbled in her mind.

Mrs. Murray agrees there was a lengthy delay in calling the police, but lays that delay at the doctors' door. "They had much to talk about," she says, "on how it could have happened, no doubt having to do with how many tablets they had prescribed for her." Yet Dr. Greenson's earliest statements to the police, and his correspondence, say flatly that the first he knew of a crisis was the call from Mrs. Murray at 3:30 A.M.

There is a great difference, actually and in the ordinary perception of a witness, between midnight and half past three. If Mrs. Murray did realize Marilyn was dead or in serious trouble at midnight, and if she did not call Dr. Greenson then, what did occur between the late evening and the early hours of the morning?

That mystery may well now be resolved, thanks to the discovery of new witnesses with startling, fresh information.

* * *

Arthur Jacobs, the head of the company which handled
Marilyn's public relations, was never questioned about what
happened on the night of her death. He is dead, but his
widow, Natalie, offers a firsthand account that completely
changes the story.

As we have seen, the Jacobs were close to Marilyn. They
spent a great deal of time with her in the last months, nursing
her through her troubles and listening to her unhappy story of
love for the President and of meetings with Bobby Kennedy.

Natalie Jacobs will never forget the night of August 4,
1962. It was the eve of her birthday, and she and Arthur went
to a concert at the Hollywood Bowl that Saturday night. They
sat under the stars listening to Henry Mancini's orchestra, and
piano duets by Ferrante and Teicher.

It was a fine night, and Natalie was in love. She and Arthur
were not yet married, and this was a rare peaceful evening
undisturbed by the demands of Hollywood clients. Then, toward the end of the concert, the peace was interrupted.
Someone—she thinks one of the staff of the Hollywood Bowl—
came to Jacobs with a message. It was from Pat Newcomb,
Natalie believes, and the news was that Marilyn was dead.

"We got the news long before it broke," says Natalie.
"We left the concert at once and Arthur left me at our house.
He went to Marilyn's house, and I don't think I saw him for
two days. He had to fudge the press."

Natalie Jacobs is absolutely certain the news of Marilyn's
death reached them before the concert ended. A check in the
Los Angeles Times for that day shows that the concert had
begun at 8:30 P.M.; it certainly ended well before midnight.
Natalie Jacobs believes they had the news by 11:00 P.M.

I reminded Natalie that, according to the version given to
the police and for public consumption, Marilyn's body was
not discovered till 3:40 A.M. the next morning. She replied,
"Allow me to tell you why. My husband fudged everything—I
cannot tell you why. I was not there. I was at home. That was
his business."

With this new evidence, a great deal falls into place. It is
now obvious why the various guests at the Lawford house
heard nothing about alarming phone calls with Marilyn during
the early evening. We can now see why Lawford called two
of his guests, the Naars, only after they had returned home, to
ask them to stand by to go and check on Marilyn. And if the
truth was now to be "fudged," we can see exactly why he
called back to tell them not to bother.

It is time, too, to turn for a moment to the medical evidence. Professor Keith Simpson was keenly interested to learn that Marilyn's body was already stiff, in *rigor mortis*, when Dr. Greenson entered her room at about 3:40 A.M. Professor Simpson said, "*Rigor mortis* only shows after four to six hours, which places her death well before midnight."

Marilyn sounded befuddled when she spoke to various friends between eight and ten o'clock that Saturday night. It seems most probable that it was soon after 10:00 P.M. that she slipped into a terminal coma. It is highly unlikely, though, that she simply lay dead in her bed until Mrs. Murray's call to Dr. Greenson in the early hours.

Another piece of new evidence strongly suggests that this timing is correct, that the true drama began long before Dr. Greenson was alerted. The evidence indicates that others were present at the house long before Marilyn's psychiatrist, and that, for a while, they hoped she might survive.

In 1982, during the District Attorney's review of the case, investigators learned the entirely fresh information—never even hinted at before—that an ambulance was called to Marilyn's home that night.

The D.A.'s staff talked to a former ambulance driver named Ken Hunter, who in 1962 worked for Schaefer Ambulance, the biggest private ambulance company in the Los Angeles area. He said he attended Marilyn's home with an assistant, "in the early morning hours." He said—to the D.A.'s man at any rate—that Marilyn was dead. As the crew left, the police were arriving.

Hunter told me he saw no doctors or police. He seemed evasive and refused further contact after an initial call. He had told the District Attorney that he thought his assistant that night had been an employee named Murray Liebowitz. I traced Liebowitz, who has changed his name to Leib.

My telephone interview with Leib began with a series of silences on his part, even on whether he had once driven for Schaefer Ambulance. When I explained my interest, he said, "I don't want to be involved in this. . . . I wasn't on duty that night. I heard about it when I came to work next morning. . . . I'm not worried about anything, there's nothing to worry about. Don't bother to call me anymore."

In 1985 I talked on several occasions to the late Walt Schaefer, who was then still running the ambulance company he founded. He confirmed, with utter certainty, that a Schaefer ambulance was called to Marilyn's home. Asked whether

Murray Liebowitz was one of the crew, he said, "I know he was."

Schaefer said he learned of the Monroe call the next morning, and that the bill was subsequently paid by her estate. "We'd hauled her before," he recalled, "because of the barbiturates. We'd hauled her when she comatosed."

The ambulance company chief then added the most remarkable detail of all on the events of the fatal night. He said the ambulance "took her to Santa Monica Hospital. She passed away at the hospital. She did not die at home."

Walt Schaefer does not remember with certainty who arranged for the ambulance or whether anyone accompanied Marilyn to the hospital. His company only keeps records for five years, so there is no way of documenting the episode. Initial research at Santa Monica Hospital has borne no fruit. The staff have changed many times since 1962, and it may be that the emergency room personnel never knew who they were treating—if indeed Marilyn ever reached the hospital.

Many questions remain. Who called the ambulance? Who was able to accomplish the quiet return of a dead Marilyn to her home—before Mrs. Murray sounded the alarm at 3:30 A.M.? If this was done, how can we explain the telephone found in Marilyn's dead hand?*

Testimony suggests that several people may have been at Marilyn's home before that hour. Natalie Jacobs says Arthur Jacobs was there within an hour of leaving the Hollywood Bowl, probably by 11:30 P.M. Several people place Milton Rudin, the lawyer, at Marilyn's house in the middle of the night.

Lawford's agent, Ebbins, who says he called Rudin earlier in the evening to raise the first alarm, says the lawyer called him at four in the morning—before the police were called.

" 'I'm at Marilyn's house now,' " Ebbins quotes Rudin as saying, " 'and she's dead.' And do you know, no one has ever mentioned Rudin being at her house? He was *there*."

Interviewed in 1973, Pat Newcomb also said she heard news of Marilyn's death "around four," from Rudin, calling—she thought—from Marilyn's home.

In 1982, in a statement to the District Attorney's staff, Peter Lawford for the first time injected into his story the precise time at which he heard the death news, and how. He

---

* New information, dealt with in the Postscript, may explain the matter of the telephone.

said he was wakened at 1:30 A.M. by a phone call from
Ebbins, passing on news from Rudin that Marilyn was dead.
Lawford said he was "sure he received the verification at
1:30 A.M. because he looked at the bedside clock at the time
of Ebbins' call."

Ebbins, for his part, says he indeed tried to pass on the
news to Lawford—but not till 4:00 A.M., and *he* says he got
no response from Lawford's phone. "I called but I couldn't
get anyone," Ebbins says. "The phone didn't answer. . . ."
Had Peter Lawford gone out? And if so, what was his purpose?

Lawford's former wife, Deborah Gould, who says he confided in her about Marilyn, offers disturbing answers. "Marilyn got on the phone to Peter," says Gould, "grasping out, to
inform him that she couldn't take any more, and that it would
be best for everybody that she died, and she was going to kill
herself. Peter had been drinking a great deal, and he had a
cynical sense of humor, but maybe he didn't take her
seriously."

It may be that Peter Lawford did, after all, respond to the
troubling telephone conversation with Marilyn, though he
clearly arrived too late. It seems, indeed, that he was one of
the very first people to reach her home.

Deborah Gould quotes Lawford as responding to Marilyn's
talk of suicide with, " 'Nonsense, Marilyn, pull yourself
together; but, my God, whatever you do don't leave any notes
behind.' That was the end of the conversation," Gould says,
"as far as what he told me."

Asked whether Marilyn did leave a note, Gould says, "Yes,
she did." Asked what it said, she replies, "I don't know; the
note was destroyed." Who destroyed it? "I'm sure Peter did,
he told me he did," Gould responds.

Lawford's former wife says Lawford went to Marilyn's
house that night. According to her, "He went there and
tidied up the place, and did what he could, before the police
and the press arrived. . . ." Questioned about the alleged
destruction of the note, Gould says Lawford did it "to protect
loved ones involved."

The loved ones involved, according to Gould, were the
Kennedy brothers. "That's where Peter's role came in," she
says, "to cover up all the dirty work, and take care of
everything." Gould, quoting Lawford, says the Kennedys
ensured there would be no proper inquiry into Marilyn's
death.

49

BEFORE DAWN ON THE morning of Sunday, August 5, about 5:00 A.M., the radio crackled into life at an apartment in Hollywood used by one of the most effective and discreet security men on the West Coast. He talks now only on the written understanding that his name not be used, but five intensive interviews, and complex crosschecks, confirm his background and expertise, and indicate that he is telling the truth.

The radio call, says the security man, was a summons from Fred Otash, the Hollywood private detective whose name has been linked with surveillance of Marilyn and the Kennedy brothers. Otash, as he readily admits, was a man for hire. On this occasion, ironically, the mission called for a cover-up on behalf of the Kennedys.

It took the security man some twenty minutes to get up and drive to Otash's office. There, he says, he found Otash in the company of Peter Lawford, "squirming like a worm in a frying pan."

The briefing was intense and to the point. The security man was told that Marilyn was dead, that she had tried the night before to reach the President at the White House—he had, in fact, been at Hyannis Port over the weekend—and that she had done so in the midst of great upset over Robert Kennedy.

According to the security man, "Lawford said Monroe had been in a rage about being used and refused. She did not want to be treated as a piece of meat." The security man understood that Marilyn had left some sort of note, which had already been removed. His job, he was told, was to check her house, especially for papers or letters, that might give away her affairs with the Kennedys. He was also to try to discover potential sources of leaks, and take action to silence them.

Fred Otash, faced with the security man's statements, says, "I know that [the security man] has been saying that I called him up in the middle of the night, and that we had a meeting with Peter Lawford and discussed clearing up after Marilyn

Monroe died, and well, my response to that is, 'I will neither confirm nor deny it.' All I've got to do is say that, and I'm going to end up in front of a grand jury.''*

The consultant says he judged the assignment impracticable, but he was to be well paid—thousands of dollars were involved. He had excellent police contacts, as I confirmed, and by about nine o'clock he was able to walk into Marilyn's house with a police officer.

The policeman was from another division in the city, and had no proper business at the house. He was nervous, and the two men spent only twenty minutes on the scene. The security man therefore had no chance to perform his task, and left empty-handed. Before leaving, however, he noted an important detail—a filing cabinet in the garden room had been forcibly opened.

Bills submitted to Marilyn's estate by the A-1 Lock and Safe Company show that during the summer she had the lock changed on a filing cabinet at her home. Joe DiMaggio's friend, Harry Hall, who accompanied him to the house later on Sunday, says DiMaggio "looked for what he referred to as a book, and it was gone. All her personal notes were gone."

The security consultant, called to meet Lawford that Sunday morning, learned that "Bobby Kennedy had been at Marilyn's house sometime Saturday, and was at Lawford's house sometime in the evening. They had tried to talk her into coming to the beach house. I understood Bobby had been in town and then got out by what Lawford referred to as the Air Force. I think he left soon after Marilyn's last call."

Lawford's former wife, Deborah Gould, quotes her husband as saying the Attorney General at first tried to get Lawford to persuade Marilyn that their affair was over "a couple of days before she died." Then, says Gould, "She tried desperately to get in touch with Bobby. Peter mentioned she made calls to Pat, trying to find out where Bobby was, and found out that he was on the West Coast, in San Francisco."

Told that Lawford maintained, as late as 1973, that Robert Kennedy was on the East Coast that weekend, Gould says, "Peter is a very good actor, but a very poor liar."

Gould, quoting Lawford, says Kennedy came from San Francisco to Los Angeles that weekend. Robert Kennedy, as

*Otash was there—as he admitted after the publication of *Goddess* in 1985. His important new statements are included in the Postscript.

is well documented, was indeed in California. But did he stay in the San Francisco area, or did he go to see Marilyn in Los Angeles?

"Even Peter Pan would have had a hard time doing that," says John Bates, Kennedy's host that weekend. "It's mind-boggling." During their weekend on the Bates ranch, Robert and Ethel Kennedy and their children spent much of their time with the Bates family. Although they used a separate guest cottage, most meals were eaten communally.

Bates thinks everyone went horseback riding together sometime on Saturday, Marilyn's last day alive. He believes he would have known if Kennedy had left for long enough to reach Los Angeles and return by the early hours of Sunday.

The ranch is at Gilroy, three hundred miles northwest of Los Angeles. Certainly, the parish priest confirms, Kennedy was in Gilroy by 9:30 A.M. on Sunday, attending Mass at the Church of St. Mary.

Questioning of the Bateses aside, further checks on Kennedy's time at the ranch are difficult. The weekend arrangements were private. The Kennedys were assisted at various stages by the San Francisco office of the FBI, but the Special Agent in Charge at the time is not cooperative. The agent, Frank Price, refuses to comment on the Attorney General's movements.

If Robert Kennedy did make a trip to Los Angeles that Saturday, he must have made it by air. There are several airstrips in the vicinity able to take private aircraft. According to a number of people in Los Angeles, Kennedy did make the journey.

Ironically, information on this seems to have come from Peter Lawford himself, the man who in public was adamant that Robert Kennedy was nowhere near Los Angeles that weekend.

Marilyn's former business partner, Milton Greene, told me the matter came up when he lunched with Lawford in New York after Marilyn's death. Greene said Lawford told him Kennedy "was in town. He saw her. He left, and went to the beach, and Marilyn got on the telephone to Lawford."

Two senior policemen are quoted as saying Kennedy came to Los Angeles. According to former Mayor Yorty, Chief Parker told him the President's brother "was seen at the Beverly Hilton Hotel the night she died."

Chief of Detectives Thad Brown told several people he

believed Kennedy was in Los Angeles. Brown's brother, Finis, himself a former detective, did some work on the case. He says he talked to contacts who "said they had seen Kennedy and Lawford at a hotel the night she took the overdose. I went to Thad with the information and he said he had been informed of the fact. He did believe Kennedy was in Los Angeles that night."

Hugh McDonald, who was in charge of Homicide at the Sheriff's Department in 1962, quoted Thad Brown as saying, "Bobby was indeed at the Lawford house that night, but failed to keep a dinner engagement with her."

During the recent District Attorney's review, former Deputy DA John Dickey told investigators that, in 1962, he received information that Kennedy had been in Los Angeles, and believed it.

Two fragmentary reports, one from a police source, one from a former member of the Twentieth Century-Fox staff, Frank Neill, suggest Kennedy arrived in the city by helicopter, putting down near the studio's Stage 18, in an open space then used by helicopters serving the area near the Beverly Hilton. According to these sources, the President's brother arrived in the early afternoon.

In 1982 the District Attorney gave cursory attention to a report that Kennedy was seen arriving at Marilyn's home during the afternoon. I recently tracked that story to its source, a woman called Betty Pollard. She says her mother was playing bridge at a neighbor's home that day, when her hostess drew the players' attention to a car parking outside. Kennedy, immediately recognizable, emerged from the car and went into Marilyn's house. The hostess mentioned that she had seen him visiting on previous occasions.

If this happened as described, it must have been before 5:00 P.M., when Dr. Greenson arrived. Eunice Murray denies seeing Kennedy that day, but agrees that she went out shopping between two and four o'clock, leaving Pat Newcomb and Marilyn in the house.*

Lawford's former wife, Deborah Gould, quotes him as saying Kennedy did visit Marilyn that afternoon. He had earlier tried to sever their connection at long distance, Gould

---

*Shortly before Murray went out a mechanic, Henry D'Antonio, returned her car from the garage. He has contradicted on whether he entered the house or not, and becomes highly defensive when asked what he observed that afternoon. He refers all questions back to Mrs. Murray.

said, "because he did not want the thing to get out of proportion. One of the reasons was that he felt threatened that his enemies might get hold of information that could ruin his career. Peter mentioned 'gangster types.' "

Marilyn, says Gould, had refused to accept messages from Kennedy passed on through Lawford, and Kennedy now decided to confront her for the last time. "He came straight to see Marilyn at her home," Gould says. "Marilyn knew then that it was over, that was it, final, and she was very distraught and depressed."

It was, of course, at 4:30 that afternoon that Dr. Greenson, who had thought Marilyn in fairly good spirits the previous day, received a sudden, unexpected call from her, sounding drugged and depressed.

One of the things she was distressed about, according to a Suicide Prevention Team doctor who interviewed Greenson, was that "Marilyn had been expecting to see one of the 'very important people' that evening, but the arrangement was canceled. Something had happened."

There is one firsthand witness who claims to have sighted Kennedy in Los Angeles that day. A check of many former beach residents located Ward Wood, who lived next door to the Lawford beach house. He says he happened to be outside his house "in the late afternoon or early evening," and saw Kennedy arrive. Wood says Kennedy was not in an official car. Wood, who used to be in the automobile trade, thinks the vehicle was a Mercedes.

Lawford's ex-wife, Deborah Gould, says the delay in calling the doctors or the police—between midnight and 3:30 A.M.—was used "to get Bobby out of town." As she understood it from Lawford, "He left by helicopter to the airport."

Former *Herald Tribune* Bureau Chief, Joe Hyams, and photographer William Woodfield, teamed up for several days after Marilyn's death to dig deeper into the events of the fatal night. They hired a former policeman, who has been interviewed for this book, to help with the research. Hyams and the former policeman both say they learned that a helicopter touched down on the beach, close to the Lawford house, late that night. They discovered this in separate interviews with Lawford's neighbors.

There is nothing inherently improbable about a helicopter being used as early as 1962 to move people to or from the Lawford beach house. Checks with neighbors, and in old press clippings, reveal that Peter Lawford was infatuated with this relatively new form of transport, in those days reserved for the military and the very wealthy.

Lawford himself, in his interview with this author, cheerfully admitted that he was "chopper-happy" in those days. Neighbors at the beach regularly complained that helicopters, which were permitted to land on the beach during the Kennedy presidency, blew sand into their swimming pools.

Reporter Joe Hyams tried to track down the helicopter said to have landed at the beach on the night of the tragedy. At an aircraft rental company, he established that "a small helicopter had been rented in the night of Marilyn's death. But the company was not willing to allow me access to the records and flatly refused to tell me the name of the passenger. I was, in fact, warned off the premises."

Photographer William Woodfield, Hyam's colleague, had better luck. He had recently used a helicopter for air-to-ground shooting, while preparing an article on Frank Sinatra's luxurious private plane. The helicopter in question was one regularly chartered by Sinatra and Lawford. Within three days of Marilyn's death, Woodfield says, he revisited the pilot, who had flown him before, at Clover Field, Santa Monica. That is the nearest airfield to the Lawford beach house.

Woodfield says he went back to the pilot on the pretext of preparing a follow-up article on the use of helicopters by celebrities, an idea he had discussed when they previously met. It promised welcome publicity for the pilot and his company, and he proved agreeable. He raised no objection when Woodfield asked to leaf through the helicopter's logbook, supposedly in search of famous customers who had recently used the service.

Seated quietly with the log, Woodfield turned back a few days to the page covering the night of August 4, 1962. He found what he had hardly dared to hope for. An entry for the night of Marilyn's death showed that a helicopter had been rented to pick up a passenger at the Lawford house and to deposit him at the main Los Angeles airport.

"The time in the log," Woodfield recalls, "was sometime after midnight—I think between midnight and two in the morning. It showed clearly that a helicopter had picked up Robert Kennedy at the Santa Monica beach.

Four days after Marilyn's death, Hyams and Woodfield realized they had the makings of a remarkable story. Huddled in the little office behind Hyams' house, they placed a call to Robert Kennedy's office in Washington. They told an aide what they had learned, and asked if Kennedy would comment, "to put the story to rest." The reply came quickly. They were told, Woodfield recalls, "The Attorney General would appreciate it if you would not do the story."

Hyams did phone the story to the *Herald Tribune* desk in New York. An hour later he received a call from a senior editor, congratulating him on his research. "But although we're a Republican paper and it's an election year," said the editor, "the story would be a gratuitous slap at the President. He'd be guilty by association. So we're killing it."

Marilyn's adult life had been one long newspaper event, yet the only serious effort to report her death had been scuttled. The stage was now set for two decades of whispers and half-truths.

Today, for the first time, taking all the evidence into account, we can build a scenario for the last days and hours of Marilyn's life. It seems that for many months she engaged in intermittent sexual encounters with both the President and Robert Kennedy. For both the brothers, and for Marilyn, there had been the initial attraction between stars, each glittering prizes in the interlocking galaxies of politics and show business. The brothers, bred to the knowledge that they could have any woman they desired, at first failed to perceive that in Marilyn they were dealing with a female who was doubly dangerous.

Marilyn was dangerous in a way that less celebrated mistresses—like Judith Campbell—were not. Unless literally caught in the act, perhaps by the lens of a prying camera, allegations of an affair could easily be shrugged off. In those pre-Watergate days of assumed trust in public figures, allegations about most women would hardly need dignifying with a denial. Marilyn Monroe, however, was another matter altogether—in a real sense, her name was as potent as that of the Kennedys' themselves.

Marilyn was additionally dangerous because she was so unstable. It is doubtful that either Kennedys saw past the beauty and the intelligence to the truly shattered nature of her personality. It was one which, as her psychiatrist later admitted, would have made her a candidate for an institution—had her name not been Marilyn Monroe.

For her part, Marilyn—her grip on reality failing—may have dreamed that something permanent could come of a Kennedy relationship. Reading between the lines of some of her comments to friends, it seems she even deluded herself—after marriages to great American stars of sport and culture—that she could eventually obtain the ultimate prize, the hand of a Kennedy in marriage.

In more lucid moments, the total improbability of such a notion must have dawned on Marilyn. Meetings with the President were always sporadic; by the summer of 1962 it must have been apparent that his interest was little more than his habitual, affectionate but careless self-indulgence. Meanwhile, there was Robert Kennedy.

The Attorney General, never the womanizer his brother was, may have begun his relationship with Marilyn as a rescue mission, an attempt to steer her into emotional calm. Soon, though, perhaps initially tempted to follow his brother merely in grasping the sexual prize, Robert then fell for the flickering light of Marilyn's fragile spirit. Their affair lasted for months. Then, alarmed not least by the flood of reports that criminals were hoping to take advantage of the Kennedy follies, the Attorney General tried to sever the connection.

It was not easily done. Nose-diving into her last despair, Marilyn proved hard to discard. She became a pest, demanding constant attention and—as Robert Slatzer suggests—may have tried to hold her man by threatening exposure.

Kennedy brother-in-law Peter Lawford seems to have been assigned to contain the danger. He was a weak creature, a man seduced by turns both by his White House connections and by his association with criminals like Sam Giancana. To calm Marilyn, he chose to take her more than once to a place infested with Kennedy enemies, the Cal-Neva Lodge. It was there that she spent her last full weekend alive, floundering in drink and drugs, beyond the help of the one man who could perhaps have brought her back from the brink, Joe DiMaggio.

On the last Friday, when Robert Kennedy arrived in San Francisco, Marilyn's pleas seem to have reached a peak. Imagining perhaps that he could reason with her, the Attorney General made a hurried visit to Los Angeles, arriving soon after midday on Saturday. He probably saw her briefly at her home in Brentwood, reiterated that the Kennedy affairs could not continue, and retreated—to spend the evening either at Lawford's house, or somewhere nearby.

Unable to smother her anguish with a steady intake of sedatives, Marilyn now called in her psychiatrist, Dr. Greenson. She told him that she had expected to see Robert Kennedy that night, said she was being rejected. Greenson tried to talk her down, as one would a person teetering on some high rooftop. He left, believing he had succeeded.

Alone with her telephone and her drugs, Marilyn made a series of calls for help. Ordinary friends were either not at home, or failed to understand that this despair was different. Repeated calls to Robert Kennedy, or frantic messages to him through Peter Lawford, failed to bring Kennedy running. Like many a man or woman attempting to shed a lover, he may have believed that the kindest course was the hard stance, to hang tough, to keep his distance. And it was also safer not to risk a further visit to Marilyn's home in the light of the danger of exposing himself to his enemies.

Today it is impossible to say whether Kennedy's enemies—the agents of Sam Giancana and Jimmy Hoffa—played an active role in Marilyn's last hours. The medical evidence, as we have seen, leaves open the possibility that someone other than Marilyn administered the fatal barbiturate dose. More probably, she simply underestimated the effects of a sudden large dose taken on top of a steady intake during the day. This author does not believe that she intended to kill herself.

Late that Saturday night, probably soon after 10:00 P.M., Marilyn made her final call to the Lawford home. She was rambling and confused, and it was suddenly obvious that she was slipping into unconsciousness. It is fair to hypothesize—and one would like to believe—that word of this jolted Robert Kennedy into a decent, humane action. It may have been he, perhaps accompanied or followed by Peter Lawford, who now hastened the short distance to Marilyn's home. There they found her comatose, but not yet dead.

Here the evidence that an ambulance was called, albeit fragmentary, becomes pivotal. If the director of the ambulance company is correct, Marilyn was taken from the house still alive. She may have died on arrival at Santa Monica Hospital where, without makeup, and swathed in blankets, she may not have been recognized. This author thinks it more likely that Marilyn died *before* arriving at the hospital—that someone accompanying her, perhaps Robert Kennedy himself, was faced with an awful dilemma.

Marilyn was dead, under circumstances that could spell utter ruin for the Attorney General. Even had he never had an affair with Marilyn—and all the evidence suggests the contrary—for a Kennedy to be found with a dead Marilyn Monroe, even on a legitimate mission of mercy, would have meant certain political disaster.

The solution was to return the body to the house in Brentwood, and into the bed from which she had made her last frantic calls. Now, time was needed, above all time to allow Robert Kennedy to slip out of town, time for a cleanup operation at Marilyn's home. Only when all this had been accomplished did a call go out to Dr. Greenson, who duly came to "discover" the body sometime between 3:30 and 4:00 A.M.

As the trail followed by reporters Hyams and Woodfield indicates—and as described by Lawford to his third wife, Deborah Gould—the Attorney General left for northern California by air. Meanwhile, as he told Gould, Lawford destroyed some compromising document, probably a half-written letter rather than a suicide note, and commissioned private detective Fred Otash to sweep dust over whatever telltale tracks might remain. In any event, Otash and his associates were able to do little. By the time they were activated, early on Sunday morning, more powerful wheels had been set in motion.

Summoned from the concert at the Hollywood Bowl, Marilyn's public relations consultant, Arthur Jacobs, a man with considerable power in Los Angeles, rushed to her home. He may never have known the full story of the night's events, of the aborted ambulance journey and of Robert Kennedy's nocturnal movements, but he was the right man, as his widow puts it today, to "fudge everything." Meanwhile, someone with real power, probably Robert Kennedy himself, roused FBI Director J. Edgar Hoover. Orders went out from Washington to remove the telephone records covering Marilyn's last hours, at that time still retrievable from the telephone company.

This scenario may be wrong in certain details, but it is a fair construction from the information now available. In all probability, no serious crime was committed that night, although the return of Marilyn's body to her home was highly irregular, and Lawford's destruction of the note clearly unlawful. For Robert Kennedy, those night hours and the days that followed must have been the most harrowing of his life. If our reconstruction is essentially correct, the death of Marilyn Monroe had been his Chappaquiddick. Unlike his less fortunate brother Edward, he escaped public exposure, but only by a hair's breadth.

In 1983, on the day of his own death, the man who had directed two of Marilyn's movies, George Cukor, discussed

Marilyn's passing. It is not known what personal knowledge Cukor had of what occurred on the night of August 4, 1962, but his comments were right on the mark. "It was a nasty business," he told a companion, "her worst rejection. Power and money. In the end she was too innocent."

Part VI

AFTERMATH

"File and forget. We always have good reasons for doing nothing." Outside, the world was fast asleep.

JOHN LE CARRÉ'S *Smiley*,
in THE HONOURABLE SCHOOLBOY

50

"IF ANYTHING HAPPENS TO ME," Marilyn had said nine years earlier to Whitey Snyder, "promise me you'll make me up." She had been only twenty-seven then, busy making *Gentlemen Prefer Blondes,* and already thinking of death. To ensure he remembered, she gave her makeup man a gold clip inscribed, "While I'm Still Warm, Marilyn."

Snyder kept losing his clip over the years, but he had it in his pocket two days after her death, when he made his way to the mortuary at Westwood Memorial Park. He also took a bottle of gin with him.

It fell to Snyder and his future wife, Marilyn's longtime wardrobe assistant, Marjorie Plecher, to restore the embalmed ruin that had been Marilyn's body.

The hair, hanging straight and limp, was covered with a wig she had worn in *The Misfits.* A chiffon scarf was wound around the neck. Below it, the famous figure was no more. After the surgeon's assault, the swelling breasts were gone.

"Oh, my God," thought Plecher, "Marilyn without a bosom! She'd die." She and Snyder tore up a cushion for stuffing, found plastic bags, and made their friend a false bosom. The corpse was then dressed in a simple Pucci dress that had been Marilyn's recent favorite. "She looked beautiful," a mourner would say after the funeral, "like a beautiful doll."

With the permission of her half sister, Bernice Miracle, the funeral arrangements were made by Joe DiMaggio and Marilyn's former business manager, Inez Melson. They knew she had not liked the idea of being buried, so a wall crypt was chosen. DiMaggio paid for the crypt, which cost $800, and for the bronze casket. The public was told donations should be sent to organizations that helped needy children.

DiMaggio and Melson issued a prepared statement, letting it be known that this was to be a small funeral, "so that she can go to her final resting place in the quiet she had always sought." Only twenty-four people were invited, including the Greensons, members of the Karger family, Lee and Paula Strasberg, veteran members of Marilyn's dressing-room team, masseur Ralph Roberts, lawyer Milton Rudin, and Pat Newcomb.

One of those not invited was Frank Sinatra. "Sinatra and Ella Fitzgerald, and Sammy Davis, Jr.," Mrs. Melson recalled, "were determined to come. They had the audacity to bring security men and try to say they had permission to go to the chapel." Sinatra was not allowed in, but the poodle he had given Marilyn, the dog called Maf, spent a while at Sinatra's kennel.

Peter and Pat Lawford were not included. Lawford, who had rushed off in a helicopter to collect some of his neighbors, did not like that at all. He fulminated publicly about the fact that his wife, the President's sister, had flown from the East Coast in vain. "It seems to be a concerted effort," Lawford said, "to keep some of Marilyn's old friends from attending."

In the mortuary, Joe DiMaggio was overheard talking to one of the funeral directors. "Be sure," he said, "that none of those damned Kennedys come to the funeral."

DiMaggio spent the night before the funeral alone beside Marilyn's remains. He was on his knees for much of the time.

While the ex-husband mourned inside, some devoted followers kept vigil through the night outside the gates. Next day a relatively small crowd, about a thousand strong, gathered to watch the ceremonies.

"There were hundreds of reporters and photographers," Joan Greenson recalls. "The noise of the shutters and the motor drives on the cameras drowned out any normal conversation. At first we were not permitted to enter the chapel, the mortician informed us, because the family was with the body. I thought to myself, What family? If she'd had a family to be with, we probably wouldn't have to be here."

The chosen guests gathered at last in the chapel, facing a coffin that looked much too large. A eulogy was spoken by Marilyn's teacher, Lee Strasberg, who had not found the time to visit Marilyn the last time he had visited the West Coast.

Strasberg said of Marilyn, "She had a luminous quality, a combination of wistfulness, radiance, yearning, that set her apart and yet made everyone wish to be part of it."

A nondenominational pastor made a brief address, drawing on a verse from the Book of Psalms: "How fearfully and wonderfully she was made by the Creator!"

The music of "Over the Rainbow" was piped into the chapel—Marilyn had been a fan of Judy Garland. Then it was almost over.

Attendants solemnly slid a mass of flowers toward the foot of the coffin, and lifted the lid. As they did so, Joan Greenson recalls, "a shock of yellow hair popped out. I couldn't bear to look."

Of those who did look, Joe DiMaggio was last. Marilyn was lying, cushioned by what the press called "champagne-colored" velvet, a posy of DiMaggio's roses in her dead hands.

DiMaggio, who had wept throughout the ceremony, said, "I love you" again and again, then bent for a final cold kiss.

Held back by more police than were needed, the crowd watched as Marilyn was borne to the Mausoleum of Memories. The hearse moved slowly, incongruously flanked by security guards from Pinkerton's, in powder-blue uniforms and white gloves.

The pastor said, "Ashes to ashes," and the coffin was wheeled to a hole in the wall covered by a brown curtain. With difficulty, sweating in the heat, four men in black shoved the coffin into a waist-high vault.

The few wreaths from the famous included those from Sinatra, Jack Benny, and Spyros Skouras. There were flowers marked simply "Arthur," and more from Miller's children.

An anonymous wreath bore the full text of Elizabeth Barrett Browning's sonnet that goes:

> How do I love thee? Let me count the ways.
> . . . I love thee with the breath,
> Smiles, tears, of all my life!—and, if God choose,
> I shall but love thee better after death.

Three times a week, for twenty years, Joe DiMaggio had a pair of red roses delivered to Marilyn's crypt. In 1982, without explanation, the order was canceled.

Marilyn's friend Robert Slatzer filled the gap. He now sends white roses, under a covenant that will ensure delivery until long after his own death.

"Do you know where the poor darling is buried?" said director George Cukor. "You go into this cemetery past an automobile dealer and past a bank building, and there she lies, right between Wilshire Boulevard and Westwood Boulevard, with the traffic moving past."

At Westwood Memorial Park, a number of other celebrities have become Marilyn's neighbors in death. The ashes of Peter Lawford, most recently arrived, lie fifty feet from Marilyn's crypt. Sometimes, when the old flowers in Marilyn's urn seem too fresh to throw out, the delivery man moves them to Natalie Wood's grave, just a few paces away.

One tier above Marilyn, in the same wall, lies the body of an obscure teenager called Darbi Winters. She was murdered in 1962, just after Marilyn's death. She had only recently told her mother that, one day in the distant future, she wanted to be buried near Marilyn Monroe.

A few years ago, the owners of the vacant vault next to Marilyn's put the space up for sale for $25,000. Today the cemetery authorities will not reveal whether it has in fact been purchased.

The Monroe faithful, and the idle curious, still arrive in a steady trickle to peer at the crypt. The facing stone has been replaced once, after it had been chipped by souvenir hunters and marked indelibly with the lipstick of female kisses.

The husbands, and some of the lovers, have found their lives altered forever by their association with Marilyn.

Three years after Marilyn's death, in 1965, Joe DiMaggio stood in a ceremonial lineup for baseball hero Mickey Mantle, at New York's Yankee Stadium. Robert Kennedy came along the line, smiling and shaking hands. Rather than shake Kennedy's hand, DiMaggio quickly backed away.

"Marilyn hangs like a bat," says the singer Sammy Davis, "in the heads of the men that knew her."

Gowned in green, the goddess lies behind a marble plaque that reads simply: "Marilyn Monroe 1926–1962." She lies in the quietest place, where there are no embraces, real or rumored.

Three weeks after Marilyn's death, her mother Gladys wrote a sad but unusually lucid little letter from the Rock Haven Sanitarium where she was still confined (facing page). In a note to her guardian, Inez Melson, she said of "dear Norma Jeane":

"She is at peace and at rest now and May Our God bless her and help her always . . . I wish you to know that I gave her (Norma) Christian Science treatments for approximately a year. Wanted her to be happy and joyous. God Bless you all. . ."

Mrs Gladys P. Eley
12013 Honolulu Ave,
Verduga City
Cal.

My Dear Friend Mrs Melson.
I am very Greatfull
for your kind and
gracious help
toward Bernice and
my self and to dear
Norma Jeane. She is
at peace and at rest
now and May Our
God bless her & help
her always.

I wish you to know
that I gave her (Norma)
Christian Science
treatments for aprox-
imatily a year. Wanted

Her to be happy & ②
Joyous. God Bless you
all for your Goodness.

Loving
Gratitude
Mrs Gladys L. Eley

On a dark night a few months later, Marilyn's mother escaped from the sanitarium. Clutching a bible and a Christian Science manual, she climbed down a rope of knotted sheets and wandered off across suburban Los Angeles.

She was found in a Baptist Church, and a clergyman talked to her before she was returned to confinement. "People ought to know," the mother had said of her famous offspring, "that I never did want her to become an actress in the first place. Her career never did her any good."

A month before she died, sitting with the head of the studio at Twentieth Century-Fox, Peter Levathes, Marilyn offered a sad commentary on herself.

"I'm a failure as a woman," she said. "My men expect so much of me, because of the image they've made of me and that I've made of myself, as a sex symbol. Men expect so much, and I can't live up to it. They expect bells to ring and whistles to whistle, but my anatomy is the same as any other woman's. I can't live up to it."

Within days of that conversation Marilyn asked *Life* reporter Richard Meryman, "Do you know the book *Everyman*?" Meryman replied that he did.

"Well," Marilyn told him, "I want to stay just in the fantasy of Everyman."

Dean Martin's former wife Jeanne offers this view on Marilyn and other idols of our time. "I call them the Poster People," Martin says. "They're the most durably famous, yet in many cases they have nothing to them. You find them only through the roles they played in their films. I am not an uncompassionate person, but look at the way they were. The Montgomery Clifts, and the Marilyn Monroes, Elizabeth Taylor and David Bowie. In life they attract each other. They meet socially, they rush straight at each other, but they have nothing that means anything to mortals. History jettisons them forward into time, and I find their portraits on my son's bedroom wall, pale and beautiful, but lost to reality."

Marilyn Monroe, however, was more than a Poster Person—although she had once been just that on the wall of John Kennedy's hospital room. Certainly Marilyn was a mass of paradoxes, a sex symbol who found no happiness in love, an actress who was terrified each time she stepped onto a sound stage. She was an ardent pursuer of learning who never learned to live with herself, who toppled in the end into something very close to madness.

Marilyn's legacy, for all that, is made of more solid stuff

than fantasy. "Everyman," to whom she offered her last public aspiration, remains bewitched by a woman of astonishing achievement. Marilyn, a fugitive from a deprived childhood, battled her way to world prominence with more than sex. She did it with sheer hard work, and an innate brilliance that shines out of even the most inane movies with which Hollywood chose to launch her. For a dozen years her presence on and off the screen made millions laugh and cry, and they show no sign of forgetting.

In this fickle century that invented "stardom," only Charlie Chaplin has been memorialized and chronicled more than Marilyn Monroe, a fact that would probably amaze and amuse her. Fittingly, Marilyn's brittle, too-long laughter follows us down the decades of an era that some call the Age of Anxiety. In that odd telegram to Robert Kennedy, weeks before she died, she described herself as one of the few remaining earth-bound stars. "All we demanded," Marilyn said in the telegram, "was our right to twinkle." She more than earned that right, and Everyman has made her a goddess.

Part VII

POSTSCRIPT—1986

"Nobody has ever testified under oath as to these allegations. I believe that all the continuing questions should be confirmed, explained, or proven to be not true. . . ."

MIKE ANTONOVICH, Los
Angeles County Board of
Supervisors, October 1985.

"As public prosecutors we cannot support a grand jury investigation concerning matters of historical interest by artificially cloaking them in the guise of a criminal enquiry."

IRA REINER, Los Angeles
District Attorney, November
1985.

1985
OPEN—AND SHUT

"SHE COMMITTED SUICIDE by barbiturates; that is the reality, and there is nothing very special about it except for the fact that she was Marilyn Monroe." So spoke Los Angeles Police Chief Daryl Gates, announcing the public release of police documents on Marilyn's death. It was September 23, 1985. "Permit me to express a faint hope," said California Attorney General John Van de Kamp, "that Marilyn Monroe be permitted to rest in peace."

The release of documents was no spontaneous gesture. Gates had earlier denied me the papers. Now, knowing that I had obtained them anyway from a confidential source, he caved in to pressure from ABC Television's *20/20* program.

The released file contained rather less than what was available to readers of *Goddess*. (In a hilarious exercise in bureaucratic futility, officials blacked out—in the police version—telephone numbers that were reproduced in this book.) Gates hoped the release of the file would "put to rest speculation that Monroe was murdered"—a speculation not indulged in *Goddess*. It was a vain hope.

In the months to come, Marilyn's fate was rarely out of the headlines. For this author and his publisher, it meant a windfall of publicity that no money could buy. *Goddess* became a best-seller. It was also the trigger for two episodes—a shameful public circus involving the Los Angeles County grand jury, and a scandal over the cancellation of a television program. Ironically, and sadly symptomatic of our times, the cancellation of the *20/20* television report caused more furor than the aborted jury process. The cancellation occurred in a wave of innuendo suggesting intervention by the Kennedy family. And thus, for millions of Americans, the Monroe Show of '85 became The Show that Never Was.

The Censoring of 20/20

In midsummer of 1985, at a restaurant in Manhattan, Ene Riisna, a producer for ABC Television's *20/20*, met with a representative of Macmillan, my American hardcover pub-

419

lisher. Riisna and another senior producer, Stanhope Gould, read an early proof copy of this book and swiftly decided that the Monroe–Kennedy angle would translate into "a first-class television news story."

Both producers are distinguished—Gould has won four Emmy awards for his investigative work. In the seventies, his program on Watergate was the television production that did most to make Watergate a national issue.

Gould and Riisna did not plan to base their story solely on the documentation of Marilyn's affairs with the Kennedy brothers. That would hardly astonish the American people.

In Gould's words, "It was the documentation, coupled with the mob angle, that made it a major story—the fact that the President and Attorney General of the United States had put themselves in a position to have the nation's most powerful criminals eavesdrop on their affairs with the nation's most famous actress, and were exposed to blackmail. That's one hell of a story. . . ."

Gould and Riisna knew they would have that story if their own cross-checking and research produced positive answers to three questions: Did the affairs really happen? Did the mob obtain compromising bedroom tape recordings? Did Robert Kennedy become even more seriously compromised by visiting Marilyn in Los Angeles just hours before she died?

Executive Producer Av Westin wanted a major scoop to open the program's fall season. He told his producers, "Go to it!"

From June to September, 20/20's resources were put to work, with teams working across the United States and in Europe. The reporter was Sylvia Chase, a twenty-year veteran of TV journalism, whom Westin describes as "an absolute bear on facts. If Sylvia says it's true, it means that she's personally checked it out and sourced it three or four times."

Four months, and a quarter of a million dollars later, the 20/20 journalists were triumphant. They had corroborated the information in this book—and, in the wiretapping area, taken it further. Their program was edited to run at about half an hour, twice as long as an average item.

In mid-September huddled in a cutting room on New York's Columbus Avenue, the producers viewed their work with Executive Producer Westin. He was impressed but ill at ease. Westin wanted major cuts, including references to other episodes in which John Kennedy left himself open to blackmail—the affair with Judith Campbell, the Hollywood starlet also involved with Mafia boss Sam Giancana; and Kennedy's wartime relations with Inga Arvad, a Dane suspected of spying for the Germans.

The producers did not object to the cuts, yet Westin still seemed troubled. A program this "sensitive," he said, would have to be seen by "the Fourth Floor," the executive of ABC News. Meanwhile, the Monroe program was post-poned for a week.

The first executive viewing was by Robert Siegenthaler, Vice President for News Practices. Siegenthaler, himself a former producer, suggested minor commentary changes. As the tail end of a hurricane swept through the streets outside, 20/20's producers felt only relief. Their storm, however, was about to break.

Later, over a lunch of pizza, Roone Arledge, the President of ABC News, his Senior Assistant, David Burke, and Vice President Richard Wald viewed the Monroe program behind closed doors. The producers and reporter Sylvia Chase were unceremoniously left to cool their heels outside.

Within hours 20/20 boss Westin told them, "They don't want it to go out at all. What would be the minimum you could go with and get it on air?"

Over the next four days, working into the night, the team cut the story to thirteen minutes. During office hours, while researchers sought new sources for what was already multiply sourced, Westin and his producers engaged in a grotesque diplomatic dance with their own executives.

At one meeting, Vice President Wald said he personally had changed his mind. He would recommend, after all, that the program be shown. Roone Arledge, the chief executive, imperiously refused to meet the journalists.

According to Wald, it would have been fine simply to report the contents of *Goddess*—it was the producers' corroborative investigation that was the problem.

Arledge, as President of ABC News, said publicly that, given more hard data, he might yet run the piece. In private he had warned, "I don't want Sylvia Chase or anyone else coming in here with some little extra bit of information."

The struggle at ABC became national news. On October 3, the date on which the report was to air, *Daily News* columnist Liz Smith wrote, "I just hope ABC isn't going to let itself be a party to suppressing the history of 1962 . . . that, in my opinion, is not the function of a network with a great news-gathering arm. . . ."

Westin was determined that the final decision must be seen to be the President's. The *20/20* team continued last-minute preparations. At 6 P.M., as reporter Chase sat in the Make-up Department, word came that Arledge had canceled. The Monroe item was replaced by a piece on drug-sniffing police dogs.

All newspapers reported the debacle. Arledge's explanation was that the piece had been merely "gossip-column stuff" . . . "A sleazy piece of journalism." In protest, *20/20*'s most celebrated commentators—Barbara Walters, Hugh Downs, and Geraldo Rivera—publicly came out in support of the journalists.

Downs, one of the most respected figures on American television, issued a damning riposte. Arledge's "sleaze" was for Downs "more carefully documented than anything any network did during Watergate."

"What disturbs me," said Downs, "is the implication that people I respect more than any others in this business, who knew what the Monroe segment was and that it was accurate, were all overruled. . . . A dead president belongs to history, and he belongs to accurate history."

Following the ABC dispute a rival program on Monroe, made by the BBC and American independent producers, was broadcast repeatedly across the United States. It was seen by a vast audience and was nominated for three British Academy of Film and Television Arts awards.

Sylvia Chase and Geraldo Rivera are no longer with ABC. Others considered resignation, then went back to work. Amidst the bitterness, there was acid humor. At *60 Minutes,* *20/20*'s opponent at CBS, a sign appeared on the office bulletin board: "Support-Your-Staff-of-the-Year-Award—Roone Arledge."

Roone Arledge is a longtime, close friend of Robert Kennedy's widow, Ethel. His Assistant, David Burke, is a former Kennedy strategist. Jeff Ruhe, an Arledge aide, is married to one of Robert Kennedy's children.

The *20/20* staff was at first told that Arledge and Burke were distancing themselves from the decision on the Monroe segment. They stepped in ruthlessly when no other executive intervened.

Arledge denied that the Kennedy connection influenced him. "I wouldn't censor anything," he said, "because it would offend a friend. I've already offended half the friends I have."

20/20 producer Stanhope Gould offers the most generous explanation. "The program would have been heavily scrutinized," he says, "even without Roone's connections. It's as though, in England, the BBC got the goods on the Queen. The Kennedy name is an icon in this country, and television, the medium with the real power, had never told the full story."

Others take the more sinister view, that the ABC executives kowtowed to the Kennedy old guard. At one point, reporter Chase recalls, she was accused of being unfair to the Kennedy side. Why, she was asked, were there no interviews with Kennedy spokesmen, denying the reports about Marilyn Monroe? Chase had pressed hard to get comments from Senator Edward Kennedy, the official family standard-bearer, or from Kennedy brother-in-law Stephen Smith. Neither responded, and the senator's spokesman treated Chase with open hostility.

The timing of 20/20's calls to the Kennedy office may be significant. ABC executive concern escalated immediately after Chase's first call to the senator's office in Washington.

During the ABC fracas, Chase received a call from Dick Tuck, a Democrat campaigner who serves as a friendly contact with correspondents. He told Chase that Goddess was "just ridiculous hearsay, supposition," then tried to persuade her that one witness's story was inaccurately reported. Chase had already confirmed the information by interviewing the witness—twice—and told Tuck so.

Shortly afterward, at a diplomatic reception, 20/20 producer Riisna met former Kennedy aide, author William Haddad. Haddad seemed unaware that she had been a producer of the Monroe program. "He told me," Riisna later told me, "that he had been asked to analyze your book, Goddess, in order that it could be refuted." Asked who exactly had made this request, Haddad replied, "Just some friends. . . ."

Haddad has confirmed that while a Kennedy aide, he collated information to counter the Marilyn allegations. I told him I would welcome any information that might rebut key points in the story. Haddad promised to offer some, but I received no further word.

At ABC, Executive Producer Av Westin still stands by his journalists. He told me, "The piece was sourced well. The journalism in it was first-rate, and it should have been run." Because of Arledge's action, some twenty million citizens were deprived of the opportunity to see that journalism. Rightly or wrongly, few are likely to believe that the Kennedy family's connections with Arledge and Burke had nothing to do with the decision.

Meanwhile, on the other side of the country, officialdom was crushing a development that could have resolved the mysteries surrounding Marilyn's death.

The Grand Jury Fiasco

This is a short, sad footnote to history. In September 1985, in Los Angeles, Marilyn's friend Robert Slatzer wrote a letter to Mike Antonovich, of the Los Angeles County Board of Supervisors, about the new evidence in *Goddess*. Slatzer noted information that Marilyn had been removed from her home alive, by ambulance, and that some people knew she was dead or dying some five hours before Dr. Greenson was summoned to "discover" her dead in bed.

Slatzer felt that some witnesses had told less than the truth. He appealed to the county supervisors to have the surviving witnesses questioned—for the first time ever—under oath.

The Los Angeles Board of Supervisors had tried once before to have Marilyn's death investigated. It was at the Board's request, in 1982, that the then District Attorney John Van de Kamp ordered a review of the evidence. The conclusion then was that in spite of "factual discrepancies and unanswered questions . . . the cumulative evidence available to us fails to support any theory of criminal conduct."

In 1985, in the pages of *Goddess*, fresh information was available. This time the supervisors asked the grand jury—the body empowered to decide whether there are grounds for prosecution—to look into the new information. The request was referred to the jury's Criminal Justice Committee.

Two weeks later grand jury foreman Sam Cordova said the Justice Committee had signed an agreement to investigate Marilyn's death. District Attorney Ira Reiner denounced Cordova's statement as "irresponsible almost beyond description" and untrue.

That was on a Friday. On Monday, jury foreman Cordova was removed by a superior court judge. The new foreman said of the Monroe investigation, "I am reluctant to see it go forward." It did not—the grand jury decided against reopening the investigation.

Cordova claimed the District Attorney had been telling the grand jury what to do. Other jury members said "Reiner had preempted the issue." Almost all the jury's information had come from the same D.A.'s officials who—in 1982—recommended that the case remain closed.

In 1985, the Marilyn case foundered in a morass of personality conflict and political bias. Sam Cordova was a controversial jury foreman. District Attorney Reiner, a liberal Democrat, frequently confounds prediction. This time he performed as one would expect and opposed any new inquiry.

The Board of Supervisors, which sent the case to the grand jury, is Republican—by a margin of 3 to 2. Mike Antonovich, the board's moving force on Monroe, is a conservative Republican running for the U.S. Senate.

There was little sign, during the fracas, that anyone was interested in the evidence. I discovered, after it was all over, that neither the grand jury foreman nor the Board of Supervisors had yet seen *Goddess*, the publication that led to calls for new inquiries.

A good deal was learned during the past year by the journalists of ABC Television, the British Broadcasting Corporation—and by myself. There is new material on the Kennedys' affairs with Marilyn, on the malign surveillance by their enemies, and on Robert Kennedy's actions on the day she died. For the record, here it is.

Marilyn and the Kennedy Brothers—Walking on the Water

A key source for Marilyn's affair with the late President Kennedy is Pete Summers, a senior Kennedy adviser in 1960 and a man instrumental in bringing the Democratic Convention to Los Angeles. Summers now reveals that the affair was a matter for grave concern to Kennedy advisers, concern that began at the height of the convention.

"There were a number of celebration parties going on," says Summers. "Marilyn was at one—at the Beverly Hilton where there was a private celebration with dancing. She was there, and I saw Jack, right after telephoning his wife on the East Coast, go out and start dancing with Marilyn."

Summers says, "We didn't know how serious this affair would be—platonic or otherwise." On a visit to the Lawford beach house he found out.

"I had to go and see Jack," Summers recalls. "He came out of the shower, putting on his tie, and started talking. And a few minutes later Marilyn came out of the shower with just a towel around her. She had clearly been in there, in the shower, with him. It was obvious, but neither of them seemed worried about it."

Summers and other Kennedy advisers were worried. He says, "I had buddies in the media that started asking me about it. I told the President, and I told Bobby, that we could have something very explosive here that could blow us out of the water. . . . Bobby made a real strong admonition to Jack on this. He was getting out of line. He was no longer, you know, just Senator Kennedy. He was more and more under the zoom. This was something that could destroy us.''

During the presidency, as Marilyn's affair with John Kennedy ran its sporadic course, the brother-in-law's house came in useful again. Peter Lawford's last wife, Pat Seaton, could not be interviewed till after her husband's death, in 1984. She offers corroboration on the more colorful uses of the bathroom at the beach house. ''Peter told me there was an affair with JFK,'' Seaton says. ''When we went through the house, he showed me the onyx bathtub and said, ''Jack and Marilyn fucked in here.' ''

Marilyn's rendezvous with the President in March 1962, at Palm Springs, is now further documented. Producer ''Bullets'' Durgom, Lawford's close friend, recalls ''flying down to join the party in a private plane. On the way to the airport I was told there would be someone else on board, but I was not supposed to recognize them. She was wearing a wig and all that, but of course I knew. It was Marilyn, and when we got there, a car picked her up and took her off.''

Marilyn's friend and masseur, Ralph Roberts, provides detail. Marilyn often used a false name while traveling. On the Palm Springs trip, with Roberts's connivance, she called herself ''Tony Roberts,'' a mix of the masseur's name and that of another friend.

Actress Terry Moore, former wife of Howard Hughes, says Marilyn told her of her affairs with both Kennedys and that her hopes knew no bounds. ''She even imagined herself as a future First Lady with one or the other of them.''

During his presidency John Kennedy borrowed a house in Florida from Josephine Paul, celebrated as the first woman to head a member firm on the New York Stock Exchange, widow of a former ambassador to Norway. Mrs. Paul was ''scandalized'' by the goings-on in her house on some of the President's visits. Sometimes he would arrive with two male friends and a bevy of young women. The German housekeeper learned it was unnecessary to make up separate rooms for the women.

According to one of Mrs. Paul's friends, who contacted me following the publication of *Goddess*, Marilyn was one of the female guests. Mrs. Paul complained, ''They are flying Marilyn Monroe to my home for Bobby, and that is not why I let them have the place.''

Robert Kennedy's image as the faithful husband, the puritan of the three brothers, has long gone unquestioned. During the writing of *Goddess* I looked no further than the relationship with Marilyn—the subject of my book. ABC and BBC producers established that the President's brother had extramarital affairs with at least four women. One was the wife of a key Kennedy aide. Robert Kennedy was, after all, human.

The Attorney General's press secretary, Ed Guthman, told me he was almost certain Kennedy did not meet Marilyn till six months before her death. Guthman, it turns out, was right.

During the years of research I stayed in touch with Marilyn's business manager, Inez Melson. Aged and sick, she often spoke of a locked file cabinet in the garage, unopened since Marilyn's death. In 1985, after Melson's death, I at last examined its contents.

In a jumble of papers I found two letters written by Marilyn the day after meeting Robert Kennedy. They are unsigned carbon copies, but undoubtedly authentic.

On February 2, 1962, in a letter to her former father-in-law, Isadore Miller, Marilyn wrote:

> Last night I attended a dinner in honor of the Attorney General, Robert Kennedy. He seems rather mature and brilliant for his 36 years, but what I liked best about him, besides his Civil Rights program, is he's got such a wonderful sense of humor.

On the same day Marilyn wrote to "Bobbybones," Arthur Miller's fourteen-year-old son Robert. She thanked him for recommending a book. "Is it *Lord of the Flies* or the *Fleas*?" Marilyn asked. "I would love to read something really terrifying."*

Then Marilyn turned to her latest news:

> "Oh, Bobby, guess what. I had dinner last night with the Attorney General of the United States, Robert Kennedy, and I asked him what his department was going to do about Civil Rights and some other issues. He is very intelligent, and besides all that, he's got a terrific sense of humor. I think you

---

*William Golding's book, published in 1954, was being turned into a film in 1962.

would like him. Anyway, I had to go to this dinner last night as he was the guest of honor, and when they asked him who he wanted to meet, he wanted to meet me. So I went to the dinner and I sat next to him, and he isn't a bad dancer, either. But I was mostly impressed about how serious he is about Civil Rights. He answered all of my questions and then he said he would write me a letter and put it on paper. So I'll send you a copy of the letter when I get it because there will be some very interesting things in it, because I really asked many questions. First of all he asked if I had been attending some kind of meetings (ha ha!). I laughed and said, "No, but these are the kind of questions that the youth of America want answers to and want things done about." Not that I'm so youthful, but I feel youthful. But he's an old 36 himself which astounded me because I'm 35. It was a pleasant evening, all in all."

Marilyn wrote the Millers, Robert and his grandfather, the day after the dinner with the Attorney General, the evening she had prepared for by boning up on politics with Danny Greenson, her psychiatrist's son. The dates of her letters make it clear that her relationship with the Attorney General spanned only the last six months of her life, almost to the day.

Two fresh interviews indicate that after Kennedy's return from a world tour, the meeting he had requested led to romance.

Lawford's friend, "Bullets" Durgom, recalls an interruption while dining at the beach house in 1962. "Suddenly, unexpectedly," he recalls, "Marilyn and Robert Kennedy came in. They took one look around them, saw there were several people there, and left. It was just 'Hi!' and 'Bye!' We looked at each other and said, 'Well, okay . . .' I guess they felt it was the wrong place for them to be seen together. And they left."

Peter Dye, Lawford's neighbor at the beach, says, "She told me she was nuts about him . . . I get the impression he felt the same way. But she was infatuated, and scared of him at the same time."

Marilyn, an emotional mess, was now involved with both brothers. Both called her in California, Eunice Murray now admits. The New York maid, Lena Pepitone, says Robert Kennedy called "many times."

Meetings were secret but not always secure. "There was some sort of problem," said the President's close friend, Senator George Smathers. "As I recall it, Marilyn got drunk on a plane when she was going to meet Bobby. . . . They were trying to quiet her down, but she told them, "I'm going to meet Bobby. . . ."

The President, says Smathers, "expressed some concern to me about his brother's relationship with Marilyn." Here was an ironic reversal. The philandering President—who had been cautioned at the 1960 convention by his younger brother— was now worrying about Robert's involvement.

Three weeks after he met Marilyn, at the end of February, the Attorney General flew back from his world tour to find a memorandum from J. Edgar Hoover. It warned that another presidential mistress, Judith Campbell, was in regular touch with mobster Johnny Roselli. Hoover had also discovered that Campbell was seeing both the President and Roselli's boss, Sam Giancana. It is generally accepted that Hoover now warned the President against further contact with Campbell.

Compelling evidence suggests that both the Kennedys failed to respond seriously enough—in terms of their relations with either Campbell or Monroe. On the one hand, Campbell's phone contacts with the White House ceased. On the other hand, Campbell herself insists she remained in touch with the President for at least three months longer.

Many weeks after Hoover's warnings about her, Campbell was in Beverly Hills, climbing into Eddie Fisher's limousine with actor Alain Delon and the President's friend, actress Angie Dickinson. Campbell quotes Dickinson as exclaiming, "You're Judy Campbell? John has told me so much about you!"

Before leaving for Mexico in February, Marilyn had taken a drive with her old friend, Hollywood correspondent Sidney Skolsky. "She talked about the President again," Skolsky recalled. "She said she'd told him about me. She said she was going to dinner at the White House in March, and she'd be taking me with her."

Come March, no more was said about the White House visit. Yet the President did not balk at having Marilyn flown down to meet him in California, within forty-eight hours of Hoover's warning about Campbell.

In May 1962 Robert Kennedy played an aggressive role in bringing Marilyn to New York to sing at his brother's Birthday Salute.

The then Chairman of the Executive Committee at Fox, Milton Gould, recalls receiving an imperious call from Robert Kennedy. "I explained to Kennedy," says Gould, "why we

couldn't do it. He got very angry and abusive and banged the
phone down on me. He called me a 'no-good Jew bastard,'
which I don't like very much. . . . He made it clear to me in
subsequent meetings that he resented what I'd done. He never
forgot.''

Gould, a lawyer, claims that later in the sixties, when
Lyndon Johnson wanted to appoint him to the federal bench,
Kennedy opposed it.

Was the extent of the Kennedy folly simply to play the
lover carelessly, heedless of the peril? Today, through the
patina of the Kennedy myth, research reveals the shape of an
even more dangerous scenario.

It seems possible that Mafia boss Sam Giancana was not
simply a shadowy gangster pursued at the Kennedys' long-
range orders. Kennedy brother-in-law Peter Lawford certainly
saw Giancana during the presidency. "Peter's conduct in Las
Vegas, with Sam Giancana," says Dean Martin's former wife,
Jeanne, "was just mind-boggling . . . a total disregard for
what people might think.''

Was there a moment, before or during the presidency,
when John or Robert Kennedy personally encountered the
Mafioso? According to one new source, they did. There may
even have been a quarrel, over a woman.

In 1962, probably in the summer, Peter Lawford and a
friend met at New York's Drake Hotel. The friend was Taki
Theodoracopulos, British-educated son of a Greek shipowner.
Today, after reporting experience in Vietnam, he is a columnist for *Esquire* and *Interview* magazines, as well as Britain's
Spectator. During the Kennedy presidency he moved in society circles, playing world-class tennis and mixing with the
famous—including the Kennedys.

During the meeting at the Drake, says Theodoracopulos,
Lawford introduced him to Sam Giancana. They were to meet
again, and Theodoracopulos came to know the Mafia leader
quite well.

"Sam Giancana was always talking about the Kennedys,"
says Theodoracopulos, "and Lawford responded like a man
who knew they all knew each other. . . . It was clear that
Giancana had, at some point, met both brothers." Theodoracopulos says he heard Lawford and Giancana "talk
fondly about past shenanigans with the First Family . . . they
talked about the girls Mooney [Giancana's nickname] used to
produce for the Kennedys. Mooney was proud of it, very
proud of his Kennedy connections.''

Allowing for exaggeration on Giancana's part, we may still not know the full extent of Kennedy indiscretion. Privately, Judith Campbell says the President *knew* that during this affair, she was also seeing Sam Giancana. It did not deter him. On Giancana's part, there may have been some old-fashioned jealousy. According to Campbell, "Sam was after me to leave Jack," once she began having sexual relations with the mafioso. "Sam was not too thrilled," she recalls of the 1962 period. ". . . I could tell by his silence that he didn't like it."

Taki Theodoracopulos recalls something else about the night Lawford introduced him to Giancana. Lawford mentioned there had been "some kind of altercation. Bobby had made a pass at Sam's girl. . . . Everybody reminded Kennedy who Mooney was and that Mooney didn't look kindly upon any-body touching his girl. . . . It happened, Lawford told me, in California."

Professor Robert Blakey, former Chief Counsel of the Assassinations Committee, believes that womanizing was the President's "fatal flaw." FBI sources, and his own daughter, suggest that—in Giancana, too—it was a weakness serious enough to make him neglect mob business.

Perhaps the Kennedys and the Mafia boss were grotesquely linked by the same fatal flaw, by passing passions that led to disproportionate disaster.

Less than a year after Marilyn's death, in June 1963, Giancana brought an injunction against the FBI to stop the Bureau's relentless surveillance. In the process, in court in Chicago, the mobster laid himself open to cross-examination. Justice Department lawyers had been waiting for such an opportunity for years. Yet, at the last moment, the government waived the right to cross-examine—on the personal orders of Robert Kennedy.

Why did Robert Kennedy withdraw at the last minute? "The reason," says Kennedy biographer John Davis, "was that by now Robert Kennedy knew too much about Sam Giancana. . . . He pulled back for the sake of his brother's and his government's reputations."

More to the point, Giancana knew too much about the Kennedys. By organizing massive vote-stealing in Illinois, he had helped Kennedy win the presidency in the first place. He knew about the plots to kill Castro. As for womanizing—by brothers who exploited their public image as family men—

Giancana was freighted with devastating knowledge—most of it involving Hollywood women.

Mob influence had removed the President's name from the divorce suit against starlet Judy Meredith. Then there was Judith Campbell. And, by that time, Giancana knew only too much about the Kennedys and the most famous name of all, a dead woman called Marilyn Monroe.

Giancana knew, and Teamsters' leader Jimmy Hoffa knew. And J. Edgar Hoover knew—perhaps more, and earlier, than we have understood.

The Monroe Tapes—What Became of Them?

With the publication of *Goddess* it became clear that hidden microphones produced smear material on Marilyn and the Kennedy brothers. For the first time the wiretappers and technicians began talking, and new information became available, new clues to what really occurred in the last hours of Marilyn's life.

Who was behind the bugging? The easy answer has always been that it was Jimmy Hoffa, because the wiretapper he regularly employed, Bernard Spindel, was deeply involved. Yet Spindel's widow insists, "Bernie certainly said he had tapes, including tapes made the night Marilyn died. But he did not tell me he himself made them, nor that the work was done for Hoffa."

Spindel, like a few others at the top of a profession in its infancy, was an electronic mercenary. He installed bugs for politicians, removed those planted by their enemies. He gave lectures to the police on bugging devices. One associate personally observed Spindel working with intelligence operatives, apparently from the CIA. Robert Kennedy had once tried personally to woo him away from Teamsters' boss Hoffa, and according to his longtime technician, Earl Jaycox, Spindel sometimes worked for Mafia boss Sam Giancana.

Spindel was an indispensable expert. He was also a volatile figure, a dangerous man to be holding dangerous secrets. Earlier in this book (see page 294), we noted how Giancana had been overheard—on a room bug installed by the FBI—discussing his bitterness against the Kennedys and his frustrated efforts to get Robert Kennedy off his back.

The same conversation, according to congressional transcripts I have obtained, included discussion on bugging devices between Giancana and his Hollywood henchman, Johnny Roselli. It ended with an apparent reference to Robert Kennedy. The mobster's dialogue is reported here for the first time:

Giancana: What I want is something really small.

Roselli: All right, here's one you can put on a wall. I got a guy out there, that is what he brought me.

Giancana: You can't take a big mike like that and put it in a flat. . . .

Roselli: Sure, if you can take it apart.

Giancana: If you take it apart, you might not get the volume as clear as—

Roselli: Well, you play with it, you get an electronics guy. . . . One thing, let me tell you what it is. The CIA has it. . . .

Giancana: Like a cigarette.

Roselli: The FBI out there . . . has got a portable, it takes conversations way out . . . I told them, for Christ's sakes, report on that thing . . . CIA . . . I got another kind you . . . A guy in L.A. who's got an electronic cap kind of a thing, and he showed me that . . . so I got to find out what the smallest thing is. If you put it in there, you got a receiver? And receive it when you are set up?

Giancana: Maybe a block, two blocks, three blocks . . .

Roselli: How big was your receiver?

Giancana: Like a . . . the box was only this big, maybe three inches by three inches. We were talking "blah, blah, blah." It picked it up. Think about it.

Roselli: Yeah. I'll work on it. Bobby is in Washington.

This conversation took place in December 1961, by which time the President's bedroom activity had already been monitored. As reported in this book, John Danoff, a technician working for Hollywood detective Fred Otash, listened in as John Kennedy made love to Marilyn at Thanksgiving 1961, in Peter Lawford's California beach house.

Recently, Danoff went into greater detail. "When I located the strongest signal," he said, "about five hundred yards from the house, I maintained my position. . . . To my amazement I started to recognize the voices—because of the President's distinct Bostonian accent and Marilyn Monroe's voice. . . . Then you heard them talking and they were going about disrobing and going into the sex act on the bed. . . ."

Danoff says he took the tapes, according to routine, to his boss, Fred Otash. Otash let him believe the client was Joe

DiMaggio but added, "What you don't know won't hurt
you." Otash, who had previously denied any personal involvement in the bugging operation, now admits Danoff is telling
the truth.

In interviews for ABC and the BBC, Otash told how, in
1961, he received a call from Bernard Spindel, requesting a
meeting in Florida. "I got on a plane," he recalled, "and I
met Hoffa and Spindel. What they wanted was for me to start
developing a real, in-depth derogatory report file on Jack and
Bobby Kennedy."

Otash agreed. As a former police officer, he says, "I had
access to information as to the President's movements and
Bobby Kennedy's, and when we had information they were
going to be in town, that's when the bugs were all activated.
There were four of five in place at the Lawford house."

Spindel helped conceive the operation, but he was East
Coast–based. In California Otash hired his own specialist.
He is a consultant who had served politicians, Las Vegas
casino operators, and government agencies for many years.
Unlike Spindel, he has always shunned publicity and has
admitted his role only on the condition—by written agreement—
that he not be named.

The consultant's career vividly reflects the risks run by
powerful men who resort to covert surveillance. For years,
one of his main customers was multi-millionaire Howard
Hughes, then busy manipulating politicians to benefit his vast
interests in defense, aviation, and Hollywood. In 1962, while
hired by Republicans during Richard Nixon's campaign for
the governorship of California, the consultant discovered that
Robert Kennedy had ordered surveillance of Republican headquarters. "We were watching his people watching the Republicans," says the consultant, "and I personally observed the
resulting tapes being flown East and going through the gates
of Robert Kennedy's home in Virginia."

The bugs at the home of Peter Lawford, says the consultant, were installed before the interest in Marilyn. The devices had been planted earlier, when the consultant attended a
large social occasion at the house.

So it was, in late 1961, that Otash and the consultant found
themselves reviewing a tape recording of the President making love to Marilyn Monroe. The consultant had bugged
Robert and Edward Kennedy before, at a San Francisco apartment, during the presidential campaign. The job had been on
behalf of Jimmy Hoffa—and the consultant had regretted it.

He did not like Hoffa, and suspecting that the Monroe tapes were also commissioned by him, he turned squeamish. The consultant claims, and Otash confirms, that one tape of the President with Monroe was destroyed.

On other occasions Otash himself had no such qualms. He admits that "twenty-five or thirty" tapes were shipped to Bernard Spindel. The recordings were a tangible threat to the presidency, in the hands of middlemen with direct connections to the mob—Spindel, who worked for Hoffa, and sometimes Giancana. Giancana's man in Hollywood, Johnny Roselli, knew both Otash and his operative Danoff.

In March 1962, just as Robert Kennedy began his entanglement with Marilyn, he became the specific target of the bugging. Marilyn's friend, Arthur James, received a message from the mob's East Coast friend, Carmine DeSapio, asking him to lure Marilyn away so that bugging equipment could be installed in her home. James refused, but the bugs went in, anyway.

Detective Fred Otash, in his new disclosures, said, "In the last months of Marilyn's life, Bernie Spindel came out to California and wanted me to engineer the wiring of her home, the placing of illicit devices in the bedroom and wiretaps on the phone . . . and I said. 'No, I didn't want to be any part of that.' He said, "Well, can you give us some support, some personnel?' And I said, 'Yes, I can.' "

Otash continued to play a key role. He offered facilities and field operatives, whom he has named; and he continued to send the results to Spindel.

For the first time, Otash and others have described what the microphones picked up. "There were more tapes made on Robert Kennedy and Monroe," Otash says, "than there had been on Marilyn and the President." The tapes contained the sounds of lovemaking—and of quarrels.

"On one tape I heard," Otash told me, "she was screaming, just screaming on and on at him. Because according to her, he had promised to get divorced and marry her. She kept bringing that up, and it led to fights." It was from his operatives—and from a police source, Otash says—that he learned of Marilyn's claim that she was pregnant.

Spindel's technician Earl Jaycox, who had earlier admitted only to seeing tapes, now admits that Spindel played him recordings of Marilyn's 1962 telephone conversations with both Kennedy brothers. There were calls to the White House and to Robert Kennedy at the Justice Department. "When she was calling looking for Jack," says Jaycox, "there was a male secretary she spoke to quite frequently . . . Kenny was the name, I think." President Kennedy's personal assistant was Kenneth O'Donnell.

"Marilyn was almost always agitated on these calls," says Jaycox, "very agitated. . . . She was acting like a betrayed woman."

There was talk of a rendezvous at a location in Virginia and of Robert Kennedy having failed to meet Marilyn at Lake Tahoe. The calls to the President, Jaycox says, seemed designed to worm information out of him about his brother's intentions. "Jack Kennedy would talk to her rather calmly," Jaycox recalls. "He covered pretty well for his brother." Robert Kennedy, in contrast, "would get infuriated and hang up on her."

It is claimed that tapes were made the very day Marilyn died, and there is no logical reason to reject the notion that the microphones were active that day. Otash says they showed that Robert Kennedy did visit Monroe in the afternoon, that the couple made love, then began a violent argument. It led to an outburst in which Marilyn said, in effect, "I feel passed around—like a piece of meat. You've lied to me. Get out of here. I'm tired. Leave me alone." Kennedy left.

The hours that followed ended in Marilyn's death. For a moment, we turn from the electronic ear to the human beings involved on the night of Saturday, August 4. Renewed research has harvested additional clues.

Subterfuge in the Night

Peter Lawford, the Kennedys' brother-in-law, was a drunk and a drug user, but the Kennedys have cause to be grateful. He refused to reveal what he knew about Marilyn, not out of loyalty to Robert but out of an almost obssessive devotion to the President's memory. However, Lawford did tell one reliable source something of what happened the night Marilyn died.

In the early seventies, ABC News producer Jørn Winther spent time with Lawford while making a documentary about Marilyn. It was agreed that Lawford would not be asked to discuss the Kennedy connection. At the end of the production, though, sitting alone with Winther in a screening room, Lawford discussed the fatal night, and efforts to get Marilyn down to the beach house.

"Lawford told Marilyn that Bobby Kennedy was going to

be there," Winther recalls, "and that Warren Beatty* and Natalie Wood would maybe be dropping in. Marilyn said, 'Who else?' and Lawford mentioned some ladies whose names she said she recognized as high-priced call girls. She got very upset about that and asked how he dared invite her when those women were going to be there. And she hung up. . . . Lawford talked to her once more, after she had taken the pills, and he phoned the lawyer, Milton Rudin. . . ."

This report matches something I was told by one of Lawford's neighbors. She had been given a similar account by Lawford's friend, producer "Bullets" Durgom, who admits having been a guest at the beach house that night.

Detective Otash, who knows Durgom, quotes him as saying in 1985 that "Bobby was very worried about Monroe getting spaced out and shooting her mouth off. He told Peter, 'Get her to your place. She won't talk to me now. You get her to the beach.' "

Interviewed in 1986, Durgom denied any knowledge of this. He said Robert Kennedy was not there but that Marilyn was expected. "The one thing I remember clearly," he adds, "is Pat Newcomb coming in, at maybe 9:30. She stood on the step and said, 'Peter, Marilyn's not coming. She's not feeling well.' "

Durgom says that "at about 10:00 or 11:00 Lawford tried to call Marilyn and could not get through." As a result, after a call to Marilyn's lawyer, Milton Rudin, "the lawyer and somebody else went over to the house . . . and it was too late."

Erma Lee Reilly, Lawford's servant for many years, says—as do supper guests Joe and Dolores Naar—that there was "no word of worry over Marilyn" until she left around 10 P.M. Robert Kennedy was not there when she was in the house.*

Juliet Roswell, a former employee of Marilyn's press agent, Arthur Jacobs, corroborates Jacobs' wife's statement: that Marilyn was known to be seriously ill or dead well before midnight. "I went out there," he told her, "at 11:00."

Dolores Naar, who had left the Lawford supper party with her husband before 11:00 P.M., says she is "very clear" that Lawford phoned soon after that to say "Marilyn's doctor" had given her a sedative and she was resting.

What happened between late evening and 3.30 A.M., when housekeeper Eunice Murray finally telephoned psychiatrist Greenson? Greenson's daughter Joan believes that when the

*See p. 387

alarm was first raised, it was decided not to call in her father.
Meanwhile, there had been activity at Marilyn's house.

Controversy swirled around the 1985 statement by the owner
of California's largest ambulance company, Walter Schaefer,
that an ambulance was called while Marilyn was still alive.
He identified the ambulance crew as Ken Hunter and Murray
Leib.

Leib still denies being on duty that night, but former driver
Hunter has recently been quoted as saying he and Leib picked
up Marilyn "in a comatose state."

Another Schaefer driver, James Hall, has stated—initially
in a paid newspaper interview—that he was on the ambulance
crew that night. He places the time as "3 A.M. or after." He
says Marilyn's assistant, Pat Newcomb, "distraught," was
already there when he arrived, and that Marilyn was not yet
dead. Newcomb denies arriving till much later and says no
ambulance men were present when she did reach the house.

Hall says he and his colleagues attempted resuscitation but
were interrupted by the arrival of a man who identified himself as a doctor. The presumed "doctor" took command,
gave Marilyn an injection, then pronounced her dead. Hall
says the police arrived as the ambulance crew were leaving.

Hall's story receives some corroboration from his family.
His father, Dr. George Hall, a retired police surgeon, says his
son told him of the incident at the time. Hall's former wife
and sister say the same.

There can be no doubt an ambulance was called, an ambulance never mentioned in any press or surviving police report.
No less than seven former employees of Schaefer's, one now
a company vice-president, recall hearing about the call in
1962.

Marilyn's regular doctor, Hyman Engelberg, says talk of
an ambulance is "pure imagination." However, he also says
he thinks the time the alarm was raised "must have been
around 11:00 or 12:00."

Engelberg told both ABC and a District Attorney's investigator that he himself was called in between 2:30 and 3:00
A.M., considerably earlier than the 3:50 A.M. time reflected in
the 1962 police report.

Mrs. Murray, the housekeeper, caused a sensation in 1985.
While being interviewed by me for the BBC, she delivered
herself of the version usually offered for public consumption.
Then, as the camera crew were starting to clear up, she said

suddenly, "Why, at my age, do I still have to cover this thing?"

Mrs. Murray then astonished us by saying that Robert Kennedy had indeed visited Marilyn on the day she died, and that a doctor and an ambulance had come while she was still alive. She said much the same to the ABC team.

Mrs. Murray did say these things. However, while the reporter she spoke with felt she was trying to tell the truth, there were contradictions and inconsistencies in her interviews.

Four years ago, however, Mrs. Murray appeared entirely lucid. In 1982, in a conversation with researcher Justin Clayton, she said she had "found Marilyn's door ajar" at about midnight. As Clayton vividly recalls, Mrs. Murray then "stopped dead, suddenly raised her hand to her mouth, and said, "I mean, I found the door locked. . . ." In 1985, referring to her interviews with the police in 1962, Mrs. Murray told me, "I told whatever I thought was . . . good to tell."

One of the policemen called to Marilyn's home was Marvin Iannone, now Chief of Police in Beverly Hills. He refused to answer questions when approached in 1986. Former Sergeant Robert Byron, however, the homicide detective called in that night, granted me his first interview ever.

Byron was roused from his bed around 5 A.M., and it took him forty-five minutes to reach Marilyn's house. He says the only people present were the attorney, Milton Rudin, Dr. Engelberg, and Eunice Murray. "Engelberg," Byron recalls, "told me he'd had a call from the housekeeper who said Marilyn was either dead or unconscious. He came on over and found Monroe dead. The lawyer said very little. He didn't want to discuss much about it." The psychiatrist, Dr. Greenson, was no longer at the house by the time Sergeant Byron arrived.

Byron and his superior, Lieutenant Grover Armstrong, Chief of Detectives in West Los Angeles, conducted the main interviews. As the reports show, they had some difficulty reconciling the accounts of Mrs. Murray, Dr. Engelberg, and Dr. Greenson, especially with regard to timing. They felt strongly enough to write in one report that Mrs. Murray was "possibly evasive."

Byron, a veteran policeman, had been a homicide detective for five years. "My feeling was that she had been told what to say," Byron recalls, "that it had all been rehearsed beforehand. She had her story, and that was it."

As for Dr. Engelberg and Milton Rudin, Byron says, "As

far as those two were concerned, it was a negative result. . . . They were telling me what they wanted me to know. That was my feeling at the time. I was thrown by their attitude."

"All in all," Byron remembers, "I got some wild answers. There was a lot more they could have told us. . . . I didn't feel they were telling the correct time or situation, but we did not do what we'd normally do, and drag them into the station."

The investigation was not pursued further, Byron explains, because there were no signs of violence at the scene and because the autopsy clearly reflected barbiturate poisoning. The memory of those interrogations, though, still rankles.

Byron says he heard, from police sources at the time, "that Robert Kennedy had come to see her. . . ." That was outside the scope of his investigation. There is now, however, corroboration for Robert Kennedy's departure from Los Angeles.

Following up the lead that Kennedy had left by helicopter, I interviewed the family of the late Hal Conners, who frequently flew to the beach for Peter Lawford. Conners's daughter, Patricia, remembers her father staying out late the night Marilyn died. "Next morning," she says, "I remember saying, 'Did you hear Marilyn Monroe died?' and he didn't really answer at all."

Conners's chief pilot, and vice-president of the Los Angeles Air Taxi Service, was James Zonlick. Zonlick, traced in Florida, recalls an occasion when Conners picked up Robert Kennedy at the beach under unusual circumstances.

"Hal told me about it about three days later," Zonlick remembers. "We got a call from the police department because there had been complaints from the neighbors about the late hour. This was the only night trip we made in there. I got the impression it was around 9:30 P.M., or perhaps as late as 11 P.M. Hal had picked Robert Kennedy up at the beach house and left him at Los Angeles International Airport. . . . He was a little pleased that we'd handled that VIP sort of person."

Ed Connelly, who also flew for Conners, has a similar memory. "He had landed on the Santa Monica Beach without lights," says Connelly. "It was mysterious . . . uncharacteristic for Hal to do that sort of thing. He was almost giggly about it." Neither Zonlick nor Connelly, both now pilots for major airlines, can recall exactly when the flight occurred. Zonlick, however, believes it was probably in the second half of 1962—the right time frame.

There is confirmation, from two sources, that Peter Lawford

that night commissioned a security man to clear up evidence of the Kennedy connection at Marilyn's house. Detective Fred Otash, who earlier refused to confirm or deny involvement, now admits it. He is aware of the irony, that a man involved in bugging the Kennedys should now act on their behalf.

Otash says wearily, "Well, Lawford came to me. I was the guy in town who sorted out personal problems for the rich and famous. I'd helped Lawford before, over a drug problem he had with the Sheriff's Department. My services were for hire, and I said we'd do our best."

Lawford told his last wife, Pat Seaton, that he employed Otash on several occasions, including the night of Marilyn's death.

Urgent action was taken to contain the damage Otash's knowledge might cause. Otash says, and an associate confirms, that Secret Service agents that year "muscled" him into handing over his file on Kennedy activity in Los Angeles.

There were other urgent measures to protect the Kennedys. It is no coincidence that photo agency files contain not a single picture of Marilyn with either Kennedy brother, not even of the very public meeting with the President on the night she sang "Happy Birthday" at Madison Square Garden.

Globe Photos did have at least two pictures of Marilyn with the President that night. "In one of them," says a former senior executive of Globe, "he was looking up at her. You could see the admiration in his eyes—it was a great picture. . . ."

About a fortnight after Marilyn's death two men flashing FBI badges visited Globe's offices. "They said they were collecting material for the presidential library," says the former executive. "They asked to see everything we had on Monroe. I had a stock girl look after them, and then—afterward—we found that everything was gone, even the negatives. . . . Believe me, over the years that loss must have cost us thousands of dollars. They took the lot."

"It became so sticky," said Marilyn's housekeeper, Mrs. Murray, in 1985, "that the protectors of Robert Kennedy, you know, had to step in there and protect him. Doesn't that sound logical?" On the evidence, it does indeed.

The stickiest part of all remains the mystery of the last hours in Marilyn's life. Faced with contradictions in the evidence of those actually involved, we turn back—with all caution—to the greatest threat of all to Robert Kennedy: the Monroe tapes.

The Eavesdroppers' Version

Fred Otash, who shipped the tapes from the West Coast to Bernard Spindel in New York, says Marilyn was "half bombed out of her mind on pills" by the time Kennedy left her home in late afternoon. This assertion fits with Dr. Greenson's comment that Marilyn appeared "somewhat drugged" when he arrived—responding to her sudden summons—about 5 P.M.

Otash insists that from then on, rather than Marilyn reaching out to Kennedy that evening, *he* tried to get her to come to the Lawford beach house. Marilyn's response, Otash says, was "Stop bothering me. Stay away from me."

Otash's colleague, the security consultant, recalls how a shaken Lawford described the situation. "It's specific in my mind," he says. "Marilyn had done a turnabout. Lawford said Marilyn had called the White House, trying to reach the President, saying, 'Get your brother away from me—he's just using me. . . .' "

Otash and the consultant, the California end of the bugging connection, say they learned nothing of the final night hours, the hours obscured by conflicting stories about the discovery of the body, the ambulance episode, and Robert Kennedy's hurried departure. Others, though, close associates of the man who received the tapes, Bernard Spindel, tell a troubling story. One, traced only in recent months, says he listened to the recordings.

In 1985, during negotiations over television rights, I found myself meeting with Mark Monsky, a vice-president of NBC Television News. Monsky told me that while he had never investigated the Monroe case himself, he had been told about it by a long-standing and reliable contact. The contact was a man who had provided technical services to the government—not in the electronic area—since the early sixties. Monsky said the contact had known Spindel and thus had knowledge of the Monroe tapes. After considerable difficulty the contact was persuaded to meet me.

At a first meeting, in New York's Metropolitan Club, I was not even permitted to know the man's name. In due course I did learn it but cannot reveal it, for reasons I hope the reader will understand. Like the security consultant in California, he is still professionally active. His career—and perhaps his personal safety—depends on his anonymity.

The man spoke on the Monroe matter reluctantly and refused offers of high payment to tell his story publicly. He has now told me his story on numerous occasions, at intervals of several months and always consistently. The contact says he visited Bernard Spindel at his home in Holmes, New York, "not long after his first heart attack," which occurred in 1967. He recalls sitting in the living room as Spindel ate crackers and sipped ginger ale. They were alone.

Spindel told him that in 1962 he had been "hired to get the goods on RFK." The equipment installed in Marilyn's home had included a minute "grain-of-rice" microphone, almost invisible when set in a wall or woodwork, the pride and joy of Spindel's latest engineering. It transmitted to a tape bank situated some distance away and below ground, perhaps in a basement. Spindel had developed a system for recording extremely slowly so that one long reel could cover some fifteen hours of recorded sound.

Somebody, presumably one of Otash's minders, came regularly to collect the "take." At least one of Marilyn's two phones were wired, and a bug also transmitted from her bedroom. According to the new source, Spindel played him some forty minutes of tape, all of it covering activity at Marilyn's home on the day she died.

The tape reflected two visits by Robert Kennedy. "First," he says, "you could hear Marilyn and Kennedy talking. It was kind of echoey and at a distance, as though the sound was in a room next to the site of the transmitter, perhaps in some sort of hallway." Marilyn's bedroom was, in fact, around a corner from a large vestibule opening off the front door.

The source says both Marilyn's and Kennedy's voices were easily recognizable. Like Otash—and it is worth noting that the source and Otash do not know each other—the source says there was a heated argument. "Their voices grew louder and louder," he recalls. "They were arguing about something that had been promised by Robert Kennedy. Marilyn was demanding an explanation as to why Kennedy was not going to marry her. As they argued, the voices got shriller. If I had not recognized RFK's voice already, I am not sure that I would have known it was him at this point. He was screeching, high-pitched, like an old lady. . . ."

Kennedy's anger, the source claims, was because he had learned that some form of bugging was taking place. "He was asking again and again, "Where is it? Where the fuck is it?"—apparently referring to a microphone or a tape recorder. Whether or not Marilyn knew—and the possibility adds a new element to the mystery—she failed to answer. The episode ended, says the source, with the sound of a door slamming.

The tape resumed—and the source has no way of knowing whether Spindel had edited the recording—with Kennedy's return, this time accompanied by Peter Lawford. The source says he would not have been familiar with Lawford's voice, but relied on Spindel's identification. "There were these three distinct voices," he says, "at first echoey again. RFK was saying words to the effect, 'We have to know. It's important to the family. We can make any arrangements you want, but we must find it.' Apparently, he was still looking for the recording device. Then they apparently came close to where the transmitter was."

"There was a *clack, clack, clack* on the tape," the source recalls, "which Bernie said he thought was hangers being pushed along a rail. They were still searching for whatever they were after. And there was a flopping sound—maybe books being turned over. Sometimes the tape was clear, sometimes not so clear. Kennedy was again screeching, and Lawford was saying, 'Calm down, calm down. . . .' Monroe was screaming at them, ordering them out of the house."

The next part of the recording is described by the source as containing "thumping, bumping noises, then muffled, calming sounds. It sounded as though she was being put on the bed."

The source says the final portion of the recording included a discussion between Kennedy and Lawford about Kennedy's return to the San Francisco area. He says it was arranged that a call would be made to Marilyn's number once Kennedy had left the area. The last sound on the tape was that of a telephone ringing and then being picked up. The person who did so, however, said nothing at all. As Spindel interpreted it, the purpose was to create a toll slip "establishing" that Marilyn, still alive, had answered the phone at a time Robert Kennedy was provably somewhere else. Spindel's implication was that Marilyn was dead by the time Kennedy left the house.

Some arrangement of this sort might explain the fact that according to Dr. Greenson, Marilyn had the phone "clutched fiercely" in her hand when he discovered her dead. The matter of the telephone remains troubling. Two pathologists, consulted on this point, felt that a person dying of a barbiturate overdose would be "far more likely" to relax and *let go* of the telephone as they drifted into terminal sleep. One pathologist said that—if asked to speculate—he found it more likely that the phone had been placed in the hand after death. After death, with the onset of rigor mortis, the muscles of the hand would naturally contract around the instrument.

The source on the Spindel tape is the only person who claims to have actually heard it in its entirety. Two others offer partial corroboration of its existence. One, Bill Holt, was an explosives and electronics expert who worked for Spindel's company after his death in 1971. Now a security consultant, Holt confirms Spindel's association with the main source. He also says he was told about the tape by yet another Spindel employee, Michael Morrissey.*

Holt quotes Morrissey as saying Spindel played him the tape and that it did reflect a visit to Marilyn's house by Kennedy and Lawford. There was an argument, and sounds indicating that Marilyn had fallen down.

Morrissey, now a Washington lawyer, admits Spindel played him a tape—but only for a few seconds. He says he remembers hearing only a bang or a thump, as if someone were falling heavily.

Several other Spindel associates quote the wiretapper as talking about the tapes.'' Dr. Henry Kamin, Spindel's doctor and friend, says Spindel told him of the tapes and insisted that there had been some sort of violent incident. Earl Jaycox, the technician working for Spindel in 1962, says the same. Jaycox says his employer was ''very nervous'' about it.

Whatever their true content, what became of the tapes? At dawn on December 15, 1966—four years after Marilyn's death—a posse of police and District Attorney's investigators, armed with a search warrant, descended on Spindel's home in New York State. They confiscated a great deal of material, mostly electronic equipment, and Spindel formally claimed that one purpose of the raid had been to remove evidence on Marilyn and Kennedy.

A Freedom of Information Act suit in 1985 obtained both CIA and FBI reports, heavily censored, dated soon after the raid on Spindel's house. They show that both agencies were

*In 1975, during a Senate inquiry into CIA involvement with other Government agencies, Morrissey admitted briefing a federal official on what was described as electronic assassination equipment.

receiving information on Spindel and his alleged Monroe information (see p. 447).

Spindel's lawyers quickly sued to recover the items seized from the wiretapper's home. Specifically, they submitted an affidavit demanding the return of Spindel's "confidential file containing tapes and evidence concerning circumstances surrounding, and causes of death of Marilyn Monroe, which strongly suggests that the officially reported circumstances of her death are erroneous."

Spindel told John Neary, a *Life* reporter, "Hogan [the New York District Attorney] really did Kennedy a favor by pulling the raid. They stole my tapes on Marilyn Monroe and my complete file."

Court records show that during the raid Spindel objected to the removal of certain files. They were sealed before being handed over, and appear on a signed inventory as "2 Sealed Folders—Confidential Communications."

Research has failed to discover what officials did with the missing material. A suit by Spindel's widow, including a demand for the return of the material, did not succeed. The FBI says its New York investigative file on Spindel has been routinely destroyed.

One of the lawyers who dealt with Spindel's suit, Arnold Stream, says, "I cannot reveal what my client told me regarding the tapes. It is still privileged information, even though he is dead. I believed he told me the truth, in general and on this specific matter. . . . I am satisfied the tapes did exist and that copies were in the possession of the District Attorney." Stream explains that he was unable to pursue the matter further in court, as the judge ruled that the question of the tapes was irrelevant to the case as charged—a wiretapping unrelated to Marilyn Monroe.

The shadow of Marilyn pursued Robert Kennedy until his own death, also in Los Angeles, six years later. Two weeks after she died, Assistant Director Courtney Evans once again had to brief Kennedy, as Attorney General, on a Mafia allegation concerning "an affair with a girl."

The reference to "a girl in El Paso," as printed in the FBI memorandum of August 20, 1962 (see page 449), makes little sense. Robert Kennedy may, as he claimed, never have been to El Paso, Texas. In 1986, however, I obtained the surveillance information that had originally reached the FBI, as noted by a congressional committee. Meyer Lansky, the Ma-

FBI document on wiretapper Bernard Spindel. For the first time both the FBI and the CIA have released part of their files, heavily censored, referring to Spindel and his allegations about Marilyn and Robert Kennedy.

fia "finance minister," had been overheard by an FBI microphone talking with his wife Teddy about:

> Bobby Kennedy who has seven kids and is carrying on an
> affair with a girl in *???* (*possibly El Paso*) [author's italics].
> Teddy says it's all Frank Sinatra's fault and he is nothing but a
> procurer of women for those guys. Sinatra is the guy that gets
> them all together. Meyer says its not Sinatra's fault and it
> starts with the President and goes right down the line.

As reproduced here, it seems that the FBI monitors, listening to a fuzzy recording, were not at all sure of the location of
the woman linked to Robert Kennedy. Given their uncertainty,
is it unreasonable to guess that the reference "El Paso" was
in fact to "Lake Tahoe"? This makes more sense of the
second paragraph of the August 20 report, referring to Marilyn.

Mafia boss Lansky was overheard on Wednesday, August
1, just three days before Marilyn's death. Robert Kennedy
had been in Los Angeles until the previous Friday, and the
available record does not say where he spent the weekend.
Marilyn, however, was reportedly at Lake Tahoe.

In his report to J. Edgar Hoover, on Kennedy's response to
the Lansky wiretap, Evans wrote, "He said he appreciated our
informing him of it, that being in public life the gossip mongers
just had to talk. He said he had at least met Marilyn Monroe,
since she was a good friend of his sister, Pat Lawford, but
these allegations just had a way of growing beyond any semblance of the truth."

On the very day the Assistant Director wrote the memorandum on p. 449, August 20, 1962, FBI surveillance microphones picked up an ominous conversation between three
syndicate figures. They were discussing what one of them
called "a dangerous situation," in which he and his associates
were likely to be prosecuted. He feared this was inevitable but
spoke of one tactic that might force the administration to hold
off. It clearly involved pressure on the Kennedy brothers—
and specifically on Attorney General Robert Kennedy—and the
weapon to be used was scandal over Marilyn Monroe.

"They will go for every name," the syndicate figure said.
"Unless the brother—it's big enough to cause a scandal against
them. Would he like to see a headline about Marilyn Monroe
come out? And him? How would he like it? Don't you
know? . . . he was been in there plenty of times. It's been a hard

UNITED STATES GOVERNMENT

Memorandum

TO: Mr. Belmont

FROM: C. A. Evans

DATE: 8/20/62

SUBJECT: ▮▮▮▮▮▮▮▮ b7c
ANTI-RACKETEERING

Robert F. Kennedy

The Attorney General was contacted and advised of the information we had received alleging he was having an affair with a girl in El Paso. He said he had never been to El Paso, Texas, and there was no basis in fact whatsoever for the allegation.

He said he appreciated our informing him of it; that being in public life the gossip mongers just had to talk. He said he was aware there had been several allegations concerning his possibly being involved with Marilyn Monroe. He said he had at least met Marilyn Monroe since she was a good friend of his sister, Pat Lawford, but these allegations just had a way of growing beyond any semblance of the truth.

(4)

92-51387-310
NOT RECORDED
170 SEP 14 1962

23 SEP 14 1952

SEP 1 4 1962

A fortnight after Marilyn's death, a dry report by FBI assistant Director Courtney Evans, after briefing Robert Kennedy on Mafia interest in the Kennedys' womanizing. The latest intelligence, picked up by FBI surveillance microphones, had come from underworld "finance minister" Meyer Lansky—just days before Marilyn's death.

affair—and this ——— ———— [female associate of Marilyn] used to be in all the time with him—do you think it's a secret?''

Documents uncovered so far do not show whether there actually was an attempt to blackmail the Attorney General over Marilyn. His general assault on the Mafia, of course, continued as long as he remained in office, until 1964. In that year, however, the mystery surrounding his activity in Marilyn's last days became dangerously public.

On July 8, 1964, J. Edgar Hoover wrote to Kennedy to tell him of the publication of a booklet by a right-wing activist, Frank Capell. ''His book,'' Hoover wrote, ''will make reference to your alleged friendship with the late Miss Marilyn Monroe. Mr. Capell stated that he will indicate in his book that you and Miss Monroe were intimate, and that you were in Miss Monroe's home at the time of her death.''

The record does not show whether or how the Attorney General responded to this news. Frank Capell was an extreme right-wing activist who began inquiries—with the overt aim of embarrassing Robert Kennedy—from the moment of Marilyn's death. A look at Capell offers an insight into the dirty side of American politics in the early sixties—and a revelation about the policeman who was first on the scene when Marilyn died.

That policeman, former Sergeant Jack Clemmons, is a sometime Director of Fi-Po, the Fire and Police Research Association, an organization that had the stated aim of informing the public of ''the subversive activities which threaten our American way of life.'' Subversive activity, in 1962, referred to communism, the Red Menace. Clemmons agrees that he met Capell shortly before Marilyn's death. Capell, a former sheriff's investigator, that year founded *Herald of Freedom*, a propaganda pamphlet that viciously attacked American liberals, and especially Robert Kennedy, for years to come.

A month after Marilyn's death, says Clemmons, he went with Capell to visit Maurice Ries. Ries, an anthropologist who had previously worked for the State Department in some intelligence capacity, was associated with a Hollywood group called the Motion Picture Alliance for the Preservation of American Ideals. Its founders included, says Clemmons, John Wayne, writer Borden Chase, and Ginger Rogers's mother. In the McCarthy era the Alliance had been active in the persecution of Hollywood's left-wingers.

Ries and Capell asked Clemmons to help them in exposing Robert Kennedy's relationship with Marilyn, and his activity at the time of her death. The sergeant agreed to pump police sources. Capell, meanwhile, enlisted the help of West Coast friends, including lawyer Helen Clay. Interviews with Clay and a former colleague show that they made some real discoveries. A policeman was sent in to ferret through Chief Parker's papers on the case. A former Lawford security guard, and a man in the car hire business, gave information on Kennedy's activity. A telephone company contact provided a detailed list of Marilyn's calls—including ones to the Justice Department on August 3 and August 4, the day of her death.

Right-wing extremist Frank Capell was supplied with some of this material. In September 1964, when Robert Kennedy was running for election as senator for New York, Capell published a poisonous little book called *The Strange Death of Marilyn Monroe*. It cited hearings of the House Committee on Un-American Activities, and of its equivalent in the California State Senate, to "identify" Marilyn's doctor, Hyman Engelberg, as a former communist. Others close to Marilyn, like her coach Paula Strasberg and her friend Norman Rosten, were given similar labels. Robert Kennedy was portrayed as an Attorney General who let communism run rampant in the United States. Capell said, virtually in as many words, that Robert Kennedy had had Marilyn killed, with the help of the communist conspiracy, to protect his reputation.

Capell's book, obviously politically motivated garbage, failed to hurt Robert Kennedy. Kennedy's enemies, however, continued plotting to damage him because of Marilyn. When Capell's book was published, Teamsters' Jimmy Hoffa and wiretapper Bernard Spindel made contact with Fred Otash, the Hollywood detective who had been deeply involved in the bugging operations. As Otash's correspondence shows (see p. 452), Hoffa wanted the detective to cooperate in preparing a public exposé.

Hoover's warning to Kennedy about Capell almost certainly led to the bugging of Capell's telephone. In their book, *The Final Days*, Watergate reporters Woodward and Bernstein revealed that President Nixon, seeking to prove that the Kennedy administration had been as adept at skullduggery as his own, asked Legal Counsel Fred Buzhardt to obtain a list of past wiretapping operations from the Justice Department. Frank Capell's name appeared on a list of people whose phones had been bugged, apparently with Robert Kennedy's approval.

During a *60 Minutes* television interview in 1984, Richard Nixon said Robert Kennedy had "used the wiretaps for what I would say were questionable national security purposes. For

September 15, 1964

Mr. Bernie Spindell
R.F.D. 2
Holmes, New York

Dear Bernie:

To say I am disappointed in you is an understatement. You
called me in Canada and asked me to arrange to get together
with you on behalf of your client J.H.. I go out of my way
and go to New York from Canada in order to assist you, and
after sitting down and discussing with you and he, it is agreed
that I would enter into the investigation on you and J.H.'s
behalf. You promised over three weeks ago to send me all the
information that needed verifying, and as of this date I have
not heard from you by telephone or by letter.

A man called me yesterday, named Frank Capell, the author of
"The Strange Death of Marilyn Monroe", and we had a long talk.
Either you want me to assist you in this thing, or you do
not. I do not care one way or another, but do not talk out
of both sides of your mouth and take up my time and cause me
to run up an airplane bill and hotel bill on some kind of a
lark.

Waiting to hear from you one way or another.

Respectfully,

FRED OTASH

O/d

example, they wiretapped one reporter that they found was writing a book on Marilyn Monroe that might have some derogatory comments about Kennedy in it. . . .''

The year after Capell's book was published, both he and Sergeant Clemmons fell foul of the law. With others, both were indicted by a grand jury for conspiring to libel California Senator Thomas Kuchel. Capell was found guilty and fined. The charge against Clemmons was dropped, but he resigned from the police force. An internal report commented that ''his outside political interests detracted from his job interest.''

It was, presumably, a fluke of history that gave Clemmons, a committed right-winger, the role of being the first police officer on the scene. That aside, his persistent trumpeting that Marilyn was murdered, based on his observations at the scene, is of little worth. Clemmons had no experience as a homicide detective.

Capell's role as investigator, given his right-wing zealotry, was hopelessly flawed.

Bernard Spindel almost certainly did have compromising recordings. He played the ''last hours'' tape to his associate as late as 1967—after the raid on his home. He said that he had given copies to others for safekeeping. One set, he confided, had gone to the late George Ersham, an employee of the arms firm Smith and Wesson, a man with reported links to the CIA.

Perhaps rightly, Spindel felt himself persecuted by Robert Kennedy because of his affiliation with Teamsters' leader Hoffa. However, that gave the wiretapper strong motivation to use the tapes for his own malicious ends.

The specter of scandal over Marilyn posed a threat to Robert Kennedy to the very end. Ralph de Toledano, Washington reporter and Kennedy critic, says he was approached in spring 1968 by a senior executive of the American automobile industry looking for propaganda to use against Kennedy in the presidential campaign. He represented, says de Toledano, a ''bipartisan group determined to stop Kennedy.''

The company executive, whom de Toledano will not name, wished to purchase the Monroe tapes, if copies had survived. A retired Army colonel, E. Dennis Harris, hired to locate them, reported that they did exist. He said they were authentic and could be purchased for the right price. ''The plan,'' says de Toledano, ''was that the tapes were to be transcribed and mailed to the editors of every newspaper in the country.'' Negotiations were in their final stage in June that year, when Robert Kennedy was killed.

The truth the tapes might have revealed may or may not have died with Spindel. As this edition went to press, however, a new discovery—in government archives—gave the mysteries of Marilyn's last days a new and serious dimension.

Marilyn Monroe—Security Risk?

On a sunny morning at Easter 1986, when most people were headed away from the capital for the holiday, four men sat discussing Marilyn Monroe at FBI headquarters in Washington. Around the table was a Bureau team of three, a representative of the Office of Legal Counsel, an Assistant U.S. Attorney, and the Chief of the FBI's Classification and Appeals Affidavits Unit, Robert Peterson. With them sat my attorney, James Lesar, a veteran of Freedom of Information suits designed to prise documents out of government archives.

The meeting was a milestone in researchers' efforts to discover what documents the FBI really holds on Marilyn Monroe. In 1980 the Bureau had referred to its Monroe references as "voluminous," yet persistent applications had obtained only a handful of material. This did show that since 1955, the FBI had kept a "105" file on Marilyn, a designation that technically applies to "foreign counterintelligence matters." In practice, under J. Edgar Hoover, it provided a pretext to investigate any person who did anything remotely political.

Marilyn's "105" file related to her contacts with people the Bureau regarded as left-wing, dating from her relationship with playright Arthur Miller and his associates. The FBI informed me, three years ago, that the file contained thirty-one pages, of which only thirteen could be released—and those with portions heavily censored.

The withholding was justified under three main categories: protection of privacy; of agency sources; and under the "B-1" exemption. B-1, though used to cover many foreign-affairs subjects, is meant to cover matters of national security.

Even District Attorney's investigators, looking into the Marilyn case in 1982, had been unable to see certain FBI material. The reason, they were told, was that it reflected monitoring of Marilyn's activity in Mexico in February 1962, six months before her death.

In Mexico, as reported in this book, Marilyn was escorted by a man the FBI has been watching doggedly for more than half a century, Frederick Vanderbilt Field. Field had left the United States a decade earlier, wearied by a long persecution for his communist sympathies and by a spell in prison for refusing to give congressional investigators the names of his communist friends.

By 1962, Field was one of a group of some twenty-five expatriate Americans, including members of the Hollywood Ten, filmmakers whose careers had been destroyed during the McCarthy era. These people were Field's close friends, and he married a Mexican wife who had modeled for the artist— and communist—Diego Rivera. In the eyes of the Legal Attaché's office at the Mexico City embassy, the local FBI base, Field was a target for permanent surveillance.

With that in mind, my lawyer applied for release of FBI documents on Field, narrowing the request to the year in which he met Marilyn Monroe. To thwart FBI censorship in the name of Field's privacy, Field himself supported the application. Meanwhile, with Peter Lawford's death in 1984, his files, too, became vulnerable to the Freedom of Information Act. The Field and Lawford suits bore fruit, after complex legal maneuvering, with the release of two hidden documents from Marilyn's "105" file.

The two documents, dated March 6 and July 13, 1962, appear in both the Lawford and Field files. (See pages 456 and 457, headed, "MARILYN MONROE—SECURITY MATTER—C [Communist]".) The reports originate with the FBI in Mexico and are addressed to the Director and other FBI offices. As the reader can see, the actual content of the reports is obliterated by the censor's pen. Even so, for the stubborn researcher, they came as a breakthrough—above all the July document, dated just three weeks before Marilyn's death.

It was a fair guess that the March report, filed three days after Marilyn's departure from Mexico, dealt with her friendship with leftists like the Fieldses. But why a report as late as July? And why, as FBI correspondence revealed, had several pages of the documents been withheld altogether?

In March 1986 the FBI agreed to participate in a curious procedure permissible under the Act. In the meeting at FBI headquarters my attorney faced Peterson, the FBI's Unit Chief for appeals. Armed with the blacked-out documents, he was permitted to question Peterson, who had before him the origi-

2/26/86 *L678 REP/RWS*

CONFIDENTIAL

APPROPRIATE AGENCIES
AND FIELD OFFICES
ADVISED BY ROUTING
SLIP(S) OF *Classification*
DATE: 10-5-76

UNITED STATES GOVERNMENT

MEMORANDUM

TO: DIRECTOR, FBI   DATE: 3/6/62

FROM: LEGAT, MEXICO (100-0)

SUBJECT: MARILYN MONROE
    SM - C

[large redacted blocks]

CONFIDENTIAL

(7)   Bureau
    (1 Liaison Section)
    (2 New York)
    (2 Los Angeles)

REC-15   MCI-22   105-40018-2

EX-114

12 MAR 12 1962

Mexico City 1 cc

DO NOT DESTROY
COPY - see Routing
on Copy

ALL INFORMATION CONTAINED
HEREIN IS UNCLASSIFIED EXCEPT
WHERE SHOWN OTHERWISE

OPTIONAL FORM NO. 10

UNITED STATES GOVERNMENT

Memorandum

TO : Director, FBI   CONFIDENTIAL   DATE July 16, 1962

FROM : Legat, Mexico City (100-new) (RUC)

SUBJECT: MARILYN MONROE
SECURITY MATTER - C

REC-8 105-40010

Bureau
(1 - Liaison Section)
(2 - Los Angeles)
3 - Mexico City

CONFIDENTIAL

nal, uncensored file. For more than an hour the FBI man—
like a card player flashing part of his hand—gave cautious
answers to my attorney's questions. It seems a silly game, but
the rewards were ample.

Unit Chief Peterson explained that much of the censorship
was designed to protect an intelligence source—a human
being, rather than an electronic device, who had supplied the
information. That person, who was the source of all the
information, was evidently close to Fred Field during Marilyn's stay and also had direct contact with Marilyn.

A number of people had such access. Field introduced
Marilyn to a number of his own left-wing friends. Eunice
Murray, Marilyn's companion—who had herself once been
married to a U.S. labor activist—had a brother-in-law in
Mexico City, Churchill Murray. He arranged a party at which
Marilyn met diplomats and government officials. Meanwhile
there was twenty-six-year-old José Bolaños, the Mexican
filmmaker who became Marilyn's lover in Mexico.

Fred Field advised Marilyn to stop seeing Bolaños, who he
saw as a "man of left-wing pretensions, deeply mistrusted by
the real left." The relationship, however, continued until she
died. Then, according to press reports, Bolaños rebuffed
police efforts to question him. When I interviewed him, he
admitted that he had traveled to Los Angeles after the Mexico
meeting, and that he and Marilyn had secret meetings at an
apartment there. Bolaños also said that—in a telephone call
on the night she died—Marilyn told him "something that will
one day shock the whole world." At the time of the interview, in 1983, I did not take him too seriously. Today,
having glimpsed FBI's Security file in Marilyn, one wonders.

The FBI says that to reveal its source for the Mexico
documents could cause embarrassment—even today—to the
Mexican government. In 1962, Mexican security officials
worked closely with U.S. intelligence, and some censorship
in the new Marilyn documents has been requested by an
agency other than the FBI. That agency, almost certainly, is
the CIA.

Along with the free-lance eavesdroppers, U.S. agents had
been watching the Kennedy brothers as they dallied with
Marilyn. Former FBI Supervisor William Kane says he recalls, "from internal doings at the time," that reports came in
of "the presence of Robert Kennedy's car parked in her
driveway." Another source has named a senior FBI official, a
former Assistant Director, as having directed surveillance.

For J. Edgar Hoover, spying on the Kennedy's was nothing new. He had listened delightedly, as far back as World War II, to the FBI tapes of John Kennedy, then an ensign in Naval Intelligence, making love with Inga Arvad, a suspected enemy agent. Already, in 1962, Hoover had ordered surveillance of Kennedy's lover, Judith Campbell. It would have been an odd omission *not* to be watching the Kennedys with Marilyn, so the existence of the Mexico file is not startling—the content is.

Four documents were discussed at this year's FBI briefing on the file. They cover the period from Marilyn's February visit to Mexico to the summer of 1963. Three reports summarize her association with Field and his friends, concern that she was meeting them, and—an awful notion—the impression that Arthur Miller's socialist ideas had rubbed off on Marilyn Monroe.

The fascinating part of the material concerns the Kennedy brothers. The March 6 document reports that Marilyn "spent time with Robert Kennedy at Lawford's home," and that they discussed political issues. Field, now 81, well remembers Marilyn confiding that—along with a number of liberal causes—she and Robert Kennedy discussed the Kennedys' desire to fire J. Edgar Hoover. José Bolaños, for his part, says Marilyn told her of long, heated discussions with the Attorney General about American policy toward Cuba. Pressed for detail, Bolaños remains tight-lipped.

It is the FBI briefing on the July 13 report, though, that is most disturbing. The document, and an accompanying Domestic Intelligence Division note, reports something the source had heard directly from Marilyn herself. She is quoted as saying she had "attended a luncheon at Peter Lawford's residence" with one of the Kennedy brothers. The conversation, says the report, had included discussion of "significant questions." One subject, to quote the FBI briefer verbatim, had been "the morality of atomic testing."

As reported in the FBI briefing, the luncheon had been "a few days" before July 13, which has to mean either in the first two weeks of that month or—at the earliest—in late June. The FBI report indicates that the Kennedy brother meeting Marilyn had been the President. Initial inquiry shows no day in the relevant time frame when John Kennedy could have been in Los Angeles—he made an official visit to Mexico at the end of June. Research for this book suggests that the President did on occasion travel covertly. At least once—according to the widow of Marilyn's press agent, Arthur Jacobs—he flew secretly to meet Marilyn in California. The record, though, makes it more likely that the luncheon was with Attorney General Robert Kennedy.

FBI files show that Robert was in Los Angeles from the afternoon of June 26 till the morning of June 28. As reported earlier, he did see Marilyn during that visit. He would decide to fly west again two weeks later, to Nevada, with the Chairman of the Joint Chiefs of Staff, General Maxwell Taylor. His specific purpose was to witness an atomic test.

The atom bomb was the major international issue in 1962. Indeed, there has been no year when the nuclear issue was more immediately serious. The Test Ban Treaty would not be signed till the following year. In the spring, following anti-nuclear demonstrations, the United States had set off the first explosion in the megaton range and had begun a series of controversial firings of the Polaris missile. The first week of July, in the Nevada desert, saw the first known detonation of a hydrogen bomb on U.S. territory. More tests followed in the next fortnight, and it was one of these that Robert Kennedy observed.

Late June 1962 was only sixteen weeks away from the moment the world came closest to nuclear war, the Cuban Missile Crisis. Fidel Castro, expecting another U.S. invasion, was making urgent appeals to the Soviet Union for help. In early July Nikita Khrushchev made his fateful decision to ship ballistic missiles to Cuba. Already U.S. aircraft were photographing Soviet vessels en route to Havana, and the surveillance would shortly discover that long-range missiles were being delivered.

This was the period in which, according to the new information in Marilyn's FBI security file, one of the Kennedy brothers—more probably Robert—discussed atomic testing with the actress. There is no suggestion in the file so far released—nor by this author—that either Kennedy blurted out state secrets to Marilyn. The point is that any private conversation by the Attorney General or the President on this subject would have been of the utmost interest to Soviet intelligence.

It is clear from the author's interviews with Marilyn's contacts in Mexico—Frederick Field and José Bolaños—that Robert Kennedy did discuss important issues, including Cuba, with Marilyn. Bolaños says he last saw Marilyn in early July, the very time she reportedly mentioned her conversation with a Kennedy brother about atomic tests. That same month

Frederick Field, a man prominently identified as a communist and involved with communist sympathizers in Mexico, was on a visit to the United States—staying at Marilyn's New York apartment. Field's FBI file shows that in June and July he was under intense surveillance. One document shows that the FBI was specifically on the lookout for any contact between Field and Marilyn.

In the circumstances, and at this crucial time, J. Edgar Hoover's vigilance was justified. In the light of the latest FBI releases—and we do not yet have complete access to the file—Marilyn's contact with the Kennedy brothers had made her a potential danger. However naively, Marilyn liked to see herself as a supporter of the Left. According to José Bolaños, she had had "a blinding row" with Robert Kennedy over Cuba, one that led him to tell her that she was "turning communist."

Whatever it was that Marilyn prattled on about in her talks with the Kennedys—whether to actual communists or in the Mafia milieu of the Cal-Neva Lodge, a group of men with their own malign interest in Cuba—she was a potential risk. However innocuous the brothers' comments, their enemies could use them to advantage. Their famous plaything was a volatile woman, running to her psychiatrist every day, the wrong woman to be on intimate terms with the President and the Attorney General.

Marilyn Monroe, weeks before her death, was a security risk—and the fault was the Kennedys'.

Former Los Angeles Police Chief Tom Reddin, who succeeded the chief in office when Marilyn died, said the new FBI material "explains why the real file hasn't surfaced yet. There was not only a major embarrassment for the Kennedys but also, apparently, a national security implication."

Reddin says he was told "in house," in 1962, that a major report had been written, following an inquiry by the police Intelligence Division. An Intelligence Division file, Reddin says, "should be kept in perpetuity." Where is it now? Reddin points out that the present Chief, Daryl Gates, was the immediate successor to James Hamilton, the 1962 commander of the division. "Gates has to have been close," says Reddin. "He must know something."

The local authorities have said new investigation can only be justified if there are grounds to suspect murder. There is no statute of limitation on murder. Assistant District Attorney Ronald Carroll, who ran the "threshold inquiry" in 1982, now says, "We would have looked further if we had known, back then, of the statement that some individuals knew Monroe was dead five or six hours before the police were called." Carroll agrees, too, that there was only superficial inquiry into allegations that Monroe's last hours were secretly tape-recorded.

Since Carroll's inquiry, the man who conducted Marilyn's autopsy, Thomas Noguchi, has said there should be a new official investigation. He has long since voiced his suspicion that the scene of death was "disturbed." In October 1985, an ABC's *Eyewitness News*, Noguchi said there was evidence that should be looked into.

"She had a bruise on her back or near the hip that has never been fully explained," Noguchi told his interviewer. "We did not look into the collaborative [sic] evidence . . . and before we had a chance to study the stomach contents, the contents of the intestines—the specimens were no longer available. It might gave the impression to the public that we have something to hide."

"Murder?" asked Noguchi's interviewer. The man whose original finding was "probable suicide" now looked straight into the camera, nodded, and said, "Could be."

Later, speaking to reporters seeking clarification, Noguchi said of the bruise on Marilyn's body, "There is no explanation for it, and it is a sign of violence." He said he could not be positive the actress was not murdered by injection. The former coroner added, "I feel an inquiry or evaluation of the new information should be made, instead of the door being closed."

Mike Antonovich, of the Los Angeles County Board of Supervisors, insists that the "Numerous inconsistencies and new discoveries—including the issue of timing and the mysterious ambulance episode—should be investigated. If the autopsy surgeon believes there was possibly violence, he should be asked formally to explain what he means."

John Van de Kamp, who was District Attorney when the case was reviewed in 1982, is now Attorney General of the State of California. He could order the case reopened, possibly by appointing a special prosecutor. The District Attorney could also do so, using the Bureau of Investigations, and so could Police Chief Gates. All seem committed to keeping the case closed.

It is the reporter's role to report, not to press officials to hold investigations. The end of this report must be to record the failure of the authorities—in 1962 or since—to hold a full and open inquiry into the death of a citizen. Truth has been a casualty of that failure.

The public, then, is left to rely on the word of the reporter. A recent *Time* editorial pointed out that "Journalists appear to give answers, but essentially they ask a question: 'What shall we make of this?' " The same article reminded us that "the right to know and the right to be are one."

This reporter leaves it to his readers to decide what to make of the shabby story he has told. In this era of canned news and dwindling press efforts to truly inform, the Marilyn Monroe case may serve a purpose more important than her dying. May it move people to insist, urgently, on their right to know.

BIBLIOGRAPHY

On Marilyn Monroe

Agan, Patrick. *The Decline and Fall of the Love Goddesses*. New York: Pinnacle, 1979.

Anderson, Janice. *Marilyn Monroe*. New York: Hamlyn, 1983.

Capell, Frank A. *The Strange Death of Marilyn Monroe*. Herald of Freedom, 1966.

Carpozi, George, Jr. *The Agony of Marilyn Monroe*. London: World Distributors, 1962.

Conover, David. *Finding Marilyn: A Romance*. New York: Grosset & Dunlap, 1981.

Conway, Michael, and Mark Ricci. *The Films of Marilyn Monroe*. Secaucus, N.J.: Citadel, 1973.

Dougherty, James E. *The Secret Happiness of Marilyn Monroe*. Chicago: Playboy, 1976.

Franklin, Joe, and Laurie Palmer. *The Marilyn Monroe Story*. New York: Rudolph Field, 1953.

Goode, James. *The Story of the Misfits*. New York: Bobbs-Merrill, 1963.

Greenson, Joan. Unpublished manuscript by the daughter of Marilyn Monroe's last psychiatrist.

Guiles, Fred Lawrence. *Norma Jean: The Life of Marilyn Monroe*. New York: Bantam, 1969.

——. *Legend: The Life and Death of Marilyn Monroe*. New York: Stein & Day, 1984.

Hoyt, Edwin P. *Marilyn: The Tragic Venus*. Radnor, Pa.: Chilton, 1965, 1973.

Hudson, James A. *The Mysterious Death of Marilyn Monroe*. New York: Volitant, 1968.

Hutchinson, Tom. *The Screen Greats: Marilyn Monroe*. New York: Exeter, 1982.

Kobal, John, ed. *Marilyn Monroe: A Life on Film*. London: Hamlyn, 1974.

Lembourn, Hans Jørgen. *Diary of a Lover of Marilyn Monroe*. New York: Bantam, 1979.

Lytess, Natasha, with Jane Wilkie. *My Years with Marilyn*. Unpublished manuscript (Zolotow Collection, University of Texas, Austin).

Mailer, Norman. *Marilyn*. New York: Warner, 1973.

——. *Of Women and Their Elegance*. New York: Simon & Schuster, 1981.

Martin, Pete. *Will Acting Spoil Marilyn Monroe?* New York: Doubleday, 1956.

Mellen, Joan. *Marilyn Monroe*. New York: Galahad, 1973.

Monroe, Marilyn. *My Story*. New York: Stein & Day, 1974.

Moore, Robin, and Gene Schoor. *Marilyn & Joe DiMaggio*. New York: Manor, 1977.

Murray, Eunice, with Rose Shade. *Marilyn: The Last Months*. New York: Pyramid, 1975.

Pepitone, Lena, and William Stadiem. *Marilyn Monroe Confidential*. New York: Pocket Books, 1979.

Robinson, David, and John Kobal. *Marilyn Monroe: A Life on Film*. New York: Hamlyn, 1974.

Rosten, Norman. *Marilyn: An Untold Story*. © 1967, 1972–3. Extracts reprinted by permission of Harold Ober Associates, Inc.

Sciacca, Tony. *Who Killed Marilyn?* New York: Manor, 1976.

Shaw, Sam. *Marilyn Monroe as the Girl: The Making of "The Seven Year Itch" in Pictures*. New York: Ballantine, 1955.

Skolsky, Sidney. *The Story of Marilyn Monroe*. New York: Dell, 1954.

Slatzer, Robert. *The Life and Curious Death of Marilyn Monroe*. New York: Pinnacle, 1974.

Smith, Milburn. *Marilyn*. New York: Barven, 1971.

Spada, James, with George Zeno. *Monroe: Her Life in Pictures*. New York: Doubleday, 1982.

Speriglio, Milo. *Marilyn Monroe: Murder Cover-Up*. Van Nuys, Calif.: Seville, 1982.

Speriglio, Milo. *The Marilyn Conspiracy*, New York: Pocket, 1986.

Stern, Bert. *The Last Sitting*. New York: Morrow, 1982.

Wagenknecht, Edward, ed. *Marilyn Monroe: A Composite View*. New York: Chilton, 1969.

Weatherby, W. J. *Conversations with Marilyn*. New York: Ballantine, 1976.

Zolotow, Maurice. *Marilyn Monroe*. New York: Harcourt Brace, 1960.

General

Adams, Cindy. *My Friend the Dictator*. New York: Bobbs-Merrill, 1967.

——. *The Imperfect Genius*. New York: Doubleday, 1980.

Alleged Assassination Plots Involving Foreign Leaders. Interim Report of the Select Committee to Study Governmental Operations, with Respect to Intelligence Activities. U.S. Senate. Washington, D.C.: U.S. Government Printing Office, 1975.

Allen, Maury. *Where Have You Gone, Joe DiMaggio? The Story of America's Last Hero*. New York: Dutton, 1975.

Arnold, William. *Frances Farmer, Shadowland*. New York: Berkley, 1978.

Bacall, Lauren. *By Myself*. New York: Knopf, 1979.

Bacon, James. *Hollywood Is a Four-Letter Town*. New York: Avon, 1976.

——. *Made in Hollywood*. Chicago: Contemporary, 1977.

Bentley, Eric, ed. *Thirty Years of Treason, Excerpts from Hearings before the House Committee on Un-American Activities, 1938–1968*. New York: Viking, 1971.

Berle, Milton. *An Autobiography*. New York: Delacorte, 1974.

Blair, Clay, Jr., and Joan. *The Search for J.F.K.* New York: Putnam, 1976.

Blakey, Robert G., and Richard N. Billings. *The Plot to Kill the President*. New York: Times Books, 1981.

Bonanno, Joseph, with Sergio Lalli. *A Man of Honor: The Autobiography of Joseph Bonanno*. New York: Simon & Schuster, 1983.

Bosworth, Patricia. *Montgomery Clift*. New York: Harcourt Brace Jovanovich, 1978.

Brashler, William. *The Don: The Life and Death of Sam Giancana*. New York: Ballantine, 1977.

Bryant, Traphes, and Frances Spatz Leighton. *Dog Days at the White House*. New York: Macmillan, 1975.

Capote, Truman. *Music for Chameleons, New Writing*. New York: New American Library, 1975.

——. *The Dogs Bark, Public People and Private Places*. New York: Signet, 1980.

Chapman, Gil and Ann. *Who's Listening Now?* San Diego: Publishers Export, 1967.

Clinch, Nancy Gager. *The Kennedy Neurosis*. New York: Grosset & Dunlap, 1973.

Cogley, John. *Blacklisting: (Movies, Vol. 1, and Radio & Television, Vol. II)*. Fund for the Republic, 1956.

Cohen, Mickey, as told to John Peer Nugent. *In My Own Words: The Underworld Autobiography of Michael "Mickey" Cohen*. Englewood Cliffs, N.J.: Prentice-Hall, 1975.

Collier, Peter, and David Horowitz. *The Kennedys*. New York: Summit, 1984.

Corrigan, Robert W., ed. *Arthur Miller: A Collection of Critical Essays*. Englewood Cliffs, N.J.: Prentice-Hall, 1969.

Dallas, Rita, with Jeanira Ratcliffe. *The Kennedy Case*. New York: Popular Library, 1973.

Davies, Deborah. *Katharine the Great: Katharine Graham and The Washington Post*. New York: Harcourt Brace Jovanovich, 1979.

Davis, Sammy, Jr., *Yes*. New York: Farrar, Straus & Giroux, 1967.

——. *Hollywood in a Suitcase*. New York: Morrow, 1980.

De Gregorio, George. *Joe DiMaggio: An Informal Biography*. New York: Stein & Day, 1981.

Demaris, Ovid. *The Last Mafioso*. New York: Times Books, 1981.

De Toledano, Ralph. *R.F.K.: The Man Who Would Be President*. New York: Putnam, 1967.

——. *J. Edgar Hoover: The Man in His Time*. New Rochelle, N.Y.: Arlington, 1973.

Dick, Bernard F. *Billy Wilder*. Boston: Twayne, 1980.

Dunleavy, Stephen, and Peter Brennan. *Those Wild, Wild Kennedy Boys!* New York: Pinnacle, 1976.

Easty, Edward Dwight. *On Method Acting*. Orlando, Fla.: The House of Collectibles, 1981.

Epstein, Morella and Edward Z. *Lana*. New York: Dell, 1971, 1982.

Exner, Judith, as told to Ovid Demaris. *My Story*. New York: Grove, 1977.

Farberow, Norman L., and Edwin S. Schneidman, eds. *The Cry for Help*. New York: McGraw-Hill, 1961.

Feinman, Jeffrey. *Hollywood Confidential*. Chicago: Playboy, 1976.

Field, Frederick Vanderbilt. *From Left to Right, An Autobiography*. Westport, Conn.: Lawrence Hill & Co., 1983.

Fisher, Eddie. *Eddie: My Life, My Loves*. New York: Berkley, 1981.

Frank, Gerold. *Judy*. New York: Harper & Row, 1975.

Gage, Nicholas. *The Mafia Is Not an Equal Opportunity Employer*. New York: McGraw-Hill, 1971.

Gehman, Richard. *Sinatra and His Rat Pack*. New York: Belmont, 1961.

Giancana, Antoinette, and Thomas C. Renner. *Mafia Princess*. New York: Morrow, 1984.

Goodman, Ezra. *The Fifty-Year Decline and Fall of Hollywood*. New York: MacFadden, 1962.

Graham, Sheilah. *Confessions of a Hollywood Columnist*. New York: Morrow, 1969.

——. *My Hollywood*. London: Michael Joseph, 1984.

Guiles, Fred Lawrence. *Marion Davies*. New York: McGraw-Hill, 1972.

Gussow, Mel. *Darryl F. Zanuck: Don't Say Yes Until I've Finished Talking*. New York: Dacapo, 1971.

Hamblett, Charles. *The Hollywood Cage*. New York: Hart, 1969.

Harris, Radie. *Radie's World*. New York: Putnam, 1975.

Head, Edith, and Paddy Calistro, *Edith Head's Hollywood*. New York: Dutton, 1983.

Hougan, Jim. *Spooks: The Haunting of America—The Private Use of Secret Agents*. New York: Morrow, 1978.

Hunt, Irma. *The Presidents' Mistresses*. New York: McGraw-Hill, 1978.

Huston, John. *An Open Book*. New York: Knopf, 1980.

Hyams, Joe. *Mislaid in Hollywood*. New York: Wyden, 1973.

Israel, Lee. *Kilgallen*. New York: Dell, 1979.

Johnson, Dorris, and Ellen Leventhal, eds. *The Letters of Nunnally Johnson*. New York: Knopf, 1981.

Kanin, Garson, *Hollywood*. New York: Bantam, 1976.

Kennedy, Robert F. *The Enemy Within*. New York: Harper & Row, 1960.

Kiernan, Thomas. *Sir Larry*. New York: Times Books, 1981.

Klurfeld, Herman. *Winchell: His Life and Times*. New York: Praeger, 1976.

Knef, Hildegard. *The Gift Horse*. New York: McGraw-Hill, 1970.

LaGuardia, Robert. *Monty: A Biography of Montgomery Clift*. New York: Avon, 1977.

Lambert, Gavin. *On Cukor*. New York: Putnam, 1972.

Lasky, Victor. *It Didn't Start with Watergate*. New York: Dial, 1977.

Leary, Timothy. *Flashbacks: An Autobiography*. Los Angeles: Tarcher, 1984.

Life Goes to the Movies. New York: Times-Life Books, 1975.

Logan, Joshua. *Movie Stars, Real People, and Me*. New York: Delacorte, 1978.

Madsen, Axel. *Billy Wilder*. Bloomington: Indiana University Press, 1969.

Manchester, William. *The Glory and the Dream: A Narrative History of America*. Boston: Little Brown, 1974.

Martin, Ralph G. *A Hero for Our Times*. New York: Macmillan, 1983.

Martin, Robert A., ed. *Theater Essays of Arthur Miller*. New York: Viking, 1978.

Marvin, Susan. *The Women Around R.F.K.* New York: Lancer, 1967.

Masters, George, and Norma Lee Browning. *The Masters Way to Beauty*. New York: Dutton, 1977.

Mazzola, Reparata, and Sonny Gibson. *Mafia Kingpin*. New York: Grosset & Dunlap, 1981.

Meaker, M. J. *Sudden Endings*. New York: Doubleday, 1964.

Mellen, Joan. *Pyramid Illustrated History of the Movies*. New York: Pyramid, 1973.

Messick, Hank. *The Mob in Show Business*. New York: Pyramid, 1973.

Michaelis, David. *The Best of Friends: Profiles of Extraordinary Friendships*. New York: Morrow, 1983.

Miller, Arthur, *The Misfits*. New York: Dell, 1957.

———. *Death of a Salesman*. New York: Viking, 1961.

———. *After the Fall*. New York: Viking, 1961.

———. *I Don't Need You Any More* (stories). New York: Viking, 1967.

———. *Collected Plays, Vol II*. New York: Viking, 1981.

Miller, William "Fishbait," as told to Frances Spatz Leighton. *The Memoirs of the Congressional Doorkeeper*. Englewood Cliffs, N.J.: Prentice-Hall, 1977.

Moldea, Dan E. *The Hoffa Wars*. New York: Paddington Press, 1978.

Mordden, Ethan. *Movie Star: A Look at the Women Who Made Hollywood*. New York: St. Martin's, 1983.

Morella, Joe and Edward Z. Epstein. *Lana: The Public and Private Lives of Miss Turner*. New York: Dell, 1971, 1982.

Muir, Florabel. *Headline Happy*. New York: Holt, 1950.

Navasky, Victor. *Kennedy Justice*. New York: Atheneum, 1971.

Negulesco, Jean. *Things I Did and Things I Think I Did: A Hollywood Memoir*. New York: Linden, 1984.

Newfield, Jack. *Robert F. Kennedy: A Memoir*. New York: Berkley Medallion, 1969, 1978.

Noguchi, Thomas T., with Joseph DiMona. *Coroner*. New York: Simon & Schuster, 1983.

O'Grady, John, and Nolan Davis. *O'Grady*. Los Angeles: Tarcher, 1974.

Olivier, Laurence. *Confessions of an Actor*. New York: Simon & Schuster, 1982.

Otash, Fred. *Investigation Hollywood* Chicago: Regnery, 1976.

Paar, Jack. *P.S. Jack Paar*. New York: Doubleday, 1983.

Parish, James Robert. *The Fox Girls*. New York: Arlington House, 1971.

Parks, Lillian Rogers, with Frances Spatz Leighton. *My Thirty Years Backstairs at the White House*. New York: Avon, 1961.

Parmet, Herbet S. *Jack, The Struggles of John F. Kennedy*. New York: Dial, 1980.

——. *JFK, The Presidency of John F. Kennedy*. New York: Dial, 1983.

Parsons, Louella. *Tell It to Louella*. New York: Putnam, 1961.

Payne, Graham, and Sheridan Morley, eds. *The Noel Coward Diaries*. Boston: Little, Brown, 1982.

Peary, Danny. *Close-Ups*. New York: Galahad, 1981.

Powers, Thomas. *The Man Who Kept the Secrets: Richard Helms and the CIA*. New York: Knopf, 1979.

Reid, Ed. *The Grim Reapers*. Chicago: Regnery, 1969.

——. *Mickey Cohen: Mobster*. New York: Pinnacle, 1973.

Report of the Select Committee on Assassinations. U.S. House of Representatives, Ninety-fifth Congress. Washington, D.C.: U.S. Government Printing Office, 1979.

Rivkin, Allen, and Laura Kerr. *Hello, Hollywood*. New York: Doubleday, 1962.

Robinson, Edward G. *All My Yesterdays*. New York: Hawthorn, 1973.

Rosten, Leo. *Captain Newman, M.D.* New York: Harper & Row, 1961.

Saunders, Frank, with James Southwood. *Torn Lace Curtain*. New York: Pinnacle, 1984.

Scheim, David E. *Contract on America: The Mafia Murders of John and Robert Kennedy*. Silver Spring, Md.: Argyle, 1983.

Schickel, Richard. *The Stars*. New York: Dial, 1962.

Schlesinger, Arthur M., Jr. *A Thousand Days, John F. Kennedy in the White House*. Boston: Houghton Mifflin, 1965.

——. *Robert Kennedy and His Times*. Boston: Houghton Mifflin, 1978.

Sciacca, Tony. *Kennedy and His Women*. New York: Manor, 1976.

——. *Sinatra*. New York: Pinnacle, 1976.

——. *Screen Greats Vol. II*. New York: Starlog Press, 1980.

Selznick, Irene Mayer. *A Private View*. New York: Knopf, 1983.

Shaw, Arnold. *Sinatra: Twentieth-Century Romantic*. New York: Pocket Books, 1969.

Sheridan, Walter. *The Fall and Rise of Jimmy Hoffa*. New York: Saturday Review Press, 1972.

Signoret, Simone. *Nostalgia Isn't What It Used to Be*. New York: Harper & Row, 1978.

Skolsky, Sidney. *Don't Get Me Wrong, I Love Hollywood*. New York: Putnam, 1975.

Smith, Joseph Burkholder. *Portrait of a Cold Warrior*. New York: Putnam, 1976.

Spindel, Bernard B. *The Ominous Ear*. New York: Award House, 1968.

Stempel, Tom. *Screenwriter: The Life and Times of Nunnally Johnson*. San Diego: A. S. Barnes, 1980.

Strasberg, Susan. *Bitter Sweet*. New York Putnam, 1980.

Sullivan, William C., with Bill Brown. *The Bureau: My Thirty Years in Hoover's F.B.I.* New York: Norton, 1979.

Summers, Anthony. *Conspiracy*. New York: McGraw-Hill, 1980.

Talese, Gay. *Thy Neighbor's Wife*. New York: Doubleday, 1980.

Teresa, Vincent. *My Life in the Mafia*. St. Albans: Panther, 1974.

Thomas, Bob. *Winchell*. New York: Doubleday, 1971.

Thompson, Nelson. *The Dark Side of Camelot*. Chicago: Playboy, 1976.

Tierney, Gene, with Mickey Herskowitz. *Self Portrait*. New York: Wyden, 1979.

Ungar, Sanford J. *F.B.I.* Boston: Little, Brown, 1976.

Wagenknecht, Edward. *As Far as Yesterday, Memories and Recollections*. Norman: University of Oklahoma Press, 1968.

——. *Seven Daughters of the Theater*. Norman: University of Oklahoma Press, 1964.

Walker, Alexander. *The Celluloid Sacrifice*. New York: Hawthorn, 1967.

Wallace, Irving; Amy Wallace; David Wallechinsky, and Sylvia Wallace. *The Intimate Sex Lives of Famous People*. New York: Dell, 1982.

Warner, R. H., Chief Special Agent, General Telephone Co. *Wireless Electronic Surveillance, Handbook for Investigators*.

Wilkie, Jane. *Confessions of an Ex-Fan Magazine Writer*. New York: Doubleday, 1981.

Wills, Garry. *The Kennedy Imprisonment*. New York: Pocket Books, 1981, 1982.

Wilson, Earl. *The Show Business Nobody Knows*. New York: Bantam, 1971.

——. *Show Business Laid Bare*. New York: Putnam, 1975.

——. *Sinatra*. New York: Signet, 1976.

——. *Hot Times: True Tales of Hollywood and Broadway*. New York: Contemporary Books, 1984.

Winters, Shelley. *Shelley*. New York: Ballantine, 1980.

Wofford, Harris. *Of Kennedys and Kings*. New York: Farrar, Straus & Giroux, 1980.

Yeats, W. B. *Selected Poetry*. New York: Macmillan, 1983.

Zolotow, Maurice. *Billy Wilder in Hollywood*. New York: Putnam, 1977.

NOTES

IN THE FOLLOWING notes, books are indicated by the author's name, or name and a short title if there is more than one book by the same author. All books referred to in the notes are fully cited in the two preceding bibliographies. All interviews are indicated by the abbreviation *int.* and were conducted by the author, unless otherwise designated.

Chapter 1

3   August 4, 1962, scene: int. Natalie Jacobs, 1985.

3   Coverage: *Hollywood Citizen-News,* Dec. 31, 1962.

3   District Attorney inquiry: int. Assistant District Attorney Ronald Carroll and Investigator Alan Tomich, 1983.

4   Mailer: int., 1985.

5   Last interview: Richard Meryman, *life,* Aug. 3, 1962.

5   Geminis: Weatherby, 112.

5   Mother today: *Film Comment,* Sept. 1982; *National Enquirer,* 1982; int. James Haspiel, 1983.

5   Gladys' birth: marriage certificate, in Slatzer, 351.

5   MM birth: certificate, in Slatzer, 347.

5–6 Mortenson: *Photoplay,* Dec. 1962; *Los Angeles Daily News* and *The Register,* Feb. 13, 1981 (on death of a Mortensen); corr. MM genealogist Roy Turner, 1983.

6   MM denies Mortenson: Hedda Hopper, int. transcript, March 10, 1953 (Zolotow collection). See also Dougherty, 73; Skolsky, *Don't Get Me Wrong,* 220.

6   Gifford: Guiles, *Norma Jean,* 7.

6   Gable: Guiles, *Norma Jean,* 38; int. Hildi Greenson, 1983; *Empire News* (London), May 9, 1954.

6   Official form: int. Marjorie Stengel, 1983.

6   Forebears: data supplied by Monroe genealogist Roy Turner; Guiles, *Norma Jean,* 16; *Empire News,* May 9, 1954.

6   Genetic risk from syphilis: int. Dr. Burke Cunha, infectious disease specialist, and Dr. Yehudi Felman, clinical professor of dermatology, both of New York City.

7   Della "smothered" MM: Arthur Miller, in Guiles, *Norma Jean,* 14.

7   Mother "not mad": int. Inez Melson, 1983.

7   "Atheist Jew": int. Hildi and Joan Greenson, 1983.

7   Psychiatrists: corr. Dr. Ruth Bruun, Dr. Bertel Bruun, and Dr. Valérie Shikhverg, all of New York, 1985.

8   Shikhverg: corr. and int. 1985.

Chapter 2

9   "Arrival at school": *Empire News*, May 16, 1954.
9   Hecht: *Empire News*, May 2–Aug. 1, 1954.
9   Controversy: George Carpozi, *New York Post*, June 21, 1974; *Los Angeles Herald-Examiner*, Sept. 1, 1954.
10 Dougherty marriage: Dougherty; Lytess; Wilkie, 126ff, 172ff; *Empire News*, May 16, 1954.
13 MM in factory: *Empire News*, May 16, 1954.
13 Conover: Conover, opening chapters; int. David Conover, 1983; *Modern Screen*, July 1954; George Belmont, int. Monroe, *Jours de France*, 1960.
13 Figure (fn.): Palmer, 12; Donald Zec, London *Daily Express*, Aug. 6, 1962; int. Billy Travilla, 1983.
14 Acting: *Empire News*, May 23, 1954.
14 MM explores Hollywood: *Empire News*, May 23, 1954.

Chapter 3

15 MM on Norma Jean: *Empire News*, May 16, 1954.
15 "Faithful": *Empire News*, May 16, 1954.
15 Dougherty trust: Dougherty, 86.
16 MM in 1960: Jaik Rosenstein, *Hollywood Close-Up*, May 17, 1974.
16 De Dienes: Dougherty, 93–95; corr. André de Dienes, 1984; Jack Smith, *Los Angeles Times*, Aug. 8, 1962; Mailer, *Marilyn*, 76ff.; Hudson, 36.
17 Conover: int, 1983; int. Robert Markel, formerly of Grosset & Dunlap, 1984.
18 Lembourn: Lembourn; corr. Mrs. Norman Nordstrand, 1984; *New York Times*, June 3, 1979; James Haspiel, *Films in Review*, Aug./Sept. 1979.
18 Jean-Louis: int., 1983.
18 MM on men in Hollywood: *Empire News*, May 16, 1954.
19 "Call-girl": Adams, *Imperfect Genius*, 253; Strasberg, in *Swank*, Aug. 1980; int. Cindy Adams, 1985.
19 Pepitone: int., 1984; Pepitone and Stadiem, 80.
20 Halsman: *Popular Photography*, June 1953 and Jan. 1956.
20 First sex: Skolsky, *Don't Get Me Wrong*, 222.
20 Shearer: *Parade*, Aug. 5, 1973.
20 (MM version): *Empire News*, May 9, 1954.
21 Feury: int., 1983.
21 Rosenstein: *Hollywood Close-Up*, May 17, 1974.
22 Greenson: corr. colleague, 1960.
22 Nightmare: Dougherty, 34.
22 Freud: *New York Times*, Science Supplement, Jan. 24, 1984.
23 "George": *Empire News*, May 9, 1954; Monroe, 19.
22 Greene: int., 1984.
23 Kinsey: Kinsey *et al.*, *Sexual Behavior in the Human Female*, Philadelphia: W.B. Saunders & Co., 1953, 282ff.
23 Dougherty: Dougherty, 37.
23 MM interest in sex: Monroe, 28.
23 "Something else": Wilkie, 127.
23 Mitchum: Wilson, *Show Business Nobody Knows*, 299; int. Wilson, 1984.

24 MM and babies: *Empire News*, May 16, 1954.
24 Diaphragm: Dougherty, 36.
25 Carmen: int., 1983.
25 Child?: Pepitone and Stadiem, 75; int., 1984; int. Amy Greene and Jeanne Carmen, 1983–84.
26 Leonardi: Wilson, *Show Business Laid Bare*, 61; int. James Haspiel, 1984.
26 Painkillers: Zolotow, *Marilyn Monroe*, 26.
26 Rosenfeld: int., 1984.
26 Monroe on future child: *Empire News*, May 16, 1955; Monroe, 31.
26 Suicide: *New York Post*, Aug. 7, 1962.
27 MM in Las Vegas: Dougherty, 99.
27 Dougherty (fn.): *Los Angeles Daily News*, July 15, 1984.

Chapter 4
28 Slatzer meeting: int., 1983; Slatzer, 86.
28 Slatzer *bona fides* (fn.): see chapter 11.
29 Zahn: corr. and int., 1983–84.
29 Hughes: *Los Angeles Times*, July 29, 1946; (fn). Wilson, *Show Business Nobody Knows*, 308; Wilson, *Hot Times*, 72; int. Terry Moore, 1985.
30 Different names: int. James Haspiel, 1984.
30 Lyon: Parsons, 213; *Los Angeles Herald-Examiner*, Aug. 6, 1962; *Los Angeles Daily News*, June 13, 1953.
30 Screen test: Zolotow, *Marilyn Monroe*, 50
31 MM on contract: *Empire News*, May 30, 1954.
31 Zahn: int., 1983.
31 Name: Wilson, *Los Angeles Daily News*, June 13, 1953.
32 Shawhan: int., 1983.
32 Skolsky: int., 1983; Skolsky, *Don't Get Me Wrong*, 213; Goodman, 53; John Sherwood, *Los Angeles Herald-Examiner*, Oct. 17, 1962.
33 Carnovsky: Zolotow, *Marilyn Monroe*, 61ff.
33 Burnside: London *Observer*, May 6, 1984.
34 School reports (for 1942): Los Angeles City High School District files, in Slatzer, 354.
34 Occult: *Los Angeles Daily News*, Aug. 18, 1962; int. Susan Strasberg and Kenny Kingston, 1983; David Robinson *Town*, Nov. 1962; Joe Hyams, *New York Daily News*, Aug. 18, 1962; int. Gordon Heaver, Robert Slatzer, and Eli Wallach, 1983–84, int., 1985.
34 Literature: Zolotow, *Marilyn Monroe*, 66, 251; *Life*, April 7, 1952; Bill Burnside, London *Observer* May 6, 1984; Knef, 256; Winters, 293.
34 Lincoln: int. Milton and Amy Greene, Joshua Logan, Brad Dexter, and James Haspiel, 1983–84.
34 Sandburg: int. Henry Weinstein, 1984; *Look*, Sept. 11, 1962; Weatherby, 141; int. Amy Greene, and Ted Strauss, 1983–84; Alan Levy, "A Good Long Look at Myself," *Redbook*, Aug. 1962; Winchell, *Los Angeles Herald-Examiner*, Aug. 6, 1962.
34 "The people": *Life*, Aug. 3, 1962.

35   Vesalius: int. Rupert Allan, 1983; Zolotow, *Marilyn Monroe*, 46.

Chapter 5
36   Chaplin, Jr., affair: int. Lita Grey, former wife Chaplin, Sr.,
       1983; int. Arthur James, 1983; int. Nan Morris, widow of
       Edward G. Robinson, Jr.
37   Slatzer: int. Robert Slatzer and Will Fowler, 1983.
37   Wohlander: Wilson, *Show Business Laid Bare*, 61, int. Wilson,
       1984.
37   Bodne: Theresa Garofalo, int. Mrs. Bodne, 1984.
37   Nudity dream: *Empire News*, May 9, 1954; Monroe, 16.
37   Reading Freud: Zolotow, *Marilyn Monroe*, 10.
38   Policeman: *Parade*, Aug. 5, 1973; Monroe, 70; "So Far to Go,"
       Redbook, June 1952; *Hollywood Citizen-News*, June 3, 1952;
       Graham, *Confessions*, 137.
38   Guardian's husband: Guiles, *Norma Jean*, 41.
38   Skolsky disbelief: Skolsky, *Don't Get Me Wrong*, 222.
38   Carroll meeting: int. May Mann, 1983; int. Robert Slatzer, 1983;
       Guiles, *Norma Jean*, 93.
39   MM on men in Hollywood: *Empire News*, May 30, 1954.
39   MM casting couch story: *Empire News*, May 23, 1954.
39   Churchill: corr. and int. Tommy Zahn, 1983.
39   Rosenstein: *Hollywood Close-up*, May 17, 1974.
40   MM and Lyon: int. Sheilah Graham, 1985.
41   Schenck: int. Marion Marshall Wagner, 1983.
41   Taps: int., 1983.
41   Bacon: int., 1983; Bacon, *Hollywood Is a Four-Letter Town*, 125.
42   Chasin: int., 1983.
42   Minardos: int., 1983.
42   *Let's Make Love* party: int. Rupert Allan, 1983; Guiles, *Norma
       Jean*, 304.
43   Greene: int., 1984.
43   Romanoff: int., 1983.
43   Weatherby: Weatherby, 142.
43   Older men: Jaik Rosenstein, *Hollywood Close-up*, May 17, 1974.
43   MM on Schenck: *Empire News*, June 6, 1954.

Chapter 6
44   Lytess: Lytess; Wilkie, 126ff., 172ff., Natasha Lytess, *Screen
       World*, Nov. 1953; Bill Tusher, *Movie Mirror*, Mya 1957.
45   Pepitone: int., 1984; Pepitone and Stadiem, 192.
45   Muir: int. Robert Slatzer, 1983.
45   Skolsky: int. Steffi Skoksky, 1983.
45   MM on "lesbian": Weatherby, 108; *Empire News*, June 13,
       1954; Monroe, 76.
45   Lytess: Lytess, 4.
46   Karger affair: int. Anne Batté and Bennett Short, Patti Karger,
       Terry Melton, Elizabeth Karger, Vi Russell, and Richard Quine,
       1983.
47   MM on affair: *Empire News*, June 13, 1954; Monroe, 78.
48   Watch: int. Elizabeth Karger, 1983; *Empire News*, June 20, 1954;
       Monroe, 83.

49 "Bitchy": Skolsky, *Don't Get Me Wrong*, 223.
49 Lytess: Lytess, 4.
49 Taps: int., 1983.
50 MM and Cohn: *Empire News*, June 6, 1954.
50 Variation on Cohn story: Hoyt, 54ff.
50 Krekes: Conway and Ricci, 29.
50 MM sees movie: int. Anne Batté, 1983.

Chapter 7
51 Lytess: Lytess, 6.
51 Starr: int., 1983.
52 *Photoplay* event: Adele Fletcher, *Photoplay*, Sept. 1965.
52 Wilson: int., 1984; Wilson, *Show Business Nobody Knows*, 306.
52 Rosenfeld: int., 1984.
53 Hyde (dentist and cosmetic surgery): int. Elizabeth Karger and James Haspiel, 1983.
53 Lytess and *Asphalt Jungle*: Lytess, 7.
53 Padded bosom: int. James Bacon, 1983.
53 Huston: int., 1983; Huston, 286.
54 Johnson: Johnson and Leventhal, 202.
54 Romanoff: int., 1983.
54 Wilder: int., 1983.
54 Kanin: Kanin, 355ff.
55 Bacon: int., 1983.
55 MM leaves Palm Springs: int. Patti Karger, 1983.
55 MM on Karger: Guiles, *Norma Jean*, 118.
55 Marry Hyde?: *Empire News*, June 27, 1954; Monroe, 104.
55 Craft: int., 1983.
55 Lytess on Hyde: Lytess, 12.
56 MM mourning Hyde: int. Amy Greene and Maureen Stapleton, 1984–83.
56 Johnson: Johnson and Leventhal, 210.
56 Suicide attempt: Lytess, 14.
56 Suicide Prevention Center: Report to Coroner, Aug. 1962, supplied by Dr. Norman Farberow.

Chapter 8
56 Bernheim: int., 1983.
57 Knef: Knef, 255.
57 *Asphalt Jungle* reviews: Conway and Ricci, 40.
58 U.C.L.A.: Robert Cahn, *Collier's*, Sept. 8, 1951.
58 Paar: Paar, 85.
58 Lytess and studio joke: Lytess.
59 Chekhov: Weatherby, 41; Alan Levy, "A Good Long Look at Myself," *Redbook*, Aug. 1962; Monroe, 133.
59 Cahn: *Collier's*, Sept. 8, 1951.
60 *Look and Life:* int. Rupert Allan, Roy Craft, and Ted Strauss, 1983.
61 Winters: Winters, 98, 292; Adams, *Imperfect Genius*, 258; int. James Haspiel, 1985.
61 Einstein joke: int. Eli Wallach, 1984.
62 Howard: int., 1983.

62   Kazan declines interview: corr., 1984.

62   Kazan: int. Milton Greene, Eli Wallach, Alain Bernheim, and Milt Ebbins, 1983–84.

63   Kazan and Communist Party: *Current Biography*, 1972.

63   Allan: int., 1983.

64   Cameron Mitchell: Zolotow, *Marilyn Monroe*, 93.

64   "Weeping": Robert Levin, *Redbook*, Feb. 1958.

64   Lytess: Lytess, 14; Wilson, *Hot Times*, 73; int. Wilson, 1984.

65   Miller letter: Guiles, *Norma Jean*, 132.

65   MM on Miller: Parsons, 230.

65   Lytess: *New York Post*, July 8, 1956.

65   Stapleton: int., 1983.

65   Miller letter: Guiles, *Norma Jean*, 132.

66   Bacon call: Bacon, *Hollywood Is a Four-Letter Town*, 129.

Chapter 9

66   Gardner: Hy Gardner, *New York Herald Tribune*, Aug. 8, 1962.

66   Nude calendar: Tom Kelley, *Man*, March 1955; Hedda Hopper, *Los Angeles Times*, Sept 9, 1963; Natalie Kelley Grasco, *Movie Stars Parade*, July 1953; Tom Kelley, *Filmland*, Feb. 1954; Skolsky, *Don't Get Me Wrong*, 217; Aline Mosby, UPI, March 13, 1952; Aline Mosby, *Santa Monica Evening Outlook*, Aug. 6, 1962; int. Johnny Campbell, Sonia Wolfson, and Theo Wilson, 1983.

68   *Playboy:* Talese, 78ff.; *Playboy*, Dec. 1953.

68   MM and pornography: *Penthouse*, Oct. 1980; *Apple Knockers and the Coke Bottle* video; *Confidential*, March 1955; int. Steffi Skolsky, 1983.

69   MM and "father": Dougherty, 73; int. Inez Melson, 1983; Skolsky, *Don't Get Me Wrong*, 220; int. Ralph Roberts and Pat Newcomb, 1985; corr. Ralph Roberts, 1984; Guiles, *Norma Jean*, 136; int. Amy Greene and Henry Rosenfeld, 1984.

70   Henaghan: *Redbook*, June 1962; *Motion Picture*, July 1955.

70   Johnson: *Los Angeles Daily News*, May 3, 1952.

71   Appendectomy: int. Dr. Marcus Rabwin, 1984; corr. Mrs. Rabwin, 1984; Graham, *Confessions*, 133.

72   DiMaggio call: Zolotow, *Marilyn Monroe*, 143.

Chapter 10

75   DiMaggio background: di Gregorio; Allen; Gay Talese, "The Silent Season of a Hero," *Esquire*, July 1966.

75   Reluctance on book: Melvin Durslag, *Los Angeles Times*, 1982.

76   DiMaggio sees picture: Carpozi, 73; Allen, 171; Spada, 36; int. Roy Craft, 1983.

76   MM and DiMaggio meet: *Empire News*, July 18, 1954; Allen, 173; Carpozi, 72.

78   Bragging: int. Wilson, 1984.

79   Williams: *Los Angeles Mirror*, March 10, 1953.

79   Minardos affair: int. Nico Minardos, 1983.

81   DiMaggio and press: Skolsky, *Marilyn*, 62.

81   Travilla: int., 1983.

82   "Act dumber": *New York Daily News*, in Conway and Ricci, 87.

Chapter 11

82 Slatzer: int., 1982–85.
83 Slatzer *bona fides:* Snyder, in Slatzer, *xxi;* int. Noble "Kid" Chissell, Gordon Heaver, Dr. Sanford Firestone, Lee Henry, Doral Chenoweth, and Ron Pataki, 1983–85.
85 Walking shot: int. James Haspiel, 1985.
85 Reporter on Toots Shor's: Carpozi, 81.
85 Neill: int., 1983.
85 Hairdresser: int. Gladys Whitten, 1983.
86 Snyder: int., 1983.
86 Male jealousy: *Hollywood Citizen-News,* Sept. 4, 1952.
87 Kilgallen: *New York Journal-American,* Aug. 28, 1952.
87 Slatzer and books: *New York Journal-American,* Sept. 17, 1952.
87 Firestone: int., 1985.
88 Moore: int., 1983–85; *Los Angeles Times,* Feb. 15, 1983.
88 Fowler: corr., 1985.
88 Chissell: int., 1982.
90 Russell: int., 1983.
90 Skolsky: Skolsky, *Marilyn,* 62; *Modern Screen,* Oct. 1953.
90 Progress as star: *Movieland,* Dec. 1952.
91 Ray Anthony: int. Lionel Newman and Leo Gill, 1983; *Movieland,* Dec. 1952; *Marilyn,* song by Starlight Songs Inc., 1952.

Chapter 12

91 Grauman's: int. Jane Russell, 1983; Spada, 74.
92 Whitten: int., 1983.
93 Noonan: int. Jane Russell, 1983.
93 Snyder and Plecher: int., 1983.
93 Lytess gifts: Lytess.
93 Travilla affair: int., 1983; Billy Travilla *bona fides* confirmed in int. Don Feld, 1985.
96 Robinson: int. Arthur James and Nan Morris, 1983.
97 Siegel: int., 1983.
98 Greene: int., 1984.
98 Gardel: int., 1983.
98 Death of McKee: death certificate, located by Roy Turner; Guiles, *Norma Jean,* 165.
98 *Photoplay* Award: int. Billy Travillaa; Bacon, *Hollywood Is a Four-Letter Town,* 139.
98 *New York Times:* Barbara Jamison, July 12, 1953.
99 Negulesco: int., 1983; *Flashback,* Marbella Film Institute, 1983; CBS TV "Eyewitness." Aug. 10, 1962; Negulesco, 417ff.
99 Johnson: Pete Martin, 126.
99 Confused: Kanin, 358.
99 Bacall: Bacall, 208.
99 Johnson: Johnson and Leventhal, 106.
99 "Sloth": *Newsweek,* People section, Oct. 31, 1960.
100 Premiere: Johnson and Leventhal, 205ff.
100 Bacall: Bacall, 208.

Chapter 13

101 Apartment: Kendis Rochlen and Charles Park, *Los Angeles Mirror,* Jan. 19, 1954.

101   Skolsky: Skolsky, *Marilyn*, 65.
101   Mike DiMaggio: Carpozi, 91.
101   DiMaggio attitude: *Photoplay* Awards; Bacon, *Hollywood Is a Four-Letter Town*, 139; Zolotow, *Marilyn Monroe*, 172; Guiles, *Norma Jean*, 163.
102   Lytess: Lytess; int. George Masters and Henry Rosenfeld, 1983–84; Wm. Burnside notes, 1985.
102   *River of No Return:* int. Whitey Snyder, 1983; *Collier's*, Oct. 16, 1953; Bacon, *Hollywood Is a Four-Letter Town*, p. 134.
103   Mitchum: int. Wilson, 1984; Goodman, 228; Barry Rehfeld int. Robert Mitchum, in *Esquire*, Feb. 1983.
103   Accidents: *Los Angeles Times*, Aug. 13 and 20, 1953; *Santa Monica Evening Outlook*, Aug. 9, 1962; int. Norman Bishop, 1984; Winter, 428ff.; Zolotow, *Marilyn Monroe*, 189.
105   Rettig: Guiles, *Norma Jean*, 168.
105   Intruding reporters: Kendis Rochlen, *Los Angeles Mirror*, Jan. 19, 1954.
105   Belser: int., 1984.
106   Wedding plans: *Los Angeles Times*, Jan. 5 and 6, 1954; *Los Angeles Daily News*, Jan. 5, 1954; *Hollywood Citizen-News*, Jan. 5, 1954; Monroe, 139.

Chapter 14
106   Wedding: *Los Angeles Mirror*, *Los Angeles Times*, *New York Times*, Jan. 15, 1954.
107   Phone calls: Skolsky, *Marilyn*, 80; Parsons, 228; int. Kendis Rochlen, 1983.
107   Ring: Sidney Skolsky, *New York Post*, March 9, 1954.
107   Nude pictures (fn.): Guiles, *Norma Jean*, 112.
108   Paso Robles: AP, Jan. 16, 1954.
108   Skolsky interview: Sidney Skolsky, *Hollywood Citizen-News*, Feb. 1, 1954.
108   Patterson: int., 1983.
109   Far East trip: Sidney Skolsky *Photoplay*, May 1954; *Time*, Feb. 15, 1954; *Empire News*, Aug. 1, 1954; *Los Angeles Times*, Dec. 14, 1953; int. Amy Greene, 1984. 96 Size of crowd: Skolsky, *Don't Get Me Wrong*, 213.
111   Injury: *Los Angeles Times*, Jan. 30, 1954; int. Amy Greene and member of Karger family circle, 1983–84.
111   Weber: Allen, 198.
111   Rosenfeld: int., 1984.
111   Whitten: int., 1983.
111   Stapleton: int., 1983.
112   Miller: Skolsky, *Don't Get Me Wrong*, 213.

Chapter 15
112   DiMaggios in San Francisco: Gay Talese, "Silent Season of a Hero," *Esquire*, July 1966; *Movieland*, Aug. 1954.
113   MM at hotel: Skolsky, *Hollywood Citizen-News*, March 9, 1954.
113   DiMaggio and Oscar: Skolsky, *Marilyn*, 82.
113   *No Business Like Show Business:* Sidney Skolsky, *New York Post*, April–July, 1954; Lionel Newman int., 1983.

114 DiMaggio marriage: Aline Mosby, *Los Angeles Herald-Express*, Oct. 1954; Sidney Skolsky, *Photoplay*, Aug. 1954; Graham, *My Hollywood*, 113; int. Jet Fore and Amy Greene, 1983–84; Capote, *Chameleons*, 240.

114 Dexter: int., 1983.

115 Monroe testimony: *New York Daily News* and *Los Angeles Times*, Oct. 28, 1954.

115 Travilla: int., 1983.

116 Monroe nudity: Wilson, *Show Business Laid Bare*, 62; int. Wilson, 1984.

116 DiMaggio not on set: *Los Angeles Mirror*, Oct. 6, 1954.

116 Wilder: int., 1983.

116 Monroe and nude scene: int. Billy Wilder; Wilson, *Show Business Laid Bare*, 62.

116 Godiva: I.N.S., Sept. 15, 1954.

116 Brando: Sidney Skolsky, *New York Post*, Aug. 7, 1954.

117 Winchell: *Los Angeles Herald-Examiner*, Aug. 8, 1962.

118 Krasner: *Globe*, Dec. 22, 1981.

118 Whitten: int., 1983.

118 Amy Greene: int., 1984.

118 Snyder: int., 1983.

118 Monroe and sportswriters: *Life*, Sept. 27, 1954.

118 Monroe weeps and sequel: Zolotow, *Marilyn Monroe*, 214.

119 Separation: *Los Angeles Times: Los Angeles Mirror, Daily News, NANA, Houston Chronicle, Los Angeles Examiner, Hollywood Citizen-News*, Oct. 4–10, 1954.

119 Craft: int., 1983.

119 Whitten: int., 1983.

119 Travilla: int., 1983.

120 Hyams: Hyams, 141.

120 DiMaggio detectives: *Los Angeles Times*, Feb. 28, 1957; Irwin evidence; J. E. Leclair, *Confidential*, Sept. 1955.

121 Fox detectives: int. John Daley, former IRS agent, 1983.

121 Patti Karger: int., 1983.

121 Steffi Skolsky: int., 1983.

121 Dexter: int., 1983.

122 Sinatra: *Time*, Aug. 29, 1955; Gehman, Sciacca (*Sinatra*), Shaw, Wilson (*Sinatra*).

122 Divorce hearing: *New York Daily News, Los Angeles Times, Santa Monica Evening Outlook*, Oct. 27 and 28, 1954.

123 DiMaggio and reconciliation: *Los Angeles Herald-Express*, Oct. 28, 1954.

123 Monroe eve of divorce: *Los Angeles Herald-Express*, Oct. 26, 1954.

123 Refuge at Sinatra apartment: Jim Henaghan, *Motion Picture*, July 1955.

123 Winchell: *New York Mirror*, Aug. 8, 1962.

Chapter 16

124 Skolsky and DiMaggio meeting: Skolsky, *Don't Get Me Wrong*, 224.

124 Lesbian rumors: int. Steffi Skolsky, 1983.

125   Hal Schaefer: int., 1984; int. Lionel Newman, 1983.
127   Schaefer suicide attempt: int. Milt Ebbins and Sheila Stewart, 1983; *Los Angeles Herald-Examiner,* Oct. 6, 1954.
128   Press and Schaefer: Louella Parsons, *Los Angeles Herald-Examiner,* Oct. 6, 1954, Aline Mosby, *Hollywood Citizen-News,* Oct. 7, 1954; *Los Angeles Herald-Examiner,* Oct. 6, 1954.
128   DiMaggio reconciliation?: *Los Angeles Herald-Express,* Oct. 28, 1954; *Los Angeles Examiner,* Nov. 5, 1954.
128   Wrong Door Raid: *Confidential,* Sept. 1955; Report of the (California) State Interim Committee on Collection Agencies, Private Detectives and Debt Liquidators (Senate Resolution 21, 1957); *Los Angeles Times,* Feb. 17, 20, 27, 28, March 1, 2, 14, 21, and 27, 1957; *Beverly Hills Citizen,* Sept. 11, 1958; *Hollywood Citizen-News,* March 9, 1957; int. Hal Schaefer, Sheila Stewart, James Bacon, Brad Dexter, Fred Blasgen, Fred Otash, John Daley, Gloria Romanoff, 1983–84, Bacon, *Hollywood Is a Four-Letter Town,* 141; Otash, 73–84.
131   Monroe condition: *Los Angeles Times,* Oct. 6, 1954; AP Oct. 4, 1954.
131   Krohn: int. Dr. Lee Siegel and colleague's int. Dr. Krohn, 1983.
132   Monroe operation: I.N.S. Nov. 4 and 8, 1954; *Los Angeles Daily News,* Nov. 8, 9, 1954; *Hollywood Citizen-News,* Nov. 8, 1954; *Los Angeles Examiner,* Nov. 9, 1954; Motion Picture Editor, I.N.S., Nov. 13, 1954; *Los Angeles Times,* Dec. 13, 1954.
132   DiMaggio inquiries: int. Inez Melson, 1983.
132   *Itch* party: Sidney Skolsky column, *Hollywood Citizen-News,* Nov. 9, 1954; *Life,* Nov. 29, 1954.
133   Zonk alias: int. Milton Greene, 1983.

Chapter 17
137   Relationship with Greenes: int. Milton and Amy Greene, 1983–84, int. Rupert Allan, 1983.
137   Monroe's aspirations: *Los Angeles Mirror,* March 10, 1953.
139   Stay at Greenes: Helen Bolstad, *Photoplay,* Sept. 1955; Dorothy Manning, *Photoplay,* Oct. 1956.
139   Dumping of friends: int. Steffi Skolsky, 1983; Lytess.
140   Monroe's interests at Greenes': Mailer, *Of Women and Their Elegance;* int. Milton and Amy Greene, 1983–84.
141   Edometriosis: int. Dr. Lee Siegel, 1983; Robert Berkow, M.D., *The Merck Manual,* Merck Sharp Dohme Research Laboratories, N.J., 1977; Dr. Michael Carrera, *Sex,* London: Mitchell Beazley, 1981.
142   WAIF: int. Jane Russell, 1983.
142   New York press conference: I.N.S., Jan., 1955; Louella Parsons, *Los Angeles Herald-Examiner,* Jan. 11, 1955; *New York Daily News,* Jan. 7, 1955; UPI, Jan. 6, 1955; Carpozi, 119.
144   Pink elephant: int. Milton Greene, 1983; *Photoplay,* Sept. 1955; Michael Todd, Jr., and Susan Todd, *A Valuable Property,* New York: Arbor House, 1983.
145   Berle as lover (fn.): Berle, 266.
145   "Person to Person": transcript of program, April 8, 1955; int. Amy and Milton Greene.

145 Haspiel: int. 1984–85.
145 Height: 1956 passport application, released under FOIA, 1984.
146 Monroe's 1955 reading: Zolotow, *Marilyn Monroe,* 251.

Chapter 18
147 Monroe and Collier: int. Amy Greene, 1984; Capote, *Music for Chameleons,* 227; *Time* and *Newsweek,* May 9, 1955.
147 Actors Studio and Strasberg: Adams, *Imperfect Genius,* 254–79; Strasberg, Zolotow, *Marilyn Monroe,* 236*ff.;* Lee Strasberg, Swank, Aug. 1980; Paula Strasberg,
148 *Los Angeles Herald-Examiner,* Aug. 10, 1962; Parsons, 229; int. Kevin McCarthy and Maureen Stapleton, Eli Wallach, and Susan and John Strasberg, 1983. Monroe sketches: Zolotow, *Marilyn Monroe,* 265; W. J. Weatherby corr., 1984; int. Susan Strasberg, 1983. Monroe bequest: int. Jim Haspiel, 1984.
151 Monroe and Rostens: corr. and int. Norman Rosten, 1984; Norman Rosten, 1952. Sonnets: Slatzer, 136. Manhattan: Zolotow, *Marilyn Monroe,* 253. Yeats: *Selected Poetry.* Patricia Rosten: Peary, 321; Norman Rosten, *Newsday,* Aug. 1, 1982.

Chapter 19
157 Miller response: corr., 1982–84.
158 Miller background: Arthur Miller, "A Boy Grew in Brooklyn," *Holiday,* March 1955; Allan Seager, "The Creative Agony of Arthur Miller," *Esquire,* Oct. 1959; Samuel Freedman, *New York Times,* Oct. 23, 1983; Jim Cook, "Inside Story of a Romance," *New York Post* and *Los Angeles Mirror-News,* July 1956; Robert Martin; Tony Schwartz, "Miller's Return to the 'U,' " *New York Times Magazine,* Dec. 2, 1973; Josh Greenfeld, "Writing Plays Is Absolutely Senseless," *New York Times Magazine,* Feb. 13, 1972; "It's Miller Time—Again," *Los Angeles Times* Calendar, June 10, 1984; Profile, London *Observer,* Oct. 14, 1956; Ira Wolfert, "Arthur Miller, Playwright in Search of His Identity," *New York Times,* 1953; Murray Schumach, "Arthur Miller Grew in Brooklyn," *New York Times,* 1949; Dan Sullivan, "Arthur Miller, Harvest Time," *Los Angeles Times,* Oct. 5, 1980.
159 *Time:* Robert Ajemian, int. Arthur Miller, April 1956.
160 "Triangle" in plays: Zolotow, *Marilyn,* 259.
160 Marilyn and Miller reunion: Zolotow, *Marilyn,* 263. April contact: Robert Ajemian, int. Arthur Miller.
160 Leonardi: *New York Post,* July 8, 1956.
160 Marilyn dinner parties: Robert Ajemian, int. Arthur Miller;int. Maureen Stapleton, 1983.
161 MM on political freedom: Alan Levy, "A Good Long Look at Myself,"*Redbook,* Aug. 1962.
161 Close friend: Alan Levy, *Redbook,* Aug. 1962.
161 DiMaggio's reading: Meaker, 39.
161 Miller's intellect: Parsons, 232.
161 Rosten: Norman Rosten, 36.
161 *Time:* Robert Ajemian int. Arthur Miller.
163 Kargers in New Jersey: int. Bennett Short and Anne Batté, 1983.

163   DiMaggio pursuit: Wilson, *Show Business Nobody Knows,* 312; int. Wilson and Henry Rosenfeld, 1984. Row: Zolotow, *Marilyn,* 243. Haspiel: int. 1984.

163   Marilyn joke: int. Patti Karger and Bennett Short, 1983. Karger in New York: Guiles, *Norman Jean,* 202. Rosenfeld: int. Henry Rosenfeld and Norman Rosten, 1984.

164   Rainier scheme: int. Gardner and Fleur Cowles, and Milton and Amy Greene, 1983–84. Call to Kelly: Graham, *Confessions,* 135.

165   Brando: int. Milton and Amy Greene; *Movieland,* Dec. 1954; George Barris int. MM, *New York Daily News,* Aug. 17, 1962. Sex appeal: int. Pete Martin, *Saturday Evening Post,* May 5, 1956. Photograph: collection of Amy Greene. Phone calls in last days: corr. and int. Ralph Roberts, 1983–84.

166   Wilson interview: *New York Post,* Oct. 2, 1955; int. Wilson, 1984.

166   Marriage discussion: Jim Cook, *New York Post,* July 8, 1956.

166   *Anna Christie:* int. Maureen Stapleton, 1983. Lytess: Bill Tusher, *Movie Mirror,* May 1957. Kim Stanley: *American Film,* June, 1983.

167   Strasberg praise: Logan, 43; int. Joshua Logan, 1984.

167   Dressing room: Dorothy Manning, *Photoplay,* Oct. 1956; Sidney Skolsky, *New York Post,* Aug. 2, 1955.

167   Contract: Zolotow, *Marilyn Monroe,* 266; int. Amy Greene, 1984.

167   Olivier press conference: *Time,* Feb. 20, 1956; Kiernan, *Sir Larry,* 257; Manning: *Photoplay,* Oct. 1956.

168   "Schizoid": Olivier, 205.

168   Psychiatric care (during 1954): Carpozi, 114; and Zolotow, *Marilyn Monroe,* 207

169   Gottlieb: int., 1985.

169   Corday: int., 1983.

169   Drug equipment: Otash, 80; int. Fred Otash, 1983.

169   Psychiatric care: Stopped: Zolotow, *Marilyn Monroe,* 226. Greene: int., 1983. Haspiel: int. 1984.

169   Miller: Robert Ajemian int. Arthur Miller.

169   Wilder: Goodman, 227.

169   Rosenfeld: int., 1984.

170   Fletcher: *Photoplay,* Sept. 1965.

170   Leonardi: *New York Post,* July 15, 1956.

170   Notebook: Richard Gehman, *American Weekly,* May 1, 1960.

170   Pills: int. Milton and Amy Greene, 1983–84.

170   Strasberg help: Adams, *Imperfect Genius,* 263; int. John Strasberg, 1984.

171   *Time:* May 14, 1956.

171   Goodman: Goodman, 231.

171   Rosten: int. 1984; Norman Rosten, *Newsday,* Aug. 1, 1962.

Chapter 20

172   Reception: *Time,* May 14, 1956.

172   *Bus Stop:* int. Joshua Logan and Milton Greene, 1983–84; Logan, 42.

173   Adler row: Robert Ajemian int. Arthur Miller.

173 Lytess: Lytess, 27.
173 Paula Strasberg: int. Susan and John Strasberg; Adams, *Imperfect Genius*; Strasberg, 75.
174 "Iron fence": int. Rosie Steinberg, 1983.
174 Murray incident: Carpozi, 133
174 Tranquilizers: Guiles, *Norma Jean*, 229.
174 Limousine: Adams.
174 Illness: *New York Times*, April 13, 1956.
175 Press: int. William R. Woodfield, 1984.
175 *Time* interview: int. Brad Darrach, 1984.
176 Newcomb: int. Pat Newcomb and Rupert Allan, 1983–84.
176 Lange: Hoyt 176.
177 Psychiatrist: int. Milton Greene, 1983.
177 Reviews: *New York Times, New York Herald, New York Herald Tribune*, Sept. 1, 1956.
177 Award: Graham, *Confessions*, 114.
177 Logan: int., 1984; int. Wilson, *New York Post*, Sept. 1956.

Chapter 21
177 "Mr. and Mrs. Leslie": Goode, 17; Jim Cook, *New York Post*, July 8, 1956; Robert Ajemian int. Arthur Miller, April 1956.
178 Mann: int. May Mann, 1983.
178 House Un-American Activities Committee: Transcript of proceedings for June 21, 1956, U.S. Government Printing Office, 1956; Feinman, 170ff.; Huston, chap. 11; Bentley; Cogley. McCarthy: Richard Rovere, "The Frivolous Demagogue," *Esquire*, Aug. 1958; George Will, *New York Times*, June 15, 1984. Miller session: Jim Cook, *New York Post*, July 13, 1956. Winchell: undated column, June 1956. Steinbeck: John Steinbeck, "The Trial of Arthur Miller," *Esquire*, June 1957; Weatherby, 125; *Los Angeles Times*, June 22, 1956, July 1, 1956, June 1 and 19 1957; *New York Daily News*, June 22 and July 26, 1956; *Los Angeles Herald-Examiner*, May 29, 1957; *Hollywood Citizen-News*, Feb. 18, 1957. Walter: Robert Martin, 291.
179 Marilyn on HUAC: *Newsweek*, July 2, 1956; *Los Angeles Times*, Aug. 8, 1958. In Washington: int. Eli Wallach, 1984; Guiles, *Norma Jean*, 247; Signoret, 290; int. Henry Rosenfeld, 1984. Skouras threat: Signoret, 290; *Life*, Aug. 3, 1962; Weatherby, 54.
180 Greenson: int. Danny Greenson, 1984.
180 Strasbergs and "communism": Adams, *Imperfect Genius*, 172ff., 242; Capell, 43.
180 FBI releases: 1956 segment of Monroe documents released to author, 1983, and to Robert Slatzer, 1980.
180 Hoover: Wallace *et al*, 628.
180 Rosten call: Norman Rosten, 34.
181 Repairman: *Newsweek*, July 2, 1956.
182 Wedding: *New York Daily News*, June 22 and 27, 1956; *Los Angeles Time*, July 2 and 3, 1956; *Los Angeles Herald-Express*, June 28, 1956; *Los Angeles Herald-Examiner*, June 30, July 3 and 4, 1956; *Los Angeles Mirror-News*, June 30, 1956; Zolotow, *Marilyn Monroe*, 287ff.; *Westchester News*, July 3, 1956.

182   Miller's parents: Flora Rheta Schreiber, "Remembrance of Marilyn," *Good Housekeeping,* Jan. 1963; *Life,* July 16, 1956.
183   Jewish ceremony: Susan Wender, "Marilyn Enters a Jewish Family," *Modern Screen,* Nov. 1956.
183   Greene: int., 1983–84.
184   Rosten: Norman Rosten, 38.
184   Ring: Guiles, *Norma Jean,* 252.
184   "Hope": Wagenknecht, *Seven Daughters of the Theater,* 202.

Chapter 22
185   "Gershwin": Harris, 186.
185   Press coverage: London *Daily Mail,* March 21, June 13, July 13, 14, 1956; London *Daily Herald,* April 27, 1956; London *Daily Mirror,* May 14, 1956. Bicycle: London *Daily Sketch,* July 16, 1956.
185   Millers at home: London *Daily Mail,* July 16 and 17, 1956; AP, July 14, 1956.
186   Coward: Payne and Morley, 308.
186   Olivier and Monroe meetings: Winters, 299; Harris, 183.
186   *The Prince and the Showgirl:* Olivier, chap. 10; Kiernan, *Sir Larry,* 257; *Time,* May 14, 1956; int. Joshua Logan, John Huston, Billy Wilder, 1983–84.
187   "Count?": Johnson and Leventhal, 206.
187   "Amateur": *Los Angeles Mirror,* Dec. 3, 1956.
187   Cardiff: London *Sunday Dispatch,* series in Nov. 1956.
187   Monroe on Olivier: Weatherby, 61.
187   Lateness: Harris, 188.
187   "Child": Parsons, 232.
188   Miller journey: McKnight notes (Zolotow collection); Maurice Zolotow, "Who Runs Marilyn Monroe?" *Los Angeles Herald-Examiner,* Dec. 12, 1956.
188   Greene: London *Sunday Dispatch,* Nov. 8, 1956; Maurice Zolotow, *Los Angeles Herald-Examiner;* int. Milton Greene, 1983–84.
188   Greene ousted: *Los Angeles Times,* April 12 and 17, 1957; *New York Times,* April 12, 1957; Guiles, *Norma Jean,* 263–73; Zolotow, *Marilyn Monroe,* 303.
188   Coward: Payne and Morley, 358.
189   Queen: *Daily Sketch,* Oct. 30, 1956.
189   Apology: London *Daily Mail,* Nov. 17, 1956.
189   Definition of love: Zolotow, *Marilyn Monroe,* 265.
189   Note incident: Guiles, *Norma Jean,* 260; int. Bob Josephy and James Haspiel, 1984; Miller, *After the Fall,* 114.
190   Greene affair: Zolotow, *Marilyn Monroe,* 227; Davis, *Suitcase,* 238; int. Milton Greene, 1984.
190   Press and sleeping: *New York Daily News,* July 16, 1956; Guiles, *Norma Jean,* 259; int. Milton Greene, 1984.
191   Sitwell: London *Daily Mail,* July 16, 1956; *Newsweek,* Aug. 6, 1956; *Los Angeles Herald-Examiner,* Aug. 6, 1962.
191   Leigh miscarriage: Strasberg, 85.
191   Monroe pregnant? Alan Arnold, publicity director of *Prince,* in *Sunday Dispatch,* Nov. 1956; Louella Parsons, *Los Angeles Herald-Examiner,* Aug. 2, 1957.

191 Tynan: Kiernan, *Sir Larry*, 259ff.

Chapter 23

192 Marilyn on marriage: int. Richard Meryman, *Life*, Nov. 4, 1966.
192 Jamaica: AP, Jan. 15, 1957; Carpozi, 145.
192 Apartment: Guiles, *Norma Jean*, 271; int. James Haspiel, 1984; Zolotow, *Marilyn Monroe*, 314.
193 Piano: Zolotow, *Marilyn Monroe*, 14.
193 Apartment: Elsa Maxwell, *American Weekly*, May 12, 1957.
193 Marilyn on marriage: *Movieland*, March 1957; *Redbook*, Feb. 1958; Parsons, 232; Alan Levy, "A Good Long Look at Myself," *Redbook*, Aug. 1962; Lester David int. June 1957, pub. This Week, *Los Angeles Times*, April 12, 1964; Adele Whitely Fletcher, *Photoplay*, Sept. 1965.
193 Nicknames: *Look*, Oct. 1, 1957.
193 Collected plays: Corrigan, 5.
193 Miller: *Redbook*, Feb. 1958.
193 N.Y. activity: *Look*, Oct. 1, 1957.
194 Father: Flora R. Schreiber, *Good Housekeeping*, Jan. 1963.
194 Stepmother: Alan Levy, "A Good Long Look at Myself," *Redbook*, Aug. 1962; int. Lionel Newman and James Haspiel, 1983–84.
194 Domesticity: int. Maureen Stapleton and Norman Rosten, 1983–84; Norman Rosten, 54.
194 McCarthy: int., 1983.
195 Miller: "Marilyn Stands by Her Man," *Movieland*, July 1957.
195 Marilyn summoned: Carpozi, 146.
195 Slatzer: corr. Slatzer; *Confidential*, May 1957.
195 DiMaggio: Roderick Man, London *Daily Express*, July 16, 1956.
195 Note: Norman Rosten, 50.
196 Amagansett: N. Polsky, "And the Lord Taketh Away," *Modern Screen*, Nov. 1957; Zolotow, *Marilyn Monroe*, 312; *Look*, Oct. 1, 1957.
196 Premiere: *Los Angeles Times*, This Week, Dec. 11, 1960.
196 Superintendents: Joe Hyams, *New York Herald Tribune*, July 3, 1957.
196 Baby: *Los Angeles Times*, This Week, April 12, 1964; int. Danny Greenson, 1984; Norman Rosten, 46; Wagenknecht, *Seven Daughters of the Theater*, 208; London *Observer*, Oct. 14, 1956.
197 Miscarriage: N. Polsky, "And the Lord Taketh Away," *Modern Screen*, Nov. 1957; "Let My Baby Live,"*Movie Stars Parade*, Nov. 1957; Louella Parsons, *Los Angeles Herald-Examiner*, Aug. 2, 1957; UPI, Aug. 1, 1957; AP, Aug. 1, 1957; Zolotow, *Marilyn Monroe*, 316; Graham, *Confessions*, 141; Carpozi, 148; Norman Rosten, 72.
198 Pepitone: int., 1984; Pepitone and Stadiem, 27 and 48.
198 Estate: int. Bob Josephy, 1984; Hollis Alpert, *The Dreams and The Dreamers*, New York: Macmillan, 1962; *Look*, Oct. 1, 1957; Harris, 191; Norman Rosten, 66ff.; author's research on Diebolds, 1984; Patricia Rosten on Marilyn, Peary, 321.
199 Marilyn and nature: int. Inez Melson, 1983; Miller, "Please Don't Kill Anything," *Stories by Arthur Miller*, 1967.

199   Boys in park: int. James Haspiel, 1985.
199   Nasturtiums: int. Rupert Allan, 1983.
200   Rosten: corr. and int. Norman Rosten, 1984; Norman Rosten, 75
        and 55; "A Friend Remembers Marilyn," *Newsday*, Aug. 1,
        1982.
201   "Help": Norman Rosten, flyleaf.

Chapter 24
201   Beaton: Cecil Beaton, *The Face of the World,* New York: John
        Day, 1957.
201   *Life* issue: Arthur Miller, "My Wife Marilyn," *Life*, Dec. 22,
        1958.
201   Clift: Bosworth, 297; LaGuardia, 191.
202   Arrival: *Los Angeles Times* and *Los Angeles Herald-Examiner,*
        July 9, 1958; This Week, *Los Angeles Times*, Oct. 5, 1958.
202   *Some Like It Hot:* Zolotow, *Marilyn Monroe,* 320; Guiles, *Norman Jean,* 285; LaGuardia, 192.
202   Obscenity: int. Billy Wilder, 1983; Guiles, *Norma Jean,* 287.
203   Champagne: *New York Daily News,* Feb. 3, 1960.
203   Arrogance: Carpozi, 152.
203   Shearer: *Parade,* Dec. 7, 1958.
203   Wilder: *Parade,* Dec. 7, 1958; int., 1983.
204   Rosten letter: Norman Rosten, 76.
204   Doctors: Carpozi, 150.
204   Wilder and Miller: int. Billy Wilder, 1983.
205   Rosten letter: Norman Rosten, 77.
205   Pregnancy ends: *Los Angeles Herald-Examiner,* Oct. 18 and Nov.
        17, 1958; *Los Angeles Times,* Nov. 1 and Dec. 18,1958; AP,
        Dec. 18, 1958; Carpozi, 153; Norman Rosten, 71.
205   Marriage founders: Norman Rosten, 79; Strasberg, 125; Adams,
        Imperfect Genius, 267; int. Maureen Stapleton and Martin Ritt,
        1983.
207   Miller at work: Allan Seager, "The Creative Agony of Arthur
        Miller," *Esquire,* Oct. 1959.
207   British interview: David Lewin, London *Daily Express,* May 6,
        1959.
207   Khrushchev: Fisher, 172; Guiles, *Norman Jean,* 292; int. Hildi
        Greenson, 1983.
208   Sukarno: int. Joshua Logan, 1984; AP and UPI, May 31, 1956;
        int. Gloria Romanoff and Robert Slatzer, 1983; Smith, chap.
        14; Powers, 341; *Alleged Assassination Plots Involving Foreign
        Leaders;* int. Marshall Noble, formerly U.S. State Dept., dealing with Far East Public Affairs, 1985; Adams, *Dictator,* 160;
        int. Joseph Shimon, 1985; author's correspondence with Smith,
        1984.
208   Monroe and Sukarno: Norman Rosten, 72; corr. Joseph B. Smith,
        1984.

Chapter 25
209   Dressing room: Norman Rosten, 79.
209   Leading man: Joe Hyams, "The Frenchman Who Rescued Marilyn," *New York Herald Tribune,* This Week, Aug. 21, 1960.

210 Marilyn on Montand: Joe Hyams, *New York Herald Tribune; Look*, 1960.

210 Miller on Montand: Joe Hyams, *New York Herald Tribune; Look*, 1960.

210 Montand and Marilyn: Signoret, chap. 11.

210 Waiting: *Life*, Aug. 15, 1960.

211 Marilyn and doctors: int. with doctors and family of psychiatrist, Dr. Ralph Greenson, 1983–84.

211 Censor: int. Frank McCarthy, 1983.

212 Minardos: int. Nico Minardos.

212 List: Winters, 294.

212 Like DiMaggio: Bacon, *Hollywood Is a Four-Letter Town*, 142.

212 Affair begins: Graham, *Cofessions*, 142; int. James Bacon and Wilson, 1983–84, Bacon, *Hollywood Is a Four-Letter Town*, 143.

212 Airport meeting: Graham, *Confessions*, 143; Skolsky, *Don't Get Me Wrong*, 229; Bacon, *Hollywood Is a Four-Letter Town*, 144; Guiles, *Norma Jean*, 324; Carpozi, 157.

213 Montand refuses calls: original wire service reports of Hedda Hopper int. with Montand, Aug. 31, 1960; *Los Angeles Times*,, Sept. 1, 1960 and Aug. 7, 1962.

213 Buchwald: *Los Angeles Times*, Sept. 18, 1960.

213 Second reporter: Vernon Scott, UPI, Sept. 2, 1960.

213 Signoret on Marilyn: *Los Angeles Mirror-News*, Nov. 16, 1960; Signoret, 303.

Chapter 26

214 Greenson: Leo Rosten; notes of Dr. Robert Litman, 1982; drafted of Maurice Zolotow article from int. Dr. Greenson, 1973; *Medical Tribune*, Oct. 24, 1973; Lloyd Shearer, "Marilyn Monroe, Why Won't They Let Her Rest In Peace?" *Parade*, Aug. 5, 1973; Curriculum Vitae of Greenson, corr. and int. Dr. Greenson's widow, Mrs. Hildi Greenson, daughter of Joan, son Danny, and secretary Susan Alexander, 1983–85; corr. with of one of Dr. Greenson's professional colleagues, who cannot be named here; int. Dr. Robert Litman, Dr. Norman Farberow, and Dr. Norman Tabachnick, Los Angeles Suicide Prevention Center psychiatrists in Aug. 1962; conversations with Dr. Maurice Lazarus and Paul Moor, 1983.

214 Greenson and Sinatra: int. Kitty Kelley, 1985.

215 "Best script": *New York Post*, Nov. 20, 1959.

215 Greenson iterim opinion: int. and documents at Los Angeles Suicide Prevention Center, 1983–84; corr. Greenson.

Chapter 27

217 *Misfits:* Goode; Alan Levy, "A Good Long Look at Myself," *Redbook*, Aug. 1962.

218 Valentine: int. John Huston and Eli Wallach, 1983–84; Huston, 286ff.

218 Infidelity discussion: Weatherby, 13.

218 Dexter meeting: int., 1983.

219 Haspiel: int., 1985.

219   Cartier-Bresson: Goode, 101.
219   McIntyre: *Esquire*, March 1961.
220   Marilyn on Gable: *Cosmopolitan*, Dec. 1960.
220   Gable on Marilyn: int. George Chasin, 1983; Bacon, *Hollywood Is a Four-Letter Town*, 145.
220   Nembutal intake: draft of Maurice Zolotow article, 1973; int. John Huston and Whitey Snyder, 1983.
220   Row: *Los Angeles Examiner* and *Mirror*, Oct. 19, 1960.
220   Allan: int. Kathy Castle, 1984.
221   Makeup man's room: int. Whitey Snyder, 1983.
221   Lugging typewriter: Kathy Castle int. Mary Malone, 1984.
221   Strasberg: Adams, *Imperfect Genius*, 278.
221   Allan: int. Rupert Allan, 1983.
222   "Dyin'" speech: Goode, 122.
222   Suicide attempt?: int. Kendis Rochlen, reporter and friend of Gable, 1983; int. Eli Wallach, 1984.
222   Stomach pump: *Esquire*, March 1961.
222   Sheet: Strasberg, 135.
222   Brando and Sinatra calls: int. Rupert Allan, 1983.
222   Parsons: Carpozi, 163.
222   Suicide rumor: *Cosmopolitan*, Dec. 1960.
222   Ring into river: *Redbook*, 1962.
222   Wilson: int. Wilson, 1984.
222   Weatherby: Weatherby, 37–52.
223   Miller birthday: Goode, 245; Hamblett, 330.
223   Divorce: *Los Angeles Mirror* and *Examiner*, Nov. 11, 1960; *New York Times, New York Journal-American*, Nov. 12, 1960; *New York Post*, Nov. 14, 1960; *Los Angeles Herald-Examiner*, Dec. 26, 1960; *Time*, Nov. 21, 1960.
223   Chipped tooth: int. James Haspiel, 1985.
224   Gable death: *New York Journal-American*, Nov. 17, 1960; *New York Post*, Nov. 18, 1960.
224   Mrs. Gable's reactions: int. Kendis Rochlen and Ross Acuna, 1983.
224   Marilyn reaction: Skolsky, *Don't Get Me Wrong*, 230.
224   *Misfits* reviews: *Film Scripts* No. 3, edited by George P. Garrett, O. B. Hardison, Jr., and Jane R. Gelfman, New Appleton Century-Crofts, 1972, p. 203; Conway and Ricci, 157.
224   Miller: LaGuardia, 220; Goode, 300.
224   Marilyn "finding self": *Los Angeles Times*, Nov. 30, 1960.
225   Slatzer: picture in possession of Slatzer, seen 1983.
225   Minardos and Greene: int. 1983–84.
225   Montand: *Los Angeles Times*, London *Sunday Dispatch*, Nov. 13, 1960; *Los Angeles Mirror*, Nov. 16, 1960; *New York Journal-American*, Nov. 18, 1960; *Hollywood Citizen-News*, Dec. 14, 1960; int. Pat Newcomb 1983–84; Pepitone and Stadiem, 163.
226   DiMaggio: Mailer, *Marilyn*, 290; int. Marjorie Stengel, 1983; Pepitone and Stadiem, 165.
226   Will: Guiles, *Norma Jean*, 342.
226   Capsules: Guiles, *Norma Jean*, 344.
226   Strasberg incidents: Adams, *Imperfect Genius*, 264; Strasberg, 156.

226   Divorce: *Hollywood Citizen-News*, Jan. 21, 1961; *El Correo-Ciudad Juárez, La Prensa, El Universal, Exelsior*, Jan. 22, 1961.
227   Haspiel: int., 1984.
227   *Misfits* review: Anderson, 178.

Chapter 28
227   Payne Whitney: Carpozi, 174ff.; *Life*, Aug. 1966; Strasberg, 156; int. Pat Newcomb, 1983; Norman Rosten, 92; int. Gloria Romanoff, 1983.
228   Kris Sessions: Monroe files in Melson archives.
228   Marilyn letter: *San Francisco Chronicle*, June 1, 1984; *Los Angeles Times*, Jan. 6, 1984; facsimile in Speriglio, 248; *Los Angeles Times, New York Post, New York Daily News*, Feb. 9, 1961; *New York Mirror*, Aug. 6, 1962.
228   Hospital change: *Hollywood Citizen-News, Los Angeles Times*, Feb. 2, 1961; *Los Angeles Herald-Examiner*, Feb. 12, 1961; *Los Angeles Herald-Examiner* and *New York Journal-American*, March 6, 1961; Norman Rosten, 93.
229   DiMaggio: *Santa Monica Evening Outlook*, Jan. 11, 1961; *Hollywood Citizen-News*, Apr. 1, 1961; *Newsweek*, April 4, 1961; *Los Angeles Mirror*, April 20, 1961; *Hollywood Citizen-News*, July 25, 1961; *Los Angeles Examiner*, Aug. 10, 1961.
230   *Rain: New York Post* Feb. 9, 1961; Guiles, *Norma Jean*, 348ff.
230   *Freud: Los Angeles Mirror*, April 20, 1961; Huston, chap. 27; int. John Huston, 1983.
230   Gynecological operation: *Hollywood Citizen-News*, May 25, 1961; Richard Cottrell, "I Was Marilyn Monroe's Doctor," *Ladies Home Companion*, Jan. 1965.
230   Gall bladder: *New York Post*, June 29, 1961; *Los Angeles Herald-Examiner, Los Angeles Mirror, New York Times*, June 30, 1961; *Ladies Home Companion*, Jan. 1965.
231   Stengel: int., 1983.
231   Drugs: Marjorie Stengel, in LaGuardia, 197.
232   Masters: int. George Masters, 1983; and Masters and Browning, 75; Tierney, chap. 14; Bacon, *Hollywood Is a Four-Letter Town*, 259; Parmet, *Presidency*, 110.
232   Carmen: int., 1983; checks on Carmen's press file, and at Doheny apartment.
232   Apartment: int. Joan Greenson, 1983; Greenson, 12.
233   Bust enlargement: int. Jeanne Carmen and Jeanne Martin, 1983.
233   Relationship with Greensons: int. Greenson family, 1983–84, Greenson, 11ff.
236   Telegram: courtesy of Hildi Greenson.
236   Heaver: corr. and int. Gordon Heaver, 1983–84.

Chapter 29
239   District Attorney's observation: int. Gary Wean, 1983.
239   Hronek: obituary, *Los Angeles Times*, Feb. 25, 1980; int. Frank Hronek's widow, son, and former colleagues, 1983.
240   Kennedys and sex: Ralph Martin, 34, 94; Blair, 145–54, 166–70, 435, 631ff., 641, 645, 666; Ralph Martin, 54, 50, 43, 55, 77,

199, 313ff., 491; Sciacca, *Kennedy and His Women*, 156; Dunleavy and Brennan, 76ff.; Bryant and Leighton, 24; int. Milton Ebbin, 1983.

241   JFK on RFK: Schlesinger, *Robert Kennedy*, 598.

241   Father of Year: *Los Angeles Times*, Dec. 17, 1960.

241   Schlesinger: 1983.

241   Garbo: Michaelis, 177.

241   Dietrich: int. Joshua Logan, 1984.

242   Lawford background: Stephen Birmingham, *Cosmopolitan*, Oct. 1961; Helen Markel, *Good Housekeeping*, Feb. 1962; obituary of Lady Lawford, *Los Angeles Times*, Jan. 24, 1972; Twentieth Century-Fox publicity sheet, undated, early fifties. Spankings: Lady Lawford, *American Weekly; Los Angeles Herald-Examiner*, July 9, 1950.

242   Lawford home: *Los Angeles Times*, April 15 and June 8, 1978.

242   Lawfords and alcohol: *Los Angeles Times*, Jan. 9, 1984; *Herald Tribune*, Aug. 9, 1984; int. Deborah Gould and Peter Lawford, 1983. Pat L.: Saunders and Southwood, 118; int. Frank Saunders, 1984.

243   Jeanne Martin: int., 1984.

Chapter 30

244   Kennedy surgery: Blair, 650ff.; Martin, 96.

244   Monroe poster: Priscilla McMillan, Collier and Horowitz, 204.

244   Feldman: Blair, 549; int. former Mrs. Jean Feldman, 1983.

244   Dobish: int., 1983.

244   Bernheim: int., 1983.

244   Slatzer: int., 1983.

244   James: int., 1984.

245   Russell: int., 1983.

246   Gene Kelly: int. Alain Bernheim and Peter Lawford, 1983; Peary, 77.

246   Lawford denials of Kennedy affair: int., 1983; *Star*, Feb. 24, 1976; London *Observer*, July 15, 1973.

246   Monroe meets JFK 1961: int. District Attorney's office, 1983.

246   Gould: *Los Angeles Herald-Examiner*, June 26, 1976; int. 1983. Rowan: Ted Landreth, int., 1985.

247   Summers: int., 1983.

247   Markel background: *New York Times*, Nov. 27, 1968.

247   Markel: int. 1984, Helen Markel, who provided copies of Monroe-Markel correspondence. (Monroe letter of March 29, 1960 enclosed a partial letter written first—both are quoted together here.)

250   Joan Greenson: Greenson, 17.

250   Nehru: Skolsky, *Marilyn*, 60.

250   Castro: Monroe-Markel correspondence.

250   SANE: *Valley Times*, March 22, 1960 (culled by FBI Los Angeles office and kept in their files).

250   Nightmare: *Redbook*, Aug. 1962.

250   Marilyn delegate: UPI, April 13, 1960.

251   "Attend convention": *Hollywood Reporter* (undated), before convention.

Chapter 31

251 Joseph Kennedy: Schlesinger, *Robert Kennedy*, 205–11.
251 Karger: int. Patti Karger, 1983.
251 Roberts: int., 1983.
251 Coliseum speech: Ralph Martin, 335; Parmet, *Presidency*, 31.
252 Acuna: int, 1983.
252 Carmen: int., 1983.
252 Summers: int., 1983.
252 Weatherby: Weatherby, 53, 55; int. W. J. Weatherby, 1982.
252 Buchwald: *Los Angeles Times*, Nov. 9, 1960.
253 Weatherby meetings: Weatherby, 86; int. W. J. Weatherby, 1982.
254 Carlyle: Ralph Martin, 402.
254 Shalam: int., 1984.
254 Wilson: int. Wilson, 1984; Wilson, *Show Business Laid Bare*, 65.
254 Ebbins: int., 1983.
255 Strasberg: Paula Strasberg, in int. James Haspiel, 1983.
255 Skolsky: int. Skolsky, 1983; (on his death) int. Steffi Skolsky; Skoksky, *Don't Get Me Wrong*, 233.
255 Bacon and Starr: int., 1983.
256 Rosenfeld: int., 1984.
256 Newcomb: int., 1983–84.
256 Smathers: int., 1983.
256 Smathers' background: Blair, 578–95; Schlesinger, *Robert Kennedy*, 493.
257 Tretick: int., 1985.
257 Carmen: int., 1983, following up int. with Los Angeles District Attorney's office, 1982.
258 Marilyn and Benny: *Los Angeles Daily News*, Sept. 20, 1953; int. Whitey Snyder, 1983.
259 July and October visits: *Los Angeles Times*, July 3, 1961; confirmed in Fisher, 202; *Los Angeles Times*, July 7, 1961, and Oct. 4, 1961.
259 John Kennedy visit: *New York Times*, Nov. 17, 19, 20, 21, 1961; *Los Angeles Times*, Nov. 19, 20, 1961; *Santa Monica Evening Outlook*, Nov. 20, 1961.
259 Watson: int., 1983; corroborated in details of Hilton reception in contemporary coverage.
260 Snyder (fn.): int, 1983.
260 Guthman: int. Edwin Guthman, 1985.
260 Evans: int., 1984.
261 FBI files: letter, David Flanders, Chief, Freedom of Information Division, Privacy Acts Branch, Records Management Division, to Robert Slatzer, May 29, 1980.

Chapter 32

261 Sinatra on Marilyn: *Redbook*, Aug. 1962.
262 First meeting?: int. Milton Greene, 1983.
262 *Misfits* company: Goode, 92; *Sierra*, 1960.
262 Cal-Neva: visit and int. Bethel van Tassell, local historian, and Wayne Ogle, former maintenance manager, 1983–84.
262 D'Amato: Exner and Demaris, 116 and 205; Blakey and Billings, 251–379.

263 Lawford: *Star*, Feb. 17, 1976.

263 Giancana ownership?: Giancana and Renner, 113–225; review of Assassinations Committee, investigators' notes of FBI reports, 1982; *New York Times*, Feb. 2, 1984; *Dallas Morning News*, Feb. 20, 1981.

263 Sinatra withdrawal: Edward A. Olsen, official of Nevada Gaming Control Board, in Oral History contribution, 1967–69, held at University of Nevada; Arnold Shaw, 317ff.; Brashler, 261ff.; Gage, 86ff.

263 Kennedys and Cal-Neva: int. Wayne Ogle, maintenanace manager, 1983–84.

263 Lawford and Cal-Neva: int. Peter Lawford, 1983; Lawford's interview with Los Angeles Police Department, Oct. 10, 1975.

263 Dog: Guiles, *Norma Jean*, 343; Pepitone and Stadiem, 171 and 183; int. Lena Pepitone, 1984.

263 Use of house: Guiles, *Norma Jean*, 353.

263 Masters: Masters and Browning, 52; int. George Masters, 1983.

264 Greenson: corr. with professional colleague, obtained by author, 1984.

264 Sands: wire story of June 7, 1961, in Wilson, *Show Busines Laid Bare*, 63; Fisher, 203.

264 Greenson: corr. with a professional colleague, obtained by author, 1984.

264 Yacht: int. Jeanne Martin and Gloria Romanoff, 1983.

265 Pepitone: int., 1984; Pepitone and Stadiem, 199ff; int. Marjorie Stengel and George Masters, 1983.

265 Prowse: Arnold Shaw, 297ff.

265 Sinatra sees Marilyn till death: int. Gloria Roamnoff and Norman Rosten, 1983–84.

265 Photographs: Murray, 25; int. Eunice Murray, 1982.

Chapter 33

266 Cohen: background: Reid, *Mickey Cohen;* Cohen and Nugent; Martin and Lewis: Cohen and Nugent, 113. Sinatra: Gehman, 178; Cohen and Nugent, 228.

266 Villa Capri: Cohen and Nugent, 190; Reid, *Mickey Cohen*, 107.

266 District Attorney's surveillance: int. Gary Wean, 1983.

267 Recordings: int. Gary Wean, 1983; Morella and Epstein, *Lana*, 241.

267 Piscitelle and LoCigno (background): *Los Angeles Times*, Dec. 12, 1961 and later articles.

267 Corroboration: int. Jack Tobin, 1983; int. Virgil Crabtree, former Asst. Chief in California of Intelligence Division, U.S. Treasury Dept., 1983.

268 Cohen and Giancana: int. Jack Tobin; Blakey and Billings, 186ff.; 195ff.; 283, 303, 326ff., 377ff.; Cohen and Nugent, 39.

268 Cohen: Messick, 118.

268 Schenck: Messick, 120ff.

268 Karger: int., 1983.

268 Shimon: int., 1983.

268 Hall: int., 1983; checks on Hall's reliability with senior law enforcement official.

269 Campbell: Exner and Demaris. Exner is Campbell's married name today; *Alleged Assassination Plots,* 129; int. Prof. Robert Blakey, 1985.

269 Safire: *Dallas News* (New York Times News Service), Jan. 7, 1976.

270 Meredith: Exner and Demaris, 198; int. Fred Otash, 1982–83; Otash on "Tomorrow Show," NBC-TV, in *Los Angeles Herald-Examiner,* Nov. 26, 1976; Anthony Cook int. Peter Fairchild, 1983; Vicki Loewy int. Judy Meredith, 1983; review of Assassinations Committee investigators' notes of FBI reports, 1982.

270 Smith: Edward Tivnan int. Sandy Smith, 1983.

271 Roselli: Exner and Demaris, 206; Blakey and Billings reference; review of Assassinations Committee investigators' reports notes of FBI, 1982.

271 O'Hare: FBI report, July 18, 1961, files CG 139–105 & CG 92–349, released to Mark Allen, 1983; Brashler, 204; Giancana and Renner, 214; Blakey and Billings, 251.

272 McGuire: int., 1983.

273 Blakey: Blakey and Billings, 391.

273 Smathers: int., 1983.

273 Kane: int., 1983.

274 Evans: int., 1984–85.

Chapter 34

275 Clay: int., 1983.

275 Close calls: int. Gloria Romanoff, 1983.

276 Greenson: corr. with colleague, Aug. 20, 1962.

276 Newcomb: int., 1983.

276 MM promiscuity: int. Dr. Norman Tabachnick, former member of Los Angeles Suicide Prevention Team, 1983; Maurice Zolotow int. Dr. Greenson. Agent: int. Marty Philpott, 1984.

277 Greenson: continuation of Aug. 20, corr.

277 Doctors/Nurses: Monroe's address book; in Melson files.

277 DiMaggio visit: int. Mrs. Greenson and daughter Joan, 1983; Greenson, 35.

278 House: Greenson manuscript, 44; Murray, 33ff.

278 House-hunting problem: Graham, *Confessions,* 148.

278 House: author's visit to house, 1983.

278 Purchase: Murray, 49; *Redbook,* Aug. 1962; int. Milton Greene and Henry Rosenfeld, 1983.

Chapter 35

279 Marilyn prepares for dinner: int. Danny Greenson, 1984.

279 Robert Kennedy visit: Murray 85; Los Angeles visit confirmed by corr. John F. Kennedy Library, Oct. 17, 1984.

280 Habit of note-making: int. Billy Travilla, 1983.

280 Field: int., 1983.

280 Romanoff: int., 1983.

280 Melson: int., 1983–84; original document held by Melson, copied for author.

280 Kennedy Library: corr. of March 18, 1983, from William Johnson, Research Archivist, to Edward Tivnan.

280   Stephen Smith: int., 1984; corr., July 16, 1984.
282   Kennedy, Sr., stroke: *New York Times*, Dec. 20, 1961; Dallas, and Ratcliffe.
283   Novello: int., 1983.
283   Guthman: Maurice Zolotow int. Edwin Guthman, *Chicago Tribune*, Sept. 1973.
283   Gould: int., 1983.
284   Joan Greenson: int., 1983; Greenson, 78.
284   "General": *Life*, Jan. 26, 1962, 76.
284   Greenson interview: *Chicago Tribune*, Sept. 1973.
284   Litman: int., 1983; original notes and subsequent reports filed at Los Angeles Suicide Prevention Center.
285   Tabachnick: int., 1983.
285   Curphey: Florabel Muir, *New York Daily News*, Aug. 6, 1962; *Los Angeles Herald-Examiner*, Aug. 6, 1962.
285   Farberow: int., 1983.
285   Rosenfeld: int., 1983.
285   Roberts: int., 1982–84.
285   Anne Karger: int. Elizabeth Karger, Vi Russell, and Robert Slatzer (who had talked with the late Fred Karger), 1983.
286   Hall: int., 1984.
286   Sherman: int., 1983.
286   Mrs. James: int., 1983.
286   Dye: int., 1983.
287   Washington: int., 1983.
287   Pepitone: int., 1984.
287   Murray: Murray, 86; int., 1982–83.
287   "Two or three times": *Chicago Tribune*, Sept. 1973.
287   Jeffries: Ted Landreth int. Norman Jeffries, 1983.
287   Culver City: int. Robert Warner, 1983, Chief Special Agent, General Telephone Company in 1962; Ted Landreth, int. former Lt. Ron Perkins and Bob Conlon, former head of detectives, both formerly with Culver City Police, 1983.
288   Pepitone: int., 1984.

Chapter 36

288   Miller, Sr.: Flora R. Schreiber, *Good Housekeeping*, Jan. 1963; Miller letters in Monroe archives of Inez Melson.
288   Marilyn upset by Miller remarriage: Johnson and Leventhal, 201.
288   Miller remarriage and child: *Los Angeles Times*, Feb. 22, 1962. Child: *New York Times*, Sept. 29, 1962.
289   Weinstein: int., 1984.
289   Masters: int., 1983.
289   Mexico visit: *Excelsior*, Feb. 21, 23, 27, March 2 and 3, 1962; *La Prensa*, Feb. 22, 23, March 2, 3, Aug. 6, 9, 1962; *Novedades*, Feb. 22, 23, March 2, 3, Aug. 6, 7, 9, 12, 1962; Murray, chaps. 6 and 7; Field, 295ff.
289   Revealing picture: eventually published in *Hustler*.
290   Field: int., 1983.
290   Bolaños: int., 1983; *cf.* Mexico visit; Mary Powers, int. Jorge Barragan and Indio Fernandez, 1984; *San Francisco Chronicle*,

Aug. 8, 1962; Florabel Muir, *New York Daily News*, Aug. 8, 9, 10, 1962.

291 Photograph of embrace: Camera Press Ltd., shot at Golden Globe Awards, March 5, 1962.

291 "Drunk": *Los Angeles Times*, Aug. 6, 1962; Hudson, 104.

291 Opinions on Bolaños: int. as indicated; Mary Powers int. Indio Fernandez, 1984.

291 Institute: *Novedades* and *La Prensa*, March 2, 1962.

291 New check: Louella Parsons, *Los Angeles Herald-Examiner*, Aug. 11, 1962.

291 Adoption?: Guiles, *Norma Jean*, 356; *Motion Picture*, Oct. 1963.

291 Yearning for babies: int. Whitey Snyder, Marjorie Plecher, and Arthur James, 1983; Murray, 40.

291 Departure: int. George Masters, 1983; *La Prensa* and *Excelsior*, March 3, 1962.

Chapter 37

292 Hoffa investigation: Kennedy, 161, 84ff.; Sheridan; Jack Tobin and Gene Blake, *Los Angeles Times*, May–Nov. 1962.

293 Enemy Within: corr. Budd Schulberg, 1984; Schulberg introduction to Sheridan; Budd Schulberg, "The Man," *Playboy*, Jan. 1969; *Los Angeles Times*, Feb. 11, Sept. 23, 1961, Feb. 18, 1962.

293 Anonymous calls and letters: *Los Angeles Times*; FBI documents, Hoover's O & C. files, March 23, 24, and 31, 1961, obtained under FOIA, 1984. See also FBI file 77-51387-90; FBI file 94-37374-61, obtained under FOIA by Prof. Herbert Parmet, 1978.

293 PT 109: FBI documents; Pamet, *Struggles*, 110.

293 Adulterer: corr. FBI on letter dated Nov. 12, 1961, file 94-39374-71, obtained under FOIA, 1983.

293 Marilyn seen by Wald: int. Curtis Harrington, Mrs. Connie Wald's former assistant, 1983.

293 FBI surveillance: Blakey and Billings, 376, 383; Giancana and Renner, 247ff., citing verbatim FBI documents; unpublished notes and transcripts of FBI surveillance reports, obtained through source, 1983.

293 Lawyers complain: Gage, 83.

293 McMillan: int. Dougald McMillan, 1983; Howard Kohn, *Rolling Stone*, Mar. 19, 1981.

294 Roselli and Giancana overheard: Blakey and Billings, 382; Giancana and Renner, 250; unreleased FBI surviellance documents, obtained through source, 1983.

294 Campbell discoveries: Exner and Demaris, 379, 57, 251.

294 O'Donnell: Parmet, *Presidency*, 127.

294 Kennedys in California: *Los Angeles Times*, March 23–28, 1962.

294 Sinatra break: Peter Lawford, *Star*, Feb. 17, 1976; Schlesinger, *Robert Kennedy*, 496.

294 MM on decision: int. Sidney Skolsky, 1983; Skolsky, *Don't Get Me Wrong*, 51ff.

295 Monroe at Palm Springs: int. Eunice Murray, 1982–83; Murray, 87; int. Philip Watson and Ralph Roberts, 1983–85.

Chapter 38
297 James: int. 1983.
297 DeSapio links: Scheim, 381; Sheridan, 530; Schlesinger, *Robert Kennedy*, 199, 204, 370ff.
297 Remodeling: Murray, 68ff.; int. Ray Tolman, 1983.
298 Danoff: int., 1983; int. John Dolan, formerly of Dolan-Whitney Agency, 1983; int. John Daley, 1983.
298 Otash: int. (first), 1982; Otash, 242.
298 Dolan: int., 1983.
298 Piscitello: int., 1983.
299 Campbell and DiMaggio: Exner and Demaris, 225.
299 DiMaggio and Cal-Neva: int. Paul D'Amato, 1984; Bob Dean, *Photoplay*, May 1961.
299 Balletti: int., 1983.
299 Spindel: Spindel, *Life*, May 20, 1966; *Collier*'s, June 24, 1955; *Daily News*, July 1ff., 1968.
299 Spindel and Kennedy: Hougan, 115; Spindel, 215, 121ff.; refs. in Sheridan.
300 Jaycox: int., 1982–83.
300 Bug in Justice Department: FBI memorandum, Evans to Belmont, Aug. 2, 1961, and March 13, 1962, from Hoover's O & C files.
300 Kelly: *People v. Spindel et al.*, Indictment No. 4817-½ 1966, trans. Kelly testimony, 2379; int. John Constandy, Arnold Smith, Mrs. Kelly, and William Kane, 1983; Kennedy, *xiii*, 321.
301 Kelly lunch: int. Dan Moldea, 1983.
301 Shimon: int., 1983.
302 Hoffa: *Playboy* int., Dec. 1975.
302 O'Brien: int., 1983.
302 Burns: int., 1983.
302 Otash: int. (second), 1983.
303 "Checked out": int. Eunice Murray, 1982–83; Murray, 49ff.
303 Booth calls: *Redbook*, Aug. 1962.
303 Slatzer: corr. and int., 1982–85.
303 James: int., 1983.
303 Rosten: int., 1984; Norman Rosten, 97.
304 Skolsky: int. Steffi Skolsky, 1983.
305 "Lost": Skolsky, *Don't Get Me Wrong*, 234.

Chapter 39
305 Polo Lounge: Stempel, *Screenwriter*, 171; Johnson and Leventhal, 207.
305 *Something's Got to Give:* int. Henry Weinstein and Ted Strauss, 1983–84.
306 Walter Bernstein, *Esquire*, July 1973; *Los Angeles Times* Calendar, July 22, 1973.
306 Absenteeism: *Los Angeles Herald-Examiner*, June 9, 1962.
307 Virus: Murray, chap. 12; int. Dr. Lee Siegel, 1983; *Los Angeles Times*, May 10, 1962.
307 Masters: int., 1983.
307 Travilla: int., 1983.

307 Greenson visits: Greenson bill submitted to estate, in Slatzer, 369.
307 Greenson and Marilyn: Greenson corr. with colleague; Greenson, 67.
307 Jean-Louis: int., 1983.
308 Kennedy birthday: *New York Times,* May 19 and 20, 1962; int. Henry Weinstein, 1984.
308 Rehearsals: Greenson, 68ff.; int. Fred Field, Danny Greenson, Milt Ebbins, Peter Lawford, 1983–84.
308 Gala performance: as rendered in *The Legend of Marilyn Monroe,* TV documentary by Wolper Prod., 1967.
310 Activity after gala: Flora R. Schreiber int. Isadore Miller, *Good Housekeeping,* Jan. 1963; *Los Angeles Herald-Examiner,* Aug. 6, 1962; Schlesinger, *Robert Kennedy,* 590.
310 Nude swim: int. William Read Woodfield, 1984; *New York Herald Tribune,* May 25 and 27, 1962; *Los Angeles Herald-Examiner,* May 26, 1962; *Time,* June 1962, *Life,* June 22, 1962; int. Ed Wehl, 1983; *Sir,* Oct. 1962; int. Evelyn Moriarty, 1983; Evelyn Moriarty, *Motion Picture,* July 1963.
311 Playboy: *Playboy,* Jan. 1964, 190, and Jan. 1969, 164.
311 Calendar: *Modern Man,* March 1955; Hedda Hopper, *Los Angeles Times,* Sept. 9, 1953.
311 Marilyn birthday: *Motion Picture,* July 1963; *Los Angeles Times,* Aug. 6, 1962, int. Danny Greenson; Greenson, 71ff.; *New York Daily News,* Aug. 18, 1962.
312 Stand-in doctor: Murray, 107.
312 "Questions": Murray, 107.
312 Nose: int. Dr. Michael Gurdin and Dr. Alfred Conti, 1983; Conti bill to estate, June 7, 1962.
313 Marilyn acting: Walter Bernstein, *Esquire,* July 1973.
313 Greenson returns: int. Hildi and Joan Greenson, 1983.
313 Firing: *Variety* and *Hollywood Citizen-News,* June 8, 1962; *Los Angeles Herald-Examiner* and *Los Angeles Times,* June 9, 1962; *New York Times* and *Los Angeles Times,* June 10, 1962; *Los Angeles Herald-Examiner,* June 12, 1962; *Variety,* June 20, 1962; *Time,* June 22, 1962; *New York Times,* Aug. 12, 1962; Gussow, 243.
314 Thrity-six: "A Good Long Look at Myself," Alan Levy, *Redbook,* Aug. 1962; Strasberg, 155.
314 *Life:* Aug. 3 and 17, 1962.
314 Barris pictures: *New York Daily News,* Aug. 1962; estate papers, in Slatzer, 371.
314 *Vogue:* estate papers, in Slatzer; *Vogue,* Sept. 1982; Stern; int. Pat Newcomb, 1983; corr. Leif-Erik Nygårds, 1984.
314 *Life* interviews: corr. and int. Richard Meryman, 1984; *Life,* Aug. 3 and 17, 1962.

Chapter 40
317 "Two loves": *Vogue,* Sept. 1982.
317 *Something's Got to Give:* Murray, 90.
317 Marilyn and Kennedy party: int. Susan Strasberg, 1983; *New York Times,* May 20, 1962; Ralph Martin, 403; int. Ralph Roberts and James Haspiel, 1985.

318 Meyer: *Washington Post,* Feb. 23, 1976; Davies, 164, 230; *New Times,* July 9, 1976; corr. Mrs. Truitt, 1984.

318 MM and President and pills: int. Los Angeles law enforcement sources, 1983.

319 Leary: int. Timothy Leary, 1983; Leary, 128, 155, 179, 191.

320 Janiger: int., 1983.

320 MM in New York: Guiles, *Norma Jean,* 370.

320 Weatherby: int., 1983; Weatherby, 151ff.

320 Weinstein: int., 1984.

321 Murray: Murray, 107.

321 Jeffries: Ted Landreth int. Norman Jeffries, 1983.

321 Telegram: Western Union message, June 13, 1962, supplied by Kennedy Library, 1984.

321 Robert Kennedy in Los Angeles: itinerary and memoranda in FBI file 77-51387-260, obtained under FOIA, 1983; Murray, 86–112; int. Mrs. Murray, 1982–83; Ted Landreth int. Norman Jeffries, 1983.

321 Lawford: int., 1983; Los Angeles law enforcement source, 1983.

323 Doctors: bills, in Slatzer, 367–69.

323 Cal-Neva: int. Peter Lawford, George Jacobs, Julius Bengtsson, Joe and Ray Langford, Clarice Astle, Wayne Ogle, Gloria Romanoff, Mae Shoopman.

324 "Complete woman": *Novedades,* Feb. 23, 1962.

324 Barris: Theo Wilson, *New York Daily News,* Aug. 16, 1962 int. George Barris and Theo Wilson, 1983.

325 James: int., 1983.

325 Woodfield: int., 1984.

325 Otash: int., 1983.

325 Abortion and Sweden: *Los Angeles Times,* Aug. 6, 1962.

325 Phone records: retired law enforcement source, 1983.

326 Selsman: Ted Landreth int. Michael Selsman, 1983.

327 Drugs and fantasy: correspondence of Dr. Brian Wells, Maudsley Hospital Drug Dependence Unit, Beckenham, England, 1986; int. Dr. Guy Neald, 1985.

327 Jacobs: int., 1985.

Chapter 41

327 MM calls: Schlesinger, *Robert Kennedy,* 590.

327 Special number: int. with Murray, 1982.

327 Phone records: retired law enforcement source, 1983.

328 Kennedy itinerary: FBI file 77-51387-260, obtained under FOIA, 1983.

328 Slatzer: int., 1982–83; Slatzer. 1ff.

328 Threat (fn.): int. Thom Montgomery, 1985.

329 Diary: Goodman, 227; Bacon, *Hollywood Is a Four-Letter Town,* 137; int. Susan Strasberg and Amy Greene, 1983–84; *American Weekly,* May 1, 1960; int. Jeanne Carmen, 1983.

330 Field: int., 1983.

330 Bolaños: int., 1983.

332 Chasin: int., 1983; *New York Times,* July 14, 1962.

332 Wofford: Wofford, 405.

332 CIA briefs Robert Kennedy: *Alleged Assassination Plots,* 132.

332   Hoffa prosecution: Sheridan, 206; *New York Times*, May 19, 1962.

332   Hoffa murder plan: Sheridan, 217; Moldea, 148. Date: Sheridan, 210–17.

333   McGrath: *Fort Worth Star-Telgram*, Oct. 1, 1978. Abbreviated: Blakey and Billings, 382.

333   Sinatra reports: Messick, 198; int. Dougald McMillan, 1983.

333   No Giancana prosecution: *Alleged Assassination Plots Report*, 132 and 133n.2.

333   Delay movie?: FBI memorandum, Evans to Belmont, July 3, 1962, referring to discussion in Los Angeles, file 77-51387-274, obtained under FOIA, 1983.

334   Greenson birthday: Greenson, 81; Norman Rosten, 101.

334   Carmen: *Los Angeles Times*, Aug. 7, 1962.

334   Roberts: int., 1982.

334   Engelberg: doctor's bill, in Slatzer, 367; Ted Landreth conversation with Engelberg's son Michael, 1983.

334   Studio bosses: int. Pat Newcomb, 1983.

334   Strasberg: int. Steffi Skolsky, 1983; *Hollywood Citizen-News*, July 27, 1962; Monica Gruler int. Mrs. Rand, of Rand Travel Agency, 1983; Weatherby, 120; int. Joan Greenson, 1983.

334   Jeffries: Ted Landreth int. Norman Jeffries, 1983.

334   Marilyn's insomnia: int. James Haspiel, 1983.

334   Pier: Monica Gruler int. Beryl Brunkow and George Gordon, 1984.

334   Tahoe: int. Eunice Murray, Joe and Ray Langford, Ed Pucci, Julius Bengtsson, 1983–84; Ted Landreth int. Dora Foley and Ken Rotkoph, 1983; Sidney Skolsky, *Hollywood Citizen-News*, Aug. 6, 1962; Robert Slatzer int. Jeron Criswell; int. Paul D'Amato, 1984.

335   Aircraft: *American Weekly*, Sept. 2, 1962.

335   Flight: int. the former Barbara Lieto and Dan Arney, 1983.

336   Firestone: int., 1983.

336   Marilyn by pool: Ted Landreth int. Ken Rotkoph, 1983.

336   Roberts: int., 1983.

337   Hall: int., 1984; corroborated by int. Paul Sann, formerly of *New York Post*, 1985.

337   Johnson: Johnson and Leventhal, 210.

337   Monette: *New York Daily News*, Aug. 14, 1962; Allen, 197.

337   Marilyn letter: Guiles, *Norma Jean*, 376, and *Legend*, 250.

338   Ries: Heidi Sorensen, int. Pamela Ries, 1983; *Los Angeles Times*, Aug. 8, 1962.

338   Roberts: int., 1985.

338   Slatzer: int., 1983; Slatzer, 228, 233, 241.

338   Wiretapping: int. John Dolan, 1983.

338   D'Amato: int., 1984.

338   Will: Wilson, *Show Business Nobody Knows*, 316.

339   Greenson: letter to Norman Rosten, Aug. 15, 1962.

339   *Life*: *Life*, Aug. 3, 1962.

339   Kennedy: July 26: FBI file 77-51387-284, obtained under FOIA 1983; *Los Angeles Times*, July 26, 1962; hotel bill, in Capell, 58; corr. Kennedy Library, 1984.

339   Threat: FBI file 77-51387-285, memorandum from Hoover to
        Chief, U.S. Secret Service, July 26, 1962.
339   July 30 call: police log, obtained by author, 1983; Report to Los
        Angeles District Attorney, Dec. 1982, 17.

Chapter 42
343   Phone friend: Weatherby, 107.
343   Calls: int. Henry Rosenfeld, Maureen Stapleton, Bob Josephy,
        and Lena Pepitone, 1983–84.
343   Kelly: *Los Angeles Times* and *Los Angeles Herald-Examiner*,
        Aug. 6, 1962.
343   Skolsky: *Hollywood Citizen-News*, Aug. 6, 1962.
343   Thompson and Styne: int., 1983–84.
343   Sinatra dinner: int. Gloria Romanoff, 1983.
343   Snyder and Plecher: int., 1983.
344   Kingston: int., 1983.
344   Krohn: int., 1983.
344   Roberts: int., 1982–83.
344   James: int., 1983.
344   Rosten call: police log; int. Norman Rosten, who thought the call
        was Aug. 4; Rosten letter to Greenson, Aug. 11, 1962; Norman
        Rosten, 120.
345   Karger: int. Elizabeth Karger and Vi Russell, 1983.
345   Slatzer call: int. Robert Slatzer, Lee Henry, Doral Chenoweth,
        Dr. Sanford Firestone, 1983.
345   Lawford confirms: Wilson, *Show Business Laid Bare*, 86.
346   Kennedy in California: FBI report, SAC to Hoover, Aug. 6, 1962;
        Evans to Belmont, Aug. 22, in FBI file ff-51387-274, obtained
        under FOIA; *San Francisco Chronicle*, Aug. 4, 1962.
346   Bates: int., 1983; Anthony Cook int. John Bates, 1983.
346   Muir: Ted Landreth int. Elizabeth Fancher, 1983.
346   White House announcement: *New York Times*, Aug. 4, 1962.
346   Marilyn on President's visit: int. Sidney Skolsky, 1983; Skolsky,
        Don't Get Me Wrong, 236.
346   Kilgallen: Israel, 327.
347   Nursery: int. Eunice Murray, 1982; John Goka of Frank's, 1983.
347   Visit north?: int. Ed Pucci and Barbara Lieto, 1983; Ted Landreth
        int. Dora Foley, 1983.
347   Newcomb dinner: Pat Newcomb, *Los Angeles Herald-Examiner*,
        Aug. 15, 1962; int., 1983; int. with District Attorney's team,
        1983.
347   Liquor order: Don J. Briggs Inc. creditor's claim on estate, in
        Slatzer, 366.
347   Leon: int., 1983. Career: *Saturday Evening Post*, Aug. 11,
        1962.

Chapter 43
348   Carmen: int., 1983.
348   James: int., 1983.
349   Weather: *Los Angeles Herald-Examiner*, Aug. 4, 1962.
349   Murray: int., 1982–84; Murray, 123.
349   Miller, Sr.: *Good Housekeeping*, Jan. 1963.

349   Jeffries: Ted Landreth, int. Norman Jeffries, 1983; MM probate file, showing Jeffries paid Aug. 4.

349   Phones: *Life*, Nov. 4, 1966.

349   Roberts: int., 1983.

349   Skolsky: int. Steffi Skolsky, 1983.

349   Flanagan visit: int. Don Feld, 1985.

350   Greenson: two letters, to Norman Rosten, Aug. 15, 1962, and to colleague, Aug. 20, 1962.

350   Newcomb on rage: int., 1984.

351   Strasberg: Strasberg, 113.

351   Martin: int., 1984.

351   Suicide Prevention Team: int. Dr. Robert Litman, Dr. Norman Farberow, and Dr. Norman Tabachnick, including access to original notes and files, 1983.

352   Greenson plans: int. Hildi Greenson, 1983.

352   Murray overnight: Murray, 129.

352   DiMaggio, Jr.: police report of interview, Aug. 10, 1962, DR 62-509-463; *Los Angeles Times*, Aug. 8, 1962.

352   Music: *New York Daily News*, Aug. 6, 1962.

352   Dusk: *Los Angeles Herald-Examiner*, Aug. 4, 1962.

352   Question on Nembutal: Greenson corr. to colleague, Aug. 20, 1962.

352   Drugs: Toxicologist's list, Aug. 6, Coroner's file 81128. See also police Death Reports, containing confused information; District Attorney's Report, 1982, 25; int. Dr. Lee Siegel, 1983; Engleberg bill, in Slatzer, 367; Mortuary Death Report, Aug. 5, 1962, in Coroner's file.

353   Oxygen: int. Eunice Murray, 1982–83; Murray, 127.

353   Carmen: int., 1983.

353   Rosenfeld: int., 1984.

353   Guilaroff: int., 1983; Wilson *Show Business Laid Bare*, 84.

354   Bolaños: int., 1983.

354   Roberts: int., 1982.

354   Call to Greensons: Greenson corr.; Greenson, 82.

355   Smashed pane: *Santa Monica Evening Outlook*, Aug. 6, 1962.

355   Police pictures: obtained by author, 1983.

355   Call to police: police log, in Sgt. Byron's follow-up Report, Aug. 6, police file no. 62-509-463.

356   Clemmons: int., 1982–85.

Chapter 44

356   Ramirez: int., 1983.

356   Woodfield and Hyams: int., 1983–84; Hyams, 138; *Show Business Illustrated*, Feb. 1962.

356   Bacon: int., 1983; *Los Angeles Herald-Examiner*, Oct. 9, 1979.

357   Hockett: int., 1982.

357   Gray: *Los Angeles Herald-Examiner*, Aug. 6, 1962; int. Harry Tessel, 1983.

357   Wiener: int., 1982; *Los Angeles Times* Calendar, Aug. 22, 1982.

357   Unless otherwise identified, all news events and quotations following the death are taken from coverage, Aug. 6–19, 1962, of: *New York Herald Tribune, Los Angeles Herald-Examiner*,

Los Angeles Times, San Francisco Chronicle, New York Daily News, Santa Monica Evening Outlook, Hollywood Citizen-News.

358 Miller comment: *New York Post,* Aug. 7, 1962.
358 DiMaggio: int. Harry Hall, 1984; int. Inez Melson, 1983.
358 Butterfly: Strasberg, 157.
358 Greene: int. Amy and Milton Greene, 1983–84.
359 Wilder: int., 1983.
359 Greenson: int. Hildi and Joan Greenson, 1983; int. William R. Woodfield, 1964.
359 George Jacobs: int., 1983.
360 Sandals: int. Sherry Houser, 1983.
360 Zolotow: int., 1983.
360 Saunders: int., 1984; Saunders and Southwood, 130.
360 Kennedy at church: Anthony Cook int. Father John Dwyer, 1983.
360 Bates: int. 1983; Anthony Cook, int. John Bates, 1983.
360 RFK and CIA Director McCone: FBI report 77-54397-30, Courtney Evans to J. Edgar Hoover, Aug. 22, 1962.
361 JFK and drugs: *New York Daily News,* Aug. 6, 1962.
361 Noguchi: int., 1984; Noguchi, chap. 3.
361 Brown: int. Virgil Crabtree, 1984.
361 Parker: int. Mrs. Parker, 1983.

Chapter 45
362 Autopsy detail: Los Angeles Coroner's file 81128, especially Anatomical Summary; int. Dr. Thomas Noguchi, John Miner, and Eddy Day, 1983–84.
362 Noguchi controversy: *New York Times,* Nov. 13, 1982; *New York Times,* June 23, 1984.
362 Marilyn in death: picture obtained from police file, 1983.
363 Toxicology: Reports of Dr. Ralph Abernathy, Aug. 6 and 13, 1962, in Coroner's file 81128.
363 Foster: int. 1985 (pathologist at St. Bartholomew's Hospital, London, M.D., Ph.D., M.R.C. Path.).
364 Curphey: text of statement to press, Aug. 17, 1962.
364 Glass: District Attorney's Report, 1982, p. 26; *San Francisco Chronicle,* Aug. 6, 1962.
364 House sealed: *New York Herald Tribune,* Aug. 6, 1962.
365 Melson: int., 1983.
365 Note on bottle picture (fn.): photograph in possession of James Haspiel.
365 Medical examiners and coroners contacted: By D.A., 1982: Dr. Boyd G. Stephens (San Francisco) and Dr. Kornblum. For author: Prof. Keith Simpson, senior Home Office forensic pathologist, Emeritus Prof. Forensic Medicine, London University; Dr. Christopher Foster, pathologist and biochemist, St. Bartholomews Hospital (London); Dr. Henry Siegel (formerly New York City Dep. Chief. Med. Examiner); Dr. Patrick Besant-Matthews (Dallas); Prof. Earl Rose (Iowa); Dr. Joseph Davis (Dade Co. Med. Examiner, Florida); Dr. Joseph Jachimczyk (Chief Med. Examiner, Harris Co., Houston); Dr. John Coe (Hennepin Co. Med. Examiner, Minneapolis); Lee del Cortivo

(Chief Toxicologist, Suffolk Co., N.Y.); Dr. Bertram Fuchs (gastroenterologist, Mineola, New York).

366   Breaking open capsules: Guiles, *Norma Jean*, 344.
366   Meal?: int. Eunice Murray and Pat Newcomb, 1983–84; Slatzer int. Newcomb, 1973; Murray, 130.
366   Curphey press conference: *Los Angeles Herald-Examiner*, Aug. 18, 1962.
367   Destruction of specimens: int. Dr. Thomas Noguchi, 1984; Noguchi, 74.
368   Injection checks: int. Dr. Thomas Noguchi, John Miner, Eddy Day; District Attorney's Report 1982, 4.
368   Marilyn and enemas: int. Amy Greene, 1984; confirmed by John Miner in 1962; int. Jeanne Carmen, 1983 (on constipation).
368   Gould: int., 1983.
370   Right-wing tract: Capell.
370   Mailer: int., 1984; Mailer, *Marilyn*, 367.
370   Messick: int., 1983; Messick, 201, 207; FBI file 44-17593, on Ratterman, Kentucky sheriff candidate.

Chapter 46

372   Noguchi: int., 1984.
372   Bacon: int., 1983.
372   Hyams: *New York Herald Tribune*, Aug. 6, 1962.
373   Brown: int. Kenneth McCauley, "Pete" Scenderup, 1983.
373   Phillips: int., 1983.
373   McCauley request: report to McCauley, Aug. 27, 1974, by Lt. Selby, Homicide Special Section, in recovered part of police file obtained by author.
374   1975 inquiry: commissioned by Police Chief Davis, report sent Oct. 14, 1975, by Daryl Gates, then Assistant Chief, Director of Operations; report obtained by author, 1983.
374   Finck: note found in police file, 1983.
374   Gates: corr. Dec. 20, 1984.
374   Phillips: int., 1983.
374   Yorty: int., 1983.
375   Carroll: "The Death of Marilyn Monroe, Report to the District Attorney," by Ronald H. Carroll, Assistant District Attorney, and Alan. B. Tomich, Investigator, Dec. 1982.
375   Dickey: inquiry's existence discovered during research in District Attorney's office, 1982; Anthony Cook int. John Dickey, 1983.
375   Hronek: int. Gary Wean and Jack Egger, former colleagues, 1983; int. Mrs. Hronek and Steve Hronek, 1983.
376   Marilyn buys tape recorder: Norman Rosten, 107; int. Robert Slatzer, 1983.
376   Miner memorandum: District Attorney's Report, Dec. 1982; int. John Miner, 1983–84.
377   "Pressure": *New York Daily News* and *San Francisco Chronicle*, Aug. 12, 1962.
377   Greenson interview: made in 1964, in files of William R. Woodfield.

Chapter 47

378   Farberow on phone: *San Francisco Chronicle*, Aug. 7, 1962.

378 Murray: *Los Angeles Herald-Examiner* (late edition), Aug. 6, 1962.

378 Light and door: WOR Radio broadcast (11:00 A.M. Sunday, New York time), Murray, 135; int. Eunice Murray, 1982–83.

378 "Mystery call": *Los Angeles Times* and *Los Angeles Herald-Examiner*, Aug. 7, 1962.

378 "Disturbed": *New York Daily News*, *Los Angeles Herald-Examiner*, Aug. 7, 1962; *San Francisco Chronicle*, Aug. 8, 1962.

379 Ebbins and Lawford: *Los Angeles Herald-Examiner*, Aug. 8, 1962.

379 Lawford interview: *New York Herald Tribune*, Aug. 8, 1962.

379 "Mystery solved": *Hollywood Citizen-News*, Aug. 8, 1962.

379 "No calls received" (police): *Hollywood Citizen-News*, Aug. 10, 1962; int.

380 Byron report: Follow-up report, timed 4:15 P.M., Aug. 6, in surviving police file. Byron, 1986.

379 General Telephone employees: John Gurak and Bob Warner, of GTE Security, and a retired employee, 1983.

380 Two weeks later: see also District Attorney's Report, 1982, 17.

381 Muir: Hudson, 88.

381 Hyams discovery: Hyams, 142; int. Joe Hyams and former colleague, 1983.

381 Warner: int., 1983.

381 Funk: int., 1983; int. Mrs. Tiarks, 1983.

382 FBI report: Document 66-1700-39, ADIC (LA) to Acting Director, July 6, 1973.

382 Another senior agent: int., 1985.

382 Litman: int., 1983.

383 Brough: int., 1983.

383 Tobin: int., 1983–84.

383 Kennedy and Hamilton: Kennedy, 8, 264, xiii, xiv; int. Robert Hamilton, 1984.

384 Brown: int. Virgil Crabtree, 1983.

384 Reddin: int., 1985.

384 Schiller: int., 1983.

Chapter 48

385 Lawford: int., 1983.

385 Police doubt Murray: Re-Interview of Persons Known to Marilyn Monroe, police case 62-509-463, Sgt. Byron and Lt. G.Armstrong reporting, Aug. 10, 1962, retrieved by author from police files, 1983.

387 Lawford leaves: Police case 62-509-463 continuation sheet.

387 Hyannis Port: Lawford: *Los Angeles Herald-Examiner,*Aug. 10, 1962, Newcomb; *Los Angeles Herald-Examiner*, Aug. 15 and 16, 1962 (by Dorothy Manners and Alfred Robbins).

387 Farberow: int., 1983.

387 Lawford guests: *Los Angeles Herald-Examiner*, Aug. 8, 1962.

387 Naar (Joe and the former Dolores): int., 1983.

387 Wood: int. Robert Slatzer, 1983. Friend of MM: int. Lana Wood, 1984, and James Haspiel, 1985.

387 Beatty: int., 1983.

388 Durgom: int., 1983.

388 Lawford, 1975: police report of Lawford interview, Oct. 16, 1975.

388 Lawford, 1982: briefing by official sources, 1983.

389 Litman: int., 1983.

389 Ebbins: int., 1983.

389 Rudin, 1962: Continuation page of Re-Interview of Persons Known to Marilyn Monroe, police case 62-509-463, Sgt. Byron & Lt. G. Armstrong reporting, Aug. 10, 1962, retrieved by auhor from police files, 1983.

389 Rudin declines interview: corr., 1983.

389 Murray on Rudin: Murray, 131; int. Eunice Murray, 1982–83.

389 Memoir: Murray.

390 "Sixth sense": Murray, 134; int. Eunice Murray, 1982–84.

390 Lawford's explanation: Wilson, *Show Business Nobody Knows*, 316.

390 Mrs. Murray and "midnight": *Los Angeles Herald-Examiner*, Aug. 6, 1962; *New York Daily News*, Aug. 6, 1962; Greenson corr. to friend Aug. 15, 1962, and to colleague; int. Eunice Murray, 1982.

392 Jacobs: int. Natalie Jacobs, 1985.

392 Concert: *Los Angeles Times*, Aug. 4, 1962.

393 Simpson: int., 1985.

393 Ambulance: District Attorney's Report, 1982, 16; int. Ken Hunter, Walt Schaefer, Murray Leib, 1985.

394 Ebbins on Rudin: int., 1983.

394 Newcomb: int., 1983–84; Robert Slatzer int. Pat Newcomb, 1973.

395 Gould: int., 1983.

Chapter 49

396 Security man: int., under formal agreement, 1983–84.

396 Otash: int., 1983.

396 Lock company: estate papers, in Slatzer, 361–62.

398 Bates: Anthony Cook int. John Bates, 1983. Also int., 1983.

398 Kennedy at church: Anthony Cook int. Father John Dwyer, 1983.

398 Price: Anthony Cook int. Frank Price, 1983.

398 Lawford on Kennedy not in Los Angeles: London *Observer*, July 15, 1973, quoting Lawford as saying Kennedy had been on the East Coast.

398 Greene: int. Milton Greene, 1983–84.

398 Yorty: int., 1983.

399 Finis Brown: corr. and int., 1983.

399 McDonald: int., 1984.

399 Dickey: briefing on District Attorney's Report, 1983.

399 Landing at Fox: int. Frank Neill, 1983, and former policeman on pension, who requires anonymity.

399 Pollard: int., 1983.

399 Murray afternoon activity: int., 1983; Murray, 127ff.

399 D'Antonio (fn.): int., 1983.

400 Marilyn "expecting to see V.I.P.": int. of Dr. Norman Tabachnick, 1983.

400　Wood: int., 1983.

400　Hyams and Woodfield: int., 1983–84; Woodfield re-int., 1985; Hyams, 143ff.

400　Lawford and helicopters: int. Peter Lawford, Milt Ebbins, Lynn Sherman, Sherry Houser, and other neighbors. See also Ted Landreth int. James Gavin, pilot; files of *Santa Monica Evening Outlook; Time,* Aug. 12, 1966.

401　Woodfield's earlier article: traced to *American Weekly,* Sep. 2, 1962.

405　Cukor: as reported to author, 1983, by Robin Thorne, who had taken notes.

Chapter 50

409　Snyder and Plecher: int., 1983.

409　"Doll": *New York Herald Tribune,* Aug. 9, 1962.

409　Melson: int., 1983.

410　Funeral: unless otherwise indicated, descriptions are from *New York Herald Tribune, Los Angeles Times, Santa Monica Evening Outlook, San Francisco Chronicle, New York Daily News,* Aug. 8 and 9, 1962. See also from printed *Services for Marilyn Monroe* (with guest list).

410　DiMaggio on Kennedys: int. Emily Stevens, 1983.

410　Joan Greenson: Greenson, 86.

411　"Over the Rainbow": Monroe entry, Robert B. Dickerson, Jr., *Final Placement,* Guide to Deaths and Funerals of Notable Americans, Algonac, Mich.: Reference Books Inc., 1982.

411　Roses: int. Robert Slatzer, 1985; *Los Angeles Times,* Sept. 29, 1982; *Los Angeles Herald-Examiner,* Feb. 15, 1983; *Orange County Register,* Oct. 1, 1982.

411　Cukor: Lambert, *On Cukor,* 180.

412　Lawford and Wood remains: conversation, Patricia Seaton, 1985; *People,* Aug. 1982.

412　Winters: int. James Haspiel, 1985.

412　Vault for sale: *Los Angeles Daily News,* Aug. 5, 1982.

412　DiMaggio and RFK: Gay Talese, "Silent Season of a Hero," *Esquire,* July 1966.

412　Davis: Davis, *Suitcase,* 240.

412　Mother's letter: sent to Inez Melson, Aug. 22, 1962, in Melson files.

415　Mother's escape: Whit Preston, *Photoplay,* Oct. 1963.

415　Levathes: int., 1985.

415　Meryman: *Life,* Aug. 17, 1962.

415　"Poster People": int. Jeanne Martin, 1984.

Postscript

419　Gates: *San Francisco Chronicle,* Sept. 24 , 1985.

419　Van de Kamp: *Los Angeles Times,* Sept. 24, 1985.

419　Gates's denial: corr. Dec. 20, 1984; int., Sylvia Chase, 1985.

419　Rest speculation: *UPI,* Sept. 24, 1985.

419　*20/20* furor: int., Riisna, Gould, Chase, Westin, Siegenthaler, 1986.

420　Chase "bear": *Datebook* (San Francisco), Dec. 22, 1985.

421   Arledge "more data": Liz Smith column, *New York Daily News*, Oct. 4, 1985.

421   Smith: Liz Smith column, *New York Daily News*, Oct. 3, 1985.

422   Arledge—"gossip": *The New York Times*, Oct. 5, 1985.

422   Arledge—"sleazy": Liz Smith column, *New York Daily News*, Oct. 4, 1985.

422   Celebrities protest: *Rolling Stone*, Dec. 5, 1985; Liz Smith column, *New York Daily News*, Oct. 7, 1985; *The New York Times*, Oct. 5, 1985; *People*, Oct. 21, 1985.

422   Downs: *The New York Times*, Oct. 5, 1985; *People*, Oct. 21, 1985.

422   Executive links to Kennedys: *People*, Oct. 21, 1985.

422   Arledge on offending friends: *New York Post*, Oct. 5, 1985.

423   Tuck: int., Sylvia Chase, 1986.

423   Haddad: int., Riisna & Haddad, 1986; corr., Haddad, Mar. 4, 1986.

424   Slatzer letter: Sept. 23, 1985, to Mike Antonovich.

424   Grand Jury furor: int., Dawnson Oppenheimer, spokesman for Antonovich, and Asst. D.A. Ronald Carroll, 1986; research of Jordan Cohn; Motion of Board of Supervisors, County of Los Angeles, Oct. 8, 1985; Antonovich press statement, Oct. 8; Memorandum of D.A. Ira Reiner to Supervisors, Nov. 7, 1985; *Los Angeles Herald*, Oct. 29, 30, 31, 1985; *Los Angeles Daily News*, Oct. 26, 29, and Nov. 1; *New York Post*, Oct. 8 and Dec. 4; *San Francisco Chronicle*, Oct. 29; *Los Angeles Times*, Oct. 29; *South China Morning Post*, Nov. 4.

424   D.A. Report 1982: The Death of Marilyn Monroe—Report to the District Attorney, Dec. 1982.

425   Summers: int., 1986.

426   Seaton: int., 1985.

426   Durgom: int., 1986.

426   Roberts: int., 1985.

426   Moore: int., 1983 and 1985.

426   Paul: reader's corr., 1985; int. members Paul family, 1986; *Current Biography*, 1957; *The New York Times*, Nov. 26, 1967.

427   Guthman: int., 1985.

427   Monroe letters: located by author in Monroe business files, 1986— shortly to be placed in suitable place of learning.

427   Dinner: Murray, 1985; Los Angeles visit of Robert Kennedy confirmed by corr. John F. Kennedy Library, Oct. 17, 1984.

428   Danny Greenson: int., 1984.

428   Durgom: int., 1986.

428   Dye: int., 1985.

428   Murray: int., 1985.

428   Smathers: int., 1983.

429   Hoover memo: Blakey/Billings, 380.

429   Campbell "longer contact": Exner & Demaris, 251.

429   Dickinson: Exner & Demaris, 280.

429   Skolsky: Skolsky, 234; int., 1983.

429   Monroe trip to California: int., Eunice Murray, 1982–83; Murray, 87; int., Philip Watson and Ralph Roberts, 1983–85.

429   Gould: int., 1986.

430   Lawford sees Giancana: int., Lawford, 1983; int., Martin, 1984.
430   Theodoracopulos: int., 1986; *Princes, Playboys, & High-Class Tarts*, by Taki, Princeton: Karz-Cohl Publishing, 1984. *Spectator*, Oct. 19, 1985.
431   Campbell on President knowing: int., Ovid Demaris (her biographer), 1986.
431   Campbell on Giancana re. President: Exner-Demaris, 255.
431   Blakey: Blakey-Billings, 391.
431   Giancana's weakness: Giancana-Renner, 246.
431   Giancana not questioned: *The Kennedys, Dynasty and Disaster 1848–1984,* by John Davis, New York: McGraw-Hill, 1985, 406.
432   Meredith: *Goddess,* p. 270–71.
432   Mrs. Spindel: int., 1986.
432   Spindel & CIA: int., Dick Butterfield, 1983–86.
432   Kennedy woos: Spindel, 215; testimony of James Kelly, Mar. 8–12, 1965, Bernard B. Spindel Tax Proceedings Docket 3102-63, 2668-64. And *Goddess,* Chapter 38, p. 262.
432   Jaycox re. Giancana: int., Jaycox, 1986.
433   Giancana-Roselli conversation: FBI surveillance documents, Dec. 6, 1961, obtained from congressional source.
433   Danoff: int., 1985.
433   Otash: ints., 1985; author reinterviewed Otash in summer '85 and has been briefed on colleagues' interview, also 1985.
434   Consultant: int., under formal agreement, 1983–84.
435   Roselli: int., Otash, 1983–85; int., John Danoff, 1983– 85.
435   James: int., 1983–85; (DeSapio—*cf. Goddess,* p. 297.
436   Winther: int., 1986.
437   Otash re. Durgom: int., 1985.
437   Durgom: int., 1986.
437   Reilly: int., 1985.
437   Roswell: int., 1985.
437   Naar: int., 1983; re-int., Dolores, 1986.
437   Joan Greenson: int., 1986.
438   Schaefer: int. (repeatedly), 1985.
438   Hunter re. "comatose": Speriglio, *Conspiracy,* 59.
438   Hall: int., 1986; The Death of Marilyn Monroe—Report to the District Attorney, Dec., 1982, 13.
438   Hall relatives: int., Dr. George Hall (father), Lynn (sister), Kitty (ex-wife), 1986.
438   Seven employees: int., Joe Zilinski, Carl Bellonzi, Tom Fears, Sean O'Bligh, Joe Tarnowski, Edgardo Villalobos, Murray Leib, 1985–6.
438   Engelberg: int. by Los Angeles, D.A.'s investigator, 1982, and by Sylvia Chase, 1986.
438   Murray: int., 1985 (by author for BBC & separately); and by Sylvia Chase, 1985.
438   Clayton: int., Murray, 1982, witnessed by Marie Pollak, described in corr., 1985.
439   Iannone: int., 1986.
439   Byron: int., 1986.
439   "evasive": *cf. Goddess,* p. 385.

440   Conners: int., Michael and Patricia Conners, 1985.
440   Zonlick: int., 1986; *Rolling Stones*, Dec. 5, 1985.
440   Connelly: int., 1986.
441   Otash initial statement: *cf. Goddess*, p. 396.
441   Otash now: int., 1985.
441   Seaton: int., 1985; *Los Angeles Times*, Sept. 29, 1985.
441   Globe Photo: int. former executive, who requested anonymity, 1986.
442   Monsky: conversation and meeting with contact, 1985.
444   Photo "clutched": Greenson corr., August 1962.
444   Pathologists: Prof. Gee, Home Office Pathologist (U.K.), int., 1986; and Dr. Christopher Foster, St. Bartholomew's Hospital (U.K.), on contraction of muscles: int. 1986.
445   Holt: int., 1983.
445   Morrissey: int., 1985.
445   Morrissey *fn.*: *The New York Times*, Jan. 23, and 24, 1975.
445   Kamin: int., 1986.
445   Jaycox: int., 1986.
445   Spindel raid: Spindel, 221; int., Mrs. Spindel, 1982–86; *World Journal Tribune*, Dec. 18 and 20, 1966; Newark *Star-Ledger*, Dec. 21, 1966.
445   CIA and FBI: CIA memo, Feb. 20, 1967; two FBI documents, Mar. 13, 1967 (as well as Jan. 28, 1965), obtained under FOIA, 1985.
446   Suit: Court files: *The New York Times*, Dec. 21, 1966.
446   Neary: int., 1983, drawing on notes of Jan. 1967 int., Spindel.
446   Court records: affidavit of Peter Andreoli, in *People of the State of New York v. George Varis, John Connors, Richard Rutherford, Bernard Spindel*, Indictment No. 4817-½ 1966; inventory of Dec. 15, 1966.
446   Mrs. Spindel: int., 1982–86; and by Frank Capell, July 20, 1973.
446   FBI destruction: letter, SAC Paul Daly to author's attorney, Feb. 8, 1984.
446   Stream: int., 1985.
446   Evans briefing: FBI document 77-51387-310, Evans to Belmont, Aug. 20, 1962.
446   Original version of surveillance: House Select Committee on Assassinations JFK Exhibit F-624, suppressed in HSCA press handout, Sept. 28, 1978, as described in *Fort Worth Star-Telegram*, Oct. 1, 1978.
448   Syndicate conversation: FBI surveillance documents, Aug. 20, 1962, for Vol. 7 of 13 files on organized crime. Vol. 7, which originated in L.A., was obtained from a congressional source.
448   Kennedy's whereabouts: FBI file 77-51387 and researcher Ranftel's check with Henry J. Gwiazda II, Curator of Robert F. Kennedy Collection in John F. Kennedy Library, April 7, 1986.
448   Hoover letter: FBI file 77-57387, letter of July 8, 1964, to Attorney General.
450   Clemmons: int., 1982–85; (Fi-Po) *Power of the Right*, by William Turner, Ramparts Press, 1971, 224.

450 Ries: int., Clemmons, 1982–85; *Toward Soviet America* (chapter notes: Maurice Ries), Elgin Publications, California; *New York Post*, Oct. 4, 1985.

451 Clay: int., 1983; and int., Bobbie Butigan, 1983–86; Capell files, lodged with John Birch Society, Belmont, Mass.

451 Capell book: *The Strange Death of Marilyn Monroe*, by Frank A. Capell, Herald of Freedom, 1964.

451 Engelberg "communist": Capell, *supra*. 33, citing Senate Fact Finding Committee of Un-American Activities of the State of California Report, 1948; and testimony of Dr. Oner Barker & Dr. Louise Light, in Report of same Committee, 1955; and of Elizabeth B. Cohen, in Hearings of U.S. House Committee on Un-American Activities, May 28, 1954.

451 Strasberg & Rosten: Capell, pp. 43, 44.

451 Hoffa-Otash contact: corr. of Sept. 15, 1964, Otash to Spindel, provided to author by Otash.

451 Bugging of Capell: *The Final Days*, by Bob Woodward and Carl Bernstein, New York: Avon Books, 1976, p. 40.

451 Nixon: transcript of *60 Minutes*, Vol. XVI, No. 31, CBS TV, April 15, 1984, p. 6.

453 Capell & Clemmons indicted: Bridgewater, N.J. *Courier-News*, July 20 and Aug. 4, 1965.

453 Police report on Clemmons: Confidential L.A. Police *Investigation re: Article in "Oui" Magazine*, Oct. 22, 1975, p. 4.

453 Clemmons's experience: Police Report *supra*., p. 4.

453 De Toledano: int., 1982–83–85; de Toledano, *Hoover*, 309.

454 Lesar/FBI briefing: report to author by attorney Lesar, Mar. 28, 1986.

454 FBI on "voluminous" refs: letter, David Flanders, Chief, Freedom of Information Division, Privacy Acts Branch, Records Management, to Robert Slatzer, May 29, 1980.

454 105 file: FBI releases, revealing 1955 inception of file 105-40018 on Monroe, obtained by Robert Slatzer, 1980, and the author, 1983 (31 pages); letter of May 2, 1983, to attorney James Lesar from James K. Hall, Chief, FOI Privacy Acts Section, Records Management Division.

454 D.A. unable to see FBI material: int., Assistant D.A. Ronald Carroll, 1983; The Death of Marilyn Monroe—Report to the D.A., Dec., 1982, p. 2.

455 Field: int., 1983–86; Field autobiography, see Bibliography.

455 Lawford and Field releases: (Lawford) FBI "see" refs. to Peter Lawford, serials Jan., 1960 to Sept., 1962; (Field) serials from Legat., Mexico City, 100-2278.

455 Monroe documents: 105-40018-2, to Director FBI, from LEGAT, MEXICO, Mar. 6, 1962; & 105-40018-3, to Director FBI, from LEGAT, MEXICO, July 13, 1962.

458 Murray: (husband) Murray int. with Maurice Zolotow 1973, related to author by Zolotow, 1983; Speriglio, *Cover-up*, 236; (Churchill) Murray, 53, 64.

458 Bolaños: *cf. Goddess*, pp. 290–91, 330, 354, int., 1983; research of Mary Powers, 1983–84.

458 Rebuffs questioning: New York *Daily News*, Aug. 8, 9, 10, 18, 1962.

458 Kane: int., 1983.

459 Arvad: Parmet, *Struggles*, p. 92.

459 President's movements: research of Robert Ranftel in files of *The New York Times, Washington Post,* and calls to John F. Kennedy Library, April 1986.

460 Jacob's widow: int., Natalie Jacobs, 1985.

460 Atomic tests and Cuba, 1962: research of Robert Ranftel in files of *The New York Times, Washington Post,* and calls to John F. Kennedy Library, April 1986; *Thirteen Days,* by Robert Kennedy, New York: W.W. Norton, 1969; *The Brink: Cuban Missile Crisis, 1962,* by David Detzer, New York: Thomas Y. Crowell, 1979.

461 Field FBI file: FBI file 100-2278-418 to 436, on Frederick F. Field.

461 Reddin: int., 1986.

461 "blinding row": int., Bolaños, 1983.

461 Gates succeeds Hamilton: checked by researcher Ranftel's call to Gates's office, April 7, 1986.

461 Carroll: int., 1986; (superficial inquiry into bugging) The Death of Marilyn Monroe—Report to the D.A., Dec., 1982, 18.

462 Noguchi: (scene "disturbed") int., 1984; (1985 statements) int., ABC-TV affiliate, San Diego, California, Oct. 30, 1985; *New York Post,* Oct. 31, 1985, *Los Angeles Herald Examiner,* Nov. 1, 1985; *Reuter,* Nov. 1, 1985.

462 Antonovich: comment for author's use, March, 1986.

463 *Time:* Essay, by Roger Rosenblatt, *Time,* July 2, 1984.

INDEX

PHOTO CREDITS
(Listed in Order of Appearance.)

Giancana . . . UPI/Bettmann.

Jimmy Hoffa . . . UPI/Bettmann.

The bugging expert . . . Stan Wayman/*Life* magazine © 1966 Time Inc.

The last birthday . . . MND Collection.

Drinks with the President's brother-in-law . . . Courtesy of Ted Allan.

Three months before the end . . . MND Collection.

A place to die . . . Photo file.

Death in a bottle . . . Photo file.

The floor is heaped with scripts . . . Photo file.

Marilyn in death: Confidential source.

About the Author

Anthony Summers went from Oxford University to newspaper reporting and then to the British Broadcasting Corporation. His journalism covered the world, from Vietnam and Lebanon to the events that convulsed America in the sixties and seventies. His previous books, *The File on the Tsar*, on the disappearance of the last Russian imperial family, and *Conspiracy*, on the assassination of President Kennedy, brought him critical acclaim and, for *Conspiracy*, the Golden Dagger Award for the best nonfiction work on crime in 1980. He is married, with one son, and lives in Ireland.